SCHOOL FINANCE

SCHOOL FINANCE
Its Economics and Politics

Second Edition

Austin D. Swanson
State University of New York at Buffalo

Richard A. King
University of Northern Colorado

Computer Simulations programmed by
Scott R. Sweetland
State University of New York at Buffalo

Addison
Wesley
Longman

An imprint of Addison Wesley Longman, Inc.

New York • Reading, Massachusetts • Menlo Park, California • Harlow, England
Don Mills, Ontario • Sydney • Mexico City • Madrid • Amsterdam

School Finance: Its Economics and Politics,
Second Edition

Longman, 10 Bank Street, White Plains, N.Y. 10606

Acquisitions editor: Virginia L. Blanford
Production editor: Ann P. Kearns
Editorial assistant: Michael Lee
Cover design: Edward Smith
Text art: Fine Line Illustrations
Production supervisor: Edith Pullman
Compositor: Atlis Graphics & Design, Inc.

Library of Congress Cataloging-in-Publication Data

Swanson, Austin D.
    School finance: its economics and politics / Austin D. Swanson,
Richard A. King; computer simulations programmed by Scott R.
Sweetland.—2nd ed.

        p.   cm.
    Includes bibliographical references and index.
    ISBN 0-8013-1516-6

    1. Public schools—United States —Finance.   2. State aid to
education—United States.   3. Federal aid to education—United
States.   4. Education—Aims and objectives—United States.
I. King, Richard A. (Richard Auld). Date.   II. Sweetland, Scott
R.   III. Title.
LB2825.S739   1997   96-17355
379.1'22'0973—dc20   CIP

2345678910—MA—0201

Contents

Foreword

Swanson and King's *School Finance: Its Economics and Politics,* Second Edition, places the financing of schools in the context of a mixed capitalist economy with political power allocated among several levels of government. American values of democracy and equality of opportunity are emphasized. As a good produced by the public sector, education is somewhat unique. While private sector pricing can be used for school construction and the noninstructional aspects of schools, no such benchmark exists for the instructional component. Thus, the political power system seeks to determine adequate and efficient spending and the degree of equality desired; mechanisms of judicial review, family choice of schooling, and school-based decision making are used to avoid the pitfalls of centralized power. Improved teacher quality and remuneration, and altered teaching and learning through educational technologies, are seen as means toward reforming the delivery of schooling, its governance, and its financing.

The first edition of the Swanson and King text stood out for the ease with which it could be read. Students in my classes and students and colleagues at other universities commented on the fact that it was easily the most readable school finance text available. It can be given to a master's student to review the topics in school finance, yet the chapter exercises that require synthesizing material in the text prove challenging to doctoral students.

It is a thought-provoking book. The topics covered are comprehensive but not overwhelming. Primary issues are detailed, and important concepts are highlighted to assist the student. The second edition enhances the readability of the first edition with chapter introductions and summaries. The usefulness of the computer simulations, new in this second edition, will depend on the computer expertise prerequisite to the course. Nonetheless, all students, regardless of computer background, can stand the exposure to the potentials for computer usage in understanding school finance concepts and making applications to administrative problems.

The text presents a plethora of viewpoints on each major issue. The reader needs to determine where he or she wishes to stand given the evidence. Like the first edition, the second edition is a trail blazer in the content of the basic course in school finance for principals and other administrative staff in schools and school districts.

Eugene P. McLoone
President-Elect, American Education
Finance Association
Emeritus, University of Maryland

Preface

Changes in international, national, state, and local conditions continually challenge educational leaders to examine traditional policies and practices. The second edition of *School Finance: Its Economics and Politics* examines contemporary school finance policy and evaluates its ability to meet the challenges of a new millennium. In this edition, we have retained the strengths of the first edition while incorporating new developments and understandings.

One critic of the first edition noted that "The text's major strength [is] the authors' success . . . in relating economic and political issues, challenges, and opportunities to school finance." Another reviewer wrote, "The authors explain complex and sophisticated ideas in an absolutely interesting and understandable way." Another characterized it as "a carefully researched and well written book." A reviewer in a professional journal praised the readability of the first edition by writing, "Although it is not meant to be leisure or casual reading, it is enjoyable and well worth the school business official's time."

The second edition is intended as a primary text for graduate courses in public school finance and the economics of education. The first edition was also used successfully in courses on educational politics and policy analysis; the second edition should be equally useful in that context and

as a general reference for analysts of education policy. Several features distinguish this book from other texts on the market:

- It emphasizes the importance of political as well as economic forces in shaping school finance policy.
- It links changes in school finance policy to the changes in priority given to some widely held social values in explaining the intricacies of school finance and the sources of the difficulty in correcting many of the inequities and inefficiencies of contemporary school systems.
- It explores the financial implications of the school reform movement.
- It includes many cross-national references.
- It provides computer simulations to illustrate the impact of alternative school finance policies on districts of varying characteristics (a new feature of the second edition).

The strategy of this book is to respect the importance of economic theory in analyzing the impact of existing and alternative policies. At the same time it recognizes that such theories do little to help us understand the forces shaping school finance legislation and the process through which

ix

financial policy is implemented. To understand fully what has happened in the development of school finance policy, and what is likely to happen, we must also study the field by drawing on concepts of political science. In this text we strive for a balanced approach. We use paradigms of both the economist and the political scientist.

ORGANIZATION OF THE BOOK

Schools in nearly all nations have been strongly affected by the current conflict over social, political, and economic ideologies. It is within the contemporary context of ferment and change that we examine the relevance of traditional theories and practice of school finance and evaluate possible policy alternatives. Drawing on political and economic models, Part I begins with a discussion of the educational decision-making process in a political-economic system divided between public and private sectors. We then shift the discussion to the impact of public and private values on decisions made about education. We emphasize the values of equity, liberty, fraternity, efficiency, and economic growth. We demonstrate how changes in priorities given to values lead to corresponding changes in public policy. The shift in public priorities from equity and fraternity in the 1960s and 1970s to efficiency, accountability, economic growth, and liberty in the 1980s and 1990s serves as a case in point. Part I concludes with a brief description of the history and existing structure of school governance and finance in the United States.

In Part II we examine the origin of the resources used in support of education. We begin with an overview of the federated tax structure in the United States and discuss criteria that can be used for evaluating taxation policies. Because of the property tax's historical importance in the financing of public education, and because a thorough understanding of it is necessary for competent administration of most school districts, we single out this revenue source for detailed treatment. Part II concludes with a discussion of non-

tax resources for education. These include borrowing, investments, foundations, partnerships with other organizations, and the use of volunteers.

Part III addresses the merits and structure of general and categorical aid programs at state and federal levels. We discuss several constructs for measuring educational need, wealth or revenue-generating ability, and the fiscal effort school districts make in relation to state policy. We discuss strategies for monitoring the use of aid monies and their impact, including program and financial audits. We discuss federal finance policy within the context of several themes that have provided a historical rationale for federal involvement in public education.

In Part IV, we evaluate existing school finance structures and decision-making strategies for the use of resources, using as criteria of success several objectives of public policy. We weigh the equity, efficiency, and adequacy of various school finance plans on the basis of opinions rendered in judicial challenges to their constitutionality in state and federal courts. We also examine these issues using the criteria and methodologies of policy analysts. We examine evidence concerning the efficiency of public and private schools, as provided by studies using constructs generally associated with economics. These include educational production functions and cost-benefit and cost-effectiveness analysis. These studies have revealed relationships between inputs and outputs of the educational process that are sometimes surprising.

In Part V we examine the implications for school finance policy of new and proposed reforms in education governance and the delivery of instruction. We analyze the financial implications of inducing marketlike incentives into the public school structure through school-based management and family choice plans. We examine the potential of merit pay, career ladders, and other strategies for relating compensation to performance and skills in light of demands for higher standards. We discuss models for integrating state-of-the-art information and communication technologies into instruction systems, along with assessments of their impact on staffing (and thus financial) decisions.

As we enter the third millennium, there will be dramatic changes in the financing of elementary and secondary schools. The changes will reflect the organizational changes that will take place in response to new value priorities and changing social, economic, political, and technological conditions. We conclude in Part VI with a discussion of the challenges these changes pose for school finance policy and an assessment of some of the more promising alternatives before us.

The activities and computer simulations included with nearly all chapters are designed to help students apply and extend the school finance concepts we discuss in the text. A range of suggested activities, including numeric problems and interviews with administrators or policy makers, enables instructors and students to choose among various strategies to reinforce the content of the chapter. These activities satisfy the curiosity of advanced users of the text without frustrating those who are new to the field.

The text is designed to be fully comprehensible without the use of the computer simulations. If students use the simulations, however, they will have greatly enriched experiences and will understand the concepts more fully through experimentation. The simulations introduce spreadsheets as a tool for educational administrators and policy analysts—and as a technique for learning school finance concepts. The initial simulations rely on basic spreadsheet commands for adding a column or row to a given table and entering appropriate mathematical formulae into the newly created cells. In later chapters, we introduce more sophisticated procedures such as graphing and regression analysis. Students are encouraged to conduct additional what-if analyses after completing those in the text. The further activities accompanying the simulations also encourage students to relate the simulations to concepts introduced in the text or to apply their newly acquired spreadsheet skills to analyze real administrative or policy problems.

ACKNOWLEDGMENTS

The ideas and conceptualizations presented in this text have evolved over the years. They have been shaped and sharpened by the insights and criticisms of colleagues past and present. Paul R. Mort first stimulated our interest in school finance as a field of study several decades ago at Teachers College, Columbia University. His genius and mentorship provided a firm foundation on which to build understanding of the forces shaping school finance policy and the conditions to which school finance policy must respond.

As authors of this text, we assume full responsibility for its content. Many colleagues and independent reviewers assisted us, however, by developing related manuscripts, sharing documents, or critiquing early drafts of the manuscript. We acknowledge the helpful insights of many individuals. We are especially indebted to Scott Sweetland, Center for Education Resources and Technology, State University of New York at Buffalo, for the skill and insight he provided in making the concept of computer simulations a reality. Others who provided us with valuable assistance included: Mary Ann Anderson, Millcreek Township School District, Pennsylvania; Daniel J. Brown, University of British Columbia; William Crocoll, Chittenden South School District, Vermont; Frank Engert, University of Maine at Farmington; Vivian Hajnal, University of Saskatchewan; Thomas H. Jones, University of Connecticut; Barbara Y. LaCost, University of Nebraska; Bettye MacPhail-Wilcox, North Carolina State University; Betty Malen, University of Maryland; Eugene P. McLoone, University of Maryland; John A. McMahon, University of British Columbia; David A. Nyberg, State University of New York at Buffalo; Edward J. Willett, Houghton College; Catherine C. Sielke, Western Michigan University; William E. Sparkman, Texas Tech University; Thomas A. Surratt, University of South Carolina; Thomas C. Valesky, University of South Florida at Fort Myers; Deborah A. Verstegen, University of Virginia; and J. D. Willardson, Brigham Young University. We greatly appreciate the work of Carol Norris,

State University of New York at Buffalo, and Barbara Swetzig, University of Northern Colorado, in preparing manuscript drafts and anticipating potential production difficulties. The editorial skills of Virginia L. Blanford, of Longman Publishers USA, were invaluable in preparing the manuscript for publication.

We would like to thank the reviewers of this manuscript for their helpful comments:

Robert Arnold, Illinois State University
Richard V. Hatley, University of
   Missouri–Columbia
Theodore J. Kowalski, Ball State University

Eugene P. McLoone, University of Maryland
Kenneth M. Matthews, University of
   Georgia
Paul A. Montello, Georgia State University
William K. Poston Jr., Iowa State University
Nancy Schilling, Northern Arizona
   University

Finally, we acknowledge former students who have challenged us in past teaching and have inquired into school finance policy dilemmas. Anticipating the needs of future students provided our inspiration to write a textbook for their use in understanding school finance policy and practice.

WEBSITE

Visit our Website at:
http://www.EdTech.UnivNorthCo.Edu/SchFin/text.html

PART ONE

Establishing a Context for Studying School Finance Policy

Expenditures for education are the largest single budgetary component of state and local governments in the United States. Nearly 5 percent of the nation's gross domestic product is spent for all levels of educational services—3.7 percent at the elementary and secondary levels alone. By the turn of the millennium, $320 billion (in constant 1991–1992 dollars) will be spent annually on precollegiate schools (National Center for Education Statistics, 1993b). These schools are attended by fifty million children and they employ over five million professional educators and support personnel (National Center for Education Statistics, 1993a). No matter how one looks at it, schooling involves a highly significant portion of the nation's human and economic resources; education is big business. But education is much more than "big business." Education deals with matters that relate to the heart and soul of the individual citizen and, at the same time, is critical to the political and economic welfare of the nation and its security.

To ensure that both individual and societal demands for schooling are met, decisions about the provision of education are made in both the public and private sectors. Decisions are made in the public sector through political processes by governments; whereas, decisions are made in the private sector by individuals through markets. Politics—the process by which values are allocated within society—differs from economics—the study of the allocation of scarce resources within society. Economics is concerned with the production, distribution, and consumption of commodities. Achieving efficiency in the use of resources is the objective of economics—where efficiency is defined as securing the highest level of societal satisfaction at the least cost of scarce resources.

Obviously, one's value priorities strongly influence one's judgment as to what is an efficient allocation of material resources. Thus there is a continuing interaction between economics and politics. Public finance of education is one point of interaction. Decisions about the public finance of education will be made in political arenas; but the decisions made in those arenas will have strong economic implications for individuals and for businesses as well as for communities, states, and the nation. Individuals and businesses will respond independently to political decisions by deciding whether or not to participate in government programs or to supplement or substitute for government programs by purchasing services provided through the private sector.

In this first part of the text, we set the stage for studying school finance issues by examining the political and economic processes for making decisions about the provision of educational services, individual and societal values that influence the nature of educational programs and how they are financed, the evolution of the current governance structures within which those decisions are made, and some of the major issues related to school finance confronting us today.

REFERENCES

National Center for Education Statistics. (1993a). *Digest of educational statistics.* Washington, DC: U. S. Government Printing Office.

National Center for Education Statistics. (1993b). *Education in states and nations: Indicators comparing U. S. states with the OECD countries in 1988.* Washington, DC: U. S. Government Printing Office.

CHAPTER 1

Education Decision Making in a Mixed Economy

Primary Issues Explored in This Chapter:

- *Private and public sector decisions:* What economic and political processes are used in forming decisions about investments in education and about the nature of the educational services to be provided?
- *Human capital theory:* Why are people motivated to invest in their own development, and in that of their children, to improve marketable knowledge and skills?
- *Education as both a private and a public good:* Do the benefits that derive from schooling accrue solely to the individual? Or are there also societal benefits that justify public support?
- *Economic decisions:* In what ways do households and businesses influence decisions about what goods and services are produced, how these commodities are produced, and for whom the goods and services are produced?
- *Political decisions:* Why are policies required to govern individual and societal behavior? And what theories and models assist our understanding of public policy-making processes?
- *A political-economic model:* How might the dynamic interaction of values and decisions about the provision of educational services be depicted?

It is not possible to fully understand the financing of elementary and secondary schooling without also understanding how decisions about school finance are made and how public and private resources are transformed into the realization of societal and individual aspirations for education. This chapter describes the functioning of the economic and political arenas in which those decisions are made and implemented. The chapter also addresses issues of when and how governments should become involved in the process. We begin with a discussion of the theory of human capital, which considers expenditures on education a long-term investment and links that investment to the economic well-being of a nation. This theory provides one of the major rationales for placing education high on the public policy agenda.

THE THEORY OF HUMAN CAPITAL

Classical economists attributed physical output to three factors of production: land, labor, and capital. Modern economists have either treated land as a constant or subsumed it under capital, leaving labor and capital as the variables in their formulas for predicting the gross production of an economy and for assessing its efficiency. Labor represents the human resource that goes into production. Capital refers to produced means of production, such as machinery, factory buildings, infrastructure, and computers.

In their analyses, modern economists had typically measured only the quantitative aspects of the two factors of production (that is, aggregate man-hours and aggregate machine-hours used in production). In effect they considered each factor to be qualitatively homogeneous. Theodore Schultz (1963, 1981), who received the Nobel Prize in economics in 1979 for his work with developing countries, challenged this assumption. He claimed that it is essential to see the heterogeneity of labor and capital and how they complement one another in production. He noted that particular forms of material capital increase the demand for particular human skills. Schultz's work sparked a renewed interest in human capital theory and focused attention on the economic importance of education. The human capital approach assumes that schooling endows individuals with knowledge and skills that enable them to be more productive and thereby receive higher earnings. This is, of course, beneficial to the individual. The accumulation of benefits all workers derive is beneficial to society as a whole through greater total production, higher tax yields, and spillover benefits that contribute to a generally improved quality of life for all.

Schultz (1963, p. viii) observed that the concepts commonly in use at the time to "measure capital and labor were close to being empty in explaining the increases in production that occur over time." He was referring to the fact that quantitative increases in labor and physical capital explained less than one-third of the rate of economic growth in the United States between 1929 and 1957 and that the trend of their explanatory power was downward.

Schultz attempted to explain the cause of the remaining two-thirds of growth, called "the residual." Schultz drew an analogy between additions of stock to physical capital and increases in the amount of education available in the population at large. Schultz's (1963) thesis was that traditional measures of labor and capital understated the true investment. He concluded that the unexplained economic growth "originates out of forms of capital that have not been measured and consists mainly of human capital. . . . [T]he economic capabilities of man are predominantly a produced means of production and . . . most of the differences in earnings are a consequence of differences in the amounts that have been invested in people" (pp. 64–65).

Schultz was not the first to observe the relationship between earnings and personal skills. Indeed, the concept of human capital has been recognized as an essential force for economic progress since the beginning of economics as a field of study. In his *Wealth of Nations,* published in 1776, Adam Smith included this concept in his definition of fixed capital. In referring to the acquired abilities of all members of the society, he wrote (Smith, 1993):

> The acquisition of such talents, by the maintenance of the acquirer during his education, study, or apprenticeship, always costs a real expense, which is a capital fixed and realized, as it were, in his person. Those talents, as they make a part of his fortune, so do they likewise of that of the society to which he belongs. The improved dexterity of a workman may be considered in the same light as a machine or instrument of trade which facilitates and abridges labour, and which, though it costs a certain expense, repays that expense with a profit. (p. 166)

Smith (1993, p. 98) concluded, "The difference between the wages of skilled labour and those of common labour is founded upon this principle."

Despite the early recognition of the concept of human capital, and of education as a formal means for developing it, the investment aspects of education were almost completely neglected by economists through the nineteenth and the first half of the twentieth centuries (Blaug, 1970). Alfred Marshall, in his *Principles of Economics* (1948; first published in 1890), rejected the notion of including the acquired skills of a population as part of the wealth or capital of an economy. He did this because of the difficulties presented in measuring it. He did, however, accept Smith's analogy of an educated person being like an expensive machine. He claimed that the motives that induce people to invest principal capital *in* their children's education are similar to those that inspire the accumulation of material capital *for* their children (Marshall, 1890/ 1961, p. 619). Marshall also supported the spending of public and private funds on the education of the masses. He felt that without it there would be an underinvestment in education as long as the financial means to acquire education were unequally distributed among the population.

In the twentieth century, Maynard Keynes linked national output to the behavior of households and enterprises as distinct economic agents. The precise nature of the goods purchased by these two agents was irrelevant to his purpose. This led to the widely held view that the contrast between consumption and investment depends on which agent makes the decision to purchase, rather than the type of good being purchased. Thus, national income accounting, an outgrowth of Keynesian macroeconomics, treats education as consumption. This is because it is an expenditure made by households or by government acting on their behalf using taxes collected from them (Blaug, 1970).

The current interest in human capital theory brings us full circle. In it, education is again treated as investment. Proponents of the theory, such as Schultz (1963), Becker (1964), Dennison (1962), and Kuznets (1966), have found satisfactory means for measuring investment in human capital. Their work has firmly established the importance of education as a vehicle of economic development and national economic policy.

EDUCATION: A PUBLIC AND A PRIVATE GOOD

It is consistent with human capital theory to view education as both a public and a private good because it brings important benefits for society as well as the individual. If public benefits were simply the sum of individual benefits, this would not constitute a problem; but this is not the case. Frequently there are substantial differences between societal and individual interests. As noted by Marshall, full public interest would not be realized if provision of education were left solely to private vendors and to the ability of individuals to pay for education. Conversely, it is unlikely that the full private or individual interest would be satisfied if education were left solely to public provision.

Private Goods

Private goods are divisible and their benefits are left primarily to their owners. If individuals desire a particular item or service, they can legally obtain it by negotiating an agreed-upon price with the current owner. The new owner can enjoy the item or service, but those unable or unwilling to pay the price cannot. A good is private if someone who does not pay for it can be excluded from its use and enjoyment. This is known as the exclusion principle. Such goods are readily provided through the market system, that is, the private sector.

The private (or individual) benefits of education, whether it is provided by the public or the private sector, include the ability to earn more money and to enjoy a higher standard of living and a better quality of life. As part of this, educated persons are likely to be employed at more interesting jobs than are less educated persons. Schooling opens up the possibility of more schooling. This in turn leads to even better employment possibilities. Long-term unemployment is much less likely. Similarly, educated persons, through knowledge and understanding of the arts and other manifestations of culture, and with greater resources at their disposal, are likely to have more options for the use of leisure time and are likely to use such time in more interesting ways. As informed consumers, they are likely to get more mileage out of their resources. Finally, better-educated persons are likely to enjoy a better diet and have better health practices. This is likely to result in less sickness and a longer productive life.

Public Goods

Public goods are indivisible, yielding large and widespread benefits to the community and to society as a whole. Because these benefits are such that they cannot be limited to individuals willing to pay the price, it is unlikely that they would be provided fully through the market system in a satisfactory fashion. In other words, "public" or "collective" goods are those that violate the exclusion principle. The public (or societal) benefits of publicly and privately provided education include enlightened citizenship, which is particularly important to a democratic form of government. In projecting a common set of values and knowledge, schools can foster a sense of community and national identity and loyalty among a diverse population. A public school system can provide an effective network for talent identification and development, spurring the creation of both cultural and technological innovations and providing the skilled workforce required for the efficient functioning of society. This results in more rapid economic growth, higher tax revenues, and a generally more vital and pleasant quality of life for everyone.

Conflicting Concerns

Structuring the decision-making process for education becomes particularly complex because education is both a public and a private good. Procuring educational services incurs costs and produces benefits that accrue to individuals independently. At the same time, it incurs social costs and produces benefits that accrue to society collectively. Levin (1987) concluded that there is a potential dilemma when schools are expected to provide both public and private benefits:

> Public education stands at the intersection of two legitimate rights: the right of a democratic society to assure its reproduction and continuous democratic functioning through providing a common set of values and knowledge and the right of families to decide the ways in which their children will be molded and the types of influences to which their children will be exposed. To the degree that families have different political, social, and religious beliefs and values, there may be a basic incompatibility between their private concerns and the public functions of schooling. (p. 629)

A century earlier, Marshall (1890/1961, p. 216) had observed, "There are few practical problems in which the economist has a more direct interest than those relating to the principles on which the expense of education of children should be divided between the State and the parents."

If education were clearly a private good, it could be provided through the market without governmental intervention. But having many attributes of a public good, education is provided through publicly controlled institutions as well as through the market. Education as presently provided in schools to groups of students or under individually developed plans resembles private free market provision in that any individual can be excluded. Yet taxes rather than user fees have been determined to be appropriate because of the social products and benefits described above. Pure private provision by user fees would probably mean that education services would be less available than is socially desirable. Public provision by taxation is called for when social benefits exceed private benefits. When private benefits predominate, then user fees or full-cost tuition becomes appropriate.

The next section describes how resource allocation decisions are made through the market. The section following that describes political processes through which such decisions are made by governments.

DECISION MAKING IN THE MARKETPLACE

Any society has to make certain fundamental economic decisions:

> *What* commodities are to be produced and in what quantities;
> *How* goods are to be produced; and,

For whom goods are to be produced. (Samuelson, 1980, p. 16)

People in a capitalistic economy prefer to make such decisions through unrestrained or self-regulating markets. Figure 1.1 illustrates the circular flow of a monetary economy between two sets of actors, households and producers (or enterprises, using Keynes's term). It is assumed that households own all resources (capital), whereas producers have the capacity of converting resources into finished goods and services. Households may own land and capital outright or as shareholders in a corporation. They also control the availability of their individual labor.

The Private Sector

The households and the producers each have something the other wants and needs. Producers need the resources controlled by households in order to produce finished goods and services. Households need the goods and services provided by the producers for survival in the case of food and shelter and for improved quality of life in the case of many other goods. To facilitate the exchange, markets provide a means of communication. Producers (e.g., private schools) acquire the resources they need through resource markets by making money income in the form of wages, rents,

interest, and profits available to households (which include persons qualified to be teachers, bus drivers, maintenance workers, etc.). Households in turn use the money acquired through the sale of resources to purchase finished goods and services (e. g., private schooling) in product markets. It is these sales that provide producers with money to purchase resources from the households. And so the cycle continues.

Through markets, households and producers negotiate prices to be paid for resources and finished goods and services. The outcomes of these negotiations ultimately determine the three economic issues raised above. Resources are scarce and unevenly distributed among households, while household wants are unlimited. This means that each household must prioritize its wants and satisfy as many of them as possible within the constraints of the resources it controls and the value of those resources. The value or price of resources (and products) depends upon supply and demand.

Figure 1.2 illustrates the interaction between supply and demand as related to the number of teachers schools employ and the amount they pay for their services. The demand curve shows that there is an inverse relationship between the level of teacher salaries and the number of teachers that school districts are willing to employ. Conversely,

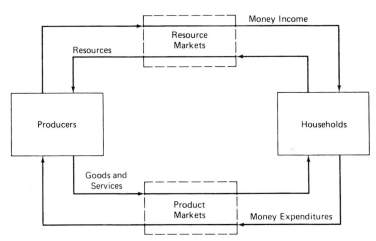

Figure 1.1. The Circular Flow of Resources in a Monetary Economy

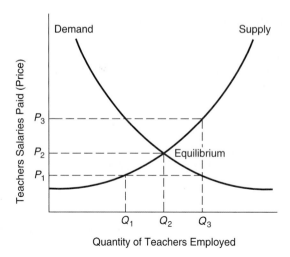

Figure 1.2. Supply and Demand Curves

the supply curve shows that the number of persons willing to take jobs as teachers is high when salaries are high and is low when salaries are low. Thus, if salaries are at P_1 as illustrated in Figure 1.2, there is a gap (Q_1 to Q_3) between the number of persons willing to work at that wage and the number of teachers school districts desire to employ. To close the gap, school districts must raise salaries to P_3 in order to attract the desired number of teachers (Q_3) or must strike a compromise whereby the number of teachers to be employed is reduced to Q_2, for example, and must raise the salaries it is willing to pay to P_2. This requires a shift in strategy for organizing schools in the district. One strategy is to substitute technology for teachers. As teacher salaries increase, technological substitutes become relatively less expensive. Thus, fewer teachers in large classes using sophisticated instructional technology may produce results similar to those of more teachers in small classes using little information technology. Alternatively, rather than purchase instructional technology, a district may provide low-cost teacher aids to assist teachers in managing their large classes.

In the private sector, producers will only produce that on which they can make a reasonable profit. Profit depends on the amount of a good or a service that is sold, the price, and the cost of production. If the demand for a product is not sufficient to sell all units produced at a price above the cost of production, the producer can make no profit. Under such circumstances, the producer has three options: reduce the cost of production through adopting more efficient means, shift production to another product that can be sold for a profit, or go out of business. When conditions permit an above-average profit for producing a given good, more producers are attracted into the field. The number of units produced increases to the point where supply equals demand. Competition forces prices down, returning the rate of profit to a normal range.

Each dollar controlled by each consuming household is a potential vote to be cast in favor of the production of one good or service over another or the product of one producer over the product of a competitor. The influence of a household over producers is directly proportional to the value of the resources controlled by the household. This poses ethical dilemmas about the distribution of wealth. The rich can make expenditures for improving the quality of their lives while the poor lack basic necessities. Also, development of highly efficient, low-cost technologies leads to reduction in the demand for labor, causing reductions in wages or widespread unemployment.

The Public Sector

We do not rely solely on market mechanisms to make economic decisions, however. Over 40 percent of our gross national product (GNP) is distributed according to political decisions made by governments, for example, municipalities and school districts. Important differences distinguish governmental units from households and producers in the ways they answer economic questions and the criteria they use in determining their answers. Downs (1957, p. 282) identified government as that agency in the division of labor that has as its proper function the maximization of social welfare. When results generated by free markets are ethically or economically unsatisfactory, government can be used as a tool of intervention to set things right (p. 292). Governments have the unique power to extract involuntary payments, called taxes, from households and producers alike. And the federal government controls the money supply on which both public and private sectors depend. Governmental programs and agencies are not profit oriented and they rarely go out of business. When they do go out of business, it is the result of political decisions and not of market forces, although conditions in the market may influence the political decision. Efficiency has not traditionally been an overriding objective of the public sector, as it is in the private sector. But growing numbers of persons think that it should be.

Figure 1.3 inserts government (the public sector) into the center of the circular flow of a monetary economy. Government interacts directly with both consumers and producers. Taxes flow from both and publicly provided goods and services flow to both. The government burden of taxes rests ultimately on consumers and producers. However, the government in purchasing goods and services (unless the purchased commodity is unique to the government, like battleships) buys in the existing markets like everyone else. So goods and services

come from the circular flow. Goods and services produced by governments that are final and collective, like defense and police, do not go into the flow, because collective goods are not distributed through the market. That is, they go to everyone or to no one. Other governmentally produced goods and services, like highways and education, do go into the flow because they are consumed individually and are intermediate products for final goods and services provided through the market.

In a free market economy, prices serve as signals to producers and consumers alike. In education, all producers and consumers, whether public or private, face the same factor prices. For example, the cost is the same regardless of sector for a given quality teacher or aid or for school supplies. Taxation is compulsory and reduces total demand in the private sector. When government budgets are balanced at full employment, government purchases do not affect overall prices. Prices for the specific goods purchased, however, may increase due to the change in demand. If the government is reckless in printing money (which only the federal government can do) or in borrowing for current operations (which, again, only the federal government can do), the resulting inflation from excess demand will distribute the burden of

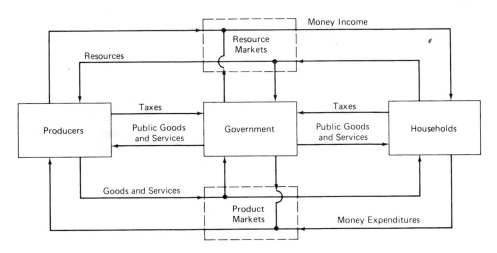

Figure 1.3. The Circular Flow of Resources, including Government (the public sector)

government in an unknown manner through inflation. Borrowing by governments can be justified only for assets lasting more than a year and, in the case of the federal government, when the economy is at less than full employment and needs stimulating.

Public sector decisions are political. Ideally, political power is distributed evenly among the electorate, that is, one person, one vote. Because the rich are better able to buy political influence through legal and illegal means, the ideal is only approximated and never realized. In the private sector, influence is distributed in direct proportion to the amount of resources controlled. Thus, the rich have much influence and the poor have little. Because of the difference in the distribution of influence over decisions made in the public and private sectors, there are marked differences between the sectors in the answers given to the three economic questions raised above. The greater relative power of the poor in the public sector when compared with the private sector leads to an equalitarian bias in decisions made in the public sector. The private sector has a libertarian bias to permit the exercise of individual preferences to the degree permitted by constrained resources.

In making decisions about education, natural tensions exist between households, members of the teaching profession, and society. To the extent that decisions are made in the private sector, individuals and families can maximize their personal aspirations within the limits of their economic resources and according to individual value preferences. Professionals are free to provide or to withhold services and to determine the nature of those services. But when decisions are made through the political process, individuals and groups of varying value orientations must negotiate a single solution. Their value preferences are likely to be compromised in the process.

Proponents of decentralizing and privatizing the educational bureaucracy (discussed in the next chapter), school-based decision making (discussed in Chapter 14), and family choice of schooling (discussed in Chapter 15) share the view that too many educational decisions are being made by

government. Some proponents believe that this has led to an unwarranted emphasis on social values such as equity, making the realization of a variety of privately held values through public education difficult. Others believe that governmental operation of public schools has resulted in the inefficient use of the resources committed. In contrast, supporters of governmental operation of schools fear that educational services will be even more inequitably distributed than they are now if schooling enterprises are privatized.

POLITICAL DECISION MAKING

Any functioning group, whether it is the United States government, a state government, a business or industry, a voluntary or charitable association, a local school district, or a school, needs to agree on a set of rules under which it will operate. These rules are called "policies." Policies include statutes in the case of government when they are formally adopted through a prescribed legislative process and local school board decisions that govern behavior of employees, students, and members of the general public. Rules and regulations generated by a government agency, including school officials, under authorization of a law are also considered policy.

The state and federal constitutions specify the formal procedures to be followed in adopting laws. But laws are usually written in quite broad terms and must be interpreted in order to be implemented. The interpretation begins with the bureau within the executive branch of government given the responsibility for administering the law, for example, state education departments and the U. S. Department of Education. Decisions made by bureaucrats to guide actions at lower levels of authority, and written in the form of regulations, are as much policy as the laws themselves. State law specifies general procedures to be followed by local school districts in formulating policy, although variation is permitted within prescribed limits. School districts may specify procedures to be followed by schools in setting policy. Or they may let the schools establish their own procedures subject to district review and approval. Private organizations may go through formal incorporation, which specifies a corporate procedure to be followed in making decisions. Or they may agree on a set of bylaws to guide corporate decision making. In the public sector, policies are usually (and preferably) written. Policies may, however, be informal, unwritten, and unstated agreements (norms) by which members of an organization bind their actions.

While constitutions, laws, charters, bylaws, and so forth spell out the formal steps to be followed in arriving at group decisions (that is, policy), the human interactions in carrying out those steps are not specified. Often these interactions involve elaborate strategies, power plays, and intrigue employed by individuals and subgroups bonded by common interests to shape an organization's (or government's) decisions. These interactions, whether simple or elaborate, can be referred to as "politics." Indeed, Hodgkinson (1983, p. 141) has referred to politics as "administration by another name." The nature of both the structure of the policy-making process and the politics employed within the structure are believed to influence policy outcomes (Dye, 1987).

There is no overarching general theory of political decision making. But there is a "grab bag" of heuristic theories and contrasting methods (Wirt and Kirst, 1982). Heuristic theory is a method of analytically separating and categorizing items in experience. Among the most useful theories for understanding policy relating to school governance are institutionalism, incrementalism, group theory, elite theory, rationalism, and systems theory. These theories and models are complementary to one another. Each emphasizes a particular aspect of the policy-making process. Taken together, they provide a rather complete picture of the total process. While these theories were developed primarily to describe policy formulation at the national level, they are fully applicable at the state level and can provide much insight in understanding the process of policy making at the school district and school building levels as well.

Institutionalism

Institutionalism focuses on the structure of the policy-making process (Elazar, 1972; Grodzins, 1966; Walker, 1981). Unlike most of the rest of the world, where education is a function of the national government, education governance in the United States is characterized by the primacy of state governments, with delegated power to school districts. On the positive side, this arrangement has produced educational systems that are quite diverse, dynamic, and responsive to local conditions. On the negative side, the structure has resulted in gross financial and curricular inequities. Some districts operate schools that are unequaled in quality throughout the world. Others operate schools that are an embarrassment to the profession and to the nation. The devolved nature of school governance has impeded state and federal efforts during the past several decades to equalize educational opportunities in terms of finance, curricular provision, and the integration of students and staff with respect to race and ethnicity.

But the structure of educational governance has changed over the years, and it continues to change. The change is reflected in Table 1.1, which shows the gradual increase of state and federal participation in the financing of public education and

TABLE 1.1. Revenue Sources for Public Elementary and Secondary Schools, 1920–1993

Year	Total Revenue in Thousands[a]	Sources as Percentage of Total		
		Local	State	Federal
1920	$970,121	83.2	16.5	0.3
1930	$2,088,557	82.7	16.9	0.4
1940	$2,260,527	68.0	30.3	1.8
1950	$5,437,044	57.3	39.8	2.9
1960	$14,746,618	56.5	39.1	4.4
1970	$40,266,923	52.1	39.9	8.0
1980	$96,881,165	43.4	46.8	9.8
1990	$207,752,932	46.6	47.3	6.1
1993	$258,800,000	47.4	45.6	6.9

[a]In current dollars. (SOURCE: National Center for Education Statistics [1995]. *The Condition of Education* 1995. Washington, DC: U.S. Department of Education.)

the decrease in reliance on local resources. Although financial support for schools is now shared nearly equally between state governments and school districts, schools are still operated by school districts. But state and federal grants-in-aid have become significant factors of influence in shaping district policies.

The growing participation by state and federal governments in the financing of schools parallels their growing interest in and influence over educational policy in general. State governments have become particularly active in the prescription of basic curricula, monitoring student progress through mandatory testing programs and the certification of teachers (Darling-Hammond & Barry, 1988; Elmore & McLaughlin, 1988). State education departments and the U. S. Department of Education have increased in size and influence (Moore, Goertz, & Hartle, 1983; Murphy, 1982).

According to Wirt and Kirst (1982, p. v), "The 1970s will be remembered as an era when the previous hallmark of American education—local control—became fully a myth." Local superintendents have lost their once-preeminent position in setting the school district agenda and controlling decision outcomes. The discretionary range of superintendents and school boards has been narrowed at the top by federal and state action and at the bottom through collective bargaining with employee unions. The more recent trend toward school-based management is narrowing the range even further. Nevertheless, local school districts continue to exert a considerable, though declining, amount of influence on educational policy (Odden & Marsh, 1989).

Other structural changes in political institutions are taking place that will have an impact on the decision-making process and the ultimate nature of the decisions made. Small districts have consolidated, and large districts have decentralized. Progress is being made toward the professionalization of teaching. The practice of letting parents choose the schools their children attend is gaining in popularity. The adoption of policies such as educational vouchers and tax credits will further change the face of educational governance, increasing the role of private providers. The recent changes in the school governance structures in Chicago (Hess, 1991) and Kentucky (Guskey, 1994) are dramatic examples of the contemporary belief that the nature of the decision-making structure of an institution influences the quality of its decisions and the efficiency of its operations.

Systems Theory

The most comprehensive of the models represents an application of systems theory to the political process. A system is made up of a number of elements that are interrelated. An open system, characteristic of political systems, draws resources from its environment, processes them in some fashion, and returns the processed resources to the environment. All systems tend toward entropy, or disorganization, and they must consciously combat this tendency in order to maintain equilibrium. A key function for combating entropy is feedback, that is, continual monitoring of a system's internal operations and its relationship with the environment. Accurate feedback is particularly critical to a system's health in that the system depends upon the environment for resources without which the system would shrink and die. Equilibrium is maintained by modifying or adapting system structures and processes based on analysis of feedback (cybernetics). Maintaining equilibrium is a dynamic process leading to growth and evolution of the system in harmony with its environment.

Easton (1965) adapted general systems theory to political systems. His model, illustrated in Figure 1.4, conceptualizes public policy as a response of a political system to forces from the environment. Environmental pressures or inputs come in the forms of (1) demands for public action through interest groups and (2) support of government by individuals and groups through obeying laws, paying taxes, and accepting outcomes of elections. The inputs are processed through the political system and transformed into policy outputs. Political systems consist of sets of identifiable and interrelated

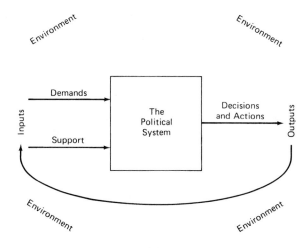

Figure 1.4. A Simplified Model of a Political System. (SOURCE: D. Easton. [1965]. *A Systems Analysis of Political Life.* Chicago: University of Chicago Press, p. 32. Copyright 1965 by University of Chicago Press. Reprinted by permission.)

institutions and activities at all levels, such as those associated with the U. S. Congress, state and county legislatures, common councils, town councils, village boards, school boards, commissions, authorities, and courts. Feedback in a political system is both formal and informal. Formal feedback is provided through elections, referenda, hearings, and policy analysis. Informal feedback occurs through personal interactions with constituents and others.

Incrementalism

Lindblom (1959) described the public policy process in the United States as a continuation of past government activities with only incremental modifications. He insightfully labeled the process "muddling through." While some deplore his exaltation of the process, one of his most ardent critics credits him with presenting "a well considered theory fully geared to the actual experience of practicing administrators" (Dror, 1964, p. 153).

Lindblom (1968, p. 32) took issue with the popular view that politics is a process of conflict resolution. He argued that "governments are instruments for vast tasks of social cooperation" and that "conflicts are largely those that spring from the opportunities for cooperation that have evolved once political life becomes orderly." Within this context, he described the play of power as a process of cooperation among specialists. It is gamelike, normally proceeding according to implicitly accepted rules. "Policy analysis is incorporated as an instrument or weapon into the play of power, changing the character of analysis as a result" (Lindblom, 1968, p. 30).

The focus of the play of power is on means (policy), not ends (goals or objectives). This, according to Lindblom, is what permits the political system to work. Because of the overlap in value systems among interested groups and the uncertainty of the outcome of any course of action, partisans across the value spectrum are able to come to agreement on means where agreement on ends would be impossible.

Since agreement on goal priorities is impossible in a pluralistic society, according to Lindblom (1968, p. 33), the type of analysis appropriate to the political process is termed "partisan analysis." It is analysis conducted by advocates (organized interest groups) of a relatively limited set of values or ends, such as teacher associations, taxpayer groups, and religious and patriotic organizations. Comprehensiveness is provided by the variety of partisans participating in the political process. The responsibility for promoting specific values thus lies in the hands of advocates of those values (pressure groups and lobbyists), and not in the hands of some "impartial" analyst (as would be the case with rationalism, to be discussed later).

The net result of this advocacy process is incremental rather than revolutionary changes in policy. In light of our grand state of ignorance about the relationships between public policy and human behavior, Lindblom viewed incremental policy decisions as being well justified. Incrementalism permits the expansion of policies that prove successful, while limiting the harm caused by unsuccessful policies. Within the context of strategic planning, incrementalism can assure that each increment leads toward desired goals, while minimizing organizational disruption. Incrementalism preserves the system while changing it.

In the next two sections we discuss group theory and elite theory. Both provide explanations of how incrementalism may work in practice.

Group Theory

Truman (1951), a leading proponent of group theory, saw politics as the interaction among groups (as opposed to individuals) in the formulation of public policy. Individuals band together into formal or informal groups, similar to Lindblom's partisans, to confront government with their demands. The group is the vehicle through which individuals can influence government action. Even political parties are viewed as coalitions of interest groups. Elected and appointed officials are seen as being continually involved in bargaining and negotiating with relevant groups to work out compromises that balance interests.

Group theory, as portrayed by Dye (1987), is illustrated in Figure 1.5. Public policy at any point in time represents the equilibrium of the balance of power among groups. Because the power alignment is continually shifting (e.g., toward Group B, in Figure 1.5, as it gains supporters or partners in coalition on a particular issue), the fulcrum of equilibrium also shifts, leading to incremental changes in policy (in the direction desired by Group B, as illustrated).

Stability in the system is attributed to a number of factors. First, most members of the electorate are latent supporters of the political system and share in its inherent values, similar in concept to Easton's input assumptions. This latent group is generally inactive, but can be aroused to defend the system against any group that attacks it. Second, there is a great deal of overlap in the membership of groups; a given individual is likely to be a member of several. This tends to have a damp-

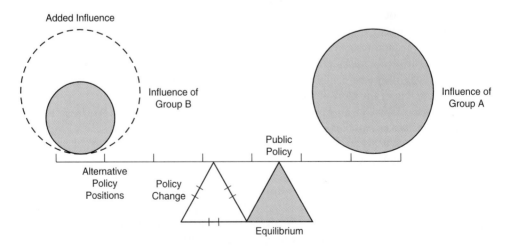

Figure 1.5. Group Theory Model. (SOURCE: T. R. Dye. [1987]. *Understanding Public Policy* [6th ed.]. Englewood Cliffs, NJ: Prentice Hall, p. 27. Reprinted by permission of Prentice Hall, Inc., Englewood Cliffs, NJ.)

ening effect with respect to any group taking extreme positions because, while the group may be focused on a single issue, its membership is much more broadly oriented. The third factor promoting system stability results from group competition. No single group constitutes a majority in American society. Coalitions are easily formed to counter the influence of any group appearing to gain undue influence. As a result, the political process is characterized by evolution, as in incrementalism, rather than revolution.

Elite Theory

Elite theory focuses on actions by a select group of influential elite citizens. Elite theory (Dye & Zeigler, 1981) characterizes the general public as apathetic, ill informed, and uninterested in public policy—not unlike the characterization of the latent group in group theory. This leaves a power vacuum that is happily filled by an elite. The elites do more to shape the opinion of the masses on public issues than the general public does to shape the opinions of the elite, although influence is reciprocal (e.g., civil rights legislation, Dye, 1987, chap. 3). According to this theory, the elites develop policy among the trappings of democratic government.

Elites tend to come from upper socioeconomic levels. They are not necessarily against the general welfare of the masses, as evidenced in the case of civil rights legislation. But they approach the welfare of the masses through a sense of noblesse oblige. While not agreeing on all issues, the elite share a consensus on basic social values and on the importance of preserving the system. The masses give superficial support to this consensus, which provides a basis for elite rule. When events occur that threaten the system, elites move to take corrective action. According to elite theory, changes in public policy come about when elites redefine their own positions, sometimes as a result of external pressures. Because elites maintain a conservative posture with respect to preserving the system, policy changes tend to be incremental.

Rationalism

Adherents of rationalism seek to shape the policy-making process so as to assure the enactment of policies that maximize social gain. According to Dror (1968), the assumptions of pure rationality are deeply rooted in modern civilization and culture and are the basis of certain economic theories of the free market and political theories of democracy. He characterized the pure rationality model as having six phases that are organized sequentially in Figure 1.6:

1. Establishing a complete set of operational goals, with relative weights allocated to the different degrees to which each may be achieved.
2. Establishing a complete inventory of other values and of resources, with relative weights.
3. Preparing a complete set of alternative policies open to the policy maker.
4. Preparing a complete set of valid predictions of the costs and benefits of each alternative, including the extent to which each will achieve the various operational goals, consume resources, and realize or impair other values.
5. Calculating the net expectation of each alternative by multiplying the probability of each benefit and cost for each alternative by the utility of each, and calculating the net benefit (or cost) in utility units.
6. Comparing the net expectations and identifying the alternative (or alternatives, if two or more are equally good) with the highest net expectation. (p. 132)

In theory, rationalism involves all individual, social, political, and economic values, not just those that can be converted to dollars and cents. In reality, measurement difficulties make inclusion of values other than economic values unlikely. Thus, this model elevates economic efficiency above other potential societal objectives, such as equity and liberty.

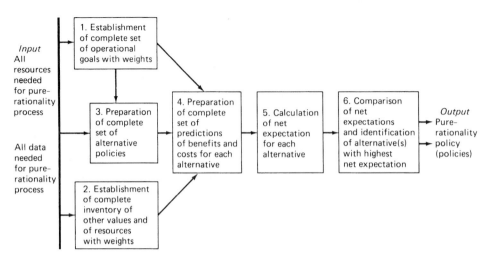

Figure 1.6. The Phases of Pure-Rationality Policy Making. (SOURCE: Y. Dror. [1968]. *Public Policymaking Reexamined.* San Francisco: Chandler, p. 134.)

Political realists argue that decisions in the public sector, including public education, are made on the basis of political rationality rather than economic rationality. To them, rationalism is at best irrelevant and can be downright dysfunctional to the political process (Schultz, 1968). To "know" all that would be required to select a policy "rationally," that is, all of society's value preferences and relative weights, all available policy alternatives, and the consequences of each alternative, is what Lindblom (1959, p. 88) termed "superhuman comprehensiveness." In essence, rationalism attempts the impossible by quantifying all elements of the political process and human behavior and expressing the decision-making function in mathematical terms (Lavoie, 1985). Wise (1979) referred to persistent bureaucratic rationalization when the relationship between means and ends is not known as "hyperrationalization," that is, an effort to rationalize beyond the bounds of knowledge. While imperfect, the representative legislature (e.g., school boards and Congress) is a political mechanism for approximating "all of society's value preferences and relative weights."

Rational techniques that are based on economic principles and procedures should be an important factor in budget development. However, Cibulka (1987) found that rationalism played a relatively small role even here. Wildavsky (1964) also argued that pure rationality is an illusion. He emphasized the political nature of the budgetary process:

> If one looks at politics as a process by which the government mobilizes resources to meet pressing problems, then the budget is the focus of these efforts. . . . In the most integral sense, the budget lies at the heart of the political process. (pp. 4–5)

Similar conclusions resulted from studies of factors influencing school district resource allocation decisions by Bigenwald (1977), Demmin (1978), and Hitzges (1988). They found socioeconomic status, crises, and aggressive professionals and laity were determining forces in budget construction.

Rationalism was a key principle behind the comprehensive centralized planning schemes of socialist and communist countries. With the collapse of many of the latter, and with the routine failure of five-year plans in socialist—mostly developing—countries, rationalism has lost much of its credibility (Agarawala, 1984; Carlson & Awkerman, 1991; Weiler, 1980).

Nevertheless, rationalistic philosophy has had an important impact on policy analysis, and indirectly on policy decision making. Its bias of economic efficiency is a value that is all too frequently neglected in the traditional political process. The spirit of rationalism has fostered such management devices as Planning Programming Budgeting Systems (PPBS), Zero Based Budgeting (ZBB), Management by Objectives (MBO), and Operations Research (OR), as well as cost-benefit and cost-effectiveness analysis. The terms "accountability" and "assessment" are now a part of the schooling vernacular, and teacher, pupil, and program evaluations are accepted procedures. Local school boards and state and federal governments are adding to their long-standing concerns over the quantity and quality of school inputs a similar concern over school outputs through mandatory evaluation and testing programs, that is, "standards-based education." They do all of this with the intent of introducing greater economic rationality into decisions about education and schooling.

Unlike incrementalism, which focuses on means, rationalism requires agreement on outcomes, which is unlikely in pluralistic organizations (e.g., state and federal governments and large urban school districts). Because of the reduced number of conflicting interest groups at the school level (this may also be the case with small, homogeneous school districts), such agreement is frequently obtained, and rationalism can become functional at that level.

SHOULD GOVERNMENTS INTERVENE?

To this point, we have sketched the functioning of the economic and political systems separately and have indicated likely differences in decisions made in the two sectors. Each sector is capable of answering the policy issues posed. But as already noted, as individuals and as a society, we would probably be quite unhappy with the results if *all* decisions were made through either sector acting alone. Given the general preference of a capitalis-tic society for the private sector as a venue for making decisions, we would like now to address the matter of when governments should intervene in private-sector decision making and how they should intervene.

Eckstein (1967) identified four situations where market mechanisms fail and where government intervention is necessary: collective goods, external economies (that is, divergence between private and social costs or benefits), extraordinary risks, and natural monopolies. We discussed education as a collective or public good earlier.

External Economies

The market works well when the prices charged reflect the total costs involved in producing goods or services. There are instances, however, where a producer can escape paying the full cost of production, with the consumer benefiting in terms of lower prices, or where a producer cannot charge the full value of what is produced. These are known as external economies, or diseconomies. When external economies occur, the good or service is not fully provided by the private sector; education is a case in point. While there are profit incentives to provide for educational programs with a specific focus, such as occupational education and college preparation, there are few profit incentives to provide for universal education in the private sector—especially for the poor and the disabled.

External economies are illustrated by paper manufacturing. Without environmental protection legislation, paper manufacturers were likely to dump highly toxic waste generated by the manufacturing process into adjacent rivers and streams, killing wildlife and fouling the air. Requiring the detoxification of waste before returning it to the environment increases the cost of production and raises the cost of paper to the consumer. Before protective legislation, manufacturers were able to escape paying a portion of the true costs of production. Part of the price was paid by those living in the environs of the mill in the form of low quality of life and low property values because of the pollution.

Similarly, when pupils drop out or are forced out of school, there is a high probability that they will become wards of society in one form or another. They are much less likely to be regularly employed than are persons who complete their schooling and are more likely to receive governmental assistance in the form of unemployment insurance payments, welfare, and medicaid. School dropouts are also more likely to turn to lives of crime and be incarcerated in penal institutions. The resources some school districts save by not fully educating such persons are lost many times over by society at large in providing social services later in life. These are financed largely at the federal and state levels.

Until intervention by federal and state governments, many persons with severe mental and physical disabilities were denied access to schooling because of the high cost of special education. This meant that they were institutionalized for their entire lives. Now, having access to schooling, many are able to work and live independently or with minimal supervision. The increased expenditures for education are paying dividends in terms of lower costs for social services and a better quality of life for persons with disabling conditions.

Extraordinary Risks

"Extraordinary risks" refers to situations where the probable payoff on investment is low. The development of atomic energy, space exploration, and cancer research are examples. Investments in research on learning, teaching, and curriculum may also fall into this category. The growing global economy requires investment in retraining low-skilled workers to prevent the development of a permanent underclass as a result of free trade agreements.

Natural Monopoly

A natural monopoly is an enterprise enjoying a continually falling cost curve. In other words, the cost of producing a unit becomes less and less as the number of units produced or served increases. Thus, because of economies of scale, the largest firm has a distinct competitive advantage, eventually driving smaller firms out of business. Electricity, gas, and water utilities are examples. The technology governing most businesses and industries is such, however, that economies of scale are realized only up to a point. Then diseconomies of scale set in, that is, the cost per unit increases as the number of units produced or serviced increases. This produces a U-shaped cost curve, nullifying any advantage of large firms over small ones and preserving competition.

Many mistakenly believe that there are substantial economies of scale in providing educational services. Such misperception is a primary motivation of school consolidation policies. But in reality, economies of scale affect only the very smallest of schools and school districts, as demonstrated in Chapter 13. Despite this, schooling has been organized as a near public monopoly.

Other Reasons for Intervention

Governmental intervention also takes place for other reasons. The federal government has assumed a responsibility for controlling business cycles and inflation, and to a limited extent, the redistribution of wealth. Schooling and training frequently become means through which such control is exercised. All governments use the power of eminent domain: They can force the sale of private property for public use, as in the construction of interstate highways—or schools.

IF THERE IS GOVERNMENT INTERVENTION, HOW MIGHT IT OCCUR?

Once the decision for intervention is made, there are numerous modes of intervention. Public schools are currently owned and operated by government. So are police and fire departments and the United States armed forces. Ownership is not the typical type of governmental intervention, however. Governments may also oversee the public interest through regulation, licensure, taxation, subsidies, transfer payments, and contracts.

Most communication systems, utilities, and intercity transportation enterprises in the United States are privately owned, yet they are carefully monitored and regulated. Restaurants are regularly inspected for health code violations. Governments license professionals, although most professionals work in the private sector, an important exception being teachers. Private schools and home schooling are regulated by state government.

Governments can attempt to influence human behavior by changing the price paid for specific items through subsidies or taxation. Governments discourage the consumption of cigarettes, alcoholic beverages, and gasoline through excise taxes that increase the cost to consumers with the intent of reducing demand. On the other hand, the government may pay subsidies to farmers to encourage them to increase (or decrease) production of specific products, or to businesses to enable them to remain in operation in the face of foreign competition. Similarly, subsidies and scholarships that reduce the cost of higher education encourage families and individuals to pursue education beyond high school. Complete subsidization makes universal elementary and secondary education possible.

Governments also contract for services from private companies. Federal, state, and local governments rely on contractors to build their buildings, highways, and parks. While the federal government coordinates space exploration, privately contracted vendors conduct research and development and manufacture space vehicles. During periods of rapid enrollment increases, school districts may rent or lease space from private vendors. Instead of providing their own services, many school districts contract with private vendors for transportation, cleaning, and cafeteria operations. Recently some school districts have contracted for the operation of individual schools, for specific administrative services, and in a couple of cases, for the administration of the entire business of the district.

The government meets many of its responsibilities through transfer payments to individuals. Social Security, Aid for Dependent Children (i.e.,

welfare), unemployment insurance, food stamps, and educational vouchers are examples. Through transfer payments, the government can equalize the distribution of resources while permitting the individual maximum discretion as to how to use the funds. For example, prior to Social Security, elderly indigents were institutionalized in facilities owned and operated by local government—as are schools. Now, with monthly payments from the Social Security system, recipients have many options open to them, such as living in their own homes, smaller apartments, retirement communities in the Sun Belt, residences for the elderly, and nursing homes, as well as living with relatives. The public policy of providing all citizens with at least a subsistence living standard is realized without prescribing their lifestyles. The GI Bill, which paid the tuition of World War II and Korean War veterans to postsecondary institutions without limitation to public institutions, is an example of education vouchers. A few states are beginning to make limited use of vouchers at the elementary and secondary level.

A POLITICAL-ECONOMIC MODEL OF EDUCATION DECISION MAKING

In studying the merits of alternative decision-making structures for education, it is useful to examine the issues needing to be addressed according to the interests and expertise of the potential decision makers, that is, individuals (or families), the teaching profession, and society. Regardless of who makes the decisions, there are five broad areas in which educational policy must be formulated (Benson, 1978):

1. Setting goals and objectives for the educational enterprise
2. Determining for whom educational services are to be provided
3. Determining the level of investment in population quality (for example, education) to promote economic growth and the general welfare

4. Allocating resources to and among educational services

5. Determining the means by which educational services are to be provided

These five policy areas represent an elaboration of the three fundamental economic decisions we discussed earlier in this chapter. The five policy areas and the three categories of decision makers (society, the teaching profession, and families) are represented as a matrix in Figure 1.7.

The potential concern of each group of decision makers extends to each of the issues, although the actual level of interest and expertise of a given group will vary from issue to issue. Societal concerns are expressed by individuals and interest groups and are moderated through the political process of government, including school boards, and through the formation of coalitions, such as those now negotiating national curricula and standards and procedures for the national certification of teachers. Societal concerns take precedence over family and professional concerns for those issues in education in which there is significant spillover

Type of Issue	Decision Makers		
	Society	Profession	Family
Set Goals and Objectives			
Allocate Resources			
Produce Services			
Distribute Services			
Make Investments			

Figure 1.7. Education Decision Matrix Showing General Policy Areas and Potential Decision Makers

of benefits ("collective" or "public" goods) and in which there are redistributive considerations (shifting of wealth and benefits from one group to another).

The teaching profession (including administrators and other certified personnel) holds the technical expertise for schooling, and as employees of the education system(s), it has a vested interest in the conditions of employment. Teachers, along with other members of the polity, participate in general elections and referenda and the related political activities accompanying them. Professional educators also have a very strong impact on public policy through the lobbying activities of their unions and professional associations. Lobbyists for the National Education Association (NEA) and the American Federation of Teachers (AFT) are particularly effective at the state and national levels. At the local level, in addition to serving on various school district advisory committees, teachers and administrators greatly influence education policy through the collective bargaining process (Bacharach & Shedd, 1989; Mitchell, 1989).

Parents are the guardians of the interests and needs of individual children. The family usually has the most intimate knowledge about and caring concern for the child. It is usually through the family that the child's voice is heard (Bridge, 1976; Coons & Sugarman, 1978). In addition to participating in school board elections and referenda, individual parents may approach school board members, school administrators, or teachers directly to express their concerns. They may also align themselves with other parents holding similar concerns, forming such associations as the Parents and Teachers Association (PTA) and the Council for Basic Education (CBE), which direct their activities largely at influencing state and federal policy. Other parent groups focus on the needs of children with special conditions, such as the emotionally disturbed, physically disabled, or intellectually gifted.

Organizations such as the League of Women Voters and the American Association of University Women embrace education issues as a continuing secondary concern. Other organizations attempt to influence educational policy as a means of accomplishing ends that transcend the school. These might include taxpayers' groups or groups with a specific political agenda, such as civil rights, affirmative action, abortion rights or the right to life, environmental protection, or the promotion of patriotism, religious fundamentalism, and so forth.

The decision matrix presented in Figure 1.7 is one way of characterizing the political-economic system. As a vehicle for synthesizing the political

and economic theories discussed above, we now take that matrix and place it within Easton's (1965) simplified model of a political system. The result is Figure 1.8. The decision matrix, in its new context, is called "The Political-Economic System." Social values and goals (of multiple interest groups) are treated as "demand" inputs to the policy-making process in the new model. Other demand inputs include existing knowledge (for example, the professional expertise of teachers and administrators)

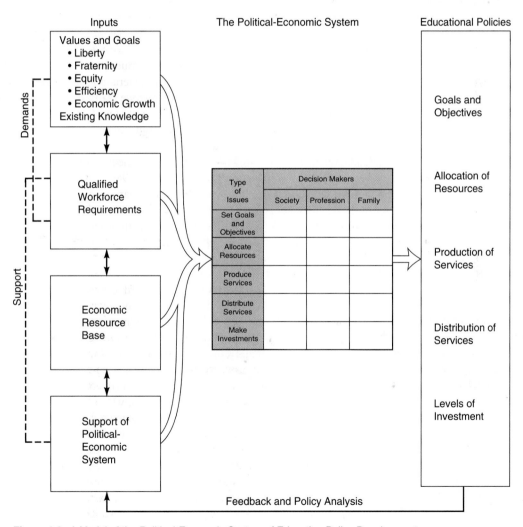

Figure 1.8. A Model of the Political-Economic System of Education Policy Development

and requirements for a qualified workforce. The latter requirement is at the same time a support input in that trained personnel (teachers and administrators) are required to implement any educational policies that are made. Indeed, the qualifications of available labor strongly influence which educational policy alternatives are feasible and which are not. Other support inputs are the economic base from which resources must be drawn to provide for implementation and the behavior of citizens in general that sustains the political-economic system. The outcomes of the process are educational policies, categorized in Figure 1.8 according to the five types of issues that were addressed through the sociopolitical process. The policies are a composite of decisions made by society, the profession, and the family.

In Chapter 2 we will return to the model and trace the evolution of power and authority over education in the United States and the resulting shift in public policy. We also use the model as a basis for comparing current power allocation patterns in the United States, England, Australia, and New Zealand. This model serves as a framework for examining alternative policies throughout the book and for developing a set of guides to school finance policy we discuss in Chapter 18.

SUMMARY

In this chapter we have described the processes by which decisions about school finance are made in the public sector by government and in the private sector by individuals and groups engaging one another in the marketplace. We began the chapter with a discussion of human capital theory. This theory offers an explanation of why individuals are motivated to invest in themselves and in their children to improve their marketable knowledge and skills. Because of the spillover benefits derived from human capital, and because many do not have sufficient resources to invest in their own education, human capital theory also provides a rationale for public intervention on behalf of those without sufficient resources. Thus, we showed that education has attributes of a private good, subject to the exclusion principle, and of a public good with indivisible benefits.

We identified five education issues that any society must answer either through the political process of government or through market transactions. These are setting goals and objectives for the system, determining for whom to provide services, deciding the level of investment in population quality, allocating resources among educational services, and determining the means by which to produce educational services. We presented a political-economic model to portray the process. This chapter provided guidelines for deciding whether a service should be provided by government or by private means. We also discussed a number of alternative strategies for governmental intervention.

In Chapter 2, we give further attention to the optimal distribution of power for making decisions about the allocation of resources to and within education functions and to the influence of value priorities on the process. Figure 1.8, a model of the political-economic system of education policy formulation, will serve as the structure for the discussion. We give particular emphasis to five value perspectives: liberty, equality, fraternity, efficiency, and economic growth. We will compare the reform movement in the United States with those in England, Australia, and New Zealand within the framework of the model.

ACTIVITIES

1. Identify the attributes of education that are in the nature of consumption and those that are in the nature of investment.
2. Identify the attributes of education that make it a public good and those that make it a private good.

   a. List separately the public and private benefits of education.
   b. Are any public benefits derived from private schools? If so: (1) What are they? (2) Can public financing of private schools be justified to the extent of the value of those public benefits?

3. Describe the process by which fundamental economic decisions about education are made.

  a. What groups are involved in making the fundamental economic decisions with respect to education listed on pp. 19–20?

  b. How might schools be organized to serve more efficiently the needs of:

- students with no severe impediments to learning?
- children with handicapping conditions?
- gifted children?
- adults?
- preschool children?

  c. What policies would be needed to facilitate the implementation of the school organizations described in activity 3b?

4. Discuss the strategies that are available to government for intervening in issues of financing, organizing, and distributing educational services.

  a. Do conditions anticipated for the 21st century justify the continuation of today's near public monopoly in the provision of elementary and secondary education? List separately the arguments supporting affirmative and negative responses to the question.

  b. What alternative structures have been proposed for organizing elementary and secondary education in the future? Which, if any, do you consider the most viable? Why?

5. Study political decision making at the local level with respect to education.

  a. Interview your superintendent of schools or members of your board of education about how education policy is developed and who influences the process in your school district.

  b. On the basis of information you gather in the above interview(s), describe situations that illustrate each of the policy-making models identified on page 11.

6. Identify aspects of education in which greater understanding is required, but in which private investment is unlikely because of uncertain payoff.

  a. Does research on teaching, learning, and curriculum development represent an activity in which the probable payoff of private investment is so low as to justify governmental involvement? List the arguments in support of your response.

  b. Ideally, how should education research be organized and financed?

REFERENCES

Agarawala, R. (1984). *Planning in developing countries: Lessons of experience* (World Bank staff working papers, No. 576). Washington, DC: The World Bank.

Bacharach, S. B., & Shedd, J. B. (1989). Power and empowerment: The constraining myths and emerging structures of teacher unionism. In J. Hannaway & R. Crowson (Eds.), *The politics of reforming school administration* (pp. 139–160). New York: Falmer.

Becker, G. S. (1964). *Human capital: A theoretical and empirical analysis, with special reference to education.* New York: National Bureau of Economic Research.

Benson, C. S. (1961). *The economics of public education.* Boston: Houghton Mifflin.

Benson, C. S. (1978). *The economics of public education* (3rd ed.). Boston: Houghton Mifflin.

Bigenwald, M. M. (1977). *An extension of Thorstein Veblen's "The Theory of the Leisure Class" to contemporary consumption of educational services.* Unpublished doctoral dissertation, State University of New York at Buffalo.

Blaug, M. (1970). *An introduction to the economics of education.* Middlesex, England: Penguin Books, Harmondsworth.

Bridge, R. G. (1976). Parent participation in school innovations. *Teachers College Record, 77,* 366–384.

Carlson, R. V., & Awkerman, G. (Eds.). (1991). *Educational planning: Concepts, strategies, and practices.* New York: Longman.

Cibulka, J. G. (1987). Theories of education budgeting: Lessons from the management of decline. *Educational Administration Quarterly, 23,* 7–40.

Coons, J. E., & Sugarman, S. D. (1978). *Education by choice: The case for family control.* Berkeley, CA: University of California Press.

Darling-Hammond, L., & Barry, B. (1988). *The evolution of teacher policy* (Report No. JRE-01). Santa Monica, CA: The RAND Corporation.

Demmin, P. E. (1978). *Incrementalism in school budgeting: Patterns and preference ordering in resource allo-*

cation. Unpublished doctoral dissertation, State University of New York at Buffalo.

Dennison, E. F. (1962). *The sources of economic growth in the United States.* New York: Committee for Economic Development.

Downs, A. (1957). *An economic theory of democracy.* New York: Harper & Row.

Dror, Y. (1964). Muddling through—"science" or inertia? *Public Administration Review, 24,* 153–157.

Dror, Y. (1968). *Public policy making reexamined.* San Francisco: Chandler.

Dye, T. R. (1987). *Understanding public policy* (6th ed.). Englewood Cliffs, NJ: Prentice Hall.

Dye, T. R., and Zeigler, H. (1981). *The irony of democracy.* Monterey, CA: Brooks Cole.

Easton, D. A. (1965). *A systems analysis of political life.* Chicago: University of Chicago Press.

Eckstein, O. (1967). *Public finance* (2nd ed.). Englewood Cliffs, NJ: Prentice Hall.

Elazar, D. J. (1972). *American Federalism.* New York: Harper & Row.

Elmore, R. F., & McLaughlin, M. W. (1988). *Steady work: Policy, practice, and the reform of American education* (Report No. R-3574-NIE/RC). Santa Monica, CA: The RAND Corporation.

Grodzins, M. (1966). *The American system.* Chicago: Rand McNally.

Guskey, T. R. (Ed.). (1994). *High stakes performance assessment: Perspectives on Kentucky's educational reform.* Thousand Oaks, CA: Corwin.

Hess, G. A., Jr. (1991). *School restructuring, Chicago style.* Thousand Oaks, CA: Corwin.

Hitzges, R. A. (1988). *Analyzing professional staff allocation decision process in selected public schools.* Unpublished doctoral dissertation, State University of New York at Buffalo.

Hodgkinson, C. (1983). *The philosophy of leadership.* Oxford, England: Basil Blackwell.

Kuznets, S. (1966). *Modern economic growth.* New Haven, CT: Yale University Press.

Lavoie, D. (1985). *National economic planning: What is left?* Cambridge, MA: Ballinger.

Levin, H. M. (1983). *Cost-effectiveness: A primer.* Beverly Hills, CA: Sage.

Levin, H. M. (1987). Education as a public and private good. *Journal of Policy Analysis and Management, 6,* 628–641.

Lindblom, C. E. (1959). The science of muddling through. *Public Administration Review, 19,* 79–88.

Lindblom, C. E. (1968). *The policy-making process.* Englewood Cliffs, NJ: Prentice Hall.

Marshall, A. (1890/1961). *Principles of economics* (9th ed.). London: Macmillan for the Royal Economic Society.

Mitchell, D. E. (1989). Alternative approaches to labor-management relations for public school teachers and administrators. In J. Hannaway & R. Crowson (Eds.), *The politics of reforming school administration* (pp. 161–181). New York: Falmer.

Moore, M. K., Goertz, M., & Hartle, T. (1983). Interaction of federal and state programs. *Education and Urban Society, 4,* 452–478.

Murphy, J. (1982). The paradox of state government reform. In A. Lieberman & M. McLaughlin (Eds.), *Educational policy-making,* The 81st Yearbook of the National Society for the Study of Education. Chicago: University of Chicago Press.

Odden, A., & Marsh, D. (1989). State education reform implementation: A framework for analysis. In J. Hannaway & R. Crowson (Eds.), *The politics of reforming school administration* (pp. 41–59). New York: Falmer.

Samuelson, P. A. (1980). *Economics* (11th ed.). New York: McGraw-Hill.

Schultz, C. L. (1968). *The politics and economics of public spending.* Washington, DC: The Brookings Institution.

Schultz, T. W. (1963). *The economic value of education.* New York: Columbia University Press.

Schultz, T. W. (1981). *Investing in people: The economics of population quality.* Berkeley, CA: University of California Press.

Smith, A. (1993; originally published, 1776). *An inquiry into the nature and causes of the wealth of nations.* Oxford, England: Oxford University Press.

Truman, D. B. (1951). *The governmental process.* New York: Knopf.

Walker, D. B. (1981). *Toward a functioning federalism.* Cambridge, MA: Winthrop Press.

Weiler, H. N. (Ed.). (1980). *Educational planning and social change.* Paris: UNESCO: International Institute for Educational Planning.

Wildavsky, A. (1964). *The politics of the budgetary process.* Boston: Little, Brown.

Wirt, F. M., & Kirst, M. W. (1982). *Schools in conflict: The politics of education.* Berkeley, CA: McCutchan.

Wise, A. E. (1979). *Legislated learning: The bureaucratization of the American classroom.* Berkeley, CA: University of California Press.

CHAPTER 2

Values, Structure, and Allocation of Power: Implications for School Finance Policy

Primary Issues Explored in This Chapter:

- *Values and finance policy:* In what ways have educational policies been influenced by values of liberty, equality, fraternity, efficiency, and economic growth?
- *Allocation of authority:* Given tensions among the above values, what trends have developed in educational policies as they relate to the centralization and decentralization of authority?
- *Governance in the United States:* In what ways might the political-economic system introduced in Chapter 1 clarify the evolution of the multi-

level governance structure and current policy debates?
- *International perspectives:* How do recent movements to transform control over education and its resources compare among the United States, England, Australia, and New Zealand?
- *Assessing and developing educational policies:* What propositions flow from the analysis of centralization and decentralization of authority to guide future school finance policy?

In Chapter 1 we described the economic and political structures within which decisions about education and its financing are made in the public and private sectors and the principal theories about how human interactions take place in the public sector. Although we referred to the role of personal and societal values in formulating decisions, we deferred a detailed discussion to this chapter. Our focus is on five societal values and the tensions they create among advocates of differing educational policies.

TENSIONS AMONG VALUES AFFECTING SOCIAL POLICY

Practically all of our activities occur within the contexts of attitudes about good and bad, right and wrong, or better and worse. Behavior is therefore a constant reflection of beliefs about how the world is structured. The actions that are taken are based, implicitly or explicitly, on these philosophical considerations (Foster, 1986).

Values Defined

Values are conceptions of the desirable (Hodgkinson, 1983; Hoy & Miskel, 1991; Parsons, 1951). A value is an enduring belief that a specific mode of conduct or state of existence is personally or socially preferable to one of the opposite or converse mode. Values are consciously or unconsciously held priorities that are expressed in all human activity. A value system is an enduring organization of values along a continuum of relative importance (Rokeach, 1973).

If values were completely stable, individual and social change would be impossible. If values were completely unstable, continuity of human personality and society would be impossible. The hierarchical conception of values enables us to define change as a reordering of priorities and, simultaneously, to see the total value system as relatively stable over time.

Metavalues

Hodgkinson (1983, p. 43) defined "metavalue" as "a concept of the desirable so vested and entrenched that it seems to be beyond dispute or contention—one that usually enters the ordinary value calculus of individual and collective life in the form of an unexpressed or unexamined assumption." He identified the dominant metavalues in administration and organizational life as efficiency and effectiveness.

Nyberg (1993, p. 196) contended that "The moral universe is the same for everyone in that it is based on concern for human dignity, decency, voluntary relations that are not oppressive, and some kind of spiritual fulfillment." The specifics differ from person to person, from group to group, from place to place, and from time to time. But the basis of concern remains consistent—a foundation on which metavalues are built. We are all similar, but each person is unique.

In making practical application of his theory about value structures, Rokeach (1973) sought to identify ideals or values that all political ideologies single out for special consideration. He hypothesized that the major variations in political ideology

are fundamentally reducible to opposing value orientations concerning the political desirability or undesirability of freedom and equality in all their ramifications. Getzels (1957, 1978) referred to national core values as "sacred." He identified four sacred values as being at the core of the American ethos: democracy, individualism, equality, and human perfectibility.

The literature on educational policy makes frequent explicit or implicit reference to these or similar values. Boyd (1984) and Koppich and Guthrie (1993) refer to equality, efficiency, and liberty as competing values of particular societal concern in making education policy in Western democracies. Wirt (1987) refers to general agreement among nations that the major values in education are quality (excellence or human perfectibility), equity, efficiency, and choice (liberty or freedom). Kahne (1994) refers to equity, efficiency, and excellence as the central concerns of education policy analysts. But he criticizes analysts for not giving equal attention to the formation of democratic communities, that is, fraternity. There is a good deal of overlap among the various lists, with freedom and equality/equity being on most.

We will focus on five metavalues or objects of policy that have been historically prominent in shaping Western societies. They are also particularly relevant to making decisions about the provision and consumption of educational services: liberty, equality/equity, fraternity, efficiency, and economic growth. With changing social circumstances, each has experienced ascendance and descendance in priority in the formulation of public policy. But none has ever lost its relevance entirely. Currently there appears to be a fundamental shift taking place in the priorities placed on these five values which underlies much of the controversy surrounding education today.

Liberty, equality, and fraternity are ethical values derived from the doctrine of natural rights expressed as early as 1690 by John Locke (1956) in his *Second Treatise of Government.* Leaders of both the American and French revolutions used Locke's arguments to justify those revolutions and in constructing their governments following victory. Liberty, equality, and fraternity are intrinsic values associated with human nature and human rights. Efficiency and economic growth are practical or derived values that enhance the realization of the former. Efficiency and economic growth have become primary objectives of public policy only during the twentieth century.

Liberty is the right to act in the manner of one's own choosing, not subject to undue restriction or control. *Equality* refers to the state, ideal, or quality of being equal, as in the state of enjoying equal social, political, and economic rights. "Equality" is used in terms of civil rights and not in terms of personal characteristics and abilities.

Nyberg (1981, pt. II) cautioned that "freedom" (or liberty) derives its meaning at least in part from the times in which it is used. He pointed out that, between 1787 and 1947, a transformation took place in the United States from "freedom as natural rights (rights *against* the government, rights of independence), to civil rights (rights to *participate* in civil government), to human freedoms (rights to the *help* of government in achieving protection from fear and want)" (pp. 97–98).

Parallel transformations have taken place in the meaning of equality. Initially equality was viewed in terms only of rights, and not of conditions; people were to be treated the same by law, custom, and tradition. When considered as such, equality was the instrument for guaranteeing liberty as originally defined. In recent times, the operational definitions of equality have expanded to include factors of condition also. It is now accepted that some persons are handicapped in enjoying liberty because of circumstances beyond their control, such as minority status, gender, poverty, and physical and psychological impairments. Within the current sociopolitical context, we emphasize the *appropriateness* of treatment. As such, "equality" has taken on connotations of "equity," "the state, ideal, or quality of being just, impartial and fair." Education has become a principal instrument of social policy for removing or reducing the liabilities of these conditions (for example, compensatory education programs). With a broadened definition of equality, equity comes into direct conflict

with the value of liberty as originally defined. This is because the policies of remediation involve not only the disadvantaged person but also all others. Liberty requires an opportunity for expression through individual freedom (for example, educational vouchers and family choice of schooling). Equity requires some curbing of individual freedom (for example, school desegregation, mainstreaming, expenditure caps).

In his international analyses, Caldwell (1993) has observed a merging of the two values of equity and excellence.

> The emerging view of equity and excellence suggests an emphasis on ensuring that each individual student has access to the particular mix of resources in order to best meet the needs and interests of that student. . . . Expressed another way, the merging of equity and excellence may involve, among other things, a shift from uniformity in resource allocation, with all decisions at the center, to different patterns of resource allocation according to the particular mix of student needs at the school level; with more decisions at the school level in determining these patterns. (p. 163)

Clune (1993) observed such a trend in the United States. He saw equity being defined in terms of a high minimum level of achievement for all pupils as the common goal for educational adequacy *and* sufficient resources to meet that goal. In other words, resource allocation is defined according to outcomes, not according to inputs.

Fraternity refers to a common bond producing a sense of unity, community, and nationhood. Building a sense of national identity is today a primary mission of schools in developing countries. This was a mission of schooling in the United States after the United States broke its identity with England and emerged from the War of Independence as thirteen independent states. Later, the school became an important instrument of the melting-pot strategists during the nineteenth century (Ravitch, 1985, chap. 14; Tyack, 1974). The schools still need to be a force welding the nation together as immigrants continue to enter the country in record numbers from all parts of the world.

Like equity, fraternity imposes constraints upon liberty. Cremin (1976) noted an inescapable and obvious relationship between the concepts of education and community (that is, fraternity). Referring to Dewey's (1916) *Democracy and Education,* Cremin wrote, "[T]here must be ample room in a democratic society for a healthy individualism and a healthy pluralism, but that individualism and that pluralism must also partake of a continuing quest for community" (p. 72). Nyberg (1977, p. 217) characterized the historical and social functions of a school as "a method by which individuals become communities, and through which these communities describe themselves."

Efficiency, the ratio of outputs to inputs, is of more recent concern in education. Efficiency is increased by increasing the probability of realizing targeted outcomes secured from available resources or by maintaining a given level of outcomes while using fewer resources. Schools are institutions functioning largely in the public sector. They therefore do not face the stringent discipline for efficient operations (internal efficiency) imposed by the market on institutions operating in the private sector (Benson, 1978, p. 14; Guthrie et al., 1988, pp. 30–33). Governments in capitalistic countries tend to deal with issues in which economic concerns are not overriding. In the educational lexicon, efficiency concerns are expressed in terms of "accountability" and "standards."

Increasing the aggregate national production of goods and services through *economic growth)* involves the development of skills needed in the workforce to support the economy so that it will expand at a desired pace. Economic growth is closely tied to human capital development, as discussed in the previous chapter. The objective of promoting economic growth, like that of promoting efficiency, is of relatively recent interest. When public education was developing in the nineteenth century, the general skill requirements of the workforce were minimal. Where special skills were required, they were usually developed through apprenticeship programs in the private sector. As entry skills required by business, industry, and the professions became more sophisticated, the connection between economic growth and educational enterprises became apparent. Public schools increasingly took on vocational responsibilities. Concern over economic growth will continue to gain in importance as a criterion for evaluating educational policy as international competition and the level of skills demanded in the labor market increase further.

Because of the conceptual inconsistencies among the five social values, it is not possible to emphasize all at the same time in public policy—or in individual lives—desirable as each may be. Priorities must be established among them by individuals and by society. This is a dynamic process, as we already noted. Priorities of individuals change with circumstances. And when there has been a sufficient shift among individuals, shifts in public priorities follow (Ravitch, 1985, chap. 5).

Agreement about priorities is not necessary for private or market sector decisions beyond the aggregation of the family. In the public sector, however, a singular decision is required that involves negotiation and compromise among interested partisans. Significant social stress may be generated in the process. The higher the level of aggregation, the more difficult agreement becomes, because more heterogeneity is introduced. Friedman (1962) analyzed the situation as follows:

> The widespread use of the market reduces the strain on the social fabric by rendering conformity unnecessary with respect to any activities it encompasses. The wider the range of activities covered by the market, the fewer are the issues on which explicit political decisions are required and hence on which it is necessary to achieve agreement. In turn, the fewer issues on which agreement is necessary, the greater the likelihood of getting agreement while maintaining a free society. (p. 24)

Major contemporary social issues, including education and its financing, revolve around the shifting priorities various groups give to the competing social objectives of liberty, equity, fraternity, efficiency, and economic growth, among others. The question of whether each can be furthered jointly through public policy is being hotly debated. The most likely scenario is that one or two values will be given top priority, as in the past, to the jeopardy of the others. Subsequently we will enter into a period of relative stability until another shift in value priorities takes place, ushering in a new phase of instability and reform.

A CHANGING VALUES HIERARCHY AND EDUCATION REFORM

The forces leading to educational reform reflect worldwide changes in social, economic, political, and technological relationships that have led to— or were caused by—shifts in the dominant value hierarchy. Collectively, these changes have been dubbed "the third wave" by Toffler (1980) and "megatrends" by Naisbitt (1982) and Naisbitt and Aburdene (1990). Drucker (1989) has referred to their amalgam as "the post-industrial society," "the post business society," and "the information age." Whatever it is called, the present age is considerably different from the one that preceded it. The magnitude of the shift has been likened to that from feudalism to capitalism or from an agriculturally based economy to industrialization. All social institutions are called upon to make appropriate adjustments; educational institutions are not being exempted.

Centralization and Decentralization of Authority

Industrialization brought with it a high degree of centralization and bureaucratization. Marion Levy (1966, p. 55), in his epic study *Modernization and the Structure of Societies,* concluded that "the degree of centralization always increases with modernization . . . and continues to increase with further modernization." Levy also directly linked the level of modernization with the level of bureaucratization and increases in the importance of government as the main focus of that centralization. Levy recognized certain dangers in centralization and bureaucratization. He admonished those who believe in democracy and the sacredness of the individual to organize bureaucracies so that impersonality, which is one of bureaucracy's special virtues, does not result in undesired consequences.

Levy noted further that less coordination and control than the minimum needed to provide social stability is neither feasible nor popular in modern societies. On the other hand, he raised the question of how much coordination and control there can be without overloading the cognitive capacities of the individuals who must plan and direct operations, or without the structures becoming so brittle that any small change within the society will fracture the whole system. In trying to apply Levy's ideas to the contemporary context, one cannot help wondering whether technological and sociological developments have negated the relationships between centralization and modernization, and whether our bureaucracies have exceeded their capacity for coordination and control (Murphy, 1983). The answer to both questions is probably yes.

One of the characteristics of the information society is a trend toward decentralization. Naisbitt (1982, p. 98) observed that "The growth of decentralization parallels the decline of industry. . . . Agricultural and information societies are decentralized societies."

Toffler (1980) identified six guiding principles of both the capitalist and socialist wings of industrial society—standardization, specialization, synchronization, concentration, maximization, and centralization.

> These principles in turn, each reinforcing the other, led relentlessly to the rise of bureaucracy. They produced some of the biggest, most rigid, most powerful bureaucratic organizations the world had ever seen, leaving the individual to wander in a Kafka-like world of looming mega-organizations. . . . Today, . . .

every one of these fundamental principles is under attack by forces of the Third Wave [the information society]. (p. 60)

Peters and Waterman (1982) studied what they considered to be America's best-run companies. They note that widely held ideas about efficiency and economies of scale have led to the building of big bureaucracies that cannot act. They argue that conventional estimates of scale economies vastly underestimate transaction costs, that is, the cost of communication, coordination, and deciding. Their "excellent companies" recognize that beyond a surprisingly small size, diseconomies of scale seem to set in with vengeance. These companies have found numerous ways to break up their organizations in order to make them fluid and to facilitate putting the right resources against the right problem. They call the process "chunking." In a more recent book, *Thriving on Chaos,* Peters (1988) questions whether "big" has ever been more efficient or more innovative.

McGinn and Street (1986) characterize centralization and decentralization as a dyad:

> Decentralization is not primarily an issue of control by government of individual citizens. Instead it is a question of the distribution of power among various groups in society. A highly participatory society—one in which all citizens actually do participate—is likely to require a competent and powerful state that actively and continuously seeks to redistribute power among groups and individuals in the society. The location of authority in local government does not protect the local citizen from tyranny, and the redistribution of power through the market mechanism in a society that currently is highly inequitable is a guarantee that inequities will persist and worsen. On the other hand, competition and markets can contribute to social justice in circumstances where there is a relatively equitable balance of powers among the participants in the competition or market. . . . A strong state

must first achieve some minimal degree of social equity so that decentralization can lead to genuine participation. (pp. 489–490)

Political Dynamics of Centralized and Decentralized Decision Making

Archer (1984) has meticulously described the differences in the political dynamics between centralized and decentralized decision making with respect to education change. She classified the actors in the change process into three categories: professional interest groups, external interest groups, and governing elites. According to Archer, in negotiating change, these groups, engage in three types of interactions: political manipulation, internal initiation, and external transactions.

The principal resource commanded by the education profession in the negotiation process is its expertise. To translate its professional goals into reality, the profession must acquire the financial means from external groups or from the political elite and the legal rights to do so from the political elite. The principal resource commanded by external interest groups is their wealth. This wealth can be used to influence the education profession to provide services of the nature desired by the external groups. The principal resource commanded by the political elite is their legal authority and capacity to bestow benefits and to impose negative sanctions. The political elite use their official powers to extract the educational services they desire and to preclude undesired outputs through a process that exchanges privileges of salary and the institutionalization of professional advice for educational services meeting their political requirements (Archer, 1984, pp. 122–123).

The negotiating strategies followed in centralized systems are quite different from those followed in decentralized ones. In a centralized system, the political elite can concentrate almost exclusively on interaction that culminates in passing legislation, decrees, or regulations. They can do this because they are generally in an unassailable

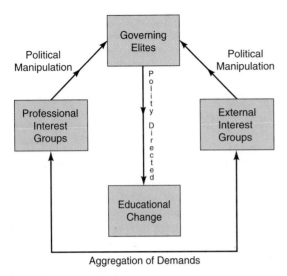

Figure 2.1. Archer's Structural Conditioning of Educational Interaction in the Centralized System. (SOURCE: Archer, M. S. [1984]. *Social Origins of Educational Systems*. London: SAGE Publications, p. 117.)

gaining positions, and the provision of educational services is not exclusively dependent on resources supplied by a central political elite. "Consequently, any change in the decentralized system involves a broader set of transactions. Every legal change introduced from the center entails negotiation with professional interest groups to insure implementation, and with external interest groups to prevent its vitiation or evasion" (Archer, 1984, p. 126).

The centralized system, as portrayed by Archer (1984), is presented in Figure 2.1; the decentralized system is presented in Figure 2.2. In the centralized system, all action by professional and external interest groups (political manipulation) focuses on the governing elite. The elite decrees what educational change will take place, if any. The only interaction among the interest groups is to aggregate their demands of the polity and perhaps to coordinate their political strategies.

In the decentralized system, educational change may be initiated internally by professional interest groups. It may be influenced by transactions conducted by external interest groups negotiated with the profession. Or change may be directed by the polity as in the centralized system. Because of the multiple routes to change in the

position. Both professional and external interest groups have few alternatives to accepting these measures. The political elite in a centralized system attempts to prevent alternative means to public provision of educational services. They refuse legal recognition of diplomas, establishments, personnel, or courses other than those under their own control. To keep the education profession from providing services outside the established system, however, the political elite must treat the profession with a certain level of generosity. The polity enacts legislation reducing local and institutional autonomy, making the system more responsive to central directives. And it promotes ideologies favoring political intervention. The political left promotes intervention on the grounds of equity and the elimination of social discrimination. The right promotes intervention on the grounds of accountability and efficiency (Archer, 1984, pp. 124–127).

In a decentralized system, the distribution of resources is less favorable to the political center. The process of negotiation becomes much more complex under these circumstances. External groups and the profession itself hold strong bar-

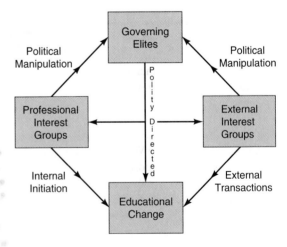

Figure 2.2. Archer's Structural Conditioning of Educational Interaction in the Decentralized System. (SOURCE: Archer, M. S. [1984]. *Social Origins of Educational Systems*. London: SAGE Publications, p. 118.)

decentralized system as compared with the centralized system, change is likely to happen more frequently—perhaps continuously. It will be more diverse in nature; but any one change will be less sweeping in impact.

Archer (1984) maintains that since political manipulation is the most important process through which change is introduced in the centralized system, the social distribution of power is of prime concern in explaining the course of educational politics. Conversely, in the decentralized system these processes of negotiation enjoy a rough parity. Thus the distribution of all these resources—wealth, power, and expertise—shapes the contours of educational politics. Archer concludes:

> Thus the social distribution of power in the centralized system and of power, wealth and expertise in the decentralized system constrain: the nature and number of people admitted to educational transactions; their initial bargaining positions and changes in them; and the volume and kinds of demands which can be negotiated at any time. (p. 131)

Shifting Value Priorities

The worldwide depression of the 1930s shattered confidence in an unregulated free-market economic system (decentralization). From that time to the present, power has been increasingly vested in government as a vehicle for providing economic as well as political stability and security. The theories of Marx, which would concentrate power in the state, were tested in Eastern Europe and in many developing countries. The West was strongly influenced by Keynesian theories of economics. It moved more cautiously toward a division of power between the state and the market. The East discovered that state bureaucracies can be as oppressive as the bourgeoisie and aristocracy that they replaced. Both East and West learned that bureaucracies are as capable of failure as are free markets.

As we approach the twenty-first century, we do so with a new respect for market mechanisms

along with an appreciation of the practical limits of governmental intervention. The strategies followed by most governments during the past fifty years in search of equity exacted a heavy toll on personal freedom and productive efficiency. There now appears to be a willingness to experiment with new strategies that respect personal as well as social privilege.

With respect to education, the trend in the 1960s and 1970s, driven by a priority concern for equity, was toward centralizing decisions at the state and federal levels. The criticism of public education during the 1980s and 1990s suggested that policies had passed the optimal point of centralization. Too much power was in the hands of the political elites and too little power in the hands of those being served (external interest groups) and those serving (professional interest groups). Paralleling trends elsewhere in society, during the past decade less attention was given to equity and fraternity as governing objectives for public educational institutions and greater attention was given to liberty (manifest, for example, in emphasizing diversity and cultural pluralism), efficiency, and economic growth. The shift in the distribution of power and authority has led to new interest in decentralizing education decision making through such devices as school-site management and family choice of schools.

EVOLUTION OF THE ALLOCATION PATTERN OF POWER AND AUTHORITY OVER EDUCATION IN THE UNITED STATES

Elmore (1993) and Weiler (1993) have suggested that the education reform debates raging throughout the world have little to do with improving the quality of teaching and learning in schools. In the final analysis, contention over centralization and decentralization is about power and its distribution (see also Archer, 1984; Slater, 1993). Institutionalism, as discussed in Chapter 1, postulates that the pattern of allocation of power and authority among interested parties influences the nature of the decisions made and the effectiveness with which they are implemented. Determining a satisfactory pattern for the distribution of power and authority is a continuing problem in determining public policy.

Elmore (1993), along with McGinn and Street (1986), has been critical of the tendency of analysts to treat centralization and decentralization as absolutes. Rather he suggests that the underlying issues should be addressed as "What should be loosely governed, and what should be tightly governed, from any given level of the system?"

> Implicit in this question is the assumption that multiple levels of government, as well as their constituencies, all have an interest in the governance of the schools, but that if they all attempt to assert equal influence over all matters of schooling, the system will collapse of its own organizational complexity. Thus the issue is not *whether* one level of government or another should influence education but rather *how much* influence of *what kind* any level of government should exert over *what factors.* (p. 51)

In Chapter 1, we presented a model of the political-economic system of educational policy development (Figure 1.8) that contained a decision matrix arraying issues needing to be determined against potential decision makers. We now return to that model and use it to describe the evolution of the allocation of authority over the making of decisions about education in the United States. In the next section, we use the model to compare current allocation patterns in England, Australia, New Zealand, and the United States. In the final section we develop guides for school finance policy based on the comparative analysis.

During the industrial age, the organization of schooling in the United States followed the same centralizing tendencies as did industry and other services of government. Schooling is now facing a restructuring similar to that of other institutions to make it compatible with the conditions of the information age.

The common school concept emerged early in the nineteenth century when agriculture dominated the United States economy and most people lived in rural areas. The common school was public. But the formal governance structure was similar to the town meeting, and the communities served were typically very small. The few cities of that period were small by today's standards and without suburbs. Even their school governance was at the ward level. School consolidation started in cities with the establishment of city school districts. From there, school districts grew along with their cities and the bureaucracies that managed them. Then centralization of rural schools began after the turn of the twentieth century. Tyack (1974) reported it this way:

> This movement to take control of the rural common school away from the local community and to turn it over to the professionals was part of a more general organizational revolution in American education in which laymen lost much of their direct control over the schools. In the cities schoolmen pioneered new bureaucratic patterns of educational organization. They sought to "free education from politics. . . ." (p. 25)

If we use Figure 1.8 as a point of reference, control over education was largely in the hands of families through a town meeting format at the origin of public education in the United States. The teaching profession was weak. The larger society as represented by the state was relatively inactive except for providing enabling legislation. The principles of liberty and equality of educational opportunity (among socioeconomic classes, but not races) were dominant within communities that were largely heterogeneous with respect to social class. Government was small. Efficiency was not yet a concern of the schools.

Despite the dispersion of control, there was a remarkable uniformity among the schools. There was a general Protestant-republican ideology that was shared among common school crusaders such as Horace Mann and Henry Barnard. The purpose of public education was seen as training upright citizens by inculcating a common denominator of nonsectarian morality and nonpartisan civic instruction. The school itself was to be free, open to all children, and public in support and control (Tyack, 1993). The key to this uniformity was not central government control but the force of common cultural beliefs in shaping institutions. Tyack (p. 5) calls this "the invisible hand of ideology."

With the growing sophistication of the teaching profession, especially its administrators, professional control and bureaucratization grew substantially during the first half of the twentieth century. This represents a shift of authority to the left in Figure 1.8 (Callahan, 1962; Tyack, 1993). States became more involved by enacting compulsory attendance laws, setting certain basic standards for teacher certification, consolidating rural schools, and providing some financing, including equalization aid. The federal government entered the scene by providing aid for vocational education. Liberty was less a concern than before. Efficiency considerations came into play for the first time; and equity concerns began to take on a statewide dimension.

Following World War II, there was a rapid expansion of suburbs and suburban school districts. Municipalities and school districts became quite homogeneous in socioeconomic status and ethnicity. The white middle class was concentrated in the suburbs. A decline in the quality of educational services in urban centers followed. During the 1950s and until through the 1970s, civil rights suits were successfully pursued in federal courts to correct the inequities that resulted (B. Levin, 1987). Litigation was followed by state and federal legislation that had the effect of making specific court decisions universal. Local decisions about the nature and distribution of educational services were constrained by national and state guidelines and mandates concerning pupil assignment and discipline, teacher employment, and curriculum.

Also in the 1970s, society's influence was enlarged with respect to the allocation of resources, again through litigation followed by legislation (Berne & Stiefel, 1983; Guthrie et al., 1988, chap. 8). States increased their participation in financing school operations, school buildings, and transportation. The federal role in school finance became a significant factor for the first time in the 1960s and 1970s. It came in the form of categorical aid grants that were focused on poor and disabled children within urban centers. State education departments grew in size and influence. There was a perceived decline in student achievement and, along with it, the credibility of the teaching profession. The principle of equity was the dominant concern during this period. It was defined in racial and ethnic as well as socioeconomic terms. Liberty and efficiency suffered as more constraints were placed on local school districts by state and federal governments. The dominant decision makers had become the state and federal governments, representing society in Figure 1.8 (Guthrie, 1980; Ravitch, 1983).

Perceived deterioration in the quality of student achievement during the 1970s became a national concern early in the 1980s. Numerous reports on the state of education were published. The current educational reform movement followed. To arrest the decline in standards, most states intervened with mandated curricula, competency examinations for both students and teachers, and stiffer requirements for teacher certification and student diplomas. This initial phase of the reform movement further constrained what remained of the discretionary authority of educational officials at the school district level. For many individuals and communities a substantial mismatch was created between aspirations for schools and the reality of these schools. The locus of authority had completed its movement from the family and the profession to society.

But legislating higher standards did not necessarily produce higher standards (Iannaccone, 1985). State governors, among others, were quick to notice. From the mid-1960s through the early 1980s, efficiency and equity had been pursued through centralized authority. Policy implementation studies of that period (Chubb & Moe, 1985, 1990; Coleman & Hoffer, 1987; Coons & Sugarman, 1978; Elmore & McLaughlin, 1988; Farrar, DeSanctis, & Cohen, 1980; McNeil, 1986; Wise,

1979, 1988) showed that federal and state governments are particularly effective in dealing with issues of equity and access. But such governments appear to be less effective in dealing with matters of efficiency and "production," that is, how schools are organized and operated. Learn from experience, there is a renewed appreciation of the concept of liberty in the United States and a tendency to pursue efficiency through decentralized authority and equity through centralized authority. This has been referred to as systemic reform.

Liberty and efficiency are back as policy concerns (Iannaccone, 1988). School-based decision making and family choice of schooling represent important tactics in an overall strategy of decentralization. These tactics return some decision-making authority to parents and teachers. This is in order to introduce marketlike forces into the public school sector for the purpose of increasing the efficiency of that sector and of providing better matches between parental expectations and the educational services provided. There is a strong desire to retain equity as a guiding principle. But many doubt that this is likely because priority is now given to liberty and efficiency.

After reviewing the evolution (successive reforms) of school governance in the United States, Tyack (1993) observed that changes in governance have generally failed to alter basic patterns of instruction. He attributed this to the fact that teachers have rarely been consulted when leaders seek to change schooling. To gain improvement in instruction, he recommended that we approach school reform from the inside out, and not from the top down. We should start with the classroom and attend to the teachers who do the steady work.

Tyack (1993, p. 25) also concluded that "the belief systems underlying much of current American education reform seem impoverished and incomplete in comparison with earlier ideologies." He found them to be narrow in sense of purpose and in measurement of success. The new emphasis is on economic competitiveness certified with higher test scores. The historical vision of the common school as an instrument for promoting active democratic citizenship is absent.

INTERNATIONAL COMPARISONS

There are a number of striking similarities in the movements to transform the control and performance of schools in the United States, England, Australia, Canada, and Japan (Beare & Boyd, 1993). A common political concern motivating reform is obtaining or maintaining international economic competitiveness. This concern is so great that national governments are taking leading roles in educational reform initiatives. This is true even in countries such as the United States and Australia, where there is no constitutional authority for such intervention. The reforms are also similar. Greater managerial authority is being devolved to schools. Parents are being allowed more discretion in selecting the schools their children attend. Countering these decentralizing forces are centralizing forces. Most countries are moving toward the development of national standards, national curricula, and national assessment.

We have reviewed the evolution of structural reform in the United States. We now look at England, Australia, and New Zealand. These nations share a common language and a similar cultural-political heritage. Canada is not included in the review because reforming education has not received the national and provincial attention given to it by the countries being considered. Canada's continuing constitutional crisis has preoccupied the national agenda. It has given the preservation of the union top priority (Lawton, 1993). Some districts in Canada, however, have gone through innovative restructuring, such as the school site management scheme in Edmonton, Alberta. The Edmonton plan is described in some detail in Chapter 14.

England

Until the Education Reform Act of 1988, the English education system was characterized as "a national system locally administered" (Department of Education and Science, 1978). Between 75 percent and 80 percent of the system's financing was provided by the national government. Administration was left to divisions of local government called

Local Education Authorities (LEAs) and to school heads. The LEAs were responsible for rationalizing the education system. They made sure that there was provision for all children, established criteria for the assignment of children to schools, and supplemented national funding. The Education Act of 1944 that structured the post–World War II system had encouraged the satisfaction of parental preferences in school assignment where possible. And parents had the right of appeal to the Secretary of State for Education if they disagreed with their LEA on a particular pupil placement decision.

Local Authorities (of which LEAs are a part) established the education budget under the 1944 Act. However, they were severely constrained by decisions made at the national level through negotiations between representatives of local authorities and the national government. Teachers' salary levels were also established at the national level, through negotiations between the national government and representatives of local authorities, on the one side, and teacher unions, on the other. The slight variations in expenditure level per pupil among LEAs were modest compared with those experienced in the United States.

School heads were given a rather free hand in organizing their schools and in designing the curriculum under the 1944 Act. National examinations provided for some curricular uniformity at the upper-secondary level. The curricular variety was (and is) matched with organizational variety. There were (and are) selective and comprehensive schools, single-sex and mixed schools, and schools sponsored by religious and other organizations. The 16–19 age cohort was (and is) accommodated in sixth forms attached to secondary schools (providing primarily an academic curriculum) and in sixth-form colleges (academic), technical colleges, and tertiary colleges (providing both technical and academic curricula). In addition, there were (and are) independent schools for those desiring an elitist education who can afford the tuition. Most church schools were (and are) maintained by the state sector. All state-maintained schools must include religious education in their curricula and conduct assemblies of Christian worship. Independent schools have never received direct state support, although the government finances scholarships enabling some poor but academically talented children and youth to attend them.

The Education Reform Act of 1988 gave the Secretary of State for Education 415 new specific powers. Subsequent legislation has added further to the secretary's authority. The act "shifted power away from LEAs to the central authority, contrary to the established tradition of avoiding too much central control" (Lawton, 1992, p. 47). Expenditure levels are now virtually set by the national government, with little effective consultation with local authorities. Variation in expenditure per pupil among LEAs is even less now than it was formerly. Teacher salaries are no longer negotiated but are set nationally by a form of continuing arbitration (Day, 1993). National curriculum and national assessment procedures are set by the School Curriculum and Assessment Authority. Membership on the authority's board of directors is determined by the Secretary of State. The National Curriculum constitutes 80 percent or more of instructional time, leaving little room for local supplement; however, the government is now trying to reduce this to 50 percent.

It is the intent of government that each of the nation's 26,000 schools be inspected once every four years in a procedure supervised by Her Majesty's Chief Inspector through the Office for Standards in Education (OFSTED). The results of school inspections and annual assessments are published for the information of parents and other interested parties. Each year schools must report to parents on their children's progress with respect to national curriculum standards.

Under recent legislation, schools are being encouraged by the national government to opt out of their LEAs and become reorganized as charitable trusts. Such schools are then funded directly by the national government rather than through their LEAs. A Funding Authority for Schools (FAS) has been established to administer payment of recurrent and capital grants to schools who choose to opt out. FAS will eventually take over the planning for sufficient spaces for the education of primary and secondary pupils, which had been a responsibility of LEAs. The national government now finances between 80 and 85 percent of primary and secondary education.

Countering the centralization actions are some actions that clearly decentralize authority. With respect to school finance, a grant that covers 85 to 90 percent of a school's operating expenses, including salaries, is made available to each school's governing body. This is based largely on enrollment and age of pupils. The authority previously held by LEAs to control pupil intake of schools has been severely curtailed. Schools can determine their own staffing patterns, make their own personnel decisions, including teachers' pay within national guidelines, and contract for support services such as building maintenance, accounting, purchasing, payroll, insurance, and auditing. Parents have gained additional representation on governing bodies and have freedom of choice among those schools that are not oversubscribed. In the case of oversubscribed schools still under the auspices of an LEA, criteria for selection are monitored by the LEA. Oversubscribed schools that have opted out of LEA control may select what applicants to admit according to criteria approved by the secretary of state for education.

The big losers in the power shuffle have been the LEAs. As a matter of fact, the 1993 Education Act anticipates the possibility that some local authorities may no longer wish to organize an education committee (that is, school board). Even if all schools within an authority opt out, the government anticipates that local authorities will have to continue to be responsible for educating pupils with special educational needs and for the provision, where necessary, of lodging and board, clothing, educational psychology and welfare services, and home-to-school transport.

In a white paper prepared by the Secretary of State for Education, John Patton (1992) identified five great themes as characterizing educational changes made by the Conservative Party since coming to power in 1979. They were higher educational quality; greater diversity in education provision; increased parental choice, influence, and control; greater school autonomy; and greater accountability by school officials.

A critic of government policy described the reforms quite differently (Whitty, 1992):

> The early analyses of the effects of the market-oriented policies of the Thatcher government . . . would seem to suggest that, far from producing a genuine pluralism and interrupting traditional modes of social reproduction, they may be providing a legitimating gloss for the perpetuation of long-standing forms of structural inequality. The Education Reform Act certainly seems more likely to produce greater differentiation between schools on a linear scale of quality and esteem than the positive diversity that some of its supporters hoped for. (p. 49)

In reference to Figure 1.8, society in England is strengthening its control over the setting of goals and objectives by mandating a core curriculum, national student assessment, national evaluation of schools, and the allocation of resources in terms of expenditure per pupil. On the other hand, the family voice in decisions about the distribution of services (the selection of schools) is enhanced. This indirectly strengthens the family's influence on all other decisions, although it appears that oversubscribed schools are selecting parents. The national government is hostile to the teaching profession and has removed much professional discretionary power over curriculum. The profession nevertheless still maintains strong influence over the implementation of the curriculum. In other respects, the influence of professionals is strengthened by the shifting to the school level of decisions about allocation of resources to the instructional process.

Australia

Traditionally, Australian schools have operated as highly centralized state systems (Butts, 1955; Hancock, Kirst, & Grossman, 1983; Partridge, 1968). There are no local education authorities (i.e., school districts). Teachers and administrators are selected, employed, and assigned by the respective state bureaucracies. The curriculum is prescribed by the states, although there is increasing coordination through the federal government.

As in the United States, the federal government has no constitutional authority to intervene in educational matters, and it directly provides less than 10 percent of the funding of government schools. However, the federal government in Australia has been the primary leader of school reform initiatives over the past fifteen years (Louden & Browne, 1993). Initial federal ventures into education were coordinated through the Australian Schools Commission, the Curriculum Development Centre, and the Commonwealth Department of Education. Federal intervention into education has been motivated largely by grave concern over Australia's economic competitiveness internationally and the belief that its future prosperity is associated with the development of a highly educated and skilled workforce. This was clearly manifested in 1987 when federal education affairs were placed under a superministry called the Department of Employment, Education, and Training.

The federal government's influence is enhanced through the use of categorical aids because a state must comply with federal mandates in order to qualify for aid. Moreover, Australian states depend directly on the federal government for significant amounts of aid for purposes other than education. Unlike state governments in the United States and provinces in Canada, state governments in Australia do not levy direct income taxes, although they have the power to do so. Income tax collection is coordinated through the federal government, and a portion of the tax collected is returned to the states through the Grants Commission. The power of the federal government to vary grants to the states and to make special grants gives the federal government very significant financial power beyond that specified in the constitution (Louden & Browne, 1993). Efficiency, pluralism, and liberty comprise the value streams directing the current federal political agenda for funding schools in Australia. Equity has dropped to a lower priority from its dominating position in previous decades.

In the 1960s, public funding was extended to private schools, first by the federal government and subsequently by state governments. This was done primarily to save the Roman Catholic schools from collapse at a time when public schools were finding it difficult to accommodate their own burgeoning enrollments. The intent was equalitarian—to upgrade the quality of education in the underfinanced Catholic sector (Hogan, 1984). For the most part, Roman Catholic parochial schools serve a nonelite working-class constituency. Elitist, high-expenditure Protestant and independent schools that cater to business and professional classes also benefited from the aid. The extent of public assistance to elite private schools, however, has been curtailed in recent years. Today the publicly subsidized private schools are providing a low-cost alternative to the public schools. Overall, 27 percent of school-aged children attend private schools. Three-quarters of these are enrolled in Catholic schools. But the non-Catholic component of the private sector is the most rapidly growing one. The percentage of enrollment in private schools is over half in the upper-secondary grades. Private schools, regardless of affiliation, now provide the standard of excellence in Australia (Anderson, 1993; Boyd, 1987).

In essence, Australia has two publicly financed systems of education—one highly centralized, the other highly decentralized. Ironically, nongovernment schools (the decentralized system) have come to serve as models for the reform of government schools (the centralized system). Government schools are perceived as being impersonal, uncaring, and institutional in character (Anderson, 1993). Teachers and principals in government schools tend to identify with the Teaching Service (the state bureau for employing teachers) rather than with the schools and communities to which they are assigned. Historically, personnel transfers have been frequent. Assignments have been made on the basis of formula and longevity, not local conditions or merit. Anderson (1993, p. 195) concluded that the value contrasts between the two sectors are fairly clear: "choice versus equity, pluralism versus social cohesion, individual responsibility versus collective responsibility through the state. The private sector is regulated by the market, the public by bureaucratic and political accountability."

The necessity to improve the efficiency of the public sector has led to similar changes in all states. Central bureaucracies have been reduced; significant authority has been devolved to schools; public involvement at the school level has been enhanced through the creation of policy formulation boards; and greater accountability requirements have been put into place at both the school and system (state) levels.

In the state of Victoria, for example, each school is governed by a council composed of teachers, parents, and community members. The councils hire the principals and have extensive authority over the allocation of financial resources provided by the state. Curriculum is coordinated at the state level through a series of "frameworks" developed with extensive involvement of teachers. The frameworks are not mandatory but serve as guides to schools (Fuhrman & Johnson, 1994). The Victorian Certificate of Education (VCE) maintains the state's role in setting standards and assessing performance of students. In grades 11 and 12, students choose which VCE studies to undertake. For each, they complete a set of work requirements negotiated with and graded by their teacher, and a set of Common Assessment Tasks (CATs) that are graded by teachers from within and outside the school. "Victoria's experience with school-based management, curriculum frameworks, and the VCE demonstrates that it is possible to fashion a system of centralized guidance and local initiative that insures high standards, supports meaningful assessments, permits curricular and pedagogical variety, and promotes collaboration and development among teachers" (Fuhrman & Johnson, 1994, p. 772).

As Tyack (1993) observed in the United States, Louden and Browne (1993) see the school as escaping relatively unscathed in Australia through all these policy changes. They anticipate

> a trend to new centralism, greater devolution of management responsibility to schools

accompanied by strengthened centralizing of policy generation, goal setting, and performance monitoring. There will be continuing tension between federal and state authorities in formulating education policies with the former being interested in central planning with the nation's economic well-being the central concern, and the latter emphasizing devolution and grass-roots considerations. (p. 133)

In reference to Figure 1.8, state governments (society) in Australia continue to make decisions for public schools concerning the setting of goals and objectives, the monitoring of accountability, and the allocation of resources. These functions are gradually being centralized even further as the foundation has been laid for a national curriculum framework and testing program (Caldwell, 1993). Decisions about the production of services are being shifted to the school level to be made by policy boards that include representatives of the teaching profession, parents, and the community served.

For private schools, state governments strongly influence the amount spent per pupil (except for the elite private schools). But the way the money is spent is determined by school trustees in consultation with their professional employees. Decisions about production of services are left largely to the discretion of private school employees within the constraints of a school's goals and objectives that are set by the school's trustees and the school budget. The family has choice of a public school (in some places, public schools) and of many private schools; most of the private schools charge low tuition, making them affordable for most families.

Anderson (1993) is pessimistic about ever again restoring the quality of Australian public schools to the point where they can successfully compete with the publicly subsidized private schools. He projects two alternative futures: either the public schools will become residual institutions for special education students and children of welfare parents, or public and private schools will be reconfigured into some form of integrated system. McGaw (1994) laments that the dominant goals of Australian education are no longer equity and effectiveness. He argues that the goal is now to strengthen the national economy, with a strong presumption that cheaper will be more efficient. McGaw contends that the Australian public would prefer defection from the public schools and a reduced call upon public provision in order that discretionary private resources may be increased, reducing the need for tax support. This is also a possible future for schools in some American cities.

New Zealand

New Zealand embarked on a program of radical educational reform in October of 1989. Although New Zealanders traditionally have cherished popular sovereignty and have preferred local government over central government, the education system had a strong centrist orientation. It was controlled and administered through the national Department of Education, three regional offices, and ten education boards. Secondary schools had boards of governors, and primary schools had school committees, all acting within policy established at the center.

A bipartisan parliamentary committee concluded in 1986 that the quality of teaching in public schools was being undermined by three conditions: provider capture (i.e., control of the education service by professional educators); grossly elaborated structures of educational administration with ineffective lines of accountability and communication; and obsolete administrative attitudes and practice (Macpherson, 1993). Education became a major issue in the national elections of 1987. Subsequently, more direct action was taken with the appointment of a task force led by Brian Picot, a senior member of New Zealand's "corporate oligarchy" and the prochancellor of Auckland University.

The Picot (1988) task force found an urgent need for greater responsiveness in public education. They reported that the administrative capacities of the system were inadequate to deal with the combined effects of new technology, changing and plural values, new cultural sensitivity, and the intensifying demands on educational services. The system was found to be overcentralized, with too many decision points, high vulnerability to pressure groups, excessive ministerial intervention, and a culture of centralism and dependence. The devolution of decision-making power, resources, and accountability was seen as an effective means by which the balance of power between the education establishment and the clients of the system could be altered. The government formally accepted almost all of the task force's recommendations in 1989 (Macpherson, 1993).

The 1989 reforms centered on the school as the unit that sustains the relationship between learner and teacher (as Tyack, 1993, had recommended for the United States). Prior to the effective date of the reforms, each school community elected a board of trustees that was responsible for developing a charter of organization to provide a structure for conducting program budgeting and accrual accounting. The charter was to reflect local needs and conditions within guidelines established by the national government. Each charter had to be approved by a streamlined Department of Education. Boards of trustees of schools were made responsible for the appointment of principals. The principals, in turn, recommend the appointment of staff. Principals also were empowered and held accountable for the day-to-day management of the school by providing educational leadership, supervising management services, planning corporately, and facilitating governance.

The reforms also abolished the ten education boards and established education service centers in their stead to provide consultative and support services to schools. They created a national education review agency to evaluate each school's use of funds to meet charter objectives. They reduced the Department of Education greatly in size and limited its responsibilities. It now serves in a policy-advising role, managing property, distributing funds, and developing national guidelines for personnel, administration, governance, and curriculum. The State Services Commission negotiated new terms of service for administrators and teachers in a somewhat uncompromising manner (Macpherson, 1993).

With respect to the decision matrix in Figure 1.8, power was concentrated before reform in the profession—especially the Department of Education. After reform, power was more widely dispersed. School assessment was placed in an independent body at the national level—a move that centralized authority outside the profession. The Department of Education retained some influence over curriculum. The principal's role was strengthened at the school level but at the price of job security. The issue of job security for principals was placed in the hands of boards of trustees. Parental influence was strengthened politically through parents' roles in selecting and serving as school trustees.

JUXTAPOSITION

The framework for allocating authority in a system of schools presented in Figure 1.8 provides a useful lens through which to observe and evaluate these events within a society over time and across societies at a given time. In this section, we discuss the experiences of the United States, England, Australia, and New Zealand in juxtaposition according to the elements and relationships suggested by the model. In the next section, we derive twelve propositions from the juxtaposition analysis that may be useful as guides in developing school finance and other education policy.

Policy makers are embarking on similar educational reform strategies regardless of their political orientations. A Conservative government initiated England's reform. In Australia and New Zealand, the initiators were Labor governments. At the national level in the United States, reform was initially led by a Republican president. But a capture of the White House by the Democrats led to virtually no change in policy. At the state level, both Republican and Democratic administrations have brought about similar reforms. Drucker (1980), in speaking generally about the paradigm shifts we are experiencing universally, wrote:

The new realities fit neither the assumptions of the Left or of the Right. They do not mesh with "what everybody knows." They differ even from what everybody, regardless of political persuasion, still believes reality to be. "What is" differs totally from what both Right and Left believe "ought to be." (p. 10)

In the preface to his book analyzing the direction of education reform in England, Lawton (1992) made a similar observation:

During the course of 1989 and 1990, I also had the opportunity of visiting a number of other countries and talking to visitors from a wide variety of education systems. It was remarkable that so many of these countries, whatever the political complexion of the government in power, were undertaking "reforms" which in England were described as "Thatcherite." Clearly something was happening politically and educationally on more than a national scale. (p. ix)

Whitty (1992), another English analyst, echoed the same theme:

The support being given to the diversification of provision to local control of schools from a variety of political perspectives, as well as in other countries with different political regimes, should certainly caution us against viewing current reforms in Britain [or the United States] as merely expression of New Right ideology, which will pass with a change of government. (pp. 48–49)

We agree wholeheartedly with both British analysts that the current educational reform movement is a worldwide event, responding to universal forces and not just parochial ones.

The United States developed a highly decentralized system of public schooling a century and a half ago to further the objectives of equality in a sparsely populated, agrarian society. As the nation grew in population and became more industrialized and urbanized, a relatively equitable rural system evolved into a highly inequitable and divisive urban-suburban system. Efforts to restore equity brought oppressiveness, impersonality, and inefficiency to the public schools.

In search of equity and efficiency, Australia and New Zealand developed highly centralized systems of public schooling. Also in the name of equity, Australia extended extensive financial assistance to the mostly underfinanced private schools. This move had the unintended consequence of enhancing aspects of liberty. While the government and nonelite private schools now operate at about the same expenditure levels per pupil in Australia (McGaw, 1994), the nongovernment schools are setting the standards of excellence and efficiency. In seeking to bring efficiency to government schools, all Australian states have moved to trim down the central educational bureaucracies and to divest authority to schools. At the same time, control over curriculum and assessment are not being devolved. To restore some of the social control over equity lost in the public financing of private schools, there is a movement toward greater public regulation of private schools. Public schools are becoming more like private schools and private schools are becoming more like public schools.

The patterns in England and New Zealand are the clearest, perhaps, because they are rooted in unitary national systems. The reallocation of power is apparent. As McGinn and Street (1986) suggested in a quotation cited earlier, it is not government verses citizens but a redressing of the balance of power among government and citizens to improve efficiency and liberty. In many respects, Australia and the United States, on the one hand, and England and New Zealand, on the other, are moving in opposite directions (Murphy, 1983). But having started at opposite ends of the spectrum, they appear to be moving toward each other (Hughes, 1987). The patterns struck by the education reform acts of England and New Zealand could well be prototypes of the educational structures that Australia and the United States are seeking.

In comparing the four countries, we see similar policies being used concurrently for similar and different ends. Local management of schools and family choice are being used in all countries to bring about greater efficiency in the system by inducing marketlike forces. In England, those in power believe that greater efficiency can best be achieved by linking these reforms to restoring a selective school system, and they are moving to that end. In the United States, largely because of constitutional protections, efficiency must be achieved while retaining at least some degree of equity. Thus, in the United States, efficiency is being pursued through school-site management and family choice within a general policy of comprehensive schools. This policy was abandoned by the Tory government in England. The situation is not as clear in Australia and New Zealand. There is considerable concern among some analysts that Australia's policy of supporting private schools is also leading toward a selective system.

Nevertheless, there is more than meets the eye in comparing English reforms with the others. In England, we have seen the capture of the reform movement and the definition of national standards and the national curriculum by supporters of a single ideological perspective. This has not happened in the other three countries. In the United States, the whole range of ideological interests is present in the reform debate. A particular interest group may have won control of a school board here and secured a legislative victory there. But because of constitutional protections, the nature of the governmental structure, and the politics of diversity, it is virtually impossible in the United States for a single ideology to have the universal impact that it has had in England. This is probably true for Australia and New Zealand as well.

In comparing the politics of British education reforms with those in the other countries, we are reminded of Lindblom's (1959) admonition to political strategists to focus on means (policy), not ends (values). Because of the overlap of value systems, the abstractness of social systems, and the uncertainty of the outcomes of any course of social action, Lindblom argued (see Chapter 1) that partisans across the value spectrum can come to agreement on means although agreement on ends would be impossible. It seems to us that the Conservative Party in England got carried away by its ideological (values) agenda. In using their political power to the fullest, the Tories have pushed relentlessly toward their ideological goals with respect to curriculum content, standards, and restoration of selective schools. In the process, they have alienated much of the population, including the teachers who will have to implement their reforms. In the long run, this approach may prove to be self-defeating. Lawton (1992) suggested that sufficient common ground exists whereby the competing parties—right and left—can agree on means even if they hold quite different values and ultimate objectives for the education system. With a change in government in the United Kingdom—and this is almost inevitable—many, perhaps most, of the reforms introduced by the Conservative Party will remain in place. But their implementation will be redirected, with greater emphasis given to equity and diversity considerations.

The education systems of the United States and England were among the most decentralized in the world. As such, it may come as no surprise to observers of the international scene that the two countries are centralizing some functions that have been traditionally left to the periphery. The fact that they are decentralizing further some functions that had been the province of school districts and local education authorities to schools and parents may, on the surface, appear to be inconsistent with their centralizing initiatives. This is not, however, necessarily the case. Cummings and Riddell (1994) warned against confusing the requirements for macro and micro levels of education policy. England and the United States appear to be centralizing macropolicy (setting a national curriculum and standards) and decentralizing micropolicy (the organization and management of schools and the placement of pupils therein).

Australia and New Zealand had highly centralized school systems—Australia at the state level and New Zealand at the national level. In Australia

further centralization is taking place in the development of curriculum frameworks and assessment, with the placement at the federal level of some new responsibility for these functions that had previously been solely the province of the states. At the same time, Australian states are shifting significant authority and responsibility to the school level and have increased parental and community participation in decision making at that level. New Zealand has maintained much responsibility for curriculum development and assessment at the national level. The role of professional educators in these functions, however, has been reduced. Authority removed from the center in New Zealand has been placed directly with school trustees and school principals. Parental and community influence has been strengthened by empowering parents and citizens to elect school trustees and to serve as such. As in England and the United States, Australia and New Zealand are maintaining control of macropolicy at the center and devolving responsibility for micropolicy.

GUIDES FOR SCHOOL FINANCE POLICY

If we analyze the situations in England, Australia, New Zealand, and the United States with the aid of the framework presented in Figure 1.8, we can suggest a number of propositions as guides to formulating school finance policy specifically and education policy generally.

Proposition 1. The optimal provision of educational services for a society requires the *distribution* of authority among government, the teaching profession, and families.

Proposition 2. Consensus on what is an optimal provision of educational services is dynamic, shifting over time in response to changes in social, economic, political, technological, and ideological contexts.

Proposition 3. The family generally holds the most intimate knowledge about and caring concern for the child and is the preferred spokesman for the welfare of the child.

Proposition 4. Societal concerns are paramount where there are significant spillover benefits from education and where there are redistributive and intergenerational considerations.

Proposition 5. The teaching profession holds the technical expertise of schooling and is best qualified for making decisions concerning the organization and administration of educational services.

Proposition 6. Centralization of authority over education policy decisions reduces the realization of individual interests, increases social stress, and makes decision making and implementation more complex.

Proposition 7. Decentralization of authority over education policy increases inequity in the allocation of human and economic resources to the provision of educational services.

Proposition 8. Decentralization of authority over education policy increases heterogeneity and reduces social integration.

Proposition 9. Policies promoting equality have their greatest impact when made at a high level of social aggregation.

Proposition 10. The policy objectives of equity and fraternity require the involvement of government in decisions related to the allocation of resources and curriculum definition.

Proposition 11. The policy objectives of liberty and efficiency can best be realized through marketlike mechanisms such as school choice and school-based decision making.

Proposition 12. Realization of the policy objective of efficiency requires that the teaching profession play a dominant role in making decisions about how education services will be produced.

A better understanding of the accuracy and implications of these propositions is essential to developing informed policy with respect to education. Analyses and evaluations of the many natural experiments that take place around the world constitute an important part of the needed research. Since most developed Western nations face similar social and economic pressures, but with different policy priorities and governance structures, we can gain important insights into relationships among governance structures, policy priorities, and policy outcomes through cross-country comparisons. Education policy makers should also continue to be alert to, and guided by, the experiences of other information-age organizations in the public and private sectors.

SUMMARY

In this chapter, we have attempted to reframe the debate over centralization and decentralization of authority so that it moves beyond simplistic doctrinally driven disputes and focuses on the core questions of what should be loosely organized and tightly controlled at various levels of the system. Agreeing on acceptable allocation patterns of authority is a dynamic process, varying over time and among cultures according to priorities given to fundamental social and personal values. The nature of values and their impact upon individual and societal decision making was discussed.

We used the framework for analyzing the allocation of authority in a system of schools developed in Chapter 1 as a vehicle for evaluating alternative patterns of power distribution. The model depicts the political-economic structure as a grid of decisions (who gets what, when, and how) and decision makers (society/government, the teaching profession, and the family/client). We applied the model to the historical evolution of education governance in the United States and to the current situations in England, New Zealand, and Australia. We suggested a number of propositions as guides to the formulation of policy concerning the design of formal structures for making decisions about education and the allocation of ultimate authority among decision makers within the structures.

In Chapter 3, we direct our attention to the United States, examining the structure it has created for the financing and governance of education and tracing the history of its development. We discuss statistics on the human and financial dimensions of the educational enterprise. We also discuss major issues education policy makers are addressing currently along with alternative policy strategies being considered for dealing with them.

ACTIVITIES

1. Examine the education decision matrix presented in Figure 1.7. Fill in each blank cell with the decisions that can best be made by each classification of decision maker for each decision type; for example, what allocation of resource decisions can best be made by society, by the teaching profession, and by the family?

2. Numerous proposals have been put forth for reforming education. Discuss each proposal listed below in reference to the model of the political-economic system of education policy development presented in Figure 1.8 (p. 21). For each, describe the change from the status quo in the allocation of decision-making authority and in the relative priorities of the five values liberty, equality, fraternity, efficiency, and economic growth:
   - family choice of public schools
   - unconstrained educational vouchers
   - tax credits for private school tuition
   - professional control over admission to the profession
   - career ladders for teachers
   - school-based decision making
   - full state funding of schooling
   - state achievement testing to determine successful completion of high school

3. If you are studying school finance with persons from other nations, compare experiences and responses to activities 1 and 2 from the perspectives of policy makers in those nations.

4. McGinn and Street (cited on page 31) wrote:

   [C]ompetition and markets can contribute to social justice in circumstances where there is a relatively equitable balance of powers among the participants in the competition or market. . . . A strong state must first achieve some minimal degree of social equity so that decentralization can lead to genuine participation.

   - Describe policies that might be pursued by a strong state to "achieve some minimal degree of social equity so that decentralization can lead to genuine participation."
   - McGinn and Street used the term "state" in a generic sense. With respect to the United States, at what level can the "minimal degree of social equity" be guaranteed most effectively: federal, state, or local? What is the rationale for your answer?

COMPUTER SIMULATION

Objectives of This Activity

- *To develop a familiarity with elementary spreadsheet skills including data entry, labeling, and printing*
- *To develop an understanding of the trends in revenue sources for public elementary and secondary schools (see Table 1.1, p. 11)*

Caution: Before beginning this simulation, make a working copy of the Computer Simulation Disk. Use your working copy in completing the prescribed simulation exercises; the original disk is held as a backup in case you inadvertently destroy a file on the working copy.

Simulation 2.1: *Revenue for Public Education*[1]

a. Load your spreadsheet software (a version of Lotus 1-2-3 for DOS and Windows or Excel for Macintosh users) and consult your software program manual for assistance in retrieving a file from the Computer Simulation Disk that accompanies this text.

b. Retrieve the file REVENUE. The table that appears on your spreadsheet presents the total revenue available for elementary and secondary education and the proportion that is accounted for by local and state revenue in various years.

c. Note that the table does not report the percentage of federal revenue. In the column to the right of the STATE column, enter a new label: FEDERAL.

d. In the new FEDERAL column, beginning on the 1920 row, enter, in turn, the percentages of federal revenue listed below opposite each year listed in the table:

[1]If you are unfamiliar with spreadsheet software, it will be necessary for you to consult an appropriate manual in executing the instructions given below and throughout the simulations.

Federal

0.3
0.4
1.8
2.9
4.4
8.0
9.8
6.1
6.9

e. Insert a new column between the STATE and FEDERAL columns and enter a new column label: LOCAL & STATE.

f. In the new LOCAL & STATE column on the 1920 row, enter a formula that will add the LOCAL percentage to the STATE percentage.

g. Copy the formula through the column.

h. Format the LOCAL & STATE column as appropriate.

i. Save your file and print the revised table.

j. **Further Activities.** What trends are evident in the proportions of revenue derived from the three levels of government throughout the century? What changes do you anticipate over the next decade? How might they impact the decisions of a local board of education?

REFERENCES

Anderson, D. S. (1993). Public schools in decline: Implications of the privatization of schools in Australia. In H. Beare & W. L. Boyd (Eds.), *Restructuring schools: An international perspective on the movement to transform the control and performance of schools* (pp. 184–199). Washington, DC: Falmer.

Archer, M. S. (1984). *Social origins of educational systems*. London: SAGE Publications.

Beare, H., & Boyd, W. L. (1993). Introduction. In H. Beare & W. L. Boyd (Eds.), *Restructuring schools: An international perspective on the movement to transform the control and performance of schools* (pp. 2–11). Washington, DC: Falmer.

Benson, C. E. (1978). *The economics of public education* (3rd ed.). Boston: Houghton Mifflin.

Berne, R., & Stiefel, L. (1983). Changes in school finance equity: A national perspective. *Journal of Education Finance, 8,* 419–435.

Boyd, W. L. (1984). Competing values in educational policy and governance: Australian and American developments. *Educational Administration Review, 2* (2), 4–24.

Boyd, W. L. (1987). Balancing public and private schools: The Australian experience and American implications. In W. L. Boyd & D. Smart (Eds.), *Educational policy in Australia and America: Comparative perspectives* (pp. 163–183). New York: Falmer.

Butts, R. F. (1955). *Assumptions underlying Australian education.* Melbourne, Australia: Australian Council for Educational Research.

Caldwell, B. J. (1993). Paradox and uncertainty in the governance of education. In H. Beare & W. L. Boyd (Eds.), *Restructuring schools: An international perspective on the movement to transform the control and performance of schools* (pp. 158–173). Washington, DC: Falmer.

Callahan, R. E. (1962). *Education and the cult of efficiency: A study of the social forces that have shaped the administration of the public schools.* Chicago: University of Chicago Press.

Chubb, J. E., & Moe, T. M. (1985). *Politics, markets, and the organization of schools* (Project Report No. 85-A15). Stanford, CA: Stanford University School of Education, Institute for Research on Educational Finance and Governance.

Chubb, J. E., & Moe, T. M. (1990). *Politics, markets, and America's schools.* Washington, DC: Brookings Institution.

Clune, W. H. (1993). The shift from equity to adequacy in school finance. *The World and I, 8:* 9, 389–405.

Coleman, J. S., & Hoffer, T. (1987). *Public and private high schools: The impact of communities.* New York: Basic Books.

Coons, J. E., & Sugarman, S. D. (1978). *Education by choice: The case for family control.* Berkeley, CA: University of California Press.

Cremin, L. A. (1976). *Public education.* New York: Basic Books.

Cummings, W. K., & Riddell, A. (1994). Alternative policies for the finance, control, and delivery of basic education. *International Journal of Education Research.* Forthcoming.

Day, G. (1993). *School Teachers' Review Body, Second report.* London: HMSO.

Department of Education and Science. (1978). *The Department of Education and Science—a Brief Guide.* London: The Department.

Dewey, J. (1916). *Democracy and education.* New York: Macmillan.

Drucker, P. F. (1980). *Managing in turbulent times.* New York: Harper and Row.

Drucker, P. F. (1989). *The new realities: In government and politics, in economics and business, in society and world view.* New York: Harper and Row.

The education reform act. (1988). London: HMSO.

Elmore, R. F. (1993). School decentralization: Who gains? Who loses? In J. Hannaway & M. Carnoy (Eds.), *Decentralization and school improvement* (pp. 33–54). San Francisco: Jossey-Bass.

Elmore, R. F., & McLaughlin, M. W. (1988). *Steady work: Policy, practice, and the reform of American education* (Report No. R-3574-NIE/RC). Santa Monica, CA: The RAND Corporation.

Farrar, E., DeSanctis, J. E., & Cohen, D. K. (1980, Fall). Views from below: Implementation research in education. *Teachers College Record,* 77–100.

Foster, W. P. (1986). *Paradigms and promises: New approaches to educational administration.* Buffalo, NY: Prometheus.

Friedman, M. (1962). *Capitalism and freedom.* Chicago: University of Chicago Press.

Fuhrman, S., & Johnson, S. M. (1994). Lessons from Victoria. *Phi Delta Kappan, 75,* 770–774.

Getzels, J. W. (1957). Changing values challenge the schools. *School Review, 65,* 91–102.

Getzels, J. W. (1978). The school and the acquisition of values. In R. W. Tyler (Ed.), *From youth to constructive adult life: The role of the school* (pp. 43–66). Berkeley, CA: McCutchan.

Guthrie, J. W. (Ed.). (1980). *School finance policies and practices: The 1980s, a decade of conflict.* Cambridge, MA: Ballinger.

Guthrie, J. W., Garms, W. I., & Pierce, L. C. (1988). *School finance and education policy: Enhancing educational efficiency, equality, and choice.* Englewood Cliffs, NJ: Prentice Hall.

Hancock, G., Kirst, M. W., & Grossman, D. L. (Eds.). (1983). *Contemporary issues in educational policy: Perspectives from Australia and USA.* Canberra, Australia: Australian Capital Territory Schools Authority.

Hodgkinson, C. (1983). *The philosophy of leadership.* Oxford, England: Basil Blackwell.

Hogan, M. (1984). *Public vs. private schools: Funding and direction in Australia.* Ringwood, Victoria, Australia: Penguin Books.

Hoy, W. K., & Miskel, C. G. (1991). *Educational administration: Theory, research, and practice* (4th ed.). New York: McGraw-Hill.

Hughes, P. (1987). Reorganization in education in a climate of changing social expectations: A commentary.

In W. L. Boyd & D. Smart (Eds.), *Educational policy in Australia and America: Comparative perspectives* (pp. 295–309). New York: Falmer.

Iannaccone, L. (1985). Excellence: An emergent educational issue. *Politics of Education Bulletin, 12,* pp. 1, 3–8.

Iannaccone, L. (1988). From equity to excellence: Political context and dynamics. In W. L. Boyd & C. T. Kerchner (Eds.), *The politics of excellence and choice in education* (pp. 49–65). New York: Falmer.

Kahne, J. (1994). Democratic communities, equity, and excellence: A Deweyan reframing of educational policy analysis. *Educational Evaluation and Policy Analysis, 16,* 233–248.

Koppich, J. E., & Guthrie, J. W. (1993). Ready, A. I. M., Reform: Building a model of education reform and "high politics." In H. Beare & W. L. Boyd (Eds.), *Restructuring schools: An international perspective on the movement to transform the control and performance of schools* (pp. 12–28). Washington, DC: Falmer.

Lawton, D. (1992). *Education and politics in the 1990s: Conflict or consensus?* London: Falmer.

Lawton, S. B. (1993). A decade of reform in Canada: Encounters with the octopus, the elephant, and the five dragons. In H. Beare & W. L. Boyd (Eds.), *Restructuring schools: An international perspective on the movement to transform the control and performance of schools* (pp. 86–105). Washington, DC: Falmer.

Levin, B. (1987). The courts as educational policy-makers in the USA. In W. L. Boyd & D. Smart (Eds.), *Educational policy in Australia and America: Comparative perspectives* (pp. 100–128). New York: Falmer.

Levy, M. J., Jr. (1966). *Modernization and the structure of societies: A setting for international affairs* (Vol. 1). Princeton, NJ: Princeton University Press.

Lindblom, C. E. (1959). The science of muddling through. *Public Administration Review, 19,* 79–88.

Locke, J. (1690/1956). *The second treatise of government.* Oxford, England: Basil Blackwell.

Louden, L. W., & Browne, R. K. (1993). Developments in education policy in Australia: A perspective on the 1980s. In H. Beare & W. L. Boyd (Eds.), *Restructuring schools: An international perspective on the movement to transform the control and performance of schools* (pp. 106–135). Washington, DC: Falmer.

Macpherson, R. J. S. (1993). The reconstruction of New Zealand education: A case of "high politics" reform? In H. Beare & W. L. Boyd (Eds.), *Restructuring schools: An international perspective on the movement to transform the control and performance of schools* (pp. 69–85). Washington, DC: Falmer.

McGaw, B. (1994). Effectiveness or economy. *Australian Council for Educational Research (ACER) Newsletter Supplement,* March.

McGinn, N., & Street, S. (1986). Educational decentralization: Weak state or strong stage? *Comparative Education Review, 30,* 471–490.

McNeil, L. M. (1986). *Contradictions of control: School structure and school knowledge.* New York: Routledge, Chapman and Hall.

Murphy, J. T. (1983). School administrators besieged: A look at Australian and American education. In G. Hancock, M. W. Kirst, & D. L. Grossman (Eds.), *Contemporary issues in educational policy: Perspectives from Australia and USA* (pp. 77–96). Canberra, Australia: Australian Capital Territory Schools Authority and Curriculum Development Centre.

Naisbitt, J. (1982). *Megatrends: Ten new directions transforming our lives.* New York: Warner Books.

Naisbitt, J., & Aburdene, P. (1990). *Megatrends, 2000: Ten new directions for the 1990s.* New York: Morrow.

Nyberg, D. (1977). Education as community expression. *Teachers College Record, 79,* 205–223.

Nyberg, D. (1981). *Power over power: What power means in ordinary life, how it is related to acting freely, and what it can contribute to a renovated ethics of education.* Ithaca, NY: Cornell University Press.

Nyberg, D. (1993). *The varnished truth: Truth telling and deceiving in ordinary life.* Chicago: University of Chicago Press.

Parsons, T. (1951). *The social system.* New York: Free Press.

Partridge, P. H. (1968). *Society, schools, and progress in Australia.* Oxford, England: Pergamon.

Patton, T. J. (1992). *Choice and diversity: A new framework for schools.* London: HMSO.

Peters, T. J. (1988). *Thriving on chaos: Handbook for a management revolution.* New York: Knopf.

Peters, T. J., & Waterman, R. H., Jr. (1982). *In search of excellence: Lessons from America's best-run companies.* New York: Warner Books.

Picot, B. (1988). *Administering for excellence,* Report of the Task Force to Review Education Administration (Brian Picot, Chairperson). Wellington, New Zealand Government Printer.

Ravitch, D. (1983). *The troubled crusade: American education 1945–1980.* New York: Basic Books.

Ravitch, D. (1985). *The schools we deserve: Reflections on the educational crises of our times.* New York: Basic Books.

Rokeach, M. (1973). *The nature of human values.* New York: Free Press.

Slater, R. O. (1993). On centralization, decentralization, and school restructuring: A sociological perspective. In H. Beare & W. L. Boyd (Eds.), *Restructuring schools: An international perspective on the movement to transform the control and performance of schools* (pp. 174–183). Washington, DC: Falmer.

Toffler, A. (1980). *The third wave.* New York: Bantam Books.

Tyack, D. B. (1974). *The one best system: A history of American urban education.* Cambridge, MA: Harvard University Press.

Tyack, D. B. (1993). School governance in the United States: Historical puzzles and anomalies. In J. Hannaway & M. Carnoy (Eds.), *Decentralization and school improvement* (pp. 1–32). San Francisco: Jossey-Bass.

Weiler, H. N. (1993). Control versus legitimation: The politics of ambivalence. In J. Hannaway & M. Carnoy (Eds.), *Decentralization and school improvement* (pp. 55–83). San Francisco: Jossey-Bass.

Whitty, G. (1992). Urban education in England and Wales. In D. Cowlby, C. Jones, & D. Harris (Eds.), *World yearbook of education: Urban education* (39–53). London: Kogan Page.

Wirt, F. M. (1987). National Australia–United States education: A commentary. In W. L. Boyd & D. Smart (Eds.), *Educational policy in Australia and America: Comparative perspectives* (pp. 129–137). New York: Falmer.

Wise, A. E. (1979). *Legislated learning: The bureaucratization of the American classroom.* Berkeley, CA: University of California Press.

Wise, A. E. (1988). Two conflicting trends in school reform: Legislated learning revisited. *Phi Delta Kappan, 69,* 328–332.

CHAPTER 3

School Governance and Finance in the United States

Primary Issues Explored in This Chapter:

- *Governance structure:* What is the history and current structure of the multilevel governance that oversees and provides resources for public education?
- *Demographics of schooling:* How have the dimensions of the educational enterprise—in terms

of enrollments, employees, and resources to support its programs—changed over the years?
- *Current and emerging issues:* What are the critical social, economic, and political issues that must be addressed through education and school finance policies?

The model of the economic-political system presented in Chapter 1 became the framework for our discussion of values and allocations of authority in Chapter 2. We suggested that the ideal balance in the distribution of authority varies from time to time and from culture to culture according to the relative priorities placed on different values.

The distribution pattern of authority can be referred to as the governance structure, and its nature directly influences the nature of the decisions made. The governance structure must change to accommodate changes in social expectations; if it does not, unrest may develop and governments may fall, either through orderly elections or through revolution. In Western democratic societies, change is usually an evolutionary or incremental process. In this chapter, we address the evolution of the structure of educational governance and finance in the United States.

A HISTORICAL SYNOPSIS OF THE DEVELOPMENT OF SCHOOL GOVERNANCE AND FINANCE IN THE UNITED STATES

In a critical analysis of public education in the United States in 1942, Henry C. Morrison (1943) referred to its structure disdainfully as "late New England colonial" (p. 258) and described the school district as "a little republic at every crossroads" (p. 75). Morrison was focusing on a characteristic of the system of American public education that makes it unique among the systems of the world—its extreme decentralization. Herein lie both its strengths and its weaknesses.

Decentralized systems seem to be more adept than highly centralized and bureaucratic systems at mobilizing the energies of their constituents and adapting curricula and instructional systems to the diversity of their constituents. Yet decentralized systems have a strong tendency to be inequitable, providing services of unequal quality. The good schools in a decentralized system tend to be very, very good; but such a system also generates—and tolerates—very poor schools. Bringing about a greater degree of equity and setting minimally acceptable social standards require intervention by higher levels of government, that is, state or federal. Such intervention has been increasingly frequent over the fifty-five years since Morrison made his analysis.

Collective concern over the formal education of the young is generally traced to the beginning of European settlement in what is now the continental United States. Massachusetts was particularly influential in setting the parameters for public education. It was the Massachusetts Colony that first required parents to train their children in reading and writing, first required towns to establish schools, first appropriated colonial funds to encourage the establishment of schools, and first permitted towns to use revenue from property taxation to support schooling. All of this happened before 1650. These events, however, must be interpreted in the light of the interrelationships between the government of the Massachusetts Colony and the Congregational (Puritan) Church. Suffrage and office holding were limited to male church members, a minority of the total population. The property tax that supported the school also supported the church and its clergy. The meetinghouse served as the school as well as the church and the town hall (Johnson, 1904). This early pattern of community control of schools leaves its press upon the organization of public education in the United States even today, although the connection between church and state is no longer permitted.

Several of the authors of the United States Constitution in 1787 had firm beliefs about the importance of an educated citizenry to the success of the new republic. But the Constitution itself is silent on the subject of education; and the Tenth Amendment assured that the powers not specifically delegated to the federal government were "reserved to the States respectively, or to the people." The founders, such as Thomas Jefferson, pursued the provision of public education at the state level. In his *Notes on the State of Virginia,* written in 1781–1782, Jefferson (1968) argued:

> Every government degenerates when trusted to the rulers of the people alone. The people themselves therefore are its only safe depositories. And to render even them safe, their minds must be improved. (p. 390)

In seeking additional funds for education from the New York State Legislature, Governor DeWitt Clinton (1826/1909) noted the importance of state sponsorship of education in a democracy:

> The first duty of government, and the surest evidence of good government, is the encouragement of education. A general diffusion of knowledge is the precursor and protector of republican institutions; and in it we must confide as the conservative power that will watch over our liberties, and guard against fraud, intrigue, corruption and violence. (p. 114)

In 1834, in a desperate effort to save Pennsylvania's newly enacted common school legislation from being repealed by tax cutters, Thaddeus Stevens (1990) stated plainly the common benefit to be realized from those tax dollars:

> Many complain of this tax, not so much on account of its amount, as because it is for the benefit of others and not themselves. This is a great mistake; it is for their own benefit, inasmuch as it perpetuates the government and insures the due administration of the laws under which they live, and by which their lives and property are protected. (p. 520)

Stevens went on to draw the connection between education and the prevention of crime, using an argument still heard today: that it is wiser, less expensive, and more humane to aid "that which goes to support his fellow-being from becoming a criminal, and to obviate the necessity of those humiliating [penal] institutions. (p. 520)"

Although the importance of education to the general welfare has been recognized traditionally, it should be noted that education was originally promoted for religious, political, and social purposes—not for economic reasons as it is today. The link between economic productivity and education had been noted by Adam Smith in his treatise on *The Wealth of Nations* in 1776, but it wasn't until the latter half of the twentieth century that economic theory (human capital theory in particular) became strongly influential in the formulation of public policy on education (see the discussion of human capital theory in Chapter 1).

Because of a desire to limit the powers of the federal government and because of the sheer infeasibility in the eighteenth and nineteenth centuries of providing human services nationally, education was made a function of the states. Even at the state level, the dispersion of the population, the primitive means of communication, and the general lack of resources made central control of education impractical. Thus, the states invented the school district as a local form of government to create and oversee schools. Cubberley (1947) commented on the spread of the school district concept nationwide:

> As an administrative and taxing unit it was well suited to the primitive needs and conditions of our early national life. Among a sparse and hard-working rural population, between whom intercourse was limited and intercommunication difficult, and with whom the support of schools was as yet an unsettled question, local control answered a very real need. The simplicity and democracy of the system was one of its chief merits. Communities or neighborhoods which wanted schools and were willing to pay for them could easily meet and organize a school district, vote to levy a school tax on their own property, employ a teacher, and organize and maintain a

school. . . . On the other hand, communities which did not desire schools or were unwilling to tax themselves for them could do without them, and let the free-school idea alone. (pp. 212–213)

Cubberley's description points to one of the difficulties of the district system once universal education became the policy of a state. The district system worked well for the willing and able, but for those who were unwilling, there was not the leadership to organize a district; and for those who were not able, there were not the resources. Inequities within the district system became apparent even during the colonial period, but with the increasing concentration of capital through industrialization and urbanization, inequities became much more severe in the nineteenth and twentieth centuries.

Attempts to address these inequities began in the nineteenth century through greater state oversight, the beginning of state aid to school districts, and the encouragement of school district consolidation. Districts that came into existence voluntarily, however, very rapidly attached loyalty to their achievements and took great pride in them. They were not responsive to criticism of their endeavors from the state and resented all constraints placed on them. Those areas that had chosen not to operate a common school were equally resistant to external compulsion to do so, especially when it involved compulsory taxation.

In an effort to establish order out of chaos, state boards of education were formed and provided with an executive officer. The first state to take such action was New York in 1812. As testimony to the sensitive nature of the position, New York's first superintendent of instruction, Gideon Hawley, served only until 1821, when the office was eliminated. A comparable office was not created again in New York State until 1854. Horace Mann, the first secretary to the Board of Education of Massachusetts, ran into similar difficulty; however, attempts to dissolve his office and the board were unsuccessful.

The first school districts to go through the process of consolidation were in cities. While New England towns and cities were coterminous with their school districts from the beginning, this was not typically true of more western cities. Buffalo, the first city to employ a superintendent of schools, serves as a good illustration. Although it had private schools before, the first school supported by taxes was established in 1818. By 1837, the city had 15,000 inhabitants and seven one-teacher school districts. That year, a superintendent of schools was appointed to supervise and to coordinate those seven schools, to establish schools in wards of the city that were without schools, and to provide for a central high school. Detroit, Chicago, and Cleveland followed similar patterns. A few cities continue to be served by more than one school district.

Extensive consolidation of rural school districts had to wait until improved means of transportation became available—well into the twentieth century. The number of school districts did not show a marked decrease until after World War II. In 1930, the number exceeded 127,000 nationwide (National Center for Education Statistics, 1980); by 1993, the number had dropped to approximately 14,550 districts (U.S. Bureau of the Census, 1993). Today, the tradition of local control remains strong, but the inequities that are inherent in such a policy are a primary cause of the current system's malaise (Kozol, 1991). Satisfying national and state educational concerns while accommodating unique local needs and priorities remains a dilemma.

The structural, organizational, and curricular changes in the public provision of educational services during the late nineteenth and early twentieth centuries reflected larger social, political, and economic changes experienced by the United States including industrialization, urbanization, and massive immigration. The net result of these developments was a rapid growth of cities. Many cities had large slums inhabited by migrants from the countryside and immigrants, largely from rural and impoverished sections of Europe. In 1820, there was only one city in the United States that exceeded 100,000 in population; by 1860, there were nine. In 1820, there were only 34 communities with populations over 5,000; by 1860, there were 229 (DeYoung, 1989).

With the coming of industrialization, a number of educational advocates became interested in the possibilities of vocational education. The federal government encouraged the development of vocational education with the Morrill Act of 1862, which provided land grants to states, the proceeds from which were to be used to establish colleges wherein agriculture, mechanical arts, and military tactics could be taught. In 1890, the federal government made money grants available for the same purpose. The federal government first made money grants available to secondary education in 1917 for the purpose of encouraging vocational programs at that level.

The early twentieth century saw the formalization of the state's role in the financing of education. At the turn of the century, state involvement was minimal, representing less than 15 percent of total expenditures and distributed primarily in the form of categorical aid. Cubberley (1905) argued for a strong state presence in the provision of educational services and the establishment of minimum provision standards. He sought school improvement through incentives for a longer school term, more teachers, and teacher supervision.

A practical design for equalizing local resources was developed by Strayer and Haig (1923) in the form of the foundation program, which continues to serve as the basis for distributing general aid to schools in most states (see discussion in Chapter 8). The Strayer–Haig formula was first enacted into law in New York State in 1924 using Mort's (1924) concept of the weighted pupil unit, a concept still incorporated into all general aid formulas (see discussion in Chapter 9). Today state financial support of elementary and secondary education approximately equals that provided by local government.

Equity among school districts and among pupils became an increasing concern during the 1950s, 1960s, and 1970s, spurred by the civil rights movement and litigation in both state and federal courts. At the federal level, the Elementary and Secondary Education Act of 1965 assumed a strategy of compensatory education to meet the special needs of "at-risk" children; other legislation championed the rights of disabled persons and affirmative action. Legislation similar to that adopted at the federal level was enacted by the states. Tyack, Lowe, and Hansot (1984, p. 219) attribute many of our problems today to the success of these programs.

> The redistribution of funds to the needy, increased educational attainment among youth from poor and minority families, new protections of student rights, willingness to address controversial issues, attempts to adapt the school curriculum to a pluralistic population, sensitivity to ethnic and linguistic differences, attempts to remedy bias by gender, efforts to desegregate schools—these were the fruit of a generation of deliberate campaigns to render schools more equal and just.

The schools had reached out to include formerly excluded populations. As schools tried to assist more heterogeneous and needy students, the task of educating all students grew harder and the results more ambiguous. When all populations were included, educational costs increased dramatically and average achievement scores dropped, giving the perception of declining standards and less efficiency. The current pressure for higher standards is due in part to the recognition that it is not sufficient only to involve formerly excluded populations in the mainstream education system; in addition, these populations must be brought up to the levels of achievement of the majority if they are to be fully participating and contributing members of society. How to do this in a fiscally prudent manner is a recurring theme of this book, and of Parts IV and V in particular.

CURRENT ORGANIZATION OF SCHOOL GOVERNANCE

Although the particulars vary from state to state, the dominant pattern of educational governance that has evolved provides five levels of influence:

the federal government, state governments, intermediate school districts, school districts, and schools. The authority for making policy is concentrated at two of these levels: the state and the school district.

State Authority

The primary level of authority is the state, as represented by the legislature, governor, state board of education, state superintendent of education, state education department, and state courts. This level is charged with establishing basic policy for the system, including its financing, and with overseeing and coordinating its components. Structural and financial considerations are usually attended to through formal legislative processes that involve the governor and the legislature, although guidance is provided through several state constitutions. Oversight of the education law with some degree of discretion is delegated to the state board of education and the chief state school officer (CSSO). State boards of education are most commonly appointed by the governors, although some are popularly elected. In New York and South Carolina they are elected by the state legislatures, and in Washington they are elected by local school board members. The CSSO oversees operation of the state education department and in most cases is the chief executive of the state school board. The CSSO is most commonly a professional educator appointed by the state board of education, although in some states the CSSO is appointed by the governor, and in others is popularly elected. State education departments are the administrative agencies that implement the education laws of the states and the policies of the state school boards.

States exercise their authority over public education through general statements in their constitutions that give state legislatures authority to establish a system of public schools. For example, the New Jersey Constitution provides that the state legislature shall provide a "thorough and efficient" system of education. For the most part, the details of school governance, that is, procedures for establishing, financing, and governing school districts, teacher certification, and so forth, are established by statutes enacted by state legislatures or through regulations promulgated by state boards of education. This permits states a great deal of flexibility in reforming school governance structures without going through the cumbersome process of constitutional amendment.

There is much diversity among the states in their ability and willingness to support public services. This diversity contributes to the overall inequity in the provision of public education as illustrated by statistics reported in Table 3.1 for the fifty states. Variation is evident on every dimension: size, wealth, expenditure, and effort. Enrollments in state school systems ranged from over 5,340,000 in California to 101,000 in Wyoming. Median household income, a measure of wealth or ability to support public services, ranged from $40,500 in New Jersey to $22,191 in Mississippi, among the 48 contiguous states. The state with the lowest per pupil expenditure for schools was Arkansas ($3,303); Mississippi was only slightly higher ($3,567). Excluding Alaska, whose figures are distorted by a cost of living that is at least 25 percent higher than in the forty-eight contiguous states, the highest-spending state was New Jersey; its $9,136 expenditure was nearly $6,000 per pupil more than the average expenditures in Mississippi and Arkansas. Again excluding Alaska, total earned income for teachers during the 1993–1994 school year ranged from $48,905 in Connecticut to $24,430 in South Dakota. The pupil : teacher ratios were most favorable in Vermont, at 12.5 to one, and New Jersey, at 13.6 to one; the least favorable ratio was in California, at 24.1 to one.

School Districts

The second level of authority is the local school district, which is charged with implementing state policy. School districts are governed by boards of education that focus on the delivery of educational services. Most school boards are fiscally indepen-

TABLE 3.1. Selected Public School Statistics Related to Membership, Household Income, Expenditure, and Staffing of State Systems

State	(1) Estimated Membership (thousands) 1994–95	(2) Median Household Income 1993	(3) Estimated per Pupil Expenditure 1994–95	(4) Average Teacher Total Earned Income 1993–94	(5) Estimated Pupil : Teacher Ratio 1994–95
Alabama	733	25,082	4,136	28,062	17.6
Alaska	122	42,931	9,320	46,903	16.8
Arizona	792	30,510	3,750	32,380	21.1
Arkansas	432	23,039	3,303	27,016	15.0
California	5,340	34,073	5,297	40,898	24.1
Colorado	641	34,488	5,101	33,118	18.5
Connecticut	503	39,516	7,545	48,905	14.6
Delaware	107	36,064	6,591	38,671	16.6
Florida	2,109	28,550	5,185	32,389	16.7
Georgia	1,271	31,663	4,595	29,705	16.4
Hawaii	183	42,662	5,050	35,920	17.9
Idaho	240	31,010	4,158	27,420	19.5
Illinois	1,919	32,857	6,502	37,814	17.0
Indiana	973	29,475	5,543	36,695	17.5
Iowa	499	28,663	5,252	28,351	15.6
Kansas	461	29,770	5,228	30,501	15.1
Kentucky	655	24,376	4,599	31,519	17.3
Louisiana	782	26,312	4,277	24,923	16.6

TABLE 3.1. Selected Public School Statistics Related to Membership, Household Income, Expenditure, and Staffing of State Systems (*Continued*)

State	(1) Estimated Membership (thousands) 1994–95	(2) Median Household Income 1993	(3) Estimated per Pupil Expenditure 1994–95	(4) Average Teacher Total Earned Income 1993–94	(5) Estimated Pupil: Teacher Ratio 1994–95
Maine	216	27,438	6,025	30,649	14.0
Maryland	791	39,939	6,249	39,350	17.6
Massachusetts	898	37,064	6,551	38,340	14.3
Michigan	1,604	32,662	6,286	44,055	19.9
Minnesota	827	33,682	5,472	35,999	17.4
Mississippi	503	22,191	3,567	24,990	17.8
Missouri	862	28,682	4,502	29,216	15.3
Montana	164	26,470	5,091	27,591	16.5
Nebraska	286	31,008	5,589	26,859	14.5
Nevada	251	35,814	4,677	34,515	18.9
New Hampshire	186	37,964	6,391	34,159	15.9
New Jersey	1,175	40,500	9,136	46,735	13.6
New Mexico	316	26,758	6,039	27,513	17.3
New York	2,791	31,697	8,217	47,016	15.1
North Carolina	1,147	28,820	4,682	28,005	16.4
North Dakota	119	28,118	5,740	24,757	14.9
Ohio	1,825	31,285	7,040	34,814	17.6
Oklahoma	611	26,260	6,846	27,646	15.3
Oregon	522	33,138	5,740	34,893	19.9
Pennsylvania	1,780	30,995	7,040	41,844	17.4
Rhode Island	147	33,509	6,846	40,789	21.0
South Carolina	642	26,053	4,292	29,112	16.5
South Dakota	143	27,737	4,321	24,430	15.1
Tennessee	866	25,102	3,920	29,134	17.7
Texas	3,680	28,727	4,894	29,176	15.1
Utah	472	35,786	3,431	28,907	21.6
Vermont	107	31,065	6,765	34,016	12.5
Virginia	1,059	36,433	5,405	31,880	14.7
Washington	934	35,655	5,724	37,152	20.2
West Virginia	310	22,421	5,887	30,366	14.8
Wisconsin	857	31,766	6,398	36,448	15.3
Wyoming	101	29,442	5,827	30,005	15.2

SOURCE: For data in columns 1, 3, and 5: NCES (National Center for Education Statistics). (1995c). *Public Elementary and Secondary Education Statistics: School Year 1994–95 Early estimates.* Washington, DC: U.S. Department of Education; for data in column 4: NCES (1995d). *Schools and Staffing in the United States: Selected Data for Public and Private Schools, 1993–94.* Washington, DC: U.S. Department of Education; for data in column 2: U.S. Bureau of the Census (1995). *Income, Poverty, and Valuation of Noncash Benefits, 1993,* Series P60-188. Washington, DC: U.S. Government Printing Office.

dent, that is, have taxing authority, although some are fiscally dependant on another unit of local government, such as a town, city, or county. School board members are typically elected in nonpartisan elections, although some board members are appointed, especially in larger cities. One of the board's most important responsibilities is to appoint a superintendent of schools to serve as chief executive officer of the school district and to supervise its professional and support personnel.

Hawaii is the only state to function as a unitary school governance unit, and with 183,000 students, it is smaller than a number of large city districts. Texas leads the states in numbers of school districts, with 1,052, all of which are fiscally independent (Gold, Smith, & Lawton, 1995). California has 1,002 fiscally dependent school districts, including 302 that are unified (provide for pupils in all grades, K–12), 593 that operate elementary schools only, and 107 that operate high schools only. Over half of California's school districts enroll fewer than 500 pupils. The number and selected characteristics of school districts by state and Canadian province are reported in Table 3.2.

A much different, but less common, policy of school district organization is typified by Maryland. Maryland's 24 fiscally dependent school districts are organized by county and the City of Baltimore. The county organization prevails in the southeast region of the country; Florida, for example, has 67 fiscally independent school districts and Alabama has 127 fiscally dependent school districts. Some western states also follow a regional pattern. Nevada has 17 fiscally independent school districts, coterminous with counties, and Wyoming has 49 fiscally independent districts (Gold et al., 1995). It is apparent that there is a rich diversity in school district organizations among the states and even within some states.

TABLE 3.2. Number of School Districts and Fiscal Authority by State and Province for the United States and Canada

State/Province	Number of Districts			Comments
	Fiscally Dependent	Fiscally Independent	Total	
Alabama	127	0	127	School district boundaries are coterminous with city and county boundaries.
Alaska	54	0	54	34 city and borough districts are dependent on local governments and 20 Regional Education Attendance Areas are dependent on the state legislature.
Arizona	4	222	226	The fiscally dependent districts serve Native American reservations that have no tax base. The fiscally independent districts consist of 88 unified or K–12 districts, 18 union high school districts, and 116 elementary districts.
Arkansas	0	315	315	
California	1,002	0	1,002	There are 302 unified, 593 elementary, and 107 high school districts. Local property taxes are limited to 1% of assessed value.
Colorado	0	176	176	
Connecticut	166	0	166	149 districts are operated by towns and 17 are regional, multitown districts.
Delaware	0	19	19	All funds, including local tax funds, are held in state accounts; the state treasurer functions as treasurer for all school districts.

TABLE 3.2. Number of School Districts and Fiscal Authority by State and Province for the United States and Canada (*Continued*)

| State/Province | Number of Districts | | | Comments |
	Fiscally Dependent	Fiscally Independent	Total	
Florida	0	67	67	School districts are coterminous with county boundaries.
Georgia	23	159	182	The fiscally independent districts are coterminous with counties; the dependent districts are city school systems.
Hawaii	1	0	1	There is a single, completely state-funded system. Hawaii has no local tax revenue for schools and no local boards of education.
Idaho	0	115	115	
Illinois	0	925	925	There are 415 unit districts (grades K–12), 400 elementary districts (K–8), and 110 high school districts (9–12).
Indiana	0	294	294	
Iowa	0	397	397	Only 358 districts have high school programs; 90 districts share grades and programs.
Kansas	0	304	304	
Kentucky	0	176	176	
Louisiana	0	66	66	There are 64 parish school systems and 2 city school systems.
Maine	211	73	284	The fiscally dependent school districts are organized as a part of a municipal government. The fiscally independent districts serve more than one municipality.
Maryland	24	0	24	School district boundaries are coterminous with county boundaries and the City of Baltimore.
Massachusetts	361	0	361	School districts include 55 academic regional school districts, three independent vocational schools, and two county agricultural schools.
Michigan	0	560	560	The state has 524 K–12 school districts, plus 36 school districts with other grade configurations.
Minnesota	0	395	395	
Mississippi	149	0	149	School districts are organized as county, municipal, or consolidated units.
Missouri	0	530	530	80 districts offer instruction through grade 8 only, while 450 offer instruction in grades K–12.
Montana	0	495	495	133 districts operate high schools; 322 districts operate elementary schools, 31 operate K–12 districts, and 9 are nonoperating elementary districts.

(Continued)

TABLE 3.2. Number of School Districts and Fiscal Authority by State and Province for the United States and Canada (*Continued*)

State/Province	Number of Districts			Comments
	Fiscally Dependent	Fiscally Independent	Total	
Nebraska	0	692	692	271 districts offer grades K–12, 22 districts offer secondary grades only (7–12 or 9–12), 399 are elementary districts offering grades K–8 or K–6.
Nevada	0	17	17	All districts are coterminous with county boundaries.
New Hampshire	175	1	176	132 are single town districts. 30 serve two or more towns. 14 districts do not operate schools. All school districts are fiscally dependent except for the capital city.
New Jersey	0	580	580	
New Mexico	0	88	88	Local revenues account for less than 3% of operating costs.
New York	5	686	691	Fiscally dependent districts are the 5 largest urban districts. 661 districts operate grades K–12; 30 districts offer other grade configurations.
North Carolina	118	2	120	School district boundaries are coterminous with 100 county and 20 city boundaries. Two city districts are fiscally independent.
North Dakota	0	260	260	119 districts serve grades K–12, 49 are elementary districts, 11 are one-room rural districts, and 9 districts are nonoperating.
Ohio	0	611	611	
Oklahoma	0	554	554	436 districts offer K–12 grades, and 118 offer K–8 only.
Oregon	0	277	277	186 districts serve grades K–12, 74 serve elementary grades only, and 17 are union high school districts.
Pennsylvania	1	500	501	One school district is nonoperating. Philadelphia is the only fiscally dependent school district.
Rhode Island	37	0	37	
South Carolina	71	20	91	
South Dakota	0	178	178	
Tennessee	139	0	139	School district boundaries are coterminous with county and city boundaries except for 14 special school districts.
Texas	0	1,052	1,052	
Utah	0	40	40	
Vermont	0	251	251	School districts are coterminous with town and city boundaries. Several towns do not operate schools and some combine resources to provide educational

State/Province	Number of Districts			Comments
	Fiscally Dependent	**Fiscally Independent**	**Total**	
				services. There are 32 union school districts, 4 unified districts, and 2 joint operating school districts.
Virginia	137	0	137	
Washington	0	296	296	247 districts serve grades K–12, and 49 districts serve other grade configurations.
West Virginia	0	55	55	Districts are coterminous with county boundaries.
Wisconsin	0	427	427	370 districts have grades K–12, 10 have grades 9–12, and 47 have grades K–8.
Wyoming	0	49	49	Wyoming has K–12 unified districts and districts providing grades K–8.
Canadian Provinces				
Alberta	0	145	145	There are 89 public school boards, 44 Roman Catholic separate school boards, and 6 other school boards; public funds are also available to independent schools.
British Columbia	75	0	75	All districts are nondenominational; public funds are available to independent schools.
Manitoba	0	53	53	All districts are nondenominational; public funds are available to independent schools.
New Brunswick	18	0	18	There are 6 Francophone and 12 Anglophone school boards; public funds are not available to private schools.
Newfoundland and Labrador	27	0	27	Sixteen school boards are integrated, 9 are Roman Catholic, 1 is Pentecostal, and 1 is Seventh Day Adventist. Local taxes were abolished in 1992. Public funds are not available to private schools.
Nova Scotia	21	0	21	All school boards are nondenominational, but one is Francophone. Public funds are not available to private schools.
Ontario	0	171	171	There are 112 public school boards, 58 Roman Catholic separate school boards, and 1 Protestant separate school board; public funds are not available to private schools.
Prince Edward Island	5	0	5	All school boards are nondenominational; four school

(*Continued*)

TABLE 3.2. Number of School Districts and Fiscal Authority by State and Province for the United States and Canada (*Continued*)

State/Province	Number of Districts			Comments
	Fiscally Dependent	Fiscally Independent	Total	
				districts are Anglophone and one is Francophone. Public funds are not available to private schools.
Quebec	158	0	158	There are 137 school boards for Roman Catholics, 18 school boards for Protestants, and 3 multidenominational school boards; public funds are available to private schools.
Saskatchewan	4	118	122	There are 100 public school boards, including four large high school divisions, and 22 Roman Catholic separate divisions. Public funds are available to private high schools.

SOURCE: Data are abstracted from S. D. Gold, D. M. Smith, S. B. Lawton, & A. C. Hyary [Eds.]. [1992]. *Public School Finance Programs in the United States and Canada, 1990–91*. Albany, NY: American Education Finance Association and The Center for the Study of States, State University of New York; and updated from S. D. Gold, D. M. Smith, & S. B. Lawton [Eds.]. (1995). *Public School Finance Programs in the United States and Canada, 1993–94*. Albany, NY: American Education Finance Association and The Center for the Study of States, State University of New York. Reprinted with the permission of the State University of New York.

The large number of school districts—even in populous states such as California, Illinois, Michigan, Massachusetts, New Jersey, New York, Ohio, Pennsylvania, Texas, and Wisconsin—results in small enrollments in many of them. Small school districts are not a phenomenon only of remote rural areas; there are also hundreds in the metropolitan counties surrounding major cities, such as New York, Los Angeles, Chicago, and Philadelphia. Fragmenting metropolitan communities into small governance units results in great diversity among school districts and municipalities in their ethnic and racial composition and in their ability to support public services. This compounds the inequities in the provision of public educational services already noted among the states.

Using 1989 census data and 1993–1994 school district information, Table 3.3 illustrates the inequity created by such fragmentation for selected school districts in the New York City (NYC) metropolitan area. Enrollment in these districts ranged from nearly one million pupils in NYC to 1,480 in Cold Spring. Median household income ranged from $29,823 in NYC to $121,275 in Scarsdale; median per capita income ranged from $13,414 in Roosevelt to $60,688 in Scarsdale. Thirty-one percent (31%) of NYC's population over the age of 20 were high school dropouts and only 22 percent held a bachelors degree or higher. This compares with 3 percent (3%) and 72 percent, respectively, in Scarsdale.

Roosevelt, in Nassau County, Long Island, had an enrollment of under 3,000 pupils, of which almost 92 percent were African American and almost 8 percent were Hispanic. Nearby Garden City had 3,000 pupils, of which almost 95 percent were white and less than 2 percent were African American or Hispanic. In the public schools of NYC, less than 18 percent were classified as white, non-Hispanic; 37 percent were African American, 36 percent were Hispanic, and 9 percent were classified as other. Only Sewanhaka had an enrollment distribution that reflected the distribution of the region as a whole. With students in the public schools of the metropolitan area separated in a similar fashion, the ideal of the common school as a socially integrated institution is difficult to realize.

NYC's per pupil expenditure was among the lowest in the metropolitan area, at $7,921. Great Neck spent over twice as much per pupil as NYC, at $16,281. Chappaqua, Cold Spring, Garden City, and Scarsdale spent at least 50 percent more per pupil than New York City. Only Roosevelt paid its teachers less than did NYC. The median teacher salary in Chappaqua, Garden City, Great Neck, and Scarsdale was at least $24,000 per year more than the median teacher salary in NYC. NYC's pupil : teacher ratio was also among the highest in the region.

School Authority

The school is the basic operating unit; but this third level, until recently, has usually been permitted little discretion, as it is constrained by policies formulated at higher levels. The range of discretion at the school level is likely to increase in the future as school-site management and governance reforms are implemented, as discussed in Chapter 14. This discretion, however, may not always be placed in professional hands. In Chicago, for example, policy making has been entrusted to school-level boards that have professional representation but are controlled by lay persons.

Intermediate Units

The intermediate units are the middle echelon in a state system, serving as arms of the state while performing services for affiliated school districts of a region. Their organization and governance vary markedly from state to state, and some state systems do not include any intermediate unit—especially those states that have organized their school districts to be coterminous with counties. Intermediate districts typically have no direct or operational authority over local school districts but may facilitate state regulatory functions. They sometimes provide certain administrative and supervisory functions, including staff development and maintenance of information networks and systems. They more often facilitate cooperation among school districts to deliver educational programs and services where substantial economies of scale can be realized, as with occupational education and education of the severely disabled.

Federal Authority

The fifth level of governance is the federal government. Although the U. S. Constitution is silent about education, leaving responsibility for it to the states, from time to time Congress does pass legislation under its authority to provide for "the general welfare," national defense, and the protection of civil rights. The Office of Education, upgraded to the Department of Education in 1979, was created in the executive branch to administer federal laws and to keep statistics. The secretary of education, who heads the Department of Education and is a member of the president's Cabinet, is appointed by the president with congressional approval.

Federal courts are arbitrators of the United States Constitution. Litigation concerning school desegregation and other education issues have invoked provisions of the Fifth and Fourteenth Amendments to the U. S. Constitution. The Fifth Amendment restrains the Federal Government from depriving any person of "life, liberty or property without due process of law." In the wake of the Civil War, the Fourteenth Amendment was adopted to extend this restraint to the states. The Fourteenth Amendment also restrains states and their agents, including school officials, from denying any person "the equal protection of the laws."

Religious and Other Private Schools

Unlike in many countries, religiously affiliated elementary and secondary schools are not permitted to receive public monies in the United States, although children attending such schools may have access to some publicly provided services. The basis for exclusion of public funds from such schools is a narrow interpretation by the federal courts of a clause in the First Amendment to the United States Constitution stating that "Congress

TABLE 3.3. Pupil and District Characteristics for Selected School Districts in the New York City Metropolitan Area

Item	Districts											
	New York City	Chappaqua	Cold Spring	Garden City	Great Neck	Hempstead	Malverne	Mt. Vernon	Roosevelt	Scarsdale	Sewanhaka	Yonkers
Enrollment[a]	992,992	3,022	1,480	3,044	5,462	5,483	1,807	9,609	2,955	3,709	6,615	20,523
Percentage White[a]	17.6	88.6	97.0	94.9	80.2	0.4	39.1	13.6	0.3	77.8	65.2	29.4
Percentage Black[a]	37.1	0.8	0.2	0.5	3.1	72.1	51.5	75.8	91.9	2.3	15.0	28.9
Percentage Hispanic[a]	36.1	1.6	0.7	1.1	6.7	26.4	7.5	8.9	7.8	2.1	9.2	37.8
Percentage other[a]	9.2	9.1	2.1	3.5	10.0	0.7	1.9	1.8	0.0	17.9	10.5	3.9
Percentage limited English[a]	15.8	1.9	0.8	0.9	2.5	13.1	2.3	4.8	6.4	5.7	2.7	15.7
1989 household income ($)[b]	29,823	107,319	111,515	74,506	66,385	32,909	49,180	34,850	45,512	121,275	47,462	36,376
1989 per capita income ($)[b]	20,186	47,197	52,447	33,224	39,316	13,374	19,071	15,835	13,414	60,688	18,331	17,484
Percentage households on public assistance[b]	13	1	1	2	2	10	5	10	14	2	4	9
Percentage age 16+ unemployed[b]	6	2	2	2	2	5	3	5	6	1	3	4
Percentage age 20+ high school dropouts[b]	31	4	4	5	9	32	17	29	26	3	20	25

Percentage age 20+ holding BA or above[b]	22	70	56	52	52	14	27	20	13	72	21	21
Percentage age 6–19 "at-risk"[b]	12	0	0	0	0	7	1	5	5	0	0	8
Annual attendance rate[a]	85.6	95.7	94.9	95.1	95.4	90.7	94.6	91.0	90.7	96.4	93.6	87.2
Pupils per teacher[a]	16	13	12	12	10	16	13	14	16	12	15	15
Median teacher salary ($)[a]	43,014	69,134	61,300	67,200	71,102	55,003	60,500[c]	60,909	39,004[d]	71,000	61,210	61,092
Expenditure per pupil ($)[a]	7,921	13,091	12,467	11,956	16,281	10,932	11,306	10,626	9,374	12,282	10,118	10,185
Combined wealth ratio[a]	1.0	2.5	3.1	3.0	3.9	0.8	1.3	0.9	0.5	3.3	1.4	1.3
Percentage enrolled in nonpublic schools[a]	23	20	24	23	16	20	23	17	16	16	17	31

[a]1993–94 school year
[b]1989 (from U.S. Census)
[c]1992–93 school year; no contract settlement for 1993–94
[d]1991–92 school year; no contract settlement for 1993–94 and 1992–93.

SOURCE: New York State Education Department. (1995). *New York the State of Learning: A Report to the Governor and the Legislature on the Education Status of the State's Schools, Vol. 2, Statistical Profiles of Public School Districts.* Albany, NY: University of the State of New York.

shall make no law respecting an establishment of religion, or prohibiting the free exercise thereof." This provision was made applicable to the states by the Fourteenth Amendment; but many state constitutions have provisions of their own which are less ambiguous, clearly stating the prohibition from the use of public funds or credit in support of *any* activity sponsored by religious groups.

Canadian provinces illustrate the variety of arrangements found throughout the world with respect to public financing of private and religious schools. It is similar to the United States, in that educational authority in Canada resides at the provincial level, with delegated powers to local school boards. Five of Canada's ten provinces fund religiously oriented school boards (see Table 3.2). Five other provinces make public funds available to private schools, including two, British Columbia and Manitoba, that have only nondenominational public schools. New Brunswick, Ontario, and Prince Edward Island have separate school boards for Anglophones and Francophones. The Canadian provinces also have differing patterns of fiscally dependent and independent authorities. In contrast with the structure in the United States, more than one school board may serve a given geographic area in Canada, for example, a public school board and a Roman Catholic school board.

THE SCOPE OF SCHOOL FINANCE

Education represents major economic, social, and cultural commitments in the United States. Table 3.4 reports the national growth in population, gross national product, and all government spending during the twentieth century. Total expenditures for all levels of government grew from 7.7 percent of the gross national product in 1902 to 41.3 percent in 1992.

Public Revenues, Expenditures, and Debt

Table 3.5 shows the size of federal, state, and local tax revenues, direct expenditures, and the number of employees since 1950. In 1950, 65 percent of all taxes were collected by the federal government. By 1992, the percentage had dropped to 56 percent. The percentage of taxes collected by states grew from 17 percent to 25 percent over the period, while local tax collections remained stable at 18 percent from 1950 through 1980, but rose to 19 percent in 1992. Although local governments collected only 19 percent of total revenue in 1992, they made 26 percent of all direct governmental expenditures and employed 59 percent of all civilian public workers (U. S. Bureau of the Census, 1975, 1995). State and local governments are able

TABLE 3.4. Growth in Population, Wealth, and Government Spending, 1902–1994

Year	Population (millions)	Gross National Product (GNP, billions)	All Government Spending	
			Billions of Dollars	Percentage of GNP
1902	79.2	22	2	7.7
1922	110.1	74	9	12.5
1932	124.9	59	12	21.3
1940	132.5	100	20	20.3
1950	152.3	288	70	24.4
1960	180.7	515	151	29.4
1970	205.1	1016	333	32.8
1980	227.8	2732	959	35.1
1990	249.9	5543	2219	40.0
1992	255.4	6026	2488	41.3
1994	260.7	6727	NA	NA

SOURCE: U.S. Department of Commerce, Bureau of the Census (1967). *Historical Statistics on Governmental Finances and Employment.* Washington, DC: U.S. Government Printing Office. Updating from U.S. Bureau of the Census (1995). *Statistical Abstract of the United States.* Washington, DC: U.S. Government Printing Office.

TABLE 3.5. Federal, State, and Local Revenues, Expenditures, and Employment, 1950–1992

	Percentage of Total				
	1950	1960	1970	1980	1992
Revenue from own sources					
Federal	65	65	62	58	56
State	17	17	20	24	25
Local	18	18	18	18	19
Total direct expenditures					
Federal	60	59	55	55	54
State	15	15	17	18	20
Local	24	26	28	27	26
Public employment					
Federal	33	27	22	18	16
State	16	17	21	23	25
Local	52	55	57	59	59

SOURCE: U.S. Department of Commerce, Bureau of the Census (1975). *Historical Statistics of the United States, Colonial Times to 1970.* Washington, DC: U.S. Government Printing Office. Updated from U.S. Department of Commerce, Bureau of the Census (1995). *Statistical Abstract of the United States.* Washington, DC: U.S. Government Printing Office.

to spend relatively more than they collect in revenue from their own sources because of intergovernmental transfers, more commonly known as state and federal aid.

Table 3.6 compares revenues, expenditures, and outstanding debt by level of government for the period 1970 through 1992. In 1970, the federal budget was "only" two billion dollars in deficit. In 1992, the deficit was $268 billion. The pattern for state and local government is quite different. Revenue for state governments exceeded expenditures for every year, reaching a surplus of $60 billion in 1990 and dropping back to $44 billion in 1992. Local governments incurred small deficits in the years reported except for 1985 (U. S. Bureau of the Census, 1995). State and local governments are typically required by their constitutions and statutes to have balanced operating budgets and can enter into long-term debt arrangements only for capital purchases. The federal government has no such constraint.

Outstanding debt has increased for all levels of government, but at a particularly alarming rate at the federal level. In 1970, the ratio of outstanding debt to revenues for the federal government was 1.8; by 1992, the ratio had reached 3.2. At the state

level, the ratio of debt to revenues grew modestly from 0.47 in 1970 to 0.5 in 1992. In other words, the debt of states is about half of their annual revenues, while the federal debt is more than three times its annual revenues. In 1970, the debt-to-revenue ratio for local governments was 1.15; by 1992 it had dropped to 0.92. Total debt of local governments is now slightly less than their annual revenues.

Figure 3.1 shows the national trends in revenue sources for public elementary and secondary education for the period 1890–1990. In 1890, 79 percent of revenues for public schools were derived from local sources, primarily the property tax. The states provided the balance. By 1979, there was a near equal division of state-local shares at about 45 percent each; the remaining 10 percent came from the federal government. Since then the federal share had declined to 6.9 percent in 1993. The state share rose to a high of 49.7 percent in 1987 and has since declined to 45.6 percent in 1993. Local share hit lows of 43.4 percent in 1981 and of 43.9 percent in 1987. Since then it increased to 47.4 percent in 1993.

In analyzing financial data over time, it is important to keep in mind the impact of inflation on the purchasing power of the dollar. For example,

TABLE 3.6. Revenue, Expenditures, and Outstanding Debt by Level of Government, 1970–1992 (in billions of dollars)

	Federal				State				Local			
Year	Revenue	Expenditures	Surplus (deficit)	Debt Outstanding	Revenue	Expenditures	Surplus (deficit)	Debt Outstanding	Revenue	Expenditures	Surplus (deficit)	Debt Outstanding
1970	206	208	(2)	371	89	85	4	42	89	93	(4)	102
1980	565	617	(52)	914	277	258	19	122	258	261	(3)	214
1985	807	1,032	(225)	1,827	439	391	48	212	402	391	11	357
1990	1,155	1,393	(238)	3,266	632	572	60	318	580	581	(1)	542
1991	1,201	1,480	(280)	3,683	661	629	32	346	612	632	(11)	570
1992	1,259	1,527	(268)	4,083	744	700	44	372	648	655	(7)	599

(SOURCE: U.S. Bureau of the Census [1995]. *Statistical Abstract of the United States.* Washington, DC: U.S. Government Printing Office, Tables 474 and 475.)

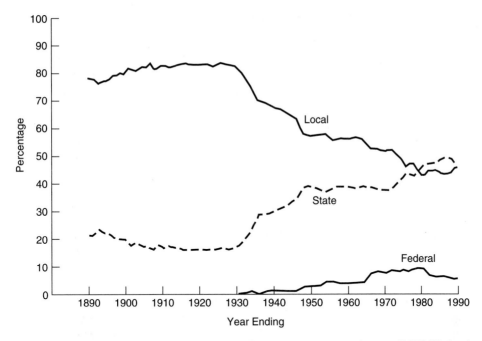

Figure 3.1. Trends in Revenue Sources for Public Education: 1890–1990. (SOURCE: NCES [National Center for Education Statistics], 1993b, p. 32.)

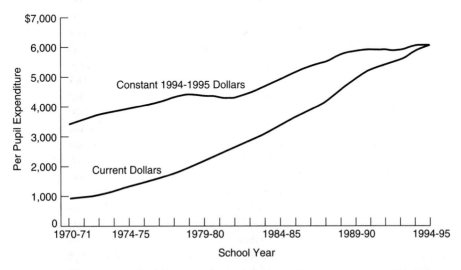

Figure 3.2. Current Expenditure per Pupil in Average Daily Attendance in Public Elementary and Secondary Schools: 1970–1971 to 1994–1995. (SOURCE: National Center for Education Statistics, *Digest of Education Statistics* [1995b]. Washington, DC: U.S. Government Printing Office, p. 49.)

per capita income in the United States increased nearly ten times in current dollars from 1960 to 1994, but the increase was two times when current dollars are converted to equivalent purchasing power of the 1987 dollar using the Gross Domestic Product Deflator (National Center for Education Statistics, 1995b, p. 46). The effect of inflation on operating expenditures per pupil for public schools since 1971 is shown in Figure 3.2. In current dollars, average per pupil expenditures increased nearly seven and one-half times from $816 in 1970 to $6,084 in 1995. Taking into account the effects of inflation, the ratio of expenditure increase drops to less than 2 to 1, that is, from $3,249 to $6,084 (National Center for Education Statistics, 1995). Expenditure increases, in general, have enabled education spending to keep pace with inflation and to allow for significant program expansions and improvements.

School Enrollment

Data for public and private school enrollments are reported in Table 3.7 for the period 1970–1992 with projections to 2005. Public school enrollments at the elementary level (K–8) were at their peak in 1970 with over 32.6 million pupils; secondary level (9–12) enrollments peaked in 1976 at 14.5 million. The subsequent decline in elementary enrollments reversed in 1985, and they have been increasing since then. Secondary enrollments began to grow again in 1991. Total public school enrollments are expected to exceed their previous high (1971) in 1997 and continue to increase to 2005 (National Center for Education Statistics, 1995e, p. 8).

Enrollment in the elementary grades peaked earlier (1965) for private schools at 4.9 million, but enrollment at the secondary level has remained relatively constant, fluctuating between 1.1 and 1.2 million. The percentage of pupils enrolled in private schools reached a high of 12.7 percent in 1983 and 1984 and has been declining since then. It is projected that the percentage will remain at its current level, 11.2 percent, through 2003. The percentage of pupils enrolled in private schools

is larger for elementary grades (12.0%) than it is for secondary grades (9.0%).

Although many public school educators fear an exodus of students from public to private schools, in reality just the opposite has been happening. The perception of private school growth may be caused by the shifting composition of private school enrollments (Cooper, 1991). In 1966, 87.5 percent of the 6,369,807 pupils in private schools were enrolled in Catholic schools; by 1989, only 47.9 percent of the 5,330,982 private school pupils were in Catholic schools. Enrollment in Catholic schools has dropped 54 percent while increasing 349 percent in non-Catholic schools. Enrollment in Evangelical schools approached one million in 1989, an increase of 793 percent since 1966. Over two-thirds of the private schools were non-Catholic in affiliation in 1989; 11.0 percent of the enrollment was in nonsectarian private schools. An estimated 220,000 children participate in home schooling. Table 3.8 reports data showing the nature of private school enrollment for the period 1965–1989.

School Employees

Local governments employ the same proportion of public workers today as they did at the turn of the century, when they collected more taxes than state and federal governments combined (Dye, 1987, p. 293). Percentages reported in Table 3.5 show that the proportion of public workers employed by the federal government has actually declined from 33 percent in 1950 to 16 percent in 1992; the proportion working for states has increased from 16 percent to 25 percent. In 1985, school districts employed 26.5 percent of all public workers— more than either state or federal governments (U. S. Bureau of the Census, 1995).

To serve the 45 million pupils in public schools in 1990, local school districts employed the full-time equivalent (FTE) of 4.4 million persons, of whom 2.3 million were classroom teachers. There were also 200,000 administrators and supervisors and 477,000 instructional support personnel, including aides, guidance counselors, and librari-

TABLE 3.7. Public and Private School Enrollments in Grades K–12, 1970–1992 with Projections to 2005

Fall of Year	Public School			Private School			Private School Enrollment as a Percentage of Enrollment		
	Total, K–12[a]	K–8[a]	9–12	Total, K–12[a]	K–8[a]	9–12	Total, K–12[a]	K–8[a]	9–12
	Actual Enrollment (in thousands)						Percentage		
1970	46,193	32,648	13,545	5,655	4,485	1,170	10.9	12.1	8.0
1971	46,575	32,518	14,057	5,378	4,252	1,126	10.4	11.6	7.4
1972	45,344	31,329	14,015	5,203	4,048	1,155	10.3	11.4	7.6
1973	44,945	30,783	14,162	4,945	3,761	1,184	9.9	10.9	7.7
1974	44,957	30,682	14,275	4,867	3,695	1,172	9.8	10.7	7.6
1975	44,520	30,017	14,503	5,001	3,821	1,180	10.1	11.3	7.5
1976	44,201	29,660	14,541	4,804	3,603	1,201	9.8	10.8	7.6
1977	43,153	28,648	14,505	5,025	3,777	1,248	10.4	11.6	7.9
1978	41,976	27,745	14,231	4,978	3,734	1,244	10.6	11.9	8.0
1979	41,651	28,034	13,616	5,000	3,700	1,300	10.7	11.6	8.7
1980	40,877	27,647	13,231	5,331	3,992	1,339	11.5	12.6	9.1
1981	40,044	27,280	12,764	5,500[b]	4,100	1,400	12.0	13.0	9.8
1982	39,566	27,161	12,405	5,600[b]	4,200	1,400	12.3	13.3	10.1
1983	39,252	26,981	12,271	5,715	4,315	1,400	12.7	13.7	10.2
1984	39,208	26,905	12,304	5,700[b]	4,300	1,400	12.6	13.7	10.1
1985	39,422	27,034	12,388	5,557	4,195	1,362	12.3	14.3	9.9
1986	39,753	27,420	12,333	5,452[b]	4,116	1,336	12.0	13.0	9.7
1987	40,008	27,933	12,076	5,479[c]	4,232	1,247	12.0	13.0	9.6
1988	40,189	28,501	11,687	5,241[c]	4,036	1,206	11.5	12.4	9.3
1989	40,543	29,152	11,390	5,355[c]	4,162	1,193	11.7	12.5	9.4
1990	41,217	29,878	11,338	5,232[c]	4,095	1,137	11.3	12.1	9.1
1991	42,047	30,506	11,541	5,199[c]	4,074	1,125	11.0	11.8	8.9
1992	42,735	30,997	11,738	5,375[c]	4,212	1,163	11.2	11.9	9.0
1993	43,353[c]	31,372	11,981	5,471[d]	4,280	1,191	11.2	12.0	9.0
	Projected Enrollment (in thousands)						Percentage		
1994	44,237	31,849	12,388	5,576	4,345	1,232	11.1	12.0	9.0
1995	45,037	32,293	12,744	5,672	4,405	1,267	11.1	12.0	9.0
1996	45,960	32,863	13,097	5,785	4,483	1,302	11.1	12.0	9.0
1997	46,797	33,420	13,377	5,889	4,559	1,330	11.1	12.0	9.0
1998	47,403	33,825	13,578	5,964	4,614	1,350	11.1	12.0	9.0
1999	47,911	34,133	13,778	6,026	4,656	1,370	11.1	12.0	9.0
2000	48,323	34,452	13,871	6,079	4,700	1,379	11.1	12.0	9.0
2001	48,684	34,681	14,003	6,123	4,731	1,392	11.1	12.0	9.0
2002	48,994	34,856	14,138	6,161	4,755	1,406	11.1	12.0	9.0
2003	49,225	34,963	14,262	6,188	4,770	1,418	11.1	12.0	9.0
2004	49,470	34,931	14,538	6,211	4,765	1,446	11.1	12.0	9.0
2005	49,651	34,703	14,948	6,220	4,734	1,486	11.1	12.0	9.0

[a]Includes most kindergarten and some nursery school enrollment.
[b]Estimated on the basis of past data.
[c]Estimate.
[d]Projected.
(SOURCE: National Center for Education Statistics. [1989]. *The Condition of Education* [Vol. 1]. Washington, DC: U.S. Government Printing Office, p. 109; and National Center for Education Statistics [1995e]. *Projection of Education Statistics to 2005*. Washington, DC: U.S. Government Printing Office, Table 1, p. 8.)

TABLE 3.8. Enrollments in U.S. Private Schools by Type, 1965–1989

| Type | Enrollment | | | | Percentage Growth/Decline |
	1965–1966	1970–1971	1980–1981	1988–1989	1965–1989
Roman Catholic	5,574,354	4,361,007	3,106,378	3,027,317	−54
Lutheran	208,209	202,362	245,812	299,502	44
Jewish	73,112	83,106	96,173	114,980	57
Evangelical[a]	110,300	254,211	759,425	985,431	793
Other religions	204,378	230,371	250,729	464,844	228
NAIS[b]	199,329	221,216	294,985	355,045	78
Others	NA	NA	122,123	340,061	NA
Home schooling	NA	NA	NA	220,000	NA
Total	6,369,682	5,352,273	4,875,625	5,807,180	−9

Note: NA = not available.
[a]"Evangelical" is a category of self-confessed born-again Christians who have indicated a fundamentalist ideal.
[b]National Association of Independent Schools.
SOURCE: The table is adapted from B. S. Cooper [1988]. The Changing Universe of U.S. Private Schools. In T. James & H. M. Levin [Eds.], *Comparing Public and Private Schools*, Vol. 1, *Institutions and Organizations*. Sussex, England: Falmer, p. 33; and B. S. Cooper [1991]. Survival, Change, and Demand on America's Private Schools: Trends and Policies. *Educational Foundations, 5,* p. 63. Reprinted with permission of *Educational Foundations.*

ans. Secretarial and clerical personnel, media specialists, bus drivers, security officers, cafeteria workers, and so forth numbered nearly 1.4 million. The percentage of total staff who were classroom teachers dropped from 70 percent in 1960 to 53 percent in 1989. The proportion of administrators in 1989 was 4.2 percent; professional support staff, just under 11 percent; and other support staff, 32 percent (National Center for Education Statistics, 1990, p. 88). The proportion of professional employees, teachers and administrators, has decreased in recent years, while the proportion of noncertified support personnel has increased (National Center for Education Statistics, 1995b).

Despite declining enrollments in public schools during the 1970s and 1980s, the total number of professional educators actually increased. This produced a continual decline in the pupil : teacher ratio from 25.8 : 1 in 1961 to 17.4 : 1 in 1995. There was a corresponding change in average class size (National Center for Education Statistics, 1995b). These statistics are reported in Table 3.9.

Teacher Salaries

Declining pupil enrollments ushered in a period of teacher surplus and weakened support for growth in teacher salaries. The trend in teachers' salaries for the years 1960–1994 are shown in Figure 3.3. Although average teacher's salaries continued to rise from $10,174 in 1973, during peak enrollments, to $36,495 in 1994, their purchasing power did not keep pace with inflation for much of the period. Stated in terms of the purchasing power of the dollar in 1994, the 1972 salary was equivalent to $33,999. From that high point, the purchasing power of the average teacher's salary declined to a low of $30,528 in 1980, when the trend was reversed (National Center for Education Statistics, 1995a, p. 158). Salaries paid in 1992 represented a new high in teacher purchasing power, $36,597; purchasing power of teachers' salaries was slightly lower in 1993 and 1994. Even though all teachers within a school district are generally paid according to a single salary schedule, secondary teachers average about $1,500 more than elementary teach-

TABLE 3.9. Trends in Pupil-Staff Ratios and Average Class Size, 1961–1995

	Pupils per Staff								Elementary[c]	Secondary[c]	
	Instruction										
	Teachers[a]										
Year	Administrators[b]	K–12	Elementary	Secondary	Teacher Aides[b]	Total[b]	Other Support[b]	Total Staff[b]	Av. Class Size[c]	Av. Class Size[b]	Av. Students Taught per Day
1960–61	829.3[d]	25.8	28.4	21.7	NA	24.1[d]	59.7[d]	16.8[d]	29	28	138
1965–66	NA	24.7	27.6	20.8	NA	NA	NA	NA	28	26	132
1970–71	697.7[e]	22.3	24.3	19.8	796.0	14.3[e]	45.1[e]	13.6[e]	27	27	134
1975–76	NA	20.4	21.7	18.8	NA	NA	NA	NA	25	25	126
1980–81	518.9	18.7	20.4	16.8	125.4	14.3	33.2	9.8	25	23	118
1985–86	584.9	17.9	19.5	15.8	128.8	14.3	29.8	9.5	24	25	94
1990–91	543.3	17.2	19.0	14.6	104.4	13.5	30.2	9.2	24	26	93
1994–95	545.1[f]	17.4	19.1	14.9	97.1	13.5[f]	28.7[f]	9.1[f]	NA	NA	NA

[a]NCES (1995b), p. 74
[b]NCES (1995b), p. 89
[c]NCES (1995b), p. 79
[d]1959–1960
[e]1969–1970
[f]1993–1994
NA = Not available.
SOURCE: National Center for Education Statistics. [1995b]. *Digest of Educational Statistics.* Washington, DC: U.S. Government Printing Office.

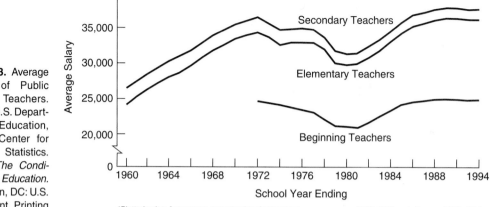

Figure 3.3. Average Salaries of Public School Teachers. (SOURCE: U.S. Department of Education, National Center for Education Statistics. [1995a]. *The Condition of Education.* Washington, DC: U.S. Government Printing Office, p. 159.)

*Plotted points for average annual salary for teachers are even years 1960–1968 and all years 1970–1994.
Plotted points for average beginning salary for teachers are even years 1972–1988 and all years 1990–1994.

ers in salaries. This reflects the greater formal education and experience of secondary teachers. The average beginning salary in 1994 was $24,661, exceeding the purchasing power of any previous period except 1972. With increasing enrollments and with increasing numbers of retirements of teachers in service, the demand for new teachers is likely to continue to be strong for the rest of the century, and teachers' salaries should continue to increase at an above average rate.

EMERGING ISSUES

All is not well with the American education enterprise. The equity and efficiency of the system are major issues being addressed by policy makers. The need for education reform gained a prominent position on the national agenda in the early 1980s and has, quite remarkably, sustained national attention ever since. In this section we identify points of national concern, and in the following section we report strategies for dealing with these concerns. Central to the whole reform movement is the public financing of educational services. Any change in the structure and procedures for educating American young people has significant implications for the financing of those services.

A Nation at Risk

There is much concern among thoughtful Americans about how well their children are equipped to compete in a world that is experiencing massive shifts in social, economic, and political interactions. With respect to education, the alarm was first sounded in our current round of reform[1] by the National Commission on Excellence in Education in its report, *A Nation at Risk* (1983). It claimed that a rising tide of mediocrity had engulfed the schools, threatening the economic competitiveness of the country and, indeed, its very survival. The theme was repeated with growing urgency in dozens of reports throughout the eighties and continued into the nineties.

In reviewing the evidence, Hodgkinson (1993a) concluded that the top 20 percent of graduates of American high schools are world-class in their preparation and that their preparation is getting better; the next 40 percent of graduates are

---

[1]This is not the first time education has been in a state of perceived crisis. After the Russians launched the first earth satellite in 1957, American education came under close scrutiny. Bestseller lists included books with such provocative titles as *Why Johnny Can't Read, What Ivan Knows That Johnny Doesn't,* and *Death at an Early Age.*

mostly capable of completing college. The bottom 40 percent are poorly served by current schooling arrangements, however, and are the target of the efforts of school reformers.

The Commission on the Skills of the American Workforce focused on the integral relationship between education and economic growth in its report, *America's Choice: High Skills or Low Wages!* (1990). The Commission admitted discomfort with emerging trends. Japan had replaced the United States as the world's economic juggernaut, and Germany, with only a quarter of the United States's population, almost equalled the United States in exports. At the same time that the United States was becoming the world's biggest borrower, Singapore, Taiwan, and Korea grew from third world outposts to premier world exporters. The Commission pointed out that American growth in productivity had slowed to a crawl (since then American productivity has grown dramatically) and that the standard of living of its people had at best stagnated (this continues to be true for most Americans). At the same time, the competitors of the United States grew in both productivity and standards of living.

The cost of the loss of ability to compete economically is for many Americans a lower standard of living than what at one time was taken for granted. The purchasing power of average weekly earnings for American workers has actually dropped by 12 percent since 1969. But the hardship has not been borne equally by all Americans. American families with the highest 30 percent in earnings had increased their share of national income from 54 percent in 1967 to 58 percent in 1987, while the bottom 70 percent lost ground (see Figure 3.4). The top 30 percent that are prospering are made up primarily of professional/technical workers, usually graduates of four-year colleges. But frontline workers have seen their wages shrink year after year. From 1972 to 1987, the relative wage of craft workers had dropped from 98 percent of that earned by professional and technical workers to 73 percent; for laborers, the fall was from 70 percent to 51 percent (see Figure 3.5).

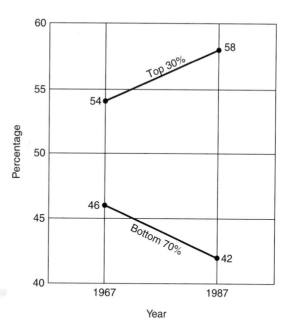

Figure 3.4. Distribution of Income in the United States 1967–1987. (SOURCE: Commission on the Skills of the American Workforce [1990].)

Another view of the situation is held by Weisman (1993). He reports that even the most sophisticated corporations in the United States have consistently failed to find a skills shortage and that there is unlikely to be such a shortage until businesses organize themselves around a management model that heightens employee involvement and allows workers to perform complex tasks.

A study of economic returns from education in Canada (Paquette, 1991) concluded that it is a perfectly reasonable decision for persons to drop out of high school if they have no intention of completing four years of college. Technology has deskilled most work to the point where there is little, if any, employment income advantage associated with the lower levels of educational attainment. Really significant differentials in earning power occur only for those holding a baccalaureate and advanced degrees. Paquette (1991, p. 475), studying Canada, concluded that "The reallocation of economic benefits from education reflects inescapably a massive deskilling of work and

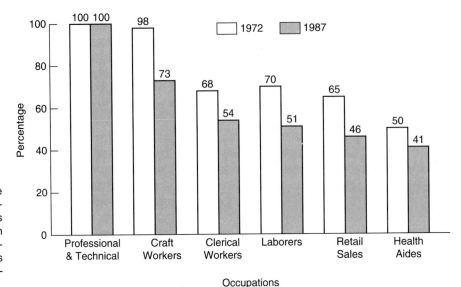

Figure 3.5. Change in Wages for Selected Occupations Relative to Each Other. (SOURCE: Commission on the Skills of the American Workforce [1990].)

rapidly increasing reliance in all sectors on 'cost-lessly replaceable' part-time and temporary help that can be hired, fired and scheduled, as well as paid, according to computer—the 'just-in-time' workers of the post-industrial age." The circumstances are quite different for most degree holders; it is only for them that the traditional benefits from further education accrue. A high school diploma, or even an associate's degree, holds little more economic significance today than completion of primary school did fifty years ago. The situation is probably similar in the United States. Other aspects of Paquette's study are reported in Chapter 13.

The United States is facing the real possibility of developing a structural underclass, and many believe that the uneven quality of the public school system is a primary cause. These fears have been supported by findings of the 1990 U.S. Census. More people are living in poverty than in 1980, and the middle class is shrinking, while the number of rich and poor is growing. The percentage of households living on less than the equivalent of $25,000 per year in current dollars has risen to 42 percent from 31 percent a decade earlier. In 1979, three-quarters of Americans were enjoying middle incomes as compared with two-thirds in 1989. At the same time, the percentage of Americans classified as having high incomes grew from 11 percent to 15 percent of the total population. Reform of education, especially in core cities, is seen by many as central to overcoming America's economic and social shortcomings—improving the lot of the 40 percent cited by Hodgkinson (1993a) as being poorly served by the current school systems.

The Commission on the Skills of the American Workforce believed that if the United States is to reverse its economic decline, it will have to transform its work organizations by reducing bureaucracy and giving frontline workers the responsibility to use judgment and make decisions. Doing this, the Commission asserted, requires the mobilization of "our most vital asset, the skills of our people—not just the 30 percent who will graduate from college, but the front-line workers, the people who serve as bank tellers, farm workers, truck drivers, retail clerks, data entry operators and factory workers" (p. 14). An essential element in the Commission's strategy for accomplishing this mobilization is the improvement of the education received by frontline workers in elementary and secondary schools, increased on-the-job training, and mechanisms for smoothing the school-to-work transition. Redesigning elementary and secondary schools to meet these ends is seen to be a responsibility of educational leadership working together with their counterparts in the community at large and in business.

The W. T. Grant Foundation (1988) also focused on the plight of the "forgotten half," the 50 percent of American youth who do not continue their education beyond high school. The study dramatically documented the shrinking opportunities for "a job with a future" for the non–college bound: non–college bound persons face a lifetime of extraordinarily high unemployment rates and steep declines in real income. The Foundation faulted the schools for having become distracted from their main mission. "Educators have become so preoccupied with those who go on to college that they have lost sight of those who do not. And more and more of the non–college bound now fall between the cracks when they are in school, drop out, or graduate inadequately prepared for the requirements of the society and the workplace" (p. 3).

The W. T. Grant Foundation (1988) pointed to the great disparity between what Americans do for the college bound and the non–college-bound. Society subsidizes college students an average of $5,000 per year, while those not going to college are frequently viewed as failures and receive little, if any, public support. The Foundation called for the development of an integrated approach to the education, training, and service needs of all youth. Further, it recommended stronger linkages between youth, adults, and their communities; access to a full array of developmental, preventative, and remedial services; and public support to ease the financial burden of raising children and adolescents.

Kozol (1991) focused on the schools themselves—especially inner-city schools. He graphically described the conditions in which many of the underclass are being educated:

[T]hese urban schools were, by and large, extraordinarily unhappy places. With few exceptions, they reminded me of "garrisons" or "outposts" in a foreign nation. Housing projects, bleak and tall, surrounded by perimeter walls lined with barbed wire, often stood adjacent to the schools I visited. The schools were surrounded frequently by signs that indicated DRUG-FREE ZONE. Their doors were guarded. Police sometimes patrolled the halls. The windows of the schools were often covered with steel grates. Taxi drivers flatly refused to take me to some of these schools and would deposit me a dozen blocks away, in border areas beyond which they refused to go. (p. 5)

Concern over Outcomes

Frequently, critics document the decline in the quality of schooling with statistics of falling Scholastic Aptitude Test (SAT) scores, comparisons with the achievement of children in other countries, high drop-out rates, violence in the schools, and the low achievement of minority children compared with that of majority children.

SAT scores did decline steadily from an average total score of 980 in 1963 to 890 in 1980 and 1981 (National Center for Education Statistics, 1991, p. 152). Scores declined for both verbal and mathematics subtests, although they dropped more dramatically for verbal tests. Since 1981, the total average score and the mathematics subscores have increased modestly, while the verbal subscores have stabilized. The average total score stood at 902 in 1994 (National Center for Education Statistics, 1995b, p. 68). The Sandia study (Huelskamp, 1993), however, concluded that "the much-publicized 'decline' in average SAT scores misrepresents the true story of SAT performance." The study attributed the decline to the fact that more students in the bottom halves of their classes are taking the SAT today than in years past. In fact, every ethnic group is performing better today than 15 years ago, as shown in Figure 3.6 (Jaeger,

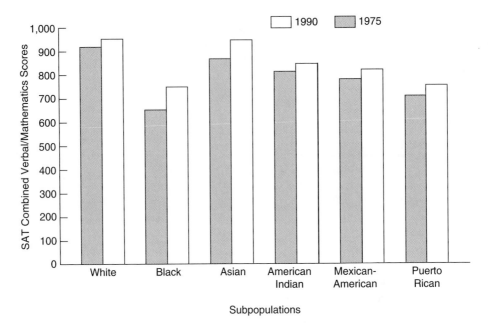

Figure 3.6. SAT Subpopulation Scores. Adapted from C. C. Carson, R. M. Huelskamp, and T. D. Woodall, "Perspectives on Education in America," Third Draft, Sandia National Laboratories, Albuquerque, NM, May 1991, p. 41, from data supplied by the Educational Testing Service and the National Center for Education Statistics. (SOURCE: R. M. Jaeger [1992]. World class standards, choice, and privatization: Weak measurement serving presumptive policy. *Phi Delta Kappan, 74,* 120.)

1992). The reason that each subgroup is improving while the overall average is declining is that lower-scoring groups represent a larger proportion of those taking the examinations today. Berliner (1993) pointed out that, of the group of current students who match the characteristics of those who took the SATs in 1975, there has been a 30 point increase, more than ten percentile ranks. More recently, Berliner and Biddle (1995) have consolidated their longitudinal analyses of student performance and have concluded that there never was a rising tide of mediocrity. Rather, they attribute the criticisms to a disinformation campaign manufactured in part by policy makers and business leaders looking to further their own political goals.

Composite scores on the American College Test (ACT) have also declined, but averages on the subscores show a different pattern than do the SAT statistics. The ACT subscores for English have remained relatively stable since 1970, while subscores for mathematics and social studies have declined sharply, and subscores for natural sciences have shown a modest increase (National Center for Education Statistics, 1991, p. 153).

The National Assessment of Educational Progress (NAEP) has not detected a decline in educational achievement over the past twenty years, although its findings do present cause for concern about the low level of average proficiency of American youth. Over the years, about 40 percent of seventeen-year-olds have been classified as performing at the "adept" level in reading, which is described as "Can find, understand, summarize, and explain relatively complicated information" (National Center for Education Statistics, 1993a, p. 202). Eighty-four percent of seventeen-year-olds perform at the "intermediate" level or better. Performance at the intermediate level is described as "Can search for specific information, interrelate ideas, and make generalizations." The percentage performing at the "advanced" level has increased from 6 percent in 1971 to 7 percent in 1990. Advanced performance is described as "Can synthesize and learn from specialized material."

While the average performance of minority groups on NAEP tests has shown improvement, it remains well below that of majority students. Over half of majority students examined in 1988 understood basic historical terms and relationships and specific government structures and functions compared to about one-fourth of African American and Hispanic students (National Center for Education Statistics, 1991, p. 142).

Of even greater concern to some analysts is the performance of American students in comparison with students in other countries. The results of a twenty-nation study published in 1992 found that American thirteen-year-olds outperformed only those from Jordan, Portugal, Brazil, and Mozambique in mathematics, and only students from those countries and Ireland in science (Rothman, 1992). U. S. nine-year-olds, who were among the highest performing of fourteen nations in science, performed near the bottom in mathematics. On the other hand, students in the United States outperformed those from nearly every other country in a thirty-two nation study of reading literacy (Rothman, 1992).

Further evidence of differences in achievement among ethnic groups was provided by an international study of mathematics achievement. Most of the populations of countries participating in the study are homogeneous, while the population of the United States is highly diversified. The highest-scoring nations for thirteen-year-olds were Taiwan (285) and Korea (285); but American children of Asian descent and trained in American schools averaged better (287) (Wainer, 1994). The United States Caucasian average score (276) would rank in the upper half of scores of European countries participating in the study. Achievement by Caucasians from the northeastern (279) and central (280) regions of the United States equalled or exceeded

achievement in the top European country. This is both good news and bad news. It is good in that it shows that American schools are working relatively well for some; it is bad in that it documents how poorly American schools are working for others. The average score for Hispanics was 245, and for African Americans, 236.

There are those who think that the criticisms of the public schools are overblown and unwarranted. "Contrary to the prevailing opinion, the American public schools are remarkably good whenever and wherever they are provided with the human and economic resources to succeed" (Berliner, 1993, p. 36; Berliner & Biddle, 1995). Berliner pointed out, for example, that today's students actually have IQs an average of fourteen points higher than their grandparents and seven points higher than their parents. The number of students scoring in the gifted range today is seven times greater than in the generation now retiring from leadership. There is also widespread agreement that our higher education system is one of our great strengths and the envy of the world (Kirst, 1993). In spite of falling average SAT scores, scores on the Graduate Record Examination (GRE) have risen 16 points for the verbal, 36 points for the quantitative, and 30 points for the analytical since 1981, even though the number of test-takers has increased by 16 percent (Hodgkinson, 1993a). Further, 40 percent of all research articles are written by American scholars; no other nation produces more than 7 percent.

Other Causes of Achievement Declines

While some statistics may suggest that schools are not doing their job as well as in the past, it is also true that their job may be more difficult than it was in the past. Some analysts place the blame for low achievement by at-risk children not so much with the schools as with the problems that the children bring to the school—particularly poverty, physical and emotional disabilities, lack of health care, difficult family conditions, and violent neighborhoods. Solving our educational crisis will require coordination of the schools' efforts with those of dealing with other community needs, including health care, housing, transportation, and social welfare (Adler & Gardner, 1994; W. T. Grant Foundation, 1988; Hodgkinson, 1993a).

During the 1980s the characteristics of American families continued to change from the traditional two-parent, two-children configuration; by 1990, barely one-quarter of households were of that variety, fewer than a decade earlier—the only classification of families to show a decline (Hodgkinson, 1991, 1993b). Households with single female heads increased by 36 percent, with single male heads by 29 percent, and households consisting of married couples without children by 17 percent. Sixty percent of all households have no children at all—a fact that makes the funding of public schools by locally levied property taxes exceedingly difficult when such levies require voter approval. Almost 50 percent of America's young people will be raised by a single parent for some years before they reach the age of eighteen. The 15 million children being raised by single mothers are in families with incomes about one-third as high as those of two-parent families (Hodgkinson, 1991, 1993b). One-quarter of American children are living in households below the poverty level, and 59 percent of all children in poverty belong to households headed by females (National Center for Education Statistics, 1991, p. 200).

The percentage of public school children from minority groups (those most likely to be ravaged by poverty) is on the rise. In 1976, minorities represented 24 percent of elementary and secondary enrollment. Projections suggest that this percentage will rise to 46 percent by the year 2020 (National Center for Education Statistics, 1991). The growth in numbers and percentages of the minority population is due only in part to their higher fertility rates as compared with that of the majority. Another important factor is an upsurge in immigration of persons from Asia and Latin America. It is estimated that approximately five million children of immigrant parents will enroll in elementary and secondary schools during the 1990s, speaking more than 150 languages (Huelskamp, 1993).

In addition to being three times as likely to be living in poverty, minority children are more likely to have other risk factors, such as coming from a single-parent household, having limited English proficiency, and having a parent or sibling (or both) who has dropped out of school. Minority children are 3.5 times as likely to have two or more of these risk factors as are white children. The effect is also intergenerational; 62-percent of children under age six who are below the poverty level have parents who did not complete high school. If one parent completed high school, the rate drops to 26 percent, and if one parent had some schooling beyond high school, to 7 percent (Poverty and Education, 1992).

School takes up only about 13 percent of the waking hours of a person's first eighteen years of life (Walberg, 1984). Children receive their initial instruction in the home and in the community, albeit informally, and those whose parents are well educated usually come to school better prepared to function efficiently in an environment of abstract learnings than do children whose parents are less well educated. Schools teaching children who already have developed good learning skills can begin their instruction at a more advanced level than can schools in which most of the children enter with poor learning skills. The pervasiveness of the problem of poor entry-level skills in American schools is recognized in the first of the eight national goals for public education set by Congress in 1993 as part of Goals 2000: "By the year 2000, all children in America will start school ready to learn."

Research in the United States on the impact of socioeconomic status (most importantly, education and income) on the achievement of children has been clouded by the issue of racial and ethnic group membership. Despite the minority focus, low socioeconomic status has emerged as the dominant factor detracting from achievement, with little, if any, effect being explained independently by minority group membership. This is not to deny that racial and cultural minority children experience discrimination, which has an additional negative impact on the development of self-esteem and realistic aspirations and expectations. Some social scientists refer to the treatment of racial and cultural minorities in the United States as functioning more like a caste system than socioeconomic differentiation (Brown, 1990; Ogbu, 1978).

Socioeconomic characteristics are only proxies for *interactions* within families and society that *tend* to be related to socioeconomic status. Home environment predicts academic learning twice as well as socioeconomic status of families (Walberg, 1984), but it is much more difficult to measure.

The interrelationships between environment and student achievement are too complex to be explained through the lens of a single discipline. Four main perspectives characterize the literature on the school performance of children from lower socioeconomic status families and racial and cultural minorities: the cultural continuity/discontinuity approach, the secondary cultural continuity approach, cultural reproduction theory, and the culture and cognition approach (Emihovich, 1994). Poor academic achievement by such children is attributed in these theories to a variety of factors, including:

- Differences between home and school in interactional, linguistic, and cognitive styles
- Effects of macroeconomic and social conditions, especially labor market forces and minority groups' beliefs about their access to employment and other social benefits
- Family values concerning the importance of education, adherence to prevailing social norms, and allegiance to community welfare rather than individual gain
- The school's perceived role in reproducing the social order to maintain class and racial barriers to social mobility
- Student resistance to learning behaviors expected by school authorities that would bestow upon the students identities that are stigmatized among their peers
- Individual variations in performance as a function of culturally influenced cognitive capacities.

Several of the above perspectives have been unified through the concept of multiple literacies:

[E]ach literacy is embedded within particular culturally organized settings, shaped by children's early experiences in the home and community environments, and influenced or modified by alternative literacies children encounter daily in schools and other social settings. In short, for children to be successful in school and society, they need to master a broad range of literacy competencies, almost in the sense of being multilingual, to cope with the diversity they can expect to encounter in written and oral formats across a wide array of situations. (Emihovich, 1994, p. 1231)

Research clearly shows that language and cultural differences in students' lives are interwoven with economic and social conditions that facilitate or impede knowledge acquisition. This bonded relationship must be taken into account in designing instructional strategies for children.

Thus, past assumptions used by educators in designing school curricula and the financial programs to support them no longer hold across the board. Children are less likely to come from majority white backgrounds. They are more likely to be members of nontraditional family types, and they are more likely to be poor. Education through high school and beyond is essential if graduates are to be employed in other than menial jobs and to enjoy comfortable standards of living. Well-paying employment opportunities increasingly require sophisticated intellectual and problem-solving skills. Educational leaders are being challenged to design new curricula that recognize the multicultural nature of students, that provide institutional support for those defined to be at risk, and that link schooling and employment.

WAVES OF EDUCATION REFORM

Response to the current problems in public education has been portrayed as coming in three waves. The first wave focused on student performance and teacher quality. The second wave focused on structural reform. Fuhrman, Elmore, and Massell (1993) have seen evidence that the reform movement is moving into a third phase, which they refer to as "systemic reform." They identify two themes that characterize this phase: comprehensive change that focuses on many aspects of the system, and policy integration and coordination around a clear set of outcomes. Greater professional discretion is being allowed at the school site under the umbrella of centralized coordination.

To bring focus to the educational reform movement, the state governors joined with President Bush in 1989 and articulated six national goals for public education (which became eight with the passage of the Educate America Act in 1994), to be realized by the year 2000. The goals were originally known as "America 2000" and were labeled "Goals 2000" by the Clinton administration. The goals focus attention on:

- Enabling children to start school ready to learn
- Increasing the high school graduation rate to 90 percent
- Improving demonstrated competency in challenging subject matter
- Making U.S. students first in the world in mathematics and science achievement
- Making every adult American literate, economically competitive, and able to exercise the rights and responsibilities of citizenship
- Freeing schools of drugs and violence, making them places conducive to learning
- Providing opportunities for professional development of teachers
- Enabling parents to be involved effectively in the schooling process.

In 1991, the National Council on Educational Standards and Testing (NCEST) was established to consider whether and how to develop new standards and tests (Ravitch, 1993). The Council recommended the establishment of voluntary national standards in key subject areas and a national system of achievement tests. The work of the National Council of Teachers of Mathematics (NCTM), in developing national standards in mathematics (published in 1989), served as a model. Following the NCTM model, the federal government funded an effort by the National Academy of Sciences to develop standards in science. Similar arrangements were negotiated with other professional groups to develop standards in history, the arts, civics, geography, English, and foreign languages. The projects were not supposed to create a national curriculum but to describe what *all* children should know and be able to do in a particular field. The principle of *federalism* does not mean the supremacy of the federal government, but rather a careful balancing of interests of the different levels of government. In this case it meant steering a course between two extremes: the familiar pattern of complete local control—in which there were no standards or widely different standards among districts—and the imposition of a federal one-size-fits-all program (Ravitch, 1993, p. 769). Developing a national system of achievement tests remains to be accomplished, but "standards will be meaningless if students continue to be tested without regard to them" (Ravitch, 1993, p. 772).

Although there was a change of presidents in 1992, there was little change in overall strategy. It should be recognized that this was a bipartisan effort from the beginning, and that, as the 1989 chair of the National Governors' Association, President Clinton was influential in shaping the America 2000 design. The National Education Goals Panel was created by the 1994 Educate America Act to monitor progress being made toward those goals and to coordinate the efforts of state and national organizations.

The bipartisan cooperation at the national level may change, however. The 1994 elections produced a much more conservative Congress than the nation had experienced in over forty years—especially in the House of Representatives. Conservative congressmen are seeking to end federal involvement in education and to abolish the Department of Education. Others among the Republican majority seek to give states more discretion over the uses to which federal funds are put by converting categorical aids into block grants. The debate has shifted from *what* the federal role in education should be to *whether* there should be any federal role at all (Jennings & Stark, 1995).

While the reform movement has experienced an unusual amount of voluntary coordination at the national level, most of the action is taking place at the state, school district, and school levels. The best example of systemic change is the State of Kentucky, where all elements of the education system have been modified, including its governance and finance. The Chicago school system is undergoing a radical form of decentralization, with policy-making authority being placed in the hands of lay-controlled boards attached to individual schools. Michigan has eliminated the local property tax as the primary source of financial support of schools and has placed almost total responsibility for financing schools with the state. Charter schools that are largely independent of school districts have been legalized in at least nineteen states, and a number of states are experimenting with limited voucher schemes. Site-based decision making and management are the order of the day, and increasingly, states and school districts are allowing family choice of schooling.

There is also increasing involvement of the private sector in the running and support of public schools. The New American Schools Development Corporation was formed by American business leaders in July of 1991 at the request of President Bush. The purpose of the corporation is to underwrite the design and implementation of a new generation of "break the mold" schools. It pledged to raise $150 million from private sources between 1991 and 1996 to finance the effort. In response to its call for proposals, 686 design teams responded, and 11 of them were selected to be supported financially for further development over a five-year period. The overriding criterion for selection was the likelihood that a design would enable all students to reach the national education goals and attain "world-class" standards (Kearns, 1993; Mecklenburger, 1992).

Members of the private sector are working in other ways to promote and to profit from school reform. Their efforts range from school-business partnerships to creating foundations and trusts to outright entrepreneurial initiatives. The most ambitious of the latter type of initiatives was launched by Tennessee businessman and media magnate Chris Whittle. His Edison Project, which was originally intended to be a network of private schools, has developed a design for a network of publicly chartered and contracted schools to operate in urban areas across the country. Because of personal financial reversals and reluctant investors, the project has been forced to scale back severely its original plans, and has opened only four for-profit public schools in the fall of 1995.

Other ventures into public education by private for-profit companies include the operation of nine Baltimore schools and Chapter One tutoring programs under contract with Educational Alternatives, Inc. (EAI) and the management of the entire Hartford, Connecticut, school district. Both EAI contracts have since been cancelled. The Minneapolis school board has hired a private firm to run its school system in place of a traditional superintendent. In Chelsea, Massachusetts, the school board has turned over the reins of control to Boston University under a ten-year contract.

Obviously there is much concern over the quality of our educational system and the implications it has for our societal well-being. The concern has generated much debate and experimentation. The issue of national goals, for example, raises a myriad of additional controversial issues, such as national standards, a national curriculum, national assessment, and national teacher certification. There are also issues of balance—between federal, state, and local governments, between political and professional authorities, and between public and private sectors. Finally, there is the issue of balance between the rights and responsibilities of parents as opposed to those of the state. Structural and financial changes will emerge from the current turmoil, but it is too early to predict just what these may be. The related issues strike at the heart of American social beliefs and traditions.

SUMMARY

In this chapter, we have described the legal basis for school governance and finance in the United States. Through statistical tables and figures the growth of the fiscal power of the federal and state governments has been shown as well as the decline of the fiscal strength of local governments. Despite these changes, local governments remain the primary provider of social services and the principal employer of public workers. Local governments are able to do this, despite their limited tax bases, because of the financial assistance provided by state and federal governments.

Financed by all three levels of governments, schools have been provided with revenues sufficient to permit expenditures to increase at several times the rate of inflation—allowing substantial program expansion and improvement, especially for children with special needs. But financial gains have been accompanied by lower average academic performance, suggesting to some that inefficiencies are present in school operations. To others, the increase in expenditures and the decline in average achievement reflect increased demands on the schools to educate a more diverse clientele.

After dramatic growth in the post–World War II period, school enrollments began to decline during the 1970s and 1980s. During the 1990s, however, enrollments are again rising, demand for teachers is very strong, and teacher salaries are increasing. Despite greater involvement by state and federal governments, the system remains decentralized in operation and, to a lessening degree, in finance.

The education system of the United States is characterized as being decentralized and as having great diversity among school districts accompanied by great inequities and unacceptably low levels of achievement by at least 40 percent of its students. Concern over these inequities has catapulted the nation into a period of continuing educational reform beginning in the early 1980s. The fiscal aspects of these concerns are addressed throughout the book, and alternative solutions are explored.

ACTIVITIES

1. To what extent should public schools receive financial support from federal, state, and local governments?
   a. What criteria did you use in arriving at your answer?
   b. Might the optimal distribution of financial support vary from state to state and from community to community? What criteria could be used to justify variations?
2. What is the basis for school district organization in your state, for example, special district, function of municipal government, fiscally dependent or independent, and so forth?
   a. What are the advantages and disadvantages of this arrangement?
   b. What, in your opinion, would be an optimal pattern of school governance? What criteria did you use in defining "optimal"?
3. Table 3.9 (p. 73) reports national statistics on the continuing decline in pupil : teacher ratios and average class size.

   a. Does this represent a decline in the efficiency of public schools, an increase in quality of educational services, or some combination?
   b. What is the rationale for your response?
   c. Measure the class size and the pupil : teacher ratio in your school. Compare your data with those of other members of the class. What significance, if any, do these differences hold?
4. What are the implications, if any, for federal educational policy of the differences among the states in financial ability and in provision of educational services, as shown in Table 3.1 (pp. 56–57)?
5. Study the patterns of academic achievement per pupil expenditure and in relation to ethnic composition of school districts in your area.
   a. What differences do you find?
   b. Can these differences be considered inequities?
   c. If the answer to (b) is yes, what policy options are available to address these inequities?

💾 COMPUTER SIMULATIONS

Objectives of This Activity:

- *To extend elementary spreadsheet skills introduced in Chapter 2*
- *To develop an understanding of changes in pupil enrollments over time*
- *To develop skill in using one approach for projecting future enrollments*

This activity uses national level data reported in Table 3.7 (p. 71), but the techniques of enrollment projection can be applied to state and local data as well. Simulation 3.1 modifies the spreadsheet table to calculate the grand total of enrollments in all public and private schools for each year, and Simulation 3.2 enables one to determine the rate of enrollment change over time as well as to project future enrollments.

Simulation 3.1: *Calculating Total Enrollment*

a. Retrieve the file ENROLL.

b. In the BOTH TYPES K–12 column on the 1983 row, enter a formula that will add the PUBLIC SCHOOL TOTAL K–12 enrollment to the PRIVATE SCHOOL TOTAL K–12.

c. Copy the formula through the column.

d. Save your file and print the revised table.

Simulation 3.2: *Projecting Enrollments*

a. Continuing with the file used in Simulation 3.1, copy the FALL YEAR label and all of the years in that column to the worksheet area directly below the revised table.

b. In the column to the right of this new FALL YEAR column, enter a new column label: K–12 ENROLL.

c. In the new K–12 ENROLL column in the 1983 row, enter the "cell reference" for the BOTH TYPES TOTAL K–12 column on the 1983 row in the revised table developed in Simulation 3.1. (The cell reference is composed of column H and row 11.)

d. Copy the "cell reference" through the column. (Notice that the row component of the reference changes.)

e. In the column to the right of the K–12 ENROLL column, enter a new column label: ENROLL CHANGE.

f. In the new ENROLL CHANGE column on the 1984 row, enter a formula that begins with the 1984 K–12 ENROLL and subtracts the 1983 K–12 ENROLL.

g. Copy the formula through the column.

h. In the column to the right of the ENROLL CHANGE column, enter a new column label: PERCENT CHANGE.

i. In the new PERCENT CHANGE column on the 1984 row, enter a formula that will divide the 1984 ENROLL CHANGE by the 1983 K–12 ENROLL.

j. Copy the formula through the column.

k. In the column to the right of the PERCENT CHANGE column, enter a new column label: AVERAGE % CHANGE.

l. In the AVERAGE % CHANGE column on the 1993 row, enter a formula that will calculate the average PERCENT CHANGE for the most recent five years (i.e., 1989, 1990, 1991, 1992, and 1993).

m. In the FALL YEAR column, beginning on the row directly below the 1993 row, enter five new row labels: 1994, 1995, 1996, 1997, and 1998, respectively.

n. In the K–12 ENROLL column on the 1994 row, enter a formula that will increase the 1993 K–12 ENROLL by the AVERAGE % CHANGE [multiply 1993 K–12 ENROLL by a factor of 1.0145 (which is the AVERAGE % CHANGE plus 1.000)].

o. Copy the formula down through rows 1995, 1996, 1997, and 1998.

p. Save your file and print the table.

q. ***Further Activities.*** Examine the newly created tables. What conclusions might be made about trends in public, private, and total enrollments? Has the rate of change in total enrollments in the nation's schools increased or decreased in recent years? What advice might you give to a board of education if district enrollment projections followed these trends? How do these projections compare with those in the text? Why may they be different? How could the projections made in Simulation 3.2 be improved?

REFERENCES

Adler, L., and Gardner, S. (Eds.). (1994). *The politics of linking schools and social services.* Washington, DC: Falmer.

Berliner, D. C. (1993). Mythology and the American system of education. In S. Elam (Ed.), *The state of the nation's public schools: A conference report* (pp. 36–54). Bloomington, IN: Phi Delta Kappa.

Berliner, D. C., & Biddle, B. J. (1995). *The manufactured crisis: Myth, fraud, and the attack on America's public schools.* Reading, MA: Addison-Wesley.

Brown, F. (1990). The language of politics, education and the disadvantaged. In S. L. Jacobson & J. L. Conway (Eds.), *Educational leadership in an age of reform,* pp. 83–100. New York: Longman.

Clinton, D. (1826/1909). Annual message to the legislature. In C. Z. Lincoln (Ed.), *State of New York—Messages from the governors,* Vol. 3 (p. 114). Albany, NY: Lyon.

Commission on the Skills of the American Workforce. (1990). *America's choice: High skills or low wages!* Rochester, NY: National Center on Education and the Economy.

Cooper, B. S. (1988). The changing universe of U.S. private schools. In T. James & H. M. Levin (Eds.), *Comparing public and private schools,* Vol. 1, Sussex, England: Falmer.

Cooper, B. S. (1991). Survival, change, and demand on America's private schools: Trends and policies. *Educational Foundations, 5,* 5–74.

Cubberley, E. P. (1905). *School funds and their apportionment.* New York: Teachers College, Columbia University.

Cubberley, E. P. (1947). *Public education in the United States.* Cambridge, MA: Riverside Press.

DeYoung, A. J. (1989). *Economics and American education: A historical and critical overview of the impact of economic theories on schooling in the United States.* New York: Longman.

Dye, T. R. (1987). *Understanding public policy.* Englewood Cliffs, NJ: Prentice-Hall.

Emihovich, C. (1994). Cultural continuities and discontinuities in education. In T. Husen & T. N. Postlethwaite (Eds.), *The international encyclopedia of education* (2nd ed., vol. 3), pp. 1227–1233. Oxford, England: Pergamon.

Fuhrman, S. H., Elmore, R. F., & Massell, D. (1993). School reform in the United States: Putting it into context. In S. L. Jacobson & R. Berne (Eds.), *Reforming education: The emerging systemic approach* (pp. 3–27). Thousand Oaks, CA: Corwin Press.

Gold, S. D., Smith, D. M., & Lawton, S. B. (Eds.). (1995). *Public school finance programs in the United States and Canada, 1993–94.* Albany, NY: Center for the Study of States.

Gold, S. D., Smith, D. M., Lawton, S. B., & Hyary, A. C. (Eds.). (1992). *Public school finance programs in the United States and Canada, 1990–91.* Albany, NY: Center for the Study of States.

W. T. Grant Foundation Commission on Work, Family and Citizenship. (1988). *The forgotten half: Pathways to success for America's youth and young families.* Washington, DC: The Commission.

Hodgkinson, H. (1991). Reform versus reality. *Phi Delta Kappan, 73,* 9–16.

Hodgkinson, H. (1993a). American education: The good, the bad, and the task. In S. Elam (Ed.), *The state of the nation's public schools: A conference report* (pp. 13–23). Bloomington, IN: Phi Delta Kappa.

Hodgkinson, H. (1993b). Keynote address. In S. Elam (Ed.), *The state of the nation's public schools: A conference report* (pp. 194–208). Bloomington, IN: Phi Delta Kappa.

Huelskamp, R. M. (1993). Perspectives on education in America. *Phi Delta Kappan, 74,* 718–721.

Jaeger, R. M. (1992). World class standards, choice, and privatization: Weak measurement serving presumptive policy. *Phi Delta Kappan, 74,* 118–128.

Jefferson, T. (1968). Notes on the State of Virginia. In *The annals of America,* Vol. 2 (pp. 563–573). Chicago: Encyclopedia Britannica.

Jennings, J., & Stark, D. (1995). Education facing new challenges. *Phi Delta Kappa Washington Newsletter, 4* (2).

Johnson, C. (1904). *Old-time schools and school books.* New York: Macmillan.

Kearns, D. T. (1993). Towards a new generation of American schools. *Phi Delta Kappan, 74,* 773–776.

Kirst, M. W. (1993). Strengths and weaknesses of American education. In S. Elam (Ed.), *The state of the nation's public schools: A conference report* (pp. 3–12). Bloomington, IN: Phi Delta Kappa.

Kozol, J. (1991). *Savage inequalities: Children in America's schools.* New York: Crown.

Mecklenburger, J. A. (1992). The breaking of the "break-the-mold" express. *Phi Delta Kappan, 74,* 280–289.

Morrison, H. C. (1943). *American schools: A critical study of our school system.* Chicago: University of Chicago Press.

Mort, P. R. (1924). *The measurement of educational need.* New York: Teachers College, Columbia University.

National Center for Education Statistics (NCES). (1980, 1993a, 1995b). *Digest of educational statistics.* Washington, DC: U. S. Government Printing Office.

National Center for Education Statistics (NCES). (1995c). *Public elementary and secondary education statistics: School year 1994–95, early estimates.* Washington, DC: U. S. Government Printing Office.

National Center for Education Statistics (NCES). (1995d). *Schools and staffing in the United States: Selected data for public and private schools, 1993–94.* Washington, DC: U. S. Government Printing Office.

National Center for Education Statistics. (1993b). *120 years of American education: A statistical portrait.* Washington, DC: U. S. Government Printing Office.

National Center for Education Statistics. (1990, 1991, 1995a). *The condition of education* (Vol. 1). Washington, DC: U. S. Government Printing Office.

National Center for Education Statistics. (1995e). *Projections of education statistics to 2005.* Washington, DC: U. S. Government Printing Office.

National Commission on Excellence in Education. (1983). *A nation at risk: The imperative for educational reform.* Washington, DC: U. S. Government Printing Office.

Ogbu, J. (1978). *Minority education and caste.* New York: Academic Press.

Paquette, J. (1991). Why should I stay in school? Quantizing private educational returns. *Journal of Education Finance, 16,* 458–477.

Poverty and education. (1992). *Education Week, 11* (16), 5.

Ravitch, D. (1993). Launching a revolution in standards and assessments. *Phi Delta Kappan, 74,* 767–772.

Rothman, R. (1992). U. S. ranks high on international study of reading. *Education Week, 12* (1), 14–15.

Smith, A. (1776/1993). *An inquiry into the nature and causes of the wealth of nations.* Oxford, England: Oxford University Press.

Stevens, T. (1900). Speech on the common school law repeal to the Pennsylvania House of Representatives, 1834. In *Reports of the Department of the Interior for the fiscal year ended June 30, 1899,* Vol. 1. Washington, DC: U. S. Government Printing Office, p. 520.

Strayer, G. D., & Haig, R. M. (1923). *The financing of education in the State of New York* (Report of the Educational Finance Inquiry Commission). New York: Macmillan.

Tyack, D., Lowe, R., & Hansot, E. (1984). *Public schools in hard times: The great depression and recent years.* Cambridge, MA: Harvard University Press.

U. S. Bureau of the Census. (1967). *Historical statistics on governmental finances and employment.* Washington, DC: U. S. Government Printing Office.

U. S. Bureau of the Census. (1975). *Historical statistics of the United States, colonial times to 1970.* Washington, DC: U. S. Government Printing Office.

U. S. Bureau of the Census. (1993). *Census of governments: Government organization and government units in 1992* (vol. 1, no. 1). Washington, DC: U. S. Government Printing Office.

U. S. Bureau of the Census. (1995). *Statistical abstract of the United States 1989.* Washington, DC: U. S. Government Printing Office.

U. S. Bureau of the Census. (1995). *Income, poverty, and valuation of noncash benefits, 1993,* Series P60-188. Washington, DC: U. S. Government Printing Office.

Wainer, H. (1994). On the academic performance of New Jersey's public school children: Fourth and eighth grade mathematics in 1992. *Education Policy Analysis Archives, 2* (10).

Walberg, H. J. (1984). Families as partners in educational productivity. *Phi Delta Kappan, 65,* 397–400.

Weisman, J. (1993). Skills in the schools: Now it is business' turn. *Phi Delta Kappan, 74,* 367–369.

PART TWO

Acquiring Resources for Schools

In Part Two, we turn to the sources of funds that have historically sustained public education and to current issues that challenge policy makers. In Part One we developed the broader political-economic context within which educational decision making occurs. Public policy making evolves as legislators and school boards respond to shifts in circumstances and the priorities that they, and the public they represent, place upon different values. We now draw upon this context, and upon the overview of the structure of school governance and finance in the United States, in presenting revenue sources. We examine basic principles of taxation and the primary revenue sources of federal, state, and local governments.

Before we look at specific taxes, we examine the federated tax structure in which different levels of government have authority to govern and to raise revenue. Federal, state, and local governments rely to varying degrees on the tax bases of wealth, income, consumption, and privilege. The intents and consequences of different taxes can be analyzed in relation to several criteria: yield, elasticity, equity, neutrality, and cost of administration and compliance. We introduce these criteria in Chapter 4 and use them to evaluate the revenue sources available to federal and state levels of government in Chapter 5, and to local jurisdictions, including school districts, in Chapters 6 and 7.

Principles of Taxation

Primary Issues Explored in This Chapter:

- *The federated tax structure:* Are there advantages and disadvantages in having multiple governance structures overseeing and raising revenue for public education?

- *Tax bases:* What forms of individual and business activities are subjected to taxes based on wealth, income, consumption, and privilege?

- *Criteria for assessing the merits of various taxes:* What insights do the criteria of yield, elasticity, equity, neutrality, and costs of administra-

tion and compliance provide policy makers in deciding which revenue sources to adopt?

- *Tax incidence and impact:* Who pays the taxes? What are the relative burdens on these groups of taxpayers?

- *Balancing values in designing tax systems:* How do policy makers weigh these criteria and the competing values of equality, liberty, fraternity, efficiency, and economic growth as they decide which taxes best meet public goals?

OVERVIEW OF THE FEDERATED TAX STRUCTURE

Public finance in the United States is influenced greatly by the separation of powers among federal, state, and local levels of government. Multiple layers, it is believed, can more efficiently and effectively finance and deliver public services. The division is not a strict one, however. There is considerable sharing of tax sources and a substantial flow of money from federal and state governments to local subdivisions such as counties, townships, municipalities, and school districts.

A highly decentralized system ties costs to the jurisdiction that provides services. Some scholars believe that a loose federation among the levels of government stimulates a stronger economy, with goods and factors of production moving freely in response to differing levels of taxes and benefits (Musgrave & Musgrave, 1989, p. 469). On the other hand, a highly decentralized tax structure tolerates inequities in the nature and extent of services provided in different tax jurisdictions. Two school districts with differing levels of property wealth or personal income, for example, have very different capacities to raise the desired revenue from these tax bases. For this reason, higher levels of government may intervene to equalize tax capacity in order to ensure that adequate public services are provided among all jurisdictions at lower levels.

Fiscal federalism has for much of the twentieth century been characterized by a trend toward greater centralization. In Chapter 3, we showed that a larger proportion of governmental revenue is now being raised at federal and state levels than in the past, and grants in aid to states and localities have increased. Despite these two trends—the centralization of revenue sources and the growth in revenue sharing from federal and state to local governments—the provision of services remains largely the responsibility of localities. This service mission continues to justify the property tax as a primary means of financial support for local schools. On the other hand, the broader-based tax systems of the federal and state governments are better suited to their mission of redistributing wealth and expanding opportunities for access to services. The federated system of governance and taxation recognizes the advantages of both centralized and decentralized units and promotes interactions among all levels.

Because local governments have no tax authority other than that granted by the state, the state is in a position to coordinate tax policy. For example, many states (as well as the federal government) permit income tax payers to deduct their local property taxes from their income tax. Several others grant income tax rebates for a portion of property taxes paid by low-income and elderly persons (see Chapter 6). Although the federal government has no constitutional responsibility to coordinate tax systems, federal provisions may also influence tax structures at lower levels. States that have income taxes rely to a large extent on federal income tax policy to reduce administrative costs and ease the burden on taxpayers as they compute their taxes and file their returns. Similarly, the reform of the federal income tax in 1986 eliminated deductions of state and local sales taxes, affecting state tax collections and policy development.

Thus, interdependence characterizes the loosely federated structure of governance and finance in the United States. It is within this framework that we present, in some detail, the tax bases and criteria for assessing the appropriateness of various revenue sources.

The Different Tax Bases

Governments measure taxpayers' abilities to pay for public services, and sometimes their actual use of those services, as the bases for their collections of revenue. Wealth, income, consumption, and privilege are the primary tax bases. Taxes on real estate, personal belongings, or inherited property reflect different forms of *wealth* at a given point in time. In contrast, *income*-based levies are a portion of the amount of money earned by an individual or business during a given tax cycle.

Taxes based on *consumption* apply to commodities purchased regardless of taxpayers' wealth or income. Excise taxes are levied on particular items, such as gasoline and cigarettes, whereas general sales and gross-receipts taxes are less selective in their application. Yet even these sales taxes usually exempt the purchase of food, housing, and other necessities rather than applying to all consumption. Taxes on legalized gambling and lotteries in some states are based on individual consumption as well as the privilege of participating in these games.

Privilege-based taxes permit individuals and businesses to engage in certain activities or make use of public facilities. For example, teachers and other professionals obtain licenses, national park patrons pay entrance fees, and ranchers pay the government for grazing their cattle on open lands. There are many privilege taxes related to transportation—vehicle owners pay registration fees, drivers obtain licenses, and specific users pay tolls for traveling on restricted-access highways.

Policy makers deliberate about the appropriate extent of reliance on these tax bases and about specific objects of taxation. Once legislators decide to tax people's economic well-being, they consider which tax objects, such as wages, income from investments, purchases, or other indicators of money flow, are the most appropriate tax mechanisms. Other policy makers prefer to tax property, accumulated capital, inventory, net worth, estates, and other measures of the stock of wealth (MacPhail-Wilcox, 1984, p. 325). The outcomes of these policy deliberations are what the government relies on to finance public services.

ASSESSING THE MERITS OF REVENUE SOURCES

Governments' reliance on these different tax bases relates to what goals are to be served by the tax policies and to several criteria for judging their appropriateness. Providing an adequate yield of money is one reason to adopt a particular revenue plan, but not the only one. Taxes serve a number of other goals, including redistributing wealth and power, creating an economic climate that supports the growth of domestic business, discouraging the consumption of certain products, and encouraging various social and economic policies. Governments may consider what group of people or businesses would be affected and in what ways by a particular tax. Five criteria for evaluating taxes—yield, elasticity, equity, neutrality, and the costs of administration and compliance—help us to understand the goals of taxation and to assess the merits of current and potential revenue sources.

Yield

The flow of revenue from a tax affects the financial health of governments. Without an adequate yield, governments may be unable to provide services, balance budgets, and avoid unnecessary debt. Among governments, only the federal government can legally run a deficit in operating its budget. Provisions in all state constitutions require state and local governments to balance budgets for current operations; they must raise sufficient revenue from other levels of government and their own tax sources to maintain services. In comparing the benefits of alternative sources, a tax with a large yield is more favorable than taxes with smaller yields.

The yield of a tax is calculated as the product of the tax base (e.g., amount of income or the value of goods purchased or property owned) and a tax rate. The tax rate is decided by a governing body or the voting public. By expanding the size of the base by encouraging economic growth or by raising the tax rate on a given base, the government can increase the yield of a tax.

Elasticity

A tax's elasticity determines the stability or flexibility of its yield in relation to movements of the economy, usually measured by changes in gross national product (GNP) or total personal income. An *elastic* tax is one in which the tax base increases at a faster rate than the rate of economic growth, or one in which the base is stable but the rate structure is progressive. In either case, the yield of an elastic tax grows more quickly than does some measure of economic change. Conversely, an *inelastic* tax is one in which the rate of revenue growth is slower than that of economic growth. If the rates of change for tax yield and the economy are the same, the revenue source has an elasticity of *unity*.

To obtain a coefficient of elasticity, one divides the percentage of change in tax *yield* between two points in time (t_1 and t_2) by the percentage change in state or national *income* during the same period:

$$\text{Elasticity} = \frac{\dfrac{\text{Yield } t_2 - \text{Yield } t_1}{\text{Yield } t_1}}{\dfrac{\text{Income } t_2 - \text{Income } t_1}{\text{Income } t_1}}$$

For example, assume that income in a given region has grown from $800 million to $1 billion, while the amount of individual income tax collections levied at a uniform rate has increased from $50 million to $70 million. In this case, the income tax is highly elastic, given the resulting coefficient of 1.6. If sales tax revenue had grown from $18 million to $22.5 million during this time frame, the resulting coefficient of 1.0 would indicate an elasticity of unity. This would contrast with the relatively inelastic property tax whose yield increased from $13.6 million to $16.66 million, with a resulting coefficient of 0.9.

The yield from a stable tax (with an elasticity coefficient of less than 1.0) grows more slowly than the rest of the economy unless there are increased tax rates. On the other hand, yield does not decline as rapidly during periods of recession. This stability provides a degree of dependability that is essential for planning and budgeting government functions. The large and predictable yield of the relatively inelastic property tax (see Chapter 6) makes it a particularly suitable revenue source for local governments:

> It is desirable to have a revenue source that does not suffer from large year to year fluctuations, especially for school districts, who have limited authority to borrow. The property tax is often viewed as being a stable revenue source, especially relative to income and sales taxes. The stability results from the relative insensitivity of property assessments to changes in cyclical economic conditions. (Netzer & Berne, 1995, p. 52)

Revenue growth associated with elastic taxes (with an elasticity coefficient of more than 1.0) during periods of economic expansion enables governments to expand programs and services and to balance budgets without the frequent adjustments in rates required by stable or inelastic taxes. But during a recession, when governmental assistance is more likely to be needed by the general population, tax yields from elastic taxes drop at a rate faster than that of the general economic decline. A tax with a relatively high coefficient of elasticity, such as the income tax, produces revenues that fluctuate with economic conditions. This flexibility, or responsiveness, may be advantageous if the economy is expanding, but it may constrain governmental services during a recession. A more stable tax offers predictable revenue yields—even in an uncertain economy.

Equity

Fairness is an important principle in tax policy. It is generally believed that all individuals in society should contribute to the public good and be treated in uniform ways. But it is also recognized that not all taxpayers are in the same financial condition when taxes are due. The determination of what taxes should be paid invokes conflicts between the principles of benefits received and ability to pay.

Equity is the most complex of the five criteria and the most difficult to measure. In dealing with its complexity; this section considers the principles that underlie the concept of equity. These principles include benefits received, ability to pay, sacrifice, and horizontal and vertical equity.

Benefits-Received Principle.   The benefits-received principle states that taxpayers should contribute to government in accordance with benefits derived from public services, just as they do when they make purchases in the private sector. For example, fees charged for municipal transportation and national parks are the same for all beneficiaries without regard to their income or wealth. To some degree it might be argued that all tax and expenditure policies within democracies reflect a benefit principle: "People, or some majority thereof, would not be willing to sustain a fiscal program if, on balance, they did not benefit therefrom" (Musgrave & Musgrave, 1989, p. 220).

However, the relationship between benefits received and taxes paid is not always clear. It is difficult to determine who benefits and to what degree from such public services as libraries and parks that are shared generally by residents (and many nonresidents) of a tax jurisdiction. Thus, for general services, including schools, ability to pay is considered a more appropriate principle in evaluating tax policy than is a benefits standard.

Ability-to-Pay Principle.   The ability-to-pay theory states that taxpayers should contribute in accordance with their economic capacity to support public services. Rather than demanding absolute equality in tax payments, the principle calls for an examination of individuals' abilities to contribute. This standard was advanced by Adam Smith as early as 1776:

> The subjects of every state ought to contribute towards the support of the government, as nearly as possible, in proportion to their respective abilities: that is, in proportion to the revenue which they respectively enjoy under the protection of the state. . . . In the observa-

tion or neglect of this maxim consists what is called the equality or inequality of taxation. (Smith, 1776/1993, p. 451)

The "revenue" to which Smith refers might include any return from property or investments. Income has become the best measure of ability to pay taxes "for it determines a person's total command over resources during a stated period, to consume, or to add to his wealth" (Eckstein, 1967, p. 60). However, it is difficult to agree on adjustments to income as appropriate recognitions of differences in abilities to pay. This creates policy dilemmas and a sense of unfairness in taxation (this is discussed more fully in Chapter 5).

The Sacrifice Principle.   In the interest of maintaining relative equity in the distribution of tax burdens, people with higher incomes are expected to pay not merely higher dollar amounts but also higher proportions of their income in taxes. This requirement is justified under the sacrifice principle. This principle ties differing abilities to pay with the economic view of diminishing marginal utility.

Under this theory, consumers seek to maximize their total satisfaction, or utility, from their income by acquiring various goods and services. For example, buying an automobile provides a large degree of utility (U_1 in Figure 4.1) in the form

of basic transportation. More benefits come from buying more automobiles, but the addition to overall utility is smaller with each new sacrifice of personal resources for transportation. Additional vehicles may give independence of movement to other family members or serve a specialized function such as recreation. At some point, however, the value of additional vehicles in terms of utility diminishes. Buying a fifth automobile brings a smaller addition to total utility than buying the earlier ones (from U_4 to U_5).

Conversely, if an automobile is taken away from an individual owning five, there is less sacrifice, or reduction in utility, than if one is taken from an individual who owns one automobile. If we apply this principle to taxation, the reduction of income by a given tax payment represents a greater sacrifice for individuals with less income. An equal-sacrifice rule then implies that individuals with different income levels should contribute different amounts to the government, in such a way that each forgoes similar amounts of utility.

Horizontal and Vertical Equity Principles.
Equality under the law is reflected in the concept of horizontal equity. Very simply, individuals with equal abilities to pay should pay the same amount of taxes (i.e., equal treatment of equals). In terms of income taxation, equivalent tax burdens should fall upon taxpayers having the same annual income.

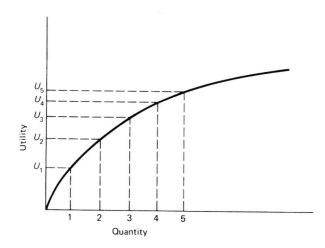

Figure 4.1. Diminishing Marginal Utility

Vertical equity (the unequal treatment of unequals) calls for differing amounts of taxes from individuals with different abilities to pay. Equity in income taxation, and its demand for fairness in the treatment of tax burdens, for example, is satisfied by unequal tax payments. Thus, those having greater ability to pay are expected to contribute more than people with less ability to pay. But all make equal sacrifices.

Neutrality

Taxes should be neutral, so that there are no undesirable side effects on the operation of the economic system: "A tax system that introduces distortions into the functioning of the economy typically imposes a loss of welfare on consumers over and above that resulting from the tax payments themselves; this extra welfare loss is the excess burden of the tax" (Oates, 1972, p. 121). A neutral or, alternatively, an efficient tax does not alter individual or business behavior in response to the tax. It does not distort consumer spending patterns, and it has neither positive nor negative effects on work incentives or choices of alternative means of production.

Taxes may alter methods of production and uses of resources, reducing the potential efficiency of both. For example, an excise tax that raises the price of products may cause a shift in consumer preferences, encouraging manufacturers to divert resources to the production of other commodities. Consumption-based taxes frequently result in reallocations of human and capital resources—due not to free market conditions but to indirect government involvement (Webb, McCarthy, & Thomas, 1988, p. 80).

Decisions of individual taxpayers about work, investments, and residential locations are often reactions to actual or perceived tax burdens. Society suffers a loss if taxes diminish the willingness of people to work, to accept more responsible positions, to gain the education necessary for professional work, or to take risks (Due, 1976, p. 258). Owners of low-rent housing in urban areas may decide to abandon the property or to allow it to deteriorate if reassessments for property improvements translate into higher tax burdens. Changes in tax structures may also influence decisions about whether to relocate. This has been one outcome of California's Proposition 13, in which property tax rates are based on valuation at the time a home was purchased rather than its current market value.

Similarly, businesses consider tax burdens when making decisions about location and investment. Differentials in sales or property taxes or in taxes on corporate income among states, counties, or municipalities may encourage businesses to move to locations that are less than optimal in terms of production efficiency. Investment incentives in tax policy affect decisions firms make about expanding into new markets. Not only do taxes alter behavior, but distortions also reduce revenue and require higher overall tax rates.

In contrast to the potential negative effects of taxation, some taxes purposely create "desirable distortions" (Levin, 1987, p. 431). Such taxes are enacted because of their economic or social effects. Sumptuary taxes deter the consumption of such products as cigarettes and liquor. Duties on imported goods protect domestic producers by making foreign products relatively more expensive. At the same time, however, consumers may pay higher prices, and product quality may fall, because domestic producers need not introduce the most efficient production techniques.

Costs of Tax Administration and Compliance

Processes for collecting a tax are necessary but are costly for governments in monetary and other ways. A good tax system should be certain, with no hidden taxes on families and businesses; it must ensure nonarbitrary administration; and its costs must be low enough to enable sufficient relative yield while also discouraging tax evasion. Similarly, processes imposed on taxpayers to determine what they owe should be understandable and should not cause a nuisance. Since the costs of compliance and administration detract from yield and acceptance by taxpayers, they should be minimized.

Individuals and businesses should have clearly stated obligations to pay taxes. Stability in government and in the private sector depends in part upon a tax system in which payments are predictable. Businesses must be certain about taxes when they make investments, and individuals must be confident that unpredictable taxes will not be levied on their incomes (Eckstein, 1967, p. 58).

Fairness in property taxation might be called into question because of exemptions granted to charitable institutions, government-owned property, veterans, and Native American reservations. Others might find fault with different assessment ratios applied to business, agricultural, and vacant property. Political pressure and outright corruption sometimes interfere with the application of the uniform procedures called for in tax codes.

Whether taxpayers accept tax burdens depends to a large extent on how easy it is to pay the taxes. Methods such as payroll deductions for income taxes, inclusion of property tax collections with home mortgage payments, and sales tax collections on goods at the time of purchase reduce the costs of compliance. In contrast, the time and expense of income tax preparation place costly burdens upon taxpayers, given the complexity of federal and state tax codes.

Enforceability is important in the structure of a good tax system. It is legal to avoid paying taxes in order to maximize after-tax income. Individuals and businesses consider tax provisions as they plan expenditures or decide upon the most advantageous investments. Tax evasion is illegal noncompliance with provisions of the tax code. All tax systems require the government to locate and place a value on taxable objects. Evasion or avoidance may result if it is easy to hide certain forms of property or income, if it is difficult for assessors to appraise them, or if it is easy to overestimate particular income tax deductions.

Audits that help ensure accurate reporting of property value or taxable income are costly in terms of personnel and technologies to government agencies, individuals, and businesses. If processes are overly intrusive, they may invoke more dissatisfaction with the tax system than the additional revenue gained through investigations is worth. On the other hand, otherwise-honest taxpayers may begin to take advantage of relaxed audit procedures.

MEASURING THE IMPACT OF TAXES AND TAX STRUCTURE

Taxpayers and governments are concerned about the economic impact of tax structures and their overall fairness. In order to understand the impact of taxes on taxpayers and the economy, we must ask questions about how taxpayers are classified, how measures of economic ability are selected, and what the relative burdens of taxes are on different groups. In this section, we discuss the concept of incidence and several measures of the impacts of taxation.

The person or business that bears the initial impact of a given tax is not always the point of ultimate *incidence,* the "settling, or coming to rest, of the tax" (Seligman, 1927, p. 2). An increased tax on a corporation, for example, may be shifted *forward* to consumers who pay higher prices for goods. Alternatively, the burden may fall *backward* on investors who derive smaller dividends or to employees who receive smaller salaries.

To understand incidence we must first define the group that is the focus of analysis. A group of taxpayers narrowly defined on the basis of race or occupation, for example, would offend the concept of equity even though all members of a given class might be taxed the same. The more appropriate classification for examining tax treatment is income, and what is of concern is the relative impact of taxation on different income groups that bear ultimate incidence.

An *indirect* tax is one in which the burden is easily transferred. For example, excise taxes on tobacco products, initially imposed on manufacturers who pay the government, are shifted wholly or in part to consumers (depending on market conditions). It is more difficult to shift a direct tax that is imposed on individuals who are meant to bear the burden (e.g., the property tax on an owner-occupied residence or a tax on personal income). But even an income tax can be shifted, as may occur when individuals are transferred to higher-income tax jurisdictions, and higher salaries are granted to offset increased tax burdens. Employers might then attempt to shift the tax burdens to consumers through higher prices. The alternative is to lower either profits or dividends to investors. We note in Chapter 5 that states may also shift or export tax burdens to residents of other states. This occurs most dramatically in the case of energy-rich states that fund their governments through severance taxes that are ultimately paid by persons in energy-consuming states.

We also need to identify the basis for the way tax burdens are related to the economic positions of taxpayers. Since taxes are ultimately paid from income, tax burdens are most often related to personal income. A *progressive* tax is one in which the proportion of income paid to the government increases as income rises. A tax system that collects $240 and $500 from taxpayers with incomes of $30,000 and $50,000, respectively, is progressive. A larger percentage of income (0.8 percent and 1.0

percent, respectively) is collected from the higher-income group. If the proportion collected decreases as income levels rise, the tax is *regressive*. For example, assuming the same amount of property tax is levied on similar homes in a given area of a community, some households may pay 8 percent of their incomes in taxes, whereas others with twice the income pay only 4 percent of their incomes. A *proportional* tax demands the same percentage of income from all income groups. The burden of a payroll tax that assesses the same flat rate on earned income (e.g., the 1.45 percent of income for medicare) is proportional.

Different relative tax burdens are evident in the state and local taxes paid in relation to family incomes in selected cities (see Table 4.1). New York City provides an example of a progressive tax system; the burden grows from 10.4 percent of income for families earning $25,000 to a larger 15.2 percent for those with an income of $100,000. In contrast, in Philadelphia, the tax system is slightly regressive; the burden falls more heavily on

TABLE 4.1. Total State and Local Taxes[a] Paid as a Percentage of Income in Selected Cities, 1992

City	Family Income[b]			
	$25,000	$50,000	$75,000	$100,000
Albuquerque, NM	5.9	6.9	7.9	8.5
Atlanta, GA	11.4	11.2	12.1	12.0
Baltimore, MD	16.3	16.5	17.1	16.7
Chicago, IL	11.8	11.9	12.4	12.1
Detroit, MI	18.9	19.4	19.7	19.3
Indianapolis, IN	8.1	7.4	8.4	8.1
Kansas City, MO	7.9	8.7	9.4	9.2
Memphis, TN	6.9	5.8	6.0	6.7
Milwaukee, WI	13.1	14.6	15.2	15.1
Newark, NJ	23.4	22.9	23.6	23.4
New York City, NY	10.4	13.2	14.9	15.2
Philadelphia, PA	15.8	15.2	15.1	14.8
Portland, ME	8.5	10.3	12.5	12.8
Salt Lake City, UT	8.2	9.4	10.1	10.0
Washington, DC	9.1	10.1	11.2	11.6
Median (51 cities)	7.9	8.6	9.7	9.9

[a]Includes state and local sales, income, auto, and real estate taxes.
[b]Mean income for family of four with two wage earners, owning their home and living in the city where taxes apply.
SOURCE: U. S. Department of Commerce, Bureau of the Census. (1995). *Statistical Abstract of the United States: 1995.* Washington, DC: U. S. Government Printing Office, Table 493.

lower-income groups. Milwaukee's tax burden, one of the highest listed, is progressive through an income of $75,000, when it becomes nearly proportional. This pattern is mirrored in the median of the cities listed in the original table. The tax burden is progressive for incomes to $75,000 and then becomes nearly proportional. In addition to these comparisons among income levels, the range in tax burdens among cities reveals differences in taxation practices. The proportion of income paid in taxes in Memphis (about 6.5%) is substantially less than that paid in Newark (about 23.5%).

The conclusions we can draw from more sophisticated comparisons of revenue sources and distributions of tax burdens depend in part on the assumptions we make about tax incidence. In his analyses of incidence, Pechman (1985) contrasts combined federal, state, and local tax burdens under eight variants, or sets of assumptions. All variants assign individual income taxes to taxpayers, and general sales and excise taxes to consumers; differences in incidence come through the treatment of corporate income, property, and payroll taxes (pp. 34–37). His least progressive variant,

3b, is reported in Table 4.2. Under this variant, property taxes are divided in such a way that taxes on land fall on landowners, whereas taxes on buildings and other improvements fall on consumers. This variant also allocates to consumers half of the corporation income tax and half of the payroll tax on employers. Under Pechman's most progressive set of assumptions, variant 1c in Table 4.2, all property taxes are assigned to owners of capital, and corporate income taxes are divided between stockholders and owners of capital.

Effective tax rates provide an expression of the amount of tax assumed to be paid *after* shifting incidence as a proportion of income. Table 4.2 compares effective tax rates for 1966 and 1985 under the two sets of incidence assumptions described above, and for the most progressive variant through 1988. With the exception of those with the lowest income, who bear a heavier burden than those in the second decile, the overall tax system is somewhat progressive. The burden was nearly proportional through the middle range of income (fourth to seventh deciles) in 1966 under each variant. By 1985, there was greater progression for the second through ninth deciles.

TABLE 4.2. Percentage of Income Paid in Federal, State, and Local Taxes under Two Incidence Assumptions, 1966 to 1988

Group (income decile)	Variant 3b (least progressive) (%)		Variant 1c (most progressive) (%)		
	1966	1985	1966	1985	1988[a]
First[b]	27.5	24.0	16.8	17.0	16.4
Second	24.8	20.1	18.9	15.9	15.8
Third	26.0	20.7	21.7	18.1	18.0
Fourth	25.9	23.2	22.6	21.2	21.5
Fifth	25.8	24.4	22.8	23.4	23.9
Sixth	25.6	25.0	22.7	23.8	24.3
Seventh	25.5	25.5	22.7	24.7	25.2
Eighth	25.5	26.2	23.1	25.4	25.6
Ninth	25.1	26.7	23.3	26.2	26.8
Tenth	25.9	25.0	30.1	26.4	27.7
All deciles	25.9	25.3	25.2	24.5	25.4

[a]Projected from 1985 on the basis of estimates of changes in effective federal tax rates.
[b]Includes only the sixth to tenth percentiles.
SOURCE: J. A. Pechman. [1985]. *Who Paid the Taxes, 1966–85?* Washington, DC: Brookings Institution, Table 5–2, p. 68, with revisions obtained from author; reprinted with the permission of the Brookings Institution; J. A. Pechman. (1989b). *The case against the value added tax.* Statement before the U. S. Senate Finance Committee, p. 7.

Under the most progressive set of assumptions, which Pechman (1989b) accepts as the most realistic, there has been a substantial decline in the burden of the highest-income decile. In 1985, effective rates were 17.0 percent for individuals earning less than $7,300 and 26.4 percent for those earning over $60,000. The burden was similar in 1966 for the lowest-income group (16.8 percent), but the burden was much higher (30.1 percent) for the highest-income decile in 1966. Changes in effective rates between 1966 and 1985 favored wealthy taxpayers. The rate for those with the top 5 percent of income declined from 32.7 percent to 26.0 percent, and the rate for those with the top 1 percent of income declined even more dramatically, from 39.6 percent to 25.3 percent. Pechman attributes this decline to reductions in personal income tax rates (from a cap of 70 percent to 50 percent in this time period) and to reductions in effective corporate rates from 32.8 percent to 16 percent.

Estimates for effective tax rates in 1988 for the most progressive assumptions, reported in Table 4.2, reveal the effects of the increases in Social Security tax rates (which are highly regressive) since 1985 and revisions in income taxation brought by the Tax Reform Act of 1986. These latter changes in the personal income tax eliminated the tax advantages of some tax shelters and raised personal exemptions and the standard deduction. Despite lower rates, collections from the corporate income tax increased under the Tax Reform Act, which redefined the tax base and removed loopholes (Pechman, 1989b). Overall, tax burdens declined somewhat in the first three income deciles and increased in the top seven, making the tax system more progressive between 1985 and 1988. However, despite restoration of some of the progressivity between 1966 and 1985, the highest income decile continues to benefit from lower effective rates than those they paid in 1966. Greater progressivity was also found in simulations of changed tax burdens between 1986 and 1987 in both federal and individual state systems (Galper & Pollock, 1988).

Shifts in burdens among income groups are also evident in Table 4.2. The aggregate tax burden has not changed over the two decades; the average proportion of income paid in taxes remained about 25 percent. However, burdens on middle- and upper-income groups (fifth to ninth deciles) have grown, whereas those borne by people in the lowest four deciles and in the highest-income group declined. Thus, a shifting in tax burdens occurred at both extremes of incomes.

Consideration of the presence of income transfers provides additional insight into understanding relative tax burdens. Welfare, food stamps, Social Security, unemployment compensation, and other such social programs have the effect of shifting monies from higher-income groups to poorer families, thus making the tax system less regressive (or more progressive). Pechman's analyses that include transfer payments show that families in the lowest three deciles receive more transfers than they pay in taxes, whereas those in the other deciles pay more taxes than they receive in transfers. He concludes that the "tax-transfer system is, therefore, highly progressive" (Pechman, 1989a, p. 23).

TRADEOFFS AMONG VALUES AND CRITERIA

Weighing the advantages and disadvantages of various proposals for new taxes or for reform in current tax structures involves value judgments that must be resolved in the political arena. The values of equality, liberty, fraternity, efficiency, and economic growth discussed in Chapter 1 are affected by modifications in tax systems. The development of tax policy is an evolutionary process that seeks balance among these often-conflicting values: "Taxation is an art and a technique as well as a science, and it always needs to be judged against the conditions of time and place" (Groves, 1974, p. 24).

Conflicting goals of taxation demand tradeoffs among these values and among the criteria discussed in this chapter. The goal of maximizing revenue yield by raising a given tax rate, for example, must be balanced against the principle of neutrality and its goal of minimizing social and economic disruptions. Similarly, a reform proposal designed to improve equity by shifting the burden to high-income groups may inadvertently be a strong incentive for some taxpayers or businesses to behave differently. Reforms driven by equity goals may also add excessive administrative or compliance costs. Increased import duties may be justified by the goals of protecting domestic producers and promoting economic development. But they can be criticized for reducing the incentive for production efficiency.

In reality, legislative bodies operate somewhere between a deliberate consideration of just and equitable taxation in relation to these goals and what Johns, Morphet, and Alexander (1983, p. 94) call the "eclectic principle." This approach, referred to as a "social expediency theory" of taxation, recognizes that taxes are obtained most easily when they affect groups least likely to object: "Pluck the goose that squawks the least." Politicians recognize the political liability of raising taxes on groups that squawk loudly. However, the consequences can be minimized by increasing taxes gradually rather than in big jumps and by making a strong case that tax increases are essential to maintain or dramatically improve services (Gold, 1994, p. 6).

When legislators entertain proposals to tip the balance among tax sources, the politics of public policy making is played out to its fullest. Diverse interest groups, including public school personnel, place pressure on policy makers when a tax bill is being considered. Governmental agencies and special interest groups such as teachers' unions and school board associations seek revenue to raise salaries or sponsor new programs. Some organizations promote policies to shift tax burdens in order to induce greater equity in tax structures without raising revenue. Industries may desire favorable tax treatment and reduced burdens to stimulate investments and economic productivity. The same groups that argue for reform in tax policy are likely to resist changes that would negatively affect their social or economic positions. Despite (or perhaps because of) these diverse forces, revenue systems of state and federal governments change very slowly, and a delicate balance is achieved among burdens placed on various tax bases.

The result is a mix of revenue sources that differs among the levels of government and that is unique to each state. The particular taxes that fuel the federal and state governments are the subject of the next chapter.

SUMMARY

The principles of taxation we have enumerated in this chapter shape the mosaic of tax policies that define the means by which the government derives funds from private-sector households and businesses for use in the public sector. The federated system of governance and finance in the United States illustrates that some forms of taxation are better suited to some jurisdictions than to others. There is not a distinct division of authority over tax policy among levels of government in a federated system, and changes in tax structure and administration at one level affect policy and yield at other levels.

Policy makers must continually assess the potential of various tax bases—including wealth, income, consumption, and privilege—for raising the necessary revenue to deliver public services while also maintaining a fair system of taxation. We can understand policy intents and consequences better by using the criteria of yield, elasticity, equity, neutrality, and costs of administration and compliance. Taxes are designed to raise revenue, but also serve various economic and social goals that affect individuals and businesses. Tax policy development is extremely complex because of the underlying real and perceived threats to equality, liberty, fraternity, efficiency, and economic growth: "Relief for one class of citizens may mean overburden for another, and how these tensions are balanced by tax policies affects the social and economic progress of individuals and the nation" (MacPhail-Wilcox, 1984, pp. 318–319). The effectiveness of the tax system depends to a large extent upon the actual and perceived fairness with which all taxpayers are treated. People who have analyzed tax incidence and relative burdens conclude that the overall revenue system in the

United States, particularly when transfers of monies to poor people are considered, is progressive.

We turn next to the merits of various tax sources in relation to the goals of taxation and the criteria presented in this chapter. Chapter 5 devotes primary attention to federal and state tax policy. The property tax and other revenue sources for local school districts provide the foci for Chapter 6 and 7.

ACTIVITIES

1. What are the justifications, if any, for permitting each level of government to draw on any available tax base for obtaining necessary revenue? For what reasons might each level be limited to one or several particular taxes?

2. In what ways might several of the values introduced in Chapter 1 and the principles of taxation presented in this chapter be considered when designing mechanisms for coordinating tax structures and policies among federal, state, and local governments?

3. Record per capita income and tax receipts from selected sources in a given state over the past ten years and calculate the elasticity of these taxes relative to income growth. If you use an electronic spreadsheet your calculations will be much easier.

4. Define the concept of neutrality as it relates to tax systems, and debate the advantages and disadvantages of using tax policy to influence the economic and social behavior of individuals and private-sector businesses.

REFERENCES

Due, J. F. (1976). Alternative state and local tax sources for education. In K. Alexander & K. F. Jordan (Eds.), *Educational need in the public economy* (pp. 257–298). Gainesville: University Presses of Florida.

Eckstein, O. (1967). *Public finance* (2nd ed.). Englewood Cliffs, NJ: Prentice Hall.

Galper, H., & Pollock, S. H. (1988). Models of state income tax reform. In S. D. Gold (Ed.), *The unfinished agenda for state tax reform* (pp. 107–128). Denver: National Conference of State Legislatures.

Gold, S. D. (1994). *Tax options for states needing more school revenue.* Westhaven, CT: National Education Association.

Groves, H. (1974). *Two hundred years of thought in Great Britain and the United States.* Madison: University of Wisconsin Press.

Johns, R. L., Morphet, E. L., & Alexander, K. (1983). *The economics and financing of education* (4th ed.). Englewood Cliffs, NJ: Prentice Hall.

Levin, H. M. (1987). School finance. In G. Psacharopoulos (Ed.), *Economics of education: Research and Studies* (pp. 326–436). Oxford, England: Pergamon Press.

MacPhail-Wilcox, B. (1984). Tax policy analysis and education finance: A conceptual framework for issues and analysis. *Journal of Education Finance, 9,* 312–331.

Musgrave, R. A., & Musgrave, P. B. (1989). *Public finance in theory and practice* (5th ed.). New York: McGraw-Hill.

Netzer, D., & Berne, R. (1995). Discrepancies between ideal characteristics of a property tax system and current practice in New York. In D. H. Monk, *Study on the generation of revenues for education, Final report* (pp. 31–47). Albany, NY: State Education Department.

Oates, W. E. (1972). *Fiscal federalism.* New York: Harcourt Brace Jovanovich.

Pechman, J. A. (1985). *Who paid the taxes, 1966–85?* Washington, DC: Brookings Institution.

Pechman, J. A. (1989a). *Tax reform, the rich and the poor* (2nd ed.). Washington, DC: Brookings Institution.

Pechman, J. A. (1989b). The case against the value added tax. Statement before the U. S. Senate Finance Committee.

Seligman, E. R. A. (1927). *The shifting and incidence of taxation.* New York: Columbia University Press.

Smith, A. (1776/1993). *An inquiry into the nature and causes of the wealth of nations.* Oxford: Oxford University Press.

U. S. Department of Commerce, Bureau of the Census. (1995). *Statistical abstract of the United States: 1995.* Washington, DC: U. S. Government Printing Office.

Webb, L. D., McCarthy, M. M., & Thomas, S. B. (1988). *Financing elementary and secondary education.* Columbus, OH: Merrill.

CHAPTER 5

Revenue Sources for Federal and State Governments

Primary Issues Explored in This Chapter:

- *Revenue for government:* To what degree do state and federal governments rely on the primary tax sources and intergovernmental transfers to support public services, including education?

- *Assessing the merits of federal and state taxes:* What are the advantages and disadvantages of personal and corporate income taxes, excise and sales taxes, lotteries, severance taxes, estate and gift taxes, and payroll taxes in relation to the criteria discussed in Chapter 4?

- *Achieving a balanced tax system:* Why is it important for government to rely upon multiple, broad-based revenue sources?

We discussed the financial contributions of state and federal governments to public education previously (see Chapter 3). As these governments' shares of school resources grew rapidly during the 1960s and 1970s, and as the public's dissatisfaction with property taxation intensified during the 1980s, educators became increasingly interested in the revenue sources that fueled state and federal governments.

In this chapter we continue our discussion of taxation. We turn from the general principles discussed in Chapter 4 to a review of the primary revenue sources through which federal and state governments support schools and other public services. We will not say much here about local governments. We discuss their reliance on property taxation and other revenue in Chapters 6 and 7.

PRIMARY REVENUE SOURCES

The total revenue raised by all levels of government in 1992 was $2.262 trillion. Included in this grand total is the $1.185 trillion that financed state and local governments (U.S. Department of Commerce, 1995, Table 474). Federal, state, and local levels of government rely on specific sources of revenue to very different degrees in raising these monies.

The proportions of revenue collected from intergovernmental transfers and from each level of the government's own tax sources are presented in Table 5.1. Grants-in-aid flow from federal to state governments to provide about one-fifth of states' revenue. Similar transfers from federal and state levels to local levels comprise about one-third of the total revenue of school districts, municipalities, and special districts. For school districts alone, state and federal aid represents about 53 percent of their total receipts (see Table 1.1). These intergovernmental transfers grew through the twentieth century, but as is shown in Table 5.1, between 1980 and 1992 there was a decline in transfers to states and local governments. We will say more about this trend in Chapters 8 and 10.

Property taxation provides no federal funds and negligible state funds and has declined in relative importance at local levels. The importance of property taxes diminished from 37 percent to about a quarter of total revenue for all local government units during the 1970s. Although the property tax remains the primary source readily available to school districts, reliance on it has been questioned, and many states and localities want other sources of revenue to replace it. For example, Michigan voters voted for a sales tax increase from 4 percent to 6 percent to offset local property tax revenue that was lost under a 1993 legislative action (see Chapter 6).

The federal government derives the bulk of its revenue from individual income taxation. States' reliance on income tax has grown from 10 percent to 14 percent of their total tax receipts, whereas the proportion from taxes on sales and gross receipts

has fallen from 30 percent to 22 percent. These consumption-based taxes, however, remain the most important sources of state revenue. The corporation income tax is declining in the proportion of total revenue relative to other sources at both federal and state levels. In contrast, user charges and miscellaneous other revenues are growing in importance at all levels of government. At the local level, user fees and sales taxes grew in importance proportionally as the shares raised by intergovernmental transfers and property taxes diminished.

The international comparison of tax receipts presented in Table 5.2 provides a useful perspective for understanding the degree to which the United States (including all levels of government) relies upon available tax sources in relation to other nations' policies. Canada taxes personal income more heavily than does the United States. The United States relies on this source to about the same degree as does Sweden. Japan, Italy, and the United Kingdom place relatively heavier burdens upon corporate income taxes. Five nations collect a higher percentage of tax receipts from social security than does the United States. Four of these countries are located in Europe; in Europe payroll collections are generally high enough to pay for national health care and other social programs. All nations but the Netherlands place a heavier burden

TABLE 5.1. Revenue for Federal, State, and Local Government (percentage of total revenue)

	Federal			State			Local		
Source	1970	1980	1992	1970	1980	1992	1970	1980	1992
Taxes									
Property	0.0	0.0	0.0	1.1	1.1	0.9	37.1	25.6	26.5
Individual income	43.7	43.2	37.8	10.1	13.4	14.1	2.2	1.9	1.7
Corporate income	16.0	11.5	7.9	4.5	4.7	3.0	0.0	0.0	0.3
Sales or gross receipts	8.7	5.7	5.1	30.3	24.5	21.9	3.4	4.7	5.1
Total taxes[a]	68.4	62.1	52.3	46.0	49.5	43.8	42.7	33.3	35.0
Charges and miscellaneous	8.3	11.9	15.3	10.1	11.6	14.5	14.6	17.1	20.1
Intergovernmental	0.0	0.4	0.2	22.5	23.1	21.8	33.7	39.5	33.3
Other revenue	33.3	25.6	32.2	21.4	15.8	19.9	9.0	11.2	11.6
Total revenue	100.0	100.0	100.0	100.0	100.0	100.0	100.0	100.0	100.0

[a]Includes taxes not listed separately.

SOURCE: U. S. Department of Commerce, Bureau of the Census. (1987). *Statistical Abstract of the United States: 1988.* Washington, DC: U. S. Government Printing Office, Table 430, p. 257; U. S. Department of Commerce, Bureau of the Census. [1995]. *Statistical Abstract of the United States: 1995.* Washington, DC: U. S. Government Printing Office, Table 474, p. 299.

TABLE 5.2. Distribution of Total Government Tax Receipts for Selected Countries, 1992 (percentage of total)

Country	Individual Income	Corporate Income	Social Security	General Consumption[a]	Excise Tax on Specific Goods and Services[b]	Other Revenue[c]
Canada	39.6	4.8	16.5	14.3	10.0	14.8
France	13.8	3.5	44.6	17.6	8.2	12.3
Germany	28.0	4.0	38.4	16.5	9.3	3.8
Italy	27.2	11.6	31.3	13.2	10.7	6.0
Japan	25.3	17.1	32.8	4.8	7.5	12.5
Netherlands	24.8	6.6	38.8	15.4	8.1	6.3
Sweden	36.0	2.4	28.8	15.9	9.6	7.3
United Kingdom	28.4	7.6	17.8	19.7	13.3	13.2
United States	34.3	7.2	29.9	7.6	7.4	13.6

[a]Primary value-added and sales taxes.
[b]For example, alcohol, tobacco, and gasoline.
[c]Includes property taxes, other payroll taxes, and miscellaneous taxes not shown separately.
SOURCE: U. S. Department of Commerce, Bureau of the Census. (1995). *Statistical Abstract of the United States: 1995*. Washington, DC: U. S. Government Printing Office, Table 1383, p. 860.

on employers for social security, but only Sweden places nearly the total burden for social security on employers (not depicted in Table 5.2). The proportion collected from employers ranges from 7.3 percent in the Netherlands to 27.5 percent in France. In contrast, in the United States, the burden on employers is 16.8 percent.

The United States makes relatively lighter use of consumption-based taxes than all countries but Japan. The European nations generally have higher consumption taxes than others. They place a value-added tax on goods in all stages of production. All countries except Japan prefer general-application consumption taxes over taxes on specific goods. The category of "other revenue" in Table 5.2 includes property tax receipts. Property taxes produce varying proportions of revenue in these countries. The Advisory Commission on Intergovernmental Relations (ACIR) (1992, p. 27) in 1989 reported a range in property tax collections from 9.1 percent at state and local levels in Germany to 100 percent of local revenue in the United Kingdom. Italy and Sweden do not use this revenue source. Property tax generated 31.7 percent of state and local revenue in the United States. Differences among nations in reliance on the taxes included in Table 5.2 reflect the structure of their economies, including the degree of fiscal centralization, the importance of the corporate sector, and varying tax policies and attitudes (Musgrave & Musgrave, 1989, p. 322).

Revenue for the Federal Government

Trends in revenue collections of the United States government are evident in Table 5.3. Individual income taxation increased from $90.4 to $588.5 billion dollars between 1970 and 1995. However, its relative importance declined somewhat, contributing 47 percent and 44 percent of total receipts, respectively, in those years. Reliance on corporate income taxation also diminished relative to other sources, from 17 percent to 11 percent of total federal collections during 1970–1995.

Payroll tax collections, including Social Security and unemployment insurance, grew dramatically during this time. The proportion of total federal revenue gained from these payroll taxes rose from 23 percent to 36 percent. Whereas federal tariffs once provided the bulk of revenue, in 1995 excise and custom duties together raised only 5.9 percent of total funds. With reforms in estate and gift taxes in the 1980s, these revenue sources declined in importance.

TABLE 5.3. Federal Government Tax Receipts, 1970 to 1995

Source	Amount (in billions)			Percentage of Total		
	1970	1980	1995[a]	1970	1980	1995[a]
Individual income	$ 90.4	$ 244.1	$ 588.5	46.9	47.2	43.7
Corporation income	32.8	64.6	150.9	17.0	12.5	11.2
Social security and unemployment	44.4	157.8	484.4	23.0	30.5	36.0
Excise	15.7	24.3	57.6	8.1	4.7	4.3
Estate and gift	3.6	6.4	15.6	1.9	1.2	1.2
Customs duties	2.4	7.2	20.9	1.2	1.4	1.6
Miscellaneous receipts	3.4	12.7	28.5	1.9	2.5	2.0
Total	$192.8	$517.1	$1,346.4	100.0	100.0	100.0

[a]Estimated.

SOURCE: U. S. Department of Commerce, Bureau of the Census. (1994b). *Statistical Abstract of the United States: 1994.* Washington, DC: U. S. Government Printing Office, Table 505, p. 331). U. S. Department of Commerce, Bureau of the Census. [1995]. *Statistical Abstract of the United States: 1995.* Washington, DC: U. S. Government Printing Office, Table 518, p. 334.

Revenue for State Government

Because public schools depend heavily upon states' general funds for their support, sources of revenue available to state legislatures is of particular interest to educators. The fifty states vary greatly in the extent to which they rely upon the primary revenue sources.

Table 5.4 shows that states collect more money from consumption-based taxes than from income-based taxes. The combined revenue from general sales taxes and specific excise taxes on motor fuels, alcohol, and tobacco products in 1992 was $150.4 billion. This amount is larger than the total collected from individual and corporate income taxes in that year, $126.2 billion. However, between 1970 and 1992 there was a change in the relative proportions of total collections these taxes accounted for. General sales tax collections increased only slightly (from 30 percent to nearly 33 percent of the total), whereas personal income taxes increased sharply (from 19 percent to 32 percent) during this time period. In addition, excise taxes on motor fuels, vehicle and license fees, and alcohol and tobacco products declined in relative importance. This decline in proportionate collections reflects the nature of the tax base. Excise

taxes are typically applied per unit (e.g., per gallon of gasoline), whereas general sales and income tax bases reflect the value of the item or earnings.

The faster rate of growth in income taxes reflects in part their larger elasticity and in part a general preference among states for imposing income-based rather than consumption-based taxation. The rate of change in amounts collected just from personal income taxes (a 1,037 percent increase, from $9.2 billion in 1970 to $104.6 billion in 1992) exceeded that of general sales taxes (an increase of 659 percent, from $14.2 billion in 1970 to $107.8 billion in 1992). With an elasticity of about unity, sales tax revenue grows at about the rate of change in inflation. Thus, rates were altered, and the scope of coverage was expanded to encompass additional goods and services, in order to stimulate the 659 percent growth in revenue (ACIR, 1995, pp. 89–94). At the same time, income tax rates were indexed to slow the rate of growth to approximate that of inflation—suggesting that the rapid change we have noted is due largely to factors other than the generally larger elasticity of income taxes. States expanded the use of income taxes. Indeed, four states adopted income taxes during this time period: New Jersey, Ohio, Pennsylvania, and Rhode Island. We might conclude from the faster

TABLE 5.4. State Government Tax Receipts, 1970 to 1992 (in millions)

Source	Amount (in millions)			Percentage of Total		
	1970.	1980	1992	1970	1980	1992
General sales and gross receipts	$14,177	$ 43,168	$107,757	29.6	31.5	32.8
Individual income	9,183	37,089	104,609	19.1	27.1	31.9
Motor fuels	6,283	9,722	22,250	13.1	7.1	6.8
Corporation net income	3,738	13,321	21,566	7.8	9.7	6.6
Motor vehicle and operators' licenses	2,728	5,325	10,660	5.7	3.9	3.2
Alcohol and tobacco products	3,728	6,216	9,717	7.8	4.5	3.0
Estate and gift	996	2,035	4,456	2.1	1.5	1.4
Other taxes	7,129	20,199	47,365	14.9	14.7	14.4
Total	$47,962	$137,075	$328,380	100.0	100.0	100.0

SOURCE: U. S. Department of Commerce, Bureau of the Census. (1993). *State Government Finances, 1992.* GF/92-3. Washington, DC: U. S. Government Printing Office, Table 1; U. S. Department of Commerce, Bureau of the Census. [1994a]. *State Government Finances, 1991–1992,* Preliminary Report. GF/92-5P. Washington, DC: U. S. Government Printing Office, Table 1; ACIR. (1994). *Significant Features of Fiscal Federalism, Volume 2: Revenues and Expenditures.* Washington, DC: Advisory Commission on Intergovernmental Relations, Table 35.

rate of growth in income taxes evident in Table 5.4 that income taxation may become a more important state revenue source for states in the future. On the other hand, the 1994 decision of Michigan voters to have a sales tax rather than an income tax suggests a preference for consumption-based taxation (see Chapter 6).

The proportionate reliance on different tax sources presented in Table 5.5 illustrates the varied pattern of states' tax policies. The yield of state tax collections varies with states' populations. It ranges from $565 million in South Dakota to $46.1 billion in California. All but five states derive revenue from general sales taxation. Those states with this consumption-based tax range in the general sales tax's percentage of the total collections from just below 20 percent in New York to nearly 60 percent in Washington State. All states collect excise taxes on such specific goods and services as motor fuel and tobacco and alcoholic beverages, but these revenues contribute relatively small amounts of revenue. The District of Columbia and forty-three states support public services through personal income taxes. These amount to as much as 67 per-

cent of total tax collections in Oregon. Although all but four states levy corporate income taxes, the yield from these is low relative to other tax sources.

In addition to the primary taxes presented in Tables 5.4 and 5.5, states rely upon other sources—including inheritance taxes, severance taxes, lotteries, and various user fees—to different degrees. These sources and other taxes account for a large proportion of revenue in many states: Alaska, Montana, and Wyoming rely heavily on severance taxes; Delaware relies on user charges and license fees; and Nevada relies on taxes on gambling. The varied proportions of tax collections in Table 5.5 illustrate clearly the great variation in states' reliance on the primary tax bases. But they do not reveal to what degree the states make use of potential tax sources.

There are several ways to depict the efforts of states to generate tax revenue from their available resources. The Advisory Commission on Intergovernmental Relations (ACIR), created by Congress to monitor and recommend improvements in tax practices and policies, reports (1) the proportions of family incomes that are spent on

TABLE 5.5. Sources of State Government Tax Collections, 1992

State	Total Collections (million)	Percentage of Total Collections						
		General Sales and Gross Receipts	Motor Fuels	Alcohol and Tobacco Products	Individual Income	Corporation Net Income	Motor Vehicle License Fees	Other Taxes[a]
AL	$4,218	26.4	7.8	4.0	29.3	3.9	3.5	25.1
AK	1,603	0.0	2.7	2.6	0.0	12.5	1.5	80.7
AZ	4,827	43.3	7.7	1.9	25.7	4.7	4.0	12.7
AR	2,748	37.6	11.2	3.4	30.9	4.6	4.2	8.1
CA	46,128	32.4	4.9	2.2	36.9	9.8	2.9	10.9
CO	3,533	25.9	10.2	2.4	45.6	3.5	2.9	9.5
CT	6,059	34.5	6.0	2.7	30.8	9.8	2.9	13.3
DE	1,340	0.0	5.4	1.6	37.1	9.6	1.4	44.9
FL	14,412	57.8	7.5	6.0	0.0	4.8	3.7	20.2
GA	7,267	37.0	6.2	2.7	42.4	5.2	1.2	5.3
HI	2,710	47.8	2.7	2.5	33.5	2.5	1.5	9.5
ID	1,391	31.6	9.5	2.0	38.5	4.9	3.5	10.0
IL	13,463	31.5	7.7	2.7	34.0	7.2	4.5	12.4
IN	6,476	42.9	8.4	2.2	34.0	6.0	2.4	4.1
IA	3,602	28.0	9.3	3.1	39.2	5.4	6.3	8.7
KS	2,802	34.2	9.0	5.1	29.8	7.1	3.9	10.9
KY	5,081	26.9	7.1	1.3	33.0	5.3	2.9	23.5
LA	4,250	29.9	11.1	3.5	20.4	5.5	2.0	27.6
ME	1,664	34.5	8.6	5.3	35.5	4.2	3.1	8.8
MD	6,502	24.3	7.1	1.8	44.7	3.3	2.3	16.5
MA	9,903	20.0	5.5	2.1	53.9	7.6	2.5	8.4
MI	11,279	32.5	6.6	3.3	28.7	15.3	4.6	9.0
MN	7,450	29.4	6.2	2.9	40.3	5.7	5.3	10.2
MS	2,494	47.4	12.7	3.4	17.6	5.9	2.5	10.5
MO	5,131	37.4	7.5	2.0	35.9	4.5	3.9	8.8
MT	950	0.0	12.8	3.0	33.8	6.1	4.3	40.0
NE	1,890	35.1	11.8	2.9	34.5	5.5	2.9	7.3
NV	1,817	49.1	7.3	3.5	0.0	0.0	3.7	36.4
NH	856	0.0	10.8	5.8	8.1	11.2	6.0	58.1
NJ	12,803	31.6	3.2	2.7	32.0	6.6	2.5	21.4
NM	2,238	43.9	8.2	1.6	19.9	3.5	4.8	18.1
NY	30,110	19.9	1.6	2.8	49.5	8.4	1.9	15.9
NC	9,010	24.1	9.6	2.2	39.8	7.1	3.1	14.1
ND	755	34.0	10.0	2.5	15.8	5.1	4.6	28.0
OH	12,115	31.0	9.3	2.4	36.4	5.3	4.0	11.6
OK	3,874	25.1	8.8	3.2	31.4	3.8	10.5	17.2
OR	3,313	0.0	8.2	3.0	67.0	4.6	7.4	9.8
PA	16,270	27.7	4.3	3.0	28.8	10.0	2.7	23.5
RI	1,276	30.5	7.4	3.6	37.5	3.8	4.0	13.2
SC	3,936	36.9	7.3	3.5	35.8	3.6	2.0	10.9

TABLE 5.5. Sources of State Government Tax Collections, 1992 (*Continued*)

State	Total Collections (million)	General Sales and Gross Receipts	Motor Fuels	Alcohol and Tobacco Products	Individual Income	Corporation Net Income	Motor Vehicle License Fees	Other Taxes[a]
		Percentage of Total Collections						
SD	565	51.2	14.6	4.1	0.0	6.2	4.5	19.4
TN	4,526	55.6	14.5	3.2	2.1	6.5	3.5	14.6
TX	17,031	50.4	11.5	5.7	0.0	0.0	4.1	28.3
UT	1,988	40.4	6.9	2.2	39.3	3.8	2.3	5.1
VT	763	20.1	7.3	4.1	35.6	4.1	4.7	24.1
VA	7,025	22.4	9.0	1.6	47.3	3.9	3.6	12.2
WA	8,468	59.3	7.4	3.2	0.0	0.0	2.4	27.7
WV	2,352	33.9	8.8	1.7	26.0	7.7	3.4	18.5
WI	6,911	28.3	7.5	2.7	42.0	6.3	3.0	10.2
WY	646	28.3	5.9	1.1	0.0	0.0	6.0	58.7
Total	$327,822	32.8	6.8	2.9	31.8	6.6	3.3	15.8

[a]Includes taxes and license fees not shown separately.
SOURCE: U. S. Department of Commerce, Bureau of the Census. (1993). *State government finances, 1992.* GF/92-3. Washington, DC: U. S. Government Printing Office, Table 6.

taxes, and (2) data comparing the degree to which states make use of the available tax capacities. This latter method of assessing relative efforts is more sensitive to the diversity of tax sources and the ability of states to shift burdens to non-residents.

The ACIR's Representative Tax System (RTS) provides an index of each state's tax base, using the national average rate for each of twenty-seven commonly used levies. Fiscal capacity is the relative per capita tax revenue a given state would raise if its tax system made use of all these levies. Measurements of capacity are useful in monitoring trends in states' fiscal health and providing perspectives on regional economic trends. Tax effort, which is measured as a state's actual tax revenue relative to its hypothetical fiscal capacity, indicates the overall tax burden placed on that base. Measures of effort can be used to compare the degree to which states use available tax bases. These measures of capacity and effort could be used to target aid to states having less ability to raise revenue from their

own sources. Or they could be used to target federal aid through grant formulas that reflect tax efforts. Policy makers can easily determine whether a state is "underutilizing" or "overworking" particular tax sources relative to the national average. However, the Advisory Commission on Intergovernmental Relations cautions analysts about interpreting these "descriptive" data: "They are not meant to imply that a state should or should not have a particular tax effort or revenue mix. Furthermore, state rankings in fiscal capacity do not imply better or worse services or revenue systems, or more or less efficiency in taxation" (ACIR, 1993, p. 9).

In Table 5.6 we give states' actual tax revenues from state and local sources expressed as percentages of personal incomes in 1992, and ACIR's indices of states' tax capacities and efforts in 1991. These data provide information about individual states and reveal regional differences. For example, Wisconsin's capacity is 10 percent below the national average, but the effort index of 118 shows that its capacity is taxed well above

TABLE 5.6. Regional Variation in Tax Revenue as a Percentage of Personal Income and in Tax Capacity and Effort

States by Region	State and Local Taxes as Percentage of Personal Income (1992)	Capacity (1991)			Effort (1991)		
		Score	Rank	1988–1991 Change	Index	Rank	1988–1991 Change
New England							
Connecticut	11.3	130	4	−13	99	18	9
Maine	11.8	95	24	−3	102	11	−3
Massachusetts	10.8	117	9	−12	101	13	7
New Hampshire	9.6	110	11	−16	84	43	18
Rhode Island	11.1	89	38	−10	115	5	11
Vermont	12.1	105	15	0	97	21	−3
Mideast							
Delaware	11.3	125	6	1	80	49	−4
Washington, DC	14.7	123	7	0	157	1	3
Maryland	10.0	106	14	−3	103	9	−5
New Jersey	11.2	119	8	−5	112	6	11
New York	14.7	103	16	−6	156	2	4
Pennsylvania	10.6	96	23	2	95	25	−2
Great Lakes							
Illinois	10.1	102	19	3	100	14	−2
Indiana	9.7	90	36	3	93	31	0
Michigan	11.1	94	26	−1	107	8	−5
Ohio	10.2	93	28	2	96	23	−1
Wisconsin	12.2	90	36	0	118	4	−1
Plains							
Iowa	11.1	93	28	10	100	14	−13
Kansas	10.1	93	28	2	100	14	−4
Minnesota	12.1	101	20	−3	112	6	0
Missouri	8.8	91	32	1	85	42	−1
Nebraska	10.7	95	24	5	99	18	1
North Dakota	10.3	91	32	5	92	33	1
South Dakota	9.1	86	42	8	83	44	−12
Southeast							
Alabama	8.7	81	48	5	81	47	−3
Arkansas	9.7	78	49	4	82	45	−2
Florida	9.8	103	16	−1	86	40	4
Georgia	9.8	91	32	−3	95	25	6
Kentucky	10.6	83	43	2	100	14	12
Louisiana	10.4	89	38	6	89	37	−1
Mississippi	9.4	68	51	3	92	33	−2
North Carolina	10.2	93	28	2	87	38	−6
South Carolina	9.8	83	43	4	90	36	−6
Tennessee	8.3	82	45	−2	82	45	−1
Virginia	9.5	103	16	−1	91	35	0
West Virginia	10.6	77	50	−1	102	11	14

TABLE 5.6. Regional Variation in Tax Revenue as a Percentage of Personal Income and in Tax Capacity and Effort (*Continued*)

States by Region	State and Local Taxes as Percentage of Personal Income (1990)	Capacity (1991)			Effort (1991)		
		Score	Rank	1988–1991 Change	Index	Rank	1988–1991 Change
Southwest							
Arizona	11.6	94	26	−5	103	9	7
New Mexico	11.6	87	40	4	96	23	−3
Oklahoma	10.0	87	40	−2	93	31	4
Texas	10.1	97	22	1	87	38	−1
Rocky Mountain							
Colorado	9.8	109	12	2	86	40	−3
Idaho	10.7	82	45	6	94	29	−3
Montana	10.9	91	32	6	78	50	−24
Utah	10.9	82	45	4	94	29	−12
Wyoming	12.5	134	3	11	81	47	−13
Far West							
Alaska	17.4	178	1	19	119	3	−8
California	13.2	115	10	−1	95	25	1
Hawaii	14.1	146	2	32	95	25	−17
Nevada	9.4	128	5	−7	73	51	4
Oregon	11.3	100	21	9	97	21	−2
Washington	10.9	108	13	10	99	18	−3
U. S. Average	10.8	100			100		

SOURCE: ACIR. (1994). *Significant Features of Fiscal Federalism, Volume 2: Revenues and Expenditures.* Washington, DC: Advisory Commission on Intergovernmental Relations, Tables 51, 98–99, pp. 92–93, 182–183.

average. This effort is also apparent in the 12.2 percent of personal income that is collected in state and local taxes. In contrast is New Hampshire, a state whose capacity is 10 percent above the national average. This state's effort lags at 16 percent below average, and it collects a lower than average 9.6 percent of income in taxes. Nevada and Wyoming also exhibit low effort despite their large tax capacities; New Hampshire does not employ sales taxes and the other states do not make use of personal income taxation.

The states with the highest relative capacities are Alaska, Hawaii, Wyoming, Connecticut, Nevada, Delaware, New Jersey, Massachusetts, and California. Those exerting the highest efforts are New York, Alaska, Wisconsin, Rhode Island, Minnesota, New Jersey, Michigan, Maryland, and Arizona. Washington, D.C., also has high capacity and effort. Alaska, the state with the highest relative capacity, also appears to exert one of the highest levels of effort. This state's collections of 17 percent of personal income, a large proportion although it has no sales or income taxes, are derived primarily from severance taxes on the extraction of natural resources. Thus, the point of incidence of this tax is not the residents of the state but out-of-state businesses and individuals that are consumers of energy and products made from extracted minerals. The revenue gained through these taxes enables Alaska to make annual rebates available to residents instead of charging them income taxes.

In general, states in the Great Lakes and Plains regions have higher than average effort relative to capacity. Many states in New England and the Far West exhibit capacities relatively higher than their rankings in tax effort. Many states in the Southeast, Arkansas, Alabama, and Tennessee in particular, exhibit low capacity and low relative effort. With a few exceptions, states in the mideast are higher than average on both measures. Interestingly, the relationship between capacity and effort does not appear to be an indirect one as might be expected. Thus, states with higher relative capacities are able to provide the same services at lower levels of effort than other states. Indeed, many of the wealthier states appear to be willing to expand services, and may improve their quality, by exerting higher relative efforts than other states. Many of these states exert greater effort to offset the large costs associated with their urbanization.

Table 5.6 also indicates the change in RTS scores over the period from 1988 to 1991, revealing changes in the economy and state tax systems over time. Although large relative shifts in fiscal capacity, or health, are evident in the positive increases noted in Hawaii, Alaska, Wyoming, Iowa, and Montana, these states also evidence a negative relative tax effort change. In contrast are New Hampshire and Rhode Island, which experienced negative changes in capacities but large positive shifts in tax effort. The former states chose not to increase tax efforts to improve or expand public services commensurate with their rapid growth in capacities, whereas the latter states exerted larger tax efforts than might have been expected in view of the relative declines in fiscal capacity.

Changes in state tax policies in recent years offer insights into directions that other state legislatures may follow in the future. In 1993, the tax reforms included the following: Arkansas, Ohio, and Washington included new services within the base of the sales tax. Iowa, Minnesota, Missouri, Nebraska, and Ohio made their income taxes more

progressive by adding new brackets or changing the definition of income subject to taxes. Wisconsin increased its standard deduction for low-income taxpayers, and Minnesota expanded the earned-income tax credit. Illinois repealed an unpopular tax on nursing homes and increased cigarette taxes to replace lost revenue. Hawaii, Utah, and West Virginia enacted new health care provider tax programs. And New Hampshire enacted a broad-based business enterprise tax, making corporate taxation more equitable. Nebraska enacted a state lottery. Nine states increased motor fuel taxes. Fifteen states increased cigarette taxes; Massachusetts voters raised the rate from 26 cents per pack to 51 cents per pack (Mackey, 1993).

Changes in personal income taxes dominated the 1994 reforms. New Jersey, Michigan, Arizona, and New Mexico cut tax rates. Massachusetts, New Mexico, New York, and Pennsylvania expanded or created new programs for easing the burden on low-income taxpayers. Six other states targeted tax relief to the elderly or to families. New York and South Carolina postponed scheduled tax cuts to maintain revenue flow. There were other reforms: Michigan raised its sales tax rate from 4 percent to 6 percent and enacted a state-level property tax to offset lost local tax revenue. Pennsylvania will reduce its corporate net income tax from the nation's highest rate, 12.25 percent, to 9.99 percent over three years. Kentucky and Missouri increased gasoline tax rates, whereas New Mexico cut its rate. And Michigan and Idaho increased cigarette taxes (National Conference of State Legislatures, 1994). The total revenue change from all reforms and from improving economic conditions in 1993 and 1994 brought net tax increases of $4.1 billion and $3.8 billion in state tax revenue for fiscal years 1994 and 1995, respectively.

MERITS OF SPECIFIC TAXES

Comparisons of governments' revenue sources detailed above reveal that governments rely on some tax sources heavily (e.g., individual income taxes and sales taxes), whereas others yield relatively small amounts (e.g., excise taxes and estate taxes). The criteria described in Chapter 4 help us to understand the advantages and disadvantages of these taxes that lead policy makers to greater reliance on some revenue sources than others. Because income taxes and sales taxes are so prevalent in tax systems, we will discuss them in some detail. Then we turn to lotteries, severance taxes, estate and gift taxes, and payroll taxation.

Personal Income Taxation

All taxes are ultimately paid from individual income. Income is the most widely accepted measure of ability to pay, and taxes on earnings are generally considered the most equitable of the major tax sources. A progressive personal income tax has long been thought to moderate disparities in welfare, opportunity, and economic power arising from unequal distributions of income (Simons, 1938, pp. 18–19).

In colonial America, a "faculty" (meaning ability to pay) tax was collected in varying amounts depending on people's skills and occupations. Although this tax countered the effects of duties on goods, which imposed higher relative burdens on lower-income consumers, income-based taxes were discontinued for many years. The new nation relied upon tariffs to finance the activities of the federal government, until the revenue demands of the Civil War necessitated a temporary income tax.

Industrialization and various social movements in the late 1800s revived interest in progressive taxes. An amendment to an 1894 tariff bill would have imposed a federal income tax, but the U. S. Supreme Court declared it unconstitutional (*Pollock* v. *Farmers' Loan and Trust Co,* 1895). The court's concern, which related to the proposed unequal distributions of revenue among states, was clearly addressed in the Sixteenth Amendment to the U. S. Constitution. Ratified in 1913, this amendment empowered Congress to collect taxes on "incomes, from whatever source, without apportionment among the several states, and without regard to any census of enumeration."

The first federal income tax was "born of a partisan movement to achieve social justice" (Waltman, 1985, p. 6). It was a response to regressive tariffs and included a sufficiently large personal exemption to relieve people with low incomes. A flat 1 percent tax applied to incomes above $4,000, and a graduated tax was levied on incomes above $20,000. Through the 1900s, the tax expanded to cover people of nearly all incomes. A more progressive rate structure and higher overall burdens financed the military expenses of two world wars, several police actions in Southeast Asia, and an expanding federal government. During the 1960s, the highest rate was 91 percent on income over $400,000.

Public demands for tax relief in the 1980s initially reduced federal tax rates from 14 percent to 11 percent at the bottom of the income scale and from 70 percent to 50 percent at the top. The Tax Reform Act of 1986 reduced the fourteen income brackets to two income divisions with taxes of 15 percent and 28 percent, respectively, eliminated deductions for state sales tax payments and for interest other than home mortgages, and removed the distinction between ordinary income and capital gains. A temporary 5 percent surcharge made the highest rate 33 percent on earnings between $78,400 and $162,700. Then changes in 1990 created a three-bracket schedule with rates of 15 percent, 28 percent, and 31 percent. The Revenue Reconciliation Act of 1993 increased the highest rate to 36 percent for joint returns of over $140,000 and for single-taxpayer incomes of over $115,000. A 10 percent surtax on incomes over $250,000 created a marginal rate of 39.6 percent, thus establishing a five-bracket income tax (ACIR, 1995, pp. 21–22).

The individual income tax is a graduated tax. It collects a higher percentage from those with higher incomes, in the District of Columbia and in thirty-three of the forty-four states taxing income (see Table 5.5). For example, Iowa relies on seven brackets, which range from 0.4 percent on income below $1,060 to 9.98 percent on incomes over $47,700 (ACIR, 1995, p. 49). Five other states (CT, IL, IN, MI, and PA) apply a flat rate to all incomes; four states (CO, ND, RI, and VT) levy a percentage of taxable income determined by federal income tax procedures; and two states (NH and TN) have a very limited tax on interest and dividend earnings. Seven of the income tax states derive over 40 percent of their tax receipts, including as much as 67 percent in Oregon, from the income tax. Another seven states do not employ any form of personal income taxation.

Over 4,000 localities, of which 2,830 are in Pennsylvania, levy an income tax in eleven states (ACIR, 1995, p. 70). In these states, in addition to many cities, counties in Indiana, Kentucky, and Maryland, and school districts in Iowa, Kentucky, Ohio, and Pennsylvania collect income taxes.

Merits of Personal Income Taxation. A substantial amount of money is raised by federal and state governments through the income tax (see Tables 5.3 and 5.4). This yield was highly elastic until indexation in the mid-1980s. This indexation linked growth in revenue produced to the rate of inflation. The coefficient of elasticity of the federal income tax was estimated by Galper and Pollock (1988, p. 125) to have declined from 1.95 to 1.80 following the 1986 reforms. This shows that this tax grows at a rate much greater than that of increases in national income. The rampant inflation of the 1970s raised family incomes in current dollars, pushing people into higher tax brackets and higher taxes. But at the same time their actual purchasing power declined. Termed "bracket creep," these increases in tax liability were not based on real income gains. They added substantially to tax coffers without enabling legislation (MacPhail-Wilcox, 1984, p. 327).

Beginning in 1985, tax rates and personal exemptions were indexed to tie their growth to changes in the general level of prices, as determined by the Consumer Price Index. Slower growth in federal revenue resulted from the restructured and indexed tax brackets. At the same time, Social Security and military retirement benefits were raised to keep pace with the growing cost of living. Diminished yields, but larger commitments, contributed to the growing federal deficit. The

return to a more progressive structure in the 1990s reversed this trend (Gold, 1994, p. 21).

Equity goals are more fully realized through income taxation than through consumption- or wealth-based taxes (see discussion of equity in Chapter 4). Exemptions, deductions, and a progressive rate structure recognize that taxpayers have differing abilities to pay. The personal exemption, $2,500 in 1995, floats with the Consumer Price Index and applies to nearly all taxpayers and their dependents with incomes below $172,050 (married) or $114,700 (single). This exemption removes low-income earners from tax obligations entirely. Other exemptions adjust the tax base to reflect family size, blindness, and senior citizen status.

Standard deductions of $3,900 for an individual or $6,550 for a joint return in 1995 (also adjusted for inflation), or itemized deductions for persons with larger financial burdens, reduce incomes before determining tax liability. Deductions encourage donations to charitable organizations and reflect such obligations as medical expenses (above 7.5 percent of income), state income taxes, mortgage interest, and casualty losses. Adjusted gross income takes these exemptions and deductions into account in defining the tax base that is subject to the associated tax rate. Finally, credits against the amount of tax owed reduce the liability of elderly and disabled persons, encourage various investments, and offset costs of child care. Because of these exemptions, deductions, and credits, the personal income tax has been progressive over the income scale, with only slight regressivity at the very top (Pechman, 1985, p. 53). Many states' income tax policies further relieve the burden on the poor through more liberal exemptions and additional deductions. Income taxes are also the mechanism for property tax relief in thirty-four states.

These provisions help achieve the goal of vertical equity. However, adjustments to income erode the tax base and raise concerns about preferential treatment for some groups of taxpayers. What is designed to be a legitimate recognition of an individual's economic well-being or tax capacity is often termed a "loophole" by those who do not benefit or who deem the adjustment to be unfair or unjustified. For example, income tax shelters and deductions are written into the tax code. These are intended to influence the behavior of taxpayers by encouraging savings for retirement and to enable individuals to legitimately defer taxation until they are in lower income tax brackets. The effects of income tax policy thus differ from the unintended effects that are often realized when consumption or property tax policies are altered, particularly at local and state levels. Income-based taxes are considered to be more neutral in social and economic effects than are other taxes because changes in personal income taxation do not intervene in market activities as directly.

The absolute cost of income tax administration and compliance is high for both taxpayers and governments. The income tax is the only major tax in which taxpayers must assess their own tax liability. The regulations and interpretations of the tax code by the Internal Revenue Service (IRS) guide taxpayers. The cost of tax consultation services provided by private vendors is high, as are the expenses of audits and dispute resolution by the IRS and tax courts. Nevertheless, the relative cost of administration is estimated to be only about 0.5 percent of revenue (Pechman, 1983, p. 61).

The elaborate system of deductions and credits complicates the income tax and often motivates creative tax avoidance on the part of taxpayers. Taxpayers must keep detailed records and often must turn to accountants and tax consultants to prepare returns. This raises the estimated cost of compliance to 7 percent of total revenue (Musgrave & Musgrave, 1989, p. 279). On the other hand, the practice of withholding estimated tax payments through payroll deductions distributes the burden of tax payment throughout the year. Those states that base their income tax collections on a given proportion of federal tax liability streamline administrative costs and minimize people's cost of compliance. They also relinquish control over decisions about exemptions and deductions, which can greatly affect state revenue.

There are many advantages of federal and state income taxation, but its use at the local level has been criticized on a number of grounds (Due, 1970, p. 320). Income is often earned in one locality by residents of another. Multiple taxation by communities, however, creates problems and raises the costs of administration and audits. If there is strong incentive for individuals and businesses to migrate to localities with no income tax, economic distortions result.

Reform of Income Taxation.   Ever-present calls for reform in income taxation center on tax simplification to reduce its complexity and high compliance costs. The many preferences expressed through deductions and tax credits help satisfy vertical equity. They also interfere with horizontal equity, however, because they dampen taxpayer morale when other people with the same gross income ultimately pay lower taxes. Critics advocate the elimination of such adjustments, favoring a flat tax of about 15 to 20 percent of all income to improve fairness and increase yield.

Analyses of effective rates—the percentage of income paid in taxes after exemptions and deductions—reveal that revenue was lost under the federal tax system prior to reform in 1986 because of its many tax preferences. In 1985, effective rates ranged from 0.7 percent on incomes below $5,000 to 26.4 percent for incomes between $500,000 and $1,000,000 (Pechman, 1984a, pp. 16–17). In comparison, incomes over $1,000,000 were taxed at an effective rate of only 23.1 percent, far below the 50 percent rate then called for in the tax code. Eliminating all personal deductions, exclusions, and investment incentives would broaden the tax base, permitting the same revenue to be raised with lower rates and a higher personal exemption: "A personal income tax conforming strictly with the 'equal treatment' principle would apply to all income from whatever source derived, making allowances only for the taxpayer and his dependents" (Pechman, 1986, p. 45). The 1986, 1990, and 1993 reforms were partially successful in meeting this goal, and several candidates in the 1996 presidential race urged adoption of a flat tax to further simplify the tax code.

Musgrave and Musgrave (1984) would also define income broadly. They suggest including all accretion, with no consideration for whether it is saved or consumed. They call for a meaningful and consistent criterion of equity: "In the absence of such a norm, technical issues of taxable income definition applicable to particular cases cannot be settled in a consistent and equitable fashion and the ever-present pressures for loophole snatching cannot be resisted" (p. 351). The deduction of home mortgage interest rather than having a housing allowance, for example, favors higher-income homeowners over renters, who tend to have lower incomes.

Capital gains taxation has been a major source of complication and economic distortion in income taxation. In principle, each year's appreciation in value (i.e., the dollar gain that exceeds relative changes in the cost of living) should be taxed as it accrues. In practice, gains were taxed for many years only when sales of properties or stocks occurred, and at substantially reduced rates to promote investment and risk taking. Most gains escaped taxation, and ordinary income was often converted into capital gains to take advantage of reduced rates. Changes in the code in 1986 treated realized capital gains the same as ordinary income for tax purposes (without considering inflation). Strong pressure to maintain the incentive for investment, however, placed a limit on the tax rate on gains of 28 percent for individuals and 35 percent for most corporations. These limits became more important to investors as higher brackets (up to 39.6 percent) were instituted in the 1993 reform. The treatment of unrealized gains from investments, those not converted to cash, is still being debated. By delaying taxation until the gain is realized, the government is in effect granting an interest-free loan to higher-income earners (Musgrave & Musgrave, 1989, p. 337).

Many changes have occurred in income taxation since ratification of the Sixteenth Amendment. The process of reform is a political one, however, and those individuals and businesses that are treated favorably resist dramatic change. Goals of equity and economic efficiency are often set aside to accommodate other social and economic objectives. For example, wealthy taxpayers benefit greatly from the exclusion of municipal bond interest from ordinary income on the premise that one government level should not tax the financial instruments of another. At the same time, however, construction of schools and other public facilities would be more costly without tax incentives for these investments.

Corporate Income Taxation

Taxation of corporate income once contributed a quarter of federal revenue but now accounts for only 8 percent of the total. All states except Nevada, South Dakota, Texas, Washington, and Wyoming derive revenue from a form of this tax, and this revenue source accounts for over 10 percent of collections in four states (see Table 5.5). Michigan repealed its corporate income tax in 1976. It replaced it with a single business tax that is a modified value-added tax (ACIR, 1995, p. 35).

Benefits received by businesses have been tied to costs of public services for many years. Congress levied an excise tax on the privilege of engaging in business when the constitutionality of the federal personal income tax was questioned in the late 1880s. The initial 1 percent rate became a graduated tax to meet growing revenue needs. Since 1987, corporate incomes below $50,000 have been taxed at 15 percent; those with incomes between $50,000 and $75,000 have been taxed at 25 percent. Corporations earning over $75,000 pay a 34 percent tax to the government; the 1993 tax reforms increased rates (to between 35 and 39 percent) on corporations with larger incomes (ACIR, 1995, p. 23).

Rates generally apply to a corporation's taxable income, defined as sales revenue less costs of production, interest, rent payments, depreciation on capital equipment and facilities, and state and local taxes. This corporate profit is the base taxed in 45 states. Many of them also base the tax on the value of capital stock or net worth. Three states tax gross receipts. Credits and incentives reduce the tax owed and serve economic and social goals. For example, investment credits encourage businesses to acquire new equipment to raise productive efficiency, energy credits encourage conservation, and various education credits in fifteen states offset a portion of the costs of vocational training and employer-sponsored child care programs. Tax incentives help businesses contribute to employees' pension plans, hire disadvantaged persons, and participate in public-private partnerships (ACIR, 1995, pp. 78–87).

Tax policy development poses problems that are similar to those identified for personal income taxation. Each deduction and credit reduces the tax base. It is difficult to have agreement on which costs of business should be deductible expenses and which incentives are important enough to be included as credits to reduce taxes paid. The corporate tax differs from individual income because it is a tax on profits rather than on income during the year.

The effective rate, the tax as a percentage of profits before deductions and other tax preferences, has fallen. In 1965, when the corporate income tax rate was 48 percent and profits were $80.4 billion, the effective tax rate was 34.5 percent. By 1982 the effective rate had declined to 13.1 percent, but the nominal rate was 46 percent and profits were $238.3 billion (Pechman, 1984b, p. 144).

Merits of Corporate Income Taxation.   The relatively high and elastic yield of the corporate income tax offers advantages of growth potential for federal and state governments. The burden of this and other taxes on businesses is hidden from taxpayers since it is often exported from the community to other parts of the country or world (Gold, 1994, p. 15). Because it has few direct effects upon voters, and because of the widely held perception that it is a tax on the rich, corporate income taxation is politically popular. However, not all shareholders are wealthy, particularly in the case of workers whose retirement plans are invested heavily in corporations. If it is assumed that the incidence of corporate taxes falls on consumers who pay higher prices or on employees who receive reduced wages, then the basis for an assumption of progressivity disappears (Pechman, 1985, p. 57), and, indeed, this burden may be regressive. The tax burden is further compounded when individuals pay a number of times from the same income—first directly through individual income taxes on earnings, then indirectly through corporate and sales taxes on their purchases.

Costs of administration are minimal relative to yield, but interstate commerce brings problems with allocations of corporate income among states. Multiple taxation of this income is minimized among states that have adopted uniform systems for reporting income and allocating collections to respective states. Compliance costs are high for corporations that plan expenditures carefully and maintain complete records in order to minimize tax liability.

Excise and Sales Taxation

Consumption-based taxes have been an important source of support for federal and state governments, and they are gaining popularity at the local level. Excise taxes are charged either on a per unit basis (e.g., per gallon of motor fuel and distilled spirits) or on an ad valorem basis (e.g., percentage of airline ticket cost or telephone charges). These taxes on selected goods are often defended as substitutes for service charges, given the close relationship between the tax and benefits received. Many governments view gasoline taxes and vehicle registration fees, for example, as user charges to support highway maintenance, and they dedicate this revenue for that purpose.

Unlike tariffs and excise taxes on specific commodities, state and local sales taxes apply more broadly as general taxation on the retail value of many goods and services. Falling property and income tax receipts during the depression of the 1930s led states to adopt emergency sales taxes. These taxes became more entrenched during World War II, and since that time sales tax rates have risen steadily (ACIR, 1990, p. 74; Due, 1982, p. 273). Only five of the thirty-six states with a sales tax in

1962 levied a rate of 4 percent, then the highest rate. The most common rate in 1994 was 5 percent (14 states), and only Colorado had a 3 percent rate. Thirteen states levied between 3 percent and 4.9 percent, and seventeen states and the District of Columbia had a rate higher than 5 percent. Mississippi and Rhode Island had the highest rate (7 percent) in 1994 (ACIR, 1995, p. 93). Alaska, Delaware, Montana, New Hampshire, and Oregon do not rely upon general sales tax revenue (see Table 5.5).

Thirty-one states permit localities, including school districts in Louisiana, to levy a sales tax (ACIR, 1995, pp. 95–99). For example, the addition of city and county sales taxes to statewide rates results in total rates over 8 percent in eighteen large cities.

Merits of Excise and Sales Taxes.   The yield of consumption-based taxes is substantial. Sales and gross receipts taxes account for more than 50 percent of tax revenue in Florida, South Dakota, Tennessee, Texas, and Washington (see Table 5.5). All states levy an excise tax on motor vehicle fuel; in fact, eleven states raise more than 10 percent of their total revenue from this source. Tobacco products are taxed in all states, and alcoholic beverages provide tax revenue in thirty-four states. But no state grosses more than 10 percent of total revenue from these excise taxes. Taken together, consumption-based taxes account for over 45 percent of total state collections.

Growth in the amount of states' sales and excise tax revenue between 1970 and 1992 was presented in Table 5.4. Collections from selective excise taxes on motor fuels and on tobacco and alcohol products more than doubled, while there was a 660 percent increase in general sales taxes. There has also been an increase in local dependence on sales taxes (see Table 5.1). Sales and gross receipts taxes accounted for 3.4 percent and 5.1 percent of local government tax revenue in 1970 and 1992, respectively. Some of this increase in state and local taxes can be accounted for by the cost of recent educational reforms. States such as Michigan have increased general sales taxation (from 4 to 6 percent) and excise taxes on cigarettes (from 25 to 75 cents per pack) to replace revenue lost from property tax reductions.

Consumption-based taxes are less sensitive to equity goals than are income taxes, because they are levied in rem (on things) rather than in personam (on the person). The amount of tax owed does not account for the conditions of individual taxpayers except for their patterns of purchases. Manufacturers and retailers may bear the initial impact of excise and sales taxes, but the ultimate incidence is clearly upon consumers. Rates applied to the value of purchases are the same for all consumers regardless of their income level, and there are no deductions or progressive rate schedules. It is only the exemption of basic necessities—including food, shelter, and medicine—in many state plans that makes general sales taxes less regressive, because these items represent a higher proportion of the budgets of the poor. Interestingly, the prevalence of consumption-based taxes in many other nations (see Table 5.2) makes their tax systems less progressive than those that rely more heavily upon income-based taxation (Pechman, 1989, p. 14).

Individuals with the same income but with different consumption habits pay varying amounts of excise and sales taxes; thus horizontal equity is not satisfied. People with different incomes also have dissimilar spending and saving patterns. As incomes rise, consumption declines as a percentage of income. This is because people with higher incomes divert more money to housing and investments—both of which are exempt from excise and sales taxes. Because excise and sales taxes place a heavier burden upon lower-income groups with little or no tax relief, vertical equity is not satisfied. Pechman's (1985, pp. 55–56) analysis, discussed in Chapter 4, reveals that the lowest-income decile paid an effective rate of 18 percent of income in sales tax, while the highest-income group paid only 1 percent.

Sales tax policy has been sensitive to this regressivity by exempting necessities or providing a credit on the amount of income tax owed in the form of a "circuit breaker." In 1994, the District of Columbia and all but two of the forty-five sales tax states exempted prescription drugs. Twenty-six of these jurisdictions exempted food but not restaurant meals. Thirty-one states did not tax a portion of electric and gas utility costs (ACIR, 1995, pp. 89–92). Only eight states exempt telecommunication services (e.g., telephone), but thirty-five states exclude personal services (e.g., hair styling). Rent is universally excluded from the sales tax.

These exemptions are thought to improve the sales tax's equity. But having more personal services fall within general sales taxation may improve its vertical equity, because the consumption of services is more elastic with respect to income than is the consumption of goods. This is because people tend to use more services as their incomes rise (Howard, 1989, p. 88). It might be argued, for example, that applying a sales tax to legal, medical, and educational (as with taxes on tuition and fees) services would reduce its regressivity. On the other hand, the taxation of services may introduce undesirable distortions. Highly mobile companies may move to avoid taxes, and other businesses may decide to provide their own services rather than purchase them (Gold, 1994, p. 27). Nevertheless, in order to increase revenue, and perhaps to improve tax equity, a growing number of states are expanding the list of personal and business services subject to sales taxation (ACIR, 1995, pp. 89–92).

Despite their political appeal and reduced tax burdens, exemptions cause substantial revenue loss (estimated between 20 percent and 25 percent of potential tax yield), complicate retailers' collection of the tax and states' enforcement of it, and exclude many expenditures of middle- and upper-income groups (Due, 1982, p. 273). For example, placing a ceiling on the amount of tax to be collected on purchases of automobiles and other vehicles makes the tax more regressive and reduces revenue. Eliminating all exemptions, even for food and prescription drugs, would simplify administration and raise greater revenue. A preferred approach for reducing regressivity may be through a circuit breaker, the mechanism that eight states use to relieve sales tax burdens (ACIR, 1995, pp. 89–90). Some states reduce their income taxes by a flat dollar credit per family member regardless of income; others apply

a declining rate as income rises; still others provide a separate refund program. Although a cash refund may be available for people with low incomes who have no tax liability, these people may neglect to file the necessary income tax forms.

Consumption-based taxes are not neutral and often cause severe economic and social effects. The shopping habits of consumers may be affected, particularly if sales tax rates differ within a relatively small geographic area. Decisions about the location of shopping plazas and automobile dealerships may be influenced by rate differences among municipalities and counties, or even across state lines. Easing geographic rate differentials would make the tax more neutral. In addition, better controls over interstate transactions would recapture lost revenue from exemptions made for goods ordered by mail and shipped across state lines.

Higher rates on demerit goods may discourage consumption of alcohol and tobacco. These excise taxes are often justified on the basis of the costs to society that can result from excessive use of the products and on sumptuary grounds, because their consumption is considered immoral and unhealthy. If these taxes were effective, however, both consumption and tax revenue would decline (Musgrave & Musgrave, 1989).

The relatively simple tax structure of sales and excise taxes minimizes administration and compliance costs. Manufacturers pay excise taxes according to the quantity produced, and retailers charge consumers general sales taxes at the time sales are made. Computerized cash registers simplify sales tax procedures. This reduces the clerks' errors that once were a problem, particularly in states with exemptions of certain goods. The costs of auditing retailers' accounts are minimal; they are estimated to be about 1 percent of the revenue collected (Due, 1970, p. 305).

Personal Expenditure and Value-Added Taxes as Alternatives. Personal expenditure and value-added taxes (VAT) offer very different approaches to consumption-based taxation. A personal expenditure tax, also referred to as a consumption expenditure tax, is based upon an individual's aggregate spending (Courant & Gramlich, 1984; Musgrave & Musgrave, 1989). Unlike sales and excise taxation, this tax is levied on consumers rather than on actual goods and services purchased. As an alternative to the income tax, its structure may also provide exemptions or deductions, and it may have graduated rates.

Tax liability is determined by (1) adding income from all sources to assets at the beginning of the tax year; (2) increasing this amount by net borrowing and decreasing it by net investments during the year to give an indication of funds available for personal expenditures; (3) subtracting accumulated assets from this total at the end of the year, yielding the annual amount of consumption; and (4) applying the appropriate tax rate. Replacing income and general sales taxes, an expenditure tax offers the advantages of both. Including personal exemptions and deductions and having progressive rates would protect low-income groups who consume higher proportions of their income. Unlike the income tax's weakness in discouraging investments, an expenditure tax would encourage saving and discourage consumption (Pechman, 1989, p. 112). However, the costs of administration and compliance would increase greatly, given the need for annual valuations of assets.

A valued-added tax (VAT) has also been suggested as an alternative to retail sales taxation. This tax recognizes that goods increase in value at various production stages, with the final prices reflecting the sum of increments in value. Used successfully in many countries, the VAT is the basic instrument of tax coordination among nations in the European Common Market. Large deficits in the United States during the 1980s brought attention to this tax as a means to generate revenue, stimulate investments, and improve the balance of payments in international trade.

The invoice method of tax calculation in use in most countries is an indirect form of taxation in that it does not actually calculate the value and apply a tax rate to that base, as happens with income, sales, and property taxes (Tait, 1988, pp. 4–5). Instead, the rate is applied to the gross receipts of a business (i.e., output) minus the value of intermediate materials and other production costs (i.e., input). Tax liability results from applying the VAT rate to this base and then crediting against the gross tax the amount of VAT already paid by suppliers of intermediate and capital goods.

Opponents view the value-added tax as a hidden and regressive tax that has high administrative costs (Aaron, 1981; McClure, 1984, p. 185; Tait, 1988, pp. 400–403). The initial impact is upon producers, but by shifting the tax forward as prices increase, the incidence falls ultimately upon consumers. Like the general sales tax, regressivity might be reduced through exemptions for necessities or income tax credits. Such measures would moderate the VAT's regressivity, making it proportional to income for the lower half of the income distribution, but it would continue to be regressive for upper-income levels (Pechman, 1989, p. 8). Costs of administration for the government and of compliance for businesses would be much greater under a VAT than are the costs necessitated by general sales taxes.

The division of revenue among government levels would need to be considered in the development of a VAT policy. If the federal government's VAT replaced states' general sales taxes such that industrial states benefited from taxes imposed at the production stage, many other states would lose tax revenue they currently collect at retail levels. Similarly, states could forfeit revenue they currently gain from the sales of imported automobiles and other products.

For the VAT to be justified, it must be argued that the tax system is too progressive, or that substantial revenue is needed to fund a major new federal direction or to close an intolerable deficit. In today's political environment, state and local officials are concerned about a federal tax on consumption and many think that as many businesses would be helped as would be hurt. Such an environment will not support a VAT (Aaron, 1984, p. 217; Tait, 1988, p. 34). Because of its disadvantages and potential complications for the current tax structure, it is not likely that a value-added tax will be adopted in the United States.

Lottery as Taxation

A lottery has been defined as a game in which "chances to share in a distribution of prizes are sold" (Commission on the Review of the National Policy toward Gambling, 1976). A governmentally sponsored lottery is a voluntary tax that can be classified as either a consumption-based tax or a privilege-based tax. If the portion paid in prizes is considered to be a product sold by the state, then the remaining revenue, less operating expenses, is an excise tax on that product (Guthrie, Garms, & Pierce, 1988, p. 95). This revenue is an "implicit" tax collected from a portion of the proceeds (Clotfelter & Cook, 1989, p. 219). It might also be considered to be a privilege tax, like that derived from casino games in an increasing number of states, in which the government collects a fee for permitting people to participate and wager in games of chance.

Lotteries have been used throughout history to resolve disputes objectively and to raise funds for churches and governments. About fifty colleges and 300 elementary/secondary schools benefited from lottery revenue through the Civil War (Ezell, 1960). However, their revenue potential has been overshadowed by political corruption and claims that any form of gambling encourages immoral behavior, fraud, and bribery. Abuses in the late 1800s brought federal legislation against using postal services for transporting lottery materials. Although charitable organizations continued to sponsor legalized social play (e.g., raffles, bingo games) for many years, the government has been hesitant to sanction more addictive and commercialized forms (e.g., casinos) of gambling. Today's state-sponsored lotteries fall in the middle of the continuum from social, low-wage play to higher-stakes gambling (Jones & Amalfitano, 1994, p. xvii).

The lottery was revived in the mid-1960s in New Hampshire and New York. By 1992, thirty-seven states and the District of Columbia had operating lotteries. Nine states reported yield in excess of $1 billion: California, Florida, Illinois, Massachusetts, Michigan, New Jersey, New York, Ohio, and Pennsylvania (ACIR, 1994, pp. 106–107). The highest revenue producer was Florida ($2.1 billion), and its proceeds accounted for 4.8 percent of total state general revenue (p. 108). Of the $19.17 billion collected nationwide in 1991, $10.35 billion (54 percent) was paid in prizes and another $1.15 billion (6 percent) was diverted to administrative expenses, leaving $7.67 billion in tax revenue (40 percent).

Federal legislation in 1988, the Charity Games Advertising Clarification Act, permits nonprofit and commercial organizations to operate lotteries in accordance with state laws and to advertise lotteries and list prize winners in adjoining states' media (P.L. 100-625, 18 USCS 1301). Various forms of the lottery include "instant games," in which players rub off a waxy substance from tickets to determine winnings; "numbers," in which players place bets on a three- or four-digit number via computer terminals and later learn the winning numbers through the media; "lotto," which generally has players select six of thirty-six numbers and has a weekly drawing to determine winners; and "video lottery terminal" (VTL) play, which resembles slot machines in casinos. Jones and Amalfitano (1994, p. 42) note that many observers expect this latter form, which was legalized in only five states in 1991, along with interactive television lottery, to be the fastest-growing form of play in the future.

Proponents argue that the revenue gained outweighs the lottery's disadvantages. Unlike many unpopular taxes, this "painless" tax is paid only by the willing (Clotfelter & Cook, 1989, p. 215). These voluntary games provide some degree of enjoyment for participants, and the public entertainment raises state revenue without increasing other taxes. A portion of the prize money is also a revenue source, since winnings are subject to income taxation, but much revenue is lost through the exemption from withholding or reporting of cash payments up to $600. The lottery provides an example of double taxation, since the money used to purchase tickets was previously taxed as income. Because no new income is generated for society through the lottery, it might be argued that there should be no income tax on winnings.

The ease of compliance, with no tax forms to complete and with readily accessible and low-cost tickets, offers an advantage for this revenue source. However, the cost of administration is high relative to the yield, raising concerns with the inefficiency of this tax mechanism. The lottery accounts for less than 7 percent of state revenues, and the costs of marketing, printing tickets, and paying off winners are high. Operating costs consumed between 3 percent (New York and Pennsylvania) and 29 percent (Montana) of 1991 collections; this compares to less than 5 percent of other tax yields (Thomas & Webb, 1984, p. 303). As a result, the proportion of lottery proceeds that is devoted to government programs ranges from 20 percent (Montana) to 67 percent (South Dakota) of receipts.

This average tax rate, the proportion of sales that becomes revenue to states (40 percent), is higher than other excise taxes, including those charged for alcohol and tobacco products. As with other consumption-based taxes, the price of the lottery ticket is the same for all. The burden is upon the poor, who spend a higher proportion of their income for tickets. It is argued that the lottery is more regressive than general sales or excise taxes (Mikesell & Zorn, 1986). Clotfelter and Cook (1989, p. 223) concluded from their review of studies of the regressivity of this tax: "Without exception, the evidence shows that the implicit tax on lotteries is regressive." If the lottery tax rate were lower to be more comparable with other such taxes, prizes could be higher and the tax burden would be lower, but the government's share would decline.

The moral and public-policy dilemmas raised by lotteries can be cast within the criterion of neutrality as they alter people's behavior. Opponents contend that lotteries catch states in a dilemma of enticing the citizenry into previously forbidden and immoral activities in order to raise needed revenue, and that legalized gambling encourages organized crime, political corruption, and fraud by reducing the stigma of playing. In response, advocates argue that governmentally sponsored games offer a legal gambling alternative to organized crime and thus compete with it and deter it (Jones & Amalfitano, 1994, pp. 59, 64–68).

Twenty-two of the lottery states earmark the proceeds for public education, senior citizen programs, or other specific purposes. These designations encourage ticket sales and enhance political appeal. But earmarking this revenue may make little difference in overall financial support. There is evidence that previously allocated money from states' general funds are diverted to support other programs. Thus, earmarking lottery proceeds does not benefit statutory recipients (Borg & Mason, 1990; Stark, Wood, & Honeyman, 1993). Jones and Amalfitano (1994) found no evidence that the presence of a state lottery, or the earmarking of revenue for education, explained the variation among states in levels of support or effort for public education. They concluded, both from analyses of revenue effects and from the moral and policy dilemmas, that states should be more judicious in sponsoring lotteries, providing "truth in advertising" or assuring that the revenue derived from lotteries benefits private charities exclusively.

States have turned to this voluntary tax despite its regressivity, low yield, high administrative costs, and opposition from groups concerned about its social effects. The success and current popularity of lotteries, as well as the emergence of a new generation of automated and interactive games, suggest that they will continue to grow in importance as an alternative to traditional state revenue sources. Educators are cautioned, however, that this additional revenue does not necessarily benefit public schools.

Severance Taxes

Thirty-eight states collect severance taxes for the privilege of extracting natural resources from land or water (ACIR, 1995, pp. 122–129). Production, license, and conservation taxes are levied on such resources as coal, natural gas, minerals, forest products, and fish. Oil and gas production accounts for over 80 percent of these taxes. Energy-related industry also brings revenue to states and localities through rents and royalties on mineral leases for energy production on public land, corporate income taxes, and local property taxes.

Severance taxes are either at a specific rate, based on the quantity of resources removed (e.g., $0.45 per ton of coal in Missouri), or ad valorem, based on market value of the goods (e.g., 0.08 to 5.25 percent of fish products in Washington). Differing extraction processes complicate the task of valuation for tax purposes. In some cases, a very large investment must be made to extract very little mineral, as with diamonds; in others, a low-cost extraction process yields much return, as with natural gas.

Collections from severance taxes grew rapidly following the 1973 oil embargo and the subsequent deregulation of the oil and gas industries, but they fell during the 1980s. The uncertain yield of this tax is evident in its steady growth from $800 million in 1972 to $7.4 billion in 1983, then its decline to $4.1 billion in 1987, and its subsequent increase to $4.9 billion in 1993 (U. S. Department of Commerce, 1995, Table 492). Severance taxes accounted for over 50 percent of state taxation in Alaska and 39 percent of state revenue in Wyoming in 1993 (U. S. Department of Commerce, 1995, Table 492).

States, counties, and school districts with energy revenues are better able to finance public services, and they can export a large share of the tax burden to nonresidents (Cuciti, Galper, & Lucke, 1983, p. 17). In order to curtail this shifting of incidence, several reforms have been suggested to limit severance taxation to a given percentage of production value or to a certain level of total revenue per capita. State policies might require those producing counties (and school districts) to share some portion of tax revenue with energy-consuming regions. But a counterargument can be made that severance taxes are fair compensation for the environmental damage associated with many extraction processes.

Estate and Gift Taxation

The base of gift, estate, and inheritance taxes is wealth. Federal and state governments tax estates for the privilege of transferring money or other property to heirs, and many states collect an inheritance tax on the privilege of receiving a bequest. These taxes reallocate a portion of very large wealth accumulations in concert with the beliefs that a wealthy and politically powerful aristocracy might otherwise disrupt free enterprise and that large inheritances might cause heirs to lead less than productive lives (Pechman, 1989, p. 121). Many universities and private foundations have benefited from tax policies that exempt donations to charitable institutions from estate taxation.

Tax reform in 1976 joined federal estate and gift taxes under a unified rate schedule to reduce the incentive for people to give away their wealth to avoid taxation at death. Estates below $600,000 are exempt from taxation at the federal level. Furthermore, a gift tax exclusion permits annual transfers of up to $10,000 for each qualified recipient without a tax obligation on either party. Gift taxes paid during the donor's life are credited against estate taxes due at the time of death. Tax reform in 1981 increased the exemption from 60 percent to 100 percent of an estate for a surviving spouse. The rates applied to remaining taxable estates range from 18 percent for those under $10,000 to 55 percent for those over $3 million (ACIR, 1995, p. 29). The large exemptions diminish collections, which accounted for less than 1 percent of total federal revenue in 1992 (see Table 5.3).

All states benefit from a portion of the federal tax. Six states levy an additional tax on estates, sixteen states place a tax on inheritances, and six states have an additional gift tax during a donor's life (ACIR, 1995, p. 147). These death and gift taxes provided 1.4 percent of total state revenue in 1992 (see Table 5.4).

Payroll Taxation

Unlike the foregoing revenue sources, which yield money for general government expenses, payroll deductions are earmarked specifically to finance two federal insurance programs, Social Security and unemployment compensation. Initiated by the Social Security Act of 1935, programs today reduce the financial burdens of old age, premature death of family providers, medical expenses, and long-term unemployment. These required payroll taxes supplement other retirement and insurance programs available to educators.

The Old-Age, Survivors, Disability, and Health Insurance (OASDHI) program, as it has been called since the addition of health benefits in 1965, is the largest program sponsored by the federal government. The original intent of Congress was to establish a fully funded insurance program. Payroll taxes would be invested in a trust fund to guarantee future benefits. The inclusion of unemployment benefits in 1939 altered the investment approach, creating a pay-as-you-go system of financing (Davies, 1986, p. 169). Despite increased collections between 1970 and 1980 (see Table 5.3), the trust fund failed to keep pace with the demands placed on the system. In 1975 cost-of-living adjustments began to keep inflation from eroding the value of benefits. This increase reached 14.3 percent in 1980 and has declined annually, along with the Consumer Price Index, to 2.8 percent in 1995. Legislation in 1983 improved the trust fund by partially taxing Social Security benefits, accelerating tax rate increases in recent years, and gradually increasing the retirement age from 65 to 67 by the year 2017. In recent years, collections have outpaced benefit payments, and balances are not likely to be exhausted before the year 2050 (Pechman, 1989, p. 183).

Social Security began in 1937 as a 1 percent tax, collecting a maximum of $30 on the covered earnings base of $3,000 (ACIR, 1995, p. 27). The earnings base has been raised annually since 1972 to keep pace with average wages. It was $61,200 in 1995. The 7.51 percent tax collected on earnings below $45,000 in 1988 increased to 7.65 percent for 1990 and thereafter. This rate includes the 1.45 percent Medicare tax on all earned income. The total tax is over 15 percent, including the matching contributions of employers. In addition, employers pay 6.2 percent (6.0 percent beginning in 1999) of the first $7,000 of each employee's income for the unemployment compensation tax. These taxes represent a sizable annual expense for school districts in states participating in the national program. Total collections represent a very large proportion (36 percent) of federal revenue (see Table 5.3).

Payroll taxes are nearly proportional for income levels to the covered earnings base. They are regressive for upper-income groups, however, because they do not contribute beyond this point. The benefit schedule is more progressive. People with low incomes receive relatively higher proportions of the taxes they pay into the system (Davies, 1986, p. 171). And beneficiaries with incomes over $44,000 (married) or $34,000 (single) pay income taxes on 85 percent of their Social Security benefits beginning in 1994.

Increased rates and the raised earnings base in recent years eased concerns that earlier retirement ages, longer life expectancies, cost-of-living adjustments for beneficiaries, and unpredictable rates of unemployment would jeopardize the fund. It has been estimated that only two workers will support each retiree after the year 2000, in comparison with a three-to-one ratio in the mid-1980s. In order to maintain solvency and reduce regressivity, more drastic reforms may be necessary: removing ceilings on contributions, graduating tax rates, supporting health insurance (Medicare) programs with income taxes, or reducing the cost-of-living allowance.

ADVANTAGES OF MULTIPLE, BROAD-BASED TAX SOURCES

Relying exclusively upon any one of the above taxes would accentuate its disadvantages and place a large burden for supporting government services on one segment of society. Data presented in the tables of this chapter give evidence that governments choose multiple sources and depend upon specific taxes to differing degrees. Designing revenue systems that include several forms of taxation and that broaden the base from which revenue is collected offers advantages to governments.

Gold (1994) noted the importance of a balanced tax system which relies on broad-based taxes. Multiple sources help keep tax rates low for any given tax to stimulate economic development and bring stability to government, since overall revenue is not subject to fluctuations in the yields of any one tax. Furthermore, including more than one tax minimizes distortions in the economy as the defects of each tax are averaged out. A broad-based tax system is also more neutral because it minimizes distortions in location decisions and improves horizontal equity.

These advantages, and the tradeoffs among values noted in Chapter 4, explain why a number of revenue sources comprise the financial support for governments. School districts, which derive much of their revenue from higher levels of government, thus indirectly depend on multiple taxes in addition to their historical reliance on the property tax.

SUMMARY

Revenue sources detailed in this chapter provide money for federal, state, and, to some degree, local governments. Personal income taxation provides high revenue yield that responds well to the economy, contributes to vertical equity, causes minimal social and economic disruption, and has a relatively low cost of administration. However, its complexity, high compliance costs, and the perception that loopholes give unfair advantage to some taxpayers fuel calls for reforms. The simplified structures of excise and sales taxes, which have no deductions or exemptions based on taxpayers' incomes, minimize administrative and compliance costs. However, these consumption taxes result in economic distortions of true consumer preferences. Furthermore, unless provisions are made for exempting necessities or allowing income tax credits, they work against equity goals. These two primary sources of tax revenue offer federal and state governments different advantages that argue for augmenting their role in tax policy. Their weaknesses offer opportunities for tax policy reform.

Corporate income taxes, lotteries, severance taxes, estate and gift taxes, and payroll taxes also contribute to governments' resources. Because they rely upon very different tax bases, these taxes offer ways to diversify tax policy. States rely to very different degrees upon income, consumption, wealth, and privilege taxes. This is because of their particular conditions of population, geography, natural resources, economy, and tradition. In deciding which taxes to adopt, states should try to have a balanced tax system that relies on broad-based taxes.

The next chapter identifies the structure and administration of property taxation. Unlike the taxes examined in this chapter, the property tax has been the principal revenue producer for local governments and for school districts in particular.

ACTIVITIES

1. Trace the history of one revenue source, identifying the initial rationale, the changes in its provisions that may have altered the original purpose, and trends in rates and collections over time.
2. Debate the advantages of income-based taxes over consumption-based taxes in relation to criteria of yield, equity, neutrality, and costs of administration and compliance.
3. Investigate the primary state-level taxes that support schools in a selected state. What proportion is derived from each source: personal income, corporate income, excise, sales, lottery, severance, inheritance, and other taxes? What modifications might you suggest to make this state's revenue system more responsive to tax criteria of yield, equity, neutrality, and costs of administration and compliance?
4. Do states with high capacity or effort spend comparatively more on education than those with lower abilities or willingness to tax? Compare the ranks in states' capacities and efforts (Table 5.6) with their revenue per pupil for education (presented in Table 8.1 of Chapter 8).
5. Design an instrument to survey the residents or policy makers of your community or state to determine their preferences for reform in tax policy in the coming decade.

COMPUTER SIMULATIONS

Objectives of this Activity:

- *To understand the relative reliance of states on various tax sources (as in Table 5.4)*

- *To identify trends in the proportions of government tax collections over time*

- *To use spreadsheet graphic capability in the analysis of school finance policy*

Simulation 5.1, Part 1: *Preparing a Table for Graphing*

a. Retrieve the file TAXATION.

b. Copy only the column and row labels to the spreadsheet area directly below the table provided so that the label, SOURCE, is located in cell A22. Do not copy the data presented in the original table; they will be used in subsequent calculations of proportionate reliance on the taxes listed.

c. In the 1970 column on the GENERAL SALES row, enter a formula using the "formula method" that will divide the 1970 GENERAL SALES in the original table by the 1970 TOTAL in the original table.

   Note: At this juncture it is important to emphasize two major points of terminology. First, it is possible to complete step "c" with a formula such as: 14,177/47,962. However, completion of the table using this approach would require entering a new formula for every cell in the table. We recommend that step "c" be completed using what we call the "formula method" throughout this text. By this we mean the use of "cell references" in formulae rather than numeric values. For step "c," the formula in our worksheet using the "formula method" is: +B9/B18 (Lotus) or =B9/B18 (Excel).

   Second, since 47,962 should be the denominator of all formulae in the 1970 column, the cell reference for this numeric value should be "absolute," meaning that it

will remain the same no matter where the formula is copied or moved to. The typical format for an "absolute" cell reference includes dollar signs (that is, B18). However, in this case we want the row reference to remain "absolute" while the column reference is allowed to change to the appropriate TOTAL as the percent of total tax receipts is calculated for each tax for 1980 and 1992. Therefore, the recommended cell reference is: B$18—allowing the column to vary, but keeping the row "absolute."

   Software manufacturers are rather consistent in the use of terms such as "cell reference," "absolute cell reference," and "relative cell reference." If our discussion or the instructions you receive on these points is unclear, we recommend that you consult your software reference manual regarding these terms.

d. Edit the completed formula to make the row reference of the denominator "absolute" and allowing the column to vary [that is: +B9/B$18 or =B9/B$18].

e. Copy the completed formula to all of the remaining cells in the table.

f. Save your file and print the new table.

Simulation 5.1, Part 2: *Making Pie and Bar Graphs of the Proportional Composition of Total Tax Receipts for All States*

a. Continuing with the file developed in Simulation 5.1, create a "pie" chart or graph of the 1992 percentages of total state government tax receipts following the instructions listed below. Consultation with your software program manual may prove especially helpful for graphing as the specifics vary considerably among software products. Our instructions attempt to accommodate similarities among programs and to emphasize key elements.

b. Activate the "Graph" function or menu of your software program.

c. Select the "Type" of graph to be created: "Pie."

d. Select the "X" axis range of data that contains the labels or names of the different tax sources.

e. Select the range of data (i.e., "A" or "First" range) that contains the percentages of total tax receipts in the 1992 column.

f. Select the appropriate command from your menu to "View" or to look at the graph on your computer screen.

g. Using the "Options" or "Graph" menu, add "Titles" and other descriptive information to the graph as appropriate.

h. Consult your software program manual to "Save" or "Name" your graph for future use.

i. Consult your software program manual to "Print" your graph.

   Note: IBM-compatible users can print a graph that appears on the computer screen by pressing the *Print Screen* key. If this does not work, you must go to the system prompt and type, "graphics.com" and press the *Enter* key. Return to Lotus 1-2-3, view the graph on the computer screen, and press the *Print Screen* key. Once the "graphics.com" command has been executed, all graphs may be printed from the computer screen by pressing the *Print Screen* key.

j. Select a new "Type" of graph to be created: "Bar."

k. Select the appropriate command from your menu to "View" or to look at the graph on your computer screen.

l. Save and print the new graph.

m. ***Further Activities.*** Consult your software program manual for assistance and create a line graph that depicts trends in states' reliance on these revenue sources over a period of years.

Simulation 5.2: *Making Pie and Bar Graphs of the Proportional Composition of Total Tax Receipts for a Single State*

a. Retrieve the file STATETAX.

b. Activate the "Graph" function or menu of your software program.

c. Select the "Type" of graph to be created: "Pie."

d. Select the "X" axis range of data that contains the labels or names of the different tax sources. Only use one row of labels rather than two (that is: SALES, FUELS, TOBACCO, INDV., CORP., LICS., OTHER). Do not include the STATE or (MILLIONS) labels in the range.

e. Select the range of data (i.e., "A" or "First" range) that contains the percentages of tax SOURCES in the CA (California) row.

f. Select the appropriate command from your menu to "View" or to look at the graph on your computer screen.

g. Using the "Options" or "Graph" menu, add "Titles" and other descriptive information to the graph as appropriate.

h. Save and print the graph. (IBM-compatible users may want to consult Simulation 5.1, Part 2, step i.)

i. Select a new "Type" of graph to be created: "Bar."

j. Select the appropriate command from your menu to "View" or to look at the graph on your computer screen.

k. Save and print the new graph.

l. ***Further Activities.***

   1. How do the graphs of California compare to the graphs that consider all states, created in Simulation 5.1, Part 2?

   2. Repeat steps "e" through "m" for your own state.

   3. In order to compare tax policies graphically for three or four states, consult your

software program manual for assistance and create a bar graph that displays tax

sources and the percentages of total tax collections for the selected states.

REFERENCES

Aaron, H. J. (Ed.). (1981). *The value-added tax: Lessons from Europe, Studies of government finance.* Washington, DC: Brookings Institution.

Aaron, H. J. (1984). The value-added tax: A triumph of form over substance. In C. E. Walker & M. A. Bloomfield (Eds.), *New directions in federal tax policy for the 1980s* (pp. 217–240). Cambridge, MA: Ballinger.

ACIR. (Advisory Commission on Intergovernmental Relations). (1990). *Significant features of fiscal federalism, Volume 1.* Washington, DC: Advisory Commission on Intergovernmental Relations.

ACIR. (1992). *Significant features of fiscal federalism, Volume 2.* Washington, DC: Advisory Commission on Intergovernmental Relations.

ACIR. (1993). *RTS 1991: State revenue capacity and effort.* Washington, DC: Advisory Commission on Intergovernmental Relations.

ACIR. (1994). *Significant features of fiscal federalism, Volume 2: Revenues and expenditures.* Washington, DC: Advisory Commission on Intergovernmental Relations.

ACIR. (1995). *Significant features of fiscal federalism, Volume 1: Budget processes and tax systems.* Washington, DC: Advisory Commission on Intergovernmental Relations.

Borg, M. O., & Mason, P. M. (1990). Earmarked lottery revenues: Positive windfalls or concealed redistribution mechanisms? *Journal of Education Finance, 15,* 289–301.

Clotfelter, C. T., & Cook, P. J. (1989). *Selling hope: State lotteries in America.* Cambridge, MA: Harvard University Press.

Commission on the Review of the National Policy toward Gambling. (1976). *Gambling in America.* Washington, DC: U. S. Government Printing Office.

Courant, P., & Gramlich, E. (1984). The expenditure tax: Has the idea's time come? In J. A. Pechman et al., *Tax policy: New directions and possibilities* (pp. 27–36). Washington, DC: Center for National Policy.

Cuciti, P., Galper, H., & Lucke, R. (1983). State energy revenues. In C. E. McLure & P. Mieszkowski (Eds.), *Fiscal federalism and the taxation of natural resources* (pp. 11–60). Lexington, MA: Lexington Books.

Davies, D. G. (1986). *United States taxes and tax policy.* Cambridge: Cambridge University Press.

Due, J. F. (1970). Alternative tax sources for education. In R. L. Johns et al. (Eds.), *Economic factors affecting the financing of education* (pp. 291–328). Gainesville, FL: National Education Finance Project.

Due, J. F. (1982). Shifting sources of financing education and the taxpayer revolt. In W. W. McMahon & T. G. Geske (Eds.), *Financing education: Overcoming inefficiency and inequity* (pp. 267–289). Urbana: University of Illinois Press.

Ezell, J. S. (1960). *Fortune's merry wheel: The lottery in America.* Cambridge, MA: Harvard University Press.

Galper, H., & Pollock, S. H. (1988). Models of state income tax reform. In S. D. Gold (Ed.), *The unfinished agenda for state tax reform* (pp. 107–128). Denver, CO: National Conference of State Legislatures.

Gold, S. D. (Ed.). (1994). *Tax options for states needing more school revenue.* Westhaven, CT: National Education Association.

Guthrie, J. W., Garms, W. I., & Pierce, L. C. (1988). *School finance and education policy: Enhancing educational efficiency, equality, and choice.* Englewood Cliffs, NJ: Prentice Hall.

Howard, M. A. (1989, Summer). State tax and expenditure limitations: There is no story. *Public Budgeting and Finance, 9* (2), 83–90.

Jones, T. H., & Amalfitano, J. L. (1994). *America's gamble: Public school finance and state lotteries.* Lancaster, PA: Technomic.

Mackey, S. R. (1993). *State tax actions 1993.* Denver, CO: National Conference of State Legislatures.

MacPhail-Wilcox, B. (1984). Tax policy analysis and education finance: A conceptual framework for issues and analysis. *Journal of Education Finance, 9,* 312–331.

McLure, C. E. (1984). Value added tax: Has the time come? In C. E. Walker & M. A. Bloomfield (Eds.), *New directions in federal tax policy for the 1980s* (pp. 185–213). Cambridge, MA: Ballinger.

Mikesell, J. L., & Zorn, C. K. (1986, July/August). State lotteries as fiscal savior or fiscal fraud: A look at the evidence. *Public Administration Review, 46,* 311–320.

Musgrave, R. A., & Musgrave, P. B. (1984). *Public finance: Its background, structure, and operation* (4th ed.). New York: McGraw-Hill.

Musgrave, R. A., & Musgrave, P. B. (1989). *Public finance in theory and practice.* New York: McGraw-Hill.

National Conference of State Legislatures. (1994). *State budget and tax actions 1994: Preliminary report.* Denver, CO: Author.

Pechman, J. A. (1983). *Federal tax policy.* Washington, DC: Brookings Institution.

Pechman, J. A. (1984a). Comprehensive income tax reform. In J. A. Pechman et al., *Tax policy: New directions and possibilities* (pp. 13–18). Washington, DC: Center for National Policy.

Pechman, J. A. (1984b). *Federal tax policy* (4th ed.). Washington, DC: Brookings Institution.

Pechman, J. A., (1985). *Who paid the taxes, 1966–85?* Washington, DC: Brookings Institution.

Pechman, J. A. (1986). *The rich, the poor, and the taxes they pay.* Brighton, Sussex, England: Wheatsheaf Books of the Harvester Press.

Pechman, J. A. (1989). *Tax reform: The rich and the poor* (2nd ed.). Washington, DC: Brookings Institution.

Simons, H. C. (1938). *Personal income taxation: The definition of income as a problem of fiscal policy.* Chicago: University of Chicago Press.

Stark, S., Wood, R. C., & Honeyman, D. S. (1993). The Florida education lottery: Its use as a substitute for existing funds and its effects on the equity of school funding. *Journal of Education Finance, 18,* 231–242.

Tait, A. A. (1988). *Value added tax: International practice and problems.* Washington, DC: International Monetary Fund.

Thomas, S. B., & Webb, L. D. (1984). The use and abuse of lotteries as a revenue source. *Journal of Education Finance, 9,* 289–311.

U. S. Department of Commerce, Bureau of the Census. (1987). *Statistical abstract of the United States: 1988.* Washington, DC: U. S. Government Printing Office.

U. S. Department of Commerce, Bureau of the Census. (1993). *State government finances, 1992.* GF/92-3. Washington, DC: U. S. Government Printing Office.

U. S. Department of Commerce, Bureau of the Census. (1994a). *State government finances, 1991–92, preliminary report.* GF92-5P. Washington, DC: U. S. Government Printing Office.

U. S. Department of Commerce, Bureau of the Census. (1994b). *Statistical abstract of the United States: 1994.* Washington, DC: U. S. Government Printing Office.

U. S. Department of Commerce, Bureau of the Census. (1995). *Statistical abstract of the United States: 1995.* Washington, DC: U. S. Government Printing Office.

Waltman, J. L. (1985). *Political origins of the U. S. income tax.* Jackson, MS: University Press of Mississippi.

CHAPTER 6

The Property Tax in Support of Schools

Primary Issues Explored in This Chapter:

- *The property tax base:* How has benefit theory resulted in the taxation of tangible real property for supporting local services, including education?
- *Determining the amount of tax owed:* What procedures are employed for assessing the value of real property, for relieving the tax burdens of certain taxpayers, and for calculating the amount owed by individuals and businesses?
- *Tax capacity and effort:* How do states differ in the size of their property tax bases, the tax rates applied to that base, and the revenue collected?
- *Strengths and weaknesses of the property tax:* How does this revenue source measure up relative to the criteria of yield, elasticity, equity, neutrality, and costs of administration and compliance?
- *Limitations on revenue and expenditures:* What constitutional or statutory limitations, particularly those imposed through citizen initiatives, affect the abilities of states and localities to increase taxes or constrain the growth of revenue and spending?
- *Local autonomy and the property tax:* Why have communities resisted attempts to elevate the property tax from a local to a regional or state revenue source, despite the potential benefits of broader-based taxation in financing educational reforms?

The property tax has traditionally been the financial mainstay of local governments, including school districts. This tax continues to provide the bulk of local funds. At the same time, the public expresses concern about its fairness. And policy makers consider proposals to replace property taxes with broader-based income or sales taxes.

The property tax persists as the primary source of local government revenue for several reasons. It is uniquely suited to be the primary source. Its stability permits public governing boards and ad-

ministrators to accurately predict annual revenue flow as they plan for and deliver services for citizens. People also defend the property tax vigorously because of its close tie with local governmental autonomy, and because it is a visible link between public services and their costs to individuals and businesses. Because county and state administrative mechanisms have been in place for many years, the cost of tax collection is relatively low.

Despite these advantages, many people severely criticize property taxation. The public rates it as the least popular form of taxation (ACIR, 1988, p. 97). It has been described as the "most wretchedly administered tax" (Shannon, 1973, p. 27). Perceptions of unfair and differentially applied assessment policies give the property tax a poor public image. It is often the most painful tax for businesses and homeowners to pay. Challenges to continued use of property taxes cite the following disadvantages: It places a regressive burden on the poor. It contributes to the deterioration of urban housing. It cannot capture the real fiscal capacity of communities. It creates inequities in educational opportunities for children in different school districts.

We devote a full chapter to property taxation because of its historical significance in financing schools, and because of its continuing role as an important revenue source in nearly all states.

THE PROPERTY TAX BASE

Property taxes are imposed on wealth in the form of tangible personal property, intangible personal property, and tangible real property. Tangible personal property consists of such objects as machines, inventories, livestock, and equipment owned by businesses, as well as individually owned jewelry, furniture, vehicles, and personal computers. Intangible personal property—stocks, bonds, savings, and other investments—has no physical existence beyond the accounts or certificates that represent its value.

Tangibles are a more common tax base in states. This is because tangibles are easier to identify, often through licensing processes, than are intangibles. Only nine states include intangibles within local tax bases. But eighteen states tax business inventories, seventeen tax household personal property, and eighteen tax motor vehicles (U. S. Department of Commerce, 1994, pp. VI, VII). Thus, the majority of states exempt tangible and intangible personal property from taxation.

The bulk of property taxation today falls on tangible real property. This property includes land and what are referred to as "improvements" in the form of houses, commercial buildings, swimming pools, and so on. Table 6.1 shows that locally assessed real property amounted to over $5.8 trillion in 1991. This amount overshadowed the $589 billion of assessed personal property. With an additional $286 billion assessed by states, the total net assessed value available to localities was over $6.6 trillion. The growth in the real property portion of this tax base was dramatic during the 1970s. There was an increase of 335 percent between 1971 and 1981. The rate of growth slowed during the 1980s, rising 141 percent, from $2.4 trillion to $5.8 trillion. It is this portion of the tax base that is of concern in school finance. Thus, the term "property" refers to real property in the remainder of this text.

The rationale for property taxation to support local government evolved from the principle of benefits received (see Chapter 4). If there is good police and fire protection, as well as public libraries and schools, within a community, the value of properties increases. It is assumed that individuals who receive the benefits of such services should pay the associated costs. It is also assumed that benefits are roughly proportional to property values (Musgrave & Musgrave, 1989, p. 411).

In accordance with benefit theory, property owners and tenants should be willing to pay higher taxes directly, or indirectly through rent, in communities with more extensive and better-quality public services than residents of other communities. However, relationships among benefits, property values, and levels of taxation are not as direct as they once were. Owners of real estate do not necessarily benefit from local services in proportion to the ascribed values of property. Indeed, many business and rental property owners may not live within the community. Other individuals who do not reside in a given tax jurisdiction may benefit from city parks, libraries, and museums that are financed by the local property tax base. Public school choice policies may permit families to cross district lines. As this practice expands, citizens will become more concerned about relationships among educational benefits, local property tax bases, and the funds available for school programs and facilities.

TABLE 6.1. Assessed Values of Real and Personal Property, 1961 to 1991 (in billions of dollars)

Kind of Property	1961	1971	1981	1991	Percentage Change 1971–1981	Percentage Change 1981–1991
Locally assessed property	326.1	641.1	2,678.4	6,395.8	318	139
Real property	269.7	552.7	2,406.7	5,806.7	335	141
Personal property	56.5	88.3	271.7	589.0	208	117
State-assessed property	27.8	53.5	159.0	285.8	197	80
Total assessed value (net locally taxable)	354.0	694.6	2,837.5	6,681.6	309	135

SOURCE: U. S. Department of Commerce, Bureau of the Census. (1994). *1992 Census of Governments, Vol. 2: Taxable Property Values.* Washington, DC: U. S. Government Printing Office, Table C, p. XIV.

Property taxation is a general tax in that it applies to all community residents, whether or not a given household has direct beneficiaries, on the assumption of a general distribution of benefits. As such, this tax source assumes that public education serves broader public goals than would a specific charge assessed only to families with children enrolled in schools (see Chapter 1). Furthermore, the amount of property tax payments in the United States is based on the value of property owned rather than being tied to taxpayers' income, total wealth, or other measures of ability to pay. In England and some other countries, the tax is levied on the actual rental income, or the rental value in the case of owner occupancy, to better reflect taxpayers' abilities to pay. How the value of the tax base is determined affects not only the amount of revenue derived but also the perceived fairness of the tax.

PROPERTY VALUATION AND TAX DETERMINATION

We need to understand the processes used to assess property and calculate the amount of taxes owed before we discuss property taxes in relation to the criteria presented in Chapter 4.

Assessing Real Property

Counties, municipalities, special-purpose districts, and fiscally independent (see Chapter 3) school districts levy ad valorem property taxes according to the value of land and improvements. The amount of equity (the portion of the property that represents the owner's wealth) is not of concern. A bank or other holding company may have title to the larger share of the property's value, but an individual or business is liable for the full tax upon its total value.

Statutes that authorize local governments to levy taxes call for an assessment of property to determine its value. An appointed or elected official is responsible for discovering, listing, and valuing each taxable property in the jurisdiction. This official is usually at the county, city, or town level of government. Other local jurisdictions use this official tax roll. Statutes may specify an assessment cycle, a period of time (for example, 10 years in Connecticut and annually in Missouri) during which the assessor must review the value of each parcel. Others indicate a fraction (for example, one-fifth in Idaho) of the jurisdiction to be reappraised each year (U. S. Department of Commerce, 1994, p. D-1).

The ideal appraisal is a recent sales price. *Fair market valuation,* often stated as true or full value, is defined as the amount that a willing seller of property would receive from a willing buyer in an open market setting. Residential property and vacant land are generally appraised according to sales of comparable properties. But because business and industrial properties do not change hands frequently, current market values are not readily available. Their appraisals are more often based on their income-earning capacity or on the cost of replacing the property (Oldman & Schoettle, 1974, Chapter 3).

Subjectivity is the primary limitation of the following three commonly used appraisal methods. It is also the basis for many tax disputes. Relying on market data assumes that the value of a given parcel can be estimated from sales of other properties of somewhat similar age, condition, location, and style. A cost approach depends on estimates of land value, current costs of replacing buildings and other improvements, and depreciation. The income method estimates the remaining life of the property and an appropriate capitalization rate in calculating the present value of future income to be derived from the property. The limitations of each method are offset by the advantages of the others. The fairest valuations depend on appraisers who can objectively apply several methods.

Advances in technology offer opportunities for greater objectivity and more frequent valuations. Scientific appraisals rely on statistical techniques to relate the actual (or estimated) selling prices of houses and businesses with a large array of characteristics, including location, land acreage, square-footage, type of heating and ventilation system, and number of fireplaces. Current technologies make it possible to maintain assessments that are closer to full value and to reappraise all properties annually without actual inspections. Revenue from more current and accurate valuations may offset the increased cost of scientific appraisals, particularly during periods of rapidly changing real estate markets. But taxpayers may express concern about what they view as unwarranted increases in property values.

The *assessed valuation* is the value given to a piece of property by an official appraiser. It is generally a percentage of the fair market value even in states that call for full valuation. Assessment ratios, which express the relationship between assessed and full values, often differ among classifications of property. Because the same tax rate is later applied to all properties in a jurisdiction, the effect of classification schemes is to legally shift the tax burden from some groups of taxpayers to others. This differentiation of properties became widespread in the 1970s following a judicial determina-

tion that the previous assessment practices had unfairly placed additional tax burdens on businesses. At that time, many local assessors had used their own "extra-legal" (Shannon, 1973, p. 29) system of classifications to deviate from uniformity mandates. Under legitimate classification plans, assessment ratios vary according to an accepted and consistently applied criterion such as the current use of parcels.

Assessment ratios are illustrated in Table 6.2. Full market valuation is called for in twenty-three states, including Nebraska. Another eleven states, like Connecticut and Indiana, specify a single percentage of full valuation to be applied to all taxable property. The remaining sixteen states, including Arizona and Tennessee, assign different ratios to various classes. Higher ratios are common for assessments of industrial, commercial, utility, and transportation property relative to those for agricultural and residential property.

Property is valued on the basis of its "highest and best" use, in accordance with the application naturally suited to the site and likely to maximize its potential monetary return. Several assessment methods provide incentives to hold agricultural, recreational, open space, and historic land from development. A preferential assessment approach was employed by twenty-seven states in 1991 (U. S. Department of Commerce, 1994, p. IX). It gives a low assessment based on current income or use rather than on the true market value of the land. The assessment continues until the qualified use ends, without any later penalty.

A deferred-taxation approach is used by thirty-one states. It also offers a preferential use assessment, but it requires a penalty (e.g., recoupment of back taxes and interest) when land use changes. Another method is employed by fourteen states. It is a restrictive agreement whereby a contract is made between the landowner and the local government to hold land in qualified use for a specified period of time in exchange for lower assessment or deferred taxation. For example, agricultural reserves and nonprofit conservation trusts maintain farm and open land in exchange for lower or forgiven taxes.

TABLE 6.2. Assessment Ratios and Classifications of Real Property in Selected States, 1991

Arizona	13 classes: a. Mines and timber, 30%
	b. Telephone, gas, and utility services, 30%
	c. Commercial and industrial, 25%
	d. Agricultural and vacant, 16%
	e. Residential, not-for-profit, 10%
	f. Residential, leased or rented, 10%
	g. Railroad and airline, ratio of assessed value of property in classes a, b, and c to the market value of such property
	h. Historic, 5%
	i. Historic, commercial, and industrial portion, modification of class *c* ratio
	j. Historic, leased or rented portion, modification of class *f* ratio
	k. Livestock, aquatic animals, bee colonies, 8%
	l. Possessory interests (e.g., lease on transportation facilities), 1%
	m. Producing oil or gas company, 100%
Connecticut	All property at 70% of market value
Indiana	All property at 33-1/3% of market value
Nebraska	All property at 100% of market value
Tennessee	3 classes: a. Public utilities, 55%
	b. Industrial and commercial, 40%
	c. Farm and residential, 25%

SOURCE: U. S. Department of Commerce, Bureau of the Census. (1994). *1992 Census of Governments, Vol. 2: Taxable Property Values.* Washington, DC: U.S. Government Printing Office, Appendix A.

Musgrave and Musgrave (1989, p. 417) argue that sound property tax administration demands "uniform assessment at full market value." However, imprecise assessment practices and the desire to maximize taxpayer satisfaction with tax systems often justify residential assessments that are below fair market values. The public is less likely to complain about these lower assessments or to vote for a change in local politicians. Similar practices reduce business assessments to attract manufacturing or commercial activity or to discourage industry from leaving the locality. On the other hand, residential and business properties that do not receive preferential assessments must absorb the tax burdens deferred or exempted from properties receiving preferential treatment. This makes them pay higher taxes than they would if all properties were subject to the same standards. To the degree that the subjectivity of assessment practices permits easy deviation from established policies or standards, favoritism or political cronyism may result. These activities are discussed more fully as a cost of administration.

Because states' allocations of financial aid to school districts are generally tied to local property wealth (see Chapter 8), states should supervise local assessment practices. Netzer and Berne (1995) discuss the importance of interjurisdictional equalization of property values:

Equalization is necessary both for the implementation of statewide policies (in state school-aid calculations and for determining tax and debt limits) and for the determination of the tax liabilities of individual taxpayers whenever there are overlapping taxing and assessing jurisdictions, like state agency assessment of the value of utility property or school district boundaries that are not coincident with the boundaries of the assessing jurisdiction. The equalization process should be understandable, it should yield results that truly do equalize among jurisdictions, and it should be seen as essentially fair. (p. 34).

An *equalization ratio* is determined for each tax jurisdiction by a state-level equalization board. The board divides the assessed values of properties by the respective equalization ratio to get an estimate of market values. It thereby brings all assessments in a state to a common basis. The school district depicted in Table 6.3 overlaps four assessing jurisdictions, such as towns or counties. Jurisdiction A has the highest equalization ratio. This is not because it is the wealthiest town, which it is, but because of its practice of assessing properties 20 percent above market value. Jurisdiction D has the lowest assessed value, but its equalized value is higher than either B or C. The reason for this is that Jurisdiction D assesses its property at only 15 percent of market value, while Jurisdictions B and C assess parcels at 85 percent and 50 percent, respectively.

This example illustrates the role that the state may take to mitigate differences in counties' assessment practices. This intervention may reduce taxpayers' presumptions of unfairness in property

TABLE 6.3. Illustration of Equalization Ratios for Several Tax Jurisdictions within a School District

Jurisdiction	Assessed Value	Equalization Ratio	Equalized Value
A	$324,000,000	1.20	$270,000,000
B	85,000,000	0.85	100,000,000
C	45,000,000	0.50	90,000,000
D	21,000,000	0.15	140,000,000
Total	$475,000,000		$600,000,000

taxation. Moreover, using equalized values for each jurisdiction permits a fairer allocation of state funds in relation to local tax capacities. Without a system of equalized assessment ratios, tax jurisdictions may underassess properties to make their wealth appear to be lower in order to gain more state revenue.

Exemptions and Tax Relief

Local tax bases are diminished by total exclusions or partial exemptions of several classifications of property: (a) schools, universities, and governments; (b) religious and welfare organizations, including churches, chambers of commerce, fraternal organizations, and labor unions; (c) heads of households, senior citizens, veterans, volunteer fire fighters, and handicapped persons; and (d) incentives to rehabilitate housing or to attract industry. Tax relief is also granted through a credit against income tax payments to individuals whose property taxes exceed a given percentage of their income.

Exemptions are defended on the basis of desired social values. It is assumed that the benefits that nonprofit organizations provide the community offset the cost of public services that are in effect given to them without tax payments. When the Supreme Court examined claims of unconstitutional aid to religion, tax exemptions for churches survived scrutiny under the First Amendment: "Elimination of exemption would tend to expand the involvement of government by giving rise to tax valuation of church property, tax liens, tax foreclosures, and the direct confrontations and conflicts that follow in the train of those legal processes" (*Walz* v. *Tax Commission of the City of New York*, 1970).

On the other hand, exemptions are criticized because of the diseconomies they create. For example, there may be income-producing office buildings, hotels, and medical centers located on tax-exempt church and university land. Manufacturing plants that are leased by counties to private corporations may be constructed on exempt public land. Even facilities constructed on private land often fall within designated enterprise zones that receive tax breaks to encourage economic development. Industries located in these tax enclaves benefit in the short run (generally not over 10 years) from no taxation or favorable tax rates. Moreover, these businesses and other residents gain long-term benefits from the enlarged tax base that reduces future tax burdens or enables the eventual expansion of public services.

Many exemptions and tax breaks provide governmental subsidies for diverse interest groups. Other residents and businesses must then pay higher taxes. The loss of the tax base to support local governments can be substantial. The exempt portion was less than 5 percent of the gross assessed valuation in all but twelve states in 1991. For example, $3.9 billion (nearly 12 percent) of the total locally assessed value is tax-exempt in Indiana. For many large cities, the loss can be even greater. Over one-third ($438 million) of assessed property is exempt in New Orleans (U. S. Department of Commerce, 1994, pp. XI, 17, 42).

Municipalities and urban school systems suffer from policies that exempt these properties. They would benefit from state reimbursement of lost revenue, like the financial payments that the federal government provides to school districts impacted by tax-exempt military installations, public housing, and Native American reservations (see Chapter 10). In this way, individuals who do not reside in the community but who use public libraries, parks, universities, and other facilities would share the cost of exemptions. A second method to spread the tax burden requires exempt organizations to pay user charges for selected governmental services. For example, many universities make payments to municipalities to offset large public service costs and to maintain community goodwill.

Nearly all states give some individual taxpayers relief from property taxes. These "homestead exemptions" came into being during the depression of the 1930s. They were granted to homeowners regardless of income. Since then, exemptions have also been granted to elderly homeowners, veterans, and disabled persons. This relief reduces assessed valuations or provides a credit toward tax liability.

For example, Georgia homesteaders' valuations are reduced $2,000. Elderly taxpayers receive an exemption of $4,000 generally and of $10,000 on education assessments. Disabled veterans' valuations are reduced by $32,500 (ACIR, 1995, p. 138). Such exemptions are criticized because they reduce the tax base, complicate tax administration, and may provide a subsidy for individuals who are otherwise able to pay taxes (Shannon, 1973, pp. 35–37).

Circuit breakers in thirty-five states and the District of Columbia permit a credit against state income taxes for property tax payments that exceed a specified proportion of income for elderly and low-income homeowners and, in some cases, renters. For example, Pennsylvania offers relief ($500 maximum) against taxes due from homeowners and renters over sixty-five and from taxpayers with disabilities. These credits range from 100 percent for incomes under $5,500 to 10 percent for incomes greater than $13,000. They give an average benefit of $263 per household (ACIR, 1995, p. 135).

Circuit breakers, which maintain the local tax base and provide income redistribution at the state level, are preferable to general homestead exemptions. However, this approach may not help all low-income earners. Property owners and renters who have little or no taxable income for the year still qualify for rebates of property taxes paid. But as in the case of income tax credits to offset sales taxes on food and necessities, these low-income families may not file for property tax relief. Renters, who currently qualify for circuit breakers in twenty-eight states, should be eligible if it is assumed that tenants bear the full property tax burden.

Because circuit breakers do not fully ease the burden on low-income taxpayers, Aaron (1973) noted that singling out this one household expenditure (i.e., property tax) for relief may be due to its political acceptability. He advocated a housing allowance. This may be a more effective mechanism if we assume that property taxes affect housing costs. It might also be argued that exempting all taxes paid over a given fraction of income would more appropriately recognize that property and other taxes excessively burden low-income households.

Calculating the Property Tax

The technical function of assessment described above determines the value of properties in a jurisdiction, that is, the capacity of the tax base. A political decision sets the tax rate. The tax rate reflects the level of tax effort the community is willing to exert to support public services.

The local tax amount *(levy)* to be collected can be expressed as the difference between projected expenditures *(costs)* of programs for a given fiscal year and the amount of funds *(revenue)* anticipated from federal, state, and other local sources:

$$\text{Levy} = \text{Costs} - \text{Revenue}$$

This levy is divided by the aggregate *assessed value,* or in some states *equalized value,* of property in the tax jurisdiction to yield a *tax rate:*

$$\text{Tax Rate on Assessed Value} = \text{Levy/Assessed Value}$$

$$\text{Tax Rate on Equalized Value} = \text{Levy/Equalized Value}$$

Tax rates are often expressed in terms of mills. A mill is defined as one-tenth of a cent (0.001). A rate of 10 mills would thus place a 1 percent tax on the assessed value of property. This rate might be expressed in a decimal form (0.01) or, as is common in many states, as a tax of $10 for each $1,000 of assessed valuation. In other states, this rate is expressed as 10 cents per $100 of valuation. For example, the school district depicted in Table 6.3 has a total equalized valuation of $600 million. If a levy of $15 million is necessary for local support of school operations, the required tax rate is 0.025 (calculated as $15,000,000/$600,000,000). This 25-mill tax is equivalent to a rate of $25 per thousand, $2.50 per hundred, or a 2.5 percent tax on equalized values.

Calculations of tax levies in Table 6.4 apply this 25-mill tax rate to the four assessing jurisdictions (initially presented in Table 6.3). The rate for the total district divided by the four respective equalization ratios yields tax rates that can be applied to the initial assessed values. The resulting tax levies for the four jurisdictions total the required $15 million for district operations.

Once tax rates have been established for jurisdictions, a tax bill is prepared for each property. The constant tax rate is multiplied by the appraised value of each parcel on the tax roll to determine the amount of property tax owed:

$$\text{Tax Owed} = \text{Rate} \times \text{Assessed Value}$$

Calculations of property taxes for four parcels in Table 6.5 illustrate the application of this formula and the effect of exemptions such as those for homesteaders, senior citizens, and veterans. The properties have the same market value, $80,000. Because the equalization ratios are different for the two jurisdictions, however, the assessed values for parcels 1 and 2 are different from those for parcels 3 and 4. Even though parcels 1 and 3 have different assessed values and tax rates, their owners pay the same amount of taxes and have the same effective

TABLE 6.4. Illustration of Tax Rates and Levies for Tax Jurisdictions within a School District

Jurisdiction	Tax Rate on Equalized Value	Equalization Ratio[a]	Tax Rate on Assessed Value[b]	Assessed Value[a]	Tax Levy[b]
A	25.00	1.20	20.83	$324,000,000	$6,750,000
B	25.00	0.85	29.41	85,000,000	2,500,000
C	25.00	0.50	50.00	45,000,000	2,250,000
D	25.00	0.15	166.67	21,000,000	3,500,000

[a]See Table 6.3.
[b]Rounded.

tax rates. Parcels 2 and 4 benefit from exemptions and pay less taxes than parcels 1 and 3. Exemptions are applied to assessed values, and parcel 4 is assessed at a smaller ratio than is parcel 2. Therefore the effect of the exemption is greater for parcel 4, because it pays the lowest taxes and has the lowest effective tax rate.

In addition to school districts, property taxes may be levied in support of overlapping branches of local governments independently or in combination. These include county, town, and city governments; community colleges and public libraries; fire protection, water, and sewer districts; and road districts. A given piece of property is usually assessed by only one jurisdiction. However, an entity such as a school district may encompass several assessing authorities as in the example above. This makes equalization ratios necessary. It is thus possible for taxes to be collected by an authority, such as county government, other than the school district or other governmental unit that levies the tax.

The political decision that establishes a tax rate is not left entirely to government personnel. Tax rate increases are very often subject to referenda. School districts in many states may find that the public is unwilling to support government when they seek approval for expansion of programs or construction of facilities. Public support of tax rate increases cannot be taken for granted. For example,

an antitax mood was blamed for New York State voters' rejections of 33 percent of 501 school district budgets in the spring of 1994 (Lindsay, 1994b). A more positive report was made one year later. Voters approved the majority of district budgets and tax referenda in New York (80 percent), New Jersey (72 percent), and Ohio (63 percent) (Lindsay, 1995).

Variations among States in Property Tax Capacity and Effort

Disparities in property tax bases and tax rates among states and local tax jurisdictions reveal differences in abilities and willingness to tax real property. Table 6.6 gives tax capacity, effort, and revenue collected for states.

The Advisory Commission on Intergovernmental Relations (ACIR) defines "capacity" as including (a) estimated market values of residential and farm properties, and (b) net book values of commercial/industrial and public utility properties. Table 6.6 lists states' capacities in four categories of properties. Many of the states with consistently low per capita tax bases are located in the South, including Arkansas, Mississippi, and West Virginia. Relatively low residential and commercial/industrial capacities in Montana and the Dakotas are offset by very high valuations of per capita farm

TABLE 6.5. Determining Net Tax and Effective Tax Rate

	Jurisdiction B		Jurisdiction C	
	Parcel 1	Parcel 2	Parcel 3	Parcel 4
Net tax				
Market value	$80,000	$80,000	$80,000	$80,000
Equalization ratio	.85	.85	.50	.50
Assessed value	$68,000	$68,000	$40,000	$40,000
less exemption	− 0	− 5,000	− 0	− 5,000
Taxable value	$68,000	$63,000	$40,000	$35,000
by tax rate[a]	× 0.02941	× 0.02941	× 0.05000	× 0.05000
Net tax owed	$2,000	$1,853	$2,000	$1,750
Effective tax rate (per $1,000 market value)	$25.00	$23.16	$25.00	$21.88

[a]From Table 6.4. In Table 6.4, the tax rates are expressed in dollars per $1,000 of assessed value. For computation purposes, they are expressed here as a ratio.

TABLE 6.6. Property Tax Capacity and Revenue per Capita, 1991

| State | Capacity per Capita | | | | Revenue per Capita | Tax Effort | |
	Residential	Farm	Commercial/ Industrial	Public Utility		Index	Rank
Alabama	$ 287.48	$14.06	$136.75	$47.10	$ 170.78	35	49
Alaska	550.12	0.00	244.50	17.65	1,212.64	149	7
Arizona	484.37	19.31	125.36	40.06	661.86	99	24
Arkansas	252.89	35.52	128.72	55.88	244.20	52	45
California	679.55	12.79	183.30	28.50	639.38	71	39
Colorado	585.29	28.37	165.25	30.41	689.77	85	32
Connecticut	667.39	3.82	229.57	38.80	1,137.61	121	13
Delaware	517.31	13.30	324.00	48.86	311.05	34	50
District of Columbia	543.55	0.00	280.34	48.90	1,474.71	169	3
Florida	500.71	12.36	115.31	36.65	687.15	103	20
Georgia	315.73	13.26	157.60	47.55	506.41	95	26
Hawaii	1,135.32	15.01	139.12	27.00	430.46	33	51
Idaho	300.97	61.33	119.95	40.63	426.81	82	33
Illinois	358.88	24.97	203.28	49.85	785.40	123	11
Indiana	287.12	26.15	189.77	56.68	570.81	102	23
Iowa	395.81	97.89	131.83	41.54	686.28	103	21
Kansas	289.04	63.29	156.94	61.15	691.46	121	12
Kentucky	275.62	25.79	157.98	39.76	276.82	55	44
Louisiana	275.08	13.52	213.34	58.64	275.50	49	46
Maine	463.98	8.10	136.82	33.29	796.43	124	10
Maryland	505.57	7.18	135.08	40.20	616.52	90	28
Massachusetts	571.42	2.89	187.49	32.59	829.90	104	19
Michigan	345.11	8.83	199.29	42.16	893.83	150	6
Minnesota	371.88	41.71	189.70	36.09	717.89	112	17
Mississippi	238.88	26.69	118.96	42.11	344.23	81	34
Missouri	293.10	28.66	161.12	40.12	377.37	72	38
Montana	287.43	128.44	120.75	68.67	524.20	87	31
Nebraska	392.41	116.04	127.50	20.40	743.92	113	16
Nevada	460.74	10.71	154.92	52.99	455.76	67	41
New Hampshire	511.74	6.73	150.30	39.00	1,341.23	190	1
New Jersey	545.83	3.89	239.28	38.30	1,256.94	152	5
New Mexico	313.89	46.67	108.95	59.38	221.80	42	48
New York	395.47	3.39	196.45	31.07	1,100.63	176	2
North Carolina	424.40	12.63	165.21	45.45	382.18	59	43
North Dakota	214.11	165.67	105.07	27.33	505.27	99	25
Ohio	363.76	12.33	191.52	43.53	540.84	88	29
Oklahoma	252.70	35.66	173.23	57.71	250.43	48	47
Oregon	490.30	25.07	145.19	29.77	877.05	127	9
Pennsylvania	403.26	8.40	182.04	49.45	561.80	87	30
Rhode Island	375.48	2.41	133.50	17.70	879.63	166	4
South Carolina	320.58	9.78	140.21	46.09	423.42	80	35
South Dakota	251.42	156.25	96.86	27.08	579.92	109	18

(Continued)

139

TABLE 6.6. Property Tax Capacity and Revenue per Capita, 1991 (*Continued*)

| State | Capacity per Capita | | | | Revenue per Capita | Tax Effort | |
	Residential	Farm	Commercial/ Industrial	Public Utility		Index	Rank
Tennessee	265.27	17.46	153.99	16.43	329.10	73	37
Texas	310.60	25.83	209.61	51.93	679.39	114	15
Utah	405.89	18.16	132.68	32.24	416.21	71	40
Vermont	591.81	21.46	134.79	32.44	925.00	119	14
Virginia	499.94	12.94	152.34	38.69	638.34	91	27
Washington	621.86	17.96	157.99	22.11	625.11	76	36
West Virginia	199.76	9.07	132.59	109.06	272.91	61	42
Wisconsin	333.33	21.39	167.55	37.41	796.78	142	8
Wyoming	472.20	81.70	211.01	127.07	912.22	102	22
U.S. Total	$431.58	$18.88	$174.70	$40.76	$665.93	100	

SOURCE: ACIR. [1993]. *RTS 1991: State revenue capacity and effort.* Washington, DC: Advisory Commission on Intergovernmental Relations, Tables 4-25 to 4-27, pp. 100–102. RTS: representative tax system.

capacities. In contrast, the states with the highest residential tax bases, like Hawaii, California, and Connecticut, have relatively lower farm capacities. The states with the highest commercial/industrial tax capacities are Delaware, Alaska, and New Jersey. Wyoming, West Virginia, and Montana have high public utility tax bases, in contrast to Alaska, Rhode Island, and Tennessee.

If we assume that states tax themselves at the national average rate, then per capita tax capacities reveal the revenue potential that is possible from property. Not all states, however, tax their capacities at that level. Some states exceed the national average by a considerable amount. Table 6.6 also gives property tax revenue raised by states in 1991 and an index of relative tax effort. The index expresses the relationship between the actual revenue produced and each state's capacity. The District of Columbia collects the most revenue per capita. It exerts a very high effort, as do many other cities in the nation. New Hampshire, New York, and Rhode Island have the highest effort indices. Alaska is ranked relatively high in effort, but this state exports much of its energy-related property tax to other states. Connecticut exerts somewhat

less effort but collects a similarly high revenue per capita because of its high tax capacity. With their relatively low capacities and very low efforts, Alabama, Arkansas, New Mexico, and Oklahoma collect low revenue per capita from property taxes.

New England has traditionally relied more heavily on property taxes than have other regions (Gold, 1979, pp. 298–303). New England has been strongly committed to local control, a high degree of fiscal decentralization, and low levels of state-financed relief. There have been few state-imposed limitations on local taxes and spending. States in the Plains and Great Lakes area, once near the top of the nation in terms of tax burdens, have led other states in adopting circuit breakers and in shifting burdens through local income taxation and limitations on property tax increases.

Southeastern states have traditionally had low property taxes because their fiscal centralization brings more state grants-in-aid. Localities in the Southeast rely more heavily on user charges and sales taxes. Their property classification schemes and homestead exemptions reduce tax collections. States in the Rocky Mountain, Southwest, or Far West regions have less in common.

In addition to these variations in tax capacities and tax efforts among states, school districts may have extremely different property valuations, and very often tax rates. In Chapter 8 we will say more about these conditions in relation to state funding formulas.

MERITS OF PROPERTY TAXATION

The criteria we looked at in Chapter 4—yield, elasticity, equity, neutrality, and cost of administration and compliance—provide a framework for us to assess the advantages and disadvantages of property taxation as a revenue source.

Yield and Elasticity

State and local revenue from property taxation totaled nearly $179 billion in 1992. The yield had increased from $156 billion in 1990 and from $68 billion in 1980. The importance of this revenue source is evident in the amount of yield in relation to that of other taxes. Property taxes collected at state and local levels in 1992 nearly equaled states' revenue from sales and gross receipts taxes ($196 billion) and exceeded personal and corporate income taxes ($115 billion and $24 billion, respec-

tively) (U. S. Department of Commerce, 1995, Table 481). Nevertheless, states have relied less on the property tax over the years. Expressed as a percentage of state and local taxes, the property tax's share of these governments' revenue diminished from 45 percent in 1956–1957 to 36 percent in 1976–1977 and to 32 percent in 1990–1991 (U. S. Department of Commerce, 1994, p. XIV).

Even when we just examine local tax collections, we find that governments depend less on this tax. Table 6.7 shows that local tax revenue grew from $12.6 billion to $161.8 billion between 1956–1957 and 1990–1991. However, its contribution to local governments declined both in relation to total revenue received (from 43 percent to 30 percent) and in relation to total local tax revenue (87 percent to 75 percent). Property taxes also add to state revenue ($6.2 billion in 1990–91), and their proportionate contributions also declined relative to other funds states received.

The property tax is generally not considered to be an elastic tax because "as income increases, the full value of property does not increase proportionately" (Netzer & Berne, 1995, p. 52). Assessed valuations, the legal base of the tax, do not necessarily reflect market values, and coefficients of elasticity appear to be below unity. The

TABLE 6.7. Revenue from Property Taxes, 1956–1957 to 1990–1991 (dollar amounts in millions)

Year	State Governments			Local Governments		
	Property Tax Revenue	Percentage of Revenue from All Sources	Percentage of Tax Revenue	Property Tax Revenue	Percentage of Revenue from All Sources	Percentage of Tax Revenue
1956–57	$ 479	1.9	3.3	$ 12,618	43.4	87.0
1961–62	640	1.7	3.1	18,416	42.6	87.9
1966–67	862	1.4	2.7	25,186	39.0	86.6
1971–72	1,257	1.1	2.1	40,876	36.1	83.5
1976–77	2,260	1.1	2.2	60,267	30.7	80.5
1981–82	3,113	1.0	1.9	78,805	25.2	76.0
1986–87	4,609	0.9	1.9	116,618	24.8	73.7
1990–91	6,227	1.1	2.0	161,772	29.9	75.3

SOURCE: U. S. Department of Commerce, Bureau of the Census. (1994). *1992 Census of Governments, Vol. 2: Taxable Property Values.* Washington, DC: U. S. Government Printing Office, Tables A and 2.

inclusion of business properties in particular reduces the elasticity, whereas residential property assessments more closely respond to changes in the economy. For this reason, Netzer (1966, pp. 184–190) argued that elasticity is best determined by the change in property tax yield in relation to the change in the underlying tax base (the market value of properties) rather than in terms of personal income. He reported studies that examined elasticity in relation to market values or to state-equalized tax bases. These calculations revealed a somewhat elastic tax, with coefficients between 1.0 and 1.2.

Assessments respond slowly to changes in the general economy, accounting for property tax stability. This is both a strength and a weakness of property taxation. On the one hand, stability is important to local officials who must plan budgets and balance expenditures with available revenue. On the other hand, assessments are slow to respond to fluctuations in prices and incomes. Unlike income and sales tax rates, which are adjusted less frequently, property tax rates must be reexamined annually and placed before voters when changes are deemed necessary. With improvements in assessment practices and more frequent valuations of properties, rising assessments reflect growing market values, particularly during periods of inflation. As the yield grows in relation to the economy, tax rates will need to be adjusted less frequently. However, the efficiency and currency of assessment mechanisms contributed to taxpayer complaints. The complaints eventually led to legal limitations on the growth of valuations in California and elsewhere (Musgrave & Musgrave, 1989, p. 418).

Because the tax base did not expand during the depression and through the Second World War, school expenditures lagged behind the growth rate of the general economy. Growth in assessments and strong public support for education permitted increases in property tax yield and rates during the 1950s and 1960s. During this period public schooling expanded rapidly. The general economic recession during the 1970s restricted governmental growth, regardless of the tax source. Federal and state governments, with their heavier reliance on more elastic taxes, faced potentially large shortfalls. School districts that relied heavily on property taxation were in many cases relatively advantaged because of the stability of the tax and the dependability of its yield. In contrast, many school systems suffered financial losses (at least in terms of slowed annual growth) during the economic slowdown of the early 1990s due in part to their greater dependence on state revenue sources.

Equity

In an agrarian society, land ownership was closely tied to wealth, income, and power. It was also a better proxy for benefits received from the government. Real property was then a good indicator of ability to pay taxes. But in information and industrial societies, land ownership is only one form of wealth, and equal treatment under tax codes is generally measured in terms of income (see Chapter 4). Moreover, since many forms of wealth (e.g., investments and personal property) are excluded from property taxation, there is little relationship between taxpayers' incomes and how much tax they pay. Horizontal equity is thus violated, because individuals with the same income do not necessarily pay the same amount of tax.

To determine the degree to which this revenue source satisfies vertical equity—the unequal treatment of unequals—we must first consider who bears the burden of the tax and then identify its relationship with taxpayers' income. Occupants bear the taxes on housing. The property tax is a direct tax on homeowners, who may be able to recoup a portion of the taxes they pay when they later sell houses for appreciated values. It becomes an indirect tax when owners of rental property are able to raise rents and shift tax increases to tenants who cannot later recoup any portion of the taxes they paid.

Under the traditional view of incidence, tax burdens are assumed to be higher for people with low incomes. Residential taxes fall on tenants rather than property owners in the case of renters.

And property taxes on businesses fall on consumers rather than owners or stockholders. Assuming lower relative valuations of higher-priced houses and a higher proportion of income spent on housing by low-income families, a tax on residential property has been considered regressive (Netzer, 1966, p. 131).

A second approach to determining incidence considers the property tax a tax on capital, such that its incidence is upon owners. Thus, taxes on commercial and industrial property are distributed in line with income from capital rather than on the basis of consumption expenditures (Aaron, 1975). If property owners are assumed to bear the burden, then the tax is more progressive. This conclusion rests upon the presumed close relationship between ownership of capital and the distribution of income.

We discussed the overall tax burdens under these two sets of assumptions in Chapter 4 (see Table 4.2). Except for the lowest income level, which bears a relatively heavy burden, the proportion of income paid in all taxes in 1985 rose slowly with income under either set of assumptions. Even if we assume that the property tax burden itself is regressive, it does not appear to make overall tax burdens regressive. Homestead exemptions and circuit breakers based on income serve to reduce property tax regressivity in many states.

Neutrality

Property taxes are not neutral. They often discourage owners from maximizing the potential use of property, contribute to the deterioration of urban areas, influence choices of geographic location for residences and businesses, and cause disparities in educational programs.

Communities engage in "fiscal mercantilism" (Netzer, 1966, pp. 45–59) to maximize tax bases in relation to the demand for public services. Lower tax rates become incentives for individuals and businesses to migrate from cities to suburbs and from northern to southern and western states. Tax benefits and restrictive zoning regulations that define land use encourage the formation of industrial enclaves. High-income families are similarly attracted to communities with higher residential wealth. Low-income families, who do not contribute to the tax base but who increase the costs of public services, are discouraged from residing there.

The practice of valuing buildings and other improvements within the taxation of real property, as it is presently structured and administered by localities, may discourage owners from making substantial investments. Site-value taxation, which would simplify property valuation by reducing the property tax base to include only land without improvements, would make the tax more neutral. By definition, a neutral tax has little or no effect on the mix of resources (land, labor, and capital) in production processes. Scholars have long argued that taxing the land itself, without valuing improvements, would not hinder production: "the whole value of land may be taken into taxation, and the only effect will be to stimulate industry, to open new opportunities to capital, and to increase the production of wealth" (George, 1879, p. 412). This approach would stimulate the development of real estate to its full potential, particularly in deteriorating central cities, because it is in the interest of owners to maximize the use of land (Peterson, 1973). However, site-value taxes might discourage investors from keeping older buildings, single-story structures, parking lots, and other improvements that do not maximize land use.

Because land values are underassessed while improvements are overassessed, land may be withheld from its most productive use in deteriorating sections of cities. Upgrading properties in generally blighted neighborhoods does not necessarily bring larger rents. But such investments would certainly result in higher taxes given the higher assessments that accompany improvements. The over-assessment of poor neighborhoods creates tax delinquency, and many cities are slow in enforcing tax collections (Peterson, 1973, p. 10).

Yinger, Borsch-Supan, Bloom, and Ladd (1988) found strong evidence that differences in effective property tax rates are, to some extent, capitalized into the price of housing. This is the case because, all else being equal, buyers are willing to pay more for houses with low taxes than comparable houses with high taxes. Yinger et al. conclude:

> Because households compete with each other for access to housing in jurisdictions with low tax rates, jurisdictions with relatively low tax rates will have relatively high house values, and vice versa. In equilibrium, households must be exactly compensated for higher property tax rates by lower housing prices. (p. 56)

Full capitalization of the property tax would impose the same burden on each unit of housing regardless of the actual tax levied; however, effective tax rates are not fully capitalized. The studies by Yinger et al. found that the degree of capitalization ranged between 16 percent and 33 percent. These differing treatments of property taxes may influence the selection of homes and communities.

Property taxes contribute to disparities among school districts in funds available for daily operations and the construction of facilities. In most states, the level of resources available for each pupil's education depends to some degree on the wealth of the local communities and on the level of effort taxpayers exert to support schools. The more local school districts depend on the property tax for their financial support, the greater will be the disparity in funding levels among school districts. This is particularly true with regard to funds for capital improvements, which are largely dependent upon property taxation with little or no assistance from state revenue (see Chapter 7).

The property tax itself, however, does not cause many of these economic distortions. The problem lies with the fragmentation of the local governance structure. If another revenue source, say the income tax or the sales tax, had been tied traditionally to local governments, similar disparities would be evident: "large differentials in the rates of any major local tax among neighboring and competitive jurisdictions are likely to be bad rather than good" (Netzer, 1966, p. 172).

Administration and Compliance Costs

Criticism of the property tax is often centered on its administration and perceptions (or the reality) of unfairness in assessment practices. Revenue is maximized, as are taxpayer acceptance and support, if valuation and collection procedures are administered efficiently and fairly.

Unlike income taxes, individual taxpayers do not determine their liability for property taxes. Property assessment and tax calculation are the responsibility of local public officials, nearly eliminating compliance costs. However, many assessors are poorly trained in appraisal procedures, serve only part-time, and are often concerned about their reelection or advancement in the local or state political arena. Problems of tax administration are epitomized by the conflict faced by assessors who must raise assessments to keep pace with inflation and property improvements while maintaining favor in the local power structure. For this reason, progressive jurisdictions are appointing assessors as civil servants. This reflects an earlier recommendation that abandoning elections in favor of appointments on the basis of demonstrated abilities to assess properties would contribute to the professionalization of the assessment function (ACIR, 1973, p. 69).

The cost of administration is low relative to its yield and in comparison with costs of other major revenue sources. However, the low cost is indicative of deficiencies in assessment practices. The deficiencies are predominantly related to the inefficiencies of small units of government. If local assessment practices were fully disclosed and appeals procedures were improved, inequities and political interference with the system might be reduced and public confidence might be increased. It would be possible to have good property tax administration at a cost of about 1.5 percent of tax collections, an acceptable amount when compared with the administrative costs for income and sales taxes (Netzer, 1966, p. 175).

Public dissatisfaction with the increased size and cost of government generally, and with larger property assessments and tax bills more specifically, culminated in tax limitation initiatives in many states.

LIMITATIONS ON TAXATION AND GOVERNMENT EXPENDITURES

Tax and spending limitations restrict government's capacity to deliver public services with the intention of encouraging fiscal responsibility. Officials who are overzealous in their desire to meet the demands of constituents may raise taxation and indebtedness to a dangerous level. The Revolutionary War was fought to insure that the citizenry would have a voice in decisions about government taxation. Two subsequent movements addressed the large debt local governments incurred in the late 1800s and the growth in both state and local government spending and taxes in the 1970s to the present. In this chapter we discuss the limitations imposed by the more recent movement because of their direct effects on local property taxation and school district operations. But their provisions also impact states' revenues and expenditures.

Limits on Local Government Debt and Tax

State constitutions and statutes that define the structure of local governments also limit their fiscal powers. Localities are typically restricted with regard to the type of taxes or the maximum tax rates they may levy. Limits on indebtedness define the maximum percentage of the local government's property tax base that can be obligated for future payments.

Table 6.8 illustrates provisions for limiting tax rates, assessments, revenues, and expenditures of school districts in several states. The limits on tax rates in many states are expressed as a maximum millage (e.g., Oregon and Wisconsin) or cents per hundred of valuation (e.g., North Carolina). In contrast is Michigan's constitutional limit; this limit rolls back property tax rates if revenue growth exceeds the change in the cost of living. Restricting

increases in assessments also imposes controls, particularly when this strategy is used in combination with limits on tax rate increases to contain governmental growth, as occurs in Michigan. Revenue limits slow the increase in taxes from year to year, either by a specified percentage amount or in concert with some measure of inflation or income growth (e.g., in Oregon and Wisconsin). In addition to revenue limits, an expenditure limitation restricts increases in spending per pupil for schools (e.g., in Colorado).

Similar limitations in many states restrict long-term borrowing for capital outlay for constructing buildings and purchasing school buses. Open-disclosure laws require hearings and referenda prior to creating debt or raising indebtedness above a given level. Additionally, school boards of fiscally dependent districts cannot themselves incur debt.

Movements to Restrict Growth in Taxation and Spending

With the growth of municipalities during an inflationary period following the Civil War, current expenses were paid by floating debt carried forward each year rather than through increased taxes. Many jurisdictions overextended their tax bases prior to the recession of the 1870s, and states responded with measures to limit debt and public services in relation to local revenue. By 1880, ten states had limitations on taxes and one-half of the states had imposed limits on debt that cities could incur (Wright, 1981, p. 42).

A century later, public perceptions of uncontained growth and inefficiency in government stimulated a similar movement to contain taxes and expenditures. Confidence and trust in government waned in the 1970s, and people claimed that reducing revenue would force efficiency in the delivery of essential services. This tax revolt was a response to the rapid growth of federal, state, and local governments during the 1950s and 1960s: "The votes are votes against inflation and irritating regulations and government actions, not just against taxes"

TABLE 6.8. Limitations on Property Taxation and Revenue Growth for Current Expenses in Selected States

State	Type of Limitation	Provisions
Colorado	Revenue and spending	Growth in revenue and expenditures is limited by the sum of percentage changes in pupil enrollment and the rate of inflation
Michigan	Assessment	Assessed values cannot increase more than 5% or the rate of inflation, whichever is less; on resale, properties are reassessed at 50% of market value
	Tax rate	Local property tax rates are rolled back if increases in revenue exceed the rate of inflation; however, a majority of voters can override the rollback and retain the existing millage rate
North Carolina	Tax rate	Local supplemental taxes cannot exceed $0.50 per $100 of valuation; larger districts with populations over 100,000 may levy up to $0.60 per $100 of valuation
Oregon	Tax rate	Five mills
	Revenue	Boards may increase tax revenue by 6% or by the amount necessary to maintain spending at the previous-year level, subject to the five-mill limit
Wisconsin	Tax rate	Beginning in 1997–98, boards may not tax for school operations in excess of 10 mills for K–12, 6.67 mills for K–8, or 3.33 mills for high school districts
	Revenue	Districts may increase revenue from state aid and property taxes by the larger of the consumer price index (CPI) or an amount of money ($194.37 in 1994–95) that is increased annually by the CPI

SOURCE: Gold et al. (1995). *Public School Finance Programs of the United States and Canada, 1993–94*. Albany: American Education Finance Association and The Center for the Study of the States, pp. 160, 344, 483, 526, 673. Reprinted with the permission of the publisher.

(Due, 1982, p. 281). Taxation became the focal point, however, and the public called for tax and expenditure limitations of two forms: (a) Reducing the existing size of government: This limitation was premised on the beliefs that tax burdens are too heavy and that government is not a good investment. (b) Containing the growth of government: This limitation was premised on the belief that government is as large as it should be relative to the rest of the economy (Palaich, Kloss, & Williams,

1980, pp. 1–2). These two goals are illustrated by initiatives in several states.

The movement began in California in 1978. Proposition 13 was a citizen initiative to reach the first goal, that of cutting the size of government by reducing revenue and thus expenditures. This constitutional change limited local property tax rates to 1 percent of 1975–1976 fair market values and restricted annual increases in assessments to a maximum of 2 percent. Assessments would reflect current values only when property changed owner-ship or was newly constructed. Proposition 4, passed one year later by a wider margin of Califor-nia voters, illustrates the goal of containing gov-ernment growth. This measure limited growth in state and local appropriations from tax revenue to the rates of increases in the cost of living and pop-ulation. This referendum also made it possible for a simple majority of voters to adjust the spending limit of any government unit and called for full state reimbursement of the costs of mandates asso-ciated with any new or upgraded program.

The effect of these limitations on property taxes can be seen in trends in effective tax rates. Table 6.9 shows a slower growth in taxation rela-tive to the value of houses in nearly all states. Ef-fective tax rates represent tax liability as a percent-age of the market value of homes financed through the Federal Housing Authority. The average rate in the nation grew from 1.34 percent in 1958 to 1.70 percent in 1966. But with the tax revolt and the concurrent shift in revenue burdens to states, this trend was reversed. Effective rates diminished to 1.16 percent in 1986. In all but eight states, there was a higher rate in 1966 or 1977, and a smaller rate was evident by 1986. Effective rates in Cali-fornia, for example, increased from 1.50 percent in 1958 to 2.21 percent in 1977, the year prior to Prop-osition 13. Then effective rates declined to 1.06 per-cent in 1986. In a comparison of fifty major cities, Los Angeles had one of the lowest effective rates (0.63 percent) in 1992 (U. S. Department of Com-merce, 1995, Table 494). Its rate was larger only than Honolulu's (0.30 percent). Effective rates in these cities were substantially lower than those of Detroit (4.53 percent) and Milwaukee (3.83 percent).

Diminishing effective rates during the years depicted in Table 6.9 do not necessarily mean that there were declines in actual millage rates levied on appraised value or in tax amounts collected. Rapidly rising market values bring increases in tax payments (assuming similar increased assess-ments) even if millage rates remain the same or decline somewhat. For example, taxes on a house appraised in 1966 for $22,000 would be $374, applying the average effective rate of 1.70 percent.

If this same house were appraised in 1986 at $45,000, it would be taxed $522, given the national average rate of 1.16 percent. The increased tax owed reflects growth in the appraisal, despite the substantial decline in the effective rate.

Much has been written about the aftermath of Proposition 13 in California. The feared reductions in government spending and services did not mate-rialize initially. Some said the state's economy was strengthened in the short run due to tax cuts (Adams, 1984, pp. 171–174). Increased user fees for public swimming pools, golf courses, marina docking, and so on placed the burden for services directly on beneficiaries. Business property turned over at a faster rate than was anticipated, and newly raised assessments shifted the burden for property taxation from residences to businesses. With respect to schools, Proposition 13 resulted in the replacement of property tax revenue with state financial aid; this narrowed the disparities in expenditures per pupil among school districts.

On the other hand, many unintended economic effects occurred. The greatly increased dependence on state revenue resulted in a loss of local auton-omy and a weakening of citizen participation in de-cision making. Reductions in property taxes were not always passed on to consumers and renters. Beneficiaries of the revolt included businesses, large oil companies, and property owners (Due, 1982, p. 281–283). Newly constructed or newly purchased property was taxed differently from property that had not changed hands. This created inequities in effective rates for properties within neighborhoods. Californians paid higher federal income taxes because of the lower deductions they could claim for the property taxes they paid. With the shift to user fees, homeowners still had to pay for services. But they lost the federal income tax deductions for which they could have qualified if they had paid for the services through property tax.

Even with the state paying proportionately more for public education, there was a large drop in total revenue for schools relative to other states. California dropped in per pupil spending for schools from among the top ten in the nation before Proposition 13 to a low of thirty-fifth. By the end

TABLE 6.9. Average Effective Property Tax Rates[a]

State	1958 (%)	1966 (%)	1977 (%)	1986 (%)	Rank[b]
Alabama	0.56	0.66	0.74	0.39	49
Alaska	1.12	1.42	NA	0.82	41
Arizona	2.14	2.41	1.72	0.68	45
Arkansas	0.86	1.09	1.49	1.09	25
California	1.50	2.03	2.21	1.06	28
Colorado	1.72	2.20	1.80	1.09	24
Connecticut	1.44	2.01	2.17	1.46	12
Delaware	0.71	1.14	0.88	0.73	43
District of Columbia	1.08	1.37	NA	1.17	21
Florida	0.76	1.09	1.13	0.89	39
Georgia	0.84	1.30	1.27	0.90	36
Hawaii	0.62	0.81	NA	0.51	48
Idaho	1.14	1.23	1.46	0.91	35
Illinois	1.35	1.96	1.90	1.59	9
Indiana	0.84	1.64	1.66	1.28	19
Iowa	1.34	2.12	1.76	1.96	8
Kansas	1.65	1.96	1.37	1.06	29
Kentucky	0.93	1.03	1.25	1.10	22
Louisiana	0.52	0.43	0.61	0.25	50
Maine	1.50	2.17	1.65	1.21	20
Maryland	1.47	2.05	1.69	1.30	18
Massachusetts	2.21	2.76	3.50	1.08	27
Michigan	1.45	1.81	2.63	2.26	5
Minnesota	1.57	2.14	1.39	1.03	31
Mississippi	0.66	0.93	1.10	0.77	42
Missouri	1.12	1.64	1.59	0.89	38
Montana	1.32	1.70	1.31	1.32	17
Nebraska	1.90	2.67	2.48	2.21	7
Nevada	1.06	1.47	1.71	0.61	46
New Hampshire	1.81	2.38	NA	1.55	10
New Jersey	1.77	2.57	3.31	2.33	1
New Mexico	0.93	1.30	1.65	1.01	32
New York	2.09	2.40	2.89	2.22	6
North Carolina	0.90	1.31	1.35	NA	33
North Dakota	1.54	1.81	1.26	1.37	15
Ohio	1.07	1.44	1.26	1.08	26
Oklahoma	0.86	1.11	0.95	0.90	37
Oregon	1.55	1.98	2.25	2.26	4
Pennsylvania	1.50	1.88	1.85	1.37	16
Rhode Island	1.67	1.96	NA	1.49	11
South Carolina	0.48	0.60	0.82	0.70	44
South Dakota	2.01	2.64	1.79	2.31	2
Tennessee	0.97	1.37	1.40	1.04	30
Texas	1.36	1.62	1.84	1.44	13
Utah	1.05	1.52	1.03	0.93	34

TABLE 6.9. Average Effective Property Tax Rates[a] (Continued)

State	1958 (%)	1966 (%)	1977 (%)	1986 (%)	Rank[b]
Vermont	1.63	2.27	NA	NA	NA
Virginia	0.90	1.13	1.21	1.42	14
Washington	0.92	1.14	1.75	1.10	23
West Virginia	0.56	0.71	NA	0.88	40
Wisconsin	1.82	2.31	2.22	2.27	3
Wyoming	1.17	1.34	0.87	0.57	47
U.S. Total	1.34	1.70	1.67	1.16	

[a]Effective rates are for existing FHA insured mortgages only, which represent varying percentages (by state) of total single-family homes.
[b]In cases where 1986 data were not available, rank was based on data for the most recent year.
NA = not available.
SOURCE: ACIR. (1987). *Significant Features of Fiscal Federalism, 1987 edition*. Washington, DC: Advisory Commission on Intergovernmental Relations, Table 30, p. 70.

of the 1980s California's rank had stabilized at twenty-fifth (Verstegen, 1988, p. 85). The effects of this reform include a dramatic reduction in the tax base because valuations are tied to the price of property at the time it is sold. The tax burden is shifted to younger, lower-income taxpayers, making it more regressive: "The result is a property tax that violates all economic standards for horizontal and vertical equity, produces a much smaller level of tax revenues, and is under state rather than local control" (Odden & Picus, 1992, p. 158).

The 1980 Massachusetts Proposition 2½ served both to reduce taxes and to contain the growth of government. It limited property tax rates to 2½ percent of "full and fair cash value," required jurisdictions that were previously taxing above that level to reduce levies, and held revenue from real estate to a 2½ percent annual growth rate. By the early 1980s, thirty states had adopted expenditure or revenue limits. Most of these actions tied increases in tax collections to changes in the cost of living, to a fixed percentage increase over prior years, or to a fixed percentage of property value (Wright, 1981, pp. 29–30).

The movement to limit taxes and expenditures slowed in the 1980s. Only six of the twenty-four states with active revenue or spending limitations noted by ACIR (1994, pp. 14–19) had adopted the restrictions after 1982. Proposition 9, defeated by

California voters in June 1980, proposed a constitutional amendment to halve state income tax rates, to index rates to stem bracket creep, and to abolish the state's inventory tax. In the same year that the Massachusetts proposition passed, initiatives failed in another five states. In 1988, tax or expenditure limitation measures were placed before voters in three states, but they all failed.

Property tax revenue, which had fallen nationally from $66.4 billion in fiscal 1978 to $64.9 billion a year later, grew substantially each year after that. It reached $179 billion in fiscal 1992 (U. S. Department of Commerce, 1994, p. VI; 1995, Table 481). In the late 1980s, public opinion shifted once again in support of public services, especially those related to expenditures for education. Quality and excellence were desired. The public voiced its willingness to raise state and local taxes to finance improved schools. The drive to ensure adequate funds for public education brought another California initiative. Proposition 98, approved by voters in 1988, amended the state constitution such that public education would receive the larger of 40 percent of any new state revenue or the previous year's allocation increased by the rate of inflation and enrollment growth. State money that could not otherwise be spent because of spending limits imposed by Proposition 4 was also diverted to support education.

The movement may have slowed with the realization that limitations may not be effective in constraining government growth. Howard's (1989) study of the effectiveness of limitations found that they played only a minor role in constraining state revenue or expenditures:

> The overall condition of state economies and structure of state tax systems, in combination with the sensitivity of policymakers to anti-tax sentiment, have done more to limit state spending than have imposed restrictions. (p. 83)

She explained the limited effectiveness of the restrictions by noting that a large proportion of state-appropriated funds (over 50% in 6 of 17 states studied) is exempt from limitations; restrictions are less effective when they are tied to personal income growth, because state tax systems are not highly elastic; and some states that have exceeded limits have been pressured to assume financial responsibilities that had previously been met by localities.

Enactments in a number of states, including those appearing in Table 6.8, revived the movement in the 1990s (Fulton & Sonovick, 1992). Oregon voters approved a constitutional amendment to limit property taxes to fifteen mills for school districts; as this burden declines to five mills by 1996–1997, the responsibility for school finance will be shifted to the state. Six states adopted limitation measures in 1992. Florida limited tax increases for residential property, and Rhode Island limited overall state spending. Arizona and Colorado made a two-thirds vote by legislators necessary. The Oklahoma constitutional provision required a three-quarters vote either by the state legislature or by voters, in order to enact tax increases. The Colorado initiative also required voters to approve increases in spending that exceed the rate of change in population and the consumer price index (CPI), in the case of state and local governments, or the percentage change in enrollments and the CPI in the case of school districts.

The 1994 elections included over two hundred initiatives. Seventy-eight of these resulted from citizen petition drives (Lindsay, 1994a). A revenue cap approved in Florida restricted state revenue growth to that of personal income. However, this constitutional amendment exempted property taxes and lottery revenue, both of which finance schools. Nevada voters gave initial approval to an amendment that requires a two-thirds legislative vote to enact tax increases. But voters must approve amendments twice before they are effective. Voters defeated similar proposed constitutional amendments to limit increases in revenue or property valuations in Missouri, Montana, Oregon, and South Dakota.

In reviewing reasons for the success or failure of citizen initiatives in seven states, Whitney (1993) noted that "education finance measures are more likely to succeed when expenditures are tied to specific educational improvements that are carefully explained to the public" (p. vii). Distrust of local government, or the real or perceived unnecessary tax burden, leads to initiatives to curtail the growth of property tax revenue. Then local officials seek additional state assistance. The property tax was once a large source of local funds for some districts. It has declined in importance as policy makers have shifted the burden for the support of schools to the state.

PROPERTY TAXES AND STATE-LEVEL REVENUES

When the property tax is weighed against the criteria of yield, elasticity, equity, neutrality, and costs of administration and compliance, there is no overriding concern that argues for its elimination. When the financing of educational programs and facilities in communities depends heavily on property taxation, however, people do object. They argue that a shift from local to either state or regional property taxation, or the replacement of this revenue with broader-based taxes, would be more equitable. Others contend that the property tax is an important part of local community control of schools.

State Assumption of Property Taxation

For many years people have argued that continuing to place a large burden on small local governmental units to finance schools is inconsistent with the

goals of equity and efficiency in resource allocation (Netzer, 1973, pp. 13–24). Having a larger
state role in school finance would equalize educational opportunities. This goal recognizes the geographic spillovers that occur when the mobility of
labor among localities distributes the positive and
negative consequences of varying school quality
among communities. Similarly, efficiency in tax
administration may be better served through state
or regional control of tax policy rather than county
or school district control.

Judicial decisions, tax study commissions,
and other pressures to meet equity goals led many
states to deemphasize local property taxation during the finance reform movement of the 1970s.
When state governments and the federal government assumed increased responsibility for financing elementary and secondary education, this
eased the burden on local revenue (see Figure 3.1).
Greater fiscal federation promised a broader base
of support, equalization of the capacities of local
districts to finance schools, and improved assessment practices (ACIR, 1973, p. 77). Inequities per-
sisted, however. Some questioned the role of property taxation in the context of educational reforms
that would ensure higher standards for all students
and eliminate the extreme disparities in spending,
programs, and facilities depicted by Kozol (1991).
At the same time, the educational reform movement of the late 1980s and early 1990s directed
attention once again to the advantages of maintaining control over many decisions at the district or
school level. Control over fiscal affairs is an
important part of control over programs.

Having access to a substantial revenue source
is important to the autonomy of local governments.
The property tax has traditionally been the revenue
source best suited to local governments. The property taxation is symbolic of the autonomy of local
government, and any move to have the state assume
property taxes is resisted. Shannon (1973, p. 28)
contended that this revenue source "serves as the
sheet armor against the forces of centralization." Although decisions about school programs could be
made locally even if all funds were allocated from
higher levels, access to this revenue source enables

local officials to determine the total level of resources
and services to provide, at least at the margin.

Gold (1994) observed that "the real root of
inequality is reliance on *local revenue,* not the
property tax itself. Disparities would generally be
even worse if the local income or sales tax were
used instead of the property tax" (p. 9). Rather than
eliminate property taxation, states' finance policies
typically consider the amount of funds that can be
raised locally in distributions of financial aid.
These formulas thus equalize local communities'
tax capacities and bring more comparable levels of
school expenditures among districts (see Chapter
8). In effect, larger tax bases, including utilities and
industrial property, are spread among more localities. Tax-based disparities and service disparities
are thus greatly reduced.

Even in states that have assumed a large financial involvement, property tax administration remains, for the most part, a local government responsibility. But states use equalization ratios and
exercise more control over assessment practices.
Some states have explored the benefits of regional
school-taxing units, in which collections from
high-wealth districts are shared with others. This
approach improves fiscal effort uniformity and
improves taxpayer equity within regions without
turning property taxation into a state responsibility
(Clark, 1995). The Texas Supreme Court, however,
declared it unconstitutional (*Carrollton* v. *Edgewood,* 1992). It may make more sense for states to
consider the level of revenue that is collected
locally in making allocations, or to turn to state-
level resources to accomplish equalization goals.

Replacing Property Taxes
with Broader-Based Taxes

In the mid-1990s several states entertained proposals to dramatically reduce the burden on property
taxes and shift to broader-based sales or income
taxes (NCSL, 1994; Pipho, 1994). The Michigan
legislature imposed a statewide property tax to raise
$1.02 billion to offset the loss of $4.4 billion when
it repealed nearly all local support for schools.
When asked about a suitable alternative to raise

additional state-level funds, voters approved a constitutional amendment that increased the sales tax rate from 4 percent to 6 percent rather than permit an automatic increase in the state income tax, as was called for in the legislation. This amendment and the subsequent statutory changes also required a three-fourths vote by the legislature to increase the tax rate, capped annual assessment increases to the lesser of 5 percent or the rate of inflation, increased the cigarette tax from 25 to 75 cents per pack, and placed a 0.75 percent tax on the sale of homes and businesses. The initial legislative action eliminated property taxes for schools. But the burden placed on state revenue resulted in continued property taxation to finance "systemic educational reforms" (Addonizio, Kearney, & Prince, 1995).

The Wisconsin legislature raised the state share of school funds from 40 percent to 60 percent by severely cutting property taxes and turning to broader-based state revenue. Voters in Rhode Island passed a constitutional amendment that required the legislature to craft a school finance plan that would reduce property taxes while increasing state aid. In contrast, other states rejected legislative proposals to decrease the reliance on property taxation in 1994. Colorado, Nebraska, and New Hampshire are notable examples.

The choice of a suitable revenue source appears to be limited to income- or consumption-based taxes to replace the large yield of the property tax. Busch and Stewart (1992) noted that when Ohio voters were first given an opportunity in 1989 to enact local option income taxes for supplementing school support, they enacted the measures in seventeen school districts. In their study of voters' attitudes they found a slim margin of support for a local income tax over the property tax. They concluded that the income tax is a viable source of school funds. Although the income tax better relates revenue yield to ability to pay (see Chapters 4 and 5), the Michigan experience suggests that voters prefer sales taxation.

The trend in the nation since the 1800s has been to ease the burden on local tax revenue. There is little question that the recent movement among

legislatures and voters to turn from property taxation toward broader-based sales and income taxes will continue. This is true if we assume that other policies protect local school and community autonomy with regard to decisions about programs.

SUMMARY

Wealth-based taxation of real property brings a stable and productive revenue source to local governments. Its productive yield and stability have effectively countered arguments against property taxation. Its stability offers predictability, enabling local officials to plan municipal and school district programs within balanced budgets. The property tax is inelastic relative to income- and consumption-based taxes, because the assessed values used in determining tax yield respond slowly to changes in the economy. As valuation practices improve, such that the tax base more closely reflects market values, the yield will grow with fewer annual adjustments in tax rates, if we assume that property values will also keep pace with the economy.

Property tax structure and administration vary considerably from state to state. Assessment and equalization ratios, exemptions, revenue and expenditure limitations, and tax relief mechanisms affect tax bases and yields. Many of these policies, along with arbitrary assessment practices, interfere with the goals of equity and neutrality. Some provisions shift the tax burdens from one group to another. These shifts result in misallocations of economic resources and to inequities among taxpayers of different incomes. Careful policy development, including the use of circuit breakers to ease tax burdens on low-income families, makes this tax less regressive. Other provisions impact the purchase and rehabilitation of houses, the location of businesses and industry, and the development of vacant and farm land. Urban redevelopment is discouraged, while businesses and upper-income families are encouraged to migrate to localities with lower tax rates but better services.

Property taxation in most states enables localities to expand educational programs beyond the minimal offerings financed by state aid programs. However, disparities in tax bases (capacity) and in tax rates (effort) among communities often result in or exacerbate program inequities. State or regional responsibilities or standards for valuing properties might ease inequities in taxation and reduce extreme disparities in programs. If properties like utilities and industrial plants that serve broad regions were removed from the local tax base and were taxed only by the state, when the tax capacity of localities would be more evenly distributed and many of the negative social and economic effects of property taxation would be reduced.

However, these reforms must be balanced against the strong historical precedent for preserving local autonomy. Assessment practices can be improved and local governments can exercise some degree of independence if we continue to place the responsibility for setting tax rates at the local or regional level. A primary goal for states and localities in the next decade should be to strengthen the integrity of property taxation by continuing to

improve its structure and administration. As more states entertain proposals for curtailing or eliminating property taxes, a crucial policy question will be how much local autonomy will be maintained.

With the resurgence of tax and spending limitations, and with the continuing movement to ease or eliminate the burden on property taxation for school finance, education must rely more on state revenue and there must be a more equitable distribution of money among districts. Tax and spending initiatives were intended to curtail the growth of government or induce greater efficiency. They may have succeeded to some degree. But there has been a concurrent push for localities to secure new revenues to maintain or expand levels of services.

In the next chapter, we explore several strategies for tapping local resources in support of school districts. Borrowing and investments by school districts bring new money to construct facilities and ensure continuous school operations. And partnerships and volunteers offer opportunities for schools to gain new talents at minimal cost.

ACTIVITIES

1. At the same time that the state legislature is considering abolishing property taxation for supporting school operations, a school district board of education is proposing to raise the local tax rate to finance expansion of programs or facilities in your school district. During a public meeting at which you are describing the project, you are asked why the property tax is an appropriate source of revenue for this purpose. How might you respond?

2. Contact your tax assessor and inquire about the current tax rates for school districts, municipalities, and other special districts served by this tax jurisdiction. When were properties last assessed and when will they next be appraised? Which of the three methods—market data, cost, or income—are most likely to be used to appraise residential, business, and agricultural property? What proportion of appraised value is exempt from taxation? What might you recommend to improve the fairness of property assessment practices?

3. Develop a rationale for tax incentives in the form of

lower assessments to attract new industry or commercial development. Keep in mind that taxes will increase for currently operating businesses if expansions in municipal and educational services are necessitated by this new development.

4. Prepare a chart that contrasts the strengths and weaknesses of property taxation with those of income- and consumption-based taxes, referring to yield, elasticity, equity, neutrality, and costs of administration and compliance. List the five criteria along the left margin. Label three columns across the top for the primary tax bases: wealth, income, and consumption. In each cell, place the names of the primary revenue sources discussed in Chapters 5 and 6 that correlate most closely with the designated base and criterion.

5. Describe provisions in one state's constitution or statutes that limit local governments' power to tax or that contain growth in revenue or spending. Design a study to determine the perceptions of legislators and superintendents about the value of such limitations.

6. Clarify your beliefs about local control over school finances and programs and about the relationship between this autonomy and the policies that govern taxes to support schools. To what degree are these beliefs consistent with proposals for (a) shifting more control over property taxation to the state level, or (b) replacing property taxes with broader-based revenue sources?

EXERCISES

1. Express a tax rate of 23.2 mills in terms of dollars per thousand, dollars per hundred, and as a percentage of assessed valuation. Given this rate, what is the tax on a house that is assessed at $64,000?

2. Find the equalized value and the amount of property tax owed by a business that has a market value of $1.6 million, is located in a jurisdiction having an equalization ratio of 0.25, and faces a school levy of $3.50 per hundred of equalized valuation (use the decimal form or mathematical equivalent of this rate as it is commonly used in your state).

3. Two school districts, each enrolling 5,000 pupils, have aggregate market valuations of $510 million and $360 million, respectively. Assume that they are located in a state that assesses all properties at one-third of market value.

a. Determine the total assessed valuation of each school district and the amount that each district raises per pupil from a 28-mill levy.

b. How much more or less is raised in each district if the tax rate remains the same but the state assessment ratio is increased to 40 percent?

c. What tax rate in mills is needed in each district to raise $1,428 per pupil, given the assessment ratio of 40 percent?

d. Explain the source(s) of inequities in the amount of funds that these districts are able to generate per pupil from the property tax.

 COMPUTER SIMULATIONS

Objectives of This Activity:

- *To develop an understanding of the concepts of equalization ratios, exemptions, and effective tax rates and their impact on the ability of school districts to raise revenue from the property tax.*

- *To develop an understanding of the impacts of increasing the tax rate on individual tax jurisdictions and parcels of property.*

Simulation 6.1 is an application of equalization ratios to several tax jurisdictions to illustrate how these ratios affect assessed values and tax levies (as in Tables 6.3 and 6.4). Simulation 6.2 makes use of the same equalization ratios in determining taxes owed by owners of four parcels that have different exemptions (as in Table 6.5).

Simulation 6.1: *Calculating Property Tax Levies and Tax Rates*

a. Retrieve the file PROPTAX. Scroll down the spreadsheet and note that this file consists of three related tables that are separated by broken lines (-----).

b. In Table 1, enter the following EQUALIZATION RATIOS for the respective tax jurisdictions:

Jurisdiction	Equalization Ratio
A	1.10
B	0.95
C	0.80
D	0.30

c. In the column labeled EQUALIZED VALUE, create formulas to determine the equalized value given these ratios (i.e., divide

ASSESSED VALUE by EQUALIZATION RATIO). Also calculate the total EQUALIZED VALUE for the DISTRICT.

d. What happens to the EQUALIZED VALUEs if it is determined that the EQUALIZATION RATIOs of jurisdictions A and B are to be reduced by 0.05 and those of jurisdictions C and D are to be increased by 0.10? How is the total affected? Print the modified Table 1.

e. In the appropriate column of Table 2, copy the EQUALIZATION RATIOs and the original ASSESSED VALUEs for each jurisdiction. (Remember to copy these cells using the "formula method" [i.e., the cell address, for example C14], so that any future changes to the cells in Table 1 will automatically be reflected in Table 2.)

f. In Table 2, create a formula to determine the TAX RATE ON ASSESSED VALUE by dividing the district's TAX RATE ON EQUALIZED VALUE by the EQUALIZATION RATIO for each jurisdiction.

g. Calculate the TAX LEVY collected from each jurisdiction by multiplying the TAX RATE ON ASSESSED VALUE by the respective ASSESSED VALUE for each jurisdiction. (Remember, the given tax rates are expressed in mills and need to be converted to the decimal form when doing computations.)

h. In the last row of the last column of this table, create a formula to determine the TOTAL LEVY for this district.

i. *Further Activities.* What happens to the total levy when the ASSESSED VALUEs of jurisdictions are increased by $5 million each? (Input these changes in Table 1 and results will automatically be transferred to Table 2.) Alternatively, what happens to the levy on the original assessed values when the TAX RATE ON EQUALIZED VALUE in Table 2 is increased to $28? Print Tables 1 and 2 resulting from these modifications.

Simulation 6.2: *Impact of Property Tax Exemptions*

a. Scroll down the spreadsheet to find Table 3 in the file PROPTAX. Copy the EQUALIZATION RATIOs from Table 2 to the row labeled EQUAL. RATIO. (Remember to copy using the formula method.)

b. In the row labeled ASSESSED VALUE, create a formula to determine values given the market value of each parcel and the respective equalization ratios (i.e., multiply the MARKET VALUE by the EQUAL. RATIO).

c. In the row labeled TAXABLE VALUE, calculate the difference between the ASSESSED VALUE and the EXEMPTION listed.

d. Copy the TAX RATE ON ASSESSED VALUE from Table 2 using the formula method. Note that the rates are the same for the parcels within a jurisdiction, but different between jurisdictions. Why is this the case?

e. Create a formula to calculate the amount of TAX DUE from the owners of respective parcels. (Remember, the given tax rates are expressed in mills and need to be converted to the decimal form when doing computations.)

f. To determine the EFFECTIVE RATE, divide the TAX DUE by the MARKET VALUE and multiply this result by 1000 in order to state the effective tax rate in dollars per $1,000 of assessed value.

g. Increase the size of the exemption granted to parcels 6 and 8 by $2,000. Print the table, showing the new exemptions and resulting calculations. What effect does changing an exemption have on the assessed value, tax due, and effective rates?

h. *Further Activities.* After printing, alter the TAX RATE ON EQUALIZED VALUE in Table 2 to reflect a recent vote of the public to raise the property tax rate to $32 per $1000 of valuation. Print the modified Tables 2 and 3, which show resulting changes in assessed values, taxes owed, and effective rates. What effect does the new rate have on the respective parcels of property?

REFERENCES

Aaron, H. J. (1973). What do circuit-breaker laws accomplish? In G. E. Peterson (Ed.), *Property tax reform* (pp. 53–64). Washington, DC: Urban Institute.

Aaron, H. J. (1975). *Who pays the property tax: A new view.* Washington, DC: Brookings Institution.

ACIR (Advisory Commission on Intergovernmental Relations). (1973). *Financing schools and property tax relief—A state responsibility,* Report A-40. Washington, DC: Advisory Commission on Intergovernmental Relations.

ACIR. (1987). *Significant features of fiscal federalism, 1987 edition.* Washington, DC: Advisory Commission on Intergovernmental Relations.

ACIR. (1988). *Changing public attitudes on government and taxes.* Washington, DC: Advisory Commission on Intergovernmental Relations.

ACIR. (1993). *RTS 1991: State revenue capacity and effort.* Washington, DC: Advisory Commission on Intergovernmental Relations.

ACIR. (1994). *Significant features of fiscal federalism, 1994 edition, Volume 1.* Washington, DC: Advisory Commission on Intergovernmental Relations.

ACIR. (1995). *Significant features of fiscal federalism, 1995 edition, Volume 1.* Washington, DC: Advisory Commission on Intergovernmental Relations.

Adams, J. R. (1984). *Secrets of the tax revolt.* New York: Harcourt Brace Jovanovich.

Addonizio, M. F., Kearney, C. P., & Prince, H. J. (1995, Winter). Michigan's high wire act. *Journal of Education Finance, 20,* 235–269.

Busch, R. J., & Stewart, D. O. (1992, Spring). Voters' opinion of school district property taxes and income taxes: Results from an exit-poll in Ohio. *Journal of Education Finance, 17,* 337–351.

Carrollton-Farmers Branch ISD v. *Edgewood ISD.* 426 S.W.2d 488 (1992).

Clark, C. (1995). Regional school taxing units: The Texas experience. In D. H. Monk, *Study on the generation of revenues for education: Final report* (pp. 75–88). Albany: New York State Education Department.

Due, J. F. (1982). Shifting sources of financing education and the taxpayer revolt. In W. W. McMahon & T. G. Geske (Eds.), *Financing education: Overcoming inefficiency and inequity* (pp. 267–289). Urbana: University of Illinois Press.

Fulton, M., & Sonovick, L. (1992). Tax and spending limitations—An analysis. *ECS Issuegram.* Denver: Education Commission of the States.

George, H. (1879). *Progress and poverty.* Garden City, NY: Doubleday, Page.

Gold, S. D. (1979). *Property tax relief.* Lexington, MA: Lexington Books.

Gold, S. D. (1994). *Tax options for states needing more school revenue.* Westhaven, CT: National Education Association.

Gold, S. D., Smith, D. M., & Lawton, S. B. (Eds.) (1995). *Public school finance programs of the United States and Canada, 1993–94.* Albany: American Education Finance Association and The Center for the Study of the States.

Howard, M. A. (1989, Summer). State tax and expenditure limitations: There is no story. *Public Budgeting and Finance, 9,* 83–90.

Kozol, J. (1991). *Savage inequalities.* New York: HarperCollins.

Lindsay, D. (1994a, November 2). Educators buck giving the public say on taxes. *Education Week,* pp. 1, 20–21.

Lindsay, D. (1994b, June 15). N.Y. lawmakers tap surplus in approving 5% boost in school aid. *Education Week,* p. 13.

Lindsay, D. (1995, May 24). Tide turns for the better in N.J., Ohio budget votes. *Education Week,* pp. 12, 15.

Musgrave, R. A., & Musgrave, P. B. (1989). *Public finance in theory and practice* (5th ed.). New York: McGraw-Hill.

NCSL (National Conference of State Legislatures). (1994). *State budget and tax actions 1994: Preliminary report.* Denver, CO: National Conference of State Legislatures.

Netzer, D. (1966). *Economics of the property tax.* Washington, DC: Brookings Institution.

Netzer, D. (1973). Is there too much reliance on the local property tax? In G. E. Peterson (Ed.), *Property tax reform.* Washington, DC: Urban Institute.

Netzer, D., & Berne, R. (1995). Discrepancies between ideal characteristics of a property tax system and current practice in New York. In D. H. Monk, *Study on the generation of revenues for education: Final report* (pp. 31–47). Albany: New York State Education Department.

Odden, A. R., & Picus, L. O. (1992). *School finance: A policy perspective.* New York: McGraw-Hill.

Oldman, O., & Schoettle, F. P. (1974). *State and local taxes and finance: Text, problems, and cases.* Mineola, NY: Foundation Press.

Palaich, R., Kloss, J., & Williams, M. F. (1980). *Tax and expenditure limitation referenda,* Report F80-2. Denver, CO: Education Commission of the States.

Peterson, G. E. (Ed.). (1973). *Property tax reform.* Washington, DC: Urban Institute.

Pipho, C. (1994, June). Property tax bans catch on. *Phi Delta Kappan, 75,* 742–743.

Shannon, J. (1973). The property tax: Reform or relief? In G. E. Peterson (Ed.), *Property tax reform* (pp. 25–52). Washington, DC: Urban Institute.

U. S. Department of Commerce, Bureau of the Census. (1995). *Statistical abstract of the United States: 1995.* Washington, DC: U. S. Government Printing Office.

U. S. Department of Commerce, Bureau of the Census. (1994). *1992 Census of governments, vol. 2: Taxable property values.* Washington, DC: U. S. Government Printing Office.

Verstegen, D. (1988). *School finance at a glance.* Denver, CO: Education Commission of the States.

Walz v. *Tax Commission of the City of New York.* 397 U.S. 664 (1970).

Whitney, T. N. (1993). *Voters and school finance: The impact of public opinion.* Denver, CO: National Conference of State Legislatures.

Wright, J. W. (1981). *Tax and expenditure limitation: A policy perspective.* Lexington, KY: Council of State Governments.

Yinger, J., Borsch-Supan, A., Bloom, H. S., & Ladd, H. F. (1988). *Property taxes and house values: The theory and estimation of intra-jurisdictional property tax capitalization.* San Diego, CA: Academic Press.

CHAPTER 7

Expanding School Resources through User Fees, Cash Flow Management, Capital Outlay, and Partnerships

Primary Issues Explored in This Chapter:

- *User charges:* Should families and community groups that directly benefit from school-related programs, transportation, and facilities pay fees for such services?

- *Investing and borrowing funds:* What are the options for investing excess or idle funds to gain interest earnings until payroll and other payments are due? What short-term strategies are available to districts to meet financial obligations until they receive other federal, state, and local revenues?

- *Capital outlay:* How does long-term borrowing through the sale of bonds enable districts to construct facilities and purchase costly equipment?

- *Partnerships, educational foundations, and voluntarism:* In what ways might involving the community and the private sector in public schools expand resources and political support for school improvement efforts?

School officials increasingly seek nontraditional sources of support. The movement to identify new monies responds in some states to the restrictions placed on the growth of property taxes and in other states to the resistance of taxpayers to increasing local taxes to support operating budgets or expand programs. Constraints on state and federal revenue available for education, given competing demands placed on these governments, also encourage school boards and administrators to look elsewhere.

In the previous chapter we found that the property tax provides the largest amount of funds within the control of localities. But school systems are not limited to this revenue. They can expand their resource bases by collecting fees from stu-

dents and other patrons and by carefully managing cash flow, including making timely decisions to invest and borrow funds. And they can use capital outlay financing for large projects. If school systems use partnerships, foundations, and volunteers creatively, parents and communities will actively support and participate in school programs.

USER CHARGES FOR EDUCATIONAL PROGRAMS

We discussed privilege-based taxation in Chapter 4. This taxation includes fees assessed for users of specific governmental services. It is justified on the benefits-received principle; the amount beneficia-ries must pay is tied to the presumed value of the privilege. In actuality, the fee rarely covers the entire cost of the service, and other forms of taxa-tion subsidize the program. In states where these fees are permitted, schools may assess students for extracurricular activities, summer schools, before- and after-school programs, lunches, field trips, elective courses, textbooks, and supplemental sup-plies. Nonstudent users of school facilities, for example, when community groups sponsor social functions in gymnasiums, often pay charges to cover the costs of utilities and maintenance. Fees charged external groups have caused little diffi-culty for schools and we do not discuss them fur-ther. The focus of this section is the prevalence and legality of charges for student access to school pro-grams.

In 1990–1991, charges for school lunch pro-grams and other activities amounted to $3.6 million and $2.7 million, respectively, across the nation (U. S. Department of Commerce, 1993, p. 14). Ex-pressed as a proportion of all revenue received by school districts, these sources averaged only 1.6 percent and 1.2 percent of monies, with a range in the "other" category from less than 0.1 percent in New Jersey to 5.6 percent in Nebraska. User charges are typically a minor source of school sup-port. But a study of fees in seven districts sur-rounding Vancouver, Canada, revealed a wide range in fees charged students. The highest fees included $1,000 for a technical studies course, $1,500 for extracurricular activities, $110 for grad-uation, and $12,000 for an international program (Brown & Bouman, 1994). Charges for particular activities and services may offer the potential for revenue growth, but they pose challenges for policy makers and administrators.

This tax is likely to cause debates between school personnel and the public over the degree to which the burden for paying costs of programs should be shifted from taxpayers to parents and other users. Parents and the courts raise many issues: "Should schools be able to charge some stu-dents for some services, if their parents can afford to pay? Should schools be able to deny other chil-dren certain activities based on the fact that their parents cannot or will not pay? If so, what are the limits?" (Jones & Amalfitano, 1994, pp. 142–143)

These questions probe several of the criteria of taxation noted in Chapter 4. The criteria include the equity principle and its dimension of ability to pay, neutrality, and the costs of administration. In questioning their legal status, a fundamental issue is whether fees may be charged in public schools whose programs are supposed to be free and acces-sible to children of all economic levels. Another issue is the degree to which charges have any unin-tended consequences. Consequences might include the diminished participation of students and nega-tive public relations as parents oppose these addi-tional taxes. Finally, user charges create a number of difficulties in enforcing compliance and over-seeing waiver policies.

Legal Status and Inequities

Because education is a provision of state constitu-tions and statutes, federal courts defer to state authorities for resolving this and other school finance issues (see Chapter 11 and the overview of judicial decisions in Dayton & McCarthy, 1992). Challenges to fees as violations of state constitu-tions' guarantees of free public education have had mixed results. Some decisions have interpreted constitutional provisions as permitting fees for textbooks and instructional supplies. Others have denied them. As a result, thirty-four states permit at least one type of student fee. But fifteen states and the District of Columbia prohibit fees (Hamm & Crosser, 1991). In many cases, the acceptability of user fees relates to whether the activity or item of expenditure is a "necessary or integral part" of the educational program. For example, an Illinois court determined that a lunchroom supervision fee could be charged students since it supported a noneduca-tional service (*Ambroiggio* v. *Board of Education*, 1981).

Instructional programs appear at first glance to fall within this standard, because it prohibits fees for essential components of students' education. State constitutions or statutes governing education prohibit public schools from charging tuition for instructional programs during the academic year, other than for students who enroll out of district. In this case tuition charges offset differentials in local tax collections. Although charges have historically been permitted for summer school programs (*Washington* v. *Salisbury,* 1983), there are circumstances for which required fees may be challenged. The U. S. Court of Appeals for the Fifth Circuit ensured that year-round services would be available for students with disabilities. Otherwise, interrupted schooling would deny an appropriate education under what is now the Individuals with Disabilities Education Act (*Alamo Heights Independent School District* v. *State Board of Education,* 1986). A similar circumstance, discussed by Dayton and McCarthy (1992, p. 135), was posed in a challenge to the Kentucky State Department's demand that private school students pay for required summer remediation. The objection rested upon the 1990 Education Reform Act's mandate of free summer programs for students who do not pass minimum competency testing required for promotion.

Elective course fees are common. Whether such fees are permitted depends on how their educational goals are assessed. Although several decisions have upheld these fees (e.g., *Norton* v. *Board of Education,* 1976), a California review denied fees for any school-related course or extracurricular activity (*Hartzell* v. *Connell,* 1984). This decision concluded that under the state's constitution, "access to public education is a right enjoyed by all—not a commodity for sale" (p. 44), despite the financial pressures placed on districts following passage of Proposition 13.

Only eight states permit textbook fees: Alaska, Illinois, Indiana, Iowa, Kansas, Kentucky, Utah, and Wisconsin (Hamm & Crosser, 1991). Interpretations are mixed concerning the permissibility of charges for required textbooks. For example, *Cardiff* v. *Bismark Public School District* (1978) disallowed fees for textbooks in North Dakota. *Marshall* v. *School District* (1976), however, upheld a Colorado district's book fee but required financial assistance for indigent students.

Supplemental instructional materials such as workbooks, dictionaries, and paperback books have been treated differently from required textbooks; such charges are often permitted (e.g., *Sneed* v. *Greensboro Board of Education,* 1980). Other courts have held that all school textbooks and supplies are covered within the guarantees of free education (e.g., *Bond* v. *Ann Arbor School District,* 1970).

States generally do not consider extracurricular activities a necessary or integral part of educational programs. Twenty-three states assess fees for participation in clubs. Twenty-one states assess fees for athletic teams (Hamm & Crosser, 1991). In an early decision, the Supreme Court of Idaho disallowed a general fee assessed against all students—half of which supported extracurricular activities—but upheld a fee charged participants (*Paulson* v. *Minidoka County School District,* 1970). A Michigan Appeals Court permitted fees for interscholastic athletics, because these activities are not a fundamental part of the state's educational program and because a confidential waiver enabled indigent students to participate (*Attorney General* v. *East Jackson Public Schools,* 1985). One year before this ruling, the Hartzell (1984) decision denied schools the ability to assess fees for any activities.

Transportation fees may become more common as bus routes are extended to enable children to attend the schools of their choice outside neighborhoods and across district lines. In one of the few federal reviews of user fees, the U. S. Supreme Court narrowly (5–4 decision) upheld a North Dakota statute that permitted districts to charge a transportation fee (*Kadrmas* v. *Dickinson Public Schools,* 1988). Districts could waive fees for low-income families under the statute, but were not obligated to. The challenge claimed that students who were unable to pay the fee were deprived of minimum access to education, in violation of the Fourteenth Amendment's equal protection clause. Like the court's analysis in the *San Antonio* v. *Rodriguez* (1973) decision, which denied a similar argument relative to differing levels of overall finances among districts, the majority would not overturn the fee, since those who were deprived of transportation did not constitute a "suspect class," nor was there a fundamental right to education under the Constitution (see Chapter 11). Because the equal protection clause did not require free transportation, and because the state successfully defended the rational relationship between the statute and its goal of encouraging districts to provide bus service, the court permitted the fee.

State court decisions have also upheld districts' transportation fees. A Michigan court examined fees for busing to school in relation to a constitutional provision: "The legislature *may* provide for the transportation of students" (emphasis added). Interpreting this phrase to permit rather than mandate busing, the court upheld fees for this nonessential part of schooling (*Sutton* v. *Cadillac Area Public Schools,* 1982). The California Supreme Court found transportation to be a "supplemental service," unlike those activities that are a fundamental part of the education program, for which fees are not permitted. The court also denied an equal protection challenge, since the statute that permits transportation fees included an exemption for indigent students (*Arcadia* v. *Department of Education,* 1992).

User charges may be necessary to provide basic educational services or to extend extracurricular programs in districts having less money available from traditional state and local revenues. But families in these districts may be the least able to afford additional charges. These taxes are regressive in that they are not always determined by a family's ability to pay, nor are they adjusted by the number of children from a family paying fees. Furthermore, fees reflect in part the ability of communities and states to adequately fund schools. The same states with low per pupil expenditures are the ones that assess academic fees (Hamm & Crosser, 1991). Governments do not consider revenue from user charges in funding formulas. Nor do state legislatures oversee these charges. Thus, these fees may interfere with efforts to equalize financial support for schools in rich and poor districts.

Fee Waivers

In response to concerns about inequities when parents with differing abilities to pay are assessed the same charges, schools have created waiver and scholarship programs to encourage students from low-income families to participate in activities and elective courses. Total fee waivers and partial reductions through scholarships depend upon family income and family size, generally using the same criteria as those that define eligibility for free and reduced-price lunches.

There are conflicting judicial opinions in state courts about the legal status of fee waivers (Dayton & McCarthy, 1992). An adequate waiver policy, including assurances of confidentiality and a timely notice of benefits and procedures to parents, was a constitutional prerequisite for upholding fees in North Carolina (*Sneed* v. *Greensboro Board of Education,* 1980). In contrasting decisions, courts in several states, including California, denied waivers along with fees for constitutionally required education. The Hartzell (1984) decision, which denied any charge for public education programs, also found a "constitutional defect in such fees [that] can neither be corrected by providing waivers to indigent students, nor justified by pleading financial hardship" (p. 44). Local district policies may not be more restrictive than those of the state, according to a Utah court. The court disallowed a district's partial waiver of fees for books, materials, and activities. The state board's rules allowed assistance to anyone unable to pay fees (*Lorenc* v. *Call,* 1990).

Neutrality

The criterion of neutrality was presented in Chapter 4 as a consideration of social, economic, and other effects of taxation. Fees are often criticized for discouraging student participation in curricular and extracurricular activities. They diminish the education of those students who encounter fiscal barriers to opportunities for developing athletic, social, artistic, or other skills. Even with a system of waivers or scholarship assistance, disadvantaged students may feel diminished self-worth and other social stigmas that lead them to withdraw from participating in school programs. Indeed, fees may actually counter other societal efforts to create positive programs for youth in order that they may experience academic and athletic success and avoid gang-related or other disfunctional activities.

Charges may also create unnecessary negative responses from parents. Parents often view fees as imposing an unnecessary double tax. Financial gains must be considered in relation to the potential damages to a district's public-relations efforts and to diminished student participation.

Costs of Administration

The amount users pay must provide a sufficiently large yield to offset some portion of the services provided. The smaller the charge in relation to program costs, the larger the burden on the general fund or other revenue to provide the activity and pay the expenses entailed in collecting the fee. However, larger fees may increase the likelihood that students will avoid the activity, raise costs of collection, and diminish public and student support of school activities.

There are administrative difficulties in overseeing both the compliance of those expected to pay fees and the waiver policies (Brown & Bouman, 1994). Hidden costs of enforcement may appear in different forms as teachers delay activities, coaches deny practice sessions or participation in games, students are not permitted to register, principals contact parents, and office personnel send reminders and withhold report cards and transcripts. Collections may become a discipline problem if students see fees as a focus for rebellion against authority. The waiver policy itself adds another set of administrative costs and problems in advertising its benefits and procedures to parents, monitoring who qualifies, maintaining confidentiality of those who are granted waivers, and defending it to those who do not qualify.

Because of these additional costs of relying on user fees to support activities, schools may seek assistance for the expansion of programs from businesses and other donors. Later in this chapter,

we explore opportunities for schools to obtain resources through partnership activities. We now turn to ways in which schools and districts supplement traditional revenue by way of interest earnings and loans.

MANAGING CASH FLOW THROUGH INVESTMENTS AND BORROWING

The financing of school systems introduces large amounts of monies on a monthly and annual basis. Wise investment decisions lead to high yields of interest earnings when funds accumulate before expenditures are due. At other times, it is necessary to borrow funds. This may happen when anticipated revenue from local taxes or state and federal aid is delayed or is not sufficient to meet current expenditures. The first of these cash flow problems brings opportunities for investing school resources. The second makes borrowing necessary.

Nonrevenue receipts, including short-term loans and long-term bond issues (see discussion of capital outlay), do not constitute additional new monies for schools. This is because the amount borrowed plus interest must be repaid in time from anticipated revenue. Nonrevenue receipts differ from revenue receipts, which generate monies through taxes, federal and state aid payments, gifts, investment earnings, and tuition and fees. Nonrevenue monies are important to school systems because they enable finance officers to maintain an even flow of district funds to meet payrolls, payments to vendors, and other expenditures on schedule. They also constitute a growing debt owed by school districts. They amounted to $63.7 billion in 1990–1991, including $60.5 billion in outstanding long-term debt (i.e., for more than one year) and $3.2 billion in short-term debt (U. S. Department of Commerce, 1993, p. 21). The total debt was nearly double that outstanding in 1985–1986 ($37.7 billion).

Investments of District and School Funds

School districts, particularly fiscally independent districts, expand their resources by investing revenue and nonrevenue money. Schools have traditionally been able to invest funds in interest-bearing accounts to acquire additional monies for student organizations. They are investing larger amounts of monies within the control of administrators and teachers under school-site management.

Large revenue payments, especially proceeds from the property tax, are concentrated at one time of the year. Operating expenditures, however, are more evenly distributed. For example, most districts' fiscal years are from July 1 to June 30, giving benefits from property tax collections during the summer and early fall (Candoli et al., 1984, pp. 389–390). Borrowing is minimized, since money is collected early in the budget year. And a large amount of idle cash can be invested for a long period. Tax collections, state and federal aid payments, proceeds from bond issues or bond anticipation notes, and monies carried forward from one year to the next all create large cash balances and opportunities to generate additional revenue through investment in short-term bank deposits or in long-term government notes and other securities.

Investments in the form of cash deposits and securities are presented by state in Table 7.1. The state with the highest amount of holdings was Illinois in 1990–1991 (over $7 billion), outpacing California and Texas, which had the largest portfolios in 1985–1986. Rhode Island school districts had minimal investments. This table reports very small investments in Alaska, the District of Columbia, Hawaii, Maryland, North Carolina, and Virginia. However, these latter districts are financially dependent on other units of government, which may manage large investment portfolios for their school systems. The total indicated for these three school years reveals rapid growth in investments. It more than doubled from $14.9 to $29.6 billion in the eight-year period from 1977–1978 to 1985–1986 and more than tripled, to a total of $50.9 billion, by 1990–1991. Investments in twelve states grew by more than 100 percent during the recent five-year period; the national total increased by 72 percent. In comparison with the three states in which investments had declined between

1977–1978 and 1985–1986, there were seven states in which districts invested less in 1990–1991 than in 1985–1986.

Investments are an important part of *cash management.* Dembowski and Davey (1986) defined "cash management" as "the process of managing the moneys of a school district to ensure maximum cash availability and maximum yield on investments" (p. 237). The goals of monitoring cash flow include (1) *safety,* protecting the school district's assets against loss; (2) *liquidity,* the ability to convert investments to cash without such penalties as the loss of interest, so there is sufficient money available to meet daily needs; and (3) *yield,* earning the maximum return on investments. These goals may conflict. This happens when longer terms to maturity give higher interest and yield, but the lost liquidity may necessitate short-term loans to cover expenses. Similarly, some degree of risk may yield higher interest, but the safety of the public's money may be jeopardized. The failure of the Orange County, California, investment pool in 1994, for example, threatened nearly $1 billion of twenty-seven school districts' operating revenue. Counties maintain district investments in this state, and some of these districts had previously taken low-interest loans to increase the amount invested in the higher-yield fund. The county borrowed extensively to triple its investments and buy less secure derivatives. This aggressive investment strategy was partially blamed for the fund's collapse and for the county's filing for bankruptcy protection (Lindsay, 1994).

The way districts manage their cash flow also contributes to several important nonfinancial goals. Sound financial management builds trust and goodwill within the taxpaying and business community, promotes favorable business relationships with vendors and banks, and ensures the orderly conduct of the financial aspects of district operations (Dembowski, 1986). There are legal and ethical considerations, and careful cash flow strategies diminish the potential for charges of embezzlement and graft. The public visibility of spending and investment decisions compels personnel to follow procedures in law, including any limitations placed on invest-

TABLE 7.1. Cash and Security Holdings of Public School Systems[a] (in millions of dollars)

State	1977–78	1985–86	1990–91	Percentage Increase (Decrease) from 1985–86 to 1990–91
Alabama	98.7	220.9	299.6	35.6
Alaska	b	b	c	NA
Arizona	353.7	741.9	925.6	24.8
Arkansas	120.5	238.1	266.5	11.9
California	1,725.0	3,223.6	5,302.0	60.4
Colorado	342.8	615.9	1,524.8	147.6
Connecticut	8.0	3.8	20.6	442.1
Delaware	3.5	13.0	16.0	23.1
District of Columbia	b	b	c	NA
Florida	726.9	1,761.5	3,216.3	82.6
Georgia	326.3	656.2	1,776.2	170.7
Hawaii	b	b	c	NA
Idaho	44.4	107.3	153.8	43.3
Illinois	1,338.4	2,449.5	7,025.8	186.8
Indiana	458.6	559.9	635.4	13.5
Iowa	205.7	281.4	536.6	90.7
Kansas	293.0	561.1	802.1	43.0
Kentucky	82.1	181.8	161.4	(11.2)
Louisiana	315.9	851.2	885.5	4.0
Maine	7.2	55.2	53.9	(2.4)
Maryland	b	b	3.7	NA
Massachusetts	58.2	67.7	96.7	42.8
Michigan	947.4	1,375.6	2,785.1	102.5
Minnesota	490.9	830.4	2,018.2	143.0
Mississippi	92.9	225.8	276.1	22.3
Missouri	353.3	563.6	1,734.9	207.8
Montana	171.0	149.3	307.9	106.2
Nebraska	164.2	318.0	778.0	144.7
Nevada	15.9	137.0	612.9	347.4
New Hampshire	11.7	36.5	59.5	63.0
New Jersey	346.2	610.7	968.1	58.5
New Mexico	60.8	189.1	278.6	47.3
New York	550.1	1,540.1	2,905.4	88.7
North Carolina	b	b	4.0	NA
North Dakota	47.7	180.2	156.3	(13.3)
Ohio	1,013.3	1,006.2	1,764.3	75.3
Oklahoma	245.0	698.5	640.0	(8.4)
Oregon	325.7	360.0	406.5	12.9
Pennsylvania	721.9	1,489.7	3,172.9	113.0
Rhode Island	0.1	0.8	—	NA

TABLE 7.1. Cash and Security Holdings of Public School Systems[a] (in millions of dollars) (*Continued*)

State	1977–78	1985–86	1990–91	Percentage Increase (Decrease) from 1985–86 to 1990–91
South Carolina	145.4	280.1	418.2	49.3
South Dakota	75.7	120.8	170.3	41.0
Tennessee	7.8	8.5	19.5	129.4
Texas	1,356.3	4,243.6	4,615.0	8.8
Utah	183.5	302.1	93.9	(68.9)
Vermont	18.4	67.8	68.7	1.3
Virginia	b	b	c	NA
Washington	392.4	875.4	1,313.2	50.0
West Virginia	186.1	322.9	296.7	(8.1)
Wisconsin	337.0	776.5	1,121.7	44.5
Wyoming	80.5	279.1	220.4	(21.0)
Total	14,850.2	29,614.9	50,908.8	71.9

[a]Holdings of retirement funds are excluded.
[b]Holdings of dependent school systems are not reported.
[c]Zero or rounds to zero.
NA = not available.
SOURCE: U. S. Department of Commerce, Bureau of the Census (1980). *Finances of Public School Systems in 1977–78,* Series GF/78-10, Washington, DC: U. S. Government Printing Office, p. 12; U. S. Department of Commerce, Bureau of the Census [1988]. *Finances of Public School Systems in 1985–86,* Series GF/86-10, Washington, DC: U. S. Government Printing Office, p. 10; U. S. Department of Commerce, Bureau of the Census (1993). *Public Education Finances: 1990–91,* Series GF/91-10, Washington, DC: U. S. Government Printing Office, p. 12.

ments (Candoli et al., 1984, p. 48). For example, many states require collateral (e.g., FDIC [Federal Deposit Insurance Corporation] insurance on the first $100,000 of deposits) for school investments, but banks pay lower interest rates when they must maintain assets as collateral rather than diverting them to more lucrative purposes (Dembowski & Davey, 1986). Finance officers exercise caution when proposed interest rates are higher than anticipated, perhaps signaling that a bidder may be on the brink of insolvency and needs to attract investors.

Several short- and long-term investment strategies are available to school districts. Savings accounts offer the advantage of immediate liquidity. Withdrawals are possible without prior notification and interest is earned on a daily basis. However, interest earnings are lower from savings than other investments. Interest on money market accounts fluctuates with economic conditions, offering opportunities to improve yield during periods when interest rates are rising. There may, however, be limits on the number of withdrawals each month, so money market accounts are less flexible than ordinary savings accounts. Certificates of deposit also offer security but with higher interest earnings. Interest rates increase as the term lengthens for deposits. Districts gain investment flexibility when they coordinate investment terms (between one week and one year) with projected dates for expenditures. Early withdrawals bring a penalty of lost interest, making these investments less liquid.

United States government securities are among the safest long-term investments. Treasury bills offer districts high security and liquidity. The government guarantees these investments. They are sold at a discount from the stated face values. The full value of bills is paid at maturity; the difference represents the interest earned by the investor. Treasury bills have the advantage that they are liquid, because there is a strong and receptive secondary market. Other investors will purchase them on the open market before they are mature. Thus, a school district may liquidate when necessary.

Investments in federal agency securities offer similar safety. These, however, are not legal obligations of the government. For example, the Federal Land Bank, the Federal Home Loan Bank, the Banks for Cooperatives, the Federal Intermediate Credit Bank, and the Federal National Mortgage Association offer higher yield than Treasury securities because of their low marketability.

Districts may enter into repurchase agreements, referred to as "repos," to earn relatively large returns in a short period. They purchase Treasury bills or other government securities under an agreement to sell them back to the issuing bank in the future. This strategy gives districts the opportunity to invest idle funds in a safe, high-yield investment for as short a period as one day.

A cash-flow schedule (Dembowski & Davey, 1986, p. 240) tracks incoming revenue and outgoing expenditures to help district- or school-level personnel plan the most productive cash management strategy. They invest deposits as soon as they receive them. Today's electronic transfers of funds speed transactions, especially for the deposit of large state and federal aid payments. Disbursements are timed to remove cash from district and school accounts as close as possible to when payments are owed to vendors. When checking and savings accounts are maintained with a balance only large enough to meet current expenses, cash resources of separate funds can be pooled to yield potentially higher earnings from longer-term investments that require large deposits.

Such pooling is common in districts that allocate monies to the control of individual buildings. Investments are centralized, and the interest gained by pooled investments is dispersed to individual accounts in the same proportion as the original contributions. Small school districts may gain similar advantages from pooling investment funds. They may do this through a Board of Cooperative Services or another form of intermediate unit of government, in order to maximize yield and minimize paperwork for finance officers.

Obtaining Loans to Cover Shortfalls

Sound financial management often relies on short-term loans to meet current obligations before receiving anticipated funds. By borrowing, districts can avoid such potentially severe consequences as disruptions in school operations, increased costs of their future purchases of needed materials as suppliers' faith in prompt payment declines, and the deteriorated morale of their employees as payrolls and scheduled acquisitions of supplies are delayed. Short-term loans are limited to the amount of future revenue due to the district. Repayment is generally scheduled to occur within the fiscal year during which the district collects taxes or aid payments.

Several mechanisms are available to ease an interim cash deficit (Dembowski & Davey, 1986). *Revenue anticipation notes* permit districts to borrow against future revenues other than property taxes (e.g., the intergovernmental transfers discussed in Chapter 8). *Tax anticipation notes* bring needed money to meet general operating expenses before actually receiving property or local income taxes. A *budget note* that raises funds to assist with an unforeseeable emergency is repaid during the following fiscal year. *Bond anticipation notes* enable districts to initiate a construction project or obtain buses or other equipment before issuing bonds following voter approval. Entering into this long-term debt to finance capital outlay is the subject of the next section.

FINANCING CAPITAL OUTLAY

School systems require more funds than they typically have at their disposal in order to construct new facilities, renovate older buildings, and purchase buses and large equipment. Many districts would find it difficult to proceed with large projects without having authority to issue bonds to spread payments over a long period. At the same time, states regulate borrowing to ensure responsible use of this debt. They thus prevent districts from defaulting on obligations or incurring large, long-term deficits.

Capital outlay funds repay the principal and interest necessary to retire bonds that are issued to finance buildings and equipment that have useful lives extending beyond a single school year. Although systems may allocate capital outlay funds within their annual budgets to make small equipment purchases, they generally finance major projects through other sources. The local property tax base has traditionally been burdened with the repayment of the resulting long-term debt. "Long-term debt" is defined to include debt payable more than one year after the date of issue. Despite the increased reliance upon state revenue for financing annual school operations, only a few states assume responsibility for constructing the facilities within which school personnel deliver programs.

This burden on school districts is reflected in the previously cited amount of total outstanding debt in 1990–1991. Long-term debt ($60.5 billion), which includes principal and interest, made up a large proportion (95%) of the total debt owed. Districts also incurred $12.8 billion in new long-term debt, and were able to retire $5.8 billion in previously issued bonds, during 1990–1991 (U. S. Department of Commerce, 1993, p. 21). The amount of new debt is sizeable, in comparison with the long-term debt issued in 1985–1986 ($8.3 billion) or during 1977–1978 ($3 billion). The amount of debt retired doubled between these years, from $3.1 billion to $6.1 billion (U. S. Department of

Commerce, 1980, p. 12; 1988, p. 10). The growth in debt that districts assumed reflects an increase in the number of construction projects as well as larger construction costs and higher interest rates in recent years.

Districts derive funds to meet capital outlay needs primarily through state and local governments. The burden for financing elementary and secondary school construction in 1990–1991 fell most heavily on local governments. Local governments funded nearly all (98%) of the total $19.8 billion spent throughout the country (see Table 7.2). Fiscally independent school districts assumed the bulk of capital outlay costs (81% of the total). Other school systems derived funds through county, municipal, or special district governments. State legislatures contributed $428 million for capital outlay, including $374 million toward construction of facilities. The growth in this aspect of school finance is evident in the rise—from 5.0 percent in 1986–1987 to 6.4 percent in 1991–1992—in the proportion of all state and local expenditures for elementary and secondary schools that was devoted to capital outlay (U. S. Department of Commerce, 1993, p. 2). A very limited amount of federal capital outlay funds is allocated for elementary and secondary education annually. These funds primarily support school construction for areas impacted by military installations and Native American reservations (see Chapter 10).

TABLE 7.2. **State and Local Government Expenditures for Capital Outlay for Elementary and Secondary Education, 1990–1991 (in millions of dollars)**

	Total	Construction of Facilities	Other Capital Outlay
State government	428	374	54
Local governments	19,424	11,988	7,436
County	1,584	1,233	351
Municipal	1,444	1,228	216
Township	358	287	71
School district	16,009	9,212	6,797
Special district	29	28	1
Total state and local	19,852	12,363	7,489

SOURCE: U. S. Department of Commerce, Bureau of the Census (1993). *Public Education Finances: 1990–91,* Series GF/91-10. Washington, DC: U. S. Government Printing Office, Table 1, p. 2.

TABLE 7.3. Elementary and Secondary Expenditures for Capital Outlay, 1990–1991 (per pupil in dollars; others in thousands of dollars)

State	Construction	Equipment	Land and Existing Structures	Total	Per Pupil
Alabama	144,817	41,821	6,728	193,366	268
Alaska	68,776	11,142	2,618	82,563	725
Arizona	448,313	66,956	9,457	524,726	820
Arkansas	60,235	46,546	1,791	108,572	249
California	1,280,458	490,941	440,821	2,212,220	447
Colorado	224,452	72,333	3,646	300,431	523
Connecticut	—	37,751	6,218	43,969	94
Delaware	15,106	9,514	407	25,027	251
District of Columbia	30,855	17,662	—	48,517	601
Florida	991,134	289,606	418,511	1,699,251	913
Georgia	19,933	164,838	406,131	590,902	513
Hawaii	103,273	26,085	777	130,135	758
Idaho	66,361	18,800	—	85,161	386
Illinois	355,822	295,259	—	651,081	357
Indiana	280,364	160,257	22,495	463,134	485
Iowa	104,417	49,782	34,622	188,821	390
Kansas	53,593	69,889	5,889	129,371	296
Kentucky	35,907	85,162	10,793	131,862	207
Louisiana	54,195	53,938	66,068	174,201	222
Maine	62,071	50,439	28,153	140,663	652
Maryland	266,914	71,314	3,567	341,795	478
Massachusetts	239,759	32,330	—	272,089	326
Michigan	386,341	345,809	12,645	744,795	471
Minnesota	168,663	124,257	143,684	436,604	577
Mississippi	58,661	40,818	—	99,479	197
Missouri	322,261	106,857	38,322	467,440	575
Montana	18,620	28,274	422	47,316	309
Nebraska	79,731	39,293	3,856	122,880	448
Nevada	298,805	31,082	—	329,887	1639
New Hampshire	59,303	12,084	14,268	85,655	496
New Jersey	229,582	141,478	52,990	424,050	379
New Mexico	128,656	8,857	959	138,472	459
New York	838,099	274,851	33,480	1,146,430	441
North Carolina	465,498	86,629	—	552,127	508
North Dakota	8,278	11,295	—	19,573	166
Ohio	270,513	123,186	29,560	423,259	239
Oklahoma	157,414	89,090	37,278	283,782	490
Oregon	17,301	4,673	78,446	100,420	207
Pennsylvania	823,835	134,312	4,795	962,942	577
Rhode Island	472	10,646	2,779	13,897	100
South Carolina	231,448	73,970	2,536	307,954	495
South Dakota	16,651	10,319	113	27,083	210
Tennessee	127,500	61,304	4,025	192,829	234

TABLE 7.3. Elementary and Secondary Expenditures for Capital Outlay, 1990–1991 (per pupil in dollars; others in thousands of dollars) (*Continued*)

State	Construction	Equipment	Land and Existing Structures	Total	Per Pupil
Texas	284,131	366,289	553,005	1,203,425	356
Utah	68,849	55,300	6,344	130,493	291
Vermont	12,748	8,144	2,191	23,083	241
Virginia	471,366	126,818	25,540	623,724	625
Washington	498,508	177,690	64,695	740,893	882
West Virginia	39,437	35,418	17,346	92,201	286
Wisconsin	137,559	138,587	2,837	278,983	350
Wyoming	26,228	22,835	105	49,168	501
Total	11,153,213	4,852,548	2,600,913	18,606,674	451

Note: — zero or rounds to zero.

SOURCE: U.S. Department of Commerce, Bureau of the Census (1993). *Public Education Finances: 1990–91,* Series GF/91-10. Washington, DC: U. S. Government Printing Office, Tables 11, 12, pp. 17–19.

Table 7.3 presents greater detail on expenditures for capital outlay projects by elementary and secondary school systems during the 1990–1991 school year. Of the $18.6 billion spent across the nation, the largest proportion (60 percent) was devoted to constructing new facilities, including additions and site improvements. Another 26 percent went for purchases of equipment such as motor vehicles and office machines having a life expectancy of more than five years. Another 14 percent was used to acquire land and existing structures. Per pupil expenditures for capital outlay varied widely. They ranged from $94 in Connecticut, where there was negligible new construction, to $1,639 in Nevada, which has experienced rapid growth in student enrollments. Population has shifted among states. These shifts help explain the large per pupil expenditures in Arizona, Florida, and Nevada relative to lower costs in Connecticut, Rhode Island, and the Dakotas. Varying costs of construction may also account for relatively high expenditures in Alaska and Hawaii and for lower per pupil expenditures in southern states, including Kentucky, Louisiana, and Mississippi.

Despite this large and growing outlay of funds for facilities, schools in many communities are inadequate and need extensive renovation for twenty-first-century needs. A survey of facility needs by the American Association of School Administrators (Hansen, 1991) revealed that one-third of currently used schools were built before World War II. Another 43 percent were built during the expanding enrollment years of the 1950s and 1960s. Relatively few were built in the 1970s (14%) and between 1980 and 1993 (11%). About 13 percent of schools had poor learning environments. An earlier survey found that the condition of a quarter of schools was inadequate, 61 percent required major repairs, 43 percent had uncorrected environmental hazards, and more than 13 percent were structurally unsound (Education Writers Association, 1989).

Based on a sample of school officials throughout the nation, the United States General Accounting Office (GAO) (1995a) estimated that one-third of schools needed extensive repair or replacement, and that about $112 billion was required to upgrade school facilities to a "good" overall condition. Of this amount, $11 billion would help districts comply with prior federal mandates that required districts to make all programs accessible to students with disabilities and to remove or correct hazardous substances such as asbestos, lead in water or paint, materials in underground storage tanks, and radon. A subsequent GAO survey revealed that most schools do not fully use modern technology. About 40 percent of schools do not meet requirements of laboratory science even moderately well. Over one-half do not have the flexibility to implement many effective teaching strategies. And two-thirds are not equipped to meet requirements of before- or after-school care or day care (U. S. General Accounting Office, 1995b). This report also observed: "Overall, schools in central cities and schools with a 50-percent or more minority population were more likely to have more insufficient technology elements and a greater number of unsatisfactory environmental conditions—particularly lighting and physical security—than other schools" (p. 2).

The poor condition of the nation's schools may reflect the unwillingness of voters to invest in this aspect of public education. Alternatively, the inadequacy may result from the traditional methods of financing capital outlay. These have placed a heavy burden on local resources. The methods include pay-as-you-go plans, sinking funds to save for future construction projects, and issuing long-term bonds to finance projects over a period of years. Some states make loans available or assume costs partially or fully. Other approaches to acquiring needed facilities include assessing fees on developers of new housing, lease purchasing, and joint venturing. The following methods of financing capital outlay are discussed in greater detail by Ortiz (1994, pp. 38–45) and Thompson, Wood, and Honeyman (1994, pp. 558–573).

Current Revenue and Construction Funds

Districts in fifteen states receive no state-level assistance for capital outlay. Even in those states that do provide a portion of funds, localities typically pay the larger share of projects (Education Writers Association, 1989). Major projects are rarely paid from current revenue receipts. This is because of their large costs and the many other demands on annual budgets. It is possible only in

the wealthiest and largest school districts. This pay-as-you-go approach offers the advantages of avoiding interest costs and discouraging districts from making the extravagant facility improvements they might make if state allocations financed the full cost of projects. However, this approach makes large increases in property tax rates necessary in most districts in order to meet such expenditures as they are incurred. And districts must turn to saving or borrowing to keep tax rates more consistent from year to year.

"Construction" or "sinking" funds are special accounts created for accumulating reserves over a period of time in anticipation of future construction needs. Some states permit such funds. These savings accrue interest to expand the reserves even more; they encourage long-range planning for future needs as the reserves grow. The advantage of this approach is that districts accrue interest on the sinking fund and eliminate the large interest costs associated with borrowing. However, savings may not be adequate for financing remodeling of facilities or new construction as schools age or for purchasing enough buses when population grows. In addition, school boards and taxpayers are reluctant to pledge funds for uncertain future projects. This is especially true when districts do not meet current instructional needs, or when school board elections or administrative appointments alter the priorities for the use of funds.

The Issuance of Bonds

Rather than delay improvements until savings accrue, districts may sell bonds to make funds available for specific projects when they are needed. Several advantages of this form of borrowing offset the additional cost of a project due to the interest that must be paid to investors. First, the debt created is paid by the actual users in future years, consistent with the benefits-received principle discussed in Chapter 4. Otherwise it would have been paid out of taxes put into a sinking fund over a period of years before the project was begun. Second, facilities that are constructed at today's costs may actually bring savings to the district.

This is because the low-interest bonds are paid with future tax revenue, which is generally worth less because of inflation.

Districts raise over 75 percent of capital outlays to finance improvements at the local level by issuing bonds (Ortiz, 1994, p. 40). Salmon and Thomas (1981) define a *bond* as a "written financial instrument issued by a corporate body to borrow money with the time and rate of interest, method of principal repayment, and the term of debt clearly expressed" (p. 91). State statutes enable school districts and other public entities to incur debt which they pay either by future gate receipts (as may be the case for sports facilities) or by anticipated property tax revenue. Unlike home mortgages and other forms of long-term debt that rely upon the property itself as collateral, *general obligation bonds* are secured by a public entity's pledge of its "full faith and credit." Because they obligate the district, or in some cases the state, to raise taxes for repayment, and because debt obligations often have the first claim on state aid, there is little fear that the district will default on future payments. Furthermore, because the interest earned from investments on public projects is exempt from federal and state income taxation, these school district bonds are attractive to investors.

Governing boards, in the case of fiscally dependent school districts, or school district voters, in the case of fiscally independent districts (see Chapter 3 for definition), decide whether or not to issue bonds and to levy property taxes for a fixed term to pay the principal and interest. Some states conduct school bond sales themselves to take advantage of their stronger taxing power and credit rating. In this way they obtain even lower interest rates. In these cases, local districts may petition the state to participate in bond sales after voters approve of a project. Or the state may assume liability for all local bond debt (Thompson, Wood, & Honeyman, 1994, p. 568).

Bonds are marketed through a competitive bid process to bond underwriters. The underwriters in turn make them available to investors. Municipal and school district bonds are marketed at substantially reduced interest rates. The rates are low because of their high security and because the interest paid to bond holders is tax exempt, as was noted previously. On the other hand, taxes must be paid on loans to finance commercial construction projects. The cost of public sector capital projects is thus reduced. Those school districts with excellent credit ratings are further advantaged because they can market bonds at very low interest rates. Professional bond rating companies, such as Moody's Investor Service and Standard and Poor's, consider such factors as local property valuation, outstanding debt, current tax rates, and enrollment trends in informing potential investors about the relative security of a bond issue. A prospectus (Wood, 1986, pp. 568–583) communicates to the financial community the purpose of the bond issue; the type and denomination of the bond issue; full disclosure of the financial condition of the district, including outstanding debt; any pending litigation that may affect the bond sale; and other information about the school district. This information, prepared by the bond underwriter, as well as the current national economy, influences the actual interest rates paid to investors (Education Writers Association, 1989, p. 31).

Serial bonds are the most common form for financing school construction. They structure repayment so that a portion of the debt is retired on periodic (e.g., annual) maturity dates; the total debt is paid over the period of issue (e.g., 10, 20, or 30 years). Interest rates are lower for short amortization periods than for long ones. Investors and school districts alike are cautious about defining interest rates over a long period. They are cautious because fluctuations in the economy may mean either sharply lowered return for investors or excessive interest payments for districts. Districts less often use *term bonds*. Term bonds specify a particular date on which the principal and interest are due.

Callable bonds include provisions under which bonds can be reissued after a specified period of years. These bonds offer districts the opportunity to take advantage of lower interest rates in the future. Noncallable bonds protect the investor and thus carry more favorable rates. But with noncallable bonds districts are unable to control the amount of interest paid as the economy fluctuates. Callable bonds are most likely to be considered when interest rates are relatively high. Even when a school district appears to be saddled with a high interest rate on a noncallable bond issue, advanced refunding may offer the potential of lowering the total net cost of borrowing. Advanced refunding is not legal in some states. In this mechanism, new bonds are issued at a lower interest rate and funds are invested with maturity just before the original bond issue's payment date.

Issuing bonds is primarily a local mechanism for raising capital outlay funds. States, however, regulate the use of monies and the bonding process itself. Districts borrow funds to acquire land and construct new facilities, to make additions to or remodel existing buildings, and to purchase equipment; but these funds may not be diverted to school operations. Once a school board has approved plans for construction and (in most cases) received clearance from the state to proceed, it releases a public notice about the project and an open hearing is held. In fiscally independent school districts, a referendum may be required to authorize the borrowing of money and the repayment of bonds by a tax rate increase. The nature of bonds to be issued is also regulated by the state. Regulations specify acceptable types of bonds, lengths of time to maturity, and maximum interest rates.

States may specify the maximum amount of debt that can be incurred by local governments. A *debt ceiling* is often imposed to prohibit school districts from overcommitting their tax bases and to ensure favorable credit ratings in the future. The ceiling may take the form of a maximum tax rate to raise capital outlay funds or a given proportion (e.g., 6 percent) of property valuation (see Chapter 6). Many poor districts are unable to meet capital outlay needs because their limited bonding capacity restricts the amount they can raise for construction of facilities and remodeling. Debt ceilings allow wealthier districts to raise more funds through bond issues than less wealthy districts, even though these restrictions bear no relationship to districts' needs (Augenblick, 1977, p. 12).

A California statute permits school districts to create "tax districts" as a way to raise school construction funds. Tax districts encompass only unoccupied land. The landowner is often a developer who desires schools and other infrastructure. The landowner's approval for tax increases is needed but not that of two-thirds of voters, as is required for a traditional bond issue. The danger of this strategy is clear in the inability of an Orange County school district (whose operating revenue was also jeopardized in the failure of the county investment fund discussed previously) to recover money invested in a failed life insurance company (Lindsay, 1995).

State Loans and Grants in Aid

Whereas state courts and legislatures have been concerned about equalizing disparities in per pupil revenues for school operations (see discussions in Chapters 8 and 11), they have not demanded policies to ease the large inequities in facilities that result from the heavy reliance on local tax bases to finance capital outlay. Loans and direct grants have provided some state-level assistance. But the funds appropriated have not been sufficient to meet capital needs.

Localities can create a pool of state funds from which loans can be made for approved projects without needing to market bonds. Loans of state money enable many communities to have sufficient facilities despite debt ceilings that would otherwise limit available funds. Loan funds are derived from reserves in retirement programs, direct legislative appropriations, permanent funds set aside with interest used for this purpose, or state-level borrowing. Salmon et al. (1988, p. 9) reported seven states that make low-interest loans available to districts. The Education Writers Association (1989, p. 27) listed five states.

The use of loans that require repayment is thus limited. In contrast, the majority of state legislatures appropriate capital outlay funds and distribute them according to such measures of need as the cost of approved projects, the number of students or instructional units, fiscal capacity, or tax effort. Only Hawaii assumes complete support of capital outlay. Full state financing has limitations in that local control over decisions is lost, and project approval and funding restrictions constrain states' abilities to meet all their needs for facilities (Augenblick, 1977, pp. 7–8; Salmon & Thomas, 1981, p. 96). Many states have adopted an approach to helping finance school construction that is sensitive to the varying fiscal abilities of districts. A majority of states providing partial assistance do so according to a foundation or percentage-equalizing formula (see Chapter 8) that takes into account local property valuations and, in some cases, tax effort (Gold, Smith, & Lawton, 1995, pp. 48–52).

Several states permit public corporations to be formed for financing capital improvements. Building authorities were first created in the early 1900s to circumvent debt restrictions of municipalities and school districts. They are subject to their own taxing and debt limitations. Camp and Salmon (1985) reported that as many as nineteen states have experimented with building authorities. But they continue to operate at either state or local levels in only eight states. For example, New York City's Educational Construction Fund represents an innovative local approach to financing school facilities for large cities. This authority constructs buildings on school-owned land. But schools occupy only portions of the facilities, and the rental of the remaining space to businesses pays the debt. Four states operate bond banks (Education Writers Association, 1989, p. 27) to consolidate bond issues, as was described previously. They thus take advantage of lower interest rates than would be available for individual district projects. Camp and Salmon (1985) suggested that multicounty public authorities and regional bond banks may offer financial advantages and economies of scale that are similar to those gained by cooperatives for delivering educational services.

A larger state role in financing capital outlay offers a number of advantages. When poorer districts can access broader-based tax revenue for expanding and improving facilities, there is greater equalization of educational opportunities. School districts realize savings in debt service costs. This is true whether districts issue bonds using states' higher credit ratings or there are direct grants without borrowing. Furthermore, guidelines and standards for approval of projects to receive state funding often outline cost-effective construction practices, influence the design and location of school buildings, and contribute to energy conservation (Johns et al., 1983, p. 286; King & MacPhail-Wilcox, 1988).

On the other hand, a larger state role has disadvantages. For one thing, when power and control become more centralized, local citizens may support public education less. If facility designs and functions become uniform across a state, innovation and the recognition of unique local needs may be inhibited. Finally, there may be delays in addressing locally expressed needs, given the intense competition for resources at the state level (Salmon & Thomas, 1981, p. 96).

Developers' Fees, Lease Purchase, and Joint Venturing

Ortiz (1994) described several other mechanisms for expanding local resources to meet facility needs. Suburban districts—primarily in rapidly growing areas of California, Colorado, and Florida—assess an *impact fee* directly on developers of new housing and businesses. This approach differs from general property taxation throughout the district, since it places a portion of the burden (from 10 to 15 percent of construction costs) for financing new buildings and expanded services on developers as building permits are approved. These privilege-based taxes are ultimately shifted to residents or owners of commercial buildings who will benefit most directly from economic development in rapidly growing communities. As attractive as impact fees are to citizens who desire to shift this burden, Bauman (1995) warns school officials to prepare for greater scrutiny from the community and business leaders who are most affected by the fees.

Lease purchasing is a form of borrowing that has been used for many years to construct facilities for institutions that cannot incur debt (e.g., Boards of Cooperative Educational Services) and to acquire large equipment and portable classroom buildings. An underwriter generally sells leases to investors, and the district uses the proceeds to acquire needed equipment. *Joint venturing* can use many of the previously discussed forms of financing to bring several government or private agencies together with school districts, who acquire or construct, then share, facilities. Joint occupancy arrangements with other public entities maximize facility use and reduce construction costs. In particular, recreation facilities such as swimming pools and tennis courts are often constructed in concert with municipalities and senior citizens' organizations.

In the future communities will increasingly need capital outlay funds to replace or expand facilities. This is particularly true in rapidly growing communities. Other districts will remodel or close older buildings as they deteriorate. Those school systems experiencing declining enrollments will sell or convert underused buildings for other purposes. Public school facilities will increasingly house early childhood and prekindergarten activities, before- and after-school programs for students, and continuing education and community college classes for adults during evenings and weekends. Restructured elementary, middle-grades, and secondary organizational patterns, as well as new uses of instructional and information technologies (see Chapter 17), will also create pressures for remodeled buildings or for very different original construction. Localities will respond to these demands with increased taxes, calls for state assistance, impact fees, or other finance mechanisms.

PARTNERSHIPS, FOUNDATIONS, AND VOLUNTARISM

Schools have historically relied on private resources to supplement public monies. Citizens, students' parents in particular, once contributed substantial time, talent, and money through tuition and special fees, fund-raising social activities,

direct donations, and volunteer time. However, individuals and the private sector became less involved in building the resource base, other than through property taxation, in many districts during the 1960s and 1970s, for several reasons. Changes in family structures and priorities for the use of time meant fewer hours to devote to school activities. Rapidly expanding communities and centralized school systems created large distances and altered relationships between parents and school personnel. A larger and more specialized profession displaced volunteers, and states assumed a greater share of the responsibility for financing public education.

New attitudes encouraging greater privatization and entrepreneurship within public education have developed in recent years. Tax limitation efforts in many states threatened to reduce local revenue. These efforts stimulated schools to turn once again to private sources of human and monetary inputs. The private sector was concerned about economic growth and international competitiveness. It encouraged school districts to involve businesses and communities not only in acquiring resources but also in planning future educational structures and learning. The changing role of private sector businesses in supporting and even managing public schools was discussed in Chapter 3 in the context of the educational reform movement of the past several decades.

Individuals have enriched schools or financed broader reform efforts through donations and through challenge grants, which require recipients to raise matching funds. In 1990, Ross Perot's $500,000 challenge grant stimulated other fundraising to support Teach for America and its recruitment of college graduates into the profession. The largest private gift ever to public education was Walter Annenberg's $500 million pledge in 1994. A portion of this gift was in the form of challenge grants to attract matching public and private investments for school reform efforts through the New American Schools Development Corporation, the Education Commission of the States, the Annenberg Institute for School Reform at Brown University, and several of the nation's largest urban school districts (Annenberg Institute for School Reform, 1995).

In the early years of the recent movement to form partnerships, the private sector and public schools forged adopt-a-school programs. Corporations lent executives to improve school leadership and management skills. They hired teachers during the summer to acquaint them with needs of business. They sponsored career days. And they financed advertising campaigns to raise consciousness about the need for school improvement and to discourage students from dropping out. Adult and continuing education programs shared school space. And municipalities jointly financed the construction of special-use facilities. Educational foundations stimulated individuals and corporations to donate funds. And senior citizens and parents volunteered in classrooms. As the movement expanded, the private sector became more aggressive in contracting with public school boards for the operation of individual schools or for providing chief executive officers to oversee districts' operations (see Chapter 3 and Doyle, 1994).

In this section, we examine entrepreneurial activities in the form of partnerships, educational foundations, and voluntarism. These activities offer school districts opportunities for securing additional capital and human resources, both as incentives to improve instruction and as enrichments to the dialogue about curriculum and policy (see King & Swanson, 1990). These activities began as partnerships to provide individual schools needed human and financial resources. They have evolved into more meaningful public-private relationships directed at system-level restructuring and renewal efforts.

Public-Private Partnerships

Formal and informal relationships between school districts or individual schools and businesses accomplish a number of purposes. The private sector desired a better-educated work force to improve its productivity, reduce on-the-job training costs, and improve international competitiveness. Interest in school improvement derives in part from the realization that tomorrow's labor market is in schools today and that businesses can work with educators in developing needed skills: "The sharing of expertise is the bedrock for effective relationships" (Hoyt, 1991, p. 451). This investment in human capital development is explored more fully in Chapter 1. It yields returns to business and society alike.

Schools have traditionally represented a large market for the sale or donation of goods and services. Businesses profit from direct sales. Schools benefit from private sector research and development undertaken to provide more efficient products and technologies. Private sector involvement is also motivated by the tax benefits that derive from donations of money and products to public schools (Wood, 1990).

In return for its investments in schools, the private sector expects improved school performance. In contrast to school systems' desires for more resources to expand offerings and produce better results, Doyle (1989) stated that the premise often underlying business involvement is that results will produce more resources:

> Business should expect of the schools precisely what it expects of itself and what its customers expect of it: performance. Schools must be able to describe and defend what they do in terms of value added. What difference does going to school make? In what measurable ways is a student better off having gone to school? (p. E100)

School-business collaborations that yield improved schooling offer returns in the form of resources *and* results for both parties.

Public-private interactions occur in several forms. Among them are the categories of donor, shared, and enterprise activities identified by Meno (1984). *Donor activities* are directed to soliciting goods, services, and money. *Shared or cooperative activities* permit schools to pool resources with community organizations, colleges and universities, or government agencies to reduce costs. *Enterprise activities* involve school districts in many revenue-producing services: providing food preparation, data processing, and transportation services for other organizations; leasing surplus buildings for alternative community uses, athletic fields to professional athletic teams, or facility space to profit-making enterprises such as credit unions; driver education and swimming instruction, which generate user fees and service charges; and the sale of access to school markets, such as food-service rights and vending machines. This latter concept of enterprise has broadened recently with the expanded search for alternative revenue: parents and students actively solicit financial support and engage in numerous fund-raising events; Whittle's Channel One brings news programs and corporate advertising into classrooms; and districts in some states sell commercial advertising space on school walls, athletic uniforms, newsletters, and buses (Bauman & Crampton, 1995). These donor, shared, and enterprise activities enrich district and school resources in diverse ways. Each one is premised on the belief that schools and the communities they serve benefit greatly through collaborative arrangements.

Partnerships at the school level offer opportunities for directly impacting classrooms, and there are countless examples of private sponsorship of school programs. Businesses directly fund or issue challenge grants to stimulate innovations. They donate computers and other equipment, finance artistic performances, sponsor academies to model reforms and market-driven innovations, create programs for connecting families with social service agencies, encourage academic and social success for low-income children, sponsor counseling and preemployment experiences for school dropouts, and raise money to guarantee high school graduates employment or financial assistance for college.

Higher education has also formed partnership agreements with elementary and secondary schools. The Chelsea, Massachusetts, public schools turned to Boston University for assistance in implementing educational reforms. State legislation in 1989 enabled the university to manage the school system for ten years. The State University of New York College at Purchase and Westchester County public schools collaborated to increase the pool of qualified college students, foster vitality in the teaching profession, raise standards, strengthen career counseling, develop leadership, and improve teaching and learning in secondary schools (Gross, 1988). Many colleges of education have joined with public schools to create professional development schools to improve the skills of current and future teachers.

Partnerships are generally created within local school districts. State reform legislation, however, often encourages or mandates linkages between businesses and schools in analyzing and planning school improvements. In addition, several national-level efforts have encouraged business involvement in school-based activities, systemwide policy development, and state-level reform efforts. The 1993 National Partnerships in Education Program brought federal encouragement. The National Association of Partners in Education (NAPE), formed in 1988, recognized the value of public-private partnerships for educational improvement.

The Public Education Fund Network (PEFNet) includes sixty urban school districts in its effort to link many locally based nonprofit partnership organizations (Bergholz, 1992; Muro, 1995). The goals and strategies of members of this network have shifted over the years (Useem & Neild, 1995). The fund was created to seek political and financial support from business and civic leaders to help impoverished school systems. The initial tactics were providing resources, improving public relations, nurturing adopt-a-school programs, and facilitating school-based projects through mini-grants to teachers and staff development. The public relations goal in particular was critical in engendering support of civic and business leaders in an era of middle-class flight from urban schools. Concomitant with changes in educational reform efforts, the role of partnerships has evolved in many urban districts to more directly involve the private sector in district-level policy debates and whole-school change initiatives: "In a number of the longer-lived funds, their dominant role has shifted from being just a resource-provider and relatively uncritical supporter of a district to that of catalyst and agent of long-term change willing to speak frankly about the need for systemic reform" (Useem & Neild, 1995). Not only are they raising questions about the organization, conducting studies of administrative arrangements and operational efficiencies, and making recommendations for changed policies, but they are also following through with assistance in implementing reforms.

This new wave of partnership activities is typified by projects that have stimulated school restructuring, studied organizational problems, or encouraged state-level reform (Useem & Neild, 1995). Examples of restructuring with partners' involvement include the following: site-based restructuring in all 600 Los Angeles schools through the LEARN initiative; teacher-driven curricular changes and restructured schools with foci on the arts or on math and sciences in Philadelphia; the adoption of the Paideia philosophy in curriculum and teaching in Chattanooga; and the creation of a principals' study group on restructuring with funds to implement projects in San Francisco. Several partnerships have studied organizational problems and formed policy recommendations. For example, the New York City chancellor's strategic working groups brought about systemwide change in the mathematics curriculum and altered graduation requirements. The Denver-area Public Education Coalition sponsored a management efficiency audit to assess organizational health in five districts. Finally, state-level reform can be an outgrowth of partnership activities, as occurred when the Education Reform Act of 1993 was modeled after recommendations of the Massachusetts Business Alliance for Education.

A survey of fifty private-sector coalitions located in twenty-six states by the Indiana Education Policy Center (Hamrick, 1993) examined influences of partnership activities on state-level policies. Coalitions included in the study had to perceive themselves as change agents for statewide education reform and to promote their priorities for change by influencing state-level education policy makers and elected officials. The highest-ranked priorities of these coalitions were improving student performance and changing the power structure through citizen and parent involvement, revised state education governance structures, reducing or eliminating state regulations, site-based management, and teacher participation in decision making. Although these organizations represented private sector interests, school choice, vouchers, and tuition tax credits were among the lowest-rated priorities of coalitions in the nation, with the exception of those located in western states. State government representatives viewed these coalitions as effective or somewhat effective and linked their effectiveness to the groups' success in developing relations with state offices, in promoting specific legislative proposals, and in building public support. Hamrick concluded that private sector influence is strong and increasing, and that coalitions are a key strategy for exercising that influence.

A number of lessons have been learned through these and other initiatives to improve school programs. Business leaders become familiar with operations. They raise questions about the distribution of power when they examine district policies and initiate whole-school change. They are frustrated by such structural roadblocks as union contracts, teacher-hiring policies, schedules in secondary schools, and standardized test requirements (Useem & Neild, 1995, p. 7). For example, the New York City fund, which launched the New Visions Schools in 1993, eventually negotiated an agreement with the district and union to permit teachers to be hired at the school site without regard for the contract's seniority provisions (Lief, 1992). From their review of partnership activities stimulated under the Public Education Fund, Useem and Neild (1995, pp. 17, 21) concluded that having meaningful roles in these new directions depends on three key factors: (1) the superintendent's encouragement and support; (2) visible and strong support from the business community that is channeled through the fund's board or through other organizational vehicles that collaborate with the fund; and (3) the negotiating and coalition-building skills of the fund's staff members. They also noted the importance of frequent communications among participants at all stages of activities, and of delicate handling of critical assessments of districts' practices, which is "almost always done through the vehicle of a broadly representative commission or task force that is quasi-independent of the fund" (p. 19).

The advantages of these public–private partnerships are numerous: they are designed to be nonbureaucratic, nonpartisan and less politicized, flexible, innovative, and entrepreneurial. They are simultaneously inside organizations, since they have commitments to work over time with specific school systems and their administrations and teacher unions, and outside organizations, since they have independent governing boards and funding sources (Useem & Neild, 1995).

The scope and visibility of large urban projects overshadow those in smaller districts, which may indeed have less need for formalized partnerships. Inman (1984) and Mann (1987b) discussed reasons why school-business partnerships are less likely to form in rural areas than in larger, more urbanized districts. The presence of strong preexisting connections, dispersed economies, a local culture of thrift, and the unintended consequences of competition in rural communities either remove the need for alliances or make creating them undesirable. Rural school districts do not have as large an economic base. Thus contacting businesses for donations of funds or supplies may be unwise when the businesses are also asked to raise taxes to support the school system budget. Smaller districts enjoy better communications among schools, businesses, and community agencies. The lack of these linkages is often a motivation for partnerships in cities. Urban school districts are the largest beneficiaries of partnership activities in part because businesses tend to support schools located within the same community.

Partnership activities grew rapidly in the 1980s. McLaughlin (1988) report that 64 percent of 130 major corporations listed elementary and secondary education as their number 1 community affairs concern. Nevertheless, only about 3 percent of corporate contributions to education are directed to precollegiate public education (Timpane, 1984). Hess (1987) surveyed sixty-two Chicago-based funding organizations and found

they made 446 grants that totaled $7.7 million. However, this represented just 4.6 percent of their total giving. Corporate downsizing in the 1990s impacted giving. For example, Atlantic Richfield reduced its total philanthropic donations from a high of $37 million in 1983 to $12.5 million in 1993 (Sommerfeld, 1994). Despite projections by corporate leaders that charitable giving would increase along with increased profits, the Foundation Center projected that philanthropy would remain flat through the 1990s, in part because of uncertainty about the potential effects of changes in federal tax treatment of corporate giving (Sommerfeld, 1995).

The amount of business donations may reflect the limited role of business in school activities and policies. Mann's (1987a, 1987b) studies of 108 school systems, including twenty-three large cities, found that only 17 percent of the schools visited had developed relationships with all four features of "new style" business involvement: a coordinating structure, multiple purposes, multiple players, and stability. Mann (1987a) stated that the modest role of businesses in addressing school improvement needs is understandable:

> After having designed a system of limited government in order to minimize the abuse of power, after having vested most control in professionals, and after having inserted boards between the schools and their communities, why should we be surprised that no one— least of all the business community—has much power to solve problems? (p. 126)

Many partnerships avoid areas of conflict, and businesses restrict their involvement to helping schools acquire funds and materials. Business reluctance to become involved in schools, according to Timpane (1984), stems from the feeling that the sponsorship of isolated projects is not likely "to improve the performance of school systems caught in webs of programmatic, managerial, and financial control created by years of governmental inaction at local, state and federal levels" (p. 391). However, their limited partnership roles do not enable educators to take advantage of business expertise, leadership, and political clout as reform directions are forged at local and state levels.

In contrast to these reports of limited roles for business, a study of effective schools found that collaborative efforts make a large difference in school programs. Wilson and Rossman's (1986) investigation of programs and policies of 571 exemplary secondary schools revealed several common themes. These schools actively recruited human resources from the community and used aggressive public relations campaigns that relied on parent volunteers who served as promoters, communicators, and decision makers. The schools successfully attracted financial resources from individuals and businesses. Schools and communities benefited mutually. Communities made extensive use of school facilities and schools formed positive identities with their communities. What set these schools apart from other schools were the frequency of cooperation between schools and communities, the high level of participation, and the degree to which these activities were considered central to the schools' missions and programs.

Partnership activities that offer more than cosmetic changes in school programs hold much potential for school improvement. The nature and extent of partners' involvement may be an important distinguishing feature of effective restructured schools.

Educational Foundations

Privately financed, nonprofit school foundations expand the capacity of individual school fund-raising efforts. Many districts have taken advantage of this form of partnership to coordinate and encourage giving from individuals and businesses. An educational foundation may support general educational goals. Or it may create special-purpose funds to attract donations for specific school programs, athletics, or other activities, or construction of facilities. Funds from foundations finance an array of special projects, including science and computer laboratories, field trips locally and abroad, grants for teachers to improve instruction, endowed teach-

ing chairs, athletic facilities, and incentives for students to complete high school or enroll in colleges. Targeting specific groups, such as alumni, industries that employ graduates, or wealthy residents of a school district, has been an effective foundation strategy. Long-term development activities encourage estate planning to establish endowments from which future income will be derived to support teaching positions or student scholarships.

Foundations may benefit schools throughout a state or within specific school systems. Statewide reform efforts are best exemplified by the efforts of the Edna McConnell Clark Foundation in stimulating collaboration on policy changes in Kentucky (McKersie & Palaich, 1994). The largest foundation gift ever made to a single school district was the MacArthur Foundation's pledge of $40 million over ten years to the Chicago schools beginning in 1990. The I Have a Dream Foundation provides incentives for at-risk students in thirty-two cities to complete school by ensuring later support of their higher education. And the Minneapolis Five Percent Club relies upon peer pressure among businesses to stimulate giving (McLaughlin & Shields, 1987). Many smaller school districts (Ballew, 1987; Neill, 1983; Nesbit, 1987) have also created foundations to solicit and manage donations.

The previously described national Public Education Fund Network (PEFNet) succeeded the Public Education Fund, which was created in 1983 through a $6 million Ford Foundation grant. A study of the activities sponsored by fifty foundations through this network between 1983 and 1988 found they sponsored "small, high visibility" projects through minigrants to teachers (an average amount of $662). They also used public relations to support district goals (Olson, 1988). The potential of this movement is evident in the size of PEFNet's largest educational foundations: the Fund for New York City Public Education (an annual budget of $9.7 million in 1994), the Los Angeles Educational Partnership ($8.2 million), and the Philadelphia Partnership for Education ($4 million) (Bergholz, 1992; Useem & Neild, 1995).

A recent appraisal of foundation efforts urges them to assume leadership roles in initiating and supporting educational reforms: "Systemic reforms based on a convergence of policy sectors—governmental, for-profit, nonprofit, and philanthropic—will have more success than systemic reforms based on a single policy sector" (McKersie & Palaich, 1994). The initiatives cited previously as examples of the expanded roles of partnerships suggest the potential of foundations in reform efforts.

Federal and state statutes define legal structures of foundations as either charitable trusts or nonprofit corporations (Wood, 1990). Because they generally operate as self-governed entities, foundations may limit school boards and personnel to advisory roles. In this role, school personnel help external groups decide on priorities for the use of resources and the appropriateness of gifts of equipment and teaching materials. In addition, they should monitor cash flow to avoid any suspicion of fund misuse. An example is the financial mismanagement and fraud that forced the Dallas, Texas, public schools to bring legal action against the Foundation for Quality Education in the late 1970s (Wood, 1990).

Foundation activities offer businesses and individuals an opportunity to support public education without devoting large amounts of time. On the other hand, this banking or "checkwriting" mode of philanthropy (McLaughlin, 1988) falls short of broader partnership goals because it does not directly involve donors in school activities. For this reason, intermediary organizations such as PEFNet attempt to reduce the distance between donors and recipient schools. For example, when the John Hancock Insurance Company donated $1 million through the Boston COMPACT, company executives served on a committee to review teachers' proposals for the use of grants. McLaughlin (1988) concluded: "These intermediary organizations thus foster knowledge, understanding, and identification, rather than alienation or distancing from the public schools" (p. 69). This observation suggests that the nature and extent of donors' involvement, like those of volunteers, is as important to school improvement as is the amount of the donation.

Voluntarism

Parents, community residents, and other individuals directly support schools when they volunteer their time and ideas. Over sixteen percent of the adults responding to a survey conducted nationally by the Gallup Organization in 1992 reported that they volunteered services to schools during the past year. This figure was second only to the 28 percent volunteering in religious organizations (NCES, 1995, p. 308).

In enacting the 1994 Goals 2000: Educate America Act, Congress declared the importance of building closer relationships with parents. This goal expanded the list of six goals originally adopted by the nation's governors: "Every school will promote partnerships that will increase parental involvement and participation in promoting the social, emotional, and academic growth of children." Just as the role of partnerships and foundations has changed in recent years, so too has the schools' involvement of volunteers.

Brown (1995) defines school voluntarism as follows: "School voluntarism or benevolence is the donation of time, from a person external to a school, to a school itself. It implies no certain return but it requires a positive interest on the part of the donor for the welfare of the student(s)" (p. 31; original in italics). People's motivations for giving freely of their time and money vary widely, but schools stand to benefit from this altruism. Brown advocates voluntarism as an opportunity to lessen three problems facing schools: the paucity of resources available at the school level to educate children; the problem of autonomy—the inability to make school-level decisions to address local priorities; and the problem of integration—the need to provide sufficient care or social support especially for students.

Voluntarism appears in diverse forms as individuals and groups lend invaluable support for instruction, extracurricular activities, and fundraising efforts. Parents, college students, and senior citizens become involved in classrooms and field trips, reducing the pupil-adult ratio so that greater individual attention can be given to students. Booster clubs lend support to athletic teams, band and choral groups, and debate and drama activities. The Parent Teachers' Association was initiated in 1897 and is today the largest voluntary organization in the country (Brown, 1995, p. 149). It supports schools in numerous ways, including sponsoring carnivals and saving grocery receipts and coupons to acquire instructional and playground equipment.

The Dedicated Older Volunteers in Educational Service (DOVES) coordinates activities in which Springfield, Massachusetts, residents serve as tutors, mentors, guest speakers, and library assistants in the public schools (Gray, 1984). In an innovative approach, the Chapel Hill–Carrboro, North Carolina, school district benefits from substantial proceeds of stores that sell donated clothing and furniture. Each school receives a portion of the funds for discretionary purposes. Allocations are based on student enrollments as well as the number of volunteer hours posted by parents and students from the respective buildings.

In recent years voluntarism has been encouraged to create opportunities for community members to affect instructional goals and management efficiency. Advisory or decision-making committees and strategic planning teams rely upon elected representatives or persons who are appointed by school administrators because of their particular expertise or positions of leadership in the community. Residents share their expertise in in-service staff development programs. Corporations lend executives to give advice on management practices or conduct performance audits. Brown (1990) observed that additional local resources strengthen school site management: "voluntarism may be regarded as a variation on the theme of decentralization since it permits discretionary decision making with private resources in a similar way that school-based management permits flexibility with public dollars" (p. 1). In addition, by giving greater responsibility to parents and other volunteers, schools are able to close the growing distance between schools and homes (Sandfort, 1987).

Successful, institutionalized volunteer programs share a number of characteristics as described by Gray (1984). The superintendent, school board, and business leaders give strong and visible support, including the formal adoption of a policy of support which then helps school staff to overcome the traditional barriers to voluntarism. A systemwide manager coordinates volunteer services and facilitates information sharing. Building-level coordinators conduct assessments of needs and identify potential resource people. The emphasis is on people who will bring personal talents and commitments rather than on procuring money. There are many options for volunteers to assist in instruction, counseling of pupils, and school management. Collaborative, long-range planning involves volunteers in seeking ways to improve schools.

Benefits and Costs of Partnership Activities

To appraise these activities fairly, we must weigh the many benefits derived from greater involvement of the private sector and volunteers in schools against the potential costs to public education. Our discussion of partnerships, foundations, and voluntarism notes returns in such forms as enriched programs, academic learning, parental advocacy, and political support. However, some suggest that these gains are concentrated in wealthy school districts. They say that privatization may negatively affect current revenue sources and decisions about public education.

It is difficult to determine the monetary value of many partnership and volunteer activities. One writer valued volunteer efforts devoted to nonprofit organizations, including schools, as worth 50 percent more than the amount of money donated (Weisbrod, 1988, p. 132). Wilson and Rossman (1986) suggested that involving the community, opening schools to other organizations, and building political support across constituencies are more important than the financial supplements to school budgets:

It builds commitment and loyalty. It creates a special identity for the school that includes the surrounding community. The ethic of mutual caring that is created multiplies the effectiveness of the school and integrates the school into its community. (p. 708)

Opening schools to the community improves relationships and contributes to "social capital," which consists of the diverse social relationships that foster children's growth and development (Coleman, 1990). Schools, families, and society generally benefit from investments in social capital as they gain in productivity from greater investments in human capital development (see Chapter 1). Coleman and Hoffer (1987) discussed this concept as it enriches private school capabilities:

The social capital that has value for a young person's development does not reside merely in the set of common values held by parents who choose to send their children to the same private school. It resides in the functional community, the actual social relationships that exist among parents, in the closure exhibited by this structure of relations and in the parents' relations with the institutions of the community. (pp. 225–226)

In a similar manner, partnerships and voluntarism can pay large dividends in public schools regardless of the socioeconomic backgrounds of children served. Coleman (1991) asserts that social capital grows in public schools in which parents join educators to establish standards for behavior, enforce rules that are consistent among families, and support one another's children.

Brown (1995) noted the presence of "rich schools in poor neighborhoods." These have considerable amounts of physical, human, and social capital: "In general, it appears that high levels of voluntarism tend to occur under two conditions— when neighborhoods are upper middle income and/or when schools are administered to welcome and support volunteers" (p. 52). There must be efforts to make opportunities available for families of disadvantaged children to volunteer:

there is strong evidence that low-income and poorly educated parents *want* to play a role in their children's education. Indeed, these parents seek a role even when they believe that their children will fail or do poorly in school. Conventional wisdom to the contrary, parents who lack knowledge themselves do not necessarily lack interest in the schools their children attend. What's lacking, in most schools and school districts, are appropriate strategies or structures for involving low-income parents. (McLaughlin & Shields, 1987, p. 157)

As the public's feelings of responsibility for and ownership of their schools grow, the local resource base expands, schools have greater opportunities for improvement, and students are the ultimate beneficiaries. The movement to restructure schools is premised on such hopes.

On the other hand, although these many material and intangible benefits may be enticing, the literature on partnerships suggests three problem areas. Substantially increased reliance on partnerships, foundations, and voluntarism may have detrimental effects on current revenue sources, decisions about resource use, and equity goals. First of all, if citizens and businesses view requests for additional donations of goods and services from the private sector to be another tax to support schools, albeit voluntary, one consequence may be opposition to various forms of public support. If increased voluntarism means that fewer certified professionals or teaching assistants are required for program delivery and fewer office staff are needed, teacher and support staff unions may express concerns about possible displacements by unpaid workers (Brown, 1993, p. 197). Partnerships may enable school systems to further ease the burden on local taxes. Similarly, states may consider these additional local resources and reduce state aid allocations. Or school systems may factor school fundraising efforts into their distributions of money or personnel allotments among schools. These developments would reduce the incentive for districts and schools to obtain external support (King & Swanson, 1990).

Although support from traditional sources could be reduced if there was substantial private support in the future, the above concerns may be overstated. Corporate involvement is minimal in relation to the total financial support of public education. Community and individual involvement in schools is on a far lower level than would threaten traditional sources. Rather than negatively affecting support, additional monetary and human resources through partnership activities can satisfy teachers' desires for more instructional materials, smaller class sizes, and released time for team planning and participation in decision making. Because the many benefits of partnerships exceed the potential threats to current resources and staffing patterns, there is no reason to discourage schools from accepting private sector involvement.

Second, some worry that increased support of public schooling by individuals and the private sector may bring undue influence over educational decisions to the detriment of traditional school board governance. Meno (1984) warns that as nontraditional finance activities grow, educators and policy makers will have to decide whether fiscal benefits are worth the potential modifications in present practices. Indeed, greater parental involvement in decision making can lead to frustrating and time-consuming efforts to reach consensus, an erosion of trust placed in professionals, and an atmosphere of fear among teachers (Yaffe, 1994). In contrast, McLaughlin (1988) argues that corporations respect educators' expertise and that donors, primarily small businesses, are unable to influence school decisions.

Business interests will be represented in formal processes of school- or district-level decision making because of their partnership activities, just as they continue to be expressed on governing boards. It might be argued that direct and indirect pressure to alter educational policy in order to receive partnership assistance is not necessarily negative. Educators need to be comfortable in deciding whether it is advantageous to form partnerships or receive gifts, especially when they are concerned about the impacts on school policy and curricula. Schools and districts should consider the

relationship between the acceptance of goods and services and subsequent decisions about their use in order to limit conflicts of interest. This concern, however, is not sufficient reason for schools to discourage participation by the private sector.

Equity is of greater concern than the potential effects on traditional resources or decision making. Schools and school districts differ in their opportunities to form partnerships with business and in their abilities to raise funds within their communities (Monk, 1990). People anticipate that just as varying property valuations have enabled school districts to raise different levels of tax revenue, the socioeconomic statuses of communities give school districts and schools within them unequal opportunities to obtain private resources. If partnerships become a potent force for raising funds in the future, disparities in educational programs and extracurricular activities will be perpetuated. Wood (1990) discusses privatization in relation to the goal of equalizing educational opportunities:

> To allow public school districts to pursue outside sources of fiscal support, however noble in the intent to support public education, is to allow the districts to engage in *laissez-faire* self interest. . . . This agenda is indifferent to local resources or lack thereof, the educational or fiscal needs, and the allocation of resources to this goal. Within this system, every school district is capable of seeking to maximize its present assets in a manner competitive with all other school districts. (p. 60)

Even though many small and rural school districts cannot take advantage of private resources to the same degree as larger and wealthier districts, potential effects on equity goals may be overstated. McLaughlin (1988) comments that dollars made available through these activities are few in comparison with total school district budgets and do not underwrite inequalities of the scale that result in judicial challenges (see Chapter 11). If the focus of partnership assistance is entirely on individual schools, they will benefit to very different degrees. However, not all private sector supports should target the school as the recipient. Some activities and foundations are more appropriately maintained at centralized—district, regional, or state—levels to permit distributions that are sensitive to equity goals. For example, the Los Angeles Educational Partnership gives bonus points to applications for grants from teachers in inner-city schools and supports programs that benefit the district as a whole through workshops, incentive programs for students, and math/science collaboratives. These arrangements hold promise for other districts as they allocate funds among restructured schools.

School improvement depends in large part on the active involvement of communities and businesses, regardless of the amount of monetary support they are able to provide. Educators are also called to action to participate with the private sector, especially as business interests are communicated through legislatures and school boards to restructure public education. Every school and district has the potential to benefit from partners and volunteers.

SUMMARY

School districts have many opportunities to expand their resources beyond their traditional reliance on property and other local taxes. User fees apply a privilege-based charge to students for some portion of costs of services and activities. Careful planning and management of the flow of money through school district accounts at times require districts to borrow to increase their available cash. At other times it frees idle cash to be invested. Partnerships, foundations, and volunteers enhance monetary and human resources as well as offer needed political support as educators reconsider the role and structure of public education.

Sometimes state regulations or judicial interpretations of constitutional provisions permit schools to charge fees. Schools desiring to charge students for instructional materials, elective courses, extracurricular activities, transportation, and other services should consider the legal, finan-

cial, and educational implications of the fees. Fees raise concerns about inequities in access to free public education. They limit opportunities for all children to participate in curricular or extracurricular programs. And they cost money to administer. They are likely to be supported in the courts when (1) they apply to activities that are not necessary and integral to the educational process; (2) the fee policy includes a confidential waiver that enables children of low-income families to participate.

Districts can add considerably to their revenue when they plan their short- or long-term investments around the flow of revenue and nonrevenue money into the district in relation to future expenditures. It also makes sense to minimize checking account balances and to pool small accounts to maximize investments. Districts select strategies for investing periodic surplus funds according to their potential yield, the safety or amount of risk entailed, and their liquidity, or the ease of accessing funds without loss of interest.

Nonrevenue money obtained through short- and long-term borrowing helps districts maintain an even flow of funds and construct school facilities. Short-term borrowing through tax and revenue anticipation notes enables districts to pay employees and outside vendors on schedule when there is a revenue deficit. When pay-as-you-go financing is not feasible, capital outlay financing to retire general obligation bonds permits construction of facilities and remodeling and the purchase of equipment. However, basing capital outlay financing on local property valuations results in large disparities among communities in the nature of school buildings. State-sponsored loan programs, direct grants of state funds, and public bonding authorities ease the burdens on local tax bases and help districts reach goals of providing adequate, if not equal, educational opportunities.

Tax limitation and education reform movements have encouraged districts to garner private resources through partnerships, educational foundations, and volunteers. These activities gain discretionary money and other goods and services for schools. They also enrich linkages between schools, businesses, community agencies, and parents. The potential for enlarging the local resource base is substantial. And meaningful involvement of individuals and groups can improve instruction and school leadership. These activities may be beneficial in many predominantly urban and suburban districts. But some people worry that supplements to school resources may not reach relatively poor and small school systems.

The chapters that follow in Part III examine the principles and mechanisms for transferring funds raised through state and federal sources to local authorities for the operation of schools.

ACTIVITIES

1. Investigate the restrictions that state policies place on charging fees for required courses, elective offerings, and extracurricular activities in your state. If fees are permitted, determine the extent to which students pay fees to support various school programs and activities in several districts that differ by size and wealth.
2. Discuss the management of cash flow, including the timing of borrowing and investments, with a school district finance officer. What opportunities exist for school-level decisions to borrow and invest funds?
3. In what ways do state-imposed limits on borrowing and investments strengthen financial management practices? In what ways do these limitations impede the flexibility districts require to maximize the benefits of these cash flow strategies?

4. Debate the appropriateness of the state or federal government's assuming a larger role in financing capital outlay.
5. Investigate to what extent private resources supplement schools and school districts in a given locality or state. What demographic or organizational conditions present within schools appear to be related to the amount of resources gained from partnerships, foundations, and voluntarism?
6. Determine how business partnerships are involved in a given school district. To what extent do partnerships evidence the four characteristics of "new style" involvement identified by Mann (1987a): a coordinating structure, multiple purposes, multiple players, and stability?

REFERENCES

Alamo Heights Independent School District v. *State Board of Education,* 790 F.2d 1153. (5th Cir., 1986).

Ambroiggio v. *Board of Education,* 427 N.E.2d 1027 (IL App. Ct., 1981).

Annenberg Institute for School Reform (1995). *Walter H. Annenberg's challenge to the nation: A progress report.* Providence, RI: Author.

Arcadia Unified School District v. *Department of Education,* 5 Cal. Reptr.2d 545 (1992).

Attorney General v. *East Jackson Public Schools,* 372 N.W.2d 638 (MI Ct. App., 1985).

Augenblick, J. (1977). *Systems of state support for school district capital expenditure.* Report No. F76-8. Denver: Education Commission of the States.

Ballew, P. (1987, November). How to start a school foundation. *Executive Educator, 9,* 26–28.

Bauman, P. C. (1995). Searching for alternative revenues: The political implications of school impact fees. *Journal of School Business Management, 7,* 38–49.

Bauman, P., & Crampton, F. E. (1995). When school districts become entrepreneurs: Opportunity or danger? *NCSL State Legislative Report, 20.*

Bergholz, D. (1992). The public education fund. *Teachers College Record, 93,* 516–522.

Bond v. *Ann Arbor School District,* 178 N.W.2d 484 (MI, 1970).

Brown, D. J. (1990). *Voluntarism for public schools.* Paper presented at the annual conference of the American Education Finance Association, Las Vegas.

Brown, D. J. (1993). Benevolence in Canadian public schools. In S. L. Jacobson & R. Berne (Eds.), *Reforming education: The emerging systemic approach* (pp. 191–208). Thousand Oaks, CA: Corwin.

Brown, D. J. (1995). *Schools with heart: Voluntarism and public education.* Unpublished monograph. Vancouver, Canada: University of British Columbia.

Brown, D. J., & Bouman, C. (1994). *Policies on fees in public schools.* Unpublished monograph. Vancouver, Canada: University of British Columbia.

Camp, W. E., & Salmon, R. G. (1985). Public school bonding corporations financing public elementary and secondary school facilities. *Journal of Education Finance, 10,* 495–503.

Candoli, I. C., Hack, W. G., Ray, J. R., & Stollar, D. H. (1984). *School business administration: A planning approach.* (3rd edition). Boston: Allyn and Bacon.

Cardiff v. *Bismark Public School District,* 263 N.W.2d 105 (ND, 1978).

Coleman, J. S. (1990). *Foundations of social theory.* Cambridge, MA: Harvard University Press.

Coleman, J. S. (1991). *Parental involvement in education.* OERI Document #65-000-00459-3. Washington, DC: U. S. Government Printing Office.

Coleman, J. S., & Hoffer, T. (1987). *Public and private high schools: The impact of communities.* New York: Basic Books.

Davies, D. (1993). The League of Schools Reaching Out. *School-Community Journal, 3,* 37–46.

Dayton, J., & McCarthy, M. (1992). User fees in public schools: Are they legal? *Journal of Education Finance, 18,* 127–141.

Dembowski, F. L. (1986). Cash management. In G. C. Hentschke, *School business management: A comparative perspective* (pp. 214–245). Berkeley, CA: McCutchan.

Dembowski, F. L., & Davey, R. D. (1986). School district financial management and banking. In R. C. Wood (Ed.), *Principles of school business management* (pp. 237–260). Reston, VA: ASBO International.

Doyle, D. P. (1989). Endangered species: Children of promise. *BusinessWeek,* Special Supplement, E4–E135.

Doyle, D. P. (1994). The role of private sector management in public education. *Phi Delta Kappan, 76,* 128–132.

Education Writers Association. (1989). *Wolves at the schoolhouse door: An investigation of the condition of public school buildings.* Washington, DC: Author.

Gold, S. D., Smith, D. M., & Lawton, S. B. (Eds.). (1995). *Public school finance programs of the United States and Canada, 1993–94.* Albany, NY: American Education Finance Association and The Center for the Study of the States.

Gray, S. T. (1984). How to create a successful school/community partnership. *Phi Delta Kappan, 65,* 405–409.

Gross, T. L., (1988). *Partners in education: How colleges can work with schools to improve teaching and learning.* San Francisco: Jossey-Bass.

Hamm, R. W., & Crosser, R. W. (1991, June). School fees: Whatever happened to the notion of a free public education? *American School Board Journal, 178,* 29–31.

Hamrick, F. (1993, April). Private-sector coalitions and state-level education reform. *Policy Bulletin.* Bloomington, IN: Indiana Education Policy Center.

Hansen, S. (1991). *Schoolhouses in the red.* Reston, VA: American Association of School Administrators.

Hartzell v. *Connell,* 679 P.2d 35, 201 Cal. Rptr. 601 (CA, 1984).

Hess, G. A. (1987). *1985 education survey.* Chicago: Donors Forum of Chicago.

Hoyt, K. (1991). Education reform and relationships between the private sector and education: A call for integration. *Phi Delta Kappan, 72,* 450–453.

Inman, D. (1984). Bridging education to industry: Implications for financing education. *Journal of Education Finance, 10,* 271–277.

Johns, R. L., Morphet, E. L., & Alexander, K. (1983). *The economics and financing of education.* (4th edition). Englewood Cliffs, NJ: Prentice-Hall.

Jones, T. H., & Amalfitano, J. L. (1994). *America's gamble: Public school finance and state lotteries.* Lancaster, PA: Technomic.

Kadrmas v. *Dickinson Public Schools,* 487 U.S. 450 (1988).

King, R. A., & MacPhail-Wilcox, B. (1988). Bricks-and-mortar reform in North Carolina: The state assumes a larger role in financing school construction. *Journal of Education Finance, 13,* 374–381.

King, R. A., & Swanson, A. D. (1990). Resources for restructured schools: Partnerships, foundations, and volunteerism. *Planning and Changing, 21,* 94–107.

Lief, B. (1992). The New York City case study: The private sector and the reform of public education. *Teachers College Record, 93,* 523–535.

Lindsay, D. (1994). Counting their losses in wealthy Orange County. *Education Week, 14* (15), p. 3.

Lindsay, D. (1995). Calif. district goes to court after bond deal goes sour. *Education Week, 14* (30), p. 5.

Lorenc v. *Call,* 789 P.2d 46 (Utah App., 1990).

Mann, D. (1987a). Business involvement and public school improvement, part 1. *Phi Delta Kappan, 69,* 123–128.

Mann, D. (1987b). Business involvement and public school improvement, part 2. *Phi Delta Kappan, 69,* 228–232.

Marshall v. *School District,* 553 P.2d 784 (CO, 1976).

McKersie, B., & Palaich, R. (1994). Philanthropy and systemic reform: Finding a cross-sector blend of risk-taking and political will. *Education Week, 13* (32), pp. 33, 48.

McLaughlin, M. L. (1988). Business and the public schools: New patterns of support. In D. H. Monk & J. Underwood (Eds.), *Microlevel school finance: Issues and implications for policy* (pp. 63–80). Cambridge, MA: Ballinger.

McLaughlin, M. W., & Shields, P. M. (1987). Involving low-income parents in the schools: A role for policy? *Phi Delta Kappan, 69,* 156–160.

Meno, L. (1984). Sources of alternative revenue. In L. D. Webb & V. D. Mueller (Eds.), *Managing limited resources: New demands on public school management* (pp. 129–146). Cambridge, MA: Ballinger.

Monk, D. H. (1990). *Educational finance: An economic approach.* New York: McGraw-Hill.

Muro, J. J. (1995). *Creating and funding educational foundations: A guide for local school districts.* Needham Heights, MA: Allyn and Bacon.

National Center for Education Statistics (NCES). (1995). *Digest of educational statistics.* Washington, DC: Office of Educational Research and Improvement.

Neill, G. (1983). *The local education foundation: A new way to raise money for schools.* NASSP Special Report. Reston, VA: National Association of Secondary School Principals.

Nesbit, W. B. (1987). The local education foundation: What is it, how is it established? *NASSP Bulletin, 71,* 85–89.

Norton v. *Board of Education,* 553 P.2d 1277 (N.M. 1976).

Olson, L. (1988). Public-school foundation effort surpasses expectations. *Education Week, 7* (30), p. 4.

Ortiz, F. I. (1994). *Schoolhousing: Planning and designing educational facilities.* Albany, NY: State University of New York Press.

Paulson v. *Minidoka County School District,* 463 P.2d 935 (Idaho, 1970).

Piele, P. K., & Hall, J. S. (1973). *Budgets, bonds and ballots: Voting behavior in school financial issues.* Lexington, MA: D. C. Heath.

Salmon, R., Dawson, C., Lawton, S., & Johns, T. (Eds.). (1988). *Public school finance programs of the United States and Canada, 1986–87.* Blacksburg, VA: American Education Finance Association.

Salmon, R., & Thomas, S. (1981). Financing public school facilities in the 80s. *Journal of Education Finance, 7,* 88–109.

San Antonio Independent School District v. *Rodriguez,* 411 U.S. 1 (1973).

Sandfort, J. A. (1987). Putting parents in their place in public schools. *NASSP Bulletin, 71,* 99–103.

Sneed v. *Greensboro City Board of Education,* 264 S.E.2d 106 (NC, 1980).

Sommerfeld, M. (1994). ARCO cuts unsettle corporate-giving field. *Education Week, 14,* 12.

Sommerfeld, M. (1995). Corporate giving predicted to increase 3% this year. *Education Week, 15,* 7.

Sutton v. *Cadillac Area Public Schools,* 323 N.W.2d 582 (MI Ct. App., 1982).

Thompson, D. C., Wood, R. C., & Honeyman, D. S. (1994). *Fiscal leadership for schools: Concepts and practices.* White Plains, NY: Longman.

Timpane, M. (1984). Business has rediscovered the public schools. *Phi Delta Kappan, 65,* 389–392.

U. S. Department of Commerce, Bureau of the Census. (1980). *Finances of public school systems in 1977–78.* Series GF78, No. 10. Washington, DC: U. S. Government Printing Office.

U. S. Department of Commerce, Bureau of the Census. (1988). *Finances of public school systems in 1985–86.* Series GF86, No. 10. Washington, DC: U. S. Government Printing Office.

U. S. Department of Commerce, Bureau of the Census (1993). *Public education finances: 1990–91,* Series GF/91-10. Washington, DC: U. S. Government Printing Office.

U. S. General Accounting Office (GAO) (1995a). *School facilities: America's schools not designed or equipped for 21st century,* GAO/HEHS-95-95. Washington, DC: Author.

U. S. General Accounting Office (1995b). *School facilities: Condition of America's schools,* GAO/HEHS-95-61. Washington, DC: Author.

Useem, E., & Neild, R. C. (1995). Partnerships. *Urban Education, 30.*

Washington v. *Salisbury,* 306 S.E.2d 600 (SC, 1983).

Weisbrod, B. (1988). *The nonprofit economy.* Cambridge, MA: Harvard University Press.

Wilkerson, W. R. (1981). State participation in financing school facilities. In K. F. Jordan & N. H. Cambron-McCabe (Eds.), *Perspectives in state school support programs* (pp. 191–213). Cambridge, MA: Ballinger.

Wilson, B. L., & Rossman, G. B. (1986). Collaborative links with the community: Lessons from exemplary secondary schools. *Phi Delta Kappan, 67,* 708–711.

Wood, R. C. (1986). Capital outlay and bonding. In R. C. Wood (Ed.), *Principles of school business management* (pp. 559–587). Reston, VA: ASBO International.

Wood, R. C. (1990). New revenues for education at the local level. In J. E. Underwood & D. A. Verstegen (Eds.), *The impacts of litigation and legislation on public school finance: Adequacy, equity, and excellence* (pp. 59–74). New York: Harper & Row.

Yaffe, E. (1994). Not just cupcakes anymore: A study of community involvement. *Phi Delta Kappan, 75,* 697–704.

PART THREE

Allocating State and Federal Funds for Schools

We began this exploration of school finance with a discussion of the extent to which society should become involved in the provision of education. Our attention turned in Part II to revenue sources, the means by which federal, state, and local governments acquire monies to support public services. We now turn to the examination of the policies available to higher levels of government for distributing dollars to school systems. Part III explores this flow of funds from state and federal governments to finance school programs at the local level.

Chapter 8 opens with a discussion of the rationale for intergovernmental transfer payments and of differences among general, block grant, and categorical aid policies. State-level policy is the primary focus of the analysis. We discuss general models and actual state funding plans to illustrate alternative ways for structuring aid formulas. Chapter 9 refines the discussion of state policy by detailing how formulas take characteristics of pupils into account and measure local fiscal capacity and effort. We examine the role of financial incentives for improving school productivity, and financial and program accountability mechanisms. Finally, in Chapter 10 we discuss the federal government's influence on educational policy through mandates, judicial decisions, and financial incentives.

CHAPTER 8

The Rationale for Intergovernmental Transfer Payments and Models for Distributing State Aid

Primary Issues Explored in This Chapter:

- *Rationale for intergovernmental transfer payments:* Why do state and federal governments support educational programs that are delivered at the local level?
- *General, block grant, and categorical funds:* To what extent should higher levels of governments dictate the purposes of grants-in-aid and oversee their use at the local level?

- *Adequacy, division of fiscal responsibilities, ability, and effort:* In what ways do state finance policies ensure an adequate level of funds, blend state and local revenue, consider local tax capacity, and affect property tax rates?
- *General models of financial aid formulas:* What prototype structures have states adopted to guide the allocation of funds for school operations?

In this chapter we discuss policies that govern transfers of funds from state and federal governments to school districts. We explore the rationale for these grants-in-aid and the extent to which policies may dictate purposes or groups to be served. We discuss a number of models for basic school support, and their application by selected states. We contrast them in terms of how they consider local property wealth and tax effort.

JUSTIFICATION FOR TRANSFER PAYMENTS

In Chapter 4 we introduced the division and overlap of responsibilities among multiple layers of government in the United States in the context of taxation. The centralization of some responsibili-

ties at higher levels of government offers a number of advantages. On the other hand, the benefits of local control over other public services justify decentralization. The balance of responsibilities and benefits is once again reinforced if we consider the allocation of funds within this federated governance structure. Channeling money raised at federal and state levels for localities to use serves a number of purposes. These are referred to as transfer payments.

First of all, state governments are constitutionally responsible for creating and maintaining systems of public education. Implicitly, states are responsible for financially supporting the delivery of programs throughout the state. Two primary mechanisms states use are providing state aid for education and granting school districts authority to tax real property. The United States Constitution's

General Welfare clause does not place a similar burden on Congress. It permits federal intervention, however, when the national interest warrants legislative action.

Second, higher levels of government can better ensure that adequate public services, including public education, are made available throughout the nation or state. If local governments were dependent solely upon their own revenue-generating sources, they would base many decisions about the level and quality of services on expected returns to the locality rather than to the larger society. State and federal leadership and financial assistance encourage and enable localities to meet goals defined by these higher levels of government in addition to those defined locally. The state plays a particularly critical role in challenging localities to improve educational opportunities and outcomes for all students. First (1992) stressed this role in terms of the state holding school districts accountable for educational outcomes:

> The battles for equal access to education and equal treatment in U.S. schools have been fought, and to a large extent, won. The battle for equal outcomes is now being fought, as is the battle for excellence in education, but it must be excellence for all, and herein lies the importance of the states' role. (p. 134)

Third, a central government (state or federal) can take advantage of broader tax bases and economies of scale to improve schools in all localities. Allocations enable a higher basic level of education, expand educational opportunities, and broaden course offerings in communities that may have little tax base or are unwilling to raise sufficient revenue.

In many ways, state and federal leadership and financial resources can improve the general quality of education. However, the regulations that may accompany such financial aid programs are often considered unwarranted interventions into the affairs of local government. Rather than promoting efficiency and economies of scale, mandates may stifle educators' abilities to address particular needs of pupils and communities. Higher levels of government take different approaches when they design financial aid policies. They may choose to use financial incentives to shape educational programs and services, but they are reluctant to impose directives that weaken the abilities of school boards to respond to community priorities, or of school personnel to meet pupils' educational needs.

TYPES OF AID PROGRAMS

Transfer payments may be described as general, categorical, or block grant aids. *General* financial aid flows from federal and state governments with few limitations on the governing boards of municipalities and school districts. Local school boards and educators largely determine specific educational programs and related expenditures within the broad guidelines of the state. In this chapter, we describe general aid distributed through states' basic finance formulas. This general aid provides the largest proportion of support for school operations.

In contrast, *categorical* aids link grants to specific objectives of the government providing the aid. These aids thereby constrain program design and delivery. To qualify for such aid, a school district must comply with program requirements. Thus, unlike general aid, categorical grants can be used only for a certain group of students (e.g., those with disabilities), a specific purpose (e.g., pupil transportation), or a particular project (e.g., construction of a school building).

State categorical aid was once the predominant form of financial assistance. It continues to be an important way for states to communicate legislative priorities. States do this through appropriations that restrict local control. Similarly, most federal funds are designated for specified program priorities. The most important priorities are vocational education and broadening the educational opportunities of children who are economically disadvantaged or disabled. *Entitlement* programs direct funds to school districts according to the number of qualifying pupils. Competitive categorical grants require that specific program proposals be initiated by school districts and approved by the granting agency.

Program control through categorical aid brings about greater centralization of decision making and more complex administration. Legislatures decide priorities. In place of local discretion, the federal or state governments make decisions. State and federal bureaucracies oversee programs and ensure that funds are used for the purposes they intended. They develop guidelines for entitlement programs, request and review proposals for competitive grants, monitor how money is used, and require results to be evaluated.

Administering categorical aid, particularly for competitive grants, is also far more involved for local officials than administering general operating aid. Officials must maintain a separate account to restrict expenditures to designated programs and targeted groups. A large burden may be placed on project coordinators to show that grants are spent to *supplement* rather than to *supplant,* or replace, state and local revenue. Whereas general aid flows to schools each year with little administrative attention, many categorical aids call for annual applications, documentation of expenditures, and frequent program evaluations. Because the paperwork involved in administering competitive categorical aids places small and rural districts at a disadvantage in competing for funds, many categoricals are allocated as entitlement programs. In recent years other categoricals have been absorbed into block grants to reduce the burden and ease controls.

General aid and categorical grants occupy the ends of a continuum of funding types based on the degree of control by higher levels of government. *Block grants* define a middle-ground approach. State and federal block grants allow a range of services within a broad set of government purposes. Requirements for planning, implementing, and assessing programs are also less distinct than for categorical aid.

The federal government popularized the block grant approach when Congress combined a number of former categorical programs within Chapter II

of the Education Consolidation and Improvement Act of 1981 (see Chapter 10). Under this block grant, states receive funds according to their total number of pupils rather than through a competitive application process that specifies educational needs or program goals. In turn, the states develop formulas that consider enrollments as well as other measures of need when they make allocations to school districts. This block grant program initially outlined several broad purposes. Under the 1994 revisions, even greater latitude gives school district personnel discretion in program designs. Despite the eased control, block grants are often accounted for separately, as is true for more restrictive categorical aids.

Local school boards, administrators, and teachers generally prefer unrestricted grants because they minimize administrative processes and permit latitude to meet local priorities. Special interest groups and many educators are concerned about diluted programs under less restrictive approaches. They argue that policy intents should be defined at broader state and federal levels. The political reality once favored equity goals through strict categorical funding. It turned in the 1980s and 1990s to support liberty and efficiency goals through block grants and greater local initiative. Clearly, the degree of control over the use of funds differentiates these three types of approaches to aid.

State finance policies rely on a mix of general aid programs for most operating expenses and categorical ones for special purposes. The bulk of school aid flows to districts through a variation of one of the prototypes we discuss in the next section. The primary focus is state policy for distributing general aid. We discuss categorical and block grants more fully in Chapters 9 and 10.

MODELS FOR STATE FINANCE PROGRAMS

States have funding formulas that allocate general aid to districts. These formulas follow several prototypes. Formulas evolved as state legislatures assumed a larger role in ensuring that all districts can access resources to provide at least a minimal level of educational services. Formulas become increasingly complex because legislatures try to define minimal levels to ensure adequacy, while also satisfying demands for uniformity and efficiency in service delivery.

Locally levied taxes have been important for determining the amount of state transfer payments allocated to school districts. These have normally been the property tax but increasingly have been income and sales taxes. In discussing state aid mechanisms, there are four key concepts that apply to all models: the *adequacy* or level of support, defined in terms of expenditure per pupil or classroom unit; the *division of fiscal responsibility* between state and local jurisdictions; local *ability* to raise taxes in support of education, defined as property valuation or personal income per pupil; and local *effort,* defined as the tax rate that is applied to the value of property or income. We will use the general features of these prototypes, sketches of selected states' applications of several models, exercises, and computer simulation to help us understand how these four concepts relate to aid structures.

Some public school programs completely rely on local funds. Others use matching grants, flat grants, foundation programs, and various forms of tax base equalization. Still others are fully funded by the state. Even though a combination of these approaches may actually be used by states in formulating their overall school aid policies, the basic operating aid typically follows one of the prototypes. Table 8.1 lists states according to the primary approach they take to fund basic school operations, as classified by Gold, Smith, and Lawton (1995). In 1993–1994, a total of forty states were classified as having a foundation program. Four states used a percentage-equalizing approach. Two used a guaranteed tax base or yield program. Several states with a foundation plan also allocated funds to districts through one of these tax-base-equalizing models as a second tier of funding. A flat amount of aid was provided in two states. And two others fully funded school operations.

Table 8.1 also indicates per pupil revenue and the relative percentages of funds from federal, state, and local levels in 1993–1994. New Hampshire, for example, relied heavily on local revenue (89 percent) in its foundation plan. School districts in Michigan, South Dakota, and Vermont also derived over 60 percent of their revenue from local sources. In contrast, Hawaii's large percentage derived from the state (91 percent) reflected its organization as a single school district; the remaining funds came primarily from the federal government. The percentage of revenue from state-level resources was also high (over 65 percent) in Alabama, Delaware, Kentucky, and Washington. A number of finance plans divided support for schools nearly equally between state and local sources: Arizona, Colorado, Florida, Georgia, Iowa, Kansas, Maine, Minnesota, North Dakota, South Carolina, Tennessee, and Texas.

The percentage mix of state and local resources is often misconstrued in relation to the adequacy of overall revenue. People often think that the higher the percentage of state funds is, the more money is available to districts. This is not the case. Figure 8.1 graphically shows the distribution of states by the percentage of funds derived from state sources and the average revenue per pupil (using data in Table 8.1). The relationship between the two variables, which is represented by the regression line on the graph, is somewhat negative (correlation of –0.1838). This inverse relationship indicates that the higher the percentage of state money, the lower the per pupil revenue. The average revenue per pupil for the twenty states that had a percentage of state funding of over 50 percent is $5,405. This compares with $6,092 for the thirty states providing less than 50 percent of total school funds.

The same pattern was noted by Parrish and Fowler (1995) in their analyses of disparities in school resources among geographic regions. Western states, which had the lowest overall adjusted revenues per student in 1989–1990 ($3,708), also received the greatest share of support from state sources (an average of 60.5 percent). In contrast, states in the Northeast (40.4 percent) and Midwest

TABLE 8.1. Classification of States' Basic Support Programs, Estimated Percentage of Revenue by Source and per Pupil Revenue, 1993–1994

State	Finance Program[a]	Revenue		Source of Revenue		
		Per Pupil	Rank	Federal (%)	State (%)	Local (%)
Alabama	FND-R	$3,913	48	13.1	65.4	21.6
Alaska	FND-R	8,189	4	12.6	63.6	23.8
Arizona	FND	4,957	38	8.9	42.3	48.9
Arkansas	FND	4,411	44	9.4	63.1	27.5
California	FND	5,327	30	8.9	54.9	36.2
Colorado	FND-R	5,107	36	5.8	46.0	48.2
Connecticut	PCT[b]	8,652	2	4.6	39.5	55.9
Delaware	FLT[c]	6,696	11	9.1	65.1	25.8
Florida	FND-R	5,838	23	7.7	49.8	42.4
Georgia	FND[d]	5,125	35	8.4	49.4	42.2
Hawaii	FULL	6,537	13	7.1	90.9	2.1
Idaho	FND	4,027	47	8.1	60.9	30.9
Illinois	FND	5,793	24	8.2	32.9	58.8
Indiana	GTB/Y	5,950	21	5.2	52.1	42.6
Iowa	FND-R	5,497	27	5.7	48.4	45.9
Kansas	FND	5,496	28	5.5	49.7	44.9
Kentucky	FND-R	4,932	39	10.2	67.2	22.6
Louisiana	FND	4,608	43	12.3	53.6	34.0
Maine	FND-R	5,957	20	7.0	48.5	44.4
Maryland	FND	6,526	14	5.6	39.0	55.4
Massachusetts	FND-R	6,754	9	5.5	36.0	58.5
Michigan	FND-R	6,840	8	5.7	32.1	62.2
Minnesota	FND-R	6,113	18	5.1	46.5	48.5
Mississippi	FND-R	3,806	50	16.6	53.8	29.6
Missouri	FND-R[e]	5,232	34	6.6	37.5	55.9
Montana	FND[d]	5,376	29	9.2	53.8	37.0
Nebraska	FND	4,984	37	4.8	39.1	56.1
Nevada	FND-R	5,245	33	5.0	36.0	59.0
New Hampshire	FND	6,380	15	2.8	8.3	88.9
New Jersey	FND	9,814	1	4.2	41.5	54.3
New Mexico	FND-R	6,228	16	10.3	61.8	27.9
New York	PCT	8,629	3	5.6	39.2	55.2
North Carolina	FLT	5,950	22	8.9	63.8	27.3
North Dakota	FND	4,761	42	11.5	43.6	44.9
Ohio	FND-R	5,699	25	6.2	43.4	50.4
Oklahoma	FND[d]	4,397	45	7.4	63.3	29.4
Oregon	FND	5,549	26	7.3	41.0	51.7
Pennsylvania	PCT	7,526	5	6.2	41.4	52.5
Rhode Island	PCT	7,016	7	4.5	40.7	54.8
South Carolina	FND-R	4,927	40	9.6	46.9	43.5
South Dakota	FND	4,830	41	10.8	25.3	63.9
Tennessee	FND-R	4,135	46	9.8	48.9	41.3

(Continued)

TABLE 8.1. Classification of States' Basic Support Programs, Estimated Percentage of Revenue by Source and per Pupil Revenue, 1993–1994 (*Continued*)

State	Finance Program[a]	Revenue		Source of Revenue		
		Per Pupil	Rank	Federal (%)	State (%)	Local (%)
Texas	FND-R[d]	5,303	31	8.5	43.4	48.1
Utah	FND-R	3,810	49	7.1	54.9	38.0
Vermont	FND	7,204	6	5.2	32.4	62.5
Virginia	FND-R	5,271	32	6.6	34.2	59.2
Washington	FULL	6,140	17	5.9	71.0	23.0
West Virginia	FND	6,007	19	8.2	64.6	27.2
Wisconsin	GTB/Y	6,706	10	4.4	38.7	56.9
Wyoming	FND-R	6,679	12	5.8	52.2	42.1
United States		5,907		7.2	46.0	46.8

[a]States with descriptions of basic support program for years other than 1993–1994: Colorado, 1994–1995; Michigan, 1994–1995; Wyoming, 1992–1993.

FLT   Flat Grant
FND   Foundation, local effort not required
FND-R Foundation, with required local effort
FULL   Full State Funding
GTB/Y Guaranteed Tax Base/Yield
PCT   Percentage Equalization

[b]Although Connecticut considers the basic support program to be a modified foundation plan, for purposes of this table it is considered to be a percentage-equalizing program since an aid ratio is used in the calculation of basic support aid.

[c]Delaware has a separate equalization component in addition to the flat grant.

[d]States two tiers of funding; the second-tier basic support funding mechanism consists of a guaranteed tax base/yield program.

[e]Missouri incorporates a guaranteed tax base add-on into the basic support formula.

SOURCE: S. D. Gold, D. M. Smith, & S. B. Lawton (Eds.). (1995). *Public School Finance Programs of the United States and Canada, 1993–94*. Albany: American Education Finance Association and The Center for the Study of the States, pp. 10, 24. Reprinted with the permission of the publisher; National Education Association. [1995]. *1994–95 Estimates of School Statistics*. Washington, DC: Author, p. 38.

(41.5 percent) had higher levels of overall revenue ($5,317 and $4,334, respectively). States that continue to rely upon local tax bases in general have higher revenue than those that finance education primarily through state resources.

The adequacy of monies available to school systems depends on the per pupil valuation of various tax bases and on the willingness of legislators, school boards, and voters to tap these sources in support of public education. The models presented in this section take school districts' fiscal capacity and tax effort into account to varying degrees in determining state aid allocations. They also communicate the priorities placed on the values of equality and liberty in their approaches to dividing responsibilities between state and local levels.

These prototypes range in scope from complete local financing with no state assistance to full state funding of education.

No State Involvement

Even though states assumed constitutional responsibility for public education, they did not assume a large role in financing schools until the twentieth century. States created school districts in the eighteenth and nineteenth centuries to encourage the spread of formal education at a time when attendance was voluntary. Schools were financed through county or district property taxes (authorized by state government), minimal state aid, and private contributions. Equalization of opportunities

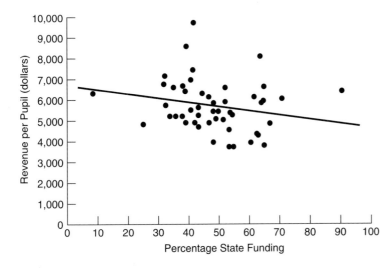

Figure 8.1. Distribution of States by Average Revenue per Pupil and Percentage of State Funding

(in terms of financial inputs) was only within, and not among, the very small and typically homogeneous school districts.

Under this arrangement, per pupil expenditures varied greatly among communities. Expenditures depended on the wealth of individuals, the capacity of tax bases, and the willingness of individuals and taxpayers to divert funds to schooling. Thus the adequacy of school programs closely reflected property assessments and tax rates (see Chapter 6). Districts with large capacity (i.e., per pupil valuations) could raise needed revenue even with low effort (i.e., tax rates). However, districts with low capacity could not finance an adequate program even with high tax effort.

These conditions were present at the turn of the century, when Cubberley (1906) advocated a state role in school finance:

> [W]hile it may be possible to maintain schools entirely or almost entirely by local taxation, the doing so involves very slight efforts on the part of some communities, and very excessive burdens for other communities ... [T]hese excessive burdens, borne in large part for the common good, should be in part equalized by the state. To do this some form of general aid is necessary. (p. 250)

Even today, when basic operating aid enables all districts to sponsor minimally adequate education, the funding of facilities is quite often reliant on local property capacity and effort. When there is little or no state involvement in financing such needs, great inequities result (see discussion of capital outlay in Chapter 7 and Kozol, 1991).

Matching Grants

One of the first forms of state aid was matching grants. These payments stimulate local taxation by requiring localities to match state contributions on an equal dollar-for-dollar basis or a proportionate match, such as requiring localities to raise $100 for each $500 of state money. Although a matching grant may effectively motivate voters to raise taxes, the total amount of funds received depends on local fiscal capacity and effort. These grants work against goals of equalizing capacity, because they favor wealthy districts that are most able to raise the required local revenue with little tax effort. Further amplifying disparities in expenditure levels among districts, they promote "inequalities in educational opportunities or burdensome local school taxes" (Burke, 1957, p. 395).

Matching grants are no longer used to provide general state aid for school districts, and this model is not listed in Table 8.1. Nevertheless, some states call for matching funds to construct school facilities, and the federal government aids vocational and technical education through matching grants. This finance strategy is also similar to the challenge grants issued by donors who desire to stimulate other fund-raising activities (see Chapter 7).

Flat Grants

States abandoned matching grants as a structure for general aid in favor of strategies that could better extend educational opportunities to districts that were unwilling to exert tax effort or had little assessed valuation. Per capita grants, which allocate money according to a count of students or teachers, ignore local fiscal capacity and effort. Initially the school census (i.e., the count of school-aged children) was the basis for apportioning funds in thirty-eight states early in the century (Cubberley, 1906, p. 100). However, pupil measures work to the disadvantage of smaller schools in rural areas because of diseconomies of scale (see Chapter 13). This is true whether a census, actual enrollment, or attendance is used. For this reason, states later allocated flat grants according to the number of teachers or instructional units. Many of today's categorical aid entitlements are flat grants.

This finance approach presumes that the state's appropriate role is to guarantee each student a minimum level of schooling, and that fairness is achieved if the state gives equal monies to all. Responding to the complete reliance on local property tax bases early in the century, Cubberley argued that the state should "equalize the advantages to all as nearly as can be done with the resources at hand" (Cubberley, 1906, p. 17). Although it was the state's duty to secure for all pupils as high a minimum of education as possible, he cautioned against reducing all to this level. Local control of schools remained a priority. States should provide only "the central support necessary to the health of the program without detriment to the local operating unit" (Mort & Reusser, 1941, p. 375).

The value of liberty is thus realized through the flat-grant approach insofar as the structure leaves to local boards or voters decisions about programs beyond the minimum. Through permissive property taxation, this model allows communities to rise above the presumed adequate base. If equality is defined in terms of minimum program standards, then the variations in total expenditures resulting from local optional taxes are not viewed as being inequitable.

Figure 8.2 illustrates the flat grant plan, as it might be applied in the hypothetical state of the computer simulation accompanying this chapter. A uniform per pupil allocation of state aid (e.g., $6,000) is supplemented by the unequal amounts raised by optional local taxes. Voters in the relatively wealthy district, Sommerset, agree to supplement the uniform state grant through a 4.41 mill levy. They add $2,719.00 of local funds to reach a desired total per pupil spending of $8,719.00. The tax rate is determined by dividing the local supplement ($2,719) by the property valuation ($617,100). Even though Ellicott and Redrock levy heavier tax rates (5.52 and 12.57 mills, respectively), their total revenues ($6,469.00 and $7,458.00) are less.[1] Clearly, the total funds available under this plan vary greatly among districts when there is a relatively large reliance on local option taxes. By increasing the size of the base allocation relative to these supplements, or by lowering the cap that might be placed on local discretionary taxes, the state can induce greater equalization of total revenue. If a state chose to disallow local leeway, the plan would have fully equalized per pupil revenue (see Figure 8.11).

Local capacity and effort are not considered in the base; the total amount of state funds available is simply divided by the number of pupils or instructional units. However, in a variation of this prototype, a variable flat-grant approach permits different funding levels according to particular needs of pupils or classes. Weighted pupil or instructional unit techniques (discussed fully in Chapter 9) enable the state to adjust the size of grants to account for varying costs of educational programs and services.

Gold, Smith, and Lawton (1995) classify two states, Delaware and North Carolina, as having a

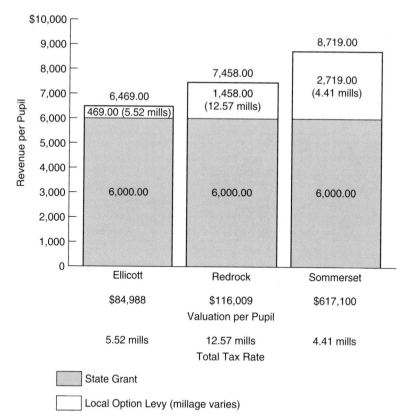

Figure 8.2. Flat Grant Model

flat grant structure as the primary school finance program. North Carolina allocates state aid through personnel allotments that specify positions to be filled. See the overview presented in Figure 8.3. These allotments vary. They reflect characteristics of teachers and class size related to particular programs. But they are not distributed in relation to any measure of local financial wealth or tax effort. Local resources, primarily from property taxation, supplement the state's basic allocations. Disparities in total spending among districts have traditionally been small because the percentage of state funds is high (64 percent in 1993–1994).

Even when the basic operations of a school district are financed through one of the other models we discuss, categorical programs are often financed through flat grants. For example, special education in Illinois is partially financed by the state through a flat grant of one-half the teacher's salary up to $1,000 per pupil, or $8,000 per teacher for physically handicapped students and a flat $8,000 for most other teachers, psychologists, and other specialists (Gold, Smith, & Lawton, 1995, p. 232). Per capita grants have also financed many federal programs, including the previously described block grant approach assumed by the former Education Consolidation and Improvement Act.

Foundation Programs

In a foundation plan, as in the flat grant model, the state legislature defines a funding level associated with a basic education. Localities are free to fund additional programs. The difference between these models is in the responsibility for financing the base or foundation level. Under a flat grant, the state alone funds the uniform per pupil or per class-

General Description

State funds are allocated according to personnel allotments based on Average Daily Membership. Minor adjustments since 1991 consider local wealth in small districts. Localities may supplement the flat grants through local option property taxation.

State Funding of Base Program

There is no required local contribution to the basic support program in this finance plan, which has remained virtually unchanged since enacted in 1933. The state fully funds what it considers to be a district's current expense requirement. Personnel allotments are based primarily on the number of students in average daily membership. The variable grants reflect state-adopted class size ratios that depend on grade level: grade K, 1:23; grades 1–9, grades 10–12, 1:28.425.

Allotments also vary according to teacher experience and training through a statewide salary schedule. Additional allotments for administrative and supervisory, teacher assistants in grades K–3, and other personnel are also determined by the number of pupils enrolled. Other positions are allocated on a district basis (e.g., superintendent).

A degree of wealth equalization has been achieved since 1991 through adjustments for districts that are in low-wealth areas. Districts that are unable to operate efficiently due to small enrollments and geographic isolation receive additional funds.

Local Support beyond the Basic Program

All but 2 of the 120 school districts are fiscally dependent. Counties levy taxes to operate and maintain facilities, hire additional personnel, and supplement state salary levels. The statewide average for local contribution to current expenses is 23.5 percent of the total annual budget. An additional tax, up to 50 cents (60 cents in districts with over 100,000 population) on $100 appraised valuation, is permitted with voter approval.

Figure 8.3. Variable Flat Grants in North Carolina. (SOURCE: H. D. Bryant & B. MacPhail-Wilcox [1995]. North Carolina. In S. D. Gold, D. M. Smith, & S. B. Lawton [Eds.], *Public School Finance Programs of the United States and Canada, 1993–94* [pp. 473–483]. Albany, NY: American Education Finance Association and The Center for the Study of the States. Reprinted with the permission of the publisher.)

room amount. In a foundation plan, the state and each school district form a partnership to finance the required program cost. The state determines the required level of local participation. Over half of the states use this approach.

Strayer and Haig (1923) devised this plan. Through it states access local revenue to share the costs of a basic education program. According to their plan, a uniform statewide tax rate "sufficient to meet the costs only in the richest district" is levied. Deficiencies in all other districts are made up by state subventions (p. 176). Under this required levy, effort is controlled and fiscal capacity dictates the relative shares of local and state funds

that apply to the foundation. Beyond the equalized guarantee, local leeway satisfies liberty interests of districts much as it did in the flat grant prototype.

An application of this model is presented in Figure 8.4. The total amounts of revenue available to districts are the same as those depicted for the flat grant model (Figure 8.2). These diagrams differ in the sources of revenue that make up the base. The guaranteed per pupil revenue (in this case, $6,000.00) appears as a horizontal line. This line is often referred to as a "Strayer-Haig line" in the foundation plan. Below this minimum foundation of spending per pupil or per instructional unit, revenue from the required local effort (RLE of 7.55 mills) blends with state funds. Districts with greater tax capacity contribute proportionately more. Thus, the poorer districts, Ellicott and Redrock, receive more state dollars per unit ($5,358.34 and $5,124.13) than does the wealthier district, Sommerset ($1,340.89). In addition to the required effort of 7.55 mills, voters in these districts approve optional taxes—just as they did under the flat grant model. Local option taxes vary substantially depending on voters' willingness to pay for program enhancements and property valuations. In this depiction, a larger effort (12.57 mills) is required in Redrock to increase spending by only $1,458.00 in comparison to the 4.41 mills levied in Sommerset to raise $2,719.00 per pupil. In-

equities are apparent in the total state and local revenues and tax rates. Sommerset has the highest revenue but the lowest total effort (11.96 mills) relative to the levies in Ellicott and Redrock (13.07 mills and 20.12 mills, respectively).

The local effort required of districts in this model is not as high as the amount that would be levied under the foundation plan conceived by Strayer and Haig. Rather than establishing a uniform statewide tax rate such that the guarantee would be fully paid by local funds in the richest district, political realities and multiple goals limit state legislatures from imposing a high levy on all districts. From a strict equalization standpoint, Sommerset would receive no state aid and the uniform levy would be 9.72 mills ($6,000.00/

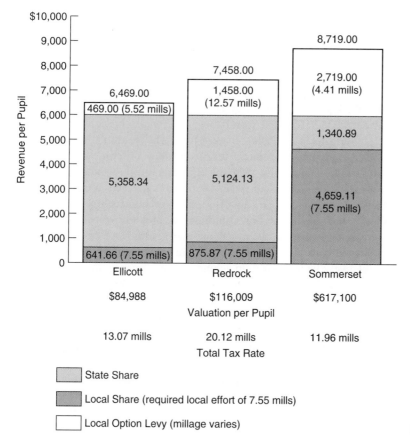

Figure 8.4. Foundation Model

$617,100). However, legislative actions result from political compromises among several priorities. Only one of these priorities is equalization (see discussion in Chapter 11). An important goal of legislatures that adopt a foundation plan is to use state aid to relieve local tax burdens and to broaden the tax base through state-level taxation. The result is therefore a lower required levy.

The foundation, or guaranteed funding, level corresponds to the state's minimum educational standards or to an educational plan that includes "all the activities the state wishes to assure the communities of least ability to support schools" (Mort & Reusser, 1951, p. 397). Establishing this guarantee is a political decision dictated by available revenue rather than a rational determination of educational needs and costs. If it is too low, there may not be enough money in those districts that have a small local tax base or in those that choose not to levy additional taxes. The state may claim that its responsibility is fulfilled. But the minimum may be insufficient to support a basic educational program. This inadequacy may become an issue in judicial reviews (see Chapter 11).

Johns, Morphet, and Alexander (1983, p. 249) suggested that the state should provide a relatively large percentage, at least 75 percent, of the guarantee. This is in order to take advantage of broader-based taxes and to recognize the heavy reliance that localities place on property taxes for capital outlay and program supplements. As Table 8.1 shows, state participation in finance plans has a wide range for foundation plans. New Hampshire, with a minimal percentage of revenue from the state (8.3 percent), contrasts with Washington's relatively large (71.0 percent) state contribution, which nearly equalizes local resources.

The required local effort (RLE) is in essence a state-imposed property tax. If the RLE is set such that the foundation level is met by local money in the wealthiest district, as conceived originally by Strayer and Haig, then the state effectively leverages property taxes to create a higher funding base than could be obtained under a flat grant program. However, state legislatures are reluctant to deny

any district state aid. The actual state implementation of this plan then diminishes the equalizing potential of the foundation plan in several ways. First, the foundation guarantee may be maintained at a high level, while the RLE is reduced. In that case, more state dollars flow to all districts, but especially to the wealthiest. Second, some states may build a foundation plan upon a flat grant guarantee. In this way even the richest districts that would otherwise receive no state funds are assured a minimum grant. Third, the local effort specified in statute or regulation is not required in nineteen states (see Table 8.1). Very often, the amount that should be raised is a "charge back" against the foundation level in districts unwilling to raise the expected local levy. Thus, there are spending disparities within the foundation amount. This is because the anticipated local funds that should be raised in accordance with the computational tax rate are deducted from the state allocations.

The yield of the optional levy builds upon the base foundation level for school operations. The foundation amount satisfies the goals of equalization. But because district voters are free to tax and spend above the foundation guarantee, liberty goals are satisfied. The resulting disparities in spending reflect not only differing tax efforts but also differing tax capacities to which rates are applied. Voter overrides are rooted in earlier finance plans that placed heavy reliance on local revenue and on continuing desires to involve the community in school finance. Rather than abandon the stimulation brought by rewards for local effort in early matching grants, finance theorists argued that local voter involvement encourages innovation and efficiency without the constraints of state-defined levels of adequacy. This "adaptability," or the propensity of districts to change with the times (Mort, 1933), enables lighthouse districts to experiment (*Fleischmann Report,* 1973, p. 87; Jones, 1985, pp. 106–107). A program adaptation, such as kindergartens in the 1950s or computer-assisted instruction more recently, may prove to be effective. Then it may be disseminated to other school systems. And then a state's foundation level may be adjusted upward so that all localities can take advantage of the program's benefits.

Forty states employ a foundation plan for basic operating expenses (see Table 8.1). The majority of these states (21) require a specific local levy for the base plan. The others permit districts to set a tax rate and then adjust the foundation level when a lower-than-expected levy prevails. The recently enacted Michigan program translates this prototype into policy. This foundation plan establishes a per pupil foundation allowance for each district. It then equalizes the locally raised property tax on nonhomestead property (see Figure 8.5). This guarantee consists of local tax revenue raised through a uniform levy (18 mills on nonhomestead property) and state revenue is distributed in inverse relation to local assessed valuation. The state earmarks 60 percent of its prior sales tax (a 4 percent rate) and 100 percent of the voter-increased sales tax (2 percent) for education. It also collects a six-mill levy on all property to pay its share (see Michigan's property tax reforms in Chapter 6 and in Addonizio, Kearney, & Prince, 1995). Local voters may supplement the equalized guarantee by approving a levy of up to three mills on all property.

Tax Base Equalizing Programs

Another approach to combining state and local revenue for school operations is found in several forms of tax base equalization. Unlike the policy of ensuring a minimum education under flat grant and foundation approaches, these plans stress local determination of a desired level of spending or taxation. Once local officials or voters set an expenditure goal, the state equalizes school districts' abilities to raise the necessary funds.

Updegraff and King (1922) argued the importance of giving localities a dominant role in finance decisions:

> Efficiency in the conduct of schools should be promoted by increasing the state grants when-

ever the true tax-rate is increased and by lowering it whenever the local tax is decreased. (p. 118)

In their view, an appropriate state role was to help school systems deliver educational programs fashioned by local educators and to neutralize the disparities in local tax bases as determinants of spending goals.

Like the foundation plan, these models contribute to states' goals of financial equalization. But they also involve localities in determining the level of state support. Even though disparities in overall spending result, the plan satisfies the standard of fiscal neutrality. Coons, Clune, and Sugarman (1970) were instrumental in articulating this concept. It has been the cornerstone of many court challenges to the constitutionality of state policies for financing public schools. *Fiscal neutrality* demands that resources for public education be a function of the wealth of the state as a whole rather than of localities. These authors identified two essential characteristics of an acceptable system of state aid:

> First, any right of subunits of the state to be relatively wealthy for educational purposes is denied. The total financial resources of the state should be equally available to all public school children. Ultimate responsibility for public schools is placed squarely with the state. Second, on the other hand, *the units should be free, through the taxing mechanism, to choose to share various amounts of the state's wealth* (by deciding how hard they are willing to tax themselves). (pp. 201–202; emphasis added)

Thus, the total level of resources available is not necessarily the same in all districts (as occurs in full state funding). Rather, a fiscally neutral system ensures that communities have the financial power to raise funds to support schools at their chosen spending levels.

Several mathematically equivalent variations of tax base equalization are evident in state poli-

General Description

Under the redesigned finance plan, basic foundation aid for general operating funds considers a locally raised property tax at a rate determined by the legislature. State revenue from a recently increased sales tax, a statewide property tax, and other sources equalizes this local tax on nonhomestead property. In addition, voters may enact local "enhancement" levies on all property to supplement the foundation guarantee.

Local/State Shares

The state guarantees each district a basic level of funding per pupil, provided the district levies a local voter-approved property tax at a millage rate set by the legislature. The number of pupils is an average of two count days, one in February of the prior school year and the other in October of the current year.

The basic foundation allowance was established at $5,000 per pupil in 1994–1995 and is anticipated to increase annually. However, not all districts are funded at this level, and the actual foundation allowance varied from $4,200 to $6,660 under a plan to level up lower spending districts without leveling down others. Lower spending districts have larger annual increases according to a sliding scale. In addition, a number of hold-harmless districts (i.e., those with higher prior spending) were permitted to retain their advantage, provided that local voters taxed themselves at a rate above the required 18-mill local levy.

The state share of a district's foundation allowance is the difference between the foundation allowance and the amount raised by the required levy on nonhomestead property. Sales tax revenue collected under the recently increased rate (from 4 to 6 percent) is the major source of state revenue. Sixty percent of the revenue from the initial 4 percent tax and all of the revenue from the additional 2 percent tax on general sales are constitutionally earmarked for the School Aid Fund. Portions of other state revenue, including a newly imposed 6-mill state property tax, the personal income tax, tobacco and liquor taxes, taxes on commercial and industrial facilities, and the lottery, as well as transfers from the state's general fund, contribute to school aid.

The property tax was not entirely eliminated in the recent legislative action to minimize reliance on this source. In addition to the state levy of 6 mills on all property, the basic program depends on a local contribution in the form of an additional local levy (requiring voter authorization) of 18 mills on nonhomestead property (i.e., other than owner-occupied residences and qualifying agricultural property). Only one-third of revenue is from these state and local property tax levies, in contrast to two-thirds of total school district funds in the past.

High-revenue districts (having a foundation allowance above $6,500 in 1994–1995) levy hold-harmless millage on all property, i.e., above the 6 mills on homestead and 18 mills on nonhomestead property.

Local Support beyond the Equalized Program

The 560 local school districts are fiscally independent. Voters can approve additional local enhancement levies, up to 3 mills on all property, that are not equalized by the state.

Figure 8.5. Foundation Program in Michigan. (SOURCE: C. P. Kearney [1995]. Michigan. In S. D. Gold, D. M. Smith, & S. B. Lawton [Eds.], *Public School Finance Programs of the United States and Canada, 1993–94* [pp. 333–346]. Albany, NY: American Education Finance Association and The Center for the Study of the States. Reprinted with permission of the publisher; C. P. Kearney [1994]. Michigan. In N. D. Theobald [Ed.], *The State of School Finance Policy Issues, 1994* [pp. 28–33]. Monograph of the AERA's Fiscal Issues, Policy, and Education Finance Special Interest Group.)

cies: percentage equalization, guaranteed tax base, and district power equalization or guaranteed yield. Six states (see Table 8.1) include one or more of these forms of tax base equalization. Five others rely on this form of equalization either as an add-on within the basic formula or as a second tier of funding that builds on the base foundation program. In *percentage equalization* formulas, local and state shares of locally determined expenditures are a function of school district wealth (taxing capacity) relative to the wealth of the state as a whole. State aid in a percentage-equalizing plan is calculated by the following formula:

$$\text{State aid ratio} = 1 - c\,\frac{(\text{school district taxing capacity})}{(\text{state average taxing capacity})}$$

The constant c, which represents the portion of expenditures to be financed by a district of average state wealth, is determined by legislation. Assuming the constant is 0.50 for the simulation included with this chapter, in which the state average valuation is \$159,591 per pupil, the formula becomes:

$$\text{State aid ratio} = 1 - .50\,\frac{(\text{school district taxing capacity})}{(\$159,591)}$$

The school district taxing capacity and the state average taxing capacity change every year according to assessment rolls and equalization ratios. The required percentage local share can be changed only through legislation. Figure 8.6 shows state and local shares for selected school districts in the computer simulation with plans having constants of 0.25, 0.50, and 0.75. For example, the model presented as Figure 8.6B assumes that 50 percent of expenditures are financed from local resources in a district of average wealth, and the remaining 50 percent are provided by the state. Calculation of the aid ratio follows the percentage equalization formula given above. This compares local property valuation with the state average valuation (\$159,591). A higher aid ratio (73.37 percent) is evident in the poorer-than-average Ellicott; Ellicott has a per pupil valuation of \$84,988. In this district, and in any other district in the state having the same valuation, the locality pays 26.63 percent of the expenditures chosen by the school board or voters. Thus, district resources provide only \$1,722.69 of the spending goal (\$6,469.00), and the tax rate is 20.27 mills (computed as \$1,722.69/\$84,988). In comparison, Redrock's aid ratio is 63.65 percent. This district receives \$4,747.12 from the state. When that is added to the \$2,710.98 raised locally from the 23.37 mill

tax, the district attains the desired per pupil spending (\$7,458.00).

If we still assume a constant of 0.50, districts with valuations exceeding the state average per pupil valuation (\$159,591) have aid ratios below 50 percent. A district having a valuation of \$319,182 does not receive state money at any level of expenditure (the aid ratio is 0.0 percent under the percentage equalization formula). Districts exceeding this valuation have negative aid ratios. This means that they would remit to the state any property tax receipts in excess of their identified spending levels. For example, Sommerset has a valuation of \$617,100 per pupil and a computed aid ratio of −93.34 percent. Given a desired spending of \$8,719.00 per pupil and the negative aid ratio, the computed state aid is a negative \$8,138.32 (\$8,719.00 × .9334). In order to collect \$16,857.32 (the sum of the spending level and the negative aid), the district must levy a tax of 27.32 mills. In toto, the district raises the equivalent of 193.34 percent of the per pupil expenditure desired by voters or the school board. The state collects the negative aid for distribution to poorer districts.

This practice of redistributing locally raised property taxes, known as *recapture*, has rarely been implemented by states. It is not only that states are reluctant to take money from districts. Political realities ensure that all districts receive some state aid. Several states, including Maine, Michigan, Utah, Wisconsin, and Wyoming, adopted recapture features at one time in either their foundation or their tax base equalizing approaches. However, provisions in the Wisconsin and Wyoming plans were found to violate the respective state constitutions (see Chapter 11). Utah's foundation plan recaptures money raised in excess of the guarantee for distribution to eligible districts. When the Kansas legislature abandoned a percentage equalization plan in favor of a foundation program and a uniform property tax statewide in 1992, a number of previously high-spending districts were subject to a revenue cap. Any amount over 10 percent of the prior year's budget had to be deducted from the state allotment (Gold, Smith, & Lawton, 1995,

a:

Equivalent forms of this model are:

Percentage Equalization, constant of 0.25; Guaranteed Tax Base, GTB of $638,364; District Power Equalization and Guaranteed Yield, $638.36 per mill levied

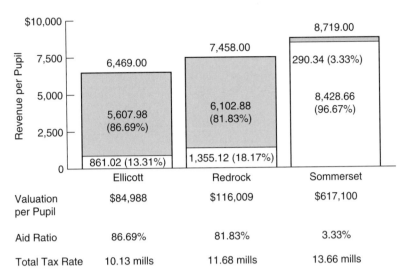

	Ellicott	Redrock	Sommerset
Valuation per Pupil	$84,988	$116,009	$617,100
Aid Ratio	86.69%	81.83%	3.33%
Total Tax Rate	10.13 mills	11.68 mills	13.66 mills

b:

Equivalent forms of this model are:

Percentage Equalization, constant of 0.50; Guaranteed Tax Base, GTB of $319,182; District Power Equalization and Guaranteed Yield, $319.18 per mill levied

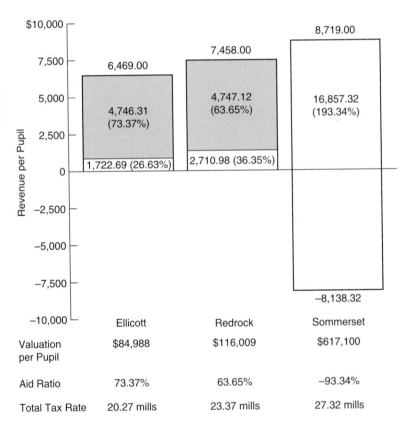

	Ellicott	Redrock	Sommerset
Valuation per Pupil	$84,988	$116,009	$617,100
Aid Ratio	73.37%	63.65%	-93.34%
Total Tax Rate	20.27 mills	23.37 mills	27.32 mills

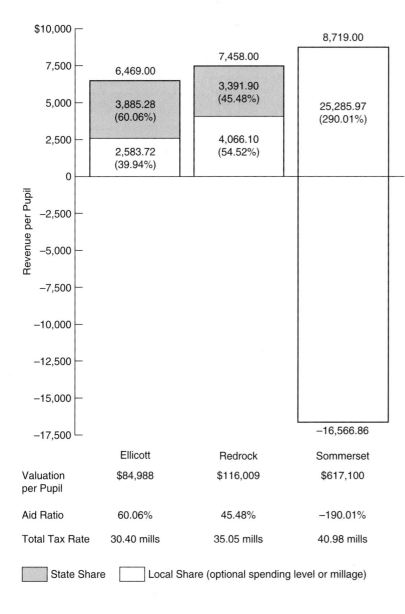

c:

Equivalent forms of this model are:

Percentage Equalization, constant of 0.75; Guaranteed Tax Base, GTB of $212,788; District Power Equalization and Guaranteed Yield, $212.79 per mill levied

	Ellicott	Redrock	Sommerset
Valuation per Pupil	$84,988	$116,009	$617,100
Aid Ratio	60.06%	45.48%	−190.01%
Total Tax Rate	30.40 mills	35.05 mills	40.98 mills

State Share ▨   Local Share (optional spending level or millage) ☐

Figure 8.6. Tax Base Equalization Models (Note: Calculations are rounded to hundredths. Any discrepancies in results between the percentage equalization, guaranteed tax base, and district power equalization models are due to this level of rounding.)

pp. 266, 601). This form of recapture was upheld by the state Supreme Court. The U.S. Supreme Court subsequently denied a petition to review the decision (*Unified School District* v. *Kansas,* 1994).

A more common policy of states when they implement percentage-equalizing schemes is to provide a *floor,* or a minimum amount of state aid for all districts. A flat grant, either as a dollar amount or a minimum aid ratio, ensures that even

the wealthiest districts receive some state assistance. Another common modification to a pure application of tax base equalization theory is placing a *ceiling,* or upper limit, on per pupil expenditures that will be aided by the state. This limits the state's total financial obligation. If the ceiling is set below what most school districts are spending, the formula will be ineffective in meeting pupils' educational needs in all districts. The plan functions like a foundation program. A ceiling has its greatest negative impact on poor districts. If states fail to recapture excess revenue and impose floors and ceilings, then power-equalizing approaches do not neutralize the relationship between wealth and spending (Phelps & Addonizio, 1981).

Figure 8.6 illustrates the effect of adjusting the constant. If the constant were reduced to 0.25 (the state meets 75 percent of the cost of schooling in the district of average wealth), virtually every district would qualify for state aid (see Figure 8.6A). The three districts' aid ratios would be 86.69 percent, 81.83 percent, and 3.33 percent, respectively. Since the state shares are larger under this lower constant than those depicted in Figure 8.6B, local contributions toward respective per pupil expenditures are reduced. The districts' tax rates thus decline to 10.13 mills, 11.68 mills, and 13.66 mills to raise the respective local shares.

In contrast, raising the constant to 0.75 (the state meets one-quarter of the cost of schooling in the district of average wealth) lowers the percentage of state aid (or increases the amount of recapture) for all districts. When the constant is 0.75 and the desired spending levels remain the same for each district (Figure 8.6C), Ellicott's aid ratio declines to 60.06 percent and its state aid diminishes ($3,885.28). And Redrock's falls to 45.48 percent ($3,391.90). More of Sommerset's money is recaptured under the negative aid ratio (–190.01 percent). This district must generate $25,285.97 in property taxes. This is 290.01 percent of desired spending; the amount that is recaptured is $16,566.86 per pupil. The respective millage rates are substantially increased, to 30.40 mills, 35.05 mills, and 40.98 mills, under this larger constant.

Lowering the value of the constant is beneficial for all districts, but especially for districts of high wealth. Of course, lowering the constant is very expensive from the state's perspective. Raising the constant lowers aid to all districts. But this policy change reduces the overall commitment of state funds and shifts the financial burden from broad-based state revenues to the local property tax. States can equalize the poorest districts with a relatively small commitment of state funds if they keep the constant high. Adjustments in the constant make it possible for any state, regardless of the revenue it devotes to schools, to afford this plan.

If voters in all three districts decided to have the same spending level—such as the $8,719.00 selected initially by Sommerset's voters—their aid ratios would dictate differing shares of state and local money. Notice that the districts depicted in Figure 8.7, in which a constant of 0.50 is once again assumed, have the same millage rate (27.32 mills). Thus, the effort is equalized along with the spending goal. This diagram makes it clearer that the policy of recapture is essential in a fully operational percentage equalization plan. Otherwise, wealthy districts retain a large advantage because they achieve their spending goals at far less effort. States must then search elsewhere for revenue to enable poorer districts to attain their desired spending levels; otherwise, inequities persist.

The New York percentage equalization plan is outlined in Figure 8.8. Fiscal capacity is defined by both real property and personal income (see discussion of fiscal capacity in Chapter 9). Each district's aid ratio considers the full property valuation and the adjusted gross income of residents relative to the state averages for those tax bases. Total operating aid is a function of the number of aidable pupil units, the aid ratio, and the expenditure level. A number of modifications in this plan illustrate deviations from the percentage equalization model. First, a flat grant floor insures that all districts receive at least a minimum ($400) in state assistance. Second, a ceiling on the amount of local spending to be equalized ($8,000) makes the plan function like a foundation plan. Finally, a save-harmless provision guarantees state funding at the level set in prior years. Thus, the amount of aid most districts receive is not a function of fiscal capacity, pupils' educational needs, or local effort alone.

Four states—Connecticut, New York, Pennsylvania, and Rhode Island—are classified in Table 8.1 as using a percentage-equalizing formula for determining state aid. This approach may also be used to fund particular programs beyond basic

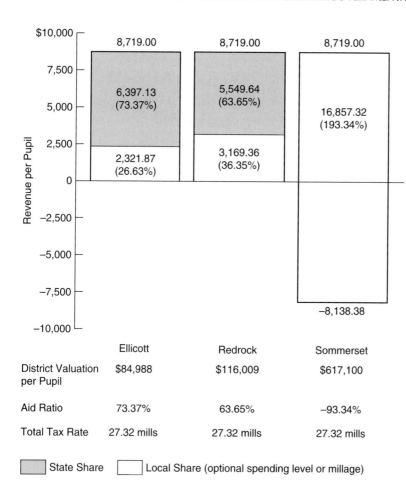

Figure 8.7. Equal Spending under Tax Base Equalization Models (Note: Calculations are rounded to hundredths. Any discrepancies in results between the percentage equalization, guaranteed tax base, and district power equalization models are due to this level of rounding.)

Equivalent forms of this model are:

Percentage Equalization, constant of 0.50; Guaranteed Tax Base, GTB of $319,182; District Power Equalization and Guaranteed Yield, $319.18 per mill levied

	Ellicott	Redrock	Sommerset
District Valuation per Pupil	$84,988	$116,009	$617,100
Aid Ratio	73.37%	63.65%	−93.34%
Total Tax Rate	27.32 mills	27.32 mills	27.32 mills

State Share ☐ Local Share (optional spending level or millage)

school operations. For example, New York uses districts' combined wealth ratios in determining support for special education programs. These four states, along with Massachusetts, provide state assistance for school construction according to a percentage-equalizing formula (Gold, Smith, & Lawton, 1995, pp. 48–52).

Guaranteed Tax Base. In this variation of tax base equalization, districts are guaranteed a state-defined valuation per pupil to achieve their spending goals. As in percentage-equalizing plans, a local district determines a spending level. Both the tax effort and amount of state aid grow proportionately along with any desired increases in expenditures. The desired budget (spending) per pupil

divided by the state guaranteed tax base (GTB) yields the tax rate the district must apply to its property valuation:

$$\text{Tax Rate} = \text{Spending/GTB}$$

The difference between the amounts that would be raised under the GTB and those that are actually raised under the local assessed valuation (AV) is funded by state resources:

$$\text{State Aid} = (\text{Rate} \times \text{GTB}) - (\text{Rate} \times \text{AV})$$

Given the same parameters as for the illustration of percentage equalization (see Figure 8.6B), each district's tax rate is computed as the desired

General Description

Operating aid depends on an aid ratio that compares the wealth of each district to the wealth of the state as a whole. Local wealth considers property valuation and per capita income. No district receives less than $400 per pupil, and a ceiling is placed on the expenditure to be equalized. Districts may spend above the ceiling, since there is no recapture provision in this percentage-equalizing plan.

Local/State Shares

The average daily attendance of resident and nonresident pupils in district-operated programs determines the total aidable pupil units (TAPU). A district may use the current year count or the average of the two most recent years plus additional weightings (e.g., high school, pupils with special educational needs as defined by scores on state examinations, and handicapped pupils served for a portion of the school week). Districts also include pupils with disabilities who are enrolled full-time in Board of Cooperative Educational Services programs. Resident pupils and applicable weights comprise the total wealth pupil units (TWPU) in the formula below.

There are 691 districts employing eight or more teachers and eligible for regular aid. Of this total, 686 are fiscally independent and 5 are fiscally dependent (the 5 largest cities). The shares of locally determined spending vary according to districts' Combined Wealth Ratios (CWR). This measure of ability to pay is the sum of two ratios: 50% of the selected equalized full valuation (SEL FV) of property per TWPU in relation to the state average, and 50% of the adjusted gross income (INC) of resident taxpayers per TWPU in relation to the state average. The selected valuation, which is the lesser of the most recent full value or 117% of the prior two-year average, eases the impact of rapid inflation of property values in some communities while placing a cap on the wealth to be equalized. Given a statewide average full value per TWPU of $303,900 and an average adjusted gross income per TWPU of $77,600 in 1993–1994:

$$CWR = \frac{(0.5 \times \text{District SEL FV/TWPU})}{\$303,900} + \frac{(0.5 \times \text{District INC/TWPU})}{\$77,600}$$

The State Sharing Ratio (SSR) for a district is the larger of the following four calculations, but not more than 0.88 or less than 0:

$$1.33 - (1.50 \times \text{CWR}) \qquad 0.78 - (0.39 \times \text{CWR})$$
$$1.00 - (0.64 \times \text{CWR}) \qquad 0.51 - (0.22 \times \text{CWR})$$

The district receives the larger of $400 per TAPU (a minimum flat grant that ensures aid to all districts regardless of wealth) or the result of the per pupil aid formula:

$$[\$3,761 + .05 \times (\text{District Expense/TAPU})] \times \text{State Sharing Ratio}$$

The District Expense in this formula is its approved operating expense (AOE); this expenditure per TAPU is between $3,761 and a ceiling of $8,000.

For example, a district of average wealth has a CWR of 1.00, and the state pays 39% of its expenditures under the third SSR formula:

$$SSR = 0.78 - (0.39 \times 1.00) = 0.39$$

The state's share is $1,574, assuming the district's per pupil AOE is $5,500:

$$\text{Aid} = [\$3,761 + .05 \times (\$5,500)] \times 0.39 = \$1,574$$

Figure 8.8. Percentage Equalization in New York. (SOURCE: R. L. Henahan [1995]. New York. In S. D. Gold, D. M. Smith, & S. B. Lawton [Eds.], *Public School Finance Programs of the United States and Canada, 1993–94* [pp. 451–471]. Albany, NY: American Education Finance Association and The Center for the Study of the States. Reprinted with permission of the publisher; F. E. Crampton [1994]. New York. In N.D. Theobald [Ed.], *The State of School Finance Policy Issues, 1994* [pp. 73–78]. Monograph of the AERA's Fiscal Issues, Policy, and Education Finance Special Interest Group.)

(Continued)

This amount is multiplied by the number of aidable pupil units (TAPU) in the district. The local share in this example is $3,926, or 71% of its chosen expenditure level. If this district is spending at or above the ceiling placed on AOE ($8,000), it receives $1,623:

$$\text{Aid} = [\$3,761 + .05 \times (\$8,000)] \times 0.39$$

A large number of districts (568) were off formula in 1993–1994. Two-thirds should have received more aid, but limited state funds inhibited the full state share. These districts received transition aid that gradually moves them on the formula. The other third received save-harmless aid which guaranteed no less than the amount of operating aid received in the base year.

The average state share was 39.2% in 1993–1994. State general fund revenue is primarily from income and sales taxation; lottery receipts are earmarked for education and provide about 10% of state school aid. Local funds are derived from property taxation; 8 counties distribute a portion of sales tax revenue to schools.

Local Support beyond the Equalized Program

Without recapture, taxes raised in many districts enable them to expend beyond the ceiling used in determining operating aid.

---

spending divided by the legislatively determined guaranteed tax base ($319,182, double the average state wealth). The tax rate in Ellicott would be 20.27 mills (calculated as $6,469.00/$319,182). It is 23.37 mills in Redrock and 27.32 mills in Sommerset. State and local shares are determined by the above formula. For example, Ellicott's state aid is $4,746.31. This is the difference between what it would raise under the GTB (0.02027 × $319,182) and the local revenue of $1,722.69 from the rate applied to the per pupil valuation (0.02027 × $84,988). The results are very similar to those obtained under the percentage-equalization model with a constant of 0.50 (any differences are due to rounding). The consequences of increasing or lowering the state GTB are evident in Figures 8.6A and 8.6C, respectively. Raising the GTB to $638,364 is equivalent to a percentage-equalization constant of 0.25. Lowering the GTB to $212,788 is the same as having a percentage-equalizing plan with a constant of 0.75.

Although percentage-equalization and guaranteed-tax-base plans are equivalent mathematically, the GTB places attention on districts' taxation rather than on their spending. In essence, the GTB plan, as illustrated in Figure 8.6B, guarantees all districts a tax base of $319,182. Those districts whose voters desire per pupil expenditures

of $8,719.00 must levy 27.32 mills ($8,719.00/$319,182), just as is depicted in Figure 8.7. If a district has above-average wealth, like Sommerset, the tax base yields a higher amount at this levy ($16,857.32). Thus the difference between this revenue and the one that would be raised by the GTB is recaptured ($8,140.17).

Like percentage-equalizing plans, ceilings are usually applied to limit the amount of state commitment. And floor funding levels ensure that all districts receive some state aid, regardless of their wealth. In such cases, the plan fully equalizes only those districts whose tax bases are less than the state GTB and whose spending is below the ceiling (Reilly, 1982).

Wisconsin relied upon a guaranteed-tax-base formula in 1993–1994. Several other states listed in Table 8.1 employed this strategy as a second tier of funding. The Wisconsin plan includes two guaranteed valuations (see Figure 8.9) according to expenditure levels. Districts spending below the ceiling ($5,453) for "primary costs" calculate state funds according to one of the three guaranteed tax bases (e.g., $310,726 for K–12 districts). Higher-spending districts also take advantage of "secondary" aid. The lower guaranteed valuation (e.g., $204,365) in this formula equalizes poorer districts' tax bases if they set high spending goals. Recapture of amounts gen-

General Description

A school district's per pupil property valuation is compared with the state's guaranteed tax base (GTB) at two different spending levels to determine state aid.

Local/State Shares

The average of pupil membership on two count days determines the number of units for aid. Full property valuation per member defines the fiscal capacity of the 427 fiscally independent districts. Aid is based on prior-year spending, membership, and property valuation.

The formula has two tiers of cost sharing, with the guaranteed valuations defined by grade-level structure and expenditure level. In 1993–1994, the per pupil GTBs for expenditures up to the "primary cost ceiling" ($5,453) and for "secondary" costs over that level were as follows:

District Type	Primary Costs	Secondary Costs
K–12	$310,726	$204,365
K–8	466,089	306,547
High school	932,178	613,095

A district receives primary and secondary aid based on the following formula, which considers per pupil tax bases:

$$\text{State Aid} = \text{District Cost} \times \frac{(\text{Guaranteed Tax Base} - \text{District Tax Base})}{\text{Guaranteed Tax Base}}$$

The total state share equals per pupil aid calculations for primary and secondary costs times average daily membership. The 227 districts spending above the primary cost ceiling in 1993–1994 received aid for those expenditures based on the lower guaranteed valuation. If secondary aid is negative because the district tax base is larger than the guaranteed base, it is subtracted from any primary aid. If total aid is negative, the district does not receive aid (referred to as a "zero-aid" district); neither is it required to pay negative aid to the state.

The state share is paid from general purpose revenue, primarily personal and corporate income taxes and sales taxes. The local share is paid through property taxes. There is a revenue growth limit on districts through 1997–1998. A two-year freeze on the growth of property taxes through 1995–1996 increased the proportion raised by state revenue. The state share (38.7% in 1993–1994) is expected to increase under these limits.

A flat grant that varies according to the district's median household income and its local levy (between $100 and $400 to 57 districts in 1993–1994) ensures at least minimum aid to all districts. A hold-harmless special adjustment aid eases the effect in reductions in aid (90% of the prior year's aid to 20 districts in 1993–1994; declines to 85% in 1995–1996 and thereafter).

Local Support beyond the Equalized Program

Without recapture, wealthy districts expand revenue raised by tax bases that exceed the state guaranteed level.

Figure 8.9 Guaranteed Tax Base in Wisconsin. (SOURCE: D. Clancy, C. Toulmin, & M. Bukolt [1995]. Wisconsin. In. S. D. Gold, D. M. Smith, & S. B. Lawton [Eds.], *Public School Finance Programs of the United States and Canada, 1993–94* [pp. 661–674]. Albany, NY: American Education Finance Association and The Center for the Study of the States. Reprinted with permission of the publisher.)

erated in districts whose tax bases exceed the GTB was called for in legislation passed in 1973. But the Wisconsin Supreme Court disallowed negative aid before it could be applied (*Buse* v. *Smith,* 1976). Thus, districts that would otherwise remit funds to the state have large amounts of revenue available for school programs. They are entitled to minimum aid (up to $400 per pupil) under the plan.

District Power Equalization and Guaranteed Yield.
The same result as that of the two preceding finance models can also be generated by focusing on local effort or tax rate in a district power-equalizing approach. Instead of guaranteeing a tax base, the state specifies and guarantees a given revenue yield for each mill of tax levied locally.

We will continue with the same parameters as those in Figure 8.6B. A state could guarantee to school districts a yield of $319.18 per pupil for each mill levied rather than a tax base of $319,182. A tax rate of 20.27 mills yields per pupil revenue of $6,469.78 (0.02027 × $319.18). This is approximately the amount of spending desired by Ellicott in the previous examples (any deviations from prior calculations are due to rounding). Similarly, a tax rate of 23.37 mills guarantees a revenue of $7,459.24, and a tax of 27.32 mills yields $8,720.00 per pupil— regardless of actual local valuation. Once the level of desired spending is determined, the associated tax rate is applied locally. The difference between this local contribution and the identified spending level is financed by the state. Unlike a foundation plan, which also involves a state-local partnership, the choice of effort is a local option, and the state's share applies to the total spending associated with that level of effort.

If a wealthy school district generates an amount in excess of the spending guarantee under a fully operational DPE model, as advocated by Coons et al. (1970), the state recaptures the excess yield. In the above example, the tax rate (27.32 mills) specified for districts spending $8,720.00 per pupil raises an additional $8,139.00 in Sommerset. This amount could be eligible for recapture. When a district returns these funds to the state, the integrity of a fiscally neutral plan—one in which all

districts choosing a given level of tax effort have the same spending level—is maintained. Although recapture (or negative aid) was once a part of power-equalizing plans in Maine, Utah, and Wisconsin, no state currently has a district power equalization plan fully implemented in its ideal form.

The effect of raising or lowering the yield that is guaranteed by the state is the same as that experienced under the previous forms of tax base equalization. Raising the guarantee to $638.36 per mill levied is equivalent to lowering the constant to 0.25 under percentage equalization, or raising the GTB to $638,364 (Figure 8.6A). This change places an additional burden on the state while easing the share to be raised locally. Lowering the guarantee to $212.79 per mill of property tax has the opposite impact. The state share is reduced and the local tax burden is substantially increased such that more revenue is recaptured from wealthy districts (see Figure 8.6C).

When recapture is not required, the district power-equalizing approach is termed a guaranteed yield plan. Georgia, Oklahoma, and Texas include a guaranteed yield plan as a second tier of funding beyond their basic foundation plans. Districts in Georgia levy a required 5 mills under the foundation plan. The state power equalizes each 3.25 mills above this levy in districts that are below the 90th percentile in property wealth per pupil. Thus, state aid is the difference between the amount of money generated by the local tax base and the amount that would be raised by the district at the 90th percentile. Tier II of the Texas plan guarantees $20.55 per pupil for each cent of tax levied above the rate required in the base plan (86 cents). Districts that raise an amount between this guarantee and $28.00 per pupil retain the revenue. Those that raise more than this amount choose one of five options for removing the excess. At least 40 percent of the state's districts do not receive Tier II aid, because they raise more than $2.55 for each cent levied (Gold, Smith, & Lawton, 1955, pp. 200, 590).

The plans of these states are linear in that there is a set increase in the guaranteed dollars per pupil for each additional mill levied. Johns, Morphet, and Alexander (1983, p. 258) identified advantages of including a number of breaking points,

---

General Description

This reward-for-effort plan guarantees a specified dollar yield for each cent of local taxes.

Local/State Shares

The 294 fiscally independent school corporations (districts) receive state aid according to a new power-equalizing formula. This formula became effective during the second half of the 1993–1994 school year. The state determines each corporation's allowable growth in spending. It then computes a tax rate according to the expenditure level by the following matrix:

Tax Rate	Cumulative Rate	Expenditure per WADM[a]
$2.99	$2.99	$ 0–3,680 ($12.31 per cent)
.46	3.45	3,681–4,035 ($7.72 per $0.01 over $2.99)
.57	4.02	4,036–4,390 ($6.23 per $0.01 over $3.45)
.67	4.69	4,391–4,745 ($5.30 per $0.01 over $4.02)
.80	5.49	4,746–5,100 ($4.44 per $0.01 over $4.69)
.91	6.40	5,101–5,455 ($3.90 per $0.01 over $5.49)

Thus, the guaranteed yield for each cent of tax levy diminishes as approved funding increases. Pupil count (WADM) is the enrollment on a given day weighted according to the number of at-risk pupils.

The local share of the guaranteed yield is calculated by multiplying the school corporation's assessed valuation by the levy corresponding to the approved spending level. The state provides the difference between the guaranteed yield and this local share. However, a minimum guarantee ranges from 2.5% to 1.25% of expenditures for the highest spenders. In 1993–1994, 182 corporations (62%) fell outside the formula and received only this minimum guarantee.

There is a six-year phase-in period to ease the transition to the guaranteed yield plan. Tax rates cannot increase or decrease more than $0.15 each year. The expenditure limit grows more quickly for low-spending districts. In 1994, the limit was the 1993 per pupil spending, increased by $11 plus one-sixth of the difference between $3,525 and the prior-year spending. Poorer corporations with high rates relative to their funding amounts are permitted larger increases ($44 per pupil plus one-sixth of the difference between $3,525 and the prior-year spending). The $3,525 is a floating per pupil expenditure floor, which all schools should reach by 1999.

Local Support beyond the Equalized Program

With no recapture, and with the six-year phase-in of equalization under the base plan, many school corporations have property tax revenue available beyond the spending levels identified in the matrix.

[a]WADM = Weighted Average Daily Membership.

Figure 8.10. Guaranteed Yield in Indiana. (SOURCE: E. Adams, C. E. Johnson, & P. Bond [1995]. Indiana. In S. D. Gold, D. M. Smith, & S. B. Lawton [Eds.], *Public School Finance Programs of the United States and Canada, 1993–94* [pp. 241–252]. Albany, NY: American Education Finance Association and The Center for the Study of the States. Reprinted with permission of the publisher; A. Rolle [1994]. Indiana. In N. D. Theobald [Ed.]. *The State of School Finance Policy Issues, 1994* [pp. 18–21]. Monograph of the AERA's Fiscal Issues, Policy, and Education Finance Special Interest Group.)

or kinks, below which a higher yield is guaranteed. Districts with tax levies above the breaking points gain revenues at a somewhat lower rate of increase. This differentiated approach levels up poorer districts' abilities to generate revenue. At the same time it discourages districts from increasing property tax rates excessively.

This concept is evident in the matrix of tax rates and expenditure levels listed in Indiana's guaranteed yield plan (see Figure 8.10). In this reward-for-effort finance program, a specified spending level is identified for each of six tax levies. For example, a school corporation with an approved expenditure of $4,000 per weighted pupil is guaranteed this yield if it taxes at a rate of $2.99 for each hundred of valuation on the first $3,680 and at a rate of $3.45 for the remaining $320 of spending. A relatively poor school corporation receives a larger proportion of this yield from the state than does its wealthier neighbors. This formula is not a true district power-equalizing plan. This is because there is a minimum percentage of spending provided by the state for all districts. Further, there is no recapture of funds raised above the guaranteed yield. However, because the guaranteed yield declines as desired spending increases, the poorest districts will be aided proportionately more in reaching approved spending levels once the plan is fully operational.

Full State Funding

The complete state assumption of all costs contrasts with the shared state–local partnership evident in foundation and percentage equalizing plans. To promote uniformity in education across school units, Morrison (1930) proposed state administration and full financial support of schools that serve public, or social, goals. He reasoned that

local autonomy should yield because education and citizenship training are state concerns.

Proponents of this approach believe that the level of funds available for designing educational programs should not in any way rely upon districts' fiscal capacity or effort. The *Fleischmann Report's* (1973) recommendation of full state funding for New York State considered its benefits:

> Full state funding makes possible, though it does not automatically provide, more effective controls over expenditures. It permits the state to invest in improvement in quality at a rate consonant with the growth of the over-all economy of the state. It eliminates the present competition among wealthy districts for the most elaborate schoolhouse and similar luxuries. (p. 56)

The simplified full state funding prototype (see Figure 8.11) illustrates that all revenue, whether from state or local sources, is equalized by the state. The relatively poorer Ellicott and Redrock districts and their wealthier counterpart, Sommerset, have the same level of funds ($7,000.00) available for each pupil. Property taxation could continue as a state-wide revenue source. But school boards and voters would not set spending levels. And they would have no power to tax to supplement the state-established

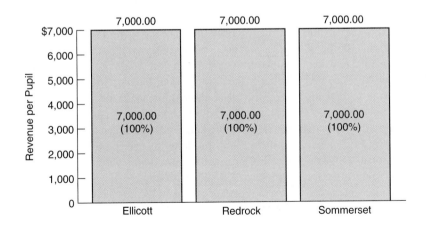

State Grant

Figure 8.11. Full State Funding Model

funding level. In this fiscally neutral plan, neither local fiscal capacity nor tax effort affects spending for schools.

Hawaii has a fully state-financed and heavily state-controlled (Thompson, 1992) educational system. Spending in Washington is fully funded by the state as a consequence of a judicial decision that the prior finance plan denied equal and adequate levels of funding in all districts (see Chapter 11). The state fully funds the basic educational program. This is briefly described in Figure 8.12. The state also funds nearly all costs of special education, bilingual education, compensatory programs, and pupil transportation. Districts may levy property taxes to exceed the formula-generated spending. But state revenue finances 71 percent of the total educational costs.

In earlier chapters we discussed the school finance reform movement, with its goal of equalizing school resources, and the subsequent movement to limit taxes and expenditures. As a result of these two movements, the foundation plans of other states, including California and New Mexico, approach full state assumption. Even with 36.2 percent of revenue coming from local resources in California, local property taxes are directly controlled by the state. The New Mexico foundation program permits districts to spend very little revenue beyond the state guarantee. Only 5 percent of local property taxes, federal impact aid, and forest reserve revenue is retained by local districts. Nearly all of these revenues become a part of the state's guaranteed funding level (Gold, Smith, & Lawton, 1995, pp. 139, 443). Despite full state control of revenue in California, New Mexico, and Washington, school districts continue to develop budgets and oversee operations.

Full state funding illustrates the tension between goals of equality, liberty, and efficiency we discussed in Chapter 2. This plan equalizes spending, attains fiscal neutrality, and shifts the burden for education finance to broader state taxes. On the other hand, more uniform finances and education policies might bring a regimented education that is inefficient and heavily controlled by an impersonal bureaucracy. Diminished local involve-

ment in policy and finance could inhibit responsiveness to unique community needs. And the restriction on fiscal flexibility would inhibit the ability of districts to support and stimulate innovations. Unless there is sufficient revenue to raise all districts at least to the level available in the highest-spending units prior to implementation of full state funding, it would be difficult for any state to fully satisfy demands in all localities. Reallocating currently available state revenue, even including all local property tax revenue, would result in leveling many districts down. This is a politically unpopular strategy.

In some states, including those in which general school operations are not fully state financed, the state assumes the full cost of various categorical programs. For example, the state fully supports the excess costs of special education in Oregon and all pupil transportation expenses in Alaska, Georgia, and Kentucky (Gold, Smith, & Lawton, 1995, pp. 111, 203, 282, 524).

SUMMARY

Transfers of funds from federal and state governments to localities ensure provision of basic public services in all communities and stimulate localities to expand programs beyond a minimum level of adequacy to meet pupils' educational needs. This revenue sharing equalizes districts' fiscal capacities through the broader tax bases available to central governments. The degree to which these transfers constrain local decision making depends on whether they are general, block grant, or categorical aids. These three approaches differ in the government level at which program goals are defined, the degree to which funds are targeted by group or purpose, the burdens placed on personnel to develop proposals and monitor programs, and the structure of fund accounting.

A blend of state and local revenue is available for school operations as general aid. We introduced four concepts for understanding state financial assistance for basic program support: the adequacy or level of support (which often reflects the blending of

General Description

The finance system equalizes educational opportunities among school districts along three dimensions: program content, staffing and compensation levels, and revenues available from state sources. A basic education allocation formula is nearly fully state-financed.

Local/State Shares

The allocation formula uses each school district's full-time equivalent (FTE) student enrollment data to calculate basic education certificated instructional, administrative, and classified staff formula units. These units are then multiplied by the district's state-recognized basic salary and benefits levels for each respective personnel group to generate the district's allotment for salaries.

The number of certificated instructional staff units varies by program: regular education, with a higher number of units allocated for K–3 grades, depending on the actual ratio of instructional staff to students (between 49 and 54.3 formula units per 1,000 FTE students), than for 4–12 (46 formula units per 1,000 FTE students); and secondary vocational programs either within a district or cooperative skills centers among districts (55.2 formula units per 1,000 FTE-eligible students). Administrative staff formula units vary in a similar manner: 4.0 units per 1,000 FTE pupils in regular programs, and 4.8 units per 1,000 FTE pupils in vocational programs and skills centers. Classified personnel account for 16.67 formula units per 1,000 pupils in regular or vocational programs.

In 292 districts, the state determines the instructional formula salary level by a statewide salary allocation schedule and each district's actual experience and education for teachers. The other 34 districts are held-harmless, with salary levels that are between 0.07 and 6.3 percent higher than the amount that would apply by the statewide salary allocation schedule. The legislature has set unique administrative and classified formula salary levels for each district. Fringe benefit levels are a fixed percentage of the respective formula salary allocations. In addition, allocations for nonemployee-related costs (e.g., books, supplies, heat) and substitute teachers are based on the number of staff formula units.

The state pays almost 100 percent of the above allotments. Certain local and federal revenues (less than 1 percent of the total) are equalized and used to fund basic education.

Local Support beyond the Basic Program

Districts may levy local property taxes for programs, activities, and support services that the state is not required to fund under its constitutional obligation. These "special levies" in 209 districts finance maintenance and operations, debt service on construction or remodeling, and transportation costs beyond the state-funded service. A local effort assistance program provides a guaranteed tax base for those districts passing this special levy with property tax rates above the state average. In addition, local taxes finance costs in excess of those provided by the state for education program enhancement, which is a block grant to meet locally identified educational needs.

Figure 8.12. Full State Funding in Washington. (SOURCE: K. E. Hoover & T. J. Case [1995]. Washington. In S. D. Gold, D. M. Smith, & S. B. Lawton [Eds.]. *Public School Finance Programs of the United States and Canada, 1993–94* [pp. 633–644]. Albany, NY: American Education Finance Association and The Center for the Study of the States. Reprinted with permission of the publisher; K. Hoover [1994]. Washington. In N. D. Theobald [Ed.], *The State of School Finance Policy Issues, 1994* [pp. 198–200]. Monograph of the AERA's Fiscal Issues, Policy, and Education Finance Special Interest Group.)

local and state revenue); the division of fiscal responsibility between state and local governments; local ability, defined as property valuation or personal income per pupil; and local effort, the tax rate that is applied to the value of property or income. If local fiscal capacity and effort alone determined the availability of financial resources to finance educational programs, there would be large variations in per pupil spending. State finance plans control and compensate for variations in these two variables. In so doing, they moderate spending disparities among districts.

The prototypes differ in their consideration of communities' abilities and efforts. Matching grants favor wealthier districts. This is because allocations respond directly to local tax capacity and effort. The state share of a flat grant does not take either local capacity or effort into consideration. But state allocations in a foundation plan control local effort and direct funds in inverse relation to fiscal capacity. Optional levies permit localities to supplement the base amount in a flat grant or foundation plan. These levies are unequalized and result in varying overall expenditures as they reflect tax capacities and rates. In the different forms of tax base equalization, state allocations respond to local effort, but capacity is fully equalized. Localities determine spending levels, and the state equalizes the ability of school districts to reach their spending goals. Because full state funding controls both fiscal capacity and effort, there is no variation in per pupil spending among school districts.

In the next chapter we discuss state finance policies. We explore the way states measure and consider the needs of pupils, the characteristics of districts, and local capacity and effort in allocations. We also discuss the potential role of financial incentives in improving school productivity, and the use of program and financial audits in determining whether states' goals in supporting school programs are realized.

NOTE

1. For illustrative purposes, calculations of revenue and mill levies are rounded to the hundredths place throughout the chapter. In reality, state funding formulas may carry calculations to four or more decimal places.

ACTIVITIES

1. Locate and compare statutes or regulations that outline the purposes and provisions of at least two state or federal aid programs. Identify language that supports your classification of these policies as general, block grant, or categorical assistance.

2. Obtain documents that describe fully the finance plan for one state and compare the basic support program with the general models presented in this chapter. What other prototype(s) is(are) used to finance special programs and services beyond the base program?

3. Review reports of school finance commissions, state agencies, or policy analysts as published in professional journals to identify strengths and shortcomings of a given state's finance system. What policy changes, if any, do these assessments suggest regarding the plan's consideration of fiscal capacity and tax effort, disparities in revenue among districts, and the adequacy of funds for education?

4. A committee of legislators and educators is considering alternative finance plans for equalizing educational opportunities while also encouraging districts to adopt innovations. Discuss the dilemma presented in the committee's charge in terms of equality and liberty goals, and present a rationale for the committee to advance one of the general finance models presented in this chapter.

5. Using the computer simulation accompanying this chapter as a guide, create an electronic spreadsheet for the formula that distributes revenue for a state's basic support program. Enter data for all districts (or a sample) and modify several of the plan's parameters to examine the effects on allocations of state aid.

EXERCISES

1. Assume that a given state has $4,394,500,000 to allocate for the education of the average daily membership of 2,350,000 pupils. (a) What is the amount of a uniform flat grant distribution? (b) If two districts supplement this state aid with a tax of 10 mills and 18 mills on their respective per pupil equalized valuations of $240,000 and $180,000, how much total revenue is available in each district per pupil? (c) What are the effects of raising the flat grant by $600 per pupil and placing a cap of 12 mills on local leeway (assume both districts then tax at this rate)?

2. A school district has a total assessed valuation of $300 million and 2,000 pupils. (a) If the state, under a foundation plan, requires a local levy of 40 cents per hundred of valuation and guarantees $2400 per pupil, how much does the state contribute? (b) If the district levies a total tax of $1.00 per hundred (including the RLE), what total per pupil amount is available, including the state transfer payment and the local option tax?

3. Assume that the district of average wealth ($220,000 per pupil valuation) contributes 48 percent of its spending in a percentage-equalizing plan. (a) Calculate state aid as a percentage of spending in three districts having per pupil valuations of $160,000, $250,000, and $520,000. (b) If each of these districts spends $4,800 per pupil, how much state aid is forthcoming? Or how much local revenue might be recaptured by the state?

 COMPUTER SIMULATIONS

Objectives of This Activity:

- *To introduce students to the hypothetical state database.*

- *To develop an understanding of the basic structures of three common formats for distributing state aid to school districts: foundation programs, percentage-equalizing programs, and guaranteed tax base programs.*

- *To conduct "what if" analyses on selected state aid models.*

Using the hypothetical state database, you are given the opportunity to change the parameters of the formula for each program. This will illustrate the impact of parameter changes on the amount of state aid received and local property tax rates for districts with differing characteristics: a district of average wealth, a poor district, and a wealthy district. You are encouraged to look for similarities and differences among the state aid programs.

Simulation 8.1: *Database Manipulation*

Software manufacturers develop software-specific command sequences that create pivot tables, extract data, or import data. Such commands may be used to facilitate efficient completion of *Part 1* of this simulation. However, we use an approach that is more generalizable and can be applied to virtually all software programs.

Part 1. Importing Data from the State Database

a. Retrieve the file DATABASE.

b. Save the file as DATA_AID.

c. **Make sure that you are in the DATA_AID file.** Copy the first column contents (from cell A1 down through A20) to the worksheet area below—beginning in cell A22.

d. Copy column D contents, the TOTAL column, in the same manner (from cell D1 down through D20—to the worksheet area beginning with cell D22).

e. Following the same procedure outlined above, copy the EXPEND PER PUPIL column contents to the worksheet area below.

f. Copy the PROPERTY VALUE PER PUPIL ($) column contents in the same manner.

g. Delete rows 1 through 21.

h. Move the TOTAL column contents to column B; EXPEND PER PUPIL to column C; and PROPERTY VALUE PER PUPIL ($) to column D.

i. Change the column widths as necessary.

j. Save your new data table.

Part 2. Determining Total and Per Pupil Property Valuation

a. Change the column B label to PUPILS.

b. Type TOTAL in the cell that is two rows below WHEATFIELD.

c. Enter a formula to compute the total number of pupils in the column [e.g., @SUM(B11...B20)=SUM(B11...B20)].

d. Type AVERAGE two rows below TOTAL.

e. Enter a formula to compute the average for the column (divide the sum by the number of districts).

f. Create a new label for column E: TOTAL PROPERTY.

g. In column E, create a formula that multiplies PUPILS by PROPERTY VALUE PER PUPIL ($). Increase the column width and copy this formula down the column to calculate each district's TOTAL PROPERTY.

h. Create a formula to compute the TOTAL PROPERTY valuation in the state.

i. Determine the AVERAGE property value per pupil by creating a formula that divides the TOTAL PROPERTY column by the TOTAL number of PUPILS. This average property valuation is used in the percentage equalization and guaranteed tax base plans (Simulations 8.3 and 8.4).

j. Format all cells in the table as appropriate.

k. Save and print the new data table.

Simulation 8.2: *Foundation Program*

Note: This file provides labels and column formatting but requires students to enter figures from DATABASE and appropriate formulas.

Part 1. Foundation Plan in One District

a. Retrieve the file FOUND.

b. In the REDROCK column, enter EXPEND PER PUPIL and PROPERTY VALUE PER PUPIL from the DATA_AID file ($7,458 and $116,009, respectively).

c. Enter STATE FUNDING LEVEL as $6,000 and STATE REQUIRED TAX RATE as $7.55.

d. Create a formula to determine REQUIRED TAX PER PUPIL.

e. State aid in a foundation plan is the difference between the state guaranteed funding level and the required local property tax levy. Create a formula to determine FOUNDATION AID PER PUPIL based on the lesser of EXPEND PER PUPIL or STATE FUNDING LEVEL.

f. In addition to the state guaranteed funding level, local voters may enact an additional tax levy. Create a formula to determine EXPEND ABOVE PER PUPIL (i.e., expenditure above the foundation program per pupil).

g. The local override tax levy is determined by dividing the amount expended above the state guarantee by the district's property value. Create a formula to determine TAX RATE FOR EXCESS.

h. Create a formula to determine TOTAL TAX RATE. Print the resulting table.

Part 2. Altering the State Guarantee and Required Local Effort

a. Copy your completed spreadsheet from *Part 1* to another file or worksheet area.

b. Copy the entire REDROCK column over into the next two columns. (Your spreadsheet should now include three identical REDROCK columns.)

c. In the second and third REDROCK columns, change the STATE FUNDING LEVEL to $7,000; in the third REDROCK column, change the STATE REQUIRED TAX RATE to $8.81. Print the resulting table.

d. Note that in the second column, only the foundation level was increased by 11.67%. In the third column, both the foundation level and the required tax rate were increased by 11.67%. The latter is the more typical legislative action. Which of the three formulations is most advantageous for REDROCK? Why?

Part 3. Foundation Plan in Three Districts

a. Copy your completed spreadsheet from *Part 2* to another file or worksheet area.

b. Change the second and third column REDROCK names to SOMMERSET and ELLICOTT, respectively.

c. In the SOMMERSET and ELLICOTT columns, enter EXPEND PER PUPIL and PROPERTY VALUE PER PUPIL from the DATA_AID file ($8,719 and $617,100, and $6,469 and $84,988, respectively).

d. Make the STATE FUNDING LEVEL equal to $6,000 and the STATE REQUIRED TAX RATE equal to $7.55 for each district.

e. Study the results. Which district receives the most state aid per pupil? Why? Which district receives the least state aid per pupil? Why? Why does REDROCK receive less state aid per pupil than ELLICOTT even though it spends more per pupil and has a higher tax rate?

f. Print the resulting table and copy it to another worksheet area below it.

g. Change the STATE FUNDING LEVEL to $7,000 for each district.

h. How did each district benefit from the changes made in the state aid formula in step g? Note that since ELLICOTT is spending below the new foundation level, its state aid is calculated on the basis of its actual expenditure per pupil. In this example, ELLICOTT has chosen to use its additional state aid for property tax relief. If, on the other hand, it had chosen to retain its tax rate at $13.07 per $1,000, it would have realized an expenditure level of $7,469.

i. Print the resulting table and copy it to another worksheet area below it.

j. **Further Activities.** Change the STATE REQUIRED TAX RATE to $8.81 for each district. Print the resulting table. Which district suffered the greatest loss in state aid per pupil because of the change in tax rate? Why? Which district suffered the smallest loss? Why?

Simulation 8.3: *Percentage-Equalizing Program*

Note: This file provides labels and column formatting but requires students to enter figures from the DATABASE and appropriate formulas.

Part 1. Percentage Equalization in One District

a. Retrieve the file EQUALIZE.

b. In the REDROCK column, enter EXPEND PER PUPIL and PROPERTY VALUE PER PUPIL from the DATA_AID file ($7,458 and $116,009, respectively).

c. Enter AVERAGE DISTRICT RESPONSIBILITY as .5 and AVERAGE STATE PROPERTY PER PUPIL as $159,591—as imputed from the DATABASE file (see Simulation 8.1, Part 2).

d. Based on the general percentage equalization formula:

$$A = 1.000 - B(C/D) \text{ where}$$

A = District Percentage State Aid
B = Average District Responsibility
C = District Property Value per Pupil
D = Average State Property Value per pupil,

create a formula to determine the DISTRICT STATE AID PERCENT.

e. Create a formula to determine STATE AID PER PUPIL by multiplying its percentage share times the locally determined expenditure level.

f. Create a formula to determine LOCAL FUNDS PER PUPIL, which is the difference between the spending level and the amount of state aid.

g. Create a formula to determine TOTAL TAX RATE by dividing the local share by the district's property valuation.

Part 2. Altering Local and State Shares in Three Districts

a. Copy your completed worksheet from *Part 1* to another file or worksheet area.

b. Copy the entire REDROCK column over into the next two columns. (Your worksheet should now include three identical RED-ROCK columns.)

c. Change the second and third column RED-ROCK names to SOMMERSET and ELLI-COTT, respectively.

d. In the SOMMERSET and ELLICOTT columns, enter EXPEND PER PUPIL and PROPERTY VALUE PER PUPIL from the DATA_AID file ($8,719 and $617,100, and $6,469 and $84,988, respectively).

e. Study the results. Note that because of its high property wealth, SOMMERSET receives a negative amount of state aid. Instead of receiving aid from the state, it pays a portion of its property tax receipts to the state; this is known as "recapture."

f. Make the EXPEND PER PUPIL for ELLICOTT the same as that for REDROCK. Compare the resulting tax rates. Why are they the same?

g. Change ELLICOTT's EXPEND PER PUPIL back to its original amount ($6,469). Print the resulting table and copy it to another worksheet area below it.

h. Change the AVERAGE DISTRICT RESPONSIBILITY to 75% for each district.

i. Study the results and compare them with the results obtained from step d, immediately above. What happened to the tax rates for all districts? Why?

j. Print the resulting table and copy it to another worksheet area below it.

k. Change the AVERAGE DISTRICT RESPONSIBILITY to 25% for each district.

l. Print the resulting table.

m. Compare the results with the tables generated by steps d and h, immediately above. Note that SOMMERSET is no longer on "recapture." How do the tax rates compare with those in the other two tables? Why aren't the tax rates all the same?

n. **Further Activities.** Design your own percentage equalization plan, adjusting the AVERAGE DISTRICT RESPONSIBILITY to illustrate what might be a fair mix of local and state shares. Print this model.

Simulation 8.4: *Guaranteed Tax Base Program*

Note: This file provides labels and column formatting but requires the operator to enter figures from the DATABASE and to create appropriate formulas.

Part 1. Guaranteed Tax Base in One District

a. Retrieve the file TAXBASE.

b. In the REDROCK column, enter EXPEND PER PUPIL and PROPERTY VALUE PER PUPIL from the DATA_AID file ($7,458 and $116,009, respectively).

c. Enter GUARANTEED PROPERTY PER PUPIL as $319,182. (Because this is twice the average value for the state of $159,591, a district of average value will receive 50% state aid.)

d. Use the formula method to determine DISTRICT EXPEND PER PUPIL by copying EXPEND PER PUPIL.

e. Create a formula to determine the TAX RATE necessary to yield a DISTRICT EXPEND PER PUPIL of $7,458 given the state guaranteed property tax base of $319,182.

f. Create a formula to determine DISTRICT YIELD PER PUPIL using this new TAX RATE and the district's actual PROPERTY VALUE PER PUPIL.

g. Use the formula method to determine STATE AID PER PUPIL, which is the difference between the district's expenditure level and local property tax yield.

Part 2. Altering the State Guaranteed Tax Base

a. Copy your worksheet completed in *Part 1* to another file or worksheet area.

b. Copy the entire REDROCK column over into the next two columns. (Your spreadsheet should now include three identical RED-ROCK columns.)

c. In the second REDROCK column, change the GUARANTEED PROPERTY PER PUPIL to $212,788; in the same row of the third REDROCK column, change the amount to $638,364. (These numbers are one-third and four times greater than the state average, permitting the district of average wealth for the state to receive 25% and 75% of its EXPEND PER PUPIL in state aid.)

d. Study the results. Under which format does REDROCK receive the most state aid? Why? Why are the district's tax rates different under each formulation?

e. Print the table resulting from step c.

Part 3. The Guaranteed Tax Base Plan in Three Districts

a. Copy the spreadsheet you completed in *Part 2* to another file or worksheet area.

b. Change the second and third column REDROCK names to SOMMERSET and ELLI-COTT, respectively.

c. In the SOMMERSET and ELLICOTT columns, enter EXPEND PER PUPIL and PROPERTY VALUE PER PUPIL from the DATA_AID file

($8,719 and $617,100, and $6,469 and $84,988, respectively).

d. Make the GUARANTEED PROPERTY PER PUPIL equal to $319,182 for each district.

e. Why are the results the same as for the table resulting from the percentage-equalizing simulation 8.3, step d, part 2? Notice that SOMMERSET is experiencing "recapture" under both formats.

f. Print the table resulting from step d, and copy it to another worksheet area.

g. Change the GUARANTEED PROPERTY PER PUPIL to $212,788 for each district.

h. Compare the results with those derived in step g above. Which format is most favorable for the three districts? Why? Which district experiences the least loss of state aid when the state guaranteed tax base is reduced? Why?

i. Print the table resulting from step g and copy it to another worksheet area.

j. Change the GUARANTEED PROPERTY PER PUPIL to $638,364 for each district. Print the file.

k. **Further Activity.** Contrast the results with those obtained in steps d and g above. Which format is most favorable for the three districts? Why? Which district experiences the greatest gain in state aid when the guaranteed tax base is increased? Why? Note that SOMMERSET is no longer in a state of "recapture" as a result of the adjustments made in step j.

REFERENCES

Adams, E., Johnson, C. E., & Bond, P. (1995). Indiana. In S. D. Gold, D. M. Smith, & S. B. Lawton (Eds.), *Public school finance programs of the Unites States and Canada, 1993–94* (pp. 241–252). Albany, NY: American Education Finance Association and The Center for the Study of the States.

Addonizio, M. F., Kearney, C. P., & Prince, H. J. (1995, Winter). Michigan's high wire act. *Journal of Education Finance, 20,* 235–269.

Bryant, H. D., & MacPhail-Wilcox, B. (1995). North Carolina. In S. D. Gold, D. M. Smith, & S. B. Lawton (Eds.). *Public school finance programs of the United*

States and Canada, 1993–94 (pp. 473–483). Albany, NY: American Education Finance Association and The Center for the Study of the States.

Burke, A. J. (1957). *Financing public schools in the United States.* (Rev. ed.). New York: Harper & Brothers.

Buse v. *Smith* (1976). 74 Wis. 2d 550, 247 N.W. 2d 141.

Clancy, D., Toulmin, C., & Bukolt, M. (1995). Wisconsin. In S. D. Gold, D. M. Smith, & S. B. Lawton (Eds.), *Public school finance programs of the United States and Canada, 1993–94* (pp. 661–674). Albany, NY: American Education Finance Association and The Center for the Study of the States.

Coons, J. E., Clune, W. H., & Sugarman, S. D. (1970). *Private wealth and public education.* Cambridge, MA: Belknap Press of Harvard University Press.

Crampton, F. E. (1994). New York. In N. D. Theobald (Ed.), *The state of school finance policy issues, 1994* (pp. 73–78). Monograph of the AERA's Fiscal Issues, Policy, and Educational Finance Special Interest Group.

Cubberley, E. P. (1906). *School funds and their apportionment.* New York: Teachers College, Columbia University.

First, P. F. (1992). *Educational policy for school administrators.* Needham Heights, MA: Allyn and Bacon.

The Fleischmann report on the quality, cost, and financing of elementary and secondary education in New York State, Vol. I. (1973). New York: Viking Press.

Gold, S. D., Smith, D. M., & Lawton, S. B. (Eds.). (1995). *Public school finance programs of the United States and Canada, 1993–94.* Albany, NY: American Education Finance Association and The Center for the Study of the States.

Henahan, R. L. (1995). New York. In S. D. Gold, D. M. Smith, & S. B. Lawton (Eds.), *Public school finance programs of the United States and Canada, 1993–94* (pp. 451–471). Albany, NY: American Education Finance Association and The Center for the Study of the States.

Hoover, K. (1994). Washington. In N. D. Theobald (Ed.), *The state of school finance policy issues, 1994* (pp. 198–200). Monograph of the AERA's Fiscal Issues, Policy, and Education Finance Special Interest Group.

Hoover, K. E., & Case, T. J. (1995). Washington. In S. D. Gold, D. M. Smith, & S. B. Lawton (Eds.), *Public school finance programs of the United States and Canada, 1993–94* (pp. 633–644). Albany, NY: American Education Finance Association and the Center for the Study of the States.

Johns, R. L., Morphet, E. L., & Alexander, K. (1983). *The economics and financing of education* (4th ed.). Englewood Cliffs, NJ: Prentice Hall.

Jones, T. H. (1985). *Introduction to school finance: Technique and social policy.* New York: Macmillan.

Kearney, C. P. (1995). Michigan. In S. D. Gold, D. M. Smith, & S. B. Lawton (Eds.), *Public school finance programs of the United States and Canada, 1993–94* (pp. 333–346). Albany, NY: American Education Finance Association and The Center for the Study of the States.

Kearney, C. P. (1994). Michigan. In N. D. Theobald (Ed.), *The state of school finance policy issues, 1994* (pp. 28–33). Monograph of the AERA's Fiscal Issues, Policy, and Education Finance Special Interest Group.

Kozol, J. (1991). *Savage inequalities: Children in America's schools.* New York: Crown.

Morrison, H. C. (1930). *School revenue.* Chicago: University of Chicago Press.

Mort, P. R. (1933). *State support for public education.* Washington, DC: American Council on Education.

Mort, P. R., & Reusser, W. C. (1941). *Public school finance: Its background, structure, and operation.* New York: McGraw-Hill.

Mort, P. R., & Reusser, W. C. (1951). *Public school finance* (2nd ed.). New York: McGraw-Hill.

Parrish, T. B., & Fowler, W. J. (1995). *Disparities in public school district spending, 1989–90.* Washington, DC: U. S. Government Printing Office.

Phelps, J. L., & Addonizio, M. F. (1981). District power equalizing: Cure-all or prescription? *Journal of Education Finance, 7,* 64–87.

Reilly, G. J. (1982). Guaranteed tax base formulas in school finance: Why equalization doesn't work. *Journal of Education Finance, 7,* 336–347.

Rolle, A. (1994). Indiana. In N. D. Theobald (Ed.), *The state of school finance policy issues, 1994* (pp. 18–21). Monograph of the AERA's Fiscal Issues, Policy, and Education Finance Special Interest Group.

Strayer, G. D., & Haig, R. M. (1923). *The financing of education in the State of New York, Report of the Educational Finance Inquiry Commission,* Vol. 1. New York: Macmillan.

Thompson, J. A. (1992). Notes on the centralization of the funding and governance of education in Hawaii. *Journal of Education Finance, 17,* 286–302.

Unified School District No. 244 v. *Kansas.* No. 94-1792. (1994).

Updegraff, H., & King, L. A. (1922). *Survey of the fiscal policies of the state of Pennsylvania in the field of education.* Philadelphia: University of Pennsylvania.

CHAPTER 9

Adjusting State Aid for Differences in Need, Wealth, Costs, and Performance

Primary Issues Explored in This Chapter:

- *Measuring educational needs:* What characteristics of pupils and programs are considered as having legitimate cost implications when allocating state funds?

- *Measuring district wealth and tax effort:* Are there advantages in blending property valuation with other measures of the ability of school districts to pay for education? How is tax effort defined to identify the extent to which available tax bases are tapped in supporting schools?

- *Cost differences among school districts:* Do char-

acteristics of districts—including size, personnel, and the cost of delivering education—warrant consideration in funding formulas?

- *Financial incentives:* What measures of school or district performance might be considered in allocations to provide rewards or incentives for school improvement?

- *Financial and program accountability:* How might districts and states monitor whether funds are being spent appropriately to achieve state and local goals?

In this chapter we continue our discussion of state school finance policy. We turn from the basic structure of finance plans to consider a number of measurement and administrative issues related to the educational and financial conditions of school systems. When state legislatures modify simple per pupil distributions of funds to all districts, their goal is to recognize financial capacities and costs fairly. Some of the costs are beyond the control of local school boards. Failure to make such modifications would diminish the funds available for classroom instruction in some districts.

School finance formulas have become very sophisticated and complex in the years since Mort

(1924) argued early in the twentieth century that states should consider the causes of variation in costs over which local communities had little or no control. Today's formulas are tailored to provide different levels of funds to enable districts to offer programs appropriate to the learning abilities and educational needs of pupils. Many states consider these additional costs within the equalized aid plan. Others address special needs through categorical funds. These funds are often allocated outside the basic funding formula. They offset costs in all districts regardless of local wealth.

Once the educational needs of pupils have been defined, states consider how to blend state and local funds to finance school operations in their policies. In Chapter 8 we discussed different ways that state finance plans incorporate contributions from local revenue sources. In addition to measuring educational need, in this chapter we explore problems of measuring districts' fiscal capacities and the effort taxpayers make to finance school operations.

Other factors in aid formulas are sensitive to variations in the costs of delivering educational programs in terms of the sparsity or density of population, the costs of living and education, and the characteristics of personnel. A number of states blend the goals of educational reform with finance policies as they provide incentives for school or district improvements. This accountability mechanism adjusts aid in accordance with performance measures. It thus differs from traditional financial and program audits. Districts and states make use of these audits to monitor the use of funds and to identify the impacts of programs on specified educational goals.

It should be noted that the measures of need, fiscal capacity, effort, and performance in state aid programs are typically approximations of the intended concepts. In many cases, they are the most valid indicator available. In other cases, because of political processes, a program uses one measure as a proxy for another closely related but not easily measured variable.

MEASURING PUPILS' EDUCATIONAL NEEDS

The scope of public education is crudely expressed in terms of the number of students served. This measure of the school district's need is closely tied to the size of the teaching force, the sizes of programs and facilities, and ultimately, the amount of money required. But state governments are also concerned about the nature and cost of programs designed to meet particular educational needs of students. They want to more accurately measure those needs that warrant state financial assistance.

Then they want to determine how best to offset all or a portion of the additional costs.

Pupil Count

Governments determine how much money they need to finance education primarily on the basis of the number of students served. Early in the century allocations relied on a full census that accounted for all school-aged children. Or else they relied on a count of those pupils who attended either a public or a private school. The first of these techniques, the full census, offered little incentive for keeping children enrolled in schools. The second one overfunded many communities that had a large percentage of pupils attending private schools.

Average daily membership (ADM), *average daily attendance* (ADA), and *enrollment counts* (ENR) in today's state aid plans provide better estimates of the costs associated with the number of pupils actually enrolled in or attending public schools. Gold, Smith, and Lawton (1995, p. 26) reported that seven states use ADA. ADA is the average number of pupils in attendance during specific weeks of the school year. Another twenty-two states use ADM. ADM is the average number of pupils enrolled over a particular period. And twelve states use ENR. ENR is the actual enrollment on a given date. Seven states base their allocations on the number of teachers or instructional units to be funded. Even this method ultimately reflects the number of pupils enrolled or in attendance. Specific dates (e.g., tenth-day enrollment) or periods of time (e.g., average attendance in the months of October and March) are often established in statute for collecting pupil counts for funding purposes. The majority (twenty-six) of the states base their funding on pupil counts during the current year. Thus school revenue is determined by the actual number of students served. The others use previous-year enrollment or attendance data. These states have accurate counts and have their revenue needs identified as the fiscal year begins.

The choice between measuring enrollment and measuring attendance has implications for politics, pedagogy, and efficiency. ADM and ENR recognize that the costs of school operations continue regardless of the actual presence of pupils, but that there may be inefficiencies if districts are not held accountable for reducing absenteeism and truancy. ADA-based funding reinforces compulsory attendance laws and the belief that pedagogical goals are maximized when absenteeism is reduced. Approaches relying on enrollments work to the financial advantage of central cities, which have higher absence rates. ADA shifts the available state aid to suburban and rural school systems.

Shifts in enrollments often create unanticipated costs that may justify state assistance. Declining enrollments would mean reduced state funding if governments did not recognize that personnel and facility costs remain somewhat fixed at least in the short run (Edelman & Knudsen, 1990). The need for an adjustment in the method of counting pupils became apparent during the rapid enrollment declines of the 1970s. This situation continues in many localities that face boom-and-bust cycles of rapid growth or decline. At least six states include a hold (or save) harmless to guarantee the same count as the previous year's pupil count and ease the impact of sudden aid reductions (Gold, Smith, & Lawton, 1995, pp. 38–43). Ala-bama, Missouri, and Nevada guarantee payment for 100 percent of the previous year's enrollment. Florida funds 50 percent of the decline in un-weighted pupils from the previous year. Some states have a policy of a rolling average of several years' pupil enrollment or attendance to cushion the impact of a reduction in resources. For example, Ohio school districts receive funding based on the current ADM or the average of the current year and the two previous years' pupil counts.

If districts are able to continue previous years' pupil counts for aid purposes, there is a more predictable resource base for planning programs and making personnel commitments. However, save-harmless clauses that result in no loss of funds may unnecessarily protect districts from confronting the critical issues of reduction in enrollment (Leppert & Routh, 1978, p. 190). They also introduce inequities by channeling funds to some districts with little need for a cushion and introduce inefficiencies by discouraging local economies (Goettel & Firestine, 1975, p. 212). Policies that include percentage reductions in student units, short terms for phasing in reductions, or an average of several years' enrollments more effectively encourage planning and efficiencies than do provisions that continue inflated pupil counts into the future.

The finance plans of fourteen states consider the rapid increases in costs associated with large growth in enrollment (Gold, Smith, & Lawton, 1995, pp. 38–43). Kentucky districts experiencing growth in the first two months of the school year receive additional funds. So do Arizona districts with increases in excess of 3 percent from the previous year. Wyoming recalculates district entitlements to compensate for growth in those districts having increases of over 10 percent during the first sixty days, or over 15 percent growth by February 14.

Grade Levels and Special Programs

The simplified models of state finance plans we discussed in Chapter 8 may create the impression that the same level of funding is tied to each pupil. In reality, the amount of aid varies considerably depending on student characteristics that policy makers agree warrant special and more expensive programs. The resulting cost differentials are due to smaller classes and more support personnel, as well as specialized equipment and instructional materials. Consistent with the concept of vertical equity (the unequal treatment of unequals), state finance policy pegs allocations to the higher costs of education at different grade levels and for specified categories of students.

Allocations in the majority of states consider *weighted-pupil* or *weighted-classroom* units. Mort conceived this approach in his refinement of early foundation plans. His weighted-pupil and typical-teacher units provided objective measures of educational need to give "extra weight to the actual number of pupils in those situations where the true per pupil cost of a given educational offering is high" (Mort, 1926, p. 15).

This method of adjusting operating aid within the base program assigns weights for grade levels and special programs relative to a base that defines the lowest-cost instruction. A typical child, usually in grades 3–6, counts as a unit of 1.0. Students in higher-cost programs are granted additional weights. In some states, weights are assigned to instructional units. These are determined by dividing the total number of students by a legislatively defined typical classroom size. In either a weighted-pupil or a weighted-classroom approach, higher weights reflect traditionally larger expenditures in secondary grades and in vocational and special education programs. The weights listed in Table 9.1 for South Carolina's foundation program correspond to the anticipated average costs of each grade level and program relative to those of fourth through eighth grades. The weights recognize, for example, that educational and support services for emotionally and orthopedically disabled children cost twice as much as those for elementary school

students who are not placed in a special program. High school students carry a weighting of 1.25. Pupils in vocational programs are assigned a slightly larger weight (1.29).

Because some children are served for only a portion of a school day, the concept of full-time equivalency (FTE) is often used to express pupil counts. For example, South Carolina's support of only half-day kindergartens means that 148 students would be considered as 74 FTEs, with a weight of 1.30, or 0.65 each. In other states, enrollment of students for one hour of a day in a compensatory or bilingual program brings 0.6 FTE. Placement of a mainstreamed pupil with a disability for a split day justifies 0.5 FTE. These FTE pupil units are used in formulas in addition to the weights earned for students' grade-level assignments.

To determine financial need under a weighted-pupil approach, the number of FTE students enrolled in or in attendance in each grade level and applicable special program is multiplied by the weights specified in the statute. The resulting products for all programs and grade levels are then totaled to obtain a composite measure of educational need. This weighted measure of pupils' needs can be entered into the general finance models we discussed in Chapter 8. In a foundation plan, for instance, the legislatively established dollar guarantee for a given year is multiplied by the total number of weighted-pupil units. Likewise, in measuring a district's fiscal capacity, its valuation is divided by the total number of weighted-pupil units.

Similarly, states that finance schools according to the number of teachers or instructional units specify varying ratios of pupils to teachers as a measure of grade level and special program needs. For example, the twelve categories for special education in the Delaware plan specify class sizes that range from four to fifteen pupils (Gold, Smith, & Lawton, 1995, p. 181).

The size of weights generally mirrors cost differences prevailing in schools (i.e., what is). They are not grounded in studies of what funding would most appropriately finance educational programs

TABLE 9.1. Weighted-Pupil Categories in South Carolina

Category	Weight
Grade levels	
Kindergarten (half-day program)	0.65
Primary (grades 1–3)	1.24
Elementary (grades 4–8)	1.00
High school (grades 9–12)	1.25
Vocational programs	
Vocational (three levels)	1.29
Special education	
Learning disabilities	1.74
Educable mentally handicapped	1.74
Trainable mentally handicapped	2.04
Emotionally handicapped	2.04
Orthopedically handicapped	2.04
Visually handicapped	2.57
Hearing handicapped	2.57
Speech handicapped	1.90
Homebound	2.10

SOURCE: J. M. Garris & R. Ginsberg (1995). South Carolina. In S. D. Gold, D. M. Smith, & S. B. Lawton (Eds.), *Public school finance programs of the United States and Canada, 1993–94* (pp. 547–563). Albany, NY: American Education Finance Association and The Center for the Study of the States, p. 551. Reprinted with the permission of the publisher.

to meet the needs of pupils (i.e., what should be). Mort (1924) recommended weights for high schools, for example, on the basis of the costs associated with the typical practice of assigning more teachers per pupil in high school grades than in elementary grades and on the basis of their higher salaries. Accepting the rationality of average practice, that procedure became the benchmark to be applied when assigning state aid. Similarly, the National Education Finance Project (Johns, Alexander, & Jordan, 1971, Chapter 6) based its indices of average per pupil cost on actual costs of grade levels and special program offerings within selected school districts rather than upon true measures of need. New York's *Fleischmann Report* (1973) addressed the disadvantage of accepting average practice in aid formulas:

> The pedagogical wisdom of weighting secondary students more heavily than elementary students is questionable; we suspect that in many instances it might be good policy to spend more money per student in the elementary grade than in the secondary, but the present weighting factor has a psychological effect of suggesting that all districts should spend more money on secondary students. (p. 64)

Thus, average costs based on past program experience may tend to drive all programs to that expenditure level.

Although they were designed to provide additional dollars to meet educational needs determined locally, weighted-unit methods may in practice create incentives to misclassify pupils, and possibly to remove them unnecessarily from regular classrooms for the sake of the additional state aid generated. Furthermore, in the absence of close monitoring, state dollars need not actually be spent in intended programs.

Another approach to accommodating higher costs is through an *excess cost reimbursement* strategy. According to this procedure, the state partially or fully aids those expenditures that exceed a given level for specified programs. By paying these costs,

states encourage local districts to expand programs to serve qualifying students, such as those enrolled in vocational or special education offerings. States aid pupils in these programs twice, first under the basic formula and second under the excess cost formula. The amount of assistance may be variable. In some states it depends on the actual cost of programs. In others it depends on local wealth and tax effort. This method enables poorer districts to provide special programs they could not otherwise afford. However, some states finance the same amount of excess cost (e.g., through a flat grant) in all school districts regardless of local wealth. Allocations of this categorical aid may then be disequalizing, since wealthy and poor districts both receive full payment. A report of the National Conference of State Legislatures (1994) noted the trend of states to increasingly earmark revenues for specific purposes, "so a growing share of state support is outside the general fund" (p. 9).

Policy makers and educators worry about the degree to which funding mechanisms create incentives to misclassify pupils. Weighted-pupil and other child-based formulas in which funds depend on a count of eligible pupils may encourage overclassification. Instructional-unit and other resource-based formulas in which the number and type of personnel drive funding have fewer incentives for misclassification. In these formulas, additional funds depend on larger numbers of pupils. On the other hand, in the case of weighted-pupil plans, a single qualifying student generates more dollars. Reimbursement plans that partially finance excess costs offer the least incentive to misclassify pupils. This is because they demand local matching funds (Hartman, 1980).

Special education programs are rarely fully reimbursed by states above the average cost of educating nondisabled students. If a state assumes full costs, as occurs in Oregon, there may be little incentive for districts to operate efficient programs. For this reason, states may require local funds to be applied to special programs. They do this by only partially reimbursing excess costs. For example, Wyoming aids 85 percent of actual special education program expenses. New Hampshire pays 80 percent of costs that exceed 3.5 times the state average per pupil expenditure. Wisconsin differentiates its reimbursement. It pays 63 percent of the costs of salaries and transportation, 51 percent of the costs of psychologists and social workers, and 100 percent of the costs of lodging and transportation for nonresident students. About twenty-one states fund programs through the basic support program, most often by weighting different categories of pupils or services (Gold, Smith, & Lawton, 1995, pp. 57–60).

Gifted and talented pupils are identified in the finance plans of forty states (Gold, Smith, & Lawton, 1995, pp. 61–62). Their needs are met through additional pupil weights, flat dollar amounts for eligible students, variable competitive grants for innovative programs, or support for residential high schools for exceptional students. For example, Arkansas provides an additional weight of 0.25 for gifted and talented pupils up to a maximum of 5 percent of the district's ADM. Michigan sponsors three programs, two of which assist intermediate school districts' support of teachers and summer institutes for gifted and talented pupils. Maximum grants of $3,000 in the third program provide districts, or cooperatives among districts, up to $50 per pupil for up to 5 percent of their enrollments. A number of states finance specialized high schools for academically gifted pupils. For example, Virginia sponsors regional and residential Governors Schools (Gold, Smith, & Lawton, 1995, pp. 129, 340, 630).

Categorical support for approved *vocational education* programs continues to be the predominant funding method. But weighted-pupil and instructional-unit approaches gained popularity during the 1970s. Delaware's finance plan calls for one classroom unit for each fifteen FTE pupils enrolled in vocational programs. Florida's weighted-pupil plan includes ten vocational-technical program categories that range in weight from 0.969 to 1.979. Michigan districts are reimbursed for up to 75 percent of the additional costs of approved programs. The Pennsylvania subsidy varies according

to districts' aid ratios under the percentage equalization formula (Gold, Smith, & Lawton, 1995, pp. 181, 191, 341, 535).

Compensatory programs serve low-income pupils, educationally disadvantaged pupils, or other categories of at-risk pupils through additional aid in twenty-eight states (Gold, Smith, & Lawton, 1995, pp. 61–62). Many states tie eligibility to family income following federal guidelines for defining Aid to Families with Dependent Children (AFDC) or for free and reduced-price lunches under the National School Lunch Program (see Title/Chapter I criteria discussed in Chapter 10). For example, Ohio's flat grants range from $103 per pupil in districts with at least fifty pupils from households receiving AFDC (or between 5 and 10 percent of all pupils) to $1,092 per pupil for districts with over 20 percent qualifying students. Minnesota's method for determining compensatory revenue gradually increases the number of pupil units per qualifying AFDC student from zero to 0.65 as the ratio of AFDC students to the total district ADM increases from zero to 11.5 percent. Other states fund remedial programs to serve eligible students. For example, in Missouri, reading programs are financed by a flat grant of $9,200 per classroom or approved teacher. Washington fully funds a remedial assistance program that is based on the number of pupils scoring in the lowest quartile on the state's fourth- and eighth-grade basic skills tests. Districts in Louisiana and North Carolina must sponsor state-funded remediation programs for students who fail parts of the statewide standardized test.

Indiana determines a more elaborate at-risk factor from the decennial census. It includes the percentages of families with incomes below the poverty level and of children whose parents do not live together within the household, and the overall population over nineteen years of age who have not graduated from high school. The different determinants of need in these compensatory and at-risk adjustments have limitations. Some at-risk measures assume a correlation between family income and educational deficiencies. Others are designed to compensate for low academic performance and may inadvertently reward schools for their poor performance.

Thirty states finance *bilingual education* programs for students with limited English proficiency through a partial excess cost reimbursement or weighted-pupil approach (Gold, Smith, & Lawton, 1995, pp. 61–62). New Jersey, for example, provides an additional weight of 0.18 for each pupil enrolled in approved programs. The Florida weights vary according to grade levels: 1.600 for K–3, 1.617 for 4–8, and 1.454 for 9–12. Alaska districts receive 4.2 percent of the value of an instructional unit in addition to the contribution eligible students make through overall enrollments. The number of pupils served in limited English proficiency programs in Rhode Island is multiplied by a state-defined per pupil cost; each district's aid ratio determines the state's share.

Early childhood education programs are financed through allocations to public schools in thirty-six states (Gold, Smith, & Lawton, 1995, pp. 61–62). South Carolina districts must offer programs for four-year-olds with significant readiness deficiencies. These programs must be developed with the collaboration of the Interagency Coordinating Council on Early Childhood Development and Education. Grants to Illinois districts enable screening programs to identify children who are potentially at risk of academic failure. They also enable programs to increase later school success, parental involvement, and linkages with community agencies. Programs for three-year-olds and four-year olds are financed in Texas, where half-day prekindergartens serve children who cannot speak and understand English or who are from low-income families.

Categorical aid finances an array of other educational programs related to pupils' needs, both to offset costs and to give incentives for districts to adopt programs. The following representative programs reveal legislative priorities. The Electronic Classroom program creates a network for delivering high school credit courses, primarily in languages and mathematics, and for staff development

opportunities in Virginia. Massachusetts and Wisconsin provide integration aid to finance voluntary inter- and intradistrict transfers of pupils to improve racial balances. Several states, including Arizona and North Carolina, finance programs to reduce high school dropout rates. Maryland's Community Center Funds enable youths and adults to use school facilities during weekends and evenings for supplementary education and leisure programs. Adult education is also financed through state assistance. In Virginia school districts are reimbursed for general adult education programs on a fixed cost per pupil or cost per class basis (Gold, Smith, & Lawton, 1995, pp. 123, 322, 331, 480, 630, 668).

Pupil counts and special programs to meet educational needs are important triggers for additional state funds. Once the cost of the educational program is determined for individual school districts, aid structures consider measures of local capacity and effort that determine the most appropriate amount of local revenue to be applied to meet those needs.

DEFINING FISCAL CAPACITY AND TAX EFFORT

In previous chapters, we have discussed the fiscal inequities caused by the extreme decentralization of the school district pattern of governance. The financial ability of districts, and the willingness of elected officials or the voters to deliver more resources to education, often dictate the amount of available funds. In Chapter 8, we discussed a number of approaches to equalizing such inequities. Basic to all except flat grants and full state funding is an accurate measure of the school district tax base.

Measurement of Fiscal Ability

Fiscal capacity "represents the resources of a government or taxing jurisdiction that are available for taxation" (Sparkman, 1976, p. 302). Fiscal ability or "wealth" of a jurisdiction is the ratio of fiscal capacity to a measure of the demand for public services:

$$\text{Fiscal ability} = \frac{\text{fiscal capacity}}{\text{demand for public services}}$$

State school finance plans have traditionally considered property valuation the measure of fiscal capacity because of the historical reliance on this tax base. They have considered the number of pupils (modified or weighted as discussed in the previous section) as the measure of demand for services:

$$\text{District fiscal ability} = \frac{\text{district property valuation}}{\text{number of weighted-pupil units}}$$

Over the years, states have developed greater sophistication in measuring both the numerator and denominator of this ratio, more accurately assessing fiscal ability and injecting greater equity into state distribution policies.

Problems in measuring fiscal capacities of large cities illustrate the shortcomings of relying upon property valuation alone. Urban areas such as Atlanta, Denver, New York, and San Francisco have relatively large commercial and industrial tax bases to draw on for school support. However, this property-based wealth is a poor representation of the local money available for schools, given competing demands for public funds and services. Because state aid flows in inverse proportion to local wealth, and localities are expected to draw upon their property tax base for the remainder, equalization formulas assume that all school districts have equal access to the property tax bases. This assumption works to the disadvantage of urban centers.

Other large cities, such as Baltimore, Buffalo, and Saint Louis, have faced large-scale migration of businesses and higher-income families to the suburbs during the past several decades. With deteriorated tax bases and diminished economic activity, these cities are less financially able to provide adequate municipal services *and* public education. At the same time, the growing concentrations of low-income families increase the percentage of children in need of high-cost education programs.

The heavier costs of services and the demands on property tax bases in cities (referred to as municipal overburden in Chapter 7) urge a broader view of fiscal capacity. Many states have modified their finance plans to

- expand property wealth measures to include other economic indicators;
- measure capacity on a per capita rather than a per pupil basis; and
- adjust the per pupil denominator in wealth measures to reflect the educational needs of school districts (Goertz, 1981; Odden 1977).

Nearly one-half of the states expand the definition of fiscal capacity beyond simply property valuation. Gold, Smith, and Lawton (1995, p. 27) reported that twenty-four states use assessed valuation only; nine states add personal income; nine states include various other revenue sources but not personal income; and five states combine property valuation, personal income, and other revenue. Three other states (Hawaii, North Carolina, and Washington) do not consider local fiscal capacity in making state allocations. Maine recently adopted a school finance plan in which personal income (adjusted for local cost of living rates) counts toward determining 15 percent of a district's state aid, and property value counts for 85 percent (Johnston, 1995). If a state includes other sources of revenue actually received by the district or various indicators of economic health that may not be subject to local taxation, it creates a more accurate picture of districts' ability and willingness to raise local revenue. Despite their complexities, such indices offer a more complete measure of capacity, according to Ladd (1975) and Gurwitz (1977).

Measures that include income strengthen state assessments of fiscal capacity. This is particularly true in districts that receive local income tax revenue. However, even when income taxes are collected, there may be difficulties with accounting applicable revenue. This is especially true in states where school district boundaries are not coterminous with county or municipal boundaries. For example, a study of income as a partial measure of capacity in New York found many problems due to inaccurate, incomplete, and untimely reporting of income tax revenue to be credited to school districts (Dembowski et al., 1982). Nevertheless, defining capacity in terms of income per pupil reflects both financial ability and pupils' educational needs (Adams & Odden, 1981, p. 152). Most indices are additive (i.e., the sum of ratios of property valuation and income to the number of weighted-pupil units) rather than multiplicative (i.e., the product of per pupil valuation and per capita income). Adams and Odden (1981) argued that a multiplicative factor would allocate more aid to low-income districts and improve the equity of the school finance system.

When both property valuation and personal income are taken into account in finance plans, cities appear poorer. This is because cities have relatively higher per pupil property values and relatively low incomes. Because they have high personal incomes, suburban districts appear wealthier. In Connecticut, for example, property wealth is adjusted through a comparison of per capita local income with the state's highest income district. This adjustment makes the computed fiscal capacity of many cities lower. They then receive higher state aid than they would receive under a property-tax-based formula (Goertz, 1981, p. 125).

Per capita rather than per pupil measures of fiscal capacity increase the denominator of the wealth : size ratio. More state aid is directed to districts with a smaller than average proportion of their population enrolled in public schools. This is often the case for large cities, especially in the Northeast. In the Northeast large numbers of children are enrolled in nonpublic schools. Including total population is a better measure of the ability of municipalities to raise revenue to support multiple public services. However, per capita factors also

direct more aid to districts with large percentages of pupils enrolled in private schools. Thus these factors do not account for the increased abilities of these districts to support the remaining pupils (Odden, 1977, p. 362). Several states, along with Connecticut, cited above, use per capita measures of capacity. Virginia's composite index, for example, includes property valuation, personal income, and taxable sales on both a per pupil and a per capita basis (Gold, Smith, & Lawton, 1995, p. 622).

We addressed the importance of correcting pupil counts according to educational needs in the previous section. Several states also modify the definition of local tax bases to reflect the needs of pupils. Adjusting fiscal capacity in this way advantages cities because of their disproportionate enrollment of students in high-cost programs. For example, New York considers the number of pupils with special educational needs and handicapping conditions in its determination of Total Wealth Pupil Units (Gold, Smith, & Lawton, 1995, p. 455).

Measurement of Effort

The amount of effort put forth to determine local contributions toward the support of school programs works in concert with fiscal capacity. Tax effort is defined as the "extent to which government is actually using the resources available to it for tax purposes" (Sparkman, 1976, p. 302). Two school districts may have the same fiscal capacity. But the one that exerts the greatest effort has the higher level of revenue for school operations.

Measures of tax effort involve a ratio of local tax revenues to some measure of fiscal capacity:

$$\text{Effort} = \frac{\text{tax revenue}}{\text{fiscal capacity}}$$

This ratio often serves as a proxy for the willingness of school boards or voters to support their schools. It often reflects such factors as the public's attitudes toward public schools and the use of taxation to support public services generally. The effect that district effort has on spending is most apparent when funding relies totally on local revenue. This often occurs in financing capital outlay (see Chapter 7) and when local option taxes are not capped in flat grant or foundation plans. It also occurs when there is insufficient state funding of any of the tax-base-equalizing plans we discussed in Chapter 8.

Expenditure levels are often used to approximate effort. But they are an unsatisfactory measure, because spending in wealthier districts is exaggerated. Wealthier districts can raise and expend large amounts of local revenue with little actual tax effort because of their large fiscal capacities. Locally determined tax rates express the ratio of revenue to property valuation. These rates are commonly used indicators of voters' sacrifice to support schools. The fairest comparison of the property tax effort among school systems is effective tax rates. If tax rates are related to full market or equalized values, differing assessment practices are taken into account (see Chapter 6).

Fiscal capacity measures may be broadened to include personal income and other indicators of economic status. Analyses of local effort may be similarly enriched. Revenue may be expressed as a percentage of personal income (per capita or per pupil) to compare effort among states—or districts where personal income data are available—in relation to ability to pay. Similarly, the Representative Tax System we discussed in Chapter 5 examines actual tax receipts in relation to available (whether used or not) tax bases to compare effort (see Table 5.6).

Local fiscal capacity and tax effort are important constructs in the reform of finance structures. Disparities in educational opportunities are most often a function of differing levels of capacity and effort. States, however, have traditionally viewed local property tax yield as the means to increase the total revenue available. It is easy to agree that local fiscal capacity and effort are important components of nearly all state finance plans. It is less clear what measures of each dimension provide fair indicators of available wealth and the public's willingness to support education.

The politics of school finance comes alive in debates about the most appropriate measures of capacity and effort within state aid formulas. Potentially large shifts in state aid accompany any change in the definitions of fiscal capacity and tax effort. Winning and losing school districts express their positions in the policy arena. Strong rationales for revisions and accurate projections of the impacts of alternative measures are essential to counter arguments made solely to protect resources granted under less effective measures.

Financial capacity and tax effort define local contributions to state aid plans designed to meet the educational needs of pupils. Very often aid formulas are further refined by several school and district characteristics that affect costs.

RECOGNIZING COMMUNITY AND SCHOOL DISTRICT CHARACTERISTICS

State finance policies consider aspects of communities that have cost implications beyond the control of local school officials. If there were no state intervention, there would be inequities in programs and finance among districts. The inequities result from the extreme differences in per pupil wealth among districts and from variations in the per pupil costs of providing equivalent educational opportunities (Johns, 1975, p. 160; Kozol, 1991). Adjustments in state aid plans most often take into account the density of the population, the cost of personnel or staff development, and the cost of living or of delivering education.

School and District Size

The sizes of districts and individual schools vary widely. Some urban districts are large both geographically and in terms of pupil enrollment. On the other hand, some rural districts cover many sparsely populated square miles. Up to a point, large and densely populated school systems may benefit from economies of scale (see Chapter 13).

For these reasons, state finance plans often include corrections of need associated with size.

Need is measured more appropriately in terms of the number of students served or in terms of the density of the general population rather than in terms of per pupil expenditures. Swanson (1966) observed that sparsely populated rural districts and densely populated cities may each have high expenditures. Their schools are costly, however, for very different reasons. Small class sizes and diseconomies of scale influence costs in small, rural districts. But costs may be as high or higher in larger systems. These systems need expanded services and personnel to serve at-risk populations. Both large urban districts and small rural schools and districts in geographically isolated areas tend to have higher per pupil costs for basic educational services than do suburban schools and districts. This is true even though suburban districts may spend as much or more, thus having a higher level of services.

States may adjust their aid on the basis of sparsity of population or the small number of pupils served by rural schools. In doing this they recognize (1) the higher costs of smaller classes; (2) diseconomies resulting from the division of some expenses (e.g., superintendent and principal salaries) among fewer students; and (3) additional salaries needed to attract teachers to remote areas, particularly in subject fields experiencing shortages. Gold, Smith, and Lawton (1995, p. 34) reported that for funding purposes, eight states adjust for sparsity of population and twelve assist districts that are declared to be small. Table 9.2 illustrates that states' adjustments for population sparsity and pupil counts within schools or school districts vary greatly. Plans may provide for additional pupil weights or instructional units, additional flat grants, or proportionately more funds to compensate for size-related costs. Adjustments may be keyed to enrollments, as in Montana and New Mexico; membership in regional districts, as in Connecticut; population sparsity and bus distances, as in Texas; or the existence of remote and necessary small schools, as in California and Washing-ton. This latter criterion enables small isolated schools to serve students close to their homes despite the high per pupil cost. States determine whether a small school is essential on the basis of such factors as the distance from another school, terrain and road conditions that create safety problems, and the length of bus routes (in miles or hours) to the nearest larger school. For example, the island of Ocracoke is located off the North Carolina coast and has fewer than forty K–12 students; it receives a special allotment.

Adjustments should not encourage the creation or continuation of unnecessary and inefficient districts (Johns, 1975, p. 202). States should ensure that educational opportunities are adequate in necessarily small schools. But state aid correction factors should apply only when mergers are not feasible. Otherwise, size adjustments may become "allocative disincentives" (Cohn, 1975, p. 216) for schools and districts to remain small. Explicit penalty and incentive structures within state aid plans provide stimuli for changing school organization when there is considerable waste of resources (Cohn, 1974, pp. 95–103). Penalties reduce state aid by a portion of the cost savings that would be realized had the district operated schools with more optimal enrollments. Under incentive systems, districts that undertake grade-level reorganization and district consolidation receive additional general aid and assistance with capital projects.

It is not just sparsely populated regions that experience higher costs. Needs and costs in large cities may also justify additional state funds. States may make adjustments for density or large size. They do this to the degree that weighted-unit and excess-cost finance plans fail to aid urban areas that have higher expenditures. These corrections recognize that demands on local tax bases for competing public services (in Chapter 4 we discussed municipal overburden) create fiscal stress in cities (Sjogren, 1981). On the other hand, individuals live in communities that offer the kinds of public services they desire and are willing to pay for (Tiebout, 1956). Some argue that state intervention is therefore unwarranted.

TABLE 9.2. Adjustment in Selected States for Small Size

State	Adjustment
California	Additional funding for necessary small schools in districts below 2501 ADA[a] according to graduated scales for elementary schools under 101 ADA and for secondary schools below 301 ADA.
Connecticut	Towns that are members of K–12 regional school districts receive a bonus grant of an additional $25 per pupil; those belonging to regional high school districts receive a bonus of $25 per pupil for those students who attend the regional high school times the ratio of the number of grades in the regional high school to 13.
Montana	Per pupil entitlements are inversely related to school size, with higher per pupil support for elementary districts with fewer than 1,000 pupils and secondary districts with fewer than 800 pupils.
New Mexico	Additional pupil units are granted by formulas for small schools, with a weight of 1.0 for elementary and junior high schools with fewer than 200 pupils; and weights of 2.0 and 1.6 for senior high schools with fewer than 200 or 400 pupils, respectively; for small districts, with a weight of 0.15 for districts below 4,000 pupils; and a weight of 0.5 for rural isolation that considers total district enrollment and the number of high schools.
Texas	Districts with under 1,600 pupils receive a small district adjustment, and additional weight is given to those of under 300 square miles. Other sparsity adjustment applies by grade level: a district offering K–12 programs with fewer than 130 pupils receives aid based on 130 ADA if it has at least 90 ADA or is 30 or more miles by bus from the nearest high school district; those with K–8 programs with at least 50 ADA or at least 30 miles by bus from the nearest high school district receive aid for 75 ADA; those with K–6 programs having at least 40 ADA or at least 30 miles by bus from the nearest high school district receive aid for 60 ADA.
Washington	Additional instructional staff units for districts with "remote and necessary" K–8 schools with under 100 FTE,[b] 9–12 schools with under 25 FTE, no high schools and between 50 and 180 FTE, and not more than 2 high schools and under 300 FTE in each school.

[a]ADA = average daily attendance.
[b]FTE = full-time equivalent.
SOURCE: S. D. Gold, D. M. Smith, & S. B. Lawton (Eds.). (1995). *Public school finance programs of the United States and Canada, 1993–94.* Albany, NY: American Education Finance Association and The Center for the Study of the States, pp. 144, 170, 389, 441, 590, 635. Reprinted with the permission of the publisher.

A few states consider this burden in their finance formulas. Pennsylvania's density factor provides a supplement based on local tax effort and population per square mile. The highest percentage of instructional expenses (19 percent) supplements other state aid in districts that tax above the median and have population of over 5,950 per square mile and over 35,000 weighted-pupil units. Other states consider the higher costs of delivering education in urban areas through corrections based on enrollment. New Mexico's cities qualify for density units if pupil counts are between 15,000 and 35,000 (0.15 weight) or over 35,000 pupils (0.023 weight). New York provides aid for special services to its five largest city school districts that are not eligible for the state assistance granted to districts participating in Board of Cooperative Educational Services (BOCES) programs (Gold, Smith, & Lawton, 1995, pp. 442, 466, 531).

Debates about the appropriateness of state aid provisions for urban areas are sensitive to the extent of participation and the amount of aid. It is difficult to determine which communities should be eligible for additional funds. States must also determine how much aid is necessary to offset only those costs that are beyond the control of school systems. These costs include maintenance related to crime and vandalism; larger salaries and benefit packages to attract teachers to difficult situations; land for school construction; desegregation; and disproportionate numbers of language-deficient, disabled, and disadvantaged students. To the degree that other formula adjustments tied to pupil needs and personnel costs already recognize these burdens, a provision based on population density may not be warranted.

Personnel Costs

Allocations of additional funds to small schools having low pupil : teacher ratios, and thus high personnel costs per pupil, emerged initially as alternate forms of sparsity correction. In addition to size factors, some states today have formulas that are sensitive to costs related to the qualifications of certified employees and that offset costs of staff development.

Early in the century, Cubberley (1906, p. 252) argued that "the real unit of cost is the teacher who must be employed to teach the school, and not the children who may or do not attend." Placing teachers in a prominent place in apportionment plans would reflect personnel costs and the efforts of communities to support schools. It was also believed that this focus on teachers, regardless of their level or their subject areas, would stimulate the development of innovative programs. Updegraff and King (1922) later refined the concept of the "teacher unit" to account for other community characteristics. Like a sparsity or density factor, different ratios of average daily attendance per teacher would compensate for costs experienced in rural and urban communities, in elementary and secondary schools, and for special subjects.

Adjustments for personnel costs now present in state policies rely primarily on the two traditional determinants of salaries. The extent of training and experience of teachers, counselors, administrators, and other certified personnel is reflected in minimum salary schedules. Some states use these schedules to fund personnel costs through formulas based on instructional units. Arizona, Minnesota, and New Mexico recognize personnel costs through formulas that account for teacher training and experience. In the New Mexico weighted-pupil formula, a matrix identifies weights associated with personnel characteristics to determine the average level of training and experience in each district (see Figure 9.1). School systems having low weights because of a concentration of teachers with bachelor's degrees and only a few years of experience generate fewer additional weighted-pupil units than do districts having many highly experienced and trained professionals. They thus receive less enhancement in state aid.

Without state assistance for this aspect of need, districts that have difficulty financing adequate salaries might deny tenure or stimulate rapid turnover as teachers gained experience and graduate degrees. This scenario is less likely when there are teachers' unions and state legislative guarantees of due process in removal procedures. The diversion of funds from other instructional and administrative budgets to raise salaries to competitive levels is more likely. This assistance may make the most sense in poorer school systems. However, the net effect of the aid is often to help wealthy districts maintain their competitive edge in attracting and holding the highest-quality teachers (Cohn, 1974, p. 16). Teachers in high socioeconomic status (SES) communities tend to have higher levels of formal training and more years of experience, and SES explains much of the variation in salaries among districts (King, 1979). In addition to a given district's relative wealth, the willingness of local communities to support education is critical in determining salaries relative to those paid in neighboring districts (Kirby et al., 1993). Thus, legislatures should examine closely the "disequalizing effect on local school finances" (Leppert et al., 1976, p. 19) brought by states assisting districts with costs incurred for salaries of personnel.

Unlike adjustments driven by training and experience, the education reforms of the 1980s brought allocations of state funds to upgrade the quality of teaching. Career ladders and performance-based merit pay plans expand or replace tra-

An instructional staff Training and Experience (T&E) index is calculated as follows:

(1) Multiply the number of FTE[a] instructional staff in each academic classification by the numerical factor in the appropriate Years of Experience column of this matrix:

Academic Classification	Years of Experience				
	0–2	3–5	6–8	9–15	Over 15
Bachelor's degree or less	0.75	0.90	1.00	1.05	1.00
Bachelor's plus 15 credit hours	0.80	0.95	1.00	1.10	1.15
Master's or Bachelor's plus 45 credit hours	0.85	1.00	1.05	1.15	1.20
Master's plus 15 credit hours	0.90	1.05	1.15	1.30	1.35
Post–Master's or Master's plus 45 credit hours	1.00	1.15	1.30	1.40	1.50

(2) Divide the total of the products obtained in (1) by the total number of FTE instructional staff. No district's factor shall be less than 1.00.

The resulting T&E index is multiplied by the total units derived from early-childhood, grades 1–12, special education, and bilingual education programs.

[a]FTE = full-time equivalent.

Figure 9.1. Training and Experience Index in New Mexico. (SOURCE: B. C. McOlash & J. P. Garcia [1995] New Mexico. In S. D. Gold, D. M. Smith, & S. B. Lawton [Eds.], *Public school finance programs of the United States and Canada, 1993–94*. Albany, NY: American Education Finance Association and The Center for the Study of the States, p. 443. Reprinted with the permission of the publisher.)

ditional criteria for salary enhancement (see Chapter 16). Various forms of aid stimulate staff development opportunities. For example, Georgia makes funds available for teachers and other employees to correct identified weaknesses, to gain skills in areas needed by the district, and to improve individual competencies. Oregon's staff development funds enable schools and districts to design programs for improving curriculum and instructional methodologies. South Dakota finances workshops for teachers, librarians, and counselors before the opening of schools. Florida directly finances teachers' participation in intensive summer in-service training programs focused on subject matter content. Oklahoma funds a teacher consultant, or mentor, to supervise, advise, and evaluate first-year teachers. Michigan sponsors professional development for administrators and teachers, a biennial educational policy institute, a statewide leadership

academy, community leadership development, and sabbatical leaves for master teachers involved in professional development (Gold, Smith, & Lawton, 1995, pp. 197, 206, 341, 517, 525, 569).

Cost of Living or Education

Like the density corrections for cities, indices tied to the cost of living or a broader cost of delivering education apply in expensive regions of states. The cost of living is typically determined by the cost of purchasing a basket of consumer goods at today's prices (Greenwald, 1994, p. 222). But Wendling (1981) argued that a cost-of-living index for educational purposes should include multiple determinants of salaries: personal characteristics, professional environment, fiscal capacity, student characteristics, school district characteristics, and regional characteristics.

States that recognize this cost factor have adopted less complex indices. For example, Ohio calculates the Cost of Doing Business Factor by county according to average weekly wages as a proxy for regional costs of providing equivalent educational services. Colorado's cost-of-living adjustment reflects the cost of housing, goods, and services; it is applied to the portion of a district's base funding that is allocated for personnel costs. The Alaska formula considers regional cost-of-living differentials. Such formula adjustments may be most essential when finance plans are almost fully state funded. For example, Florida's highly equalized foundation plan includes a Price Level Index in which cost differentials of county units are based on a three-year average of consumer prices. This index considers many factors (e.g., housing, food, transportation, health, and recreation) that influence salary levels; thus it is assumed to approximate educational costs, because a high proportion of school budgets is related to personnel (Gold, Smith, & Lawton, 1995, pp. 110, 159, 192, 497).

For several reasons, few states have adopted cost-of-living corrections. In some cases, aid adjustments for teacher characteristics relieve this need. In other cases, demands for more aid to supplement salaries receive little attention in the political arena. High-cost areas tend to be major metropolitan areas. Many believe that cultural amenities, opportunities for advanced education, and the generally higher quality of public services counter demands for additional aid. Moreover, the most fiscally able districts tend to be located in metropolitan areas. This makes high-cost aid counterequalizing.

A cost-of-education index takes into account the differences in actual costs schools face in purchasing specific instructional supplies and personnel. States assume that helping schools purchase these material inputs makes a difference in learning according to the production function we discuss in Chapter 13. A resource-cost model assesses the extent to which differences in the costs of educational services reflect variations in prices paid for comparable resources, pupils' programmatic needs, and the scale of school and district operations

(Chambers, 1980; Chambers & Parrish, 1986). These models identify educational costs by listing a uniform set of educational programs, determining the specific resource requirements (e.g., personnel time, supplies, equipment) for each of these programs regardless of the location of the school, and attaching prices that prevail within localities to each of these resources. Ideally, state aid based on such a model gives all districts the purchasing power to provide pupils access to the same kinds and combinations of resources.

Cost-of-education adjustments in Texas considered geographical variations in known resource costs due to factors beyond the control of school districts until 1994–1995. In the future the Foundation School Fund budget committee will adopt the adjustments (Gold, Smith, & Lawton, 1995, p. 589). In analyzing the former index, Monk and Walker (1991) described the difficulties in constructing valid measures:

> As progress is made toward clarifying goals for educational systems, toward gaining knowledge about educational production realities, and toward developing criteria for which modes of production are and are not acceptable, we can aspire to developing a truly comprehensive cost of education index, one that accounts for differences in a wide range of phenomena currently handled on a largely ad hoc basis within funding formulae. (p. 176)

In addition to measures of the educational needs of students and the financial conditions of districts, state aid plans may consider whether financial aid policies can induce desired program improvements.

INCENTIVES FOR SCHOOL IMPROVEMENT

States have created ways to recognize schools that successfully raise student performance or to encourage schoolwide improvement. We discuss performance-based rewards for individual teachers more fully in Chapter 16. This section describes several approaches taken by states to reward schools and districts and identifies challenges to policy makers as they seek feasible and effective incentives within school finance plans.

Cibulka (1989) advanced rational choice theory as a framework for understanding the conditions under which incentives are effective:

> Incentives are a case of voluntary contractual exchange in which the donor sets forth the terms. Both the donor and the recipient are assumed to be utility-maximizing; they strive to maximize benefits and to minimize costs to themselves. Incentives work to the extent that both the donor (in this case, state officials) and the recipients (here, the school, school district, teachers or administrators) perceive that their gains sufficiently exceed their costs so as to justify the voluntary arrangement. Each party may continue the arrangement despite less than optimal terms; indeed, suboptimality and "sacrificing" are the rule rather than the exception in political exchanges. (p. 419)

In designing an incentive structure, the state seeks to maximize the benefits for society (e.g., improving pupil performance) and provides financial incentives to motivate recipient schools or districts to achieve the performance goals. Interestingly, this perspective suggests that districts create programs that will attain rewards (both monetary and status enhancement) at the least possible cost. Similarly, the size of the state's incentive is gauged to the perceived value of benefits to be realized in a way that minimizes the burden on state resources while stimulating change at the local level.

Legislators became interested in incorporating measures of student performance in the determination of financial allocations to districts or individual schools in the context of the recent educational reform movement. States that are refining policies to tie standards to assessments are also exploring the advantages of linking these and other performance measures with the amount of funds available to schools. They believe that marketlike incentives that encourage local district and school improvement efforts in response to national and state goals can be more effective in attaining public goals than mandates and regulations.

Early modifications in state policy encouraged the adoption of performance-based pay or career ladders (e.g., Tennessee, Utah) that would reward individual teachers for assuming greater responsibilities for improving teaching (see Chapter 16). Other states (e.g., Florida) adopted a merit-schools approach to overcome objections that individual incentives work against other educational reforms designed to build effective teamwork.

In addition to incentives that recognize the performance of individual teachers and principals, several states provide awards and competitive grants for school innovations. The South Carolina School Incentive Reward Program distributes funds on a per pupil basis to schools and districts that demonstrate exceptional performance and meet criteria of gains in achievement. School personnel may spend funds in a discretionary manner for areas of need identified in school improvement plans. But these funds may not supplement salaries. The School Innovation program provides competitive planning (up to $5,000) and implementation (up to $90,000 for a three-year period) grants that stimulate innovative and comprehensive approaches for improving student development, performance, and attendance.

The Kentucky Education Reform Act (KERA) established a School Reward Trust Fund from which performance incentives would be appropriated. This legislation granted school personnel greater latitude in determining how schools are run and students are taught. It held schools accountable by dispensing bonuses based on gains in achievement, dropout and attendance rates, and trends in student transition from school to work or higher education. In addition to school-based incentives, the state rewards districts in which these performance measures exceed state goals. Rewards for school- and districtwide improvements in performance are thought to be more effective than recognition of individual teacher merit (Harp, 1995).

The Indiana School Improvement Award Program rewards individual schools for demonstrating gains in student attendance, graduation rates, and scores on statewide tests. Awards can be used for educational purposes but not for salaries or athletics. Additional weights are awarded in the Florida finance plan for students with high scores on the College Board Advanced Placement exams and who graduated from International Baccalaureate programs during the previous year.

Competitive grants awarded by California's School Improvement Program enable recipient schools to design and implement locally determined improvement projects. A school-site advisory council consisting of parents, teachers, and the principal assists in developing a plan that is submitted to the state. Once a school receives funds, the grant becomes an annual occurrence. The Vermont Reinventing Schools grants encourage schools to do fundamental educational restructuring. The Illinois school improvement program also assists educational change efforts. This program extends the possible projects to include assistance for districts or consortia of districts to plan for educational choice initiatives (Gold, Smith, & Lawton, 1995, pp. 152, 191, 237, 250, 280, 558, 615).

Systemic educational reforms are likely to grow in the future from the emerging emphasis on standards and assessments. Both Congress (Goals 2000: Educate America Act, 1994) and many state legislatures are encouraging districts to identify goals, establish model standards, and adopt innovative teaching and learning methods in tandem with the standards. Once standards and instructional delivery mechanisms are in place, assessments of student performance will be tied to the standards. It is also likely that policy makers will raise the possibility of directly relating the funds available to schools to measures of student performance on these assessments. The challenge is to design a system of financial incentives (and perhaps penalties) that will have the desired effect of encouraging individual teachers, grade levels and departments, schools, or entire districts to perform at higher levels so that their students will also demonstrate increased learning.

The dilemmas of designing effective policies are expressed in the following questions (see also Odden & Picus, 1992, Chapter 11; Picus, 1992; Richards & Shujaa, 1990):

- What *measures* of student or teacher performance are best linked to incentives: for example, achievement on state assessment tests, attendance or dropout rates, enrollments in advanced placement classes, or evaluations of teaching performance? Which measures are least likely to induce negative actions (teaching to the test, purposely encouraging poor performance in a base year to inflate later gains) or morale problems?
- Is a *structure* that provides an absolute standard (e.g., a predetermined criterion) for receiving funds more effective than a relative standard (e.g., competitions among schools or classrooms) in stimulating school improvement?
- What *organizational unit* should be the recipient of funds: e.g., district, school, grade level or department, or individual classroom?
- Should incentive money be *general or categorical* in nature? Are incentives that tie funds to specific programs or standards (i.e., categorical) likely to be more effective in achieving goals than formula adjustments that reward school improvement efforts but give latitude to local personnel for determining priorities with no subsequent monitoring or tracking of funds to specific targeted areas (i.e., general)?
- What *amount of money,* in relation to the overall school finance program, should be allocated to incentives?
- What should be the *permissible uses* of funds at the school or classroom level (e.g., salary enhancements, instructional supplies and materials, rewards for students)?
- For *how many years* should incentive money continue to flow to a meritorious school/district? Might the removal of incentive funds in subsequent years be viewed as a form of punishment?

- Are there impacts on *equity goals,* including those that seek to reduce the relationships among the financial wealth of districts, family socioeconomic status, and pupil achievement? Does incentive money enable the most effective schools (regardless of students' backgrounds) to improve teaching and learning even more, to the detriment of those schools most in need of assistance? Do incentive structures enable low-performing schools, which often serve low-income and disadvantaged students, to acquire monies for compensatory and innovative programs to enhance learning?
- Are systems of financial rewards and punishments *likely to be effective?* Have there been empirical studies to determine the effectiveness of these or similar incentive structures?
- What is the likely *duration of effects* of rewards? Are incentives effective only in the short run, or do they stimulate school improvements that continue after the supplemental funds disappear?
- What is the *political reality* surrounding systems of incentives? Are rewards and punishments popular among policy makers primarily because they give the impression that the state is taking action to improve education? Are they useful in gaining educators' acceptance of state-established reforms and standards by offering an opportunity to acquire funds to raise salaries or assist in school improvement efforts?

The effectiveness of incentives in maximizing benefits for schools and society, while minimizing unintended effects on personnel and pupils, may depend on the way states' policies address the above questions.

After a state gives aid to finance schools, the role of the state becomes one of monitoring to assure that the funds are spent according to the policy requirements and to assess the degree to which the performance goals are attained.

FISCAL AND PROGRAM ACCOUNTABILITY

Accountability in school finance policy is defined broadly as responsibility for "the results or outcomes derived from the exercise of discretionary authority by school policy makers or administrators in fiscal matters including revenue and taxation, budgeting and appropriation, and expenditure and resource management" (Hack et al, 1981, p. 252). Implicit in this statement are two aspects of accountability: assessing the appropriateness of the decisions about the distribution of resources given the degree of discretion available to the school boards and administrators; and holding the school system responsible for the effectiveness of the programs and the personnel purchased by these resources in achieving goals.

The first dimension of accountability in this definition urges policy makers and school personnel to allocate and spend funds in appropriate ways. Internal and external financial audits ensure that allocated monies are spent legally (Drake & Roe, 1994, pp. 114–116). District personnel conduct an *internal audit,* to guard against the improper administration of funds as a result of intentional or unintentional errors at the time transactions occur or are recorded. *External audits* are conducted by state and federal agencies as well as by independent accountants. These audits determine whether appropriations of state and federal funds are made in accordance with prescribed law. *Program audits* determine whether delivery systems are directed toward the goals defined by legislatures and state boards of education, that instructional programs reflect educational standards and curriculum guides, and that programs serve the particular groups of children for whom the funds are intended.

Financial mismanagement, including malfeasance or other intentional wrongdoing, or poor pupil performance may result in severe actions by state agencies. For example, evidence of mishandling funds over a six-year period in the East Saint Louis schools resulted in the State Board of Education's assumption of financial oversight of the district (Schmidt, 1994). The threat of fiscal bankruptcy due to severe debt or declining property valuations may necessitate increased taxes, budget reductions, or state actions even when there is no mismanagement of funds (Fulton & Sonovick, 1993). State education departments in Missouri and Oklahoma are empowered to annex financially distressed districts to avoid bankruptcy. Missouri's board may also reassign children from insolvent districts to solvent ones. If a fiscally distressed district in Pennsylvania is taken over by the state department of education, a special board of education oversees the actions of the local board and the superintendent until fiscal propriety is restored. Ohio districts that cannot meet the financial standards of operation are required to borrow, if they are eligible, from the state loan fund following a strict review. The superintendent of public instruction monitors these districts to ensure that academic standards are met. A more dramatic accountability mechanism is illustrated by the decision of the District Court judge who is overseeing the desegregation of the Cleveland schools to order the state superintendent to assume "total control" of the district and to close fourteen schools that were beyond repair. This takeover was ordered because internal dissension, management problems, and a $30 million budget deficit had undermined the district's ability to carry out its educational program (Bradley, 1995).

The complexity of the audit processes states require depends in part on whether state aid is structured as categorical or general (see Chapter 8). The well-defined cycle demanded of categorical grants establishes a framework for program planning, budget development, identification of pupils, expenditures for personnel and other resources to deliver services, and program evaluation and fiscal audits. In contrast, processes for monitoring expenditures of local and state money for general school operations are not program specific. State statutes and regulations that govern fiscal management outline the necessary budgeting, accounting, and auditing procedures for the local use of general operating aid. Proposals for spending are examined through public budget hearings or a state review of expenditure plans. The overall effectiveness of the use of resources is later assessed, if at all, through internal performance reviews, external accreditation processes, and statewide testing programs.

We described financing of special programs earlier in this chapter as either categorical (e.g., flat grant and excess cost reimbursements) or general (e.g., weighted-pupil formulas) aid. Categorical programs target money to groups of pupils with particular educational needs, restrict spending through special accounts, and closely monitor program content and outcomes. Following the flow of money makes it easier to identify spending patterns among schools and classrooms within a district. These financial aids tie funding to the delivery of services more closely than do weighted-unit plans and make it more difficult to integrate categorically aided services with other instructional programs. With greater flexibility in planning and budgeting, weighted-unit plans permit latitude in the delivery of instructional programs to meet locally identified pupil needs. These plans rarely call for program audits to ensure that the monies generated according to pupil placements are actually spent within grade levels or special programs. Nevertheless, schools should be held accountable for program outcomes under either of these funding approaches.

In addition to ensuring appropriate spending decisions, accountability also stresses the importance of holding policy makers and school personnel responsible for results measured against previously agreed upon performance standards. Wagner (1989, p. 122) identified four elements of the performance-contracting approach to accountability. Peterson (1992) similarly delineated four questions to be addressed by a well-functioning assessment and accountability system:

- Which goals, outcomes, or performance objectives are critical?
- What measurements, indicators or data will tell us if we are making progress toward those goals or objectives over time?
- How do we know if we are successful, mindful that circumstances differ among schools, districts, and states?

- How can information from the assessments be used by policy makers to improve decision-making in general, reward success, and intervene in situations of poor performance? (p. 110)

These questions framed the accountability mechanisms that have emerged in the past several decades. Actual and perceived declines in school performance in the 1970s, including highly visible standardized test scores, raised numerous questions and fueled efforts to improve public education if not dramatically alter it. Nearly all states portray progress (or the lack thereof) toward desired results through publications of test scores and other performance measures by building, district, and state to monitor and publicize school improvement efforts (Gaines, 1995). For example, the Texas annual categorization of exemplary, recognized, and low-performing schools ranks them according to achievement scores, dropout rates, attendance, and school size (Harp, 1994). The United States Department of Education's annual wall chart once ranked states according to a number of indicators: pupil's performance on college entrance exams (ACT and SAT); graduation rates; resource inputs, including percentage of schools with Advanced Placement programs, teachers' salaries, pupil-teacher ratios, and expenditure levels; and demographic characteristics, such as per capita income and the percentage of pupils who live in poverty, are minorities, or have disabilities. Such comparisons were criticized for presenting an incomplete picture of schooling outcomes (U.S. Department of Education, 1988), since they failed to capture comprehensive indi-cators of students' performance in areas of problem solving, creative thinking, writing, and the arts.

The National Education Goals Panel (1994) released an annual report detailing information on states' progress toward the eight goals listed in Chapter 10. This report documented gains made by the nation and individual states on measures of children's health, family-child reading, and preschool participation; high school completion; mathematics and reading achievement in grades 4,

8, and 12; international comparisons in mathematics and science achievement; adult literacy and participation in adult education; minority-group participation in higher education; drug and alcohol use; victimization of students and teachers; and student disruptions that interfere with teaching and learning. The conclusion reached in 1994 expressed frustration with the progress made thus far and encouraged effort at all levels to make greater advances:

> . . . our current rate of progress is nowhere near the levels that will be required in order to achieve the National Education Goals within the next six years. Although we have made significant improvement on four of the core indicators of progress, much greater concerted effort will be required to accelerate our pace and move the others in the desired direction. . . . Only by involving students, parents, educators, schools, higher education, and local business and community leaders as active partners will we be able to mobilize sufficient grass-roots community effort to achieve the Goals. (p. 53)

Accountability mechanisms may be designed to compare the gains in performance of groups of students, who are often sorted by race, ethnicity, socioeconomic status, or gender. For example, South Carolina and California adopted "comparison bands" within their incentive programs to analyze the performance of individual schools or districts in relation to those of units similar in terms of student characteristics (Cibulka, 1989; Peterson, 1992, p. 120). This approach more fairly recognizes the social context of schools and places attention on the results of good schooling rather than social privilege. Other techniques might permit comparisons of schools' expected scores based on prior performance to show the amount and direction of change in various measures. A well-constructed report card on school performance can enable educators and communities to assess schools' strengths and weaknesses and design strategies for school improvement.

Once high- and low-performing schools and school districts are identified, recognition or intervention is called for. Notable improvements in student outcomes should bring public recognition, incentives to continue successful practices, encouragement to diffuse ideas to other settings, and relaxed or waived state regulations, which often inhibit local innovation (U.S. Department of Education, 1988). For example, South Carolina's Flexibility through Deregulation Program provides a blanket regulatory waiver provision for relatively high-performing schools; Washington's Schools for the 21st Century Program includes regulatory relief (Fuhrman & Elmore, 1992). Deficiencies in school performance should also trigger local and state responses, including increased technical assistance and possibly funding, changes in personnel and program delivery, or consolidation with more effective units. However, despite the need for assessing and improving schools (and the rhetoric of politicians demanding such), the efforts of states and localities are often inhibited by problems with budgets, staff expertise, technologies, and internal and external political climates.

The most extreme response to poor performance under a results-based accountability system is to declare local school systems academically bankrupt. Policies enacted in a number of states between 1983 and the mid 1990s authorized state education agencies to assume district operations if pupils are academically deficient. For example, the New Jersey Education Department is empowered to dismiss and replace the school board, superintendent, and district administrators responsible for curriculum, personnel, and finance. Interventions can last up to five years or until the state decides that the deficiencies have been eliminated and local control can be restored. The Kentucky Schools-in-Crisis Program outlines a process for assessing school performance. A school that fails to improve following the third biennial assessment is declared to be "in crisis." A panel of "distinguished educators" is empowered to provide assistance and evaluation for retention, dismissal, or transfer of staff (Fuhrman & Elmore, 1992; Peterson, 1992).

When states use state technical assistance and educational bankruptcy, they assume that state-level officials can perform better than local officials. These accountability mechanisms should be most effective if their intent is to guide and assist local districts to improve school operations and use of resources consistent with other reforms that call for placing greater control over curriculum and finance at the lowest level possible (see the discussion of school-based management in Chapter 14).

SUMMARY

State finance policy allocates resources to augment the capabilities of school systems to meet pupils' educational needs. The measurement of needs has expanded greatly from simply counting students enrolled to considering student characteristics, educational goals, and resource requirements by grade levels and special programs. States adopted weighted-pupil and instructional-unit approaches to finance anticipated costs. Some also use flat grants or reimburse a portion of the excess costs of education for students with disabilities, programs for gifted and talented students, vocational offerings, compensatory education, bilingual education, early childhood education, and other such programs.

Measures of fiscal capacity and tax effort are indicators of the ability and willingness of localities to support public education. Most state aid plans include local contributions. These allocation plans are strengthened by expanded measures of capacity that include both property valuation and personal income and by effort measures that consider the local revenue actually raised in relation to that capacity.

State aid mechanisms also recognize that the cost of school operations reflects community and school district characteristics. Size adjustments respond to economies and diseconomies of scale related to population sparsity or density and to pupil enrollments. Personnel training and experience affect the costs of program delivery. State aid assists districts in meeting salary obligations and the expenses of staff development. Factors may be designed to raise funding in districts where the general cost of living and other costs of educational resources are unusually high. Policies may include incentives for school and district improvement efforts or rewards for gains in pupil performance.

The many adjustments in finance plans we have discussed in this chapter can offset legitimate costs that would otherwise burden localities or diminish the amount of funds available for instruction. However, states must guard against the possibility that formula adjustments favor politically powerful districts and interest groups. Such adjustments would divert funds from meeting legitimate needs. In addition, states should be aware that the trend to increasingly offset costs through categorical aid programs that fund excess costs in all districts may unnecessarily reduce the amount of money available to equalize poorer districts' abilities to finance educational programs.

Once aid is received through formulas discussed in Chapters 8 and 9, districts and states

monitor the use of funds and their impacts in relation to performance measures. Finance and program audit systems inform policy makers and the public about allocation and expenditure decisions in relation to broad financial and educational goals. Program-specific audits and evaluations ensure that the intended beneficiaries in special programs receive resource supplements; they determine whether the programs and services are appropriate for pupils' educational needs; and they assess pupil performance in relation to the educational goals and resources provided. Analyses of district productivity may trigger interventions. Interventions may include the takeover of severely deficient school systems by the state.

State general and categorical aid, the major source of intergovernmental financial assistance for education, has greatly expanded the capabilities of districts to meet pupils' educational needs. We turn our attention next to federal legislation and aid programs. We discuss their role in defining local district policies and curricula.

ACTIVITIES

1. Define need, capacity, and effort of school districts and list several measures of each. Discuss the contribution of these concepts to the functioning of state aid plans.

2. If enrollment measures (ADM or ENR) recognize the pupil costs associated with the number of students served, why do some states adopt ADA to count pupils? Describe the school systems that would benefit most from approaches that use enrollment rather than attendance data.

3. Differentiate a weighted-pupil strategy from a full or partial excess-cost-reimbursement approach to compensate districts for the higher costs of instructional programs required to meet pupils' educational needs. What incentives are implicit in each approach? What are the likely advantages of each method for addressing needs effectively?

4. Examine a state's policy for defining the wealth of a school district in its finance plan. Collect data and compare the effects of changing the definition (a) to

blend property valuation and income, or (b) to include per capita or per pupil measures of fiscal capacity. Which measures work to the advantage of rural, suburban, and urban school districts?

5. Debate the merit of adjustments in funding formulas depending on enrollment decline or growth measures; small-school or -district factors; density; cost-of-living or education indices; teacher experience and training factors; incentives for school improvement; and so on. How might you discover whether these modifications provide legitimate recognition of the needs and costs of school districts or whether they represent political tampering with formulas to serve the interests of particular school systems?

6. Why have some states funded schools on an instructional unit basis rather than directly recognizing the higher costs associated with highly trained and experienced teachers? Which method better reimburses districts for the actual costs of personnel?

Which one better controls class size? Which one limits local flexibility the most?

7. Discuss the questions listed in the section *Incentives for School Improvement* with a legislator, board member, or district- or school-level administrator. What might be a feasible approach for modifying your state's finance plan to direct additional resources to districts that prove they are effective in raising the levels of pupil achievement or other performance measures? What unintended conse-

quences might result if schools or districts compete for incentives?

8. Outline an accountability mechanism that would provide information about the use of state and local funds devoted to educational programs. What specific data are needed for making decisions about program modification, program continuation with increased or decreased funds, or termination? Who should be responsible for program and finance decisions?

 ## COMPUTER SIMULATIONS

Objectives of This Activity:

- *To develop an appreciation of the importance of how elements of the state aid formulas presented in Chapter 8 are measured.*

- *To understand the differential impact on the distribution of state aid when:*
  - a. *district ability is measured using property value per pupil, personal income per pupil, or some combination of these;*
  - b. *district need is measured using average daily membership (ADM) or average daily attendance (ADA).*
  - c. *district need is calculated using weights to indicate the relative costs of educating students with differing characteristics.*

The simulations for this chapter will familiarize you with variations of the basic formulas introduced in Chapter 8. For example, states are increasingly introducing personal income per pupil as a measure of school district wealth along with the traditional measure of property value per pupil. Furthermore, the measurement of pupil need varies greatly from state to state. Some states use average daily attendance (ADA) as the basic pupil count; others use average daily membership (ADM). All states provide additional funding for students enrolled in more costly educational programs (e.g., secondary pupils, pupils with disabilities, low achieving pupils, and pupils whose primary language is not English).

Using the hypothetical state database, you are given the opportunity to change the need and wealth measures used in several of the formulas presented in Chapter 8. This will illustrate the impact of measurement changes on the amount of state aid received by school districts with differing characteristics: a district of average wealth, a poor district, and a wealthy district. These are the same districts used in Chapter 8. You are encouraged to look for similarities and differences among the state aid programs.

Simulation 9.1: *Database Manipulation*

The file DATABASE includes a number of variables for each district. This section guides the student in accessing the database for particular measures related to district need.

Part 1. Creating DATA_TEC Datafile

a. Retrieve the file DATABASE.

b. Save the file as DATA_TEC.

c. **Make sure that you are in the DATA_TEC file.** Copy the first column contents (from cell A1 down through A20) to the worksheet area below—beginning in cell A22.

d. Copy column B contents, the K–6 column, in the same way (from cell B1 down through B20—to the worksheet area beginning with cell B22).

e. Copy the 7–12, TOTAL, AVG % DAILY AT-TEND, EXPEND PER PUPIL, INCOME PER PUPIL ($), and the PROPERTY PER PUPIL ($) column contents in the same way.

f. Delete rows 1 through 21.

g. Move the EXPEND PER PUPIL column contents to column F; INCOME PER PUPIL ($) to column G; and PROPERTY PER PUPIL ($) to column H.

h. Change the column widths as necessary.

i. Save your new data table and print it out.

Part 2. Creating DATA_TI Datafile

a. Save the DATA-TEC file again as DATA_TI.

b. **Make sure that you are in the DATA_TI file.** Delete columns B and C (K–6 and 7–12, respectively).

c. Delete the AVG % DAILY ATTEND and EXPEND PER PUPIL columns.

d. Change the column B label to PUPILS.

e. Type TOTAL in cell A22.

f. In cell B22, enter the formula @SUM (B11..B20) for Lotus 1-2-3 or =SUM (B11:B20) for Microsoft Excel to compute the total for the column.

g. Type AVERAGE in cell A24.

h. In cell B24, enter the formula +B22/10 for Lotus 1-2-3 or =SUM (B11-B20) for Microsoft Excel to compute the average for the column.

i. Create a new label for column E: TOTAL INCOME.

j. In column E (cell E11), create a formula that multiplies PUPILS by INCOME PER PUPIL ($). Increase the column width and copy this formula down through E20.

k. Create a new label for column F: TOTAL PROPERTY.

l. In column F (cell F11), create a formula that multiplies PUPILS by PROPERTY PER PUPIL ($). Increase the column width and copy this formula down through F20.

m. Copy the @SUM formula from cell B22 to cells E22 and F22.

n. In cells E24 and F24, create a formula that divides the totals in each of these columns by the total number of pupils.

o. Format all cells and column names in the table as appropriate.

p. Save your new data table and print it out.

Simulation 9.2: *Changing the Measure of School District Wealth in the Percentage-Equalizing Program*

In this exercise we continue to use full property value per pupil as a measure of school district tax-generating ability, and we introduce personal income per pupil as an alternative measure.

Note: This file provides labels and column formatting but requires students to enter figures from the databases and appropriate formulas.

Part 1. Aid Based on Property Value Alone

a. Retrieve the file INCOME.

b. In the REDROCK column, enter EXPEND PER PUPIL, INCOME PER PUPIL, and PROPERTY PER PUPIL amounts from DATA_TEC ($7,458 and $45,962 and $116,009, respectively).

c. Enter AVERAGE DISTRICT RESPONSIBILITY as .5. In addition, enter AVERAGE STATE INCOME PER PUPIL as $69,775 and AVERAGE STATE PROPERTY PER PUPIL as $159,591—as imputed from the DATABASE file in creating DATA_TI.

d. Based on the general percentage-equalizing formula:

$$A = 1.000 - B(C/D)$$

where

A = District Percentage State Aid
B = Average District Responsibility
C = District Property Value per Pupil
D = Average State Property Value per Pupil

create a formula to determine the DISTRICT STATE AID PERCENT based on property value only.

e. Create a formula to determine STATE AID PER PUPIL.

f. Create a formula to determine LOCAL FUNDS PER PUPIL.

g. Create a formula to determine TOTAL TAX RATE.

Part 2. Aid Based on Property Value and Income

a. Copy the entire REDROCK column over into the next two columns. (Your spreadsheet should now include three identical RED-ROCK columns.)

b. In the second and third REDROCK columns, change the STATE AID BASED ON: labels to PROP+INC and INCOME, respectively.

c. Based on the general percentage equalization formula that combines property valuation and income measures:

$$A = 1.000 - B(.5 * C/D + .5 * E/F)$$
where

A = District Percentage State Aid
B = Average District Responsibility
C = District Property Value per Pupil
D = Average State Property Value per Pupil
E = District Income per Pupil
F = Average State Income per Pupil

in the second REDROCK column, create a new formula to determine DISTRICT STATE AID PERCENT based on property value and income weighted equally.

d. Based on the general percentage equalization formula that computes state aid based on income alone:

$$A = 1.000 - B(E/F)$$
where

A = District Percentage State Aid

B = Average District Responsibility
E = District Income per Pupil
F = Average State Income per Pupil

in the third REDROCK column, create a new formula to determine DISTRICT STATE AID PERCENT based on income only. Print the resulting table.

e. Study the results. Under which formulation does REDROCK receive the greatest amount of state aid? Why?

Part 3. Comparing Capacity Measures in Three Districts

a. Copy your completed worksheet from *Part 2* to another file or worksheet area.

b. Change the second and third column RED-ROCK names to SOMMERSET and ELLI-COTT, respectively.

c. In the SOMMERSET and ELLICOTT columns, enter EXPEND PER PUPIL, INCOME PER PUPIL, and PROPERTY PER PUPIL from the DATA_TI file ($8,719 and $36,818 and $617,100; and $6,469 and $45,253 and $84,988, respectively).

d. Insert "PROPERTY" in the row labeled STATE AID BASED ON: for each district. (Remember to change the formulas as well as the labels.)

e. Study the results. Note that because of its high property wealth, SOMMERSET receives a negative amount of state aid, i.e., instead of receiving aid from the state, it pays a portion of its property tax receipts to the state; this is known as "recapture."

f. Change the STATE AID BASED ON: row label from "PROPERTY" to "PROP+INC" for each district. (Remember to change the formulas as well as the labels.)

g. Study the results. Which district benefited the most from the inclusion of income in the measurement of its tax-raising ability? Why?

h. Print the table resulting from step f.

i. Develop a rationale for basing a state's aid formula on one measure of fiscal capacity: property valuation, income, or a combination of property valuation and income.

Simulation 9.3: *Changing the Measure of School District Need from Average Daily Membership (ADM) to Average Daily Attendance (ADA)*

Part 1: Database Manipulation

In this database manipulation, we convert EXPEND PER PUPIL to EXPEND PER ADA and PROPERTY VALUE PER PUPIL ($) to PROPERTY VALUE PER ADA.

a. Retrieve the file DATA_TEC.

b. Save the file as DATA_TA.

c. **Make sure that you are in the DATA_TA file.** Erase or clear the data in the K–6, 7–12, and INCOME PER PUPIL ($) columns.

d. Move the TOTAL and AVG % DAILY ATTEND columns to columns B and C.

e. Change the column B label to (ADM) PUPILS.

f. Create a new label for column D, (ADA) PUPILS.

g. In column D, create a formula that multiplies (ADM) PUPILS by AVG % DAILY ATTEND. Copy the formula for all districts.

h. In column A below WHEATFIELD, type TOTAL. On this row in the (ADM) PUPILS and (ADA) PUPILS columns, create a formula that provides the column totals. Compare the total ADM count of pupils with the number of ADA. Which is larger? Why?

i. Move the EXPEND PER PUPIL column to column E.

j. Create a new label for column F, TOTAL EXPEND. In column F, create a formula that multiplies EXPEND PER PUPIL by (ADM) PUPILS. Copy the formula for all districts.

k. Create a new label for column G, EXPEND PER ADA. In column G, create a formula that divides TOTAL EXPEND by (ADA) PUPILS. Copy the formula down through the column.

l. Create a new label for column I, PROPERTY PER ADA. In column I, create a formula that multiplies PROPERTY PER PUPIL ($) by (ADM) PUPILS and divides the results by (ADA) PUPILS. Copy the formula down through the column.

m. Change the column widths as necessary to print the table on one page, or print it using condensed print (e.g., in Lotus 1-2-3, use right margin 132 and setup string \015; in Microsoft Excel, change margin settings or decrease font size.)

n. Save and print the data table.

Part 2. Foundation Plan Using ADM and ADA

a. Retrieve the file ATTEND.

   Note: This worksheet is the same as the one created for Simulation 8.2: Foundation Program, Step h, Part 1 except that (ADM) has been added above the REDROCK label to indicate that all of our work thus far has been based on pupils in average daily membership (ADM).

b. Copy the REDROCK column over into the next column.

c. Change the (ADM) label in the new column to (ADA).

d. In the new (ADA) column in the EXPEND PER PUPIL and PROPERTY PER PUPIL rows, enter $8,592 and $133,651 from the EXPEND PER ADA and PROPERTY PER ADA columns of the database manipulation table you created in Part 1.

e. Print and study the resulting table. Note that state aid per pupil has dropped and the local contribution has increased along with the local property tax rate when the foundation level ($6,000) remains unchanged. The number of units on which state aid is calculated is reduced by approximately 9.6 percent statewide in shifting from ADM to ADA. To prevent the aggregate level of state support from dropping, it is necessary to increase the foundation program by the ratio of ADM to ADA statewide—to $6,573. We do this in the next part.

Part 3. Adjusting the State Funding Level in Shifting from ADM to ADA

a. Copy your completed table from Part 2 to another file or worksheet area.

b. Copy the (ADA) REDROCK column over into the next column.

c. In the new column, change the STATE FUNDING LEVEL to $6,573. (For an explanation of the change, see the comments accompanying step e of Part 2.)

d. Print and study the resulting table. What advantages or disadvantages does using ADM or ADA have for REDROCK?

Part 4. Three District Comparisons

a. Copy your completed table from Part 3 to another file or worksheet area.

b. In the first REDROCK column, change the (ADM) label to (ADA). Change the amounts for EXPEND PER PUPIL to $8,592; PROPERTY VALUE PER PUPIL to $133,651; and STATE FUNDING LEVEL to $6,573.

c. In the second REDROCK column, change the REDROCK label to SOMMERSET. Change the amounts for EXPEND PER PUPIL to $9,188; PROPERTY VALUE PER PUPIL to $650,263; and STATE FUNDING LEVEL to $6,573.

d. In the third REDROCK column, change the REDROCK label to ELLICOTT. Change the amounts for EXPEND PER PUPIL to $6,853; PROPERTY VALUE PER PUPIL to $90,030; and STATE FUNDING LEVEL to $6,573.

e. Print and study the results. Compare the results with those obtained in Simulation 8.2, Part 3, step d. When district need is measured using ADA units rather than ADM units, REDROCK'S TOTAL TAX RATE increases from $20.12 per $1,000 of property valuation (using ADM) to $22.66 (using ADA), while the TOTAL TAX RATEs for SOMMERSET and ELLICOTT drop from $11.96 to $11.57 and from $13.07 to $10.66, respectively. Why is this?

Simulation 9.4: *Changing the Measure of School District Need from Average Daily Membership (ADM) to Weighted Average Daily Membership (WADM)*

Part 1: Creating the DATA_TW Datafile

a. Retrieve the file DATA_TEC.

b. Save the file as DATA_TW.

c. **Make sure that you are in the DATA_TW file.** Erase or clear the AVG % DAILY ATTEND and INCOME PER PUPIL ($) columns.

d. Create a new label for column E, 1.25 WEIGHT 7–12. (Make sure that "1.25" is in a cell by itself as a numeric value.)

e. In column E, create a formula that multiplies 7–12 by the cell that contains "1.25."

f. Edit the formula to make the "1.25" cell absolute and copy the formula all the way down through the column (see Simulation 5.1, step C).

g. Insert a column to move the EXPEND PER PUPIL column to the right one column.

h. Create a new label for column F, (WADM) PUPILS. In column F, create a formula that adds K–6 to 1.25 WEIGHT 7–12. Copy the formula down through the column.

i. Change the column D label to (ADM) PUPILS.

j. In column A below WHEATFIELD, type TOTAL. On this row in the (ADM) PUPILS and (WADM) PUPILS columns, create a formula that provides the totals for each column, respectively.

k. Create a new heading for column H, EXPEND PER WADM. In column H, create a formula that multiplies EXPEND PER PUPIL by (ADM) PUPILS and divides the result by (WADM) PUPILS. Copy the formula down through the column.

l. Create a new heading for column J, PROPERTY PER WADM. In column J, create a formula that multiplies PROPERTY PER PUPIL by (ADM) PUPILS and divides the result by (WADM) PUPILS. Copy the formula down through the column.

m. Change the column widths as necessary to print on one page or print the table using condensed print (in Lotus 1-2-3, use right margin 132 and setup string \015; in Microsoft Excel, change the margins or decrease the font size).

n. Save the table.

o. Why are expenditure and property valuations less when WADM is used in place of ADM as a measure of educational need?

Part 2. The Foundation Plan Using Weighted-Pupil Units to Measure Educational Need

a. Retrieve the file WEIGHT. Note that this file is the same as Simulation 9.3, step a, Part 2.

b. Copy the REDROCK column into the next column.

c. Change the (ADM) label in the new column to (WADM).

d. In the new (WADM) column in the EXPEND PER PUPIL and PROPERTY VALUE PER PUPIL rows, enter $6,774 and $105,369, respectively, from the EXPEND PER WADM and PROPERTY PER WADM columns in the database manipulation table created in Part 1.

e. Print and study the resulting table. Note that state aid per pupil has increased and the local contribution has decreased along with the local property tax rate. The reason for

this is that the foundation level ($6,000) remained unchanged; but in shifting from ADM to WADM, the number of units on which state aid is calculated was increased by approximately 9.5 percent statewide. To prevent the aggregate level of state support from increasing, it is necessary to decrease the foundation program by the ratio of ADM to WADM—to $5,428. We do this in the next part.

Part 3. Adjusting the State Guarantee Using WADM as the Measure of Educational Need

a. Copy your completed table from Part 2 to another file or worksheet area.

b. Copy the (WADM) REDROCK column over into the next column.

c. In this new column, change the STATE FUNDING LEVEL to $5,428. (For explanation of the change, refer to the comments made in step e of Part 2.)

d. Print and study the resulting table. In what ways might the use of WADM be viewed as being beneficial or harmful to REDROCK?

Part 4. Three District Comparisons

a. Copy your completed table from Part 3 to another file or worksheet area.

b. In the first REDROCK column, change the (ADM) label to (WADM). In that column, change the amount indicated for EXPEND PER PUPIL to $6,774; PROPERTY VALUE PER PUPIL to $105,369; and STATE FUNDING LEVEL to $5,428.

c. In the second REDROCK column, change the REDROCK label to SOMMERSET. In that column, change the amount indicated for EXPEND PER PUPIL to $7,839; PROPERTY VALUE PER PUPIL to $554,835; and STATE FUNDING LEVEL to $5,428.

d. In the third REDROCK column, change the REDROCK label to ELLICOTT. In that column, change the amount indicated for

EXPEND PER PUPIL to $5,872; PROPERTY VALUE PER PUPIL to $77,140; and STATE FUNDING LEVEL to $5,428.

e. Print and study the resulting table. Compare the results with those obtained in Simulation 8.2, Part 3, step d. When district need is measured using WADM units rather than ADM units, REDROCK'S TOTAL TAX RATE increases from $20.12 per $1,000 of property valuation (using ADM) to $20.32 (using

WADM), and ELLICOTT'S increases from $13.07 to $13.31. At the same time, the TOTAL TAX RATE for SOMMERSET drops from $11.96 to $11.90. Why is this?

f. **Further Activities.** Describe and defend a proposal for state finance policy that best combines measures of fiscal ability, pupil counts, and pupil characteristics. Refer to observations from Simulations 9.2 through 9.4 in your response.

REFERENCES

Adams, E. K., & Odden, A. (1981). Alternative wealth measures. In K. F. Jordan & N. H. Cambron-McCabe (Eds.), *Perspectives in state school support programs* (pp. 143–165). Cambridge, MA: Ballinger.

Bradley, A. (1995). "Crisis" spurs state takeover of Cleveland: Judge places district in Ohio chief's hands. *Education Week, 14,* 1, 9.

Chambers, J. G. (1980). The development of a cost of education index. *Journal of Education Finance, 5,* 262–281.

Chambers, J. G., & Parrish, T. B. (1986). *The RCM as a decision making process.* Stanford, CA: Stanford Education Policy Institute.

Cibulka, J. G. (1989). State performance incentives for restructuring: Can they work? *Education and Urban Society, 21,* 417–435.

Cohn, E. (1974). *Economics of state aid to education.* Lexington, MA: Lexington Books.

Cohn, E. (1975). A proposal for school size incentives in state aid to education. *Journal of Education Finance, 1,* 216–225.

Cubberley, E. P. (1906). *School funds and their apportionment.* New York: Teachers College, Columbia University.

Dembowski, F. L., Green, M., & Camerino, J. (1982). Methodological issues in the use of income in the allocation of state aid. *Journal of Education Finance, 8,* 73–92.

Drake, T. L., & Roe, W. H. (1994). *School Business Management: Supporting Instructional Effectiveness.* Boston: Allyn and Bacon.

Edelman, M. A., & Knudsen, J. J. (1990). An analysis of selected school aid compensation options for school districts with declining enrollment. *Journal of Education Finance, 15,* 319–332.

The Fleischmann report on the quality, cost, and financing of elementary and secondary education in New York State, Vol. I. (1973). New York: Viking Press.

Fuhrman, S. H., & Elmore, R. F. (1992). *Takeover and deregulation: Working models of new state and local regulatory relationships.* Rutgers, NJ: Consortium for Policy Research in Education.

Fulton, M., & Sonovick, L. (1993). *School-district fiscal bankruptcy—An analysis.* ECS Issuegram. Denver, CO: Education Commission of the States.

Gaines, G. (1995). *Linking education report cards and local school improvement.* Atlanta: Southern Regional Education Board.

Garris, J. M., & Ginsberg, R. (1995). South Carolina. In S. D. Gold, D. M. Smith, & S. B. Lawton (Eds.), *Public school finance programs of the United States and Canada, 1993–94* (pp. 547–563). Albany, NY: American Education Finance Association and The Center for the Study of the States.

Goertz, M. (1981). School finance reform and the cities. In K. F. Jordan & N. H. Cambron-McCabe (Eds.), *Perspectives in state school support programs* (pp. 113–142). Cambridge, MA: Ballinger.

Goettel, R. J., & Firestine, R. E. (1975). Declining enrollments and state aid: Another equity and efficiency problem. *Journal of Education Finance, 1,* 205–215.

Gold, S. D., Smith, D. M., & Lawton, S. B. (Eds.). (1995). *Public school finance programs of the United States and Canada, 1993–94.* Albany, NY: American Education Finance Association and The Center for the Study of the States.

Greenwald, D. (Ed.). (1994). *McGraw-Hill encyclopedia of economics* (2nd edition). New York: McGraw-Hill.

Gurwitz, A. (1977). *The financial condition of urban school districts: A federal policy perspective.* Santa Monica, CA: Rand Corporation.

Hack, W. G., Edlefson, C., & Ogawa, R. T. (1981). Fiscal accountability: The challenge of formulating responsive policy. In K. F. Jordan & N. H. Cambron-McCabe (Eds.), *Perspectives in state school support programs* (pp. 251–279). Cambridge, MA: Ballinger.

Harp, L. (1994). Tex. politicians wrangle over school rankings. *Education Week, 14,* 16.

Harp, L. (1995). Ky. names schools to receive achievement bonuses. *Education Week, 14,* 11.

Hartman, W. T. (1980). Policy effects of special education funding formulas. *Journal of Education Finance, 6,* 135–159.

Johns, R. L. (1975). An index of extra costs of education due to sparsity of population. *Journal of Education Finance, 1,* 159–204.

Johns, R. L., Alexander, K., & Jordan, K. F. (Eds.) (1971). *Planning to finance education,* Vol. 3. Gainesville, FL: National Education Finance Project.

Johnston, R. C. (1995). Maine governor signs school-aid bill that includes personal income in formula. *Education Week, 14,* 12.

King, R. A. (1979). Toward a theory of wage determination for teachers. *Journal of Education Finance, 4,* 358–369.

Kirby, P., Holmes, C. T., Matthews, K. M., & Watt, A. D. (1993). Factors influencing teacher salaries: An examination of alternative models. *Journal of Education Finance, 19,* 111–121.

Kozol, J. (1991). *Savage inequalities: Children in America's schools.* New York: Crown.

Ladd, H. F. (1975). Local education expenditures, fiscal capacity, and the composition of the property tax base. *National Tax Journal, 28,* 145–158.

Leppert, J., Huxel, L., Garms, W., & Fuller, H. (1976). Pupil weighting programs in school finance reform. In J. J. Callahan & W. H. Wilken (Eds.), *School finance reform: A legislators' handbook.* Washington, DC: Legislators' Education Action Project, National Conference of State Legislatures.

Leppert, J., & Routh, D. (1978). An analysis of state school finance systems as related to declining enrollments. In S. Abramowitz & S. Rosenfeld (Eds.), *Declining enrollment: The challenge of the coming decade* (pp. 187–208). Washington, DC: National Institute of Education.

McOlash, B. C. & Garcia, J. P. (1995). New Mexico. In S. D. Gold, D. M. Smith, & S. B. Lawton (Eds.), *Public school finance programs of the United States and Canada, 1993–94.* Albany, NY: American Education Finance Association and The Center for the Study of the States.

Monk, D., & Walker, B. D. (1991). The Texas cost of education index: A broadened approach. *Journal of Education Finance, 17,* 172–192.

Mort, P. R. (1924). *The measurement of educational need: A basis for distributing state aid.* New York: Teachers College, Columbia University.

Mort, P. R. (1926). *State support for public schools.* New York: Teachers College, Columbia University.

National Conference of State Legislatures. (1994). *State budget and tax actions 1994.* Denver, CO: Author.

National Education Goals Panel (1994). *The national education goals report: Building a nation of learners.* Washington, DC: U. S. Government Printing Office.

Odden, A. (1977). Alternative measures of school district wealth. *Journal of Education Finance, 2,* 356–379.

Odden, A. R., & Picus, L. O. (1992). *School finance: A policy perspective.* New York: McGraw-Hill.

Peterson, T. K. (1992). Designing accountability to help reform. In C. E. Finn & T. Rebarber (Eds.), *Education reform in the '90s* (pp. 109–132). New York: Macmillan.

Picus, L. O. (1992). Using incentives to promote school improvement. In A. R. Odden (Ed.), *Rethinking school finance: An agenda for the 1990s* (pp. 166–200). San Francisco: Jossey-Bass.

Richards, C., & Shujaa, M. (1990). State-sponsored school performance incentive plans: A policy review. *Educational Considerations, 17,* 42–52.

Schmidt, P. (1994). Ill. state board moves to take over troubled East St. Louis schools. *Education Week, 14,* p. 13.

Sjogren, J. (1981). Municipal overburden and state aid for education. In K. F. Jordan & N. H. Cambron-McCabe (Eds.), *Perspectives in state school support programs* (pp. 87–111). Cambridge, MA: Ballinger.

Sparkman, W. E. (1976). Tax effort for education. In K. Alexander & K. F. Jordan (Eds.), *Educational need in the public economy* (pp. 299–336). Gainesville: University Presses of Florida.

Swanson, A. D. (1966). *The effect of school district size upon school costs: Policy recommendations for the state of New York.* Buffalo: Committee on School Finance and Legislation.

Tiebout, C. M. (1956). A pure theory of local expenditures. *Journal of Political Economy, 65,* 416–424.

U. S. Department of Education. (1988). *Measuring up: Questions and answers about state roles in educational accountability.* Washington, DC: Office of Educational Research and Improvement.

Updegraff, H., & King, L. A. (1922). *Survey of the fiscal policies of the state of Pennsylvania in the field of education.* Philadelphia: University of Pennsylvania.

Wagner, R. B. (1989). *Accountability in education: A philosophical inquiry.* New York: Routledge.

Wendling, W. (1981). The cost of education index: Measurement of price differences of education personnel among New York State school districts. *Journal of Education Finance, 6,* 485–504.

CHAPTER 10

The Federal Role
in School Finance

Primary Issues Explored in This Chapter:

- *Justifying a federal role in education:* What national interests are evidenced in the many legislative acts that have historically brought mandates or incentives to shape education policies and curricula?
- *Programs and financial assistance:* What purposes and distribution mechanisms characterize the primary federal programs that provide assistance for vocational education, districts impacted by federal activities, national goals and educational reforms, students who are economically

disadvantaged or have disabilities, students with limited English proficiency, and educational innovations?

- *Amounts of assistance:* Do trends in allocations of federal funds reveal changes in priorities over time?
- *The future federal role in education:* Given historical shifts in the prevailing views of federalism and the desire to reduce the federal budget deficit as well as tax burdens, what directions are likely now and into the new millennium?

The federal government's role in financing public education in the United States expands the capacities of local and state governments and provides incentives for policy development. Decisions of the federal courts, the executive leadership of the president, and congressional actions very often shape priorities for the use of educational funds, regardless of their source. Some financial aid programs have carefully defined purposes. In other cases, federal grants do not indicate the specific uses of funds but assist educators in accomplishing locally established goals. In this chapter, we discuss the principles of intergovernmental transfers we discussed in Chapter 8 in relation to the federal role in educational policy and finance.

FEDERALISM AND FUNDING STRATEGIES

Several views of federalism have historically shaped debates about how much decisions made at the national level should influence state and local government policy. On the one hand, the national government empowers local school districts because it believes that they are best positioned to respond to parents, determine students' educational needs, and conceive innovations. This perspective argues for giving the affected populations the authority to make decisions about programs and services (Elazar, 1972). When local officials are accountable to the constituencies who pay for and use public services, there is greater efficiency and responsiveness (Levin, 1982). *General* grants in aid, which do not specify purposes or restrict fund use, and *block grants,* which give localities some discretion in defining priorities within broad federal purposes, are consistent with this view of federalism.

On the other hand, some argue that the extent and quality of education provided throughout the nation depend on the leadership of the federal government. This is particularly true when schools serve students who are economically disadvantaged or have disabilities. Whereas local and state resources are often committed to maintaining existing efforts, the "federal government, free of such constraints, can attempt to pinpoint its resource inputs on the margins of change" (Milstein, 1976, p. 126). Federal policies can thus target financial assistance to purposes or population groups that states and localities have been unable or unwilling to target, perhaps because of limited resources or political considerations (Verstegen, 1987, 1994). *Categorical* grants, which restrict the use of funds for particular purposes or identify the groups to be served, enable the government to influence educational priorities in line with this view of federalism. The large number of federal categorical programs developed during the 1960s and 1970s evidenced legislators' preference for focusing intervention. But the demand to return control over education to localities in the 1980s and 1990s led to the adoption of block grants. Block grants give discretion to state and local policy makers, often as former categorical aid programs are combined. But they also bring smaller federal allocations on the premise that fewer programs and regulations ease administrative costs.

Intergovernmental transfers for specific purposes recognize that local governance does not always serve broader state and national interests. Just as state intervention influences local priorities and attempts to equalize fiscal abilities, the early basis for federal aid was "to stimulate the correction of weaknesses in state school systems, particularly in those areas in which national interest had evolved" (Mort & Reusser, 1941, p. 473). Re-

sponding to constituents, the judiciary (see Chapter 11), and many influential groups, Congress determines programs and funding priorities that serve this "national interest." Policy makers often adopt the strategy of categorical aid to focus this influence. They draw on the authority granted by the general welfare clause of the U.S. Constitution (Article 1, Section 8).

An expanding federal role in public education during much of the twentieth century responded to urgent social needs and desires to equalize educational opportunities. But power was more centralized at federal and state levels as a result. A different view of federalism, initiated in the 1980s, was characterized by deregulation and decentralized decision making. The movement to diminish the federal presence and budget for education was interrupted in the mid-1990s with the adoption of eight National Education Goals. And the government reauthorized many federal programs aimed at upgrading education through the adoption of voluntary content and performance and opportunity-to-learn standards. Within two years of the increase in federal influence, the 1994 elections shifted control of Congress to the Republican Party. The Republican agenda stressed a downsized federal role and downsized financial allocations for education and social services.

Policy makers' determinations of the national interest and the prevailing view of federalism have historically shaped the nature and extent of federal involvement in public education. We categorize legislative actions within seven themes to illustrate national interests that have justified federal assistance over time.

FEDERAL EDUCATION PROGRAMS AS REFLECTIONS OF THE NATIONAL INTEREST

In defining the powers and responsibilities of the federal government, the United States Constitution is silent on the subject of education. Unlike many other countries, the United States has no national education system or strong federal-level governance body that oversees educational policy. The Tenth Amendment within the Bill of Rights leaves such responsibilities as education to the states or the citizenry. Even though the federal government can assume only the duties expressly granted by the Constitution, the implied powers under the general welfare clause and judicial interpretations of constitutional provisions (see Chapter 11) shape its role in education.

Congress influences national education policy through its power to make laws and appropriate funds. For example, the Improving America's Schools Act of 1994, which amended the earlier Elementary and Secondary Education Act, clearly communicated the national interest in education:

> The Congress declares it to be the policy of the United States that a high-quality education for all individuals and a fair and equal opportunity to obtain that education are a societal good, are a moral imperative, and improve the life of every individual, because the quality of our individual lives ultimately depends on the quality of the lives of others. (P. L. 103–382, Sec. 1001)[1]

A number of national interests are evident in the history of elementary/secondary legislation (National Center for Education Statistics, 1995a, pp. 366–376). Although there may be several underlying reasons for federal interventions, this categorization places legislative Acts within seven themes: strengthening national productivity; improving defense and international relations; promoting educational reform; expanding educational opportunities; upgrading facilities, technologies, and programs; advancing research and development; and improving nutrition, health, and safety.

Strengthening National Productivity

The Continental Congress communicated the importance of education to the developing democracy: "Religion, morality and knowledge being necessary to good government and the happiness of mankind, schools and the means of education shall forever be encouraged." By setting aside one section of land in each newly settled township from which income would be derived to support public schooling, land ordinances of 1785 and 1787 made financial commitments to promote this interest in a well-educated citizenry. This interest continues to shape federal education policy.

The government's desire to strengthen the economy clearly falls within the general welfare clause. This purpose has justified direct financial assistance to public education. These actions often coincided with economic, political, and social changes, such as wars and depressions. The Civil War and the later industrialization and urbanization stimulated government programs to improve farm and factory production. The Morrill Acts of 1862 and 1890 allocated public land from which states and territories would derive income for colleges to advance instruction and research in agricultural and mechanical arts. Today's sixty-nine land-grant colleges and universities continue to receive earnings from land holdings.

The First World War coincided with federal actions to improve food production and vocational training programs. The Smith-Lever Act of 1914 financed teacher training in agriculture and home economics and provided for extension services by home demonstration agents, 4-H leaders, and county agricultural agents. The Smith-Hughes Act, also called the Vocational Education Act of 1917, granted states funds for trade-related programs in high schools. More than weapons production motivated this first direct federal support of precollege education. The industrial revolution created a demand for skilled workers. Educators enlarged school curricula to accommodate the growing secondary school enrollments.

A large lobbying force for vocational education (Grubb & Lazerson, 1974) urged expansions in federal aid to maintain a qualified workforce, reduce unemployment, and ensure national preeminence throughout the century. The Vocational Rehabilitation Act of 1918 and the Smith-Bankhead Act of 1920 provided job training grants for World War I veterans. Unemployment during the Great Depression stimulated legislation to create the Federal Emergency Relief Administration (1933), which sponsored adult education and vocational rehabilitation; the Public Works Administration (1933), which constructed public buildings, including schools; and the Civilian Conservation Corps (1933–1943), which provided work and education for youths who restored depleted natural resources and constructed dams and bridges. World War II continued the federal government's involvement in vocational education. The 1943 Vocational Rehabilitation Act assisted disabled veterans; the George-Barden Act (Vocational Education Act of 1946) expanded support for vocational education programs.

Domestic conditions stimulated the federal role in upgrading vocational education between 1960 and 1984. Occupational training funded by the 1961 Area Redevelopment Act and the Manpower Development and Training Act of 1962 were designed to ease unemployment and poverty. An enlarged Vocational Education Act of 1963 created work-study opportunities for students, developed programs for out-of-school youth, and provided funds for the construction of area vocational schools. Grants to states from the 1966 Adult Education Act encouraged adults to continue education or job training; and the 1968 Vocational Education Act increased funds to states for new programs and established the National Advisory Council on Vocational Education.

The 1973 Comprehensive Employment and Training Act (CETA) created employment and training opportunities for economically disadvantaged and unemployed persons. In the late 1970s Congress created four set-asides that allocated 50 percent of basic state grants for programs to serve disadvantaged, disabled, postsecondary, and bilingual populations. The Perkins Vocational Education Act of 1984 (which replaced the 1963 Vocational Education Act) also made vocational education more accessible on a nondiscriminatory basis, thus advancing the national interest in expanding educational opportunities to previously underserved groups. The 1990 reauthorization of this program deleted the specified allocations for special-needs students, targeted funds to districts with higher percentages of such students, gave

local districts greater latitude, and designed program evaluations to ensure that needs were appropriately served.

Vocational education, the first direct federal assistance to schools, is described in greater detail in Figure 10.1. Of the fiscal year 1996 appropriation of $1.3 billion, a total of $1.1 billion was directed to various vocational programs, and $260 million financed adult education and literacy programs.

In addition to this direct funding of vocational education, numerous programs indirectly foster a strong economy by increasing awareness of occupational choices, encouraging students to continue formal education, reducing adult illiteracy, and creating national skill standards. The 1974 Juvenile Justice and Delinquency Prevention Act developed programs to prevent students from dropping out of school and to limit unwarranted expulsions. The Youth Employment and Demonstration Projects Act of 1977 promoted literacy training, vocational exploration, and on-the-job skills training. The wish to help elementary and secondary students understand potential careers stimulated the 1978 Career Education Incentive Act. The School Dropout Prevention and Basic Skills Improvement Act of 1990 called on secondary schools to adopt programs for youth who are at risk of failing or discontinuing formal education. The Homeless Assistance Act of 1988 had the goals of reducing adult illiteracy and improving the education of homeless children. Illiteracy was also the focus of the National Literacy Act of 1991. This act established the National Institute for Literacy and the Interagency Task Force on Literacy. The 1994 School-to-Work Opportunities Act created a system for easing the transition from high school to employment or further training. The National Skills Standards Act of 1994 stimulated the development of a voluntary system of standards and assessments for job training programs in secondary and postsecondary institutions that "will result in increased productivity, economic growth and American economic competitiveness."

The goal of strengthening the nation's productivity led to expanding federal assistance for sev-

Intent

To make the United States more competitive in the world economy by developing more fully the academic and occupational skills of all segments of the population.

Enacted

Originally the Smith-Hughes Act (1917). The Vocational Education Acts of 1946 and 1963 increased financial assistance to secondary schools. The Carl Perkins Vocational and Applied Technology Education Act was initiated in 1985 and was amended subsequently to improve educational programs leading to academic and occupational skills needed to work in a technologically advanced society, apply new technologies, and expand access for underserved populations.

Appropriation

$1.340 billion in fiscal year 1996, including basic grants to states of $973 million for vocational, $100 million for Tech-Prep education, and $260 million for adult education.

Distribution

Matching grants encourage a high level of state financial commitment. Grants flow through State Educational Agencies (SEAs); state boards for vocational education oversee the development, implementation, and evaluation of states' plans. Local advisory councils assess needs and submit proposals to SEAs. States allocate at least these percentages of basic funds: the Secondary School Vocational Education and the Postsecondary and Adult Education programs, 75%; Program for Single Parents, Displaced Homemakers, and Single Pregnant Women, 7%; Sex Equity Program, 3%; and State Programs and State Leadership Activities, not more than $8\frac{1}{2}$%. Allotments are made to districts in proportion to receipts of Elementary and Secondary Education Act (ESEA) Title I (70%) and Individuals with Disabilities Education Act (20%) funds and enrollments in vocational programs (10%).

Restrictions

Federal assistance for vocational education is categorical in that funds are targeted by purpose. States have discretion in developing state plans, but primary state projects are professional development for teachers and counselors, program improvement, and curricula development to integrate vocational and academic instruction, as well as performance standards and assessments. To promote equitable participation of special populations, district programs are coordinated with ESEA Title I, IDEA (Individuals with Disabilities Act), and programs to promote gender equity.

Figure 10.1. Federal Program No. 1: Vocational Education (SOURCES: 20 USC 2301; 34 CFR 400; Final fiscal 1996 appropriations [1996, pp. 22–23].)

eral other curricular areas in the 1980s. The purpose of the Education for Economic Security Act of 1984 was to improve the quality of mathematics and science instruction and to promote careers in these fields, as well as in engineering, computers, and foreign languages. Funds encouraged the formation of partnerships among the business community, higher education institutions, and elementary/secondary schools. Presidential awards recognized excellence in teaching, and competitive Excellence in Education grants improved program quality. The 1988 Education and Training for American Competitiveness Act cited challenges to the nation's "preeminence in international commerce" as a rationale for grants to improve the teaching of mathematics, science, foreign languages, and technologies in schools and to assist functionally illiterate adults and out-of-school youth in obtaining skills. One section of this legis-lation, the Educational Partnerships Act, prompted private and nonprofit sector resources to enrich education and students' career awareness.

Movements to strengthen the economy and American education in the 1990s brought voca-tional education under scrutiny. A study of the effects of the reauthorized Perkins Vocational Edu-cation Act suggested a need for models of out-come-based program improvement and for focused technical assistance at local and state levels (Stecher et al., 1994). A three-year federal study, the National Assessment of Vocational Education (1994), concluded that neither vocational nor gen-eral track studies adequately prepared students for work or postsecondary education, and that fewer than one-half of the vocational education courses taken were actually used on the job. The report rec-ommended substantial improvements in secondary education, including combining vocational and general tracks to create industry-based majors and designing courses around industry-oriented stan-dards. The preparation of future teachers and in-service professional development would stress the integration of vocational and academic instruction.

States and localities would gain more control over vocational education under proposals intro-duced in Congress by the Republican Party. Rather than reauthorize prior vocational education pro-grams in 1996, a broader workforce development block grant would consolidate nearly one hundred separate federal job training programs, including the Perkins Act, the Job Training Partnership Act, and other community-based programs.

Supporting and stimulating reform of voca-tional education and related areas of schools' curricula have been designed to serve the federal interest in improving the nation's economic pro-ductivity.

Improving Defense and International Relations

The government's interest in, and constitutional duty to provide for, national defense is closely related to the goal of strengthening the economy. A number of the actions we discussed in the previous section coincided with wars. But the relationship between international conflicts and changes in edu-cation policies is less than direct. Times of national crisis foster, rather than cause, expansions in the federal role: "Wars both threaten and unite a nation, creating reasons for large scale mobiliza-tion of talent and resources that tend to outweigh traditional resistance to centralized control of edu-cation" (Kaestle & Smith, 1982, p. 391).

Governmental sponsorship of military acad-emies is an example of direct federal support of defense-related education. The U.S. Military Acad-emy (established in 1802), Naval Academy (1845), Coast Guard Academy (1876), and Air Force Academy (1954) are nearly fully funded by the federal government. In addition, Reserve Officer Training Corps (ROTC) programs are federally sponsored in both high schools and postsecondary institutions.

The Lanham Act of 1941 initiated impact aid as an indirect form of educational support for dis-tricts that were financially affected by the presence of military installations. In 1950, coincident with the Korean War, the School Assistance to Federally Affected Areas augmented this aid for school oper-ations and the construction of facilities. Programs expanded in subsequent decades to include fami-lies living on Native American reservations and in federally supported low-income housing. Im-pact aid assists districts that gain additional chil-dren or suffer loss of property tax revenue due to the tax-exempt status of military bases, govern-ment buildings, and Native American reservations in accordance with the provisions outlined in Fig-ure 10.2.

Alterations to the impact aid program in 1994 targeted funds to the most severely affected dis-tricts. The formula, to be fully in place in 1997, assigned the largest weights to children living on Indian lands and those whose parents live *and* work on military installations (often referred to as *A* chil-dren). Less weight was assigned to children whose parents work for the government but do not reside on federal land (*B* children), and to those who reside in low-rent housing. Multiplying this

---

Intent

To provide financial assistance for public schools in areas affected by federal activities, due to the acquisition of real property by the government, and to help federally connected children meet challenging state standards.

Enacted

School Assistance to Federally Affected Areas enacted in 1950 for school operations and school facility construction; reauthorized as Title VIII of the Improving America's Schools Act of 1994.

Appropriation

$693 million in fiscal year 1996, including $582 million in basic support, $50 million for heavily impacted districts, and $40 million for supplemental payments for children with disabilities.

Distribution

Applications for operational funds are made through State Education Agencies. Aid is provided to school districts by a formula that assigns weights for students who live on Indian land (1.25), whose parents live and work on federal property (1.00), who reside in low-rent housing (0.10), and whose parents are employed by the federal government but do not live on federal land (0.10). The latter category includes only the most severely impacted districts after 1995 (those with over 2,000 eligible students who constitute over 15 percent of total average daily attendance). Additional weight (0.35) is granted the first two categories in districts with over 100,000 total average daily attendance (ADA) and at least 6,500 eligible pupils. Students with disabilities who qualify for both impact aid and IDEA (Individuals with Disabilities Act) services are given a weight of 1.00. The total eligible weighted-student count is multiplied by the greater of 50% of average per pupil expenditure for the state or nation or the comparable local contribution rate certified by the state. In years for which there are insufficient funds, allocations are made first to districts with high percentages of eligible students.

Restrictions

Impact aid is general rather than categorical in nature, with the exception of aid provided for children with disabilities.

Figure 10.2. Federal Program No. 2: Impact Aid (SOURCES: Improving America's Schools Act of 1994 [Title VIII]; Final fiscal 1996 appropriations [1996, pp. 22–23].)

weighted-student count by the local per-pupil expenditure determines a district's entitlement. To ease the fund reduction, districts were partially held-harmless in 1995 and 1996, receiving 85 percent of the previous year's allocation.

The historically most controversial aspect of impact aid has been payments for B children. Many of these children attend schools in districts that have lost no property to federal installations (e.g., those residing in counties bordering the District of Columbia) and may have been helped economically by their proximity to government activities. For many years, B students received a lower prior-ity in fund distribution. Attempts to discontinue this support were frustrated in the political arena because of the large amount of aid available to districts in all states. Formula revisions in 1994 tightened eligibility requirements. Assistance is granted only if a district has 2,000 or more eligible students and if they exceed 15 percent of the district's total pupil count. It was estimated that 800 districts would relinquish all impact aid once formula changes were fully implemented. In addition, the 1994 amendments limited special education funding under impact aid to children from military families and Native American reservations.

Impact aid supplements local and state resources. Districts decide the priorities for this general aid, with two primary exceptions. First, aid for children with disabilities is categorical, and regulations ensure that payments are expended for identified pupils. Second, states that successfully satisfy one of two fiscal equity standards may apply impact aid receipts, just as they consider local property taxes, to reduce the state equalization allocations to districts. The wealth neutrality test demands that at least 85 percent of local and state operating revenue (i.e., the portion included in the state equalization program) is unrelated to local wealth. Few states (including Arizona, Maine, Michigan, and Kansas) have satisfied this test. The disparity standard demands that the difference in general revenue for districts at the 5th and 95th percentiles of pupils (see federal range ratio in Chapter 12) cannot exceed 25 percent. Only Alaska and New Mexico have met this standard. These two standards were initially created to determine the "extent to which a state had removed from the local district one of the primary reasons for the federal aid—the loss of local taxable wealth" (Magers, 1977, p. 126). However, the definition of revenue to be included in the tests and the rigor of the standards have been questioned by some analysts in the context of school finance litigation and states' adoption of formulas to address equity, efficiency, and adequacy (Sherman, 1992).

A number of other federal initiatives have advanced the goals of strengthening defense or improving international relations. The Fulbright Act of 1945 and the Information and Education Exchange Act of 1948 sponsored programs to share elementary/secondary and higher education faculty between the United States and other countries. The National Science Foundation was created in 1950 to "promote the progress of science; to advance the national health, prosperity and welfare; to secure the national defense; and for other purposes." One year after the Soviet Union's launch of *Sputnik,* Congress enacted the National Defense Education Act (NDEA) of 1958. This broad program of financial assistance for science, mathematics, and foreign languages was designed to increase the supply of competent teachers and improve instruction, guidance, and the use of television and other media. The curricular emphasis was placed on potentially high achievers. School systems subsequently adopted policies to track capable students into advanced placement and honors classes.

As the Cold War evolved into an era of economic competitiveness, the national interest again stimulated education legislation. The legislation included the Education for Economic Security Act of 1984; the Education and Training for American Competitiveness Act of 1988; the Excellence in Mathematics, Science, and Engineering Act of 1990; and the 1991 National Defense Authorization Act. The Foreign Language Assistance Act of 1994, a new section of the reauthorized Bilingual Education Act (Title VII of the Improving America's Schools Act), supported the creation of model programs in elementary and secondary schools. This legislation was premised on the finding that "Multilingualism enhances cognitive and social growth, competitiveness in the global marketplace, national security, and understanding of diverse people and cultures" (P. L. 103–382, Sec. 7202).

These diverse programs to finance military academies, education for children in federally impacted school systems, exchanges of people and ideas, and improvements in math, science, and foreign language curricula relate to the nation's interests in strengthened defense and international relations.

Promoting Educational Reform

Federal actions that are designed to improve the economy and national defense often influence schools' priorities in curriculum, staff development, and financial allocations. Even without large-scale federal funds, the priorities of the federal agenda influence the goals and programs of states and school districts. In the mid-1990s, the federal role in education became more active when the government promoted systemic reform in curriculum and instruction around National Education Goals and the voluntary development of standards and assessments.

The adoption of six national goals by the nation's governors and the president in 1990 initiated a movement in many states and local communities to reform education in order to upgrade outcomes for all students. The Goals 2000: Educate America Act of 1994 expanded the list of goals to eight (inserting numbers 4 and 8 below) and made several changes in the original language of others. The goals declare that *by the year 2000:*

1. . . . all children in America will start school *ready to learn.*
2. . . . the high school *graduation rate will increase* to at least 90 percent.
3. . . . all students will leave grades 4, 8, and 12 having demonstrated *competency over challenging subject matter* including English, mathematics, science, foreign languages, civics and government, economics, arts, history, and geography, and every school in America will ensure that all students learn to use their minds well, so they may be *prepared for responsible citizenship, further learning, and productive employment* in our Nation's modern economy.
4. . . . the Nation's *teaching force will have access to programs for the continued improvement of their professional skills* and the opportunity to acquire the knowledge and skills needed to instruct and prepare all American students for the next century.
5. . . . United States students will be *first in the world in mathematics and science* achievement.
6. . . . *every adult American will be literate* and will possess the knowledge and skills necessary to compete in a global economy and exercise the rights and responsibilities of citizenship.
7. . . . every school in the United States will be *free of drugs, violence, and the unauthorized presence of firearms and alcohol* and will offer a *disciplined environment* conducive to learning.

8. . . . every school will *promote partnerships that will increase parental involvement* and participation in promoting the social, emotional, and academic growth of children. (P. L. 103–227, Title I, Sec. 102; emphasis added)

Title III of the act, entitled "State and Local Education Systemic Improvement," provided grants to participating states to develop *content standards* that define what all students should know and be able to do in specific subjects, *performance standards* that define what students need to do to demonstrate proficiency under the content standards, and *opportunity-to-learn standards or strategies* that define the conditions of teaching and learning necessary for all students to have a fair opportunity to achieve the required knowledge and skills. Inclusion of national opportunity-to-learn standards within the act sparked controversy over the degree to which the federal government should define schools' curriculum and instruction. As enacted, the voluntary opportunity-to-learn standards encompassed (1) the quality of instructional materials and technologies, teachers, professional development, and facilities; (2) assurances of nondiscrimination by gender; and (3) the extent to which curriculum, instruction, and assessments are aligned with national standards. Proponents of including the latter guidelines argued that they help overcome inequities in education and testing. Opponents, who feared continued federal intrusion into local control of the quality and nature of education (Porter, 1995), were successful in eliminating opportunity-to-learn standards in 1996.

The Goals 2000: Educate America Act is summarized in Figure 10.3. Funds available through the act helped participating states, districts, and schools prepare education improvement plans. At least 60 percent of funds in 1995 were directed to districts to develop their plans and for professional development (the remainder could be used by State Education Agencies). At least 75 percent of districts' funds supported individual school improvement initiatives. After the first year, districts received 90 percent of the aid and passed at least 85

Intent

To place in statute the eight National Education Goals; to improve learning and teaching by providing a national framework for education reform; to promote the research, consensus building, and systemic changes needed to ensure equitable educational opportunities and high levels of achievement for all students; to promote the development and adoption of a voluntary national system of skill standards and certifications.

Enacted

Goals 2000: Educate America Act of 1994.

Appropriation

$530 million in fiscal year 1996, including $340 million in state grants and $180 million in school-to-work grants.

Distribution

Participating states receive allotments in proportion to the funds received under the Elementary and Secondary Education Act (ESEA), with 50% according to the number of children from low-income families and 50% according to the total number of students. SEAs allocate at least 90% to Local Education Authorities (LEAs) to implement state and local improvement plans and to upgrade teacher preparation and professional development of current teachers; no more than 4% is for state administration expenses; the remainder supports implementation of the state plan. LEAs must allocate 85% of funds to schools for comprehensive school improvement; at least 50% of funds go to schools with a special need (e.g., low-income families, low achievement) for assistance.

Restrictions

States that voluntarily adopt the eight National Education Goals receive grants to enable state planning panels to develop reform plans and to create a state technology plan. Participating states must develop content standards to define what all students should know and be able to do in specific subjects and performance standards to define what students need to do to demonstrate proficiency. Districts develop improvement plans in line with state standards.

Figure 10.3. Federal Program No. 3: National Goals and Educational Reforms (SOURCES: Goals 2000: Educate America Act of 1994; Final fiscal 1996 appropriations [1996, pp. 22–23].)

percent of the funds through to schools. The act permitted flexibility in determining how funds would be used to achieve the National Education Goals. Waivers in regulations governing other federal programs would be granted to the extent that federal directives impeded school improvement plans.

Other provisions of the act affected educational technologies, finance, school prayer, and international exchanges of educational practices. The Office of Educational Technology was created to promote effective uses of technologies in instruction. Grants were authorized to provide states with assistance in achieving a greater degree of equity in school finance plans. Several amendments that would have promoted prayer in schools were defeated. But the legislation as passed prohibited the use of federal funds to adopt policies that would prevent voluntary prayer and meditation. An international education program was established to analyze other nations' educational systems, including organizational structures and curricula, and to promote exchanges of information about "exemplary curriculum and teacher training programs in civics and government education and economic education."

The goal of enabling all children to meet the participating states' academic content and performance standards in concert with the eight National Education Goals shaped the subsequent reauthorization of many federal programs.

Expanding Educational Opportunities

The federal government has always been interested in assuring educational opportunities for all citizens. Beginning in the 1780s, when land grants enabled schooling in territories, this interest grew with the creation of the Freedman's Bureau to advance educational opportunities for African Americans following the Civil War, the promotion of civil rights in land-grant colleges in the reauthorized Morrill Act of 1890, and enactment of the GI Bill to give veterans opportunities for higher education rather than to overburden the job market following World War II. The decades of the 1960s and 1970s raised awareness of the role that education can play in improving the social and economic positions of particular groups, resulting in large increases in financial assistance for public school programs. The 1990s movement to restructure school curricula and assessments in line with national goals stimulated reforms to upgrade the education of all students.

We discuss the primary legislative acts that finance and guide the development of programs serving children with special needs, who are often overlooked at state and local levels (Verstegen, 1987, 1994). These groups include Native Americans, economically disadvantaged children, children with disabilities, and students whose native language is not English. Many programs we discuss in this section are entitlements. This means that the available funds are allocated according to the numbers of qualifying students. Other programs are competitive and require applications that identify program goals and implementation strategies.

Indian Education.   Treaty provisions during the 1800s obligated the federal government to educate Native American children. The government initially supported church-related mission schools. It used treaty provisions and the commerce clause of the Constitution to override concerns about the entanglement with church affairs (Ryan, 1982, p. 423). By the turn of the century, financial support for sectarian schools ended. The Bureau of Indian Affairs (BIA) assumed responsibility for administering boarding schools in remote areas and day schools in population centers. Public school districts whose boundaries overlap with reservations serve the majority of Indian students today.

Federal programs to help finance Indian education in public schools began in 1934 with enactment of the Johnson-O'Malley (JOM) Act. The Indian Education Act of 1972 expanded the federal role in improving educational opportunities through research and demonstration projects that developed appropriate bilingual and curriculum materials. Public school districts serving reservations benefit from impact aid payments. But these general funds are not necessarily targeted for Native American students (see Figure 10.2.).

Funds allocated under Title IX of the Improving America's Schools Act of 1994 were to address the special educational and culturally related academic needs of American Indians and native Hawaiian and Alaskan students to enable them to meet the content and performance standards of participating states.

Education of Disadvantaged Students.   The Supreme Court's *Brown* v. *Board of Education* (1954) decision that "separate but equal" schools are inherently unequal set the stage for subsequent legislation. Federally funded programs to compensate for economic and educational deprivation evolved from the interest in expanding educational opportunities.

The Civil Rights Act of 1964 was passed as part of President Johnson's War on Poverty. It included two mandates to cease discriminatory practices. Title VI prohibited discrimination based on race, religion, or national origin in "programs and activities" receiving federal financial assistance. Title VII prohibited employment-related discrimination based on these same characteristics, as well as gender. Later enactment of Title IX of the Education Amendments of 1972 prohibited discrimination on the basis of gender in educational programs receiving federal funds. The Equal Pay Act (1963), Age Discrimination in Employment Act (1967), Education of All Handicapped Children Act (1975), Americans with Disabilities Act (1990), and the Civil Rights Restoration Act (1991) further extended protection from discrimination. The Women's Educational Equity Act of 1994 (Improving America's Schools Act, Title V, Part B) provided grants to promote effective gender-equity policies and programs and to increase opportunities for women to enter highly skilled, high-paying careers.

The 1964 Civil Rights Act instituted the policy of withholding federal funds to encourage school districts to comply with mandates. The Office of Civil Rights (OCR) was created within the Department of Education to investigate and resolve reported denials of civil rights. This strategy of influencing change through such adverse consequences as legal actions and withholding transfer payments is said to hold a *stick* of enforcement over local officials. It differs from financial incentives, often referred to as *carrots,* offered by other federal categorical aid programs. Directives, or *strings,* attached to these grants redirect state and local behavior toward national priorities.

In 1964 Congress created the Office of Economic Opportunity and financed a number of programs. These include the Job Corps to provide vocational training, Volunteers in Service to America (VISTA), Head Start, Follow Through, and Upward Bound. The commitment to early childhood education for economically disadvantaged children continues today. Over ninety programs were sponsored by eleven federal agencies and twenty offices in 1993 (U.S. General Accounting Office, 1994a). The largest program is Head Start. Head Start's goal is to provide comprehensive health, nutritional, educational, and social services for preschool children from low-income families. The Childhood Education and Development Act of 1989 expanded Head Start to include child care ser-

vices. The 1992 Ready-to-Learn Act advanced preschool education through television programs and instructional materials for teachers, parents, and child care providers.

The reauthorization of Head Start in 1994 created programs for children from birth to age three and for easing the later transition to elementary schools. The revisions also devoted 25 percent of funding to the goal of upgrading the quality of personnel and operations and created a process for identifying and improving poorly performing programs. Programs that fail to correct deficiencies within one year face potential termination of funds. The Even Start Family Literacy Program within ESEA Title I (see below) integrates early childhood with adult basic and parenting education. States must provide matching funds for programs designed cooperatively between schools and other agencies.

The progress of school districts toward desegregation was slow during the 1960s and 1970s, despite consistent rulings of federal courts to end *de jure* segregation resulting from prior state and local policies in southern as well as northern states. Congress passed the 1972 Emergency School Assistance Act (ESAA) to reward school systems that had already desegregated and to encourage others to voluntarily desegregate. However, limited funds permitted few projects, and restrictions constrained the policy options of districts. Funding for ESAA ended in 1981, when it was absorbed within the Chapter 2 block grant (see next section). The stated purpose of the 1984 Education for Economic Security Act's assistance for magnet schools that offer special curricula to attract students of different races was to reduce minority group isolation.

The Elementary and Secondary Education Act (ESEA) of 1965 greatly enlarged the federal role in educating disadvantaged children. The purpose of ESEA Title I was to provide financial assistance to districts "serving areas with concentrations of children from low-income families . . . to expand and improve their educational programs." Passing the original Title I required a number of compromises (Benson, 1978, pp. 379–382). As a result, nearly all school systems and many private schools received funds, and the allocation formula directed more aid to higher-spending states. The continuing assumption that poverty is a valid indicator of educational need means that two students with the same educational needs receive different treatment if only one of them attends an eligible school (Jones, 1985, p. 219). Funds have been targeted to schools serving children from low-income families. But remedial reading and mathematics programs for many years served pupils who scored poorly on standardized tests regardless of their family income.

Chapter 1 of the 1981 Education Consolidation and Improvement Act (ECIA) renamed and modified Title I. Parent advisory councils were no longer required. But schools needed to assure that educational programs were designed in consultation with the parents and teachers of the children served. Services for eligible nonpublic school children could no longer be delivered within parochial schools, in accordance with the Supreme Court's holding in *Aguilar* v. *Felton* (1985). Nevertheless, eligible private school students are served on an equitable basis at a neutral site by employees of public agencies. And programs remain under the control and supervision of agencies that are independent of private schools and religious organizations.

Extensive modifications in ESEA in 1988 required school-level accountability, a focus on higher-order skills, and greater parental involvement. The goal of Chapter 1 was clarified to help students succeed in the regular school program, attain grade-level proficiency, and improve achievement in both the basic and more advanced skills. The emphasis shifted from a stand-alone pullout program for disadvantaged students to one that would be coordinated with the regular school curriculum and for which the entire school would be responsible for success (LeTendre, 1991). The reforms allowed schoolwide projects when at least 75 percent of students were eligible for services, permitted greater flexibility in the use of funds, encouraged districts to adopt local standards and measures rather than norm-referenced tests for determining student performance, and urged improvements in programs that did not attain the

anticipated achievement gains. An accountability system identified schools needing program improvement when students failed to make substantial progress. A subsequent study of the accountability system's effectiveness found a number of deficiencies: Using only achievement test scores to judge program effectiveness limited the accuracy of the identification process. Focusing on annual gains in scores often neglected the needs of the schools with the lowest-achieving students. And applying pressure to increase test scores had negative effects on instruction in some schools (U.S. General Accounting Office, 1993).

Title I/Chapter 1 program effects have been scrutinized and debated more than most other federal categorical aid programs. A number of longitudinal analyses reported success in raising cognitive levels of disadvantaged children, particularly for African American and Hispanic students (e.g., National Assessment of Educational Progress, 1981; Schorr & Schorr, 1988; Smith & O'Day, 1991; Stickney & Plunkett, 1983; Stonehill & Anderson, 1982). Other studies, however, found evidence that the effects are modest and are not sustained over time (e.g., Carter, 1984; Kaestle & Smith, 1982; Millsap et al., 1992).

Several factors inhibited the potential of compensatory education. First, regular classroom teachers do not have to ensure students' success under pull-out programs. This was the primary local implementation model, but it was not mandated in the legislation. Second, students had a fragmented school experience. They learned basic skills from different texts and were taught in different styles in regular classes and remedial classes. Third, organizational and political variables impeded the effectiveness of programs: Local and state officials were reluctant to accept its major priorities. Teachers and principals failed to support programs. And program assurances and processes essential in securing resources often alienated those teachers and administrators who were not directly involved in Title I programs (Wayson, 1975). Even the 1988 reforms to bring greater flexibility as well as school-level accountability did not impact program delivery or student achievement in all settings (Herrington & Orland, 1992). In addition, the lack of full funding inhibited the program's potential. Verstegen (1992, 1995) noted that only 60 percent of eligible Title I students were served. Timar (1994) examined the history of Title I funding and its effects on schools as organizations. He observed that the regulations themselves contributed to the fragmentation: "The federal government's return on its investment was compliance with the letter of the law rather than uniformly better schools for poor children" (p. 54). His conclusions challenged policy makers to design programs and evaluations in ways that would encourage organizational coherence and integration: "Policy should create incentives and provide resources for schools to do things not only better but differently. . . . Rather than asking how policy can change students, we should first ask how policy can change schools that serve diverse student needs" (p. 65).

These research findings and recommendations shaped the comprehensive changes in the reauthorization of ESEA in the Improving America's Schools Act of 1994. The Title I designation was restored. Program requirements, use of funds, and accountability were altered. Participating states needed to establish content and performance standards in at least language arts and mathematics and assessments aligned with these standards, in order to receive future Title I grants. Schools that participated in the Goals 2000: Educate America Act (see Figure 10.3) were eligible for reform grants to assist in formulating content, performance, and opportunity-to-learn standards. This reauthorization recognized that schools with high concentrations of children from low-income families had the most urgent need for improvement. Otherwise, "achieving the National Education Goals will not be possible" (P. L. 103–382, Sec. 1001). Title I continued its distribution to schools on the basis of poverty, but it no longer restricted participation in programs to low-achieving students. The intent of Congress was to appropriate sufficient funds to enable schools to serve all eligible students by fiscal year 2004. But a rescission in 1995 and the diminished spending proposed for fiscal year 1996 jeopardized this goal.

Schools in attendance areas in which the percentage of children from low-income families is at or above the average for the district may receive funds if they have at least ten eligible children. Priority is given to schools in which poverty children account for at least 75 percent of all children in the attendance area. Annual rankings determine schools served when there are insufficient funds. New appropriations after 1996 were to be distributed under one or both of two revised allocation formulas (Riddle, 1995). One formula targeted "concentration grants" to districts with high concentrations of poverty children (over 6,500, or 15 percent of all children). The other formula, an education finance incentive program, rewarded states that had equalized spending among districts to a certain point (an equity factor) and directed aid to states in which school spending was high relative to per capita income (an effort factor). The reauthorization also advanced liberty interests in permitting Title I students to exercise choice in moving among qualifying schools and in establishing a charter school demonstration program.

Title I is the largest program of federal financial assistance for educational services. The total of $7.2 billion in 1996 was eclipsed only by the school lunch and milk allocations. Figure 10.4 summarizes the intent and provisions of this categorical aid program. The percentages of pupils who were served in remedial reading and mathematics during 1993–1994 are indicated in Table 10.1. Nearly 11 percent of all students were in reading. Somewhat fewer (7 percent) participated in mathematics programs. These students were concentrated in elementary and combined schools in central cities. But a large percentage of students in rural areas also received remediation, especially in reading.

Schoolwide reform was encouraged under the reauthorization to minimize removing Title I students from the regular classroom, to involve them in complex-thinking and problem-solving experiences, and to stimulate effective instructional strategies to increase the amount and quality of

Intent

To improve the teaching and learning of children in high-poverty schools to enable them to achieve challenging state academic content and performance standards.

Enacted

Originally Title I of the Elementary and Secondary Education Act (ESEA) of 1965; revised as Chapter 1 of the Education Consolidation and Improvement Act (ECIA) of 1981; reauthorized as Title I of the Improving America's Schools Act of 1994.

Appropriation

$7.2 billion in fiscal year 1996, including $6.7 billion in grants to states, $102 million for Even Start, and $305 million for migrant education.

Distribution

Funds flow through State Education Agencies (SEAs) to districts. The amount received is calculated by multiplying the number of eligible children (determined by family income) by 40 percent of the statewide average expenditure per pupil (no less than 80 percent nor more than 120 percent of the national average). Formulas effective in 1996 directed more funds to districts with high proportions of poverty students or to states with equalized spending among districts (equity factor) and high educational spending relative to family incomes (effort factor).

Restrictions

Categorical aid that is directed to schools having the highest concentrations of low-income children and supplements education for eligible children. All schools may benefit if the concentration is uniformly high throughout a district, and programs may be schoolwide if there is a high concentration (50% or over) of eligible students. In the past, only educationally deprived children in eligible schools received services. Under 1994 revisions, schools are given flexibility in determining how to use funds, and funds may be combined with local and state monies in a comprehensive effort to raise the quality of an entire school. Title I projects are linked to overall school reform efforts to achieve state content and performance standards developed under Goals 2000. Parents, schools, and communities design programs collaboratively and share responsibility for improved performance. Districts must maintain fiscal effort, supplement nonfederal funds, and ensure comparability of services to those in schools not receiving funds.

Figure 10.4. Federal Program No. 4: Education of Disadvantaged Students (SOURCES: Improving America's Schools Act of 1994 [Title I]; Final fiscal 1996 appropriations [1996, pp. 22–23].)

learning time. The latter could include an extended school day or year, summer programs, and other opportunities for enriched and accelerated curricula. The percentage for determining whether funds could be used for schoolwide programs was reduced from 75 percent of all students in a school to 60 percent for 1995–1996 and to 50 percent thereafter. Teachers were given greater decision-making authority and flexibility in exchange for greater responsibility for student performance. And parents were afforded meaningful opportunities to participate in their children's education.

Schools were urged to coordinate Title I programs with services for children with disabilities and limited English proficiency or who are homeless, migratory, neglected, delinquent, or at risk of dropping out, in order to "increase program effectiveness, eliminate duplication, and reduce frag-

TABLE 10.1. Student Participation in Selected Federally Financed Programs, by Level of School and Type of Community, 1993–94

	Number of Students	Percent of Students Participating in Program				
		Remedial Reading	Remedial Mathematics	Programs for Students with Disabilities	Bilingual Education	English as a Second Language
Total	41,621,660	10.9%	6.9%	6.9%	3.1%	4.0%
School level[a]						
Elementary	26,886,026	13.5	7.8	6.8	4.0	4.8
Secondary	13,757,801	5.6	5.0	6.5	1.4	2.6
Combined	977,833	13.7	9.4	14.8	1.8	1.9
Community type						
Central city	13,496,625	12.4	7.9	7.0	5.7	6.5
Urban fringe/ large town	12,953,165	8.9	5.7	6.3	2.1	4.1
Rural/ small town	15,171,870	11.2	7.0	7.2	1.2	1.2

[a]Elementary schools have grade 6 or lower and no grade higher than 8; secondary schools have no grade lower than 7; combined schools have grades lower than 7 and higher than 8.
SOURCE: National Center for Education Statistics (1995a). *Digest of Education Statistics, 1995*. Washington, DC: U. S. Government Printing Office, Table 57, p. 70.

mentation of the instructional program" (P. L. 103–382, Sec. 1112). Partnerships with businesses and the integration of school- and work-based learning were stressed to prepare students for the transition from school to work. Recognizing the many conditions outside of schools that can adversely affect academic achievement, the act also encouraged the coordination of education with the assistance for health and social service available to families.

In determining yearly progress toward goals, the act outlined three levels of performance: advanced, proficient, and partially proficient. Assessment of Title I student performance used the same instruments and included higher-order thinking skills and understandings as those instruments to be adopted by states to assess all students in relation to content and performance standards. Assessments made reasonable adaptations and accommodations for students with diverse learning needs. They permitted tests "in the language and form most likely to yield accurate and reliable information" on the knowledge of limited-English-proficient students. Schools failing to make adequate

progress toward state goals for two consecutive years would be subject to corrective actions. These include withholding funds, creating interagency agreements to provide health and other social services to remove barriers to learning, revoking the authority to operate schoolwide programs, decreasing school-level decision-making authority, reconstituting school staff, making alternative governance arrangements (e.g., charter schools), or instituting state opportunity-to-learn standards or strategies. A new system of support was to be designed by states with assistance from the federal regional technical assistance centers and regional educational laboratories. It would include support teams of personnel "knowledgeable about research and practice on teaching and learning."

State Educational Agencies (SEAs) are permitted to retain a percentage of funds from many federal programs to finance administration, coordination, training, and technical assistance responsibilities. This support grew rapidly following the initial enactment of ESEA Title I (Plunkett, 1991). It amounted to an average of 41 percent of both funding and staffing of SEAs in 1993. The level of federal support ranged widely among states, from about 10 percent to 80 percent. The percentage depended on the number and types of federal and state programs within the responsibility of SEA (U.S. General Accounting Office, 1994b). Despite this substantial support, SEAs are criticized for not providing needed programmatic leadership: "Staff sizes are small, other responsibilities already involve major time commitments, and staff members are much more comfortable with regulatory and fiscal matters than with curriculum and instruction in their dealing with school districts" (Millsap et al., 1992, pp. ix–x). Nevertheless, responsibilities for SEA oversight of district curriculum increased under the Improving America's Schools Act. In addition to guiding processes for developing content and performance standards, SEAs were placed in control of corrective actions for schools needing improvement.

Education of Children with Disabilities. Enabling the education of children with disabilities within public schools became a federal priority during the 1960s and 1970s. It continues to receive a large amount of financial assistance.

Financial aid for educational programs began in 1965 with benefits granted by Title VI of the Elementary and Secondary Education Act (ESEA) and with creation of Gallaudet College by the National Technical Institute for the Deaf Act. This federally funded residential institution was renamed Gallaudet University in 1986. It operates model elementary and secondary schools for deaf students. The 1968 Handicapped Children's Early Education Assistance Act authorized preschool programs, and the Education of the Handicapped Act (EHA) of 1970 created a Bureau of Education for the Handicapped. Several federal court decisions (e.g., *Mills v. Board of Education,* 1972) found that districts had an obligation to meet the educational needs of students with disabilities. These cases preceded congressional actions that enlarged the federal role.

Section 504 of the Vocational Rehabilitation Act of 1973 prohibited discrimination against physically, mentally, or emotionally handicapped persons in schools and other federally assisted programs. This civil rights legislation protects all children having one or more physical or mental impairments that substantially limit a major life activity. But it does not engender financial assistance. Instead, its mandate to provide a quality of educational experience for children and youth with disabilities comparable to that available to nondisabled students of the same grade and age covers many students. For example, educators make accommodations or modify facilities for students who are confined to a wheelchair but are otherwise able to learn academic material. Section 504 coverage also guarantees services for students with AIDS, attention deficit disorder (ADD), substance abuse, and some childhood diseases that do not fall within the narrower definition of disabilities of the following legislation (Anthony, 1994).

The national commitment to educate children with disabilities was stated strongly in the 1975 Education for All Handicapped Children Act, often referred to as Public Law 94-142. Its reauthorization in 1991 as the Individuals with Disabilities Education Act (IDEA) continued the assurance that children with disabilities would have "appropriate educational services which would enable them to have full equality of opportunity" (20 U.S.C. 1400) Figure 10.5 summarizes IDEA. IDEA is one of the largest federal education programs, because it provided $3.3 billion in 1996. Seven percent of the nation's students received special education services in 1993–1994. These students were about evenly divided between elementary and secondary schools and among cities, small cities, and rural areas (see Table 10.1).

Amendments to the original act expanded coverage. Related legislation promoted coordinated service delivery. Funds were added in 1986 for demonstration projects for the severely disabled, research and technology, early childhood education for children aged three to five, and early intervention services for eligible children from birth to age two. The 1988 Technology-Related Assistance for Individuals with Disabilities Act helped states to develop consumer-responsive statewide technology programs for disabled persons of all ages. Even though the 1994 reauthoriza-

---

Intent

To assure that children with disabilities from age 3 to 21 have a free appropriate public education that includes special education and related services to meet their unique needs.

Enacted

Originally the Education of All Handicapped Children Act (P.L. 94–142) in 1975; reauthorized as the Individuals with Disabilities Education Act (IDEA) of 1991; amended by the Improving America's Schools Act of 1994.

Appropriation

$3.245 billion in fiscal year 1996, including $2.324 billion for grants to states, $360 million for preschool programs, $316 million for infants and families, $91 million for personnel development, $25 million for early childhood education, $24 million for secondary and transitional services, and $14 million for innovations.

Distribution

State Education Agencies (SEAs) submit an annual program plan on behalf of school districts. Grants equal the number of children with disabilities aged 3 to 21 who receive special education and related services multiplied by a given percentage (40 percent authorized by IDEA) of the national average per pupil expenditure. SEAs may retain 25% of funds for administrative expenses, including financial and program audits; they allocate at least 75% to districts as flat grants.

Restrictions

Each eligible child has an individual education plan (IEP) that identifies present levels of educational performance, annual goals and short-term instructional objectives, special education and related services, the extent of inclusion in regular educational programs, and evaluation procedures to determine progress toward goals. State and local public agencies are responsible for ensuring that IEPs are prepared for private school children who receive special services from public agencies. There is to be coordination with Impact Aid and Elementary and Secondary Education Act (ESEA) Title I programs in districts receiving these funds.

Figure 10.5. Federal Program No. 5: Education of Students with Disabilities (SOURCES: 20 USC 1400 to 1485; 34 CFR 300; Improving America's Schools Act of 1994 [Title III, Part A]; Final fiscal 1996 appropriations [1996, pp. 22–23].)

---

tion of ESEA encouraged state and local personnel to coordinate services under Title I and IDEA, funding streams continue to be separate under these categorical programs (Verstegen, 1995). A new federal initiative, the Families of Children with Disabilities Support Act, enacted within the 1994 amendments to ESEA, also encouraged collaboration. The purpose of this legislation was to assist states to develop "a family-centered and family-directed, culturally competent, community-centered, comprehensive, statewide system" of support for families of children with disabilities. The competitive matching grants encouraged states to promote interagency coordination and create model demonstration projects.

IDEA assures that all children eligible under its provisions are entitled to a *free appropriate public education.* This principle has been the subject of litigation about schools' obligations to address the needs of children with severe disabilities. For example, there was a responsibility to educate a multiply-disabled child who was allegedly unable to benefit from special education (*Timothy W.* v. *Rochester,* 1989). The most appropriate placement may be in a private school. This education is at public expense when school programs cannot meet a child's needs. The U.S. Supreme Court ruled in 1993 that parents can be reimbursed for private school expenses even if that school is not approved by state officials and does not meet all federal regulations (*Florence* v. *Carter,* 1993).

Special education is defined in IDEA as "specially designed instruction" in accordance with the *Individualized Education Plan* (IEP) prepared for each disabled child. The child-specific nature of this education implies that it can be accomplished by regular academic instruction, vocational instruction, community living skills, transition services to prepare the student for life after public schooling, or whatever is deemed appropriate for the child's needs. Related services encompass transportation and developmental, corrective, and other supportive services to help the child benefit from special education. The services include physical and occupational therapy, audiology and speech pathology, counseling and psychological services, and medical services for diagnostic and evaluative purposes. Several Supreme Court decisions clarified the extent to which such services must be provided. The court denied a parental request for a sign-language interpreter for a hearing-impaired child who was making satisfactory academic progress (*Board of Education* v. *Rowley,* 1982). But it found the administration of a catheterization procedure to be a related service when the child would otherwise not be able to remain at school (*Irving* v. *Tatro,* 1984). Stating that "IDEA creates a neutral government program dispensing aid not to schools but to individual handicapped children," the court found that the Establishment Clause did not prohibit the district from furnishing a sign-language interpreter for a student in a sectarian school (*Zobrest* v. *Catalina,* 1993).

IDEA's regulation of a *least restrictive environment* has been a challenge to educators, for example, in determining the appropriate degree to which students with disabilities should be included in regular classrooms and activities. Removal is permitted for part of or the full school day only when "the nature or severity of the disability is such that education in regular classes with the use of supplementary aids and services cannot be achieved satisfactorily." As of 1994, the settings in which the student is educated must be specifically designated in the IEP or Section 504 plan. Several court decisions favored inclusion in the general classroom, including the *Greer* v. *Rome* (1991) holding that school officials had not adequately considered educating a Down's syndrome child in the regular classroom with supplementary services. The court's test for determining whether inclusion in the general classroom is appropriate assessed the academic benefits in both placements, such nonacademic benefits as social development, the effects on other students, and financial costs. Another review of a school-proposed segregated placement of a mentally retarded child resulted in full-time placement in a regular public school class (*Sacramento* v. *Rachel,* 1994). The child subsequently made substantial academic progress with no detrimental effects on other students when enrolled in a private school.

The *regular education initiative* called for greater social and academic integration of disabled and nondisabled students (Sage & Burrello, 1994; Skrtic, 1991). The National Association of State Boards of Education (1992) as well as Colorado, Iowa, New Mexico, Michigan, and Vermont adopted positions in support of full inclusion—educating all children in the general classroom and neighborhood school. Barriers to meeting this commitment effectively include inadequate funds for training all teachers to address children's academic and physical problems, large class sizes, too few special educators who are spread too thinly among classrooms, principals' limited knowledge and expertise in promoting inclusion in a participatory manner, and the paucity of research on the effects of full inclusion on the learning of special and regular students (Anthony, 1994).

Although the mandates of Section 504 and IDEA have successfully expanded educational opportunities for students with disabilities, states and districts worry that federal funds are inadequate. IDEA authorizes federal assistance for 40 percent of the national average per pupil expenditure. Annual appropriations, however, have not exceeded 12.5 percent of this level (Parrish & Verstegen, 1994). When expenditures for all special education and related services are considered, the burden falls most heavily on states (55.9 percent in 1987–1988) and localities (36.3 percent), with the federal share lagging (7.9 percent).

The steady growth in federal aid between fiscal year 1979 ($217 for each eligible child) and 1993 ($420) failed to keep pace with inflation, let alone the expansion over the years of schools' services for children with disabilities. Spending declined from the 1979 equivalent of $424 in 1993 dollars to a low of $350 in 1982. It then fluctuated for a decade to a high of $434 in 1991 and then slipped to $420 in 1993 (Parrish & Verstegen, 1994). The Center for Special Education Finance (1994) urged full funding of the authorization level (40 percent) and outlined a formula based on states' overall student populations. It did this in an effort to provide disincentives for the overidentification that may occur when funds flow according to the number diagnosed for special education services. A poverty-based funding adjustment would direct additional allocations to states or districts with concentrations of poor families; and a factor would reward higher levels of equalization within states.

In anticipation of IDEA's reauthorization, Verstegen (1995) reiterated the need for adequate funding to close the gap between authorizations and appropriations. She also urged greater coordination of efforts for children with disabilities:

> Beyond *tolerating* integration and coordination, a new policy atmosphere needs to be created in which these practices are clearly *fostered* and *encouraged,* across the diverse set of actors involved with national disability policy, and at all levels of the system. (p. 52; emphasis in original)

Bilingual Education.   Students whose native languages are not English received attention in 1968 with passage of the Bilingual Education Act (Title VII of ESEA amendments). Following the Supreme Court's decision that the denial of a "meaningful education" for non-English-speaking children violated Title VI of the Civil Rights Act (*Lau v. Nichols,* 1974), the Educational Opportunities Act of 1974 urged districts to provide equal opportunities regardless of language.

The Bilingual Education Act was reauthorized as Title VII of the Improving America's Schools Act of 1994. Reforms were urged to help students achieve English proficiency and master academic content and higher-order skills in order to meet promotion and graduation standards in concert with the National Education Goals. Programs may use both English and the students' native languages for instruction, and English-proficient students may be enrolled with the goal of enabling all students to be multilingual. Grants supported program improvements designed locally. District- or school-wide projects are permitted where there are concentrations of eligible students. Districts were to plan to assure parental involvement, accountability in achieving high academic standards, and coordination with other education programs and related services that were provided to children and families. The quality of staff was to be strengthened through improved training of future and current teachers and a bilingual education career ladder program. Recipients had to assure the grantor that funds would be used to build capacities to continue to offer services if the federal assistance was reduced or eliminated in the future.

Figure 10.6 describes the purpose and distribution of funds for bilingual education. Table 10.1 gives the percentages of pupils who participated in Bilingual and English as a Second Language (ESL) programs in 1993–1994. About 7 percent of pupils enrolled in one of these programs. The greatest concentration was in urban elementary schools.

Bilingual education has provoked controversy primarily in terms of how long, if at all, students should receive instruction in their native language while they learn English. Some specialists advocate teaching English as a second language (ESL), with students learning basic skills in their native languages until English is mastered. Others argue for a more rapid transition to English and enrollment in regular classes. A third group advocates an English-only approach, with no native language

---

Intent

To educate limited-English-proficient children and youth to meet challenging state content and performance standards expected of all students.

Enacted

Title VII of the 1968 amendments to the Elementary Secondary Education Act; amended by the Bilingual Education Act of 1974; reauthorized as Title VII of the Improving America's Schools Act of 1994.

Appropriation

$178 million in fiscal year 1996 for bilingual and immigrant education, including $128 million for basic grants and $50 million for education of immigrants.

Distribution

Funds are allocated on a discretionary rather than formula basis; districts apply directly to the Department of Education; state agencies have an opportunity to comment on local districts' plans. States receive up to 5% of allocations to districts for coordination and technical assistance.

Restrictions

The 1994 reauthorization permitted greater discretion for districts to design programs for eligible students. Funds are directed to systemic improvement and reform to adopt exemplary bilingual education and special alternative instruction programs, develop bilingual skills and multicultural understanding, improve English and native language skills, upgrade curriculum and technological applications, develop instructional materials and assessments, and improve the professional training of teachers.

Figure 10.6. Federal Program No. 6: Education of Students with Limited English Proficiency (SOURCE: Improving America's Schools Act of 1994 [Title VII]; Final fiscal 1996 appropriations [1996, pp. 22–23].)

---

instruction in public schools. The flexibility permitted under the reauthorized act promoted innovations in instructional approaches; the National Clearinghouse for Bilingual Education disseminated information about effective programs.

Programs to assist immigrants and refugees also benefit students with limited English language facility. The 1962 Migration and Refugee Assistance Act and the 1975 Indochina Migration and Refugee Assistance Act authorized loans and grants for education and vocational training. The Emergency Immigrant Education Program within the 1994 reauthorized Bilingual Education Act provided financial assistance for improving educational programs in districts experiencing unusually large enrollment increases due to immigration.

These civil rights mandates and categorical aid programs expand educational opportunities for diverse groups of students. Grants are targeted in states participating in many of these programs after 1994 to strengthen the capacity of schools to enable *all* students to achieve states' content and performance standards.

Upgrading Facilities, Technologies, and Programs

Federal aid has assisted school and district improvement efforts by aiding in constructing facilities, updating instructional materials and technologies, and helping personnel enrich curriculum and instruction. In 1930 Congress spent $47 million to build schools. The Disaster Relief Act of 1965 gave financial assistance to school districts "to help meet emergency costs resulting from a national disaster." The School Facilities Infrastructure Improvement Act of 1994 linked the financing of facilities, including libraries and media centers, to the achievement of the National Education Goals under ESEA Title XII. However, funding for this program disappeared under the 1995 budget rescissions.

Financial incentives have encouraged schools to develop materials and advance the use of technologies in instruction. Various Titles of the original ESEA helped state agencies and schools improve library resources, develop curricula and instructional materials, assess educational progress, and initiate innovative programs. Schools broadened their use of television and other media under the 1962 Communications Act, the 1967 Public Broadcasting Act, and the 1976 Educational Broadcasting Facilities and Telecommunications Demonstration Act. The Children's Television Act of 1990 initiated controls over advertisements and programming to address the "educational and informational" needs of children.

The use of technologies in education expanded with the information age. Congress enacted the High Performance Computing Act of 1991. This legislation established a National Research and Education Network and created standards for high-performance networks. The potential benefits of technological education brought additional funding and recognition in two parts of the Improving America's Schools Act of 1994. The Technology for Education Act (Title III) promoted technology-enhanced curriculum and instruction to support school reforms, professional development to improve teachers' use of technologies, equity in providing access to students with the greatest needs, and the schools' access to telecommunications networks. The Star Schools Act (Title III, Part B) advanced distance-learning strategies to improve interactive instructional programming via telecommunications.

The new federalism of the Reagan administration emphasized local determination of the best use of federal funds for school improvement activities. Chapter 2 of the Education Consolidation and Improvement Act (ECIA) of 1981 adopted a block grant approach to consolidate forty-three previous categorical aid programs. The goal was to give local education agencies discretion to direct funds where they judged improvements were most needed. At the same time, the act tried to minimize the federal presence, reduce paperwork, and eliminate prescriptive regulation and oversight. Block grants were available through states to public and nonpublic schools for activities related to development of basic skills, school improvement and support services, and special purposes. This funding strategy shifted grant administration to states and decentralized the responsibility for designing and implementing programs within these broad purposes to district and school personnel. However, funds were reduced over 25 percent from antecedent program levels. Redistributions of funds aided nearly all districts, to the detriment of poor and minority children that were primarily in urban districts (Verstegen, 1987).

Chapter 2 continued as Title VI of the Improving America's Schools Act for those states that participated in the Goals 2000: Educate America Act. This part of the act was entitled Innovative Education Program Strategies. It was more categorical in that it supported districts' innovations that enabled achievement of the National Education Goals and states' content and performance standards. Figure 10.7 presents this program's intent and the distribution of funds to states, districts, and private schools.

The national government has been concerned about the improvement of teachers' skills. The 1965 Higher Education Act established the Teacher Corps and fellowships for teacher preparation. The Education Professions Development Act of 1967 was designed to improve the quality of teaching and to relieve the shortage of adequately prepared educators. Nearly all of the subsections of the Improving America's Schools Act of 1994 listed professional development as an important aspect of strengthening schools' abilities to enable students to achieve challenging standards and the National Education Goals. Title II of the act initiated the Eisenhower Professional Development Program to support the efforts of states, districts, and teacher training institutions to improve the teaching and

---

Intent

To support district innovations and effective school programs that are consistent with state reforms under the Goals 2000: Educate America Act and to provide a continuing source of innovation and educational improvement.

Enacted

Initially as Chapter 2 of the Education Consolidation and Improvement Act (ECIA) of 1981; reauthorized as Title VI of the Improving America's Schools Act of 1994.

Appropriation

$275 million in fiscal year 1996.

Distribution

State Education Agencies (SEAs) apply for grants based on pupil populations, including the number of non-public school students. SEAs distribute no less than 85% of funds to school districts by formulas that consider enrollments and such high-cost factors as the number of children from low-income families and living in sparsely populated areas. SEAs may retain 15% for administrative costs.

Restrictions

SEAs have basic responsibility for the administration of funds and programs, including financial audits. However, district and school personnel have flexibility in designing programs that have the objectives of promoting school-level planning, improving instruction and staff development, increasing achievement levels of all students, and achieving factors identified in research as distinguishing effective from ineffective schools.

Figure 10.7. Federal Program No. 7: Innovative Education Program Strategies (SOURCES: Improving America's Schools Act of 1994 [Title VI]; Final fiscal 1996 appropriations [1996, pp. 22–23].)

learning of all students. This program encouraged "sustained and intensive high-quality professional development" aligned with state content and performance standards and continuous improvement throughout schools.

The government helped to improve still other aspects of education during the 1980s and 1990s. Legislation in 1984 created the National Talented Teachers' Fellowship Program, a Federal Merit Scholarship Program, and a Leadership in Educational Administration Program. The Fund for the Improvement and Reform of Schools and Teaching (1988) authorized grants to help at-risk children meet higher standards, strengthen school leadership and teaching, encourage school systems to refocus priorities, and provide entry-year assistance to new teachers and administrators. Title X of the Improving America's Schools Act of 1994

established the Fund for the Improvement of Education to promote systemic reform, including research and development related to standards and assessments, strategies for student learning, involvement of parents and the community, professional development, public school choice and site-based decision making, transitions from preschool to school or from school to work, and the integration of education with health and social services.

Several initiatives have encouraged districts to explore the benefits of increasing instructional contact time. The 1991 National Commission on a Longer School Year Act created a panel to study the relationship between time and learning. The Improving America's Schools Act of 1994 provided seed money for schools to substantially increase the amount of time spent in academic programs and to promote flexibility in schools' schedules.

The government has assumed an active role in strengthening facilities, instructional materials and technologies, and local improvement efforts through diverse funding strategies, including both categorical and block grants. Because of its interest in school improvement, the federal government sponsors research and development activities.

Advancing Research and Development

The federal government serves an important role in stimulating, financing, and disseminating the findings of educational research and development. Through grant competitions and financial incentives it establishes priorities for researchers in school systems, state and federal agencies, universities, and independent institutes. Sponsored research furthers our understanding of current practice and innovations in teaching and learning, governance and decision making, school organization and leadership, finance and program equity, uses of technologies, and alternative assessments.

When it was established in 1867, the mission of the U.S. Department of Education was limited to collecting and diffusing statistics that "show the condition and progress of education." Its redesignation as the Office of Education within the Department of the Interior one year later minimized its presence until 1953. Then the Office of Education became a division of the Department of Health, Education, and Welfare. The federal interest in educational research and development, particularly that related to science and math curricula, increased in the late 1950s with NDEA and the subsequent creation of the National Science Foundation.

This interest expanded in 1965 under ESEA Title IV. Title IV authorized the Office of Education to sponsor regional laboratories, university-based research and development centers, the Educational Resources and Information Clearinghouse (ERIC), and graduate training programs for educational research (Timpane, 1982). Other programs funded applied research and demonstration in vocational education, special education, bilingual education, and library services during the

1960s and 1970s. Field experiments were also initiated, including the planned-variation evaluation designs for Head Start and Follow Through programs, the Experimental Schools program, performance contracting to involve private agencies in instruction, and voucher plans to encourage choice among schools. The National Institute of Education (NIE) was established in 1972 to house federal research activities in an independent agency. The National Center for Education Statistics (NCES) was formed in 1974 to coordinate data collection and dissemination.

The Department of Education was created in 1979 to consolidate educational programs from several departments and agencies. It brought greater visibility. The Office of Educational Research and Improvement (OERI) within the department replaced NIE in coordinating and encouraging educational research and development. The reauthorization of OERI by the Educational Research, Development, Dissemination, and Improvement Act of 1994 established the National Educational Research Policy and Priorities Board. OERI's Office of Reform Assistance and Dissemination coordinates the efforts of the Educational Resources and Information Clearinghouses (ERIC), the twelve regional educational laboratories, the Teacher Research Dissemination Demonstration Program, the Goals 2000 Community Partnerships Program, and the National Diffusion Network. There are five National Institutes, which focus research, development, dissemination, and evaluation on the following: Student Achievement, Curriculum, and Assessment; Education of At-Risk Students; Educational Governance, Finance, Policy-Making and Management; Early Childhood Development and Education; and Postsecondary Education, Libraries, and Lifelong Education.

The various parts of the Improving America's Schools Act we discuss in this chapter refer to directions for research and development (R&D) in designing programs, identifying effective instructional strategies, and assessing performance in school reforms that enable all children to achieve the content and performance standards of states. Title XIII provided financial incentives to stimulate this R&D and created a national technical assistance and dissemination system. A network of fifteen comprehensive regional assistance centers coordinated activities with the Education Department's regional offices, the regional educational laboratories, and the state literacy and vocational resource centers. The National Diffusion Network (NDN) also received grants to carry out state-based outreach, consultation, training, and dissemination programs and to help districts implement exemplary practices.

Many of these legislative actions extended the federal role in setting the direction for educational reform. Other enactments confronted more basic concerns about children's health and safety.

Improving Nutrition, Health, and Safety

Government subsidies and programs to address students' physical well-being have ranged from support of food service to asbestos removal. The school lunch program under the Department of Agriculture responded in part to concerns with children's nutrition. But it also uses oversupplies of farm produce. The 1935 Agricultural Adjustment Act made commodities available for school lunches. And the National School Lunch Act of 1946 provided funds on an equalized percentage matching basis to support facilities and purchase food.

This effort was expanded with the School Milk Program Act of 1954. And a major commitment to the welfare of children of low-income families coincided in the 1960s with educational programs for disadvantaged children. The 1966 Child Nutrition Act delivered breakfast. And the government subsidized lunches for eligible students. Children in families that qualify for the federal food stamp or Aid to Families with Dependent Children (AFDC) programs are eligible for free lunches. Other low-income students qualify for reduced-price lunches if family incomes are within 185 percent of the nonfarm-income poverty guidelines established by the Office of Management and Budget. One-third of all students, including 43 percent of students in central cities and 33 percent of students in rural communities, qualified for free or reduced-price lunches in 1993–1994 (National Center for Education Statistics, 1995a, Table 365).

A proposal to dramatically alter school lunch and breakfast programs in 1995 suggested replacing the categorical entitlement funding with a broader family-nutrition block grant tied to welfare reform. States would spend at least 80 percent of funds to subsidize meals for low-income students. But the remainder could support other social services, including child care. This proposal illustrates the tension that exists between advocates of a strong federal role in overseeing nutrition and eligibility standards through categorical aid and those who would broaden the scope of the program through block grants to permit flexibility in directing funds to nonfood and nonschool programs.

The fight against drug abuse brought grants for disseminating information, developing community education programs, and training teachers under the Alcohol and Drug Abuse Education Act of 1970. Two years later, the Drug Abuse Office and Treatment Act established a special action office for abuse prevention to coordinate planning and policy, created a National Advisory Council for Drug Abuse Prevention, and provided community assistance grants to support mental health centers for treating and rehabilitating drug abusers. The 1986 Drug-Free Schools and Communities Act financed drug abuse education and prevention in coordination with community efforts. And the Omnibus Drug Abuse Prevention Act authorized teacher training and early childhood education programs. Schools and law enforcement agencies gained additional funding under the Anti-Drug Education and the Drug Abuse Resistance Education (DARE) Acts of 1990.

Diverse federal initiatives have raised awareness of the environment and the effects of air quality on children. The Environmental Education Acts of 1970 and 1990 provided funds for teacher training and community education, disseminated information about ecology, and created a federal Office of Environmental Education. The 1980 Asbestos School Hazard Protection and Control Act mandated inspections and plans for eliminating or containing the material, and loans assisted districts' efforts to remove hazardous asbestos. The Pro-Children Act of 1994 prohibited smoking in facilities housing child care, elementary and secondary schools, and library services for children.

The increased incidence of youth violence in schools and society prompted legislation. The Gun-Free Schools Act of 1993 required states and districts that received financial assistance under ESEA to develop policies mandating a full-year expulsion for possessing firearms on school property. District superintendents were empowered to modify this provision on a case-by-case basis. The Safe and Drug-Free Schools and Communities Act of 1994 (ESEA Title IV) supported programs that involve parents and community resources in preventing violence and the illegal use of alcohol, drugs, and tobacco.

These wide-ranging legislative actions that finance school lunches, drug abuse prevention, asbestos removal, and safe school programs promote the nation's interest in maintaining a healthy and secure populace.

In toto these seven themes capture the primary thrusts of federal involvement in public education. The many categorical programs illustrate the willingness of Congress and the executive agencies to influence and control specific dimensions of education. Those programs that receive the greatest attention of educators and the critics of federal intervention are those that receive the most funds.

TRENDS IN FEDERAL FINANCIAL ASSISTANCE

Federal spending for elementary and secondary education amounted to $35.2 billion in 1995. This represents only a portion of the federal government's commitment to education. The total of $73.8 billion spent on education broadly included another $17.7 billion for postsecondary education programs, $15.9 billion for research conducted primarily in universities, and $5.0 billion for various other education programs (National Center for Educational Statistics, 1995b, p. 6). Educational

spending accounted for about 4.5 percent of the total government budget of over $1.5 trillion.

The federal share of elementary and secondary school funds is much less than that of either state or local governments. The general trend for federal involvement, presented graphically in Figure 3.1, was one of growth until early in the 1980s. The federal share increased from under 1 percent in the 1930s to about 3 percent in 1950. At that time the government supported school lunches, vocational education, Indian education, and impacted districts. By 1970 the federal contribution had grown to 8.0 percent of total funds for schools, with support for a wide range of programs enacted in the 1960s to enlarge educational opportunities. The maximum percentage aided by federal funds was 9.8 percent of all revenue for education. This occurred in 1980 after a decade of program expansions, including education for children with disabilities. By 1987 the federal share had declined to 6.2 percent of the total as state and local revenue increased. By 1993–1994, the percentage of total elementary and secondary education revenue provided by the federal government reached 7.2 percent (see Table 8.1).

The average percentage of federal support varies among states and school districts. In 1993–1994, eight states received over 10 percent of their revenue from this source. The highest amount was 16.6 percent, in Mississippi. Federal revenue accounted for under 5 percent in six states. The lowest amount was 2.8 percent, in New Hampshire. States were affected to varying degrees by the decline in federal aid (an average of 14 percent after adjustments for inflation) between 1980 and 1990, with "four out of every five states experiencing double digit percentage reductions" (Verstegen, 1994, p. 109). There were declines of over 40 percent in Arizona, Michigan, and North Carolina. Colorado, New York, and Vermont each increased over 40 percent.

Trends in allocations for the primary elementary and secondary programs over the past three decades are ranked by 1995 outlays in Table 10.2. The table reveals priorities in federal education policy. School lunch and milk programs accounted

TABLE 10.2. Federal Outlays for Selected Education Programs for Fiscal Years 1965 to 1995 (in millions)

Program	1965	1975	1985	1990	1995[a]
School lunch and milk[b]	$623	$1,884	$4,135	$5,529	$8,169
Grants for disadvantaged	—	1,874	4,207	4,494	7,032
Education for handicapped	14	151	1,018	1,617	3,612
Head Start	96	404	1,075	1,448	3,534
School improvement programs	72	700	526	1,189	1,589
Vocational and adult education	132	655	658	1,307	1,544
Impact aid	350	619	647	816	1,088
Indian Education (BIA and JOM)[c]	108	163	203	218	436
Bilingual education	—	93	158	189	251
Education reform—Goals 2000	—	—	—	—	179

Note: Dollar amounts are not adjusted for inflation.
[a]Estimated.
[b]Includes other Department of Agriculture subsidies for school food services.
[c]Bureau of Indian Affairs and Johnson-O'Malley Act.
SOURCE: National Center for Education Statistics (1995b). *Federal Support for Education: Fiscal Years 1980 to 1995.* Washington, DC: U.S. Government Printing Office, Table C.

for the largest amount of federal aid to schools in every year except 1985. This support rose from $623 million to over $8 billion between 1965 and 1995 (reported allocations are not adjusted for inflation). Because of the rapidly growing interest in the education of economically disadvantaged students, funds for school lunches were eclipsed in 1985 by financial assistance for this interest. Enactment of ESEA in 1965 brought nearly $2 billion in aid by 1975 and steady growth to $7.0 billion, including Title I funds, in 1995. Assistance for the education of children with disabilities amounted to $14 million in 1965. This commitment increased to $1 billion by 1985 following the 1975 passage of P. L. 94–142. It increased to $3.6 billion in 1995. The financing of Head Start programs had exceeded that for exceptional students through 1985. It grew from $96 million in 1965 to $3.5 billion in 1995. Allocations for school improvement efforts amounted to a relatively large $72 million in 1965. But increases have lagged behind those for the other programs illustrated since 1975. Funding for school improvement programs, including Chapter 2 (renamed ESEA Title VI in 1994), amounted to $1.6 billion in 1995.

Sponsorship of vocational education has been an important federal activity since the early 1990s. But its relative importance in school finance

slipped between 1965 and 1995 as more of these funds were directed toward community colleges. Financial support for vocational and adult education programs grew from $132 million in 1965 to $1.5 billion in 1995. Payments to federally impacted school districts were second only to those for school lunch programs in 1965. But this aid increased more slowly than other programs, from $350 million to $1.1 billion by 1994. There was no support for bilingual education before the 1968 Bilingual Education Act. Program funds rose from $93 million in 1975 to $251 million in 1995. Passage of the Goals 2000: Educate America Act, despite the relatively low funding of $179 million in 1995, encouraged participating states and localities to design programs around national goals.

These trends reveal changes over the years not only in the national interests served but also in views of the appropriate role of the federal government in influencing educational policies and practices. Aside from continuous assistance for school lunch programs, the federal government has shifted its priorities from the defense-related impact aid and vocational education programs prior to the 1960s to equalizing educational opportunities through the 1970s. Although it diminished its support for many smaller categorical programs, Congress empowered states and localities to determine priorities for school improvement efforts through a limited block grant approach beginning in the 1980s. The newly enacted and reauthorized programs of the mid-1990s may increase the federal government's presence in financing and guiding education. But a number of economic and political considerations may constrain the federal government.

FUTURE FEDERAL FINANCIAL ASSISTANCE: AGREEING ON AN APPROPRIATE ROLE WHILE REDUCING THE DEFICIT

We have looked at an array of federal programs. Each of them might be defended as serving the national interest and furthering the general welfare. However, the scope of the federal government's sponsorship of specific programs and its general influence over local and state education has been challenged as an unwarranted intrusion into an area that is constitutionally reserved to the states or the people under the Tenth Amendment. Whereas the federal courts and Congress may have legitimate roles in guarding the access of minority groups to education and ensuring equitable treatment under the Fourteenth Amendment, the government's role in encouraging states to define standards and upgrade curricula is constitutionally more tenuous. We discussed this concern about the appropriate degree of control over education and its resources in the context of taxation in Chapter 4 and of transfer payments in Chapter 8. We raise it now as it relates to the role of the federal government in public education.

Wise (1979) analyzed the expanded presence of the federal government during the 1960s and 1970s. He concluded that the promulgation of educational policies, often in response to judicial decisions, resulted in the bureaucratization of education at all levels. He characterized the impacts on local control, institutional autonomy, and classroom activities as legislated learning and hyperrationalization:

As other and higher levels of government seek to promote equity and increase productivity in our educational institutions, important educational decisions are increasingly being determined centrally. The discretion of local officials is limited by their need to conform to policy decisions. . . . To the extent that this process causes more bureaucratic overlay without attaining the intended policy objectives, it results in what I shall call the *hyperrationalization of the schools.* (pp. 47–48; emphasis in the original)

This hyperrationalization appeared in the excessive prescription of inputs and outcomes of schools and in the proliferation of educational programs seen as solutions to the problems facing society. Policy makers and educators rationalized the need for new policies and programs. They assumed that beneficial outcomes would result from programs that differed from preexisting educational practices: "School systems that presumably previously did not have the knowledge or will or wherewithal to teach such children would, with federal funds, discover the knowledge, gain the will, and acquire the wherewithal to solve the problem" (Wise, 1979, p. 68).

Concerns about the increasingly centralized control of educational policy without demonstrable results brought deregulation and the block grant strategy early in the 1980s. The overriding issue of educational quality in relation to economic competitiveness was raised in the 1983 report of the National Commission on Excellence in Education, entitled *A Nation at Risk.* The issue remained unresolved as the presidency changed. Early in the Clinton presidency, Congress issued a challenge to states to upgrade public education in concert with the National Education Goals. This legislation, the Goals 2000: Educate America Act, was designed to give participating states flexibility to reform education following content, performance, and opportunity-to-learn standards. The intent of Congress was to assist states in bottom-up reform. But several states (including Montana, New Hampshire, and Virginia) declined to apply for grants. They cited fears of federal intrusion in education (Sharpe, 1995).

The balance of power in Congress shifted in 1995. A number of political and economic factors were expected to impede the initiatives passed one year earlier. The Republican House majority included within its Contract with America pledges to consider a balanced-budget amendment, a presidential line-item veto, term limits for members of Congress, and tax reductions. The federal role in education in the remainder of the twentieth century may be severely constrained under several of these proposals and the shift in Congressional priorities.

The agenda of the Republican-controlled Congress would repeal or amend categorical programs, combine federal programs within block grants, create a voucher program to enable nonsectarian private schools to educate low-income students, restrict Congress from enacting unfunded mandates, and limit the power of (or abolish) the Department of Education. These strategies would effectively alter the federal presence in defining educational goals and standards and in shaping curriculum and assessments. This redirection of priorities and the diminished federal presence may strengthen local, state, and parental control of education. It may also encourage national associations to assume leadership in framing the debate over educational goals, content standards, and curriculum (e.g., National Teachers of Mathematics). It may also encourage foundations to support organizations' efforts to reform education (e.g., Carnegie sponsorship of the National Board for Professional Teaching Standards).

The movement to limit federal control over education coincides with the nation's frustration with the budget deficit. It has been nearly three decades since the federal fiscal year ended with a surplus ($3.2 billion in 1969). The size of the deficit (i.e., expenditures in excess of revenue) has increased with minor fluctuations each subsequent year. The deficit amounted to $73.8 billion in 1980. It peaked at $290.4 billion in 1992, and it was estimated to be $192.5 billion in 1995 (ACIR, 1994, p.

23; U.S. Department of Commerce, 1995, Table 517). The nation's debt ceiling has been raised over these years (amounting to $4.96 trillion in 1995) to permit the government to borrow additional funds to cover the deficit.

Attempts to control this growing deficit have had little success; nor have proposals for a Constitutional Amendment to require a balanced budget. The 1985 Balanced Budget and Emergency Deficit Control Act, commonly referred as the Gramm-Rudman-Hollings legislation after its sponsors, established declining maximum levels of annual deficits and called for automatic reductions when deficit projections exceeded target amounts. Deficit reduction legislation in 1993 imposed caps on federal spending and dictated that there would be no growth in expenditures for defense, international affairs, and discretionary domestic programs through 1998. Rescissions in the fiscal year (FY) 1995 budget amounted to $574 million. They included the elimination of six education programs (Johnston, 1995). Further reductions were expected in FY 1996. The goal of balancing the federal budget somewhat conflicts with the continuing call for income tax relief.

As a result of deficit reduction, tax relief, and the view of federalism that prefers a smaller role for government, the momentum that codified the National Education Goals and would encourage states and school systems toward systemic reform may be slowed in the future. Those who question whether there should be a federal role in education at all will continue to press for reduced funding and block grants. They will also press for the elimination of the Department of Education, because it symbolizes the government's presence in an area they see as properly within the purview of the states. They insist that a more appropriate role for the federal government would be to enable and coordinate the efforts of states and schools rather than to design and closely monitor educational programs.

This view of federalism would limit the government's presence. In contrast, others fear that severe reductions in funding and eased regulations will diminish the capacities of many districts to meet pressing needs. Politically powerless groups, including the growing numbers of poor children, may once again be denied adequate and appropriate education. Proposals for tax relief are criticized for easing burdens on wealthy taxpayers. Block grant flexibility is welcomed by some state-level policy makers. Others, however, express concern that education and social programs will suffer as less money is spread more thinly to compensate for reductions in funding in other areas of state government. Thus, many educators and advocates for children with special learning needs look to the president and Congress for the leadership and funds to help states and localities deliver this important public service.

As this text went to press, the 1996 election was one year away. A division emerged in the Republican coalition that had once been solidly behind the Contract with America. Business leaders and conservative Christian groups found ideological differences. They generally agreed about weakening the federal role in favor of returning authority to states and localities and encouraging choice among schools. But they were divided about national standards, outcome-based education, and integrated services for children. Despite these disagreements, there was seemingly a strong call for changed relationships between federal, state, and local levels of government. The presidential and congressional elections would once again reflect the public's preferences about federalism and would shape future education policy accordingly.

SUMMARY

Intergovernmental transfers of funds are important strategies available to state and federal governments. These grants-in-aid permit local school personnel to expand educational programs in ways that satisfy broader societal goals. The general welfare clause enables Congress to assume a role in influencing educational priorities in a way consistent with the national interest. Seven themes derived from the history of federal education legislation capture the government's rationale for intervention and financial assistance: strengthening national productivity; improving defense and international relations; promoting educational reform; expanding educational opportunities; upgrading facilities, technologies, and programs; advancing research and development; and improving nutrition, health, and safety.

The preference for categorical funding of particular programs to achieve objectives was clearly established in vocational education programs early in the century and with enactment of NDEA late in the 1950s. It was not until Congress passed ESEA in 1965, however, that federal aid for educational programs was sufficiently large to significantly affect school offerings. This and other categorical aid programs influenced school priorities and created a new local-state-federal partnership. Federal funds peaked as a percentage of total revenue for schools in 1980–1981. At that time nearly 10 percent of all funds came from national resources. The 1980s brought reduced federal involvement, deregulation, and decentralization. A limited block grant strategy consolidated many former categorical aid programs. And the proportion of funds derived from the federal level declined.

Congress embarked on a more active federal role in education in the mid-1990s. The America 2000: Educate America Act codified the eight National Education Goals. And the Improving America's Schools Act reauthorized the major federal programs that provide financial assistance to states and districts under ESEA. This latter legislation provided the direction and funds to enable participating states to design challenging content and performance standards for *all* students. These acts called for greater integration of programs, effective strategies for using technologies in instruction, continuous professional development, alternative assessments linked with the standards, and upgraded educational outcomes.

The directions posed in these acts, along with reforms initiated within many states, promise change in education at all levels. However, the federal presence in directing and supporting systemic reforms may be diminished in the short term as congressional priorities shift in response to demands for deficit reduction, tax relief, and a balanced federal budget. The pace of reform, at least that encouraged by the federal government, may be slowed without financial incentives. The federal government's role may become one of facilitation and leadership, much as it was when the federal government provided only a limited proportion of all school revenue.

The federated governance structure for education in the United States places control primarily at the state level. It is only when national interests and prevailing views of federalism favor assistance that the federal government exercises a stronger role in public education. Maintaining a proper balance among governance levels is a continuing dilemma of intergovernmental transfers: To what degree should state and federal governments intervene to shape school policies and practices without jeopardizing the benefits of local control?

In Part III we discussed state and federal leadership and fiscal programs that supplement those available at the local level. In Part IV we look at the decisions being made about the use of these resources.

NOTE

1. The notation indicates that this legislation was the 382nd Public Law of the 103rd session of Congress.

ACTIVITIES

1. Interview school district personnel who oversee federal programs. What opportunities are present for students and teachers, and what challenges do they foresee (or did they have to overcome) in redesigning programs to meet the expectations outlined in the Goals 2000: Educate America Act and the Improving America's Schools Act?

2. Debate the advantages and disadvantages of modifying the federal role in financing education with regard to (1) increasing the proportion of revenue derived from national sources (e.g., one-third of the total) to relieve local and state tax bases, (2) redistributing current appropriations to equalize state and local fiscal capacities, or (3) permitting schools or states to exercise total control over the use of aid.

3. In what ways should federal finance policy be influenced by research on the impacts of categorical or block grant aid programs in terms of such criteria as changes in educational achievement, educational opportunities, and economic productivity?

4. Investigate thoroughly the rationale given for passing one federal aid program, its eventual provisions, and compliance with accompanying regulations. Locate hearings in the *Congressional Record,* the statute in the *United States Code,* and implementing regulations in the *Code of Federal Regulations.* Interview a state or school system program coordinator to discuss experiences with compliance. What modifications in policy do you recommend?

5. Which of the seven general themes identified in this chapter, if any, should provide the primary rationale for federal intervention and fiscal policy in education during the coming decade? Which view of federalism should guide the nature of grants and implementing regulations to influence the degree to which this theme becomes important to state policy makers and school district personnel?

6. Modify Simulation 14.1, which is a site-based budget, to assist the management of federal funds. Rows should list specific projects and associated line items, and columns should record the previous year's expenditures as well as the current year's revenue, budget, expenditures to date, and the remaining balance for each line item.

REFERENCES

ACIR (Advisory Commission on Intergovernmental Relations). (1994). *Significant features of fiscal federalism, Volume 2: Revenues and expenditures.* Washington, DC: Advisory Commission on Intergovernmental Relations.

Aguilar v. *Felton,* 473 U.S. 402 (1985).

Anthony, P. G. (1994). The federal role in special education. *Educational Considerations, 22,* 30–35.

Benson, C. (1978). *The economics of public education* (3rd ed.). Dallas, TX: Houghton Mifflin.

Board of Education of Hendrick Hudson School District v. *Rowley,* 458 U.S. 176 (1982).

Brown v. *Board of Education,* 347 U.S. 483 (1954).

Carter, L. (1984). The sustaining effects study of compensatory and elementary education. *Educational Researcher, 13,* 4–13.

Center for Special Education Finance. (1994). IDEA reauthorization: Federal funding issues. *The CSEF Resource, 2,* Palo Alto, CA: Author.

Elazar, D. J. (1972). *American federalism: A view from the states* (2nd ed.). New York: Crowell.

Final fiscal 1996 appropriations. (1996). *Education Week, 15,* 22–23.

Florence County School District v. *Carter,* 114 S.Ct. 361 (1993).

Greer v. *Rome City School District,* 950 F.2d 688 (11th Cir. 1991).

Grubb, W. N., & Lazerson, M. (1974). Vocational education in American schooling: Historical perspectives. *Inequality in Education, 17,* 5–18.

Herrington, C., & Orland, M. E. (1992). Politics and federal aid to urban school systems: The case of Chapter 1. In J. Cibulka, R. Reed, & K. Wong (Eds.), *The politics of urban education in the United States* (pp. 167–180). Philadelphia, PA: Falmer.

Irving Independent School District v. *Tatro,* 468 U.S. 883 (1984).

Johnston, R. C. (1995). Clinton signs bill cutting $574 million from education in fiscal 95. *Education Week, 14,* p. 24.

Jones, T. H. (1985). *Introduction to school finance: Technique and social policy.* New York: Macmillan.

Kaestle, C. F., & Smith, M. S. (1982). The federal role in elementary and secondary education, 1940–1980. *Harvard Educational Review, 52,* 384–408.

Lau v. *Nichols,* 414 U.S. 563 (1974).

LeTendre, M. J. (1991). The continuing evolution of a federal role in compensatory education. *Educational Evaluation and Policy Analysis, 13,* 328–334.

Levin, H. M. (1982). Federal grants and educational equity. *Harvard Educational Review, 52,* 444–459.

Magers, D. A. (1977). Two tests of equity under impact aid Public Law 81–874. *Journal of Education Finance, 3,* 124–128.

Mills v. *Board of Education,* 348 F. Supp. 866 (D.D.C., 1972).

Millsap, M., Turnbull, B., Moss, M., Brigham, N., Gamse, B., & Marks, E. (1992). *The Chapter 1 implementation study: Interim report.* Washington, DC: Office of Policy and Planning, U.S. Department of Education.

Milstein, M. M. (1976). *Impact and response: Federal aid and state education agencies.* New York: Teachers College Press.

Mort, P. R., & Reusser, W. C. (1941). *Public school finance: Its background, structure, and operation.* New York: McGraw-Hill.

National Assessment of Educational Progress. (1981). *Has Title I improved education for disadvantaged students? Evidence from three national assessments of reading.* Denver, CO: Education Commission of the States (ERIC ED 201 995).

National Assessment of Vocational Education. (1994). *Final Report to Congress.* Washington, DC: Author.

National Association of State Boards of Education. (1992). *Winners all: A call for inclusive schools.* Alexandria, VA: Author.

National Center for Education Statistics (NCES). (1995a). *Digest of Education Statistics: 1995.* Washington, DC: U.S. Government Printing Office.

National Center for Education Statistics (NCES). (1995b). *Federal $upport for Education: Fiscal years 1980 to 1995.* Washington, DC: U.S. Government Printing Office.

National Commission on Excellence in Education. (1983). *A nation at risk: The imperative for educational reform.* Washington, DC: U.S. Government Printing Office.

Parrish, T. B., & Verstegen, D. A. (1994). The current federal role in special education funding. *Educational Considerations, 22,* 36–39.

Plunkett, V. R. L. (1991). The states' role in improving compensatory education: Analysis of current trends and suggestions for the future. *Educational Evaluation and Policy Analysis, 13,* 339–344.

Porter, A. (1995). The uses and misuses of opportunity-to-learn standards. *Educational Researcher, 24,* 21–27.

Riddle, W. (1995). Education for the disadvantaged: Analysis of 1994 ESEA Title I allocation formula amendments. *Journal of Education Finance, 21,* 217–235.

Ryan, F. A. (1982). The federal role in American Indian education. *Harvard Educational Review, 52,* 423–430.

Sacramento City Unified School District v. *Rachel H., 14* F.3d 1398 (9th Cir. 1994).

Sage, D. D., & Burrello, L. C. (1994). *Leadership in educational reform: An administrator's guide to changes in special education.* Baltimore, MD: Brookes.

Schorr, L. B., & Schorr, D. (1988). *Within our reach: Breaking the cycle of disadvantage.* New York: Doubleday.

Sharpe, R. (1995). Federal education law becomes hot target of wary conservatives. *The Wall Street Journal, 133* (42), p. 1.

Sherman, J. D. (1992). Special Issue: Review of school finance equalization under Section 5(d) (2) of P.L. 81–874, the impact aid program. *Journal of Education Finance, 18,* 1–17.

Skrtic, T. M. (1991). The special education paradox: Equity as the way to excellence. *Harvard Educational Review, 61,* 148–205.

Smith, M. S., & O'Day, J. (1991). Systemic school reform. In S. H. Fuhrman & B. Malen (Eds.), *The politics of curriculum and testing* (pp. 233–268). New York: Falmer.

Stecher, B. M., Hanser, L., Hallmark, B., Rahn, M., Levesque, K., Hoachlander, G., Emanuel, D., & Klein, S. (1994). *Improving Perkins II performance measures and standards: Lessons learned from early implementers in four states.* Santa Monica, CA: RAND.

Stickney, B. D., & Plunkett, V. (1983). Closing the gap: A historical perspective on the effectiveness of compensatory education. *Phi Delta Kappan, 65,* 287–290.

Stonehill, R. M., & Anderson, J. I. (1982). *An evaluation of ESEA Title I—Program operation and educational effects: A report to Congress.* Washington, DC: U.S. Department of Education.

Timar, T. (1994). Federal education policy and practice: Building organizational capacity through Chapter 1. *Educational Evaluation and Policy Analysis, 16,* 51–66.

Timothy W. v. *Rochester, New Hampshire, School District,* 875 F.2d 954 (1st Cir., 1989).

Timpane, M. P. (1982). Federal progress in educational research. *Harvard Educational Review, 52,* 540–548.

U.S. Department of Commerce, Bureau of the Census. (1995). *Statistical abstract of the United States, 1995.* Washington, DC: U.S. Government Printing Office.

U.S. General Accounting Office. (1993). *Chapter 1 accountability: Greater focus on program goals needed.* Washington, DC: Author.

U.S. General Accounting Office. (1994a). *Early childhood programs: Multiple programs and overlapping target groups.* Washington, DC: Author.

U.S. General Accounting Office. (1994b). *Education finance: Extent of federal funding in state education agencies.* Washington, DC: Author.

Verstegen, D. A. (1987). Two-hundred years of federalism: A perspective on national fiscal policy in education. *Journal of Education Finance, 12,* 516–548.

Verstegen, D. A. (1992). Economic and demographic dimensions of national education policy. In J. G. Ward & P. Anthony (Eds.). *Who pays for student diversity? Population changes and educational policy* (pp. 71–96). Newbury Park, CA: Corwin Press.

Verstegen, D. A. (1994). Efficiency and equity in the provision and reform of American schooling. *Journal of Education Finance, 20,* 107–131.

Verstegen, D. A. (1995). *Consolidated special education funding and services: A federal perspective.* Palo Alto, CA: Center for Special Education Finance.

Wayson, W. (1975). ESEA: Decennial views of the revolution. Part II. The negative side. *Phi Delta Kappan, 57,* 151–156.

Wise, A. E. (1979). *Legislated learning: The bureaucratization of the American classroom.* Berkeley, CA: University of California Press.

Zobrest v. *Catalina Foothills School District,* 113 S.Ct. 2462 (1993).

PART FOUR

Evaluating Current School Finance Policies

In earlier parts of this text, we presented the nature of school finance policy making, governance structures, and sources of revenue currently made available to schools. This section evaluates school finance policies and uses of resources in relation to the values presented in Chapter 2 and included in Figure 1.8: equality/equity, fraternity, liberty, efficiency, and economic growth.

We consider goals of equality, liberty, and efficiency in Chapter 11 as they have been weighed in judicial decisions. We examine the role courts play in assessing states' finance plans in relation to constitutional guarantees of equal protection and the requirement that educational delivery systems be uniform, thorough, and efficient. Chapter 12 discusses issues of equity (and through equity, fraternity) from the perspectives of policy analysts. Chapter 13 focuses on education finance policies designed to further the goals of efficiency and economic growth. Many believe these conditions engender incentives that encourage greater efficiency (and effectiveness) in educational systems.

CHAPTER 11

Judicial Reviews of School Finance Policy within Evolving Standards of Equality, Efficiency, and Adequacy

Primary Issues Explored in This Chapter:

- *The role of the courts:* What is the role of the judiciary in relation to that of state legislatures in determining school finance policy and in deriving standards under which challenges to those policies are resolved?
- *Standards for judicial reviews:* How have the standards of equality, efficiency, and adequacy been derived from the equal protection clauses of federal and state constitutions and from education articles that call for state legislatures to provide public education?
- *Applying standards to state school finance statutes:* What decisions of federal and state

courts have interpreted whether statutory mechanisms to allocate funds to school systems violate state constitutional provisions—either upholding plaintiffs' claims of inequitable, inefficient, or inadequate allocations or reinforcing states' abilities to fashion policies that further the goal of local control over education despite the resulting inequities?

- *Future litigation and finance policy development:* Are there implications for the development of school finance policy, given the expanding role of the courts?

The judicial branch of government is the primary formal mechanism society has established for arbitrating the differences that arise among its members. Federal and state courts have heard challenges to school finance systems in a majority of states since 1968. Plaintiffs typically argue that state aid formulas fail to allocate funds in a manner that enables property-poor districts to deliver educational opportunities similar to those available in wealthier school systems, as directed by constitutional provisions calling for equality, adequacy, or efficiency. Defendant states contend that finance policies must tolerate disparities in spending that result from the legitimate goal of promoting local control of education, in concert with the value of liberty. In the resolution of this conflict, courts define standards of equality, adequacy, and efficiency against which school finance policy should be judged. They determine whether constitutional provisions permit variations in revenue or expenditure.

We begin this chapter by contrasting judicial decision making by the courts with the policy making role of legislatures.

THE NATURE OF JUDICIAL REVIEWS AND LEGISLATIVE RESPONSES

Judicial and legislative branches of government perform different functions in the formation of school finance policy. The state and federal aid programs we discussed in earlier chapters illustrate the products of legislative processes. The judiciary may be asked to test whether these fiscal policies satisfy societal expectations as expressed in federal or state constitutions. This external review by the courts provides a check on legislative actions. And judicial reviews often stimulate legislatures to alter school finance policy. Courts do not, however, initiate the subjects of judicial review. Instead they react to the conflicts and problems posed by members of society.

Defining the concept of equality of educational opportunity has been a national concern since the Supreme Court pronounced in *Brown* v. *Board of Education* (1954): "Such an opportunity, where the state has undertaken to provide it, is a right which must be made available to all on equal terms." Federal courts extended the reach of this principle through numerous decisions affecting other student groups. Congress responded with such legislation as Title VI of the Civil Rights Act of 1964 (race and ethnicity), Title IX of the Education Amendments of 1972 (gender), and Section 504 of the Vocational Rehabilitation Act of 1973 (disabilities). These congressional actions were intended to ease inequities in educational opportunities (see Chapter 10).

State policy changes to address inequities through school finance structures did not immediately follow the lead of the courts or Congress. Despite pressures to reform finance policy to enable districts to improve educational opportunities for students in property-poor districts, state legislatures were slow to respond. The nature of state legislative processes, characterized by "give-and-take, negotiation, and compromise" (Fuhrman 1978, p. 160), inhibited voluntary reform of states' finance structures. Even when state legislatures considered reform measures in response to pres-sure brought by impending and actual court reviews, the movement to equalize tax bases slowed as consensus-building processes shaped the actual content of policies adopted.

Judicial decision making is based on constitutional principles. It differs from legislative policy development in several ways. First, as representatives of the school districts to be affected by the proposed school finance reforms, legislators are often more concerned with protecting their school systems' interests than with promoting equity to improve all children's education. Second, redistributions of monies through finance policy changes affect nearly all districts. It is therefore essential that a majority benefit from reforms to ensure the necessary votes. Equity goals are often sacrificed because bargaining and compromise are essential so that legislators can find solutions. The solutions are premised on which districts gain and which ones lose. Finally, the resolution of school finance issues is not isolated from other concerns, such as improving highways and prisons, placed before legislators. Lining up votes on a finance proposal depends on positions taken by legislators on prior and subsequent policy issues. It does not depend solely on the merits of equalizing educational opportunities (Brown & Elmore, 1982).

Legislative processes give primary attention to school districts' interests and to consensus building. Challenges to states' school finance policies heard in the courts, on the other hand, are more likely to consider inequities in the treatment of pupils. For example, decisions subsequent to *Brown* determined that absolute equality of resources did not give all children, particularly those with disabilities (*Mills* v. *Board of Education,* 1972) or limited English-language proficiency (*Lau* v. *Nichols,* 1974), equality of educational opportunity. These decisions present the principle of *equity* as a broader concept than that of equality. They imply that *children have a right of access to instructional programs appropriate to their individual learning potentials and needs.* Equalizing educational opportunities does not necessarily mean equal dollars per pupil or equal dollars per program. In these contexts equity requires additional funds for programs that serve legitimate educational needs.

Many of the early challenges to school finance systems explored the concept of equality as it related to disparities in wealth and the impacts of those disparities on districts' abilities to adequately finance educational programs. As this standard evolved, the courts addressed the question of whether the goal of equity, as it is defined above, can be possible if there are inadequate resources to permit a thorough or efficient provision of services.

JUDICIAL REVIEWS OF SCHOOL FINANCE STRUCTURES

The law of equity permits individuals or groups to seek judicial redress when they believe that principles of fairness are not served by government policies and actions. Plaintiffs in school finance suits contend that variations in spending resulting from finance structures, as well from inadequate resources, violate federal or state constitutional provisions.

Standards for Reviews

Judicial reviews of school finance policies rely on standards created within the equal protection clauses of federal and state constitutions and by the language of education articles within state constitutions. These statements convey society's expectations for legislative policy development. Underwood and Sparkman (1991) discuss more fully the following primary approaches to school finance litigation and differences in standards for reviews by federal and state courts.

Equality. Under equal protection guarantees, people in similar situations must be treated the same. In other words, differential treatment will be upheld only if the classifications created by the law are not arbitrary or irrational. When it is alleged

that varying treatment of children or taxpayers is contrary to equal protection guarantees, a three-tiered test determines the reasonableness of the classification: strict scrutiny, sliding scale, and rational basis (Underwood, 1989, pp. 415–416).

If a state uses a "suspect classification" (e.g., race, national origin) to differentiate people for treatment, or if a fundamental right (e.g., voting privileges) is involved, courts employ a strict level of review to determine violations of equal protection. To be upheld under the *strict scrutiny test,* the classification must be necessary to further a compelling state objective. Moreover, the state must show that there are no less-intrusive methods to achieve that goal. A later section cites decisions of state courts that interpreted education as a fundamental right. The courts also found that the heavy reliance on property taxation created a suspect classification based on wealth. In this instance, the quality of students' educational opportunities in different districts may rely too heavily on the wealth of localities, rather than depending for primary or complete support on the wealth of the state as a whole. This argument was instrumental in judicial decisions in which finance plans were found to violate a standard of fiscal neutrality. The courts directed the state legislatures to equalize property tax capacities among school districts.

The judiciary exercises greater restraint when neither a suspect classification nor a fundamental right is involved. The less-stringent *rational basis test* asks whether the classification is related to a legitimate state objective. If it is, it is upheld. The U.S. Supreme Court and many state courts adopted this test as the appropriate one for judging school finance challenges. These courts reasoned that finance structures are constitutional if the policies are reasonably related to states' interests in promoting and preserving local control of education. This is the case even when there are program or fiscal disparities among districts. Underwood and Verstegen (1990) observed that a court could find a finance system unconstitutional under this test if it determined that the resulting disparities did not further a legitimate state interest: "A court could just as easily see the purpose of the funding formula to be the equitable provision of education to all children of the state, in which case disparities in funding would not be rationally related to this purpose" (p. 188).

Finally, a midlevel scrutiny requires that classifications be substantially related to an important state interest. This *sliding-scale test* has been used in cases where courts are reluctant to declare a particular class (e.g., based on gender) suspect, yet want to afford some protection (Underwood, 1989). The United States Supreme Court employed this test in its ruling that Texas could not deny free public education to the children of illegal aliens (*Plyler* v. *Doe,* 1982). Under this test, a court recognizing a wealth-based classification within the equal protection clause may still sustain the plan if it serves an important state objective. For example, the North Dakota Supreme Court adopted this level of scrutiny in its decision to uphold the finance plan: "our state equal protection cases also require consideration of the intermediate level of heightened scrutiny for important substantive rights" (*Bismarck* v. *State,* 1994, at 257).

The determination of which test is appropriate under equal protection clauses of federal or state constitutions shapes the nature of a state's burden in defending the school finance structure.

Uniformity, Efficiency, and Adequacy.
In addition to or coincident with challenges based on equal protection clauses are judicial reviews that focus on education clauses within state constitutions (McUsic, 1991; Sparkman, 1994). These articles require state legislatures to establish and maintain public education for school-age children and specify that the provision of education, among other things, be "uniform," "adequate," "thorough" and/or "efficient."

Individuals and groups challenging the legality of states' finance plans that permit revenue or expenditure disparities contend that this constitutional language requires access to equal, efficient,

and adequate educational opportunities. States respond that education articles require only the provision of a minimum or basic education program. They say that these mandates are satisfied even when finance or program disparities are permitted. Very often these conflicts center on the amount of discrepancy tolerated. This is particularly true when the lowest-spending district is unable to deliver the minimum expectations under state program standards. In such cases courts may be more concerned with the adequacy of resources, programs, and services necessary to attain desired results (i.e., efficiency) than with fiscal equity (Sparkman, 1983, p. 99).

McCarthy (1981) contrasted these standards of equity and adequacy. Whereas equity connotes fair and unbiased treatment, including unequal treatment for individuals who are not similarly situated, adequacy "connotes the state of being sufficient for a particular purpose" (p. 316). Wood (1995) stated the adequacy argument in terms of the degree to which local and state expenditures correlate with a lack of programmatic opportunity. Using this strategy, plaintiffs must demonstrate a substantive impact on students in terms of such factors as the "inability to update texts, hire teachers with advanced degrees, purchase school buses on a periodic basis, offer equal special education programs as compared with other school districts, support special education aid cuts, and so on" (p. 33).

Determinations of adequacy rest on standards of sufficiency and may be quite unrelated to the standard of equity. For example, schools within a state may provide equitable educational opportunities for students, but they may fall short of a standard of adequacy. Conversely, resources for educational programs may be declared at least minimally adequate in all schools. But there may be large disparities among districts. It is difficult to achieve an "efficient" or "thorough" educational system if these standards of equity and adequacy are not met through school finance policies.

Judicial reviews of school finance plans illustrate that courts differ in their interpretations of equality, efficiency, and adequacy standards as they test whether finance statutes violate equal protection clauses and state constitutional provisions for public education.

The Search for Appropriate Standards in Federal and State Court Reviews

Table 11.1 lists states in which challenges to school finance systems have been heard in federal and state courts between 1968 and 1995. Included in this table are the decisions of the highest level of court to have reviewed states' finance policies. It should be noted that recent lower court opinions may be heard by an appellate court in the future.

Judicial reviews upheld state support mechanisms in twenty-eight states, including previous invalidations in Minnesota and Wisconsin. Two decisions upholding states' finance structures sustained highly equalized distributions (Kansas and the 1995 Texas decision). The U.S. Supreme Court heard challenges in Texas (1973) and Mississippi (1986). The other twenty-two cases were litigated in the highest state court. Finance systems were found to be unconstitutional in eighteen states. Four of them (Arizona, Montana, Texas, and Washington) had successfully defended structures in earlier challenges. The highest state court issued rulings in fifteen of these states. The history of judicial decisions sustaining or overturning finance plans illustrates differences in interpretations of similar constitutional language and evolving judicial standards. This evolution began in the federal courts. Here plaintiffs expressed concerns about spending disparities and pupils' educational needs.

Two early reviews by federal district courts upheld the Illinois (*McInnis v. Shapiro,* 1968) and Virginia (*Burruss v. Wilkerson,* 1969) school finance systems and deferred to state legislatures as the appropriate forum for policy development. For example, the *Burruss* court discussed educational needs and the limited abilities of courts to fashion appropriate remedies to ease inequities: "the courts have neither the knowledge, nor the means, nor the

power to tailor the public moneys to fit the varying needs of these students throughout the state. We can only see to it that the outlays on one group are not invidiously greater or less than that of another" (at 574).

Alexander (1982, p. 201) noted that these cases failed because the courts lacked standards against which to assess disparities in educational opportunities resulting from variations in property wealth. He attributed the absence of "discoverable and manageable standards" (*McInnis* at 335) to a lack of definitiveness in the measurement of fiscal capacity and to an inability to determine the educational standards needed to compensate disadvantaged children. Although these early cases were not successful for plaintiffs, their arguments urged a concept of equity under which state funds would erase fiscal disparities among school districts and correct variations in educational needs.

In 1971, the California Supreme Court applied a narrower and more measurable standard (i.e., the equality of dollar inputs) than the educational needs standard employed in the earlier *McInnis* and *Burruss* challenges. A standard of equality that is measured by the needs of pupils conveys the attributes of a full-blown concept of equity (Alexander, 1982, p. 202). However, it is complex constitutionally. The question posed in *Serrano* v. *Priest* (1971) was expressed more simply in terms of discrimination on the basis of wealth. It permitted a successful challenge to the Fourteenth Amendment's equal protection clause. The state court was asked to examine inequities in expenditures that result from differing property wealth and tax burdens among school systems. The court declared that education was a fundamental right and that school district wealth created a suspect classification. It placed the burden on the state to demonstrate a compelling reason for maintaining such inequities. Because the state failed this strict scrutiny test, its finance plan was declared unconstitutional.

In saying that an operational definition of equality was satisfied by the legislature, the court adopted the concept of fiscal neutrality as defined

TABLE 11.1. Reviews of School Finance Systems by Federal and State Courts

| Year | Finance Systems Upheld | | Finance Systems Invalidated | |
	Federal Review	State Review	Federal Review	State Review
1968	Illinois			
1969	Virginia			
1971			Minnesota	California[a]
1973	Texas[a]	Arizona[a]		New Jersey[a]
		Michigan		
1974		Montana[a]		
		Washington[a]		
1975		Idaho[a]		
1976		Oregon[a]		Wisconsin[a]
1977				Connecticut[a]
1978				Washington[a]
1979		Ohio[a]		
		Pennsylvania[a]		
1980				Wyoming[a]
1981		Georgia[a]		
1982		Colorado[a]		
		New York[a]		
1983		Maryland[a]		Arkansas[a]
1984		Michigan		West Virginia[a]
1986	Mississippi[a]			
1987	Louisiana	North Carolina		
		Oklahoma[a]		
1988		South Carolina[a]		
1989		Wisconsin[a]		Kentucky[a]
				Montana[a]
				Texas[a]
1990				New Jersey[a]
1991		Oregon[a]		
1993		Minnesota[a]		Alabama
		Nebraska[a]		Massachusetts[a]
		North Dakota[a]		Missouri
				New Hampshire[a]
				Tennessee[a]
1994		Illinois		Arizona[a]
		Kansas[a]		Arkansas
		South Dakota		New Jersey[a]
		Virginia[a]		
1995		Maine[a]		Wyoming[a]
		New York[a]		
		Ohio		
		Oregon		
		Rhode Island[a]		
		Texas[a]		

[a]Case decided by United States Supreme Court or the highest state court.

by Coons, Clune, and Sugarman (1970): "The quality of public education may not be a function of wealth other than the wealth of the state as a whole" (p. 2). Following several judicial rejections of revised statutes over the next decade, a state appellate court declared in 1986 that the finance system "had reduced wealth-related disparities to insignificance and that remaining differences were justified by legitimate state interests" (*Serrano* v. *Priest,* 1986, at 616). The maximum disparity in spending among districts exceeded the original target of $100 per pupil. The court was satisfied, however, by a somewhat larger range (adjusted for inflation) within which spending fell for nearly all (93 percent) of the state's pupils. Ward (1990) observed that fiscal neutrality had been achieved "largely because of a major event outside of the education policy making arena, namely Proposition 13, which did change some institutional factors and created equality of spending in a way that the system itself could not" (p. 244; refer also to tax limitation initiatives in Chapter 6).

Using the rationale developed in *Serrano,* federal district courts held education to be a fundamental right. They found that the Minnesota and Texas finance plans violated the equal protection clause of the Fourteenth Amendment. Denying a motion to dismiss the Minnesota case, the court deferred to the state legislature to develop a satisfactory finance system (*VanDusartz* v. *Hatfield,* 1971). The lower court decision was not appealed.

The Texas decision is the only school finance dispute to be fully reviewed by the United States Supreme Court (*San Antonio* v. *Rodriguez,* 1973). In this five : four reversal of the district court, the high court's interpretation of students' interests in education differed from that of the *Serrano* review. The court stated that a child's right to a public education was not explicitly or implicitly guaranteed under the federal constitution. In its decision in *Brown,* the Supreme Court recognized that education is "perhaps the most important function of state and local governments." However, in the review of Texas school finance, the court noted that education's importance as a state and local govern-

ment service did not elevate it to the level of other fundamental interests protected at the federal level. The state's finance system enabled children to obtain at least a minimal education, and there was no absolute denial of this opportunity. In the words of the court, "no charge fairly could be made that the system fails to provide each child with an opportunity to acquire the basic skills necessary for the enjoyment of the right of speech and of full participation in the political process" (at 36–37).

Furthermore, the rights of a suspect class were not endangered under the Texas school finance formula because poor people did not cluster in districts having low property values. Without a fundamental right to an education or a finding that the finance system operated to the disadvantage of a suspect class, the court needed only to apply the less-stringent rational basis test. The court concluded that there was a rational relationship between the funding plan and the state's interest in preserving local control over schools.

The same rationale was followed in a federal district court's dismissal of a complaint about one aspect of the Mississippi finance system. The complaint claimed that distributions of state money to compensate for lost revenue from railroad lands was inequitable. The Supreme Court's review found that the court's action was proper since "such differential funding was not unconstitutional" under *Rodriguez* (*Papasan* v. *Allain,* 1986, at 275). Another challenge of a state finance system in the federal courts is discussed below. In it the Fifth Circuit upheld the Louisiana school finance statute in 1987. It is clear that a major consequence of the Supreme Court's holding in *Rodriguez* was to shift the attention of the finance reform movement from federal to state courts to resolve conflicts over state statutes and constitutional provisions.

In the sections that follow, we review state court decisions that invalidated or upheld finance systems. We do this to illustrate the evolution of judicial standards. In some cases the standard of equality, as this concept is derived from constitutional mandates for equal protection, has been the focus of judicial scrutiny. In other reviews, standards of uniformity, efficiency, and adequacy have framed the arguments. These concepts are derived from articles in state constitutions that create legislative duties to provide public schooling.

State Court Decisions Upholding Plaintiffs' Claims

Many of the early state court decisions invalidating finance plans (see Table 11.1) followed the *Serrano* rationale on the basis of equal protection clauses. Recent cases, however, have relied both on this rationale and on standards of efficiency and adequacy derived from education articles. Courts have often found that statutes permitting large resource or spending disparities among districts deny guarantees of equal protection under state constitutions. For example, the Supreme Court of Connecticut held that "the right to education is so basic and fundamental that any infringement of that right must be strictly scrutinized" (*Horton* v. *Meskill*, 1977, at 373). It declared the finance plan unconstitutional because it did not correct for large disparities in communities' abilities to finance education. The court discussed the relationship between resource availability and educational programs and concluded that disparities in expenditures were closely related to disparities in educational opportunities. The legislature responded with a finance plan that the court found satisfied its mandate to equalize resources (*Horton* v. *Meskill*, 1985).

The Wyoming Supreme Court also determined that wealth constituted a suspect class and education was a fundamental right when it struck down the state's finance plan (*Washakie* v. *Herschler*, 1980; *Campbell* v. *State*, 1995). Most recently, the court concluded that disparities created by a recapture provision, an optional mill levy, financing of capital outlay, and the distribution formula itself were not justified. It thus found the finance structure to be unconstitutional under both the state's equal protection clause and education article.

The Arkansas Supreme Court applied the less-stringent rational basis test to invalidate the finance statute (*Dupree* v. *Alma*, 1983). The court found that disparities in revenue served no legitimate state interest: "Such a system only promotes greater opportunities for the advantaged while diminishing the opportunities for the disadvantaged" (at 93). The court declared that only wealthy districts benefit from local control over finance decisions. In its analysis it gave the goal of equalizing educational opportunities greater weight than preserving local control. In 1994, a lower court concluded that the state did not provide a "general, suitable and efficient" educational system as was constitutionally required. It said the finance statute that passed as part of a reform package resulted in even greater disparities (Miller, 1994).

Like *Serrano*, these rulings focused on resource inequities and relied on equality as a standard for review. Other state courts have considered arguments that inadequate funds are available to meet pupils' needs in all districts. This adequacy standard is explicit in or derived from education articles in state constitutions. It was addressed in a series of New Jersey decisions. One month after *Rodriguez*, the state Supreme Court examined the finance plan in relation to the state constitutional requirement that the legislature ensure a "thorough and efficient" educational system. It defined this standard to include "that educational opportunity which is needed in the contemporary setting to equip a child for his role as a citizen and as a competitor in the labor market" (*Robinson* v. *Cahill*, 1973, at 295). The court's finding of unconstitutionality ushered in a lengthy period of legislative actions and judicial reviews to find an acceptable formula that would ensure both equity and adequacy.

In 1976 the court enjoined the State Department of Education from allocating aid to school districts. It thus effectively closed schools until the legislature adopted a state income tax to fuel a new finance plan. A subsequent review of progress by a lower court found disparities had "steadily widened" because of the "proclivity of the equalization formula . . . to perpetuate inequalities" (*Abbott* v. *Burke*, 1984, at 1284). The Quality Education Act of 1990 equalized tax burdens and distributed state aid more equitably. Later revisions, however, lowered the base foundation level and diverted funds from the equalization plan to provide property tax relief (Goertz, 1993).

The New Jersey Supreme Court expanded its demand for adequacy when it held the finance system to be unconstitutional only as it affected selected poor urban districts. Education in these settings was "tragically inadequate" in virtually all areas of curricula, personnel, and facilities. There were unacceptable dropout and failure rates (*Abbott* v. *Burke,* 1990, at 395–401). Three aspects of the Quality Education Act were found to limit the effectiveness of equalization aid: Basing aid on the previous year's budget perpetuated past inequities. Restricting annual increases in budgets by a specified percentage inhibited the leveling up of lower-spending districts. And paying categorical aid for special programs regardless of local wealth worked against a provision that cut off equalization aid to high-spending districts. The court ordered the act to be amended to assure funding in poorer cities at the level of property-rich districts, to guarantee state funds so spending would not depend on the ability of local school districts to tax, and to provide a level of funding that is "adequate to provide for the special educational needs of these poorer urban districts in order to redress their extreme disadvantages" (at 363). Clune (1992, p. 748) observed that this decision was unique in interpreting the state constitution as requiring a substantial amount of compensatory aid. In 1994, the court mandated unequal spending and supplemental programs and services to improve education in relation to the standard of adequacy noted previously. That is, the state had to prepare all students as citizens and competitors in the labor market (*Abbott* v. *Burke,* 1994).

Two challenges in the state of Washington also reflect the shift in courts' reviews from an equity to an adequacy standard. The Washington Supreme Court in its initial review (*Northshore* v. *Kinnear,* 1974) determined that disparities in expenditures reflecting district wealth did not violate equal protection guarantees and that children were not denied access to minimum educational

opportunities. The court reached a different conclusion several years later. It declared education was a fundamental constitutional right: "It is the paramount duty of the state to make ample provision for the education of all children residing in its borders" (*Seattle* v. *State,* 1978, at 84). LaMorte (1989) commented that the court treated the definition of an "acceptable basic education" as a prerequisite to other educational reforms. A finding that the equity standard is satisfied would depend on a prior finding that the finance plan meets the standard of adequacy. Underwood (1994, p. 145) also noted a changed judicial view of equity: "More courts are beginning to see the purpose of the funding formula to be the equitable provision of education to *all* children of the state. When this posture is taken, the court concludes that funding disparities do nothing to advance this state interest."

When legislatures enact finance plans to meet equity goals, the resulting redistributions of property tax revenue under recapture provisions (see Chapter 8) may in turn be challenged. In Montana, a newly enacted equalization plan was tested because it called for wealthy districts to remit to the state property tax proceeds in excess of the foundation funding level (*Woodahl* v. *Straub,* 1974). The state Supreme Court upheld this recapture feature. It rejected claims that the state-imposed tax discriminated against taxpayers in counties that paid more than was required to support their local schools. The court analyzed the policy under the equal protection mandate. It reasoned that the general property tax constituted "a rational method of providing for basic public education required by the Constitution" (at 777). The Wisconsin Supreme Court reached the opposite conclusion in invalidating a similar recapture provision. It held that the redistribution of property tax revenue violated the constitutional mandate for uniform taxation (*Buse* v. *Smith,* 1976). These decisions illustrate that judicial reviews under different constitutional provisions (equal protection and uniformity) may result in seemingly conflicting holdings.

Subsequent reviews of these two states' finance plans also differed. The Wisconsin Supreme Court upheld the finance structure. It found that equal opportunity for an education is a fundamental right under the state's equal protection guarantee (*Kukor* v. *Grover,* 1989). However, this right did not require absolute equality in financing. Disparities were rationally based on the goal of preserving local control even if certain districts lacked funds to provide special programs to meet all children's needs. In addition, the uniformity provision of the education article assured only that state resources would enable the "character" of instruction to be as uniform as practicable. "Character" refers to standards for curriculum, teacher certification, and numbers of school days.

In contrast, the Montana Supreme Court found that its finance plan violated the constitutional guarantee of equal educational opportunity as a result of the "failure to adequately fund the Foundation Program, forcing an excessive reliance on permissive and voted levies" (*Helena* v. *Montana,* 1989, at 690). Unequalized levies and other revenue generated 35 percent of school budgets in 1985–1986. This compared with less than 20 percent in 1950, when the state provided proportionally more revenue. In determining adequacy, the court accepted state accreditation standards as establishing a "minimum upon which quality education must be built." In response to this ruling, the legislature revised the finance system to require all districts to spend between 80 percent and 100 percent of an optimum funding level, to limit their ability to override this level, and to equalize school building funds (Fulton, 1994). These two states' decisions differed in their outcomes. But both tolerated supplemental levies only when the base foundation programs financed adequate educational programs.

A number of decisions since 1984 greatly expanded the role of the courts in finding not only school finance systems but also educational governance structures and policies to be unconstitutional. The first of these was in West Virginia. It was rooted in an earlier decision. The earlier decision had declared that the requirement of a "thorough and efficient system of free schools" made education a fundamental right (*Pauley* v. *Kelly,* 1979). But the state's highest court, the Supreme

Court of Appeals, did not declare the finance plan to be unconstitutional. Rather it directed a lower court to determine whether there was a compelling state interest to justify any discriminatory classification created by the finance plan. More significantly, the court desired an assessment of whether the failure of the school system to meet "high quality" educational standards resulted from "inefficiency and failure to follow existing school statutes" or an inadequacy of the existing system (at 878).

The trial court then examined existing levels of resources available to districts in relation to standards for facilities, curriculum, personnel, and materials and equipment. In 1982, the court found all county school systems, including those with the greatest wealth, to be deficient. It invalidated both the educational system and financing mechanisms as not meeting the thorough and efficient standard. The court ordered the development of a master plan for the "constitutional composition, operation and financing" of the state's educational system. The Supreme Court of Appeals subsequently affirmed the State Board of Education's "duty to ensure delivery and maintenance of a thorough and efficient" educational system as embodied in the "Master Plan for Public Education" (*Pauley* v. *Bailey,* 1984). Camp and Thompson (1988) noted that the judiciary had assumed a new role in delineating for the state the characteristics of a quality education: "Though the court was not trying to usurp the power of the legislature, it needed standards to evaluate the system" (p. 237).

Several other state courts pronounced that systemic reform was essential. They followed the lead of this West Virginia decision. In 1989 the Kentucky Supreme Court declared that the "*entire system* of common schools is unconstitutional" (*Rose* v. *Council,* 1989). The court placed an absolute duty on the legislature to "re-create, re-establish" the entire system of public education:

> This decision applies to the statutes creating, implementing and financing the *system* and to all regulations, etc. pertaining thereto. This decision covers the creation of local school

districts, school boards, and the Kentucky Department of Education to the Minimum Foundation Program and Power Equalization Program. It covers school construction and maintenance, teacher certification—the whole gamut of the common school system in Kentucky. (at 215)

The court specified seven competency areas, including academic content and vocational skills, that would enable students to compete in academics or the labor market. Other state courts have noted these guidelines in defining an adequate education. The court left responsibility to the General Assembly to devise a plan to ensure adequate funding. But it specified clearly that any plan relying on real and personal property taxation would have to assess all property at 100 percent of market value and would necessitate uniform tax rates throughout the state. The far-reaching Kentucky Education Reform Act (KERA) of 1990 promoted systemic reform of governance, curricula, and finance. It created a foundation formula and restricted local supplemental levies, raised the minimum mill rate for district contributions and increased the state sales tax, rewarded school improvement efforts, and reorganized the state education department (Adams, 1993).

Responding to a legislative request to clarify a lower court's decision that effectively struck down Alabama's entire public educational system, the state Supreme Court required the legislature to comply with the order to "provide school children with substantially equitable and adequate educational opportunities" (*Opinion of the Justices,* 1993, at 165). The lower court had determined that the right to education was fundamental. It stated: "the Alabama system of public schools fails to provide plaintiffs the equal protection of the laws under *any* standard of equal protection review." The court also found that the state failed to provide appropriate and special services to children with disabilities and rejected arguments favoring local control.

Two decades after the United States Supreme Court's landmark ruling in *Rodriguez,* the Texas Supreme Court ordered drastic measures to force wealthy districts to share tax bases or consolidate with poorer districts. In 1989, the court agreed unanimously that the finance system violated the constitution's mandate that there be "support and maintenance of an efficient system of public free schools" to foster a general diffusion of knowledge (*Edgewood* v. *Kirby,* 1989). In defining the term efficient, the court stated: "'Efficient' conveys the meaning of effective or productive . . . results with little waste" (at 395). The extreme range in abilities of districts (from $20,000 to $14 million in property valuation per pupil) enabled the wealthiest districts to exert far less effort. Because state allocations did not sufficiently equalize spending and resulting educational opportunities, the state Supreme Court concluded that the finance plan did not meet the constitutional mandate: "The present system . . . provides not for a diffusion that is general, but for one that is limited and unbalanced. The resultant inequalities are thus directly contrary to the constitutional vision of efficiency" (at 396).

The court required full fiscal neutrality with a "direct and close correlation between a district's tax effort and the educational resources available to it" (at 397). An efficient system does not preclude the ability of communities to exercise local control over the education of their children: "It requires only that the funds available for education be distributed equitably and evenly" (at 398). The court noted the "implicit link" between goals of equality and efficiency. An efficient system recognizes the value of local control in decisions about the amount of spending and equalizes districts' abilities to finance desired educational programs.

Legislation was passed to satisfy the court's holding. It permitted unequalized local supplements in wealthy districts and did not include the very wealthiest districts in the equalization plan. The court found this practice to insulate the most concentrated property wealth from being taxed to support schools. It required a plan to be in place to enable "substantial equality" among all districts before funds could be appropriated for public education (*Edgewood* v. *Kirby,* 1991). Although affirming its position in 1992, the court concluded that the local property tax of the revised finance system was in reality a statewide ad valorem tax which was levied in violation of the constitution (*Carrollton-Farmers* v. *Edgewood,* 1992). The legislature responded with a plan to have 101 wealthy districts lower their property wealth to $280,000 per pupil and transfer the excess to poorer districts through one of five options: merging tax bases, consolidating districts, transferring property, contracting to educate nonresident students, or writing a check to the state. Clark (1995) reported that 97 districts either purchased attendance credits from the state or supported nonresident students' education. Only one district detached property and none opted to create a regional taxing jurisdiction. Despite a previous state Supreme Court decision that prohibited the state from requiring districts to divert property taxes to another district (*Love* v. *Dallas,* 1931), this plan including these forms of recapture passed scrutiny in 1995. The state Supreme Court held that the restructured finance system did not violate the constitution: The State's reliance on local ad valorem taxes does not amount to the imposition of a state tax (*Edgewood* v. *Meno,* 1995, at 472).

An adequacy standard provided the basis for 1993 holdings in Tennessee, New Hampshire, and Massachusetts. The Tennessee Supreme Court noted that reliance on local funds inhibited poor districts' abilities to meet program standards of the 1990 state Master Plan. It said that there was "a direct correlation between dollars expended and the quality of education a student receives" (*Tennessee Small School Systems* v. *McWherter,* 1993, at 144). The court applied the rational basis test and found the system violated the state's equal protection clause because it was unjust and without any reasonable basis. Determining that the issues were "quality and equality of education" rather than equality of funding, the court concluded that the finance system was unconstitutional. Responding to a contention that substantially equal funding would "squelch innovation," the court noted: "Given the very nature of education, an adequate system, by all reasonable standards, would include innovative and progressive features and programs"

(at 156). Despite this tolerance for disparities, in 1995 the Supreme Court ordered the state to equalize teachers' salaries as a part of its finance reform. The Tennessee General Assembly then amended the Education Improvement Act to ease salary inequities (Whitney & Crampton, 1995, p. 7).

Holding that "a free public education is at the very least an important, substantive right," the New Hampshire court found its school finance system to be unconstitutional (*Claremont* v. *Governor,* 1993, at 1381). The court concluded that the constitution's encouragement of literature clause imposed a duty to "provide constitutionally adequate education" and to "guarantee adequate funding." The Massachusetts Supreme Judicial Court, the state's highest court, similarly ruled its finance system was inadequate and unconstitutional (*McDuffy* v. *Secretary,* 1993). Such deficiencies as inadequate teaching of the basics, neglected libraries, poor-quality teachers, the lack of curriculum development, the lack of predictable funding, administrative reduction, and inadequate guidance counseling contributed to the holding. These cases demonstrate that plaintiffs can prevail under a "deprivation theory" (Underwood, 1994, p. 147) if there is evidence that students do not receive the minimum level of education necessary to prepare them for responsibilities of citizenship.

A number of the judicial reviews cited referred to the condition of facilities as one of a number of indicators of adequacy or educational quality. The recent Texas Supreme Court decision upholding the revised finance plan noted continuing deficiencies and the state's duty to provide all districts with substantially equal access to the operations and facilities funding necessary for a general diffusion of knowledge (*Edgewood* v. *Meno,* 1995, at 47). Crampton and Whitney (1995) stated that Arizona was the first state whose school funding system was declared unconstitutional solely on the basis of the condition of school facilities. The state Supreme Court observed that the quality of facilities is directly proportional to the value of districts' real property (*Roosevelt* v. *Bishop,* 1994). The court noted disparities in the condition and age of buildings and the quality of classrooms and instructional equipment: "Some districts have schoolhouses that are unsafe, unhealthy, and in violation of building, fire, and safety codes" (at 808). School facilities in poorer districts in nearly all states have such deficiencies, yet few funding formulas provide equalization of local property tax revenue devoted to capital outlay (see Chapter 7).

Recent litigation favoring plaintiffs in lower courts mirrored the rationales presented in this discussion of state supreme court decisions (see Hickrod, Lenz, & Minorini, 1995). For example, a Missouri circuit court judge found that the state's finance plan was unconstitutional, inadequate, and "simply irrational" (Hatley & Shaw, 1994). Excessive disparities among districts resulted from the inadequate funding of the foundation plan, excessive reliance on local property taxes, and a "prior year" provision that capped increases in state aid in districts experiencing enrollment growth while maintaining funding for declining enrollment districts. The U.S. District Court overseeing the Kansas City desegregation plan had previously ordered the school district to levy taxes to finance remedies. The remedies included magnet schools, education-improvement programs, salary increases, and construction of new schools. The United States Supreme Court upheld this order (*Missouri* v. *Jenkins,* 1990). The district court subsequently ordered the state to finance a large share of the costs of these remedies. The U.S. Court of Appeals concluded in 1994 that the district court could appropriately tie the level and duration of funding of the Kansas City desegregation program to a goal that students would "achieve, at least, at the state average on Missouri's minimum competency tests" (Hatley & Shaw, 1994). However, the U.S. Supreme Court reversed this order. It held that substandard achievement by African American students was not a sufficient basis for requiring the state to pay desegregation costs (*Missouri* v. *Jenkins,* 1995). The court held that the district court had exceeded its authority in ordering improvements in salaries, facilities, and educational programs at state expense. It is not clear what impact this holding will have on an appeal of the prior state lower court's decision that the finance plan itself is unconstitutional.

In contrast to these rulings in favor of plaintiffs are judicial reviews in which states have successfully defended challenges to finance structures.

State and Federal Court Decisions Upholding Finance Systems

In decisions referred to previously, federal courts upheld school support mechanisms in Illinois, Virginia, Texas, Mississippi, and Louisiana. Subsequent to the United States Supreme Court's finding that there is no federal right to an education and that school finance is a matter for resolution within states *(Rodriguez),* a number of state courts have validated finance plans (see Table 11.1). Like those decisions overturning finance systems, the following holdings illustrate an evolution in standards based on equal protection clauses and education articles of state constitutions.

With a few exceptions, state courts upholding finance policies declared that education was not a fundamental interest when asked to determine whether the finance statute satisfied equal protection clauses. Justices determined that the appropriate level of scrutiny was the less-stringent rational basis test. Under this test states have successfully demonstrated a nexus between the finance plan and such goals as promoting local control over educational decisions. In 1973, the Arizona Supreme Court declared that children are guaranteed a basic right to education under the state constitution. But it did not invalidate the finance system under the strict scrutiny analysis. Instead, the court determined that the educational finance system need be "only rational, reasonable, and neither discriminatory nor capricious" (*Shofstall* v. *Hollins,* 1973, at 592). But the court reached a different conclusion in the 1994 *Roosevelt* decision cited above.

The varied arguments used in upholding finance systems are evident in the following decisions. The Michigan plan was challenged under both federal and state equal protection clauses. The court rejected the Fourteenth Amendment claim following the *Rodriguez* rationale. Holding that the state's equal protection clause did not guarantee equality of educational opportunity, nor did it forbid disparities in wealth, the court sustained the finance system, including local property tax levies used to supplement state funds (*Milliken* v. *Green,* 1973). The state Court of Appeals reiterated in 1984 that education was not a fundamental interest and that there was no denial of equal protection under the state constitution arising from unequal spending among districts (*East Jackson* v. *State,* 1984). Subsequently, the Supreme Court overturned a recapture provision, since it violated a constitutional amendment that required the state to fully fund any new program imposed on school districts (*Schmidt* v. *Michigan,* 1992). The Supreme Court of Pennsylvania examined the finance plan under the education article and concluded that, in absence of any legal harm to a district or injury to a student, there was no violation of the constitutional provision of a thorough and efficient educational system (*Danson* v. *Casey,* 1979). Recently, the Nebraska Supreme Court recognized disparities among districts. But it concluded that the plaintiffs had failed to show how the differences in spending affected educational quality or resulted in inadequate schooling or funding. Because the plaintiffs failed to state a cause of action, the court ruled that the trial court should have dismissed the lawsuit (*Gould* v. *Orr,* 1993).

In addition to these diverse rationales there is the argument that districts have a strong interest in retaining local control over educational decisions. The Oregon Supreme Court determined that the uniformity standard applied to the general education system of education, not to specific funding disparities. Because the state finance plan enabled all districts to adequately finance at least a minimal level of education, the constitution was satisfied even when it permitted districts to exercise local control over decisions about spending for programs beyond the minimum level guaranteed by the state (*Olsen* v. *State,* 1976). The court's subsequent review rested on a finding that because voters had approved a constitutional amendment that created a "safety net" for districts in financial difficulty, they had demonstrated support for allowing disparities among districts. Districts could continue to operate under the prior year's levy without voter approval.

Thus the amendment tolerated disparities in taxation and levels of funding per pupil (*Coalition* v. *State,* 1991, at 120).

The Supreme Courts of Idaho, Ohio, and Maine also concluded that education was not a fundamental right and that their finance systems furthered the states' rational interests in maintaining local control (*Thompson* v. *Engleking,* 1975; *Board of Education* v. *Walter,* 1979; *School Administrative District* v. *Commissioner,* 1995). The Idaho court reviewed disparities in spending again in 1993. It concluded that the mandate of a uniform system in the education clause required only uniformity in curriculum, not uniformity in funding (*Idaho Schools* v. *Evans,* 1993). However, one year later the court remanded the case to the district court to determine whether the constitutional obligation of thoroughness was satisfied. The issue was adequacy. The court defined *adequacy* conservatively as satisfactorily meeting state accreditation standards. Following legislative actions to direct more aid to low-wealth districts and raise appropriations substantially, one-half of the forty plaintiff districts withdrew from the lawsuit (Sommerfeld, 1994).

The Colorado Supreme Court relied on the local control argument when it reversed a state district court ruling that had found that the state's finance system violated both the federal and the state constitutions. The lower court noted in 1979 that educational needs varied among school districts because of "geographical, ecological, social, and economic factors." It noted, however, that neither the legislature nor the Department of Education had taken steps to formulate a plan to satisfy the constitution's "thorough and uniform" mandate. In overturning this decision, the Supreme Court ruled that the state constitution did not establish education as a fundamental right, nor did it require the General Assembly to develop a centralized school finance system that would restrict schools to equal expenditures per pupil (*Lujan* v. *Colorado State Board of Education,* 1982). The court upheld the state's argument that the reliance on property taxation was rationally related to its objective of fostering local control over schools: "Taxation of local property has not only been the primary means of funding local education, but also of insuring that the local citizenry direct the business of providing public education in their school district" (at 1021).

Unlike the New Jersey holding in *Abbott* that called for remedies favoring poorer cities, earlier reviews in New York and Maryland rejected plaintiffs' desires to broaden the concept of equity to include the conditions of urban districts. In addition to poor school systems in New York that challenged disparities in spending, the state's four largest cities challenged distributions of state aid on two grounds. The plan relied on an "arbitrary and inadequate" measure of local capacity, since it did not consider the general poverty of residents nor cities' higher levels of municipal and educational services. And the aid formula "arbitrarily and inequitably grants less and inadequate aid per pupil" in urban districts having the highest concentrations of pupils requiring compensatory schooling services (*Levittown* v. *Nyquist*, 1978, at 611). Goertz (1981) described four urban conditions that the state had failed to consider: municipal overburden, in which higher tax efforts are required to finance extensive public services; educational overburden, given the expense of educating disproportionate numbers of high-cost students; cost differentials, due to higher prices often paid for goods and services; and absenteeism overburden, in which revenue is lost under formulas that determine aid by average daily attendance. Cities expressed concern that state aid formulas overstated their wealth and understated their educational needs, school tax effort, and higher costs.

The state's highest court, the Court of Appeals, determined that the finance system did not offend the equal protection clauses or the state constitution's education provision (*Levittown* v. *Nyquist*, 1982). Accepting the rational basis test as the appropriate level of review, the court held that the "preservation and promotion of local control of education" was a legitimate state interest to which the finance system was reasonably related. Disparities in spending and educational opportunities did not violate the education article because there was no reference to any requirement that the education

provided in districts "be equal or substantially equivalent." Finally, the court determined that "municipal dollars flow into cities' treasuries from sources other than simply real property taxes— sources similarly not available to non-municipal school districts" (at 649). Despite the various dimensions of overburden, the court reasoned that these alternative revenue sources countered the argument that the aid distribution plan denied equal protection.

A lower court subsequently found even greater disparities among New York's districts and unmet needs in poorer districts. It nevertheless followed the "philosophical underpinning" of *Levittown* in dismissing the complaint and stating that reform "*must* come" from either the high court or the legislature (*R.E.F.I.T.* v. *Cuomo*, 1991, at 976). The Court of Appeals ultimately upheld this reasoning, stating that the disparities "have not caused students in the poorer districts to receive less than a sound basic education" (*R.E.F.I.T.* v. *Cuomo*, 1995, at 553). The state's highest court sustained the Maryland finance plan. It used justification similar to that given in the *Levittown* decision (*Hornbeck* v. *Somerset*, 1983).

Judicial reviews in the late 1980s turned once again to the equal protection clause of the Fourteenth Amendment and to state equal protection guarantees when they examined the constitutionality of finance plans. The Oklahoma Supreme Court denied a challenge by thirty-eight school districts that claimed that the finance system violated both federal and state constitutions. The court declared that education was not a fundamental right and that "equal educational opportunity in the sense of equal expenditures per pupil" was not guaranteed by the state constitution (*Fair School Finance Council* v. *State*, 1987, at 1136). Because children received an adequate basic education, they were not denied equal protection, even though there were disparities in spending among districts. This court's reasoning mirrored the U.S. Supreme Court's arguments in the *Rodriguez* decision.

Relying on a similar rationale, the Fifth Circuit Court of Appeals upheld Louisiana's school finance plan. Two school districts brought suit under the federal statute (42 U.S.C. Section 1983) that protects individuals from state denial of federal constitutional rights and under the Fourteenth Amendment's equal protection clause. Once again reinforcing that school finance is a state issue, the court applied the rational basis test and upheld the constitutionality of the state plan as being rationally related to goals of "providing each child in each school district with certain basic educational necessities and of encouraging local governments to provide additional educational support on a local level, to the extent that they choose to and are financially able to do so" (*School Board* v. *Louisiana,* 1987, at 572). The South Carolina Supreme Court employed the rational basis test under the Fourteenth Amendment to uphold the state's finance system (*Richland County* v. *Campbell,* 1988).

The North Dakota Supreme Court relied on an "intermediate scrutiny analysis" after finding important substantive rights. It applied this test to confirm the trial court's declaration that "the distribution method, as a whole, is unconstitutional" (*Bismarck* v. *State,* 1993, at 257). The Supreme Court agreed that "the present educational funding system seriously discriminates against some students and significantly interferes with their right to equality of educational opportunities" (at 262). A three-judge majority voted to invalidate the plan. It survived, however, because the constitution required a vote by four justices to invalidate a statute. The court concluded that the education clause did not require absolute uniformity, only a basic level of education in all districts.

The concept of *adequacy* is derived from state constitutions' education articles. It was an issue in several state courts' decisions to uphold school finance statutes. The Georgia Supreme Court determined that the term "adequate education" in the constitution did not "impose an obligation on the legislature to equalize educational opportunities." Nor did it prevent local districts from raising funds to improve education (*McDaniel* v. *Thomas,* 1981). The Minnesota Supreme Court discussed adequacy once it had found education was a fundamental right and the finance system, including voter-

approved tax supplements and debt service levies, satisfied the strict scrutiny test (*Skeen* v. *State,* 1993). Disparities in overall funding were not objectionable, as long as the equalized base funding level provided an adequate education. Here *adequacy* "refers not to some minimal floor but to the measure of need that must be met" (at 318). The Virginia Supreme Court accepted state minimum standards as its definition of *adequacy* in its decision that declared education was a fundamental right and upheld the finance plan (*Reid Scott* v. *Virginia,* 1994). The court held that the constitution did not mandate "substantial equality of payments or programs," but guaranteed only that the State Board of Education's Standards of Quality be satisfied. Similarly, the Rhode Island Supreme Court upheld the state finance system despite inequities. It noted that money alone does not determine whether students receive an adequate education (*City of Pawtucket* v. *Sundlun,* 1995).

In Kansas, in a very different situation, plaintiffs challenged a funding formula that fully equalized local property taxation. The state district court had previously reasoned that the constitution's mandate that the state provide for education meant that it should also control and distribute all funds, including local property taxes, "regardless of current practices or concepts of local school control." The legislature revamped school finance policies in 1992 to equalize local wealth through a statewide property tax and a recapture provision that affected property taxes collected above a given level. The Kansas Supreme Court upheld the plan (*Unified School District* v. *Kansas,* 1994). This followed the ruling in Montana in 1974 upholding a recapture feature and the 1989 Texas decision that upheld the court order to institute full fiscal neutrality, including the redistribution of wealth between wealthy and poor districts. These decisions that urged states to redistribute wealth contrast with an Illinois court's conclusion: "[The] constitution does not contain a 'fiscal neutrality' mandate and we are reluctant to read one into the efficiency clause and so limit the options of the legislature in adopting a school finance scheme" (*Committee* v. *Edgar,* 1994).

Reviews of school finance policies by lower state courts have often come to similar conclusions. A lower court in North Carolina ruled that the constitution did not guarantee each student "a fundamental right to education substantially equal" to that provided in all other districts (*Britt* v. *State,* 1987). Disparities in spending were challenged in 1994 in South Dakota. But a lower court upheld the finance plan when it concluded that the constitution did not require all districts to levy the same tax rate nor to spend equal amounts per student (*Bezdichek* v. *South Dakota,* 1994). An Oregon court of appeals upheld the state's finance plan in 1995. It said that disparities in funding and educational opportunities did not violate the state constitution's requirement of a uniform public school system (*Withers* v. *State,* 1995). In 1995 a state appeals court reaffirmed the previously cited 1979 finding of the state Supreme Court that the Ohio finance system was constitutional. It noted that the school finance plan assured adequacy, since all districts have funding to meet the basic standards (Lindsay, 1995).

These decisions upholding state plans illustrate judicial tolerance for spending disparities, particularly when a base funding level enables districts to provide an adequate educational program. The promotion of local control of educational decisions is a legitimate state interest in designing school finance policy. This is a strategy that advances the value of liberty, as discussed in Chapter 1.

IMPLICATIONS FOR SCHOOL FINANCE POLICY

This history of federal and state court holdings reveals varying degrees of judicial activism and differing standards derived from constitutional provisions when courts settle conflicts over school finance structures. These judicial decisions and the consequent legislative actions suggest a number of implications for school finance policy development.

1. *Whereas judicial reviews may stimulate school finance reform, policy development remains a legislative prerogative.*

The judiciary performs important functions. It serves as a check on legislative actions, testing whether finance structures satisfy constitutional provisions. It also serves as a catalyst for policy change (Clune, 1992). Lehne (1978) describes the courts' role in advancing finance reform issues as an "agenda-setting" rather than a "decision-making" function. The courts specify which issues will be considered rather than act as institutions that develop concrete policies. The effect of the courts on policies is obscured. But there is some evidence that judicial decisions bring greater equalization, higher levels of funding for schools generally, and a shift in power to states (Henderson, 1991; Hickrod et al., 1992). In addition, courts motivate change, whether states are under direct orders to reform unconstitutional finance systems, have cases in process, or are threatened by the possibility of judicial reviews (Fuhrman, 1978, p. 162).

Courts are reluctant to overstep their role to assume that of policy maker. A tradition of judicial deference to legislative processes assures that a representative body develops policies involving taxation and allocations of public funds. The U.S. Supreme Court, for example, despite its conclusion in *Rodriguez* that the Texas finance system satisfied legal tests, commented that "ultimate solutions must come from the lawmakers and from the democratic pressures of those who elect them" (at 59). The Idaho Supreme Court refrained from convening "as a 'super-legislature,' legislating in a turbulent field of social, economic and political policy" (*Thompson* v. *Engelking,* 1975, at 640). The Minnesota Supreme Court noted: "the determination of education finance policy, in the absence of glaring disparities, must be a legislative decision because it involves balancing the competing interests of equality, efficiency, and limited local control" (*Skeen* v. *State,* 1993, at 318). However, courts do not avoid the issues because of this deference to policy makers. The Kentucky Supreme

Court stated: "To avoid deciding the case because of 'legislative discretion,' 'legislative function,' etc., would be a denigration of our own constitutional duty" (*Rose v. Council,* 1989, at 209).

Courts recognize that there are many constitutionally permissible methods of solving the complex problems of financing a statewide school system. Clune (1992) described the dilemmas faced by courts and their limited expertise in school finance policy:

> Equalization of tax resources proved to be a devilishly complicated exercise of intergovernmental management, both with respect to spending limits and recapture from the wealthiest districts. If equalization of spending seemed more manageable, what level of spending should occur (given different needs), and how should a court give guidance to a legislature? How could a court possibly play a manageable role in setting the amount of compensatory aid for poor children and the development of more effective spending policies? (p. 732)

Many state court decisions validated finance policies when states demonstrated convincingly that local control objectives fell within the prerogative of lawmakers, despite the resulting expenditure variations. In these states, advocates of reform must work within legislative processes rather than rely upon the judiciary to further goals of equity and adequacy. For example, the Michigan reviews upheld finance structures in 1973 and 1984. The legislature nevertheless adopted a new finance system in 1993 that abolished the local property tax as a primary support mechanism. Similarly, Colorado lawmakers enacted equalization formulas in 1988 and 1994. This was despite the 1982 *Lujan* holding that stressed the importance of local control in school finance policy.

Even in states in which courts declare finance plans invalid under constitutional mandates, they typically let the legislatures form remedies. However, moving the reform agenda from the courts to the legislative arena permits individual legislators that represent special interests of school districts to shape finance policies. When principled decision making yields to political interests and compromises, the goals of equalizing wealth and educational opportunities may be sacrificed. Brown and Elmore (1982) observed that fiscal limitations and social realities may result in school finance systems that are more "rational" by some standard but not necessarily more "equitable" by the criteria of reformers and courts. Plaintiffs may demonstrate successfully to a court that disparities in funds, facilities, and capabilities of personnel due to wealth variations among school systems inhibit students' access to similar educational opportunities. But this may be only the first step in a lengthy process of reforming school finance policy.

Conflicting interpretations of similar constitutional provisions illustrate that the courts do not have a clear role in school finance reform. Sparkman (1990) concluded:

> There is a profound sense that something is at work in the courts' deliberations that is not reported in the decisions. It is clear that the courts frequently struggle with the various issues and often express concern about the disparities, but they continue to defer to the legislature with the anticipation that the political process might rectify the problems. What seems to be missing in the decisions is a discussion of the basic sense of fairness. (p. 216)

This conjecture, and the lack of any definitive trend in decisions over the years, suggests that principled decision making by the courts may be as uncertain as the politicized decision making within legislatures.

2. *Standards of equity, adequacy, and efficiency continue to evolve, both to judge policy and to guide finance policy development.*

Constitutions provide broad statements concerning the protection of individual rights and the maintenance of public school systems. In the absence of firm criteria for judicial reviews and legislative action, there are many possible approaches to designing finance structures.

Early decisions evidenced a lack of an equity standard to relate the disparities in districts' wealth or pupils' needs to constitutional provisions. The standard of fiscal neutrality was clearly advanced by the *Serrano* court, and policy makers assumed the task of defining the structure and parameters for making educational finance a function of state wealth. The court was concerned with reducing the variation in resource inputs. During the next fifteen years, several judicial reviews of policy changes took place until the court's standard was satisfied. The standard of equity has changed substantially over the years from this emphasis on redistributions of revenue to broader concerns for the quality of students' education (Benson, 1991).

Such vague standards in education articles as *uniform, adequate, thorough,* and *efficient* have frustrated courts and legislatures. A number of state courts followed *Robinson*'s lead. They placed as great an emphasis on the adequacy of school resources and programs as on equality and fiscal neutrality. Once again, policy makers were given the task of determining what level of funding and what distribution plan would satisfy such standards as *adequate* and *thorough and efficient*. Whereas the earlier *McInnis* and *Burruss* plaintiffs were unable to protect children's educational needs under the United States Constitution, the *Robinson* court accepted the argument that education must be adequate to meet the state constitution's mandate. This initial determination of whether *thorough* and *efficient* standards were satisfied depended upon analyses of the degree to which finance structures resulted in unequal resource inputs.

The subsequent review of the revised New Jersey finance system extended the standard of adequacy. It required supplemental resources for programs and services to address urban students' needs and prepare them for citizenship and work responsibilities. Compensatory aid that raised spending above that of richer districts would satisfy

the constitutional requirement of "a certain level of education, that which equates with thorough and efficient; it is that level that *all* must attain; that is the *only* equality required by the Constitution" (*Abbott* v. *Burke,* 1990, at 369). Decisions in West Virginia, Kentucky, and Alabama also broadened the analyses to include the quality of educational programs and facilities in determining whether the level of revenue was adequate to enable all districts to provide a thorough or efficient educational opportunity. Underwood and Sparkman (1991) observed that recent decisions changed the focus from equity litigation tied to spending levels to the broader concept of meeting students' needs: "Focusing on the educational product and student needs changes the question from how much is spent to *how* it is spent and with what effects" (p. 543). Federal policy reforms in the mid 1990s (see Chapter 10) demanded that all children be enabled to meet challenging state academic content and performance standards. This will heighten the scrutiny of resource adequacy by courts and legislators in relation to the products of schooling.

In contrast, decisions such as those in Wisconsin, Virginia, and Minnesota endorsed plans that assured an adequate base foundation level to enable all districts' educational programs to meet minimum standards. These reviews tolerated policies, such as voter override provisions, that resulted in disparities in total available revenue and that advantaged wealthier districts in the name of local control. Clearly, courts differ in definitions of adequacy. And legislatures that are not under judicial directives to fully equalize resources are free to adopt plans that respect the desire of local districts to supplement base funding.

The adequacy of facilities has often been cited as an indicator of students' access to equal educational opportunities. Supreme courts in Arizona and Texas observed the correlation between the quality of facilities and local property wealth. They demanded the equalization of capital outlay funds in their holdings (Crampton & Whitney, 1995). The finance policies of few states encompass this costly aspect of educational delivery at an adequate level.

Statutes in most states would probably fail to meet constitutional tests, if we assume that districts' access to capital outlay funds was deemed to fall within guarantees of uniform, efficient, or adequate educational systems.

Many courts recognize that an equitable distribution of resources alone does not improve educational programs and services. Equity is a necessary, but not a sufficient, condition for attaining equal educational opportunities. The standard of adequacy is an important criterion for judging school finance policy in relation to the constitutional provisions of equality and efficiency. Recent decisions suggest a trend toward a larger judicial role in defining standards, not only for judicial decision making but also for policy formulation.

3. *The fiscal neutrality standard is not incompatible with goals of preserving and promoting local choice of spending levels or total tax effort.*

The value of liberty is evidenced in many states' school finance policies in provisions that permit district voters to determine spending levels. The goal of maintaining local control has been accepted by federal and state courts as a legitimate interest in satisfying the rational basis test. The school finance reform movement of the 1970s and 1980s encouraged states to adopt finance plans that stressed equality over liberty. In this way they erased many of the benefits of school district autonomy. Ward (1990) observed that local voters had less discretion and school programs became more standardized: "Rather than increasing democratic participation in public decision making, the net effect of the school finance reform cases was increased centralization and bureaucratic decision making" (p. 246). The response to this movement in the 1980s and 1990s was to return control of educational decisions to communities and school district and school personnel (see Chapters 14 and 15).

In adopting the standard of fiscal neutrality, courts in California, Texas, and Kansas proclaimed that the quality of a child's education may not be a function of wealth other than that of the entire state. Legislatures may choose to fully equalize local district spending to satisfy this standard. But fiscal neutrality tolerates variations in tax effort and spending levels if the result is that districts choosing to exert the same effort have the same total per pupil revenue available. Reformers have advanced model formulas that blend the goal of fiscal neutrality with that of preserving local control (see the various forms of percentage equalization discussed in Chapter 8). States have adopted forms of these formulas. For example, rich and poor districts desiring the same expenditure per pupil must tax local property at the same rate. The state provides unequal amounts of aid to raise each district to that desired spending level. Expenditures vary among districts. But the finance system is fiscally neutral because local wealth is equalized by the state. Disparities are a function only of local decisions about educational programs.

The Texas Supreme Court concluded in *Edgewood* (1991) that the goals of equality and efficiency are both satisfied when local control is encouraged within such an equalized finance plan. The 1994 Kansas decision upheld legislative plans premised on full fiscal neutrality. Absolute equality of expenditures is not necessarily the goal of finance reform in states adopting this standard; policies need only alter the direct correlation between wealth and total spending.

4. *In the absence of legislative action to promote equity, adequacy, and efficiency, courts may assume a more activist role.*

When the New Jersey and Texas legislatures failed to agree on funding plans to satisfy standards, their state supreme courts threatened to withhold public funds for schools until the issue was resolved. Lehne (1978) discussed the *Robinson* decision in relation to the growing activism of the judiciary and the dynamic role the courts play in policy debates:

While judicial decisions have traditionally been negative statements proscribing specified actions, in recent decades, courts more frequently demand positive actions from government to achieve specified goals. The judiciary is now more likely to require the executive, the legislature, and the public to deal with an issue but also to leave them an uncertain latitude to determine exactly how to deal with it. (p. 16)

Perhaps because of the vagueness of the constitutional language calling for equal treatment, thoroughness, or efficiency, or because of legislative resistance to change and legislators' processes of negotiations and compromise, which frustrate reformers' desires to reduce inequities, courts in recent years have assumed strong roles in defining standards and designing remedies. The New Jersey court eventually fashioned a remedy that required substantial compensatory aid to ensure program adequacy in selected districts. Even more dramatically, the Alabama, West Virginia, and Kentucky rulings indicate the courts' willingness to effect change in educational governance structures and offerings, in addition to finance plans, to enable students to meet academic performance standards. Underwood (1994) concluded that the latitude to interpret vague constitutional language, particularly that of education articles, permits judicial activism and "some freedom to construe the language liberally to meet its own goals of reform" (p. 157). Similarly, using the U.S. Constitution, the United States Supreme Court in *Jenkins* directed Missouri to fund much of the desegregation plan for that state's cities. It reinforced the district court's order to impose taxes on district residents although the levies were not permitted under state law. This action indicates the willingness of the courts to fashion strong remedies to undo past inequities, despite the resulting financial burdens.

Commenting on the balance of powers between courts and legislatures, Alexander (1991) noted that the comprehensive invalidation of Kentucky's education system tended to preserve legislative autonomy:

Had the court tried to remedy the complaint by striking only selected statutes, thereby re-

quiring specific statutory revision, the court's order could have been interpreted as a more serious intrusion into legislative prerogative. By invalidating the entire system, the court was able to set forth more general guidelines by which the legislature itself could effectuate a constitutional remedy. (p. 364)

The balance of power seems to have shifted dramatically toward the courts in these states. But legislatures have the opportunity and responsibility to design educational policies in ways that ensure that students in all districts, regardless of wealth, can access adequately funded instructional programs and services appropriate to their needs and the goals of the state and nation.

SUMMARY

The courts have played important roles in defining standards and stimulating change in school finance policy. Interpretations of constitutional provisions that guarantee equal treatment and define legislative responsibilities for education establish standards for later policy development. Federal court decisions and congressional actions that focused attention on equal educational opportunities in the 1960s and 1970s led to challenges of states' school finance systems. Reformers were denied reviews under the United States Constitution. So they turned to state courts.

Differing state court interpretations of equal protection clauses depended in part upon choices of the appropriate level of judicial analysis. A strict scrutiny analysis is premised on findings that public education is a fundamental right or that disparities are a consequence of a suspect wealth-based classification. Such an analysis places a very difficult burden on states to justify spending variations among school districts. States have been more successful in satisfying the less-stringent rational basis test. They have shown that disparities under finance systems are related to a legitimate objective, such as maintaining local control over educational decisions.

Judicial reviews may also rest on the education articles of state constitutions. These provisions for establishing and maintaining public educational systems require states to satisfy standards of uniformity, thoroughness, efficiency, and adequacy. Interpretations of these standards evolved from simplistic determinations of the degree of disparity in expenditures to judgments of the adequacy of the resources available to enable all students to achieve program standards. Several recent reviews of state policies show the role of the courts has expanded in defining standards for pupil performance and declaring entire educational systems to be unconstitutional.

Judicial reviews represent one way to determine whether finance policies satisfy the goals of equality and efficiency. The next chapter continues to focus on the value of equality (and through equality, fraternity) but from the perspectives of policy analysts.

ACTIVITIES

1. Locate the original reports of at least two of the judicial reviews cited in this chapter, of which one was decided in favor of the plaintiffs and the other upheld a state's finance system. Contrast the rationales of these courts in reaching decisions. Discuss the levels of scrutiny deemed appropriate if spending disparities were challenged under equal protection clauses. Discuss the definitions of equality, adequacy, and/or efficiency if education articles were challenged.

2. What have been the roles of the legislatures and the courts in the development of educational finance policy in a selected state? Interview several individuals and read news accounts to investigate conditions that were (or may be in the future) related to an actual or threatened challenge to the finance structure. What legislative enactments, if any, responded to judicial pressure?

3. What is meant by "Education is a fundamental right"? Debate the appropriateness of elevating school finance policy issues to a strict level of scrutiny to determine violations of the equal protection clauses of the Fourteenth Amendment or state constitutions.

4. Speculate about the role of the judiciary in educational policy development in the coming decade, given the willingness of the court in West Virginia to fashion a remedy by ordering the formation of a master plan, and given the Kentucky and Alabama courts' findings that their entire public education systems are unconstitutional.

REFERENCES

Abbott v. *Burke,* 477 A.2d 1278 (1984); 495 A.2d 376 (1985); 575 A.2d 359 (N.J. 1990); 643 A.2d 575 (N.J. 1994).

Adams, J. E. (1993). School finance reform and systemic school change: Reconstituting Kentucky's public schools. *Journal of Education Finance, 18,* 318–345.

Alexander, K. (1982). Concepts of equity. In W. W. McMahon & T. G. Geske (Eds.), *Financing education: Overcoming inefficiency and inequity* (pp. 193–214). Urbana, IL: University of Illinois Press.

Alexander, K. (1991). The common school ideal and the limits of legislative authority: The Kentucky case. *Harvard Journal on Legislation, 28,* 341–366.

Benson, C. S. (1991). Definitions of equity in school finance in Texas, New Jersey, and Kentucky. *Harvard Journal on Legislation, 28,* 401–421.

Bezdichek v. *South Dakota,* Circuit Court, Civs. 91–209 (1994).

Bismarck Public School District No. 1 v. *State,* 511 N.W.2d 247 (N.D. 1994).

Board of Education v. *Walter,* 390 N.E.2d 813 (Ohio 1979); cert. denied, 444 U.S. 1015 (1980).

Britt v. *State Board of Education,* 357 S.E.2d 432 (N.C. 1987).

Brown, P. R., & Elmore, R. F. (1982). Analyzing the impact of school finance reform. In N. H. Cambron-McCabe & A. Odden (Eds.), *The changing politics of school finance* (pp. 107–138). Cambridge, MA: Ballinger.

Brown v. *Board of Education,* 347 U.S. 483 (1954).

Burruss v. *Wilkerson,* 310 F.Supp. 572 (1969); Affirmed, 397 U.S. 44 (1970).

Buse v. *Smith,* 247 N.W.2d 141 (Wisc. 1976).

Camp, W. E., & Thompson, D. C. (1988). School finance litigation: Legal issues and politics of reform. *Journal of Education Finance, 14,* 221–238.

Campbell County School District v. *State,* 907 P.2d 1238 (Wyo. 1995).

Carrollton-Farmers Branch Independent School District v. *Edgewood Independent School District,* 826 S.W.2d 489 (Tex. 1992).

City of Pawtucket v. *Sundlun,* 662 A.2d 40 (R.I. 1995).

Claremont School District v. *Governor,* 635 A.2d 1375 (N.H. 1993).

Clark, C. (1995). Regional school taxing units: The Texas experience. In D. H. Monk, *Study on the generation of revenues for education: Final report* (pp. 75–88). Albany: New York State Education Department.

Clune, W. H. (1992). New answers to hard questions posed by *Rodriguez:* Ending the separation of school finance and educational policy by bridging the gap between wrong and remedy. *Connecticut Law Review, 24,* 721–755.

Coalition for Equitable School Funding, Inc. v. *State,* 811 P.2d 116 (Or. 1991).

Committee for Educational Rights v. *Edgar,* 267 Ill.App. 3d 18 (Ill. 1994).

Coons, J. E., Clune, W. H., & Sugarman, S. D. (1970). *Private wealth and public education.* Cambridge, MA: Belknap Press.

Crampton, F. E., & Whitney, T. N. (1995). Equity and funding of school facilities: Are states at risk? *State Legislative Report, 20.* Denver: National Conference of State Legislatures.

Cubberley, E. P. (1906). *School funds and their apportionment.* New York: Teachers College, Columbia University.

Danson v. *Casey,* 399 A.2d 360 (Pa. 1979).

DeRolph v. *Ohio,* Common Pleas Court, Perry County, No. 22043 (1994).

Dupree v. *Alma School District No. 30,* 651 S.W.2d 90 (Ark. 1983).

East Jackson Public Schools v. *State,* 348 N.W.2d 303 (Mich.App. 1984).

Edgewood Independent School District v. *Kirby,* 777 S.W.2d 391 (1989); 804 S.W.2d 491 (Tex. 1991).

Edgewood Independent School District v. *Meno,* 893 S.W.2d 450 (Tex. 1995).

Fair School Finance Council of Oklahoma, Inc. v. *State,* 746 P.2d 1135 (Okl. 1987).

Fuhrman, S. (1978). The politics and process of school finance reform. *Journal of Education Finance, 4,* 158–178.

Fulton, M. (1994). Recent school finance litigation. *State Education Leader,* Education Commission of the States, *13,* 16–21.

Goertz, M. (1981). School finance reform and the cities. In K. F. Jordan & N. H. Cambron-McCabe (Eds.), *Perspectives in state school support programs* (pp. 113–142). Cambridge, MA: Ballinger.

Goertz, M. E. (1993). School finance reform in New Jersey: The saga continues. *Journal of Education Finance, 18,* 346–365.

Gould v. *Orr,* 506 N.W.2d 349 (Neb. 1993).

Hatley, R. V., & Shaw, R. C. (1994). Missouri. In N. D. Theobald (Ed.), *The state of school finance issues, 1994.* Monograph of the American Educational Research Association's Fiscal Issues, Policy, and Education Finance Special Interest Group (pp. 34–39).

Helena Elementary School District No. 1 v. *Montana,* 769 P.2d 684 (Mont. 1989).

Henderson, R. L. (1991). An analysis of selected school finance litigation and its impact upon state education legislation. *Journal of Education Finance, 17,* 193–214.

Hickrod, G. A., Hines, E. R., Anthony, G. P., Dively, J. A., & Pruyne, G. B. (1992). The effect of constitutional litigation on education finance: A preliminary analysis. *Journal of Education Finance, 18,* 180–210.

Hickrod, G. A., Lenz, R., & Minorini, P. (1995). *Status of school finance constitutional litigation.* Bloomington, IL: Center for the Study of Educational Finance.

Hornbeck v. *Somerset County Board of Education,* 458 A.2d 758 (Md. 1983).

Horton v. *Meskill,* 376 A.2d 359 (Conn. 1977); 486 A.2d 1099 (Conn. 1985).

Idaho Schools for Equal Educ. Opportunity v. *Evans,* 850 P.2d 724 (Idaho 1993).

Kukor v. *Grover,* 436 N.W.2d 568 (Wisc. 1989).

LaMorte, M. W. (1989). Courts continue to address the wealth disparity issue. *Educational Evaluation and Policy Analysis, 11,* 3–15.

Lau v. *Nichols,* 414 U.S. 563 (1974).

Lehne, R. (1978). *The quest for justice: The politics of school finance reform.* New York: Longman.

Levittown Union Free School District v. *Nyquist,* 408 N.Y.S.2d 606 (Sup. 1978); Affirmed, 443 N.Y.S.2d 843 (App.Div. 1981); Reversed, 453 N.Y.S.2d 643 (Ct.App. 1982); Cert. denied, 459 U.S. 1139 (1983).

Lindsay, D. (1995). Court upholds school-finance system in Ohio. *Education Week, 15,* 14.

Love v. *City of Dallas,* 40 S.W.2d 20 (Tex. 1931).

Lujan v. *Colorado State Board of Education,* 649 P.2d 1005 (Colo. 1982).

McCarthy, M. M. (1981). Adequacy in educational programs: A legal perspective. In K. F. Jordan & N. H. Cambron-McCabe (Eds.), *Perspectives in state school support programs* (pp. 315–351). Cambridge, MA: Ballinger.

McDaniel v. *Thomas,* 285 S.E.2d 156 (Ga. 1981).

McDuffy v. *Secretary of the Executive Office of Education,* 615 N.E.2d 516 (Mass. 1993).

McInnis v. *Shapiro,* 293 F.Supp. 327 (1968); Affirmed, *McInnis* v. *Ogilvie,* 394 U.S. 322 (1969).

McUsic, M. (1991). The use of education clauses in school finance reform litigation. *Harvard Journal on Legislation, 28,* 307–340.

Miller, L. (1994). Judge gives Ark. lawmakers 2 years to fix formula. *Education Week, 14,* 13.

Milliken v. *Green,* 212 N.W.2d 711 (Mich. 1973).

Mills v. *Board of Education of the District of Columbia,* 348 F.Supp. 866 (1972).

Missouri v. *Jenkins,* 495 U.S. 33 (1990); 515 U.S. ___, 132 L.Ed. 2d 63 (1995).

Northshore School District No. 417 v. *Kinnear,* 530 P.2d 178 (Wash. 1974).

Olsen v. *State,* 554 P.2d 139 (Or. 1976).

Opinion of the Justices, consolidation of *Alabama Coalition for Equity* v. *Hunt & Harper* v. *Hunt,* 624 So.2d 107 (Ala. 1993).

Papasan v. *Allain,* 478 U.S. 265 (1986).

Pauley v. *Bailey,* 324 S.E.2d 128 (W.Va. 1984).

Pauley v. *Kelly,* 255 S.E.2d 859 (W.Va. 1979).

Plyler v. *Doe,* 457 U.S. 202 (1982).

R.E.F.I.T. (Reform Education Financing Inequities Today) v. *Cuomo,* 578 N.Y.S.2d 969 (Sup. 1991); 631 N.Y.S.2d 551 (Ct.App. 1995).

Reid Scott v. *Virginia,* 443 S.E.2d 138 (Va. 1994).

Richland County v. *Campbell,* 364 S.E.2d 470 (S.C. 1988).

Robinson v. *Cahill,* 303 A.2d 273 (N.J. 1973); 355 A.2d 129 (N.J. 1976).

Roosevelt Elementary School v. *Bishop,* 877 P.2d 806 (Ariz. 1994).

Rose v. *Council for Better Education,* 790 S.W.2d 186 (Ky. 1989).

San Antonio Independent School District v. *Rodriguez,* 411 U.S. 1 (1973).

Schmidt v. *Michigan,* 490 N.W. 2d 584 (Mich. 1992).

School Administrative District No. 1 v. *Commissioner,* 659 A.2d 854 (Me. 1995).

School Board of the Parish of Livingston v. *Louisiana State Board of Elementary and Secondary Education,* 830 F.2d 563 (1987).

Seattle School District No. 1 of King County v. *State of Washington,* 585 P.2d 71 (Wash. 1978).

Serrano v. *Priest,* 487 P.2d 1241 (1971); 557 P.2d 929 (1976); 226 Cal. Rptr. 584 (Cal.App. 1986).

Shofstall v. *Hollins,* 515 P.2d 590 (Ariz. 1973).

Sjogren, J. (1981). Municipal overburden and state aid for education. In K. F. Jordan & N. H. Cambron-McCabe (Eds.), *Perspectives in state school support programs* (pp. 87–111). Cambridge, MA: Ballinger.

Skeen v. *State,* 505 N.W.2d 299 (Minn. 1993).

Sommerfeld, M. (1994). Idaho response to school-adequacy suit is monetary. *Education Week, 14,* 17.

Sparkman, W. E. (1983). School finance litigation in the 1980s. In S. B. Thomas, N. H. Cambron-McCabe, & M. M. McCarthy (Eds.), *Educators and the law: Current trends and issues* (pp. 96–108). Elmont, NY: Institute for School Law and Finance.

Sparkman, W. E. (1990). School finance challenges in state courts. In J. K. Underwood & D. A. Verstegen (Eds.), *The impacts of litigation and legislation on public school finance: Adequacy, equity, and excellence* (pp. 193–224). New York: Harper & Row.

Sparkman, W. E. (1994). The legal foundations of public school finance. *Boston College Law Review, 35,* 569–595.

Tennessee Small School Systems v. *McWherter,* 851 S.W.2d 139 (Tenn. 1993).

Thompson v. *Engelking,* 537 P.2d 635 (Idaho 1975).

Underwood, J. K. (1989). Changing equal protection analyses in finance equity litigation. *Journal of Education Finance, 14,* 413–425.

Underwood, J. K. (1994). School finance litigation: Legal theories, judicial activism, and social neglect. *Journal of Education Finance, 20,* 143–162.

Underwood, J. K., & Sparkman, W. E. (1991). School finance litigation: A new wave of reform. *Harvard Journal of Law and Public Policy, 14,* 517–544.

Underwood, J. K., & Verstegen, D. A. (1990). School finance challenges in federal courts: Changing equal protection analyses. In J. K. Underwood & D. A. Verstegen (Eds.), *The impacts of litigation and legislation on public school finance: Adequacy, equity, and excellence* (pp. 177–191). New York: Harper & Row.

Unified School District No. 244 v. Kansas. 885 P.2d 1170 (Kan. 1994).

VanDusartz v. Hatfield, 334 F.Supp. 870 (1971).

Verstegen, D. A. (1994). The new wave of school finance litigation. *Phi Delta Kappan, 76,* 243–250.

Ward, J. G. (1990). Implementation and monitoring of judicial mandates: An interpretive analysis. In J. K. Underwood & D. A. Verstegen (Eds.), *The impacts of litigation and legislation on public school finance: Adequacy, equity, and excellence* (pp. 225–248). New York: Harper & Row.

Washakie County School District No. 1 v. Herschler, 606 P.2d 310 (Wyo. 1980); Cert. denied, 449 U.S. 824 (1980).

Whitney, T. N., & Crampton, F. E. (1995). State school finance litigation: A summary and analysis. *State Legislative Report, 20.* Denver: National Conference of State Legislatures.

Withers v. State, 891 P.2d 675 (Ore. Ct.App. 1995).

Wood, R. C. (1995). Adequacy issues in recent education finance litigation. In W. J. Fowler (ed.), *Developments in school finance* (pp. 29–37). Washington, DC: U.S. Government Printing Office.

Woodahl v. Straub, 520 P.2d 776 (Mont. 1974).

CHAPTER 12

Using Equity and Fraternity Standards

Primary Issues Explored in This Chapter:

- **Definitions of equity:** What is the meaning of equity today? How have its meanings evolved? What implications do varying definitions of equity hold for school finance policy?
- **Analysis of equity:** What are the focus groups of equity studies? What objects should be included in equity studies? What principles should guide equity studies? How is equity measured?
- **Studies of school finance equity:** How equitable is the distribution of resources committed to ele-

mentary and secondary education among states, districts, and schools within districts? How equitable is the distribution of outputs from elementary and secondary schools among states, districts, and schools within districts?

- **Policy implications:** What changes are needed in school governance and finance to facilitate greater equity in the distribution of resources to schools and the outcomes of schools?

Courts are the formal mechanisms created by society for evaluating social policy within parameters established by constitutional and statutory authority. The previous chapter examined the assessments of school finance policy made by courts in the United States, where equality is a primary, but not exclusive, concern. In this chapter, we view the closely related concepts of equity and fraternity from the perspectives of policy makers and policy analysts who are not constrained by the same parameters and procedures as judicial reviews.

Equality and fraternity, along with liberty, are described in Chapter 2 as ethical values that influence decisions about school finance. *Equality* was defined as the state, ideal, or quality of being equal,

as in enjoying equal social, political, and economic rights. The operational definition of *equality* within the sociopolitical context also includes factors of condition. The emphasis is on the appropriateness of treatment. As such, equality has taken on the broader connotations of *equity,* defined as "the state, ideal, or quality of being just, impartial and fair" (*American Heritage Dictionary of the English Language,* s. v. "equity"). In this chapter, the term *equity* is used instead of *equality* as more accurately reflecting modern usage in reference to public policy.

Fraternity was defined as a common bond producing a sense of unity, community, and nationhood. Public policies that further the realization of equity frequently, but not always, advance the realization of fraternity. For example, policies of school desegregation were implemented to make the educational opportunities of all children equivalent. The ideas was that separate is inherently unequal. Policies of desegregation could have been advanced just as well to further fraternity. This is because a desegregated school provides a common experience for all children. It unites them at a tender age. Horace Mann used this argument in the nineteenth century when lobbying for the "common" school.

On the other hand, in seeking equality of opportunities, inputs, and outcomes of the educational process, there is a real danger of overlooking the unique talents and needs of individual students. Dewey (1916/1966), for example, encouraged educational policies that would compensate for social and economic inequalities. But he did not want to do this at the expense of educational goals tailored to the characteristics of each student and pedagogical and curricular approaches designed around individual talents, needs, and interests. Uniform and comparative measures of success can transform efforts to equalize opportunity and achievement into zero-sum games. They pit individual against individual and weaken social bonds (Kahne, 1994). Such systems can foster destructive forms of competition that undermine the development of supportive fraternal relationships. Kahne (1994) elaborates on the objectives of "democratic communitarians":

[D]emocratic communitarians endorse societies in which members share commitments to one another and work together on common projects. They strive for free and full communication, social harmony, shared interests, scientifically informed debate, experimentation, and a sense of what John Gardner (1990) refers to as a "wholeness incorporating diversity." They seek to promote the support, sense of common mission, and sense of belonging that can come out of community and avoid the envy, alienation, destructive competition, and exploitation that can result from the self-serving behavior of individuals. (p. 239)

Settings are needed in which the values of educational equity *and* fraternity (or, using the terminology of Dewey and Kahne, "democratic communitarianism") are pursued simultaneously.

During the latter half of the twentieth century, equity considerations have dominated fraternal ones in public policy debates. This has been the case even though many of the policies implemented have promoted both objectives. For example, children with disabilities are included in regular classrooms. Following the flow of the discourse, policy analysts have designed their analyses around equity constructs. Few, if any, analyses have been built around the concept of fraternity. In this chapter we will thus focus the discussion on equity. But the reader should keep in mind that with the exceptions just noted, much that has been said about equity pertains to fraternity as well. In the remainder of this chapter, we describe the dimensions of equity. We discuss a number of statistical measures that policy analysts use to evaluate the equity of school finance policies. And we review several analyses that were intended to inform policy makers.

DIMENSIONS OF EQUITY

Philosophical and Political Dimensions

Figure 12.1 represents an adaptation of Alexander's (1982) reconciliation of the philosophical and legal dimensions of equity to the practice of school finance and the relative extent of governmental involvement required for policy implementation. Definitions of equity range from the politically conservative to the politically liberal. They include commutative equity, equal-distribution equity, restitution equity, and outcome equity. School finance practices are associated with each dimension.

Commutative equity entitles a person to something on the basis of property rights alone and leaves the distribution produced by the marketplace unaltered. Such a philosophy would not support any public intervention in school finance. Some intervention is inevitable, however. Subscribers to

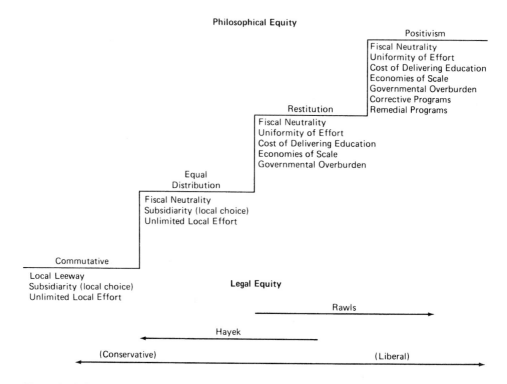

Figure 12.1. Perspectives of Equity (SOURCE: Adapted from K. Alexander. [1982]. "Concepts of Equity." In W. W. McMahon and T. G. Geske [Eds.], *Financing Education: Overcoming Inefficiency and Inequity* [pp. 193–214]. Urbana: University of Illinois Press, p. 211. Reprinted by permission.)

commutative equity would endorse the greatest possible local discretion in using local tax bases. Such a policy would move us on the continuum toward distributive equity.

Distributive equity is concerned with correcting inequitable conditions created by the design of government. This has direct relevance to school finance. This is because a primary source of inequity, the variation in the capacity of school district tax bases to produce revenue, lies in the school district structure that was created by the state. Holders of this position would endorse the concept of fiscal neutrality, particularly as it is embodied in power equalization formulas that put no restraints on local effort.

Restitution equity endorses the correction of inequitable conditions that arise from social and economic circumstances as well as those the gov-

ernment creates. Restitution focuses only on weaknesses of the system. It does not focus on the personal education needs of children. Persons accepting this view would endorse fiscal neutrality. They would also endorse uniform tax effort and adjustments for regional cost variations, economies of scale, and municipal overburden. From this perspective, full state funding would be an acceptable means of financing public schools.

Positivism equity introduces the concept of the educational needs of children. Holders of this position justify intervention designed to assist the least advantaged. They demand that unique and high-cost corrective, remedial, and compensatory programs be fully financed by the government. Alexander identified several features that would need to be included in an ideal model of education finance in order to satisfy this level of equity: adequate financing of basic education programs, complete fiscal equalization of each district's taxpaying ability, uniform tax effort, and supplemental standards for corrective and remedial education programs. The latter may also include programs that link schools and social services in ways that strengthen families' abilities to cope with social and environmental factors outside the school (Adler and Gardner, 1994; Howe, 1993; Kirst, 1994; Zigler and Finn-Stevenson, 1994).

Over time, policy analysts have gradually shifted their interest from commutative equity to positivism equity. Before the educational reform movement of the 1980s, they focused on equal distribution and restitution equity. In the early phases of the current reform movement, they gave little attention to equity considerations at all. They merely lamented over the possibility that the emphasis on excellence, high achievement standards, and efficiency might have inequitable consequences. They asked whether we can simultaneously satisfy the social objectives of equity and efficiency.

There has been a decided shift in this opinion in the 1990s. The shift was encouraged in part by the court decisions in New Jersey, Texas, Kentucky, and elsewhere (Hirth, 1994). In many instances, court decisions (see Chapter 11) declared state school finance schemes in violation of their state constitutions on the grounds of both inequity and inefficiency. In the case of Kentucky, the whole governance structure for education was nullified, not just the finance scheme. A social consensus now seems to be developing around the common goal of high minimum achievement for all children (Clune, 1994), that is, positivism equity.

Technical Dimensions

Berne and Stiefel (1984, 1992, 1994) have framed the most comprehensive conceptualization of equity in school finance from the perspective of the policy analyst. They organized their analyses around four questions:

1. What is the makeup of the *groups* for which school finance systems should be equitable?

2. What services, resources, or, more generally, *objects* should be distributed fairly among members of the groups?
3. What *principles* should be used to determine whether a particular distribution is equitable?
4. What quantitative *measures* should be used to assess the degree of equity? (p. 7)

Groups of Concern. In reference to (1), two groups have been the primary subjects of studies of school finance equity; schoolchildren and taxpayers. Alternative concepts involved in the analysis of equity for children as identified by Berne and Stiefel (1984) are shown in Figure 12.2. A portrayal of concepts related to taxpayer equity would look similar to Figure 12.2 except for the objects of analysis. In evaluating taxpayer equity, the primary interests are the tax rates and the revenue generated.

Objects. The objects to be distributed equitably among schoolchildren (2) are divided into inputs, outputs, and outcomes. Inputs are the human and material resources used in the schooling process. They may be measured in terms of dollars or actual amounts of physical resource employed. Dollar inputs are most commonly used. They may be analyzed as revenues or expenditures. Revenues may be subdivided according to source. Expenditures may be subdivided according to purpose (for example, operating expenditure, instructional expenditure). Some categories of revenues and expenditures are of greater interest than others from a policy perspective; the selection needs to be made with care. Berne and Stiefel (1984, 1992) recommended the use of price-adjusted dollars to correct for the regional variations that exist within many states and among states.

Inputs may also be measured by the actual amount of resources available. These include pupil : adult ratios; average class sizes; characteristics of teachers, such as teacher verbal ability and experience; and the number of library books. The advantage of using measures of actual resources is that the measurements are not affected by regional

Alternative for Each Component

Component of Equity Concept			
Who? The Group	*Children*		
What? The Object	*Inputs* Dollars Price-adjusted Dollars Physical Resources	*Outputs* Student Achievement Behavioral Output Measures	*Outcomes* Earning Potential Income Satisfaction
How? The Principle	*Horizontal Equity* Equal Treatment of Equals Minimize Spread in Distribution	*Vertical Equity* Unequal Treatment of Unequals More of the Object to the Needier	*Equal Opportunity* No Discrimination on the Basis of Property Wealth in School District or Other Categories Minimize Undesirable Systematic Relationships
How much? The Summary Statistic	*Univariate Dispersion* Range Restricted Range Federal Range Ratio Relative Mean Deviation The McLoone Index Variance Coefficient of Variation Standard Deviation of Logarithm Gini Coefficient Atkinson's Index Theil's Measure	*Relationship* Simple Correlation Simple Slope Quadratic Slope Cubic Slope Simple Elasticity Quadratic Elasticity Cubic Elasticity Constant Elasticity Adjusted Relationship Measure from Simple Regression Adjusted Relationship Measure from Quadratic Regression Adjusted Relationship Measure from Cubic Regression Implicit Weight Averaged Implicit Weight	

Figure 12.2. Berne and Stiefel's Alternative Concepts of School Finance Equity for Children. (SOURCE: R. Berne and L. Stiefel. [1984]. *The Measurement of Equity in School Finance: Conceptual, Methodological, and Empirical Dimensions.* Baltimore, MD: The Johns Hopkins University Press, p. 9. Reprinted by permission.)

price variations or inflation over time. The major disadvantage is that there is no satisfactory way of aggregating quantities of different resources, for example, the combined teacher experience in years and class size.

Outputs and outcomes relate to the goals and objectives of schooling. Outputs represent the im-

mediate products of the schools. They are often measured in terms of pupil achievement and behavioral changes. Outcomes include such long-range effects of schooling as lifetime earnings and quality of life.

The list of possible objects of analysis is almost infinite. There is no general agreement on what inputs, outputs, and outcomes should be equitably distributed. Objects selected for analysis need to be closely related to the stated or implied purposes of the policy being analyzed. Analyses of distribution equity and restitution equity have tended to focus on inputs. Outputs and outcomes have not been used generally in equity studies until very recently. They, of course, relate to outcome equity as depicted in Figure 12.1.

Equity Principles.   Berne and Stiefel (1984) proposed three principles that can be used to determine whether a particular distribution is equitable (3): horizontal equity, vertical equity, and equal opportunity. We introduced the concepts of horizontal and vertical equity (Chapter 4) with respect to taxation policy. *Horizontal equity* refers to the equal treatment of equals—the traditional meaning of *equality.* Vertical equity recognizes that equal treatment is not always fair and just for pupils (or taxpayers) experiencing extraordinary conditions such as poverty or physical, psychological, and mental disabilities (or high costs of living, dispersed populations, and municipal overburden). Thus vertical equity allows for the appropriate unequal treatment of unequals. Berne and Stiefel (1984, p. 17) defined *equal opportunity* in the negative as the condition in which there are no differences in treatment according to characteristics such as race, gender, or national origin that are considered illegitimate. Other analysts treat equal opportunity as a condition of horizontal equity. Until recently, virtually all studies of school finance equity have dealt only with the horizontal and equal-opportunity dimensions.

Useful Statistics.   In response to Berne and Stiefel's fourth question, Figure 12.2 lists various statistics that policy analysts use to assess the degree to which distributions of objects satisfy equity principles. We describe those most commonly used in the next section.

Unit of Analysis.   Until recently, the unit of analysis for equity studies has been the school district. Studies continue to be conducted at that level. Now

studies are likewise being conducted at the school level in response to the growing understanding that the most critical teaching and learning activities are those that involve the child. They are also in response to the increasing interest in outcome equity. School-level analyses have been made feasible by rapid advancements in computer technology. These advancements enable the collection and analysis of data at a level of detail that was not possible in the past (Berne and Stiefel, 1994).

MEASURING EQUITY

In this section we discuss two categories of statistics used for assessing equity. The most commonly used measures of dispersion of a single object are range, coefficient of variation, McLoone index, and Gini coefficient. Measures of the relationships among two or more objects include correlation coefficient, slope, and regression coefficient.[1]

To illustrate the concepts behind each statistic, Table 12.1 presents a set of values for twenty hypothetical school districts representing two hypothetical states. The districts are arranged in ascending order according to the object of interest, in this case, expenditure per pupil. Each district has 100 pupils and each state has 2,000 pupils. The mean and median expenditure per pupil for both states is $3,450. The range is the same, $2,500 to $4,400. Distributions within that range, however, vary considerably. We also give data for property values per pupil and percentage of minority students. The computer simulations accompanying this chapter permit further application of these measurements to the state database introduced in Chapter 8.

Dispersion of a Single Object

Restricted Range.   The spread between the highest- and lowest-expenditure districts in both states is $2,850 (see Table 12.1). On the surface, this would suggest comparable equity. But on closer examination, one can see that the distribution of expenditures among districts is quite different. Dis-

TABLE 12.1. Equity-related Data for Two Hypothetical States, Each with 20 Districts and 2,000 Students

	Pupils			State A			State B		
District Number	Number	Accumulative Number	Percentile	Expenditure per Pupil	Full Property Value per Pupil	Percentage Minority	Expenditure per Pupil	Full Property Value per Pupil	Percentage Minority
1	100	100	5	$3,750	$75,000	10	$3,750	$67,500	41
2	100	200	10	3,900	67,500	48	4,575	90,000	64
3	100	300	15	4,050	90,000	1	4,650	82,500	29
4	100	400	20	4,200	93,000	50	4,725	105,000	50
5	100	500	25	4,350	82,500	11	4,800	93,000	19
6	100	600	30	4,500	105,000	1	4,875	127,500	20
7	100	700	35	4,650	112,500	20	4,950	120,000	48
8	100	800	40	4,800	102,000	11	5,025	150,000	1
9	100	900	45	4,950	120,000	16	5,100	135,000	10
10	100	1,000	50	5,100	135,000	17	5,175	157,500	20
11	100	1,100	55	5,250	127,500	41	5,250	180,000	11
12	100	1,200	60	5,400	150,000	64	5,325	165,000	22
13	100	1,300	65	5,550	143,500	3	5,400	195,000	11
14	100	1,400	70	5,700	165,000	7	5,475	172,500	7
15	100	1,500	75	5,850	180,000	20	5,550	225,000	16
16	100	1,600	80	6,000	172,500	29	5,625	195,000	17
17	100	1,700	85	6,150	195,000	19	5,700	210,000	7
18	100	1,800	90	6,300	210,000	7	5,775	270,000	0
19	100	1,900	95	6,450	202,500	0	5,775	262,500	1
20	100	2,000	100	6,600	225,000	22	6,600	300,000	3

tricts in state A are evenly distributed across the range, while districts in state B cluster more closely around the median ($5,175).

One way of eliminating the distortion of outlying cases is to use a restricted range—say between the tenth and ninetieth student percentiles. The restricted range for state A is $2,250 (from $4,050 in district 3 to $6,300 in district 18). The smaller restricted range for state B ($1,050) reflects the greater equity we observed by inspection.

The restricted range provides a simple, easily understood way of comparing equity in two or more states at a given point in time. But because of the historical effects of inflation, restricted range does not provide accurate comparisons over time. To illustrate, if we make five-year comparisons, and costs double every five years, then districts would have to double their expenditures to provide the same level of services. This would increase the range for both states to $5,700. The restricted range for state A would increase to $4,500 and for state B, to $2,100. Both sets of statistics suggest that equity has suffered in both states, and especially within state A, although the actual distribution of services has not changed.

Federal Range Ratio.   To correct for the effects of inflation, the federal range ratio was developed. It divides the restricted range for the middle 90 percent of students (eliminating from consideration the top and bottom 5 percent) by the value of the object (in the case of our illustration, expenditure per pupil) for the pupil at the fifth percentile. Since both of our states have 2,000 students, we remove from consideration 100 students at the top and bottom of the expenditure range in each state, that is, districts 1 and 20. For state A, the restricted range becomes $2,550. When this is divided by the expenditure experienced by the student at the fifth percentile, $3,900, the federal range ratio is 0.65. For state B, the federal range ratio is 0.26, calculated as ($5,775 − $4,575)/$4,575. The smaller the ratio, the greater is the equity. Perfect equity (all districts with the same expenditure) results in a federal range ratio of zero. When the impact of inflation is equal for all districts, the ratio remains

unchanged even though the values of the objects of analysis increase over time.

Coefficient of Variation.   Although it is easy to compute and to understand, the range statistic is determined by only two cases in a distribution. A statistic like the standard deviation, which encompasses all cases, is preferable. The *standard deviation* measures the extent of dispersion of the cases in a distribution about its mean. In a normal distribution, about one-third of the cases fall between the mean and one standard deviation above the mean. Another one-third fall between the mean and one standard deviation below the mean. Ninety-five percent of the cases fall within two standard deviations above and below the mean. The standard deviations of the expenditure per pupil for states A and B are $888 and $587, respectively. The smaller statistic for state B indicates greater equity.

The standard deviation suffers from the same problem as the range in that it is sensitive to changes in scale. The solution is similar to that used in correcting the range to get the federal range ratio. The standard deviation is divided by the mean of the distribution, producing the *coefficient of variation.* The coefficients of variation for states A and B are 0.17 and 0.11, respectively. The smaller statistic for state B indicates greater equity. If all districts in a state spent exactly the same amount, the coefficient of variation would be zero.

The Gini Coefficient.   Economists use the *Lorenz curve* to illustrate inequalities in income. It is equally useful in illustrating inequities related to educational resources. The Lorenz curves for states A and B are shown in Figure 12.3. The horizontal axis represents the percentage of pupils and the vertical axis represents the percentage of expenditure. Perfect equity is represented by the diagonal that bisects the quadrant, that is, 25 percent of the pupils would have access to 25 percent of the total expenditures, 50 percent of the pupils would have access to 50 percent of the total expenditures, and so forth. In reality, for state A, the first 25 percent of the pupils have access to only 19.6 percent of the total expenditures. Thus, the Lorenz curve, repre-

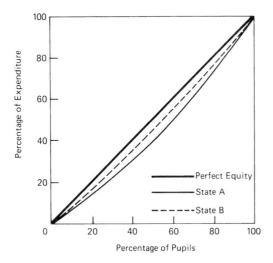

Figure 12.3. Lorenz Curve for Expenditures and Pupils for States A and B

senting the actual distribution, sags below the diagonal. The greater the area between the ideal (the diagonal line that represents perfect equity) and the actual distribution (the Lorenz curve), the greater is the inequity.

The extent of inequity is measured quantitatively by dividing the area between the Lorenz curve and the diagonal by the area of the triangle formed by the diagonal, the x axis, and the right side of the graph. The resulting ratio is known as the Gini coefficient (Berne & Stiefel, 1984, pp. 66–68). In the case of perfect equity, the actual distribution line would coincide with the diagonal. The area between the two lines would be zero, as would the Gini coefficient. In our example, the Gini coefficients for states A and B are 0.10 and 0.05, respectively. The smaller coefficient for state B represents greater equity.

The McLoone Index. The statistics discussed to this point measure attributes of the total distribution. Such statistics are appropriate in evaluating policies where the intent is to treat all individuals in the group alike. But few state finance plans are intended to accomplish this. More typically, states attempt to ensure a basic level of support above

which districts are free to spend to the extent local resources permit. Foundation and flat grant plans function in this fashion. The McLoone index is designed to assess equity under these latter assumptions (Harrison & McLoone, 1960).

The McLoone index is the ratio of the sum of the actual expenditures of all districts at or below the median expenditure for the state to what expenditures would be if all such districts actually spent at the median level. Unlike previous statistics, perfect equity is represented by 1.00, and the greatest amount of inequity is represented by zero. For states A and B, the McLoone indices are 0.855 and 0.992, respectively. The *higher* index for state B represents *greater* equity.

Relationship

All of the statistics in the previous section address equity in terms of a single object. There are instances, however, where we are interested in the relationships, or the lack of them, between two or more objects (variables). Berne and Stiefel's equal opportunity dimension represents a class of such instances. Here we are interested in the relationship between an object of distribution, such as pupil achievement or class size, and a characteristic of children, such as race or family income.

To determine the extent of fiscal neutrality, it is also necessary to resort to relationship analyses. We do this when we study the impact of percentage-equalizing and guaranteed tax base programs of the revenue produced and the district tax rates. These finance programs are not intended to eliminate differences in expenditures among pupils. Rather they are intended to uncouple the linkage between expenditures and the wealth of districts or tax rates.

Correlation Coefficient. The strength of the relationship between two variables is commonly described by the Pearson product-moment correlation coefficient. The coefficient ranges from −1.00 to +1.00. A zero coefficient indicates no relationship between the two variables—the desired state in analyses of horizontal equity, equal opportunity, and fiscal neutrality. A coefficient of 1.00 (either positive or negative) indicates a perfect correspondence between two variables; there is no unexplained variation. A positive coefficient indicates that the two variables increase in size together. A negative coefficient indicates that as one variable increases in size, the other variable decreases.

Figure 12.4 shows the scattergrams and regression lines of expenditures against percentage minority for states A and B. For state A, the plots are widely scattered, suggesting no relationship between the two variables. This is confirmed by a low correlation coefficient (-0.12) and a nearly horizontal regression line. There is a very definite pattern for state B, however. As the percentage minority increases, the expenditure per pupil decreases. This is reflected in a high and negative correlation coefficient of -0.68 and a downward-sloping regression line. In terms of horizontal equity and equal opportunity with respect to percentage minority, state A is more equitable than state B.

Slope. Figure 12.5 shows the scattergrams of expenditure per pupil against property value per pupil for states A and B and their respective regression lines. The correlation in both states is high and positive, 0.98 and 0.93, respectively. But, from an equity perspective, the situation is more serious in state A than in state B. This is because an increase in property value per pupil is associated with a much larger increase in expenditure per pupil in state A. In other words, the slope of the regression line for state A is steeper than for state B. This indicates that the equalization effect of state policy is greater in state B. The slope of a distribution measures the increase in the dependent variable (y axis), on average, associated with one unit increase of the independent variable (x axis). The slope is measured by the regression coefficient. The larger the slope, the greater the inequity. The regression coefficients for states A and B are 0.02 and 0.01, respectively.

Multivariate Methods. Despite a variety of conflicting equity goals, virtually all analyses of school finance equity have used univariate or bivariate methods as described in previous sections. A primary exception is a study by Garms (1979) which pioneered the use of multivariate techniques to permit the comparison of states or one state with itself over time. Garms pointed out that "any attempt to separately analyze the effects of multiple goals must have a way of separating the

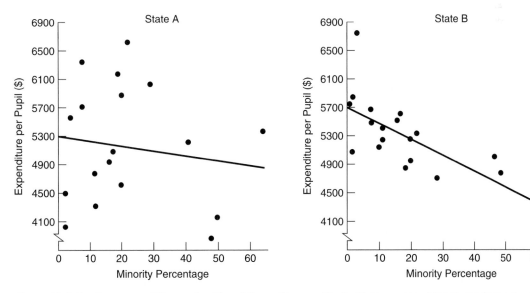

Figure 12.4. Scattergram and Regression Line of Expenditure per Pupil with Percentage Minority for States A and B

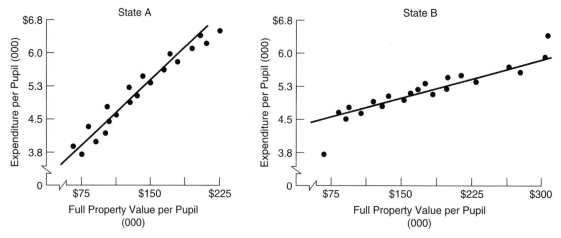

Figure 12.5. Scattergram and Regression Line of Expenditure per Pupil with Property Value per Pupil for States A and B

allocations for those goals" (p. 416). This is impossible in an accounting sense (a single allocation may be directed toward several ends). Garms therefore used multivariate statistics that enabled "the separation of provisions for differences in district wealth from differences in tax rate, and both of these from differences in provision for needs and costs" (p. 435). Garms acknowledged some problems that may limit the applicability of the method. But he said it provided a more comprehensive view of school finance systems than any method previously proposed.

More recently, Parrish, Matsumoto, and Fowler (1995) applied multivariate techniques in analyzing the disparities in public school district spending. They justified the use of multivariate analysis by explaining:

> Because the various factors on which school districts differ are correlated with each other (some, like enrollment size and urbanicity, are highly correlated), it is impossible to discern from marginal averages which of several correlated variables are most responsible for a difference. By simultaneously allowing all of the descriptive factors under study to account for variation in the dependent variable (e.g., in per pupil expenditures), it is possible to iden-

tify which are the "real" factors and which only appear to be factors because of their correlation with the "real" factors. (p. D-19)

Data envelopment analysis (DEA) is a relatively new statistical tool permitting the use of multiple inputs and outputs in analyzing the efficiency of decision units. Walters and Freeman (1993) used this approach in examining equity issues in Utah. DEA allows a richer set of variables in the assessment of comparative wealth, tax effort, and spending equity than is permitted by most other methods reviewed above (Charnes, Cooper, and Rhodes, 1978).

Equity Standards

With respect to federal policy, Berne and Stiefel (1992) recommended the use of the coefficient of variation or the McLoone index in measuring vertical equity. In computing these ratios they recommended using weighted student counts and all operating revenues or expenditures, both general and categorical. They believed that the McLoone index is the most consistent with the federal interest in vertical equity. This is because it emphasizes the weighted students who receive the fewest dollars. The coefficient of variation was favored as an alternative. It is commonly used and understood and it is consist with other more esoteric measures of disparity. They recommended the same measures for analyses of horizontal equity. Student counts should be unweighted, however, and definitions of expenditures and revenues may differ. For equal-opportunity equity, they recommend using a quadratic regression procedure (not described above).

There are no generally accepted standards of equity for the statistics we have described. Evaluations must depend largely on relative comparisons. Odden and Picus (1992) recommended the following values as a desirable level of equity: 0.10 or less for the coefficient of variation, 0.90 or higher for the McLoone index, and 0.10 or less for the Gini coefficient. They did not strongly encourage the use of the federal range ratio.

FINDINGS FROM STUDIES OF SCHOOL FINANCE EQUITY

Interest in school finance equity peaked during the decade of the 1970s and then waned until the 1990s. Beginning in the 1960s with the Civil Rights Movement and the related compensatory education programs of President Johnson's Great Society, concerns over equality of educational opportunities dominated the educational agenda. In the 1970s, attention focused on the equity of state school finance systems. Litigation was brought in over half the states, challenging the constitutionality of the systems (see Chapter 11). The 1970s was dubbed the decade of school finance reform. State after state restructured its finance system to improve its equity. States did this under court order and at their own initiative. During this decade researchers from several disciplines joined with jurists, policy makers, interest groups, task forces, and national foundations. They tried to sharpen the understanding of equity problems and to evaluate the effectiveness of the remedies attempted.

In the 1980s, national attention shifted to excellence and efficiency. Interest in equity declined but did not disappear entirely. In reviewing approximately 140 pieces of equity research between 1980 and 1987, Barro (1987) referred to them as a "holding operation" (p. 3). He found no newly developed concepts or methods of analysis. The decline in research on school finance equity paralleled a decline in the demand and funding for such studies compared to what was available in the previous decade. In the 1990s, however, there has been a renewed interest in equity. New methods of analysis have been developed.

Multistate Studies

Equity with Respect to Economic Inputs.   One might suspect—or at least hope—that with all the attention given to it during the 1970s, there would have been substantial gains in school finance equity. But this was not the case. Berne and Stiefel (1983) reviewed equity studies using data going back to 1940. They found that before the school finance reform movement, from 1940 to 1960, horizontal equity improved in most of the states. School district consolidation and increased state aid contributed indirectly to this goal. During the 1960s and 1970s, when concern over equity was an explicit issue, the trend was toward a decrease in equity.

Brown et al. (1978) also found that disparities in per pupil expenditures among districts in most states actually increased or remained constant between 1970 and 1975. The pattern was somewhat different in the nineteen states that reformed their finance structures during that period. Ten of the nineteen reduced interdistrict disparities. But four of them remained among the ten states with the greatest expenditure disparities. In 1970, reform states as a group had larger wealth-related disparities than nonreform states. By 1975, the situation was reversed.

Brown et al. (1978) took the most optimistic interpretation of their rather disappointing findings. They pointed out that the reform states were "swimming against a tide of increasing disparity" (p. 212). They said that inequities might have been even greater without reform. They attributed the lack of greater progress toward expenditure equity in part to the desire to provide property tax relief. Considerable relief was provided. It led to lower correlations between wealth-related measures and expenditures in reform states. They also noted that the six states with the least disparity in expenditures operated relatively few school systems of comparatively large size.

Using the federal range ratio and the coefficient of variation for all states except Montana, Berne (1988) analyzed changes in horizontal equity for the periods 1970–1977 and 1977–1985. For the first period, Berne found that horizontal equity improved by more than 5 percent in six states and worsened in eighteen states. For the 1977–1985 period, equity improved by more than 5 percent in fourteen states and became worse in sixteen states. For the two periods combined, 1970–1985, eleven states improved and eighteen became worse. He concluded that even though his indicator was very crude, there was some evidence that equity fared somewhat better during the more recent period. "During the first period, the general trend was towards worsening equity, while during the second period equity ups and downs were more nearly equal" (p. 177).

Carroll (1979) also provided little cause for optimism. He analyzed the impact of school finance reform in five states: California, Florida, Kansas, Michigan, and New Mexico. The results were mixed: "Reform has brought about some advances; but judged in relation to the major goals that the proponents of reform have championed, the scattered victories of reform appear somewhat hollow" (p. v). Reform reduced the linkage between district wealth and expenditure per pupil, and it increased statewide spending for education. Reform did not, however, change the distributions of revenues and instructional expenditures. In other words, taxpayer equity appears to have improved, but child equity did not.

Carroll offered two probable explanations for the ineffectiveness of the reforms in equalizing spending outcomes and opportunities: (1) States simultaneously pursued diverse and conflicting objectives such as equalizing revenues, preserving some local control over spending, trying to avoid

the political hazards of cutting back high spending districts, providing tax relief, and avoiding excessive growth in state spending for schools. (2) Each state made add-ons and adjustments to the basic plan. These policy changes had disequalizing effects. Kansas, for example, introduced income tax rebates. Florida introduced a cost-of-living adjustment. Both procedures provided more state aid to wealthy districts than to poor ones.

Hirth (1994) suggested that the situation had not improved with the passage of time. From her analysis of equity in Indiana, Michigan, and Illinois, she concluded that even though these states made valiant efforts to improve financial equity among school districts, horizontal equity had actually decreased.

Lake (1983), in a study of the public school systems in the four provinces of Atlantic Canada, found greatest equity in New Brunswick. Here the schools were fully funded by the province:

> If one focuses on Nova Scotia and New Brunswick, a policy implication of some importance arises. New Brunswick, the full provincial assumption case, made more progress toward equity than did Nova Scotia, the combined provincial/local funding case. However, in terms of sufficiency, Nova Scotia made more progress than did New Brunswick. This suggests, though it certainly does not rigorously prove, that the act of full provincial (state) assumption may help the educational community accomplish the equity goal at the expense of the sufficiency goal. (p. 460)

Bezeau (1985) used the public school systems of the United States and Canada to test relationships between equity and the centralization of governance. Unlike Lake, Bezeau found that centralization had no effect on the magnitude of expenditures per pupil. Like Lake, however, Bezeau found a small and positive relationship between centralization and greater equity.

Heinold (1983) studied the impact of federal aid on horizontal equity of revenues among states between 1960 and 1981. The coefficient of variation and the McLoone index showed movement toward greater equity among the states during the decade of the 1960s and movement away from equity during the 1970s. Federal aid enhanced equity for all years, but especially during the period from 1965 through 1976. In discussing the policy implications of his research, Heinold contrasted the situation in the United States with that in Canada:

> During the period of years analyzed, the federal government portion of the funding of elementary and secondary public education [in the United States] ranged from three to nine per cent of the total revenues. In contrast, the level of funding by the federal government of Canada was 19 per cent of the total revenues in 1978, representing an effort greater than twice that of the United States government. This increased effort on the part of Canada has been rewarded by reductions in disparities among provinces to levels below the levels of disparities among states in the United States. While progress has been made in movement toward equity among the provinces in Canada, a reverse trend in the United States has been identified by this study. (p. 473)

In analyses of the distribution of state aid earmarked for educational reform initiatives between 1980 and 1990, Verstegen (1993, 1994) concluded that the new funds benefited children unequally, "advantaging the advantaged but failing the less fortunate" (1993, p. 33). She found that the states were using a new strategy in distributing aid to school districts. It linked all new dollars to state reform strategies, 70 percent of which were distributed as *unequalized* aid. Among the states, nearly 80 percent of the variation in per pupil revenue for schools was explained by state wealth as measured by gross state product per pupil. Greater increases in funding were found in states with greater wealth and taxing capacity, growing economic activity, and lower percentages of children in poverty. Wyoming, Vermont, Georgia, and Connecticut more than doubled their state aid (adjusted for inflation). Alaska, Oregon, Michigan, Illinois,

and Montana actually distributed less state aid in inflation-adjusted dollars in 1990 than they did a decade earlier. Verstegen's studies provide additional evidence that over the decade of education reform, variations in spending across the states widened. Moreover they were significantly related to a state's ability to pay for education (1994, p. 130).

Another study of the distribution of new resources allocated to public schools over the past five years is reported by Odden, Monk, Nakib, and Picus (1995). Their conclusion is that the funds have been distributed unfairly and used ineffectively. They also conclude that the public education system needs to be restructured so that new resources can be strategically linked to improved student achievement. They find that the largest portion of increased spending had been used to hire more teachers to reduce class size and to provide more out-of-classroom services, primarily "pullout" instruction for disabled and low-achieving students. Funds were also used to increase teacher salaries. But this was not done in a fashion that would enhance teacher expertise. Large portions of increased revenues were also used to expand special education services. The authors contend that the long-term task of reform is to get schools to act more like producers of high levels of student achievement than like consumers of educational resources.

Table 12.2 reports selected equity measures of per pupil expenditures for 1989–1990 as reported by Hertert, Busch, and Odden (1994). The ranking among states corresponds quite closely for the federal range ratio (FRR), the coefficient of variation (CV), and the McLoone index (MI). Each of these is unidimensional, that is, it involves only one variable, expenditure per pupil. Only four states have a coefficient of variation less than the 0.10 standard recommended by Odden and Picus (1992): Delaware, Iowa, Rhode Island, and West Virginia. With respect to the McLoone index, nearly two-thirds of the states (33) have a ratio above their standard of 0.90. Nevada is the only state to demonstrate perfect equity on this measure, 1.00. The federal range ratio shows that for six states,

TABLE 12.2. Equity Statistics by State for Per Pupil Expenditures, 1989–1990

	Mean[a] ($)	Median ($)	Federal Range Ratio (%)	Coefficient of Variation[a] (%)	McLoone Index	Districts	Membership
Alabama	3,490	3,423	41.43	10.40	0.939	129	723,301
Alaska	7,918	6,618	174.12	43.79	0.920	54	106,289
Arizona	3,358	3,184	98.19	20.67	0.912	211	704,833
Arkansas	2,995	2,941	54.62	13.52	0.919	327	434,346
California	4,457	4,238	61.14	17.21	0.917	988	4,629,689
Colorado	4,307	4,146	51.07	13.63	0.947	176	560,878
Connecticut	6,726	6,551	55.83	13.38	0.925	166	447,787
Delaware	5,229	5,469	34.75	9.91	0.876	16	93,489
District of Columbia	6,845	n/a	n/a	n/a	n/a	1	81,301
Florida	4,758	4,697	33.39	10.26	0.927	67	1,789,925
Georgia	3,930	3,761	82.42	18.80	0.906	186	1,128,368
Hawaii	4,288	n/a	n/a	n/a	n/a	1	169,493
Idaho	3,085	2,977	55.77	17.67	0.917	115	215,462
Illinois	4,180	3,999	139.31	29.86	0.824	950	1,788,529
Indiana	4,105	4,095	52.62	14.03	0.892	299	920,686
Iowa	4,063	4,040	25.57	8.29	0.940	431	478,816
Kansas	4,139	4,154	57.90	14.69	0.896	302	430,334
Kentucky	3,022	2,845	53.36	15.95	0.938	177	630,508
Louisiana	3,617	3,587	41.65	11.17	0.921	66	779,548
Maine	4,585	4,402	59.96	15.27	0.929	225	206,590
Maryland	6,202	6,008	58.52	15.96	0.905	24	698,806
Massachusetts	5,286	4,933	108.46	23.78	0.885	327	795,051
Michigan	4,419	4,268	89.91	21.48	0.877	560	1,637,254
Minnesota	4,677	4,566	49.93	14.15	0.917	433	739,125
Mississippi	2,944	2,880	41.96	11.99	0.924	152	500,342
Missouri	3,931	3,624	138.03	27.75	0.877	542	804,680
Montana	4,282	3,763	142.40	32.16	0.904	525	147,730
Nebraska	4,451	4,541	88.77	22.38	0.816	794	264,625
Nevada	3,828	3,696	19.45	10.68	1.000	17	186,834
New Hampshire	4,795	4,683	61.09	16.31	0.892	155	165,629
New Jersey	6,560	6,325	76.25	18.49	0.887	549	1,026,741
New Mexico	3,965	3,790	56.84	17.20	0.953	87	254,937
New York	7,390	7,167	91.04	21.65	0.895	701	2,512,778
North Carolina	4,064	4,022	36.05	10.16	0.930	134	1,074,752
North Dakota	3,815	3,694	97.95	24.46	0.868	276	117,837
Ohio	4,343	4,013	109.75	24.29	0.883	613	1,764,499
Oklahoma	2,976	2,902	45.07	15.52	0.934	589	576,146
Oregon	4,862	4,682	74.34	18.59	0.893	297	472,092
Pennsylvania	5,503	5,240	98.29	20.92	0.881	500	1,621,178
Rhode Island	5,655	5,525	39.15	8.66	0.961	37	135,035
South Carolina	3,910	3,878	37.63	10.84	0.936	91	592,043
South Dakota	3,522	3,382	72.85	19.96	0.919	183	127,329
Tennessee	2,985	2,854	63.35	16.35	0.906	138	827,804
Texas	3,645	3,539	50.56	15.99	0.930	1.055	3,315,674

TABLE 12.2. Equity Statistics by State for Per Pupil Expenditures, 1989–1990 (*Continued*)

	Mean[a] ($)	Median ($)	Federal Range Ratio (%)	Coefficient of Variation[a] (%)	McLoone Index	Districts	Membership
Utah	2,606	2,500	43.53	13.35	0.963	39	435,140
Vermont	5,081	4,863	84.87	19.17	0.888	242	91,185
Virginia	4,698	4,401	66.46	21.39	0.903	133	987,414
Washington	4,336	4,198	43.36	12.55	0.955	296	809.733
West Virginia	3,549	3,536	22.63	6.79	0.953	55	323,021
Wisconsin	5,417	5,279	47.17	14.73	0.911	427	750,341
Wyoming	5,206	4,940	63.17	19.67	0.947	49	97,172

[a]Mean and coefficient of variation are weighted by membership per district.

SOURCE: L. Hertert, C. Busch, and A. Odden. (1994). School financing inequities among the states: The problem from a national perspective. *Journal of Education Finance, 19,* 253–255.

expenditure per pupil at the ninety-fifth percentile is more than double that at the fifth percentile: Alaska, Illinois, Massachusetts, Missouri, Montana, and Ohio. These states also tend to be among the most inequitable states as measured by the coefficient of variation, but not necessarily as measured by the McLoone index. In using these measures of equity, it is important to recognize that each examines a somewhat different aspect of the concept. The measure selected for evaluating the effectiveness of a particular policy should correspond closely to the intended effect of that policy.

Parrish, Matsumoto, and Fowler (1995) did a national study of the disparities in public school district spending in all school districts in the United States. They analyzed revenue and expenditure data from the 1990 Survey of Local Government Finances and nonfiscal data from the National Center for Education Statistics' Common Core of Data. They addressed questions relating to who pays, how much, and for whom. To the extent that these questions pertain to the allocation of education resources to students with comparable education needs, they are considered to be horizontal equity issues. They addressed vertical equity issues by relating expenditure differences with the differing educational needs of students. They used bivariate, multivariate, and dispersion analyses.

Critical predictors of variation in school district expenditures in the Parrish et al. study were

region (being the highest in the northeast and lowest in the west), size (an inverse relationship), socioeconomic status and education attainment (a direct relationship), percentage of minorities (a direct relationship), extent of poverty (an inverse relationship), and percentage of students in special education programs (an inverse relationship). The authors concluded that:

Students in districts enrolling the lowest percentages of students in poverty and the lowest percentages of students in need of special education services received the highest expenditures. While these trends are matters of concern from a student equity perspective, they should be considered in the context of no clear patterns of expenditure differentials for limited English proficiency and at-risk students, and a positive relationship between percentage of minority students and expenditures. (p. 11)

They found the distribution of public resources for education was substantially more equal than wealth measured by housing values. It was somewhat less varied than wealth measured by household income. They found funds allocated by states were the primary equalizing factors of resources directed to education. Some additional equalization resulted from the various federal funding programs.

Equity with Respect to Noneconomic Inputs and Outputs. There is some encouraging evidence, however, that the higher academic standards set by states as part of the education reform movement and their corresponding assessment strategies are serving to reduce, if not eliminate, the inequities in outputs experienced by at-risk children. These initiatives have been relatively inexpensive to implement. Between 1973 and 1990, the percentage of academic course taking by all students jumped from 59 percent to over two-thirds. The national dropout rate declined from 14 percent to 12 percent (Mirel & Angus, 1994). These numbers were even more impressive for minority students. Minority students are taking more and tougher academic courses than in the past. *And* they are performing better on national standardized examinations. Between 1976 and 1993, scores for African American students rose twenty-one points on the verbal section of the SAT and thirty-four points on the math section. Hispanic students showed similar progress. Also, growing numbers of minority students are taking advanced placement examinations. For African American students, the number grew from 10,000 in 1988 to more than 15,000 in 1993. For Hispanic students, the number increased from 10,000 to nearly 30,000.

Unfortunately these improvements in schooling outputs have not necessarily resulted in corresponding improvements in schooling outcomes. The percentage of African American students eighteen to twenty-four years of age enrolling in college has actually declined from 22.6 percent in the mid-1970s to 21.1 percent. At the same time, enrollment of white students has increased from 27.1 percent to 31.3 percent. Mirel and Angus (1994) commented on these overall gains:

> [F]or more than half a century, educational policy makers have made decisions based on the presumption that tougher course requirements automatically increase the dropout rate, especially among poor and minority students. Moreover, these policy makers assumed that the only way to keep the dropout rate from soaring was to make the high school curriculum less challenging and more entertaining. . . . [P]oor and minority students have been the most frequent casualties of such standard-lowering policies as allowing less rigorous courses to meet academic requirements for graduation or diluting course content in academic courses while keeping course titles the same. . . . Much of the failure of American K–12 education lies in our avoiding the formidable task of discovering how to teach difficult subjects in ways that are both accessible to young people and yet still true to the complexity and richness of the material. (pp. 40–42)

Single-State Studies

The lack of progress in bringing about greater equity in expenditures per pupil has also been confirmed, with a few exceptions, by numerous single-state studies. Hickrod, Chaudhari, and Hubbard (1983) reported on a longitudinal study of the reform adopted by the state of Illinois in 1973. They found that the state had made progress toward established equity goals of less expenditure disparity and greater wealth neutrality for a period of three years. Then a reversal began to set in. They attributed the reversal primarily to "smaller and smaller amounts of new state funds that were available after the middle of the 1970s" (p. 34).

Minnesota reformed its school finance structure in 1971. It was one of the first states to do so. Krupey and Hopeman (1983) studied the impact on equity using data for 1972–1973, 1978–1979, and 1981–1982. They found that during the first seven years of reform, the state had made progress toward reducing revenue and tax rate disparities and in making the system more fiscally neutral. As a result of subsequent legislation and the increased use of referendum levies, however, revenue disparities increased and the system became less fiscally neutral.

Oesch and Paquette (1995) compared their equity findings for the province of Ontario for 1988 and 1989 with those of Bezeau (1985) for 1965–1976. They concluded that equity as measured by coefficients of variation and Gini coefficients were generally higher during the late 1960s and the 1970s than in 1988 and 1989. This agreed with a general North American trend of increased equity in the mid 1970s. They also concluded that the Ontario equalization scheme was as good as or better than that provided by any of the equalization schemes in the United States. Interestingly, they also discovered that the panoply of categorical aids increased horizontal equity (both in expenditures and in tax neutrality) over that of the general aid plan.

Berne and Stiefel (1984) analyzed data for the state of Michigan for the years 1970 through 1978. They found that criteria of horizontal equity started and ended at about the same point but worsened during the middle of the period. With respect to equal opportunity, they found that children in wealthier districts enjoyed better educational provision. They also found inequities by region of the state and with respect to race.

Kearney and Chen (1989) continued the study of Michigan where Berne and Stiefel left off. They extended the analysis to 1985. The years 1984 and 1985 had brought about some improvements in most criteria of horizontal equity. They concluded, however, that the goal was much further from attainment in 1985 than it had been in 1979. Equality of opportunity continued to decrease over the period of the analysis.

Kearney and Anderson (1992) extended the Michigan analysis through 1989. They concluded that school finance equity in Michigan, in terms of almost any equity object, any equity principle, and any equity measure, worsened over the period 1976–1989 for both pupils and taxpayers. Frustration over the immutability of these conditions may have contributed to the radical reform adopted by Michigan in 1993. This reform virtually eliminated the property tax as a means of local support of public education (see Chapter 6).

Berne and Stiefel (1984) conducted a study of equity in New York for the fourteen-year period from 1965 to 1978. On most criteria of horizontal equity, they found improvements to about 1969. Conditions then worsened for five years and

remained level or improved slightly during the remainder of the period. As a result, there was greater inequity in educational opportunities in the latter part of the 1970s than in the 1960s. There were consistently positive correlations between indicators of levels of educational services and equalized property wealth per pupil in all of the fourteen years the study covered.

Berne and Stiefel updated their New York State study in 1990. Despite an increase in expenditures per pupil of 40 percent from 1977 through 1988 in inflation-adjusted dollars, a time series analysis of expenditure per pupil showed that equity had not improved markedly over the period. In 1991–1992, expenditures per pupil at the ninetieth percentile of spending ($9,586) were nearly twice the level at the tenth percentile ($5,034). Berne concluded that New York's public primary and secondary education system suffers from serious input and output inequities.

Berne (1994) reassessed the equity of New York State schools in 1994 using additional measures of input and introducing measures of output. Children in districts with high percentages of minority and poor children consistently experienced larger classes, less accessibility to instructional technology, and less-qualified teachers than did children in other districts. The analysis clearly established that the input inequities extended to outputs as well. Children in the highest-poverty schools were consistently among the lowest achievers on state examinations. The differences in average scores between high- and low-poverty schools were substantial.

For decades, reformers in New York State have tried to address some of these inequities. The state's school finance system has been unsuccessfully challenged in the state courts twice (*Levittown* v. *Nyquist*, 1982; *Reform Education Financing Inequities Today* v. *Cuomo*, 1991). The system is continually under study by specially appointed commissions and external consultants. And numerous changes in aid formulas by the state legislature were intended to improve equity. All of these activities, however, have taken place in a political context requiring extensive compromise to pass any legislation. The diverse population of the state is divided into 718 internally homogeneous school districts. For example, over 80 percent of the minority school population is located in the five big-city school districts of the state. The percentage of children coming from low-income families in these districts is also nearly as large. To get the votes to pass legislation meeting the needs of poor and minority children in urban centers requires concessions to school districts serving suburban and rural districts. The net result is a continuation of structural patterns of inequities.

New York illustrates the politics of equity in the absence of court-ordered reform. California illustrates that court orders do not eliminate politics from the decision-making process. They merely lead to the introduction of new political strategies. The combined effects of court-imposed school finance equalization (*Serrano* v. *Priest*) and various tax limitation measures (Proposition 13) have created a relatively equitable centralized system of school finance in California. While *Serrano* constrains the state legislature from overtly manipulating base revenue school funding to the advantage of some districts and to the detriment of others, it is not bound by the same constraints when it comes to categorical funding (Timar, 1994). As a result, categorical aids have proliferated. During the 1980s they grew in number from nineteen to seventy. In 1979–1980, categorical aids, including federal aid, represented about 13 percent of total K–12 funding. In 1991–1992, they represented over 29 percent of the total.

Timar (1994) analyzed the impact of the growth in categorical aids on equity in California. He divided such aids into three categories: compensatory, desegregation, and supplemental. He concluded that in most instances, "categorical funding decisions reflect legitimate differences in student composition or extraordinary costs among school districts; in other instances, however, they reflect differences in political control over the state budgetary process" (p. 154). He found that compensatory aid was closely related to student need. But supplementary grants and desegregation costs

bore no demonstrable relationship to unusual or uncontrollable costs. Desegregation aid went primarily to urban districts. But Timar found that the level of funding was unrelated to the number of African American and Hispanic students in the district. Supplemental aid went predominantly to suburban districts. It went there because of their suburban status. He concluded: "Clearly, in these two funding categories, educational interests are subordinated to political interests" (p. 154). These aids are creating new inequities among California school districts.

Johnson and Pillainayagam (1991) concluded that Ohio's system of financing education had not improved in either horizontal equity or equality of opportunity during the decade 1980–1989. They found that the foundation program had operated so as to maintain the relationship between local district fiscal capacity and current operating expenditures per pupil. Furthermore, the save-harmless guarantee provision under which approximately 40 percent of Ohio districts received their state aid allocation was a primary impediment to realizing greater equity of educational opportunity. It served to strengthen the relationship between current expenditures per pupil and local fiscal capacity. The only equity measure for Ohio during the decade that came close to satisfying the Odden and Picus standards was the McLoone index. This index suggested that the greatest disparity is found in the upper half of expenditure and wealth districts. Porter (1991) reached similar conclusions with respect to taxpayer equity in Ohio.

Hartman (1994) conducted a seven-year study of spending disparities among Pennsylvania school districts. He analyzed the expenditures of the fifty highest-spending school districts, the fifty middle-spending districts, and the fifty lowest-spending districts. He found that the patterns had been very stable over the seven years between 1985 and 1992.

> After seven years, a school finance equity law suit filed, much discussion and debate among policy makers, and large increases in funding

and spending levels, substantial resource disparities remain among Pennsylvania school districts; the differences continue to favor the high spending (and wealthy) school districts in the state. While some of the differences relate to cost of resources faced by districts in different locations, the remaining differences in spending represent inequity in educational opportunity. (p. 106)

In 1988, Virginia enacted a major restructuring of its school finance system intended to decrease fiscal disparities and close the gap between the best schools and the worse. An analysis by Verstegen and Salmon (1991) that compared distributions of district revenues the year before enactment with those the two years following concluded that the new system failed on all counts. When adjusted for inflation, their data showed a continuing deterioration in the level of education support for 70 percent of Virginia's schoolchildren. The linkage between revenue per pupil and ability to pay was actually strengthened.

Basing their research in conventional concepts of equity, Walters and Freeman (1993) introduced the use of data envelopment analysis (DEA) and simultaneous equations to model the impact of state aid on interdistrict spending disparity in Utah from 1975 to 1990. They found that spending disparities still existed in Utah and seemed to be getting worse. Spending disparities were primarily a function of wealth disparities among districts. They showed that while state aid policy had not achieved either fiscal or wealth neutrality in education spending, it nevertheless had some positive impact. It redistributed money in the right direction from wealthier to poorer districts. Variations in local effort appeared to have little effect on spending levels. They concluded that "while state policies have played an important role in equalizing spending, these policies have not succeeded in establishing either fiscal or wealth neutrality" (p. 153).

Although most state efforts to improve equity have failed over the long term, there have been some successes. New Mexico is one of the few states to show substantial equity among districts on both revenues and expenditures. New Mexico has assumed virtually full responsibility for school finance while retaining the district as the operating unit. No discretion is allowed to school districts in setting tax rates or determining revenues. King (1983) attributed the state's wealth neutrality to property tax limitations, uniform tax rates, and a steady increase in state financial support. Commenting on King's conclusion, Hickrod and Goertz (1983) speculated that "midwestern and northern state legislators will find these restrictions on local control too high a price to pay for greater education finance equity" (p. 3).

Verstegen (1987) analyzed data from the Texas school finance system for the period 1976 through 1986 to determine if legislative action had improved financial equity in the wake of the Supreme Court decision in 1973 (*San Antonio Independent School District* v. *Rodriguez, 1973*). She found that all measures studied (coefficient of variation, federal range ratio, restricted range, McLoone index, simple correlation, and elasticity) showed improvement, indicating greater equity over time. The improvement was even greater when the upper 5 percent of students ranked by revenue per pupil were excluded from the analysis.

The improvement was not sufficient to satisfy school districts having low property wealth, however. The Edgewood Independent School District led a new series of legal challenges to the Texas school finance system. Toenjes and Clark (1994) conducted an equity analysis of the likely impact of school finance arrangements the Texas legislature enacted in 1993 to meet the court's equity concerns coming out of the *Edgewood* (1989, 1991) decisions. The simulations they conducted revealed that the new arrangements would increase the equity of the system substantially, as measured by statistics that describe the relationship between wealth and revenue. Because of the phase-in provisions of the legislation, the full effect will not be realized until 1996–1997.

Goetz and Debertin (1992) made an early assessment of revenue equalization under the Kentucky reforms. They sought to answer these questions: Has the relationship between personal income and per pupil spending changed? Is spending within and between various districts of the state more equal? They found that the reforms were an unqualified success—at least in the short term. Funds available to all school districts increased. And the relationship between per pupil spending and the percentage of students living in poverty was reduced. Previously high correlations between per pupil revenues and tax rates, achievement scores, economic deprivation, and per capita income had also been reduced—in some instances to zero. The authors attributed the success of the reforms to the redefinition of allocation units from classrooms to individual students and to the incorporation into the funding formula of an allowance for pupils from economically deprived backgrounds.

Intradistrict Equity Studies

Equity has returned to the political agenda during the 1990s. But the emphases of analyses have shifted. Outcomes equity and equal opportunity are the focus of attention. Several studies are now giving attention to the equity of distribution of resources and outcomes within districts, even as research continues at the district, state, and national levels. All analyses have become more complicated as federal and state governments increase their use of categorical aids targeted to at-risk students as an instrument of public policy to promote vertical equity. In the past, categorical aids were small enough to be ignored or included with other revenue or expenditures in the evaluation of horizontal equity. This procedure is no longer appropriate. General education funding can continue to be used in the evaluation of horizontal equity.

Berne and Stiefel (1994) set the pattern for the study of equity within districts, just as they had for the analysis of equity within states (Berne and Stiefel, 1984). Their 1994 analysis of equity within New York City was made possible by the publication (for the first time) of detailed budgets for the

more than 800 elementary and middle/junior high schools operated by the city's thirty-two community school districts. They explored the usefulness of a variety of strategies, statistics, and measures for conducting this type of analysis.

Berne and Stiefel found that the glaring inequities in vertical equity with respect to poverty that were commonplace at the state level did not exist within New York City. Even though elementary schools budgeted and spent more resources per pupil of general education funds in lower- than higher-poverty schools, categorical aids were sufficient to bring expenditures of high-poverty schools above those of low-poverty schools. Middle and junior high schools directed greater amounts of general education funds per pupil to higher-poverty schools. High-poverty schools, regardless of grade level, had greater access to most other resources (for example, categorical aids) than did low-poverty schools.

Their analysis uncovered an alarmingly low level of per pupil general education budget for elementary and middle schools—$2,550. This compares to the almost $7,000 total per pupil budget for the district as a whole. Poorer subdistricts received more funds per pupil in nonallocated, district office, and indirect categories. But they did not usually receive more in allocated and direct categories. Berne and Stiefel concluded that this finding was consistent with the claims of many school districts serving large numbers of poor children that nonclassroom management and oversight burdens associated with programs targeted at such children are substantial. They questioned whether this practice is productive. They asked whether there might be other ways to get more resources to poor children directly with less being used to meet overhead expenses.

They also found that average teacher salaries in high-poverty subdistricts of New York City were $4,536 lower than in low-poverty subdistricts. This was because poorer students were taught by less-experienced and less-educated teachers. As a result, the teachers were paid at a lower rate. Berne and Stiefel proposed: "This raises the critical policy question of how to better allocate teacher resources within urban districts" (p. 419). These findings also suggested the methodological conclusion that "measures of dollars alone are not sufficient in an equity analysis and that to some degree the education process must be examined" (p. 419).

Hyary (1994) studied the intradistrict distribution of education resources among 1,246 New York State elementary schools in 300 school districts excluding New York City. The specific school-level resources she looked at were average annual teacher salaries, percentage of first-year teachers, percentage of teachers teaching outside their certification area, average number of students per class, number of microcomputers per 100 pupils, and number of library books per pupil. She concluded that there was considerable variation across the 300 districts in the equity of intradistrict resource distribution. Districts with high levels of intradistrict inequality tended to have relatively large enrollments, numbers of schools, and percentage of minority or poor children. She found no evidence that minority or poor children were being denied equal access to resources, however. The intradistrict inequities could have been caused by deliberate district policy targeting compensatory resources to minority or poor children. But the study design did not permit the investigation of such a possibility.

Hertert (1994) analyzed the degree of disparity in per pupil expenditures at two levels, district and school, within the state of California. She focused on unified school districts (having all grades K–12) with at least 2,500 students in average daily attendance (ADA). She did not include federal and state categorical funds in her analysis because the focus was on those fiscal resources distributed on behalf of all children (horizontal equity). She made no attempt to prorate central administration expenditures to schools because her purpose was to determine the equity of resources available and used directly by schools.

Hertert concluded that judgments on the fairness of the distributions found are a matter of per-

spective. California has a fairly equitable system across districts. Equalization across schools, however, is not so equitable. In a few of the districts she studied she found substantial variation among schools that could not be explained by school size or ethnicity. Noting that over the past several decades, a great deal of attention has been given to creating equity across districts, she concluded that these efforts might be more productive if attention were focused across schools rather than districts.

Owens (1994) studied the equity of resource allocation among elementary schools in Dade County, Florida. This is the nation's third-largest school district. It contains the city of Miami. The purpose of the study was to determine if variations in allocations were linked to racial/ethnic composition or the household income levels of the students. He measured expenditures in four ways: instructional expenditures for the basic program, including and excluding compensatory programs per unweighted pupil unit; and instructional expenditures for the basic program, including and excluding compensatory programs per pupil unit, weighted to reflect aggregate student need. Instructional expenditures were composed primarily of teachers' salaries and benefits. But they also included purchased services and classroom materials.

Owens found that instructional expenditures in some elementary schools within Dade County were much higher than in others. Unlike in the New York City and California studies, he found that these differences were related to racial/ethnic and family-income factors. Schools with high percentages of African American and low-income students and large schools had lower instructional expenditures per pupil than schools without those characteristics, for all methods of computing expenditures. Owens attributed this inequity largely to the practice of permitting senior teachers to control where they will teach. As in the New York City study, less-experienced teachers and teachers with less education were more likely to be found in traditionally minority and low-SES schools.

Discussion and Conclusions

Conceptual Considerations. There has been a marked shift in our thinking about equity during the 1990s. It is no longer a matter of equity *or* high standards; it is a matter of equity *and* high standards. While we continue to be interested in the equity of inputs into the educational process out of a sense of fairness, our ultimate concern is with student outputs and outcomes. Previously we believed almost naively that if there was equity in terms of school district inputs, equity of student achievement would automatically follow. We now know better. We have come to know that the linkages between resources and outcomes are very tenuous (Monk, 1994). Merely adding resources to a failed system will not automatically reform that system. The resources have to be organized and used effectively for the single purpose of improving student learning. While we have scattered examples of this happening, they are few and far between.

Equity studies within districts centered on schools have shown us that distribution of resources is inequitable within districts as well as among districts and states. The logical extension of this movement to school-centered studies is toward equity studies centering on programs, classrooms— and even individual children. We are moving from a concern over the equitable treatment of institutions to the equitable treatment of individuals.

Political Considerations. On the whole, the evidence leaves little room for optimism about substantial improvements in school finance equity in the absence of judicial intervention. Ironically, the greatest improvements in equity were made during the 1950s and 1960s when equity was not an explicit goal. Jones (1985) pointed to the necessity of considering allocation and distribution patterns across time, covering periods of policy reform and periods of stability, to monitor the sustained effects of efforts to change public policy.

The most likely explanation of the lack of predictability of effects of policy initiatives on equity is that equity is only one of many policy objectives

of school finance reform. Equity collides with the goals of improving adequacy and efficiency, meeting educational needs, maintaining local control, providing property tax relief, and increasing public choice (Brown & Elmore, 1982). Hickrod and Goertz (1983) observed:

> A legislative body is the appropriate forum to try to strike a balance between conflicting values such as equity and local control. It may have to be aided and abetted from time to time by the judicial branch, but it is the right place to make the decision. A compromise will be struck for these conflicting values for a given point in time with certain knowledge that that compromise is never final. The voice of the people speaks through a majority which is forever shifting through time. Each successive legislative body will change the balance point between egalitarian goals and libertarian goals and they will continue to do that so long as the democratic process is allowed to freely operate. (p. 418)

The 1980s saw a shift in favor of libertarian goals. Efficiency and standards moved to center stage. School finance reform became school reform. Few recognized that the two might be in some way connected. During the 1990s, people have seen the connection. But we still struggle to design, enact, and implement policies that will facilitate the realization of both. With constrained resources, we can realize equity of inputs only through reallocation of resources. This is a very unpopular strategy—and politically dangerous to incumbents. Leveling up poor districts, on the other hand, is very expensive and may be possible only with higher or new taxes—also unpopular and politically dangerous.

Wong (1994) provided two further explanations for the lack of progress in achieving equity in the provision of educational resources: the functional fragmentation among the three levels of government in the federal structure, and the high degree of jurisdictional fragmentation at the local level. In developing his argument, Wong proposed a topology of equity policy: social equity, territorial equity, and distributive equity. Social equity concerns the presence of special-needs populations such as those with the racial and poverty characteristics of many big-city school districts. Territorial equity concerns the great variation in fiscal capacity in taxable wealth among states and local jurisdictions. Distributive equity concerns the allocation of resources within school districts, schools, and classrooms.

Wong noted that federal policy has focused on special-needs populations and has paid little attention to territorial disparities within states. States, on the other hand, have focused their attention on equalizing interdistrict fiscal capacity but have been largely quiescent on how state aid might be used to address the needs of disadvantaged students. Local distributive decisions are based almost solely on giving each teacher an equal number of students. They have not taken into account differences in children's needs and in teacher experience, expertise, and salary. The result is substantial inequity in per pupil resources from school to school.

As big-city systems turn into predominantly low-income, minority institutions, middle-class suburban districts quickly organize themselves to ensure that the state-aid allocation formula does not undermine their interests. The politics of fragmentation . . . tend to disburse state funds widely and have produced very limited success in reducing spending disparity among districts in industrialized states with a strong minority presence. (Wong, 1994, pp. 282–283)

In the absence of judicial intervention, the possibilities of bringing about greater equity in public education appear to be remote. Even with judicial intervention, the road is long and difficult.

Structural Considerations. Levin (1994) listed what he considered to be the necessary and suffi-

cient conditions for equity in education outcomes. The necessary conditions "are to provide access to all children of a full range of appropriate programs as well as to the funding and other resources that will enable them to benefit from those programs" (p. 172). Traditional equity studies have focused on one or more of these conditions. But this approach does not lead to equity if schools are differentially effective.

In discussing the sufficient conditions of equity, Levin (1994) cited several studies that have shown large variations in outcomes of schools with apparently similar resources and student characteristics. He noted that the inefficiencies seem to be greatest among schools serving populations that are most at risk educationally. To rectify this situation, Levin's sufficient condition for achieving education equity "is that schools are maximally effective with all children in that resources are used optimally to meet their educational needs" (p. 172). Effectiveness of educational programs has not been a focus of equity studies, however. But one of the reasons for moving from input to output objectives of equity is that we realize that when input equity has been achieved, it has not necessarily resulted in output equity.

Hanushek (1994) followed a line of argument similar to Levin's when he observed that "The flaw in the traditional school finance debate is that the entire discussion centers on funding and school spending. Spending is (often implicitly) equated to school quality or performance" (p. 464). He went on to note that expenditures per pupil in constant dollars rose between 1970 and 1990 by approximately 3.5 percent per year. This significant influx of resources was allocated to (1) a dramatic increase in noninstructional expenditures, including school building administration and retirement and health benefits for educational personnel; (2) a substantial reduction in pupil : teacher ratio (by one-quarter); and (3) a real increase in teachers' salaries of 15 percent. In other words, the new resources were absorbed largely by the old, failing structure and were not allocated to programmatic innovations shown to improve student performance. Hanushek (1994) concluded that "the chances for improving the performance of the schools are closely linked to changes in the incentive structure, and these changes are at odds with much of the recent finance discussion" (p. 461).

Others also see the lack of productivity and incentives as being an impediment to the realization of equity. Behind the problem of productivity and incentives is a problem of knowledge and practice (Elmore, 1994). Porter (1994) proposed teacher, school, school district, and state accountability with serious consequences as incentives for improving productivity and reaching outcome equity. "For most teachers, schools, districts, and state systems of education there are no consequences for excellence or for failure" (p. 493). Darling-Hammond (1994) observed, "To provide such incentives, schools' success must be gauged by the quality of teaching and learning experiences they provide to all students rather than by measures of aggregate outcomes that may be substantially manipulated by changes in the students admitted or retained" (p. 195).

SUMMARY

In this chapter, we have discussed the relationship between the concepts of fraternity and equity, and the differing philosophical perspectives of equity and their horizontal and vertical dimensions. We discussed the more common criteria and methodologies used by policy analysts in measuring equity.

Early studies concentrated on horizontal equity of distributions of inputs among states and school districts. In addition, recent studies have examined distributions of outputs within districts as well as among districts and states. Studies monitoring the progress, or the lack of it, toward school finance equity goals since World War II have shown that equity gains, even as a result of judicial intervention, are short-lived. Where financial equity has been achieved, inequities in the distribution of outputs remain. To achieve equity in the distribution of outputs requires not only equity of inputs but also efficiency in the use of those resources.

The study of education equity is becoming more sophisticated. It recognizes the linkage between inputs to the education process, student outcomes, and the effectiveness of professional educators. This growing understanding is observable in recent judicial decisions and in systemic legislated reform, as in Kentucky (Pipho, 1993). There can be no equity in education where any schools function ineffectively and inefficiently. A major stumbling block to achieving effectiveness and efficiency is a lack of knowledge about the intricacies of the relationships between educational inputs, processes, and outputs. This is our focus in Chapter 13.

NOTE

1. Technical definitions are not provided in this text for standard statistics, that is, mean, standard deviation, correlation coefficient, and regression coefficient. Readers desiring such technical information are referred to a basic statistical textbook.

ACTIVITIES

1. Using data from a state or region, calculate several of the equity measures we discussed in this chapter. Which are the most relevant measures for evaluating school finance policy in that state or region? What are the implications for policy initiatives?
2. Selecting the equity measure that most closely reflects the policy objectives of the state studied in activity 1, calculate the measure for each year over a period of a decade or more. Examine the trends in relation to changes in state policy. Have the policies been effective? What changes in state policy, if any, would you propose to improve school finance equity?
3. Analyze distributions of resources among schools *within* a given school district. Discuss the resulting findings with a central office administrator. Inquire about the rationale for inequities in spending among buildings, if any. What conclusions and recommendations do you draw from this analysis?

COMPUTER SIMULATIONS

Objectives of This Activity:

- *To provide experience in the computation of various measures of equity*
- *To compare equity measures for the hypothetical state with measures for actual states as presented in the chapter*

These simulations provide the reader with experience in calculating measures of equity discussed in Chapter 12. Using expenditure per pupil data drawn from the hypothetical state database, Simulation 12.1 considers variations in the range approach to measuring equity. Subsequent simulations consider statistical and graphing approaches to the measurement of equity using the same expenditures per pupil. Statistics calculated include the coefficient of variation, the McLoone index, and the correlation coefficient. Data used in the computation of the correlation coefficients and the Lorenz curve, which is used in the determination of the Gini coefficient are also graphed. Calculation of the Gini coefficient and correlation analysis of equity measures could be more efficiently accomplished with a computer software package (such as the Statistical Package for the Social Sciences [SPSS]) than with basic spreadsheet software packages.

Simulation 12.1: *Federal Range Ratio*

Part 1. Preparing the Data Set

a. Retrieve the file EQUITY_1. This file includes two worksheets: (1) selected data from the hypothetical database state "DATA" that has been sorted in ascending order of EXPEND PER PUPIL, and (2) a template for summary of selected equity measures for the state.

b. In the CUMULATIVE PUPILS column on the BARCELONA row, enter the cell reference for PUPILS.

c. In the CUMULATIVE PUPILS column on the ELLICOTT row, create a formula that adds PUPILS to the previous number of CUMULATIVE PUPILS.

d. Copy the formula down through the column. In the last row, GETZVILLE, the number of CUMULATIVE PUPILS should be 66,090.

e. In the CUMULATIVE % PUPILS column on the BARCELONA row, create a formula that divides CUMULATIVE PUPILS by the 66,090 total pupils in the state.

f. Copy the formula down through the column. Notice that districts do not have the same number of pupils and therefore each district contributes a different percentage to the total pupils in the state.

g. Print the first completed worksheet.

Part 2. Calculating the Federal Range Ratio

a. On the MEDIAN row of the template under the column marked DATA, enter the cell reference for the EXPEND PER PUPIL of the district that contains the 50th percentile pupil of the state. Helpful hint: in the CUMULATIVE PERCENT PUPILS column, REDROCK contains pupils ranging from 28% to 63%; this expenditure represents the median for the state.

b. To calculate the range, enter the cell references on the HIGHEST and LOWEST rows of the template that correspond to the highest and lowest districts in EXPEND PER PUPIL respectively.

c. On the RANGE row of the template, create a formula that subtracts the LOWEST from the HIGHEST. This difference represents the magnitude of the range of expenditures in the state.

d. To calculate the restricted range, enter the cell references on the 90TH and 10TH PERCENTILE rows of the template for the EXPEND PER PUPIL of districts containing the 90th and 10th percentile pupils (in the CUMULATIVE PERCENT PUPILS column) respectively.

e. On the RESTRICTED RANGE row of the template, create a formula that subtracts the 10TH from the 90TH PERCENTILE. This difference between the 90th and 10th percentile expenditures represents the magnitude of the restricted range.

f. To calculate the federal range ratio, enter the cell references on the 95TH and 5TH PERCENTILE rows of the template for the EXPEND PER PUPIL of districts containing the 95th and 5th percentile pupils (in the CUMULATIVE PERCENT PUPILS column) respectively.

g. On the FEDERAL RANGE row, create a formula that subtracts the 5TH from the 95TH PERCENTILE.

h. On the FEDERAL RANGE RATIO row, create a formula that divides the FEDERAL RANGE by the 5TH PERCENTILE expenditure. The resulting decimal represents the Federal Range Ratio. Compare this statistic with those presented for states in Table 12.2. Is there greater or less equity represented by this state than by the state in which you reside?

i. Print the second completed worksheet.

Simulation 12.2. *Coefficient of Variation and McLoone Index*

a. Retrieve the file EQUITY_2. This file includes two worksheets: (1) selected data from the data worksheet used in Simulation 12.1, and (2) a template for summary of selected equity measures for the state.

b. To calculate the mean expenditure per pupil, create a new column labeled: TOTAL EXPEND.

c. In the new TOTAL EXPEND column on the BARCELONA row, enter a formula that multiplies PUPILS by EXPEND PER PUPIL. Copy the formula down through the column.

d. At the bottom of the data worksheet, create a new row labeled: TOTAL.

e. In the PUPILS column on the new TOTAL row, enter a formula that totals the number of PUPILS in the state.

f. Copy the formula on the TOTAL row to the same row in the TOTAL EXPEND column.

g. On the MEAN row of the template, enter a formula that divides the TOTAL of the TOTAL EXPEND column by the TOTAL of the PUPILS column. This result represents the average per pupil expenditure in the state.

h. On the MEDIAN row of the template, enter the cell reference that corresponds to the district that contains the 50th percentile pupil.

i. Using the district as the unit, create a formula to determine the standard deviation of EXPEND PER PUPIL on the STANDARD DEVIATION row of the template.

j. On the COEFFICIENT OF VARIATION row of the template, create a formula that divides the STANDARD DEVIATION by the state MEAN. Compare this coefficient of variation with those presented for states in Table 12.2. Is there greater or less equity represented by this state than by the state in which you reside?

k. To calculate the McLoone index, create a formula that totals the EXPEND PER PUPIL amounts that fall below the MEDIAN on the ACTUAL EXPENDITURES BELOW MEDIAN row of the template.

Note that the total will include the TOTAL EXPEND amounts from BARCELONA through SWORMSVILLE and the amount of EXPEND PER PUPIL from REDROCK times 14,289 pupils (bringing the total number of pupils considered to 50% of the state's total). Half the state's total CUMULATIVE PUPILS (66,090) is 33,045. Total CUMULATIVE PUPILS through SWORMSVILLE is 18,756. To reach the state median pupil, 14,289 pupils from REDROCK are required, the difference between 33,045 and 18,756.

l. On the MEDIAN EXPENDITURES BELOW MEDIAN row, calculate what the total would be if the MEDIAN amount were expended on each student included in step k.

m. On the MCLOONE INDEX row, create a formula that divides the ACTUAL EXPENDITURES BELOW MEDIAN by the MEDIAN EXPENDITURES BELOW MEDIAN. Compare this index with those presented for states in Table 12.2. Is there greater or less equity represented by this state than by the state in which you reside?

n. Print the completed worksheets.

Simulation 12.3: *Lorenz Curve and Data for the Gini Coefficient*

a. Copy the completed data worksheet to an area below the completed template worksheet.

b. In the new worksheet area, clear or erase the cell entries in the TOTAL EXPEND column and the TOTAL row.

c. Change the TOTAL EXPEND column label to: CUMULATIVE EXPEND.

d. In the new CUMULATIVE EXPEND column on the BARCELONA row, enter the cell reference from the completed data worksheet above in the TOTAL EXPEND column on the BARCELONA row.

e. In the new CUMULATIVE EXPEND column on the ELLICOTT row, enter the cell reference from the completed data worksheet in the TOTAL EXPEND column on the ELLICOTT row plus the cell reference from the new data worksheet in the CUMULATIVE EXPEND column on the BARCELONA row.

f. Copy the formula on the new ELLICOTT row down through the new CUMULATIVE EXPEND column. On the GETZVILLE row, the CUMULATIVE EXPEND amount will be $507,841,773.

g. Create a new column labeled: CUMULATIVE % EXPEND.

h. In the new CUMULATIVE % EXPEND column on the BARCELONA row, enter a formula that divides CUMULATIVE EXPEND by the $507,841,773 total expenditure in the state. Copy the formula down through the column.

i. Print the new completed data worksheet.

j. The graph of the Lorenz curve is based on the CUMULATIVE % PUPILS column relative to the CUMULATIVE % EXPEND column. In a state that has perfect equity, any CUMULATIVE % PUPILS would have the same CUMULATIVE % EXPEND. Refer to your software user's manual to show this relationship graphically. Helpful hints: (1) graph the CUMULATIVE % PUPILS column relative to itself to represent perfect equity, and (2) graph the CUMULATIVE % PUPILS column relative to the CUMULATIVE % EXPEND column to illustrate the actual relationship. The latter graph is the Lorenz curve.

k. Print the graph you create.

l. To compute the Gini coefficient, the area below the Lorenz curve is divided by the area below the diagonal (representing perfect equity). Determination of the coefficient is beyond the power of this software.

Simulation 12.4: *Correlation Coefficient and Scattergram*

a. Retrieve the file EQUITY_3. This file contains selected data from the data worksheet used in Simulation 12.1. Regression analysis is used to measure the bivariate relationship between expenditure per pupil and the percentage of minorities and property value per pupil. Graphical presentations of the bivariate relationships are made.

b. To explore the relationship between expenditure per pupil and the percentage of minorities in each district, we will use the regression analysis component of the spreadsheet software. In Lotus 1-2-3, use the /, Data, Regression command sequence to begin; in Excel, use the Options, Analysis Tools, Regression command sequence.

c. Select the X-Range from the column that contains data for the independent variable, PERCENT MINORITY.

d. Select the Y-Range in the column that contains data for the dependent variable, EXPEND PER PUPIL.

e. Select the Output-Range cell in the left-most column below the data table.

f. Execute the "Go" (Lotus) or "OK" (Excel) command.

g. To calculate the correlation coefficient, find the square root of "R Squared."

h. In the Y EST OF EXPEND column next to the PERCENT MINORITY column on the BAR-CELONA row of the data worksheet, create a formula that adds the "Constant" to the result of the "X Coefficient" multiplied by the PERCENT MINORITY on the BARCE-LONA row.

i. Edit the formula to "anchor" the cells that contain the "Constant" and the "X Coeffi-cient" and copy the formula down through the column.

j. Follow the same procedures, steps b through i, to arrive at the Y EST OF EXPEND using PROPERTY VALUE as the X-Range indepen-dent variable.

k. Print the completed data worksheet and the two regression outputs. What do the results indicate about the relationship between these input and output measures?

l. The graph of the bivariate relationship is based on the coordinates created by a given EXPEND PER PUPIL and the corresponding PERCENT MINORITY or PROPERTY VALUE PER PUPIL. The regression line imposed on the graph is simply the line created by the Y EST OF EXPEND. Refer to your software user's manual to create a graph of the first relationship, expenditure per pupil and per-centage of minority students in each district. Helpful hints: (1) graph the coordinates for each district contained in the data work-sheet, and (2) graph the line that connects the estimated values contained in the data worksheet.

m. Create a graph of the second relationship, expenditure per pupil and property value per pupil in each district.

n. Print the graphs you created.

o. ***Further activities.*** Obtain a data set that includes measures similar to those used in the above simulations for school districts in a state or region/metropolitan area. Calcu-late each of the measures of equity for your data. Compare the results with those obtained for states A and B in the text, the hypothetical state in this simulation, and the statistics for states reported in Table 12.2. For large data sets, and for calculation of the Gini coefficient and regression analyses, a statistical software package is suggested.

REFERENCES

Adler, L., & Gardner, S. (1994). *The politics of link-ing schools and social services.* Washington, DC: Falmer.

Alexander, K. (1982). Concepts of equity. In W. W. McMahon & T. G. Geske (Eds.), *Financing educa-tion: Overcoming inefficiency and inequity* (pp. 193–214). Urbana, IL: University of Illinois Press.

Barro, S. M. (1987). *School finance equity: Research in the 1980s and the current state of the art.* Washing-ton, DC: Decision Resources Corporation.

Berne, R. (1988). Equity issues in school finance. *Jour-nal of Education Finance, 14,* 159–180.

Berne, R. (1994). Educational input and outcome in-equities in New York State. In R. Berne & L. O. Picus

(Eds.), *Outcome equity in education* (pp. 1–23). Thousand Oaks, CA: Corwin Press.

Berne, R., & Stiefel, L. (1983). Changes in school finance equity: A national perspective. *Journal of Education Finance, 8,* 419–435.

Berne, R., & Stiefel, L. (1984). *The measurement of equity in school finance: Conceptual, methodological, and empirical dimensions.* Baltimore, MD: The Johns Hopkins University Press.

Berne, R., & Stiefel, L. (1990). *Measuring school finance equity in the 1990s: Old dogs or new tricks?* New York: New York University, Urban Research Center, Robert F. Wagner Graduate School of Public Service.

Berne, R., & Stiefel, L. (1992). Equity standards for state school finance programs: Philosophies and standards relevant to Section 5(d) (2) of the Federal Impact Aid Program. *Journal of Education Finance, 18,* 89–112.

Berne, R., & Stiefel, L. (1994). Measuring equity at the school level: The finance perspective. *Educational Evaluation and Policy Analysis, 16,* 405–421.

Bezeau, L. M. (1985). *Level and inequality of per pupil expenditure as a function of finance centralization.* Paper presented at the annual meeting of the Canadian Society for the Study of Education, Montreal, Quebec, Canada.

Brown, L. L., Ginsburg, A. L., Killalea, J. N., Rosthal, R. A., & Tron, E. O. (1978). School finance reform in the seventies: Achievements and failures. *Journal of Education Finance, 4,* 195–212.

Brown, P. R., & Elmore, R. F. (1982). Analyzing the impact of school finance reform. In N. H. Cambron-McCabe & A. Odden (Eds.), *The changing politics of school finance* (pp. 107–138). Cambridge, MA: Ballinger.

Carroll, S. J. (1979). *The search for equity in school finance: Summary and conclusions.* Santa Monica, CA: Rand.

Charnes, A., Cooper, W. W., & Rhodes, E. (1978). Measuring the efficiency of decision making units. *European Journal of Operational Research, 2,* 429–444.

Clune, W. H., (1994). The shift from equity to adequacy in school finance. *Educational Policy, 8,* 376–394.

Darling-Hammond, L. (1994). Standards of practice for learner-centered schools. In R. Berne & L. O. Picus (Eds.), *Outcome equity in education* (pp. 191–223). Thousand Oaks, CA: Corwin Press.

Dewey, J. (1916/1966). *Democracy and education.* New York: Free Press.

Edgewood Independent School District v. *Kirby,* 777 S.W. 2d 391 (1989), 804 S.W. 2d 491 (Tex. 1991).

Elmore, R. F. (1994). Thoughts on program equity: Productivity and incentives for performance in education. *Educational Policy, 8,* 453–459.

Gardner, J. W. (1990). *Building community.* Paper prepared for the Leadership Studies Program of Independent Sector, Palo Alto, CA.

Garms, W. I. (1979). Measuring the equity of school finance systems. *Journal of Education Finance, 4,* 415–435.

Goetz, S. J., & Debertin, D. L. (1992). Rural areas and educational reform in Kentucky: An early assessment of revenue equalization. *Journal of Education Finance, 18,* 163–179.

Goertz, M. E. (1983). School finance in New Jersey: A decade after *Robinson* v. *Cahill. Journal of Education Finance, 8,* 475–489.

Goertz, M. E., & Hickrod, G. A. (1983). Evaluating the school finance reforms of the 1970s and 1980s: Part 2. *Journal of Education Finance, 9,* 1–4.

Hanushek, E. A. (1994). A jaundiced view of "adequacy" in school finance reform. *Educational Policy, 8,* 460–469.

Harrison, F. W., & McLoone, E. P. (1960). *Profiles in school support 1959–60.* Washington, DC: U.S. Department of Health, Education, and Welfare [Misc. 32].

Hartman, W. T. (1994). District spending disparities revisited. *Journal of Education Finance, 20,* 88–106.

Heinold, D. (1983). Impact of federal monies on equity among states in K–12 public school finance. *Journal of Education Finance, 8,* 461–474.

Hertert, L. (1994). Equalizing dollars across schools: A study of district- and school-level fiscal equity in California. Paper delivered at the annual meeting of the American Education Finance Association, Nashville, TN.

Hertert, L., Busch, C., & Odden, A. (1994). School financing inequities among the states: The problem from a national perspective. *Journal of Education Finance, 19,* 231–255.

Hickrod, G. A., Chandhari, R. B., & Hubbard, B. C. (1983). The decline and fall of school finance reform in Illinois. *Journal of Education Finance, 8,* 17–38.

Hickrod, G. A., & Goertz, M. E. (1983). Introduction: Evaluating the school finance reforms of the 1970s and early 1980s. *Journal of Education Finance, 8,* 415–418.

Hirth, M. A. (1994). A multi-state analysis of school finance issues and equity trends in Indiana, Illinois, and Michigan, 1982–1992: The implications for 21st century school finance policies. *Journal of Education Finance, 20,* 163–190.

Howe, H., II. (1993). Thinking about kids and education. *Phi Delta Kappan, 75,* 226–228.

Hyary, A. (1994). *Intra-district distribution of educational resources in New York State elementary schools.* Paper delivered at the annual meeting of the American Education Finance Association, Nashville, TN.

Johnson, G., & Pillainayagam, M. G. (1991). A longitudinal equity study of Ohio's school finance system: 1980–89. *Journal of Education Finance, 17,* 60–82.

Jones, T. (1985). *State fiscal behavior: A study of resource allocation and distribution.* Paper presented at the annual meeting of the American Educational Research Association, Chicago.

Kahne, J. (1994). Democratic communities, equity, and excellence: A Deweyan reframing of educational policy analysis. *Educational Evaluation and Policy Analysis, 16,* 233–248.

Kearney, C. P., & Anderson, D. M. (1992). Equity measurement in school finance. In K. C. Westbrook (Ed.), *State of the states '92: Bridging troubled finance waters: Proceedings of the Fiscal Issues, Policy, and Education Finance Special Interest Group.* Annual meeting of the American Educational Research Association, San Francisco, CA.

Kearney, C. P., & Chen, L. (1989). Measuring equity in Michigan school finance: A further look. *Journal of Education Finance, 14,* 319–367.

King, R. A. (1983). Equalization in New Mexico school finance. *Journal of Education Finance, 9,* 63–78.

Kirst, M. W. (1994). Equity for children: Linking education and children's services. *Educational Policy, 8,* 583–590.

Krupey, J. E., & Hopeman, A. (1983). Minnesota school finance equity, 1973–1982. *Journal of Education Finance, 8,* 490–501.

Lake, P. (1983). Expenditure equity in the public schools of Atlantic Canada. *Journal of Education Finance, 8,* 449–460.

Levin, H. M. (1994). The necessary and sufficient conditions for achieving educational equity. In R. Berne & L. O. Picus (Eds.), *Outcome equity in education* (pp. 167–190). Thousand Oaks, CA: Corwin Press.

Levittown Union Free School District v. *Nyguist,* 453 N.Y.S. 2d 643 (1982).

Mirel, J., & Angus, D. (1994). High standards for all? The struggle for equality in the American high school curriculum, 1890–1990. *American Educator, 18,* No. 2, 4–9, 40–42.

Monk, D. H. (1994). Policy challenges surrounding the shift toward outcome-oriented school finance equity standards. *Educational Policy, 8,* 471–488.

Odden, A., Monk, D., Nakib, Y., & Picus, L. (1995). The story of the education dollar: No academy awards and no fiscal smoking guns. *Phi Delta Kappan, 77,* 161–168.

Odden, A. R., & Picus, L. O. (1992). *School finance: A policy perspective.* New York: McGraw-Hill.

Oesch, J. M., & Paquette, J. (1995). School board financial equity in Ontario: 1988 and 1989. *Journal of Education Finance, 20,* 312–331.

Owens, J. T., Jr. (1994). Intradistrict resource allocation in Dade County, Florida: An analysis of equality of educational opportunity. Paper delivered at the annual meeting of the American Education Finance Association, Nashville, TN.

Parrish, T. B., Matsumoto, C. S., & Fowler, W. J., Jr. (1995). *Disparities in public school district spending 1989–90: A multivariate, student-weighted analysis, adjusted for differences in geographic cost of living and student need.* Washington, DC: National Center for Education Statistics.

Pipho, C. (1993). School finance: Moving from equity to productivity. *Phi Delta Kappan, 74,* 590–591.

Porter, A. C. (1994). National equity and school autonomy. *Educational Policy, 8,* 489–500.

Porter, T. S. (1991). Equity and changes in tax base of Ohio's public schools: 1980–89. *Journal of Education Finance, 16,* 515–530.

Reform Education Financing Inequities Today v. *Cuomo,* 578 N.Y.S. 2d 969 Superior Court for Nassau County (1991).

San Antonio Independent School District v. *Rodriguez,* 411 U.S. 1 (1973).

Schwartz, M., & Moskowitz, J. (1988). *Fiscal equity in the United States, 1984–85.* Washington, DC: Decision Resources Corporation.

Serrano v. *Priest,* 487 P. 2d 1241 (1971).

Timar, T. B. (1994). Politics, policy, and categorical aid: New inequities in California school finance. *Educational Evaluation and Policy Analysis, 16,* 143–160.

Toenjes, L., & Clark, C. (1994). Reducing school district wealth to create equity in Texas. Paper delivered at the annual meeting of the American Education Finance Association, Nashville, TN.

Verstegen, D. A. (1987). Equity in state education finance: A response to *Rodriguez. Journal of Education Finance, 12,* 315–330.

Verstegen, D. A. (1993). Financing education reform: Where did all the money go? *Journal of Education Finance, 19,* 1–35.

Verstegen, D. A. (1994). Efficiency and equity in the provision and reform of American schooling. *Journal of Education Finance, 20,* 107–131.

Verstegen, D., & Salmon, R. (1991). Assessing fiscal equity in Virginia: Cross-time comparisons. *Journal of Education Finance, 16,* 417–430.

Walters, L. C., & Freeman, M. A. (1993). An assessment of educational spending equity in Utah using data envelopment analysis. *Journal of Education Finance, 19,* 122–156.

Wong, K. K. (1994). Governance structure, resource allocation, and equity policy. *Review of Research in Education, 20,* 257–289.

Zigler, E. F., & Finn-Stevenson, M. (1994). Schools' role in the provision of support services for children and families: A critical aspect of program equity. *Educational Policy, 8,* 591–606.

CHAPTER 13

Using Efficiency, Adequacy, and Economic Growth Standards

Primary Issues Explored in This Chapter:

- **External efficiency:** Does the United States allocate sufficient resources in support of elementary and secondary education? How does it compare in this regard to other postindustrial economies?
- **Internal efficiency:** Are schools and school districts using efficiently the resources entrusted to them for helping pupils to learn?

- **Technical efficiency:** How might schools influence students more efficiently?
- **Scale effects:** How do school and district size relate to pupil achievement and cost?
- **Policy implications:** What changes in school governance and finance policies are needed to facilitate greater efficiency in the operation of schools?

Most educators do not commonly use the term *efficiency*. We have been criticized for taking our inputs (pupils, buildings, classrooms, teaching supplies, heat, light, etc.) pretty much for granted and complaining bitterly when we believe we don't have enough. We rarely concern ourselves with the connections between those inputs, the community that supplied them, what we do in the classroom, how our former students fare after they leave us, and the impact they have on the community as a result of their school experience. In this chapter, we look at these linkages from the perspective of studies using paradigms drawn from economics.

In Chapter 11, we focused on the concepts of *equality* and *efficiency* from the perspective of the courts. In Chapter 12 we focused on *equity* from

the view of policy analysts. We found a growing recognition that most schools are operating inefficiently and that children are being harmed by those inefficiencies—especially children classified as being at risk. While the concepts of *equity* and *efficiency* are quite different, we concluded in those chapters that schooling cannot be truly equitable without also being efficient. The converse is not necessarily true.

In Chapter 2 we said efficiency and economic growth are derived values that enhance the realization of the ethical values of liberty, equality, and fraternity. Efficiency and economic growth became primary objectives of public policy only during the last half of the twentieth century. *Efficiency,* the ratio of outputs to inputs, is improved by increasing the desired outputs produced from available resources or by maintaining a given level of output while using fewer resource inputs. Improving efficiency also improves *productivity,* a similar concept.

Hanushek (1986, p. 1166) defined economic efficiency as "the correct share of input mix given the prices of inputs and the production function." *Production function* is defined as the causal relationship between inputs and outcomes. Thus, it is what goes on in schools, classrooms, and the minds of students. He cautioned against confusing *economic efficiency* and *technical efficiency.* The latter considers only the process of combining inputs to produce outcomes. It does not take into account the cost of inputs. Both concepts are important in designing educational systems, and we will consider both in this chapter.

Economic efficiency is external and internal. *External efficiency* considers contributions to national economic growth made by the scarce resources allocated by society to various sectors of production. With respect to education, we are interested in how well the economic returns we receive from investments in education compare to returns from other investment opportunities. *Internal efficiency* relates to the allocation of resources within educational enterprises in order to maximize output (for example, academic achievement, skill development, behavior, and attitudes of students) from the resources committed.

The decision matrix we discussed in Chapter 1 (Figure 1.7) posed a series of questions policy makers need to resolve. Analyses of external efficiency assist in making decisions about how much resources to commit to and among educational services and in determining the level of societal investment in population quality we need to promote economic growth. In other words, studying external efficiencies addresses the issues of how much to spend for educational services and of which kinds of services to provide in order to create the greatest aggregate economic benefit. Internal efficiency relates to the means by which educational services are produced. Studying internal efficiency is directed toward gaining the

maximum benefit from the resources committed to an institution or operation such as a school or classroom. Whereas we study internal efficiency through educational production functions and cost-benefit and cost-effectiveness analyses, we study external efficiency through rate-of-return analysis.

We begin this chapter by looking at external efficiencies. We review studies that have applied the theory of human capital (see Chapter 1) to estimating the contribution of investments in education to national economic growth. We end our discussion of external efficiency with an assessment of the adequacy of expenditures for education in the United States. In the second section we focus on internal efficiency. In reviewing evidence from studies of both the technical and economic efficiency of schools, we conclude that there are significant opportunities for redirecting resources already committed to education so as to improve the outcomes of schools substantially.

EXTERNAL EFFICIENCY

In Parts II and III, we discussed the processes by which public revenues are raised for the support of educational services and how they are distributed to school districts. We assumed that we know how much we need to spend on education. As we discussed in Part I, deciding how much to spend for educational services is largely a political process and the decisions made may not be efficient from an economic—or technical—perspective. Economic analysis can estimate the efficiency with which we are using scarce resources for educational services. But in the political process, economic efficiency is only one of many, often conflicting, objectives of social policy. Concerns for improving economic efficiency must be balanced against other social concerns. When other concerns take precedence, the policies adopted may be inefficient for good reasons. Too often, however, public policy is adopted without knowing fully its economic ramifications.

Rate-of-Return Approach

Rate-of-return analysis is one of the economist's tools for evaluating alternative investment policies. With respect to education, rate-of-return analysis is intended to inform policy makers about how much to spend on education as a sector and on specific programs within that sector (Benson, 1978, p. 91). Rate-of-return analysis compares the profit (increased earnings from additional education) to the expense of acquiring that education, including earnings forgone in the process (opportunity costs). The rate of return on investments in education has been studied at two levels, the individual and society.

In a free market, when supply and demand for persons possessing a particular set of knowledge and skills are in equilibrium, the rate of return approximates what is generally expected from other types of investments. If the rate is much higher, there is an apparent shortage of persons with these skills, permitting them to command higher wages. This encourages more people to acquire similar training and enter the workforce. This continues until wages and the rate of return drop to the levels expected. If, on the other hand, the rate of return is much lower than what can be obtained from other investments, there is a surplus of persons with similar skills—more than the market can absorb. Competition for employment drives wages down. This discourages people from acquiring such skills until supply again equals demand and the rate of return from earnings over expenditures equals the expected. (See related discussions of the interaction between supply and demand with respect to teachers' salaries in Chapters 1 and 16; and Murphy & Welch, 1989.)

Using classical rate-of-return calculations and 1980 and 1985 Canadian census data, Paquette (1991) discovered a dramatic—and disturbing— change in return on investments in education in just a five-year period. His 1980 results showed the relationship between education and earning power was a regular step function with a series of small increases in income from lower to upper categories

of education—the typical pattern observed in studies since World War II. By 1985, however, the relationship had become a relatively flat function, with giant quantum leaps at the top end of the educational attainment spectrum. His findings are portrayed in Figure 13.1. It clearly shows that while some modest income advantages persist for those with nonuniversity certificates and diplomas and for those with a university-granted certificate, really significant differentials in earning power now exist only for those with baccalaureate and advanced degrees. He concluded that with regard to average employment income, the incremental earning advantage of lower levels of educational attainment was diminishing rapidly in Canada. "On average in Canada, *additional schooling beyond the elementary level has ceased to be a rational investment in personal earning power except for those who intend to complete a post-secondary credential in a high-demand, high-reward area of study— and have the required intellectual ability, 'cultural-capital,' and fiscal resources to do so*" (Paquette, 1991, p. 474, emphasis in original). The situation is probably similar in the United States, judging from reports of the Commission on the Skills of the American Workforce and the W. T. Grant Foundation Commission on Work, Family, and Citizenship reviewed in Chapter 3.

The Paquette study considered only private rates of return, which are good guides for decisions individuals make. But in determining social policy we must consider all social costs, including those that subsidize the private costs paid directly by individuals. The price of an education in both public and private institutions is subsidized by public funds or private endowments. To calculate the social rate of return, we also include the amount of subsidization to individuals (e.g., the difference between the tuition the student pays and actual cost, scholarships, and fellowships). As a general rule, social rates of return to education are lower than private rates of return. This is an argument for having some costs of education, especially for higher education, paid in part by students' tuition and not be totally subsidized by government.

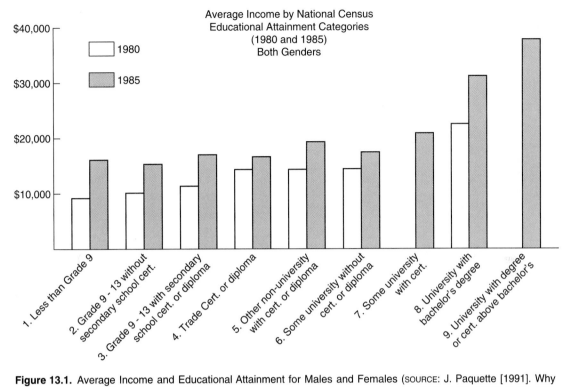

Figure 13.1. Average Income and Educational Attainment for Males and Females (SOURCE: J. Paquette [1991]. Why should I stay in school? Quantizing private educational returns. *Journal of Education Finance, 16,* 466. Reprinted with permission of the publisher.)

Becker (1960, 1964) evaluated social policy by computing the rates of return for investments in education. He estimated the social rate of return for white male college graduates in the United States as between 10 percent and 13 percent annually. Assuming that rates for college dropouts and nonwhites would be lower, he estimated that the rate for all college entrants was between 8 percent and 11 percent. Becker (1964, p. 121) concluded: "The rates on business capital and college education seem, therefore, to fall within the same range." The rates of return were higher for high school students, and they were highest for elementary students. Becker cautioned, however, that adjustments for differential ability would likely reduce or eliminate the differences in rates among levels of schooling. Estimates of rates of return from expenditures for higher education between 1939 and 1976 showed

that the returns were falling, although not by a large amount (Woodhall, 1987). This trend appears to have reversed itself dramatically during the 1980s (Murphy & Welch, 1989; Paquette, 1991) because of an increasing demand for highly trained workers and correspondingly higher wages than for workers with less training.

Psacharopoulos (1973, 1981, 1985) surveyed rate-of-return studies across nations. The findings from his 1981 study for sixty-one countries are summarized in Table 13.1. The table shows the average private and social rates of return for primary, secondary, and higher education for countries grouped according to stage of development and region. All the results, except for the social rate of return for higher education in advanced and intermediate countries, are at or above the 10 percent benchmark commonly expected from capital

TABLE 13.1. International Comparison of Social and Private Rates of Return by Education Level, Stage of Development, and Region

Region/ Country Type	Rate of Return (in percentage)					
	Social			Private		
	Primary	Secondary	Higher	Primary	Secondary	Higher
Africa	26	17	13	45	26	32
Asia	27	15	13	31	15	18
Latin America	26	18	16	32	23	23
Intermediate	13	10	8	17	13	13
Advanced	NA	11	9	NA	12	12

Note: NA = not available because of lack of a control group of illiterates.
SOURCE: G. Psacharopoulos. (1985). Returns to Education: A Further International Update and Implications. *Journal of Human Resources, 20,* 586.

investment. Returns of 8 percent and 9 percent for higher education may indicate that advanced and intermediate countries are spending at or slightly above the optimal level given the current organization of education.

The highest returns are for primary education. This is a function of the interaction between the low cost of primary education (including opportunity costs) relative to other levels and the substantial productivity differential (based on market pricing) between primary school graduates and those who are illiterate. (In the advanced countries, illiteracy has been virtually eliminated, making the calculations for that group at the primary level meaningless.) Rates of return at all levels of education tend to decline with development. This indicates the relatively greater scarcity of educated personnel in countries with low levels of economic development. For all groups, private returns exceed social returns. This is because all education is publicly subsidized. Psacharopoulos (1985) found that expenditures on the education of women were at least as beneficial as were those on men and that expenditures on the general curriculum produced higher yields than did those for vocational education (not shown in Table 13.1). The optimum investment strategy for countries appears to vary according to the level of economic development and other demographic characteristics.

Spending Levels for Education

Making international comparisons of education spending is as much an art as a science. Verstegen (1992) analyzed several studies that compared education expenditures in the United States and other developed nations. She reviewed studies that were conducted by the Economic Policy Institute, the U.S. Department of Education, the Congressional Research Service, and the American Federation of Teachers. She found that the factors that affect rankings include: the measures used (for example, aggregate expenditure, expenditure per pupil, or percentage of gross domestic product [GDP]); what is included in the definition of expenditure (or revenue); the monetary conversion procedure (for example, using purchasing power parities or market exchange rates); comparisons of expenditures made from public funds only with those from public and private sources combined; countries included; and education levels included (elementary and secondary, tertiary, or combined).

Verstegen concluded that the United States, in general, leads other developed nations in total spending on all levels of education. When only expenditures on elementary and secondary education are considered, and when expenditures are compared to GDP, the United States loses its preeminent position. For expenditures per pupil at the elementary and secondary levels, the United States ranks relatively high. When rankings are made on the basis of percentage of GDP or GDP per capita, the United States ranks relatively low.

Expenditure per pupil is an indicator of the availability, on average, of resources for each student's education. Table 13.2 shows that on this measure, the United States ranks fifth. Its leads major European countries and Japan. Expenditures for education as a percentage of GDP can be viewed as a measure of effort (similar to a tax rate). On this measure, the United States falls in the middle of major European countries, but it is still well ahead of Germany and Japan.

Table 13.3 reports investment in education in the United States for the period 1959 through 1994. Table 13.3 also gives the percentage of the total population enrolled in precollegiate and higher education. The percentage of GDP spent for all educational institutions rose steadily from 4.8 percent in 1959 to 7.5 percent in 1970 and 1975. It

then declined to 6.7 percent in 1985, rising again to 7.5 percent in 1990 and 1994. The earlier peak allocation of GDP to education (1970) corresponds to the peak in the percentage of the population enrolled in educational institutions. The 1990 and 1994 peaks in allocation of GDP to education are for a smaller population cohort than in 1970. Smith and Phelps (1995) concluded that in terms of the amount spent on education at all levels and the percentage of gross domestic product invested, the United States ranks among the highest in comparison with other large postindustrial countries.

For elementary and secondary school expenditures, the percentage of GDP rose from 3.4 percent in 1959 to 4.8 percent in 1970. Although expenditure per pupil continued to increase in constant dollars (See Figure 1.2), the percentage of GDP declined to 4.0 percent in 1985. But it has since risen to 4.6 percent. The decline in the percentage of GDP spent for precollegiate education can be attributed at least in part to the smaller per-

TABLE 13.2. Selected International Comparisons of Education Spending

Country	Total Expenditures as Percentage of GDP[a], All Levels (N = 11) Percentage	Rank	Operating Expenditures as Percentage of GDP[a], PreK–12 (N = 22) Percentage	Rank	Operating Expenditures as Percentage of GDP per Capita[b], PreK–12 (N = 22) Percentage	Rank	Expenditures per Pupil[a], PreK–12 (N = 22) $	Rank
United States	5.5	7	3.5	11	18.7	11	3,238	5
Australia	5.9	5	3.0	17	15.9	14	2,034	13
Canada	7.0	2	4.1	5	21.3	9	3,436	1
France	5.8	6	3.7	9	—	12	2,084	12
Germany (W)	4.5	10	2.7	20	15.3	17	1,941	14
Italy	4.0	11	2.9	8	15.8	20	1,816	17
Japan	5.1	8	—	—	15.4	16	1,904	15
Netherlands	6.8	3	3.4	13	15.5	15	1,824	16
Norway	6.4	4	4.3	3	22.4	6	3,307	3
Sweden	7.8	1	4.4	1	24.8	2	3,293	4
United Kingdom	4.9	9	3.5	10	21.5	8	2,502	10

[a]National Center for Education Statistics (1991). *The Condition of Education, 1991.* Vol. 1. Washington, DC: U.S. Department of Education.

[b]U.S. Department of Education (1990). *Shortchanging Education: A Case Study of Flawed Economics* (pp. 59–67). In Committee on Education and Labor, House of Representatives. Hearing on Education Funding (Serial No. 101-86). Washington, DC: U.S. Government Printing Office.

SOURCE: Adapted from D. Verstegen (1992). International Comparisons of Education Spending: A Review and Analysis of Reports. *Journal of Education Finance, 17,* 257–276.

TABLE 13.3. Percentage of Gross Domestic Product (GDP) Spent on Education and Percentage of Total Population Enrolled in Educational Institutions, 1959–1994

Year	Elementary and Secondary Schools		Higher Education		Total	
	Percentage of GDP	Percentage Enrollment of Population	Percentage of GDP	Percentage Enrollment of Population	Percentage of GDP	Percentage Enrollment of Population
1959	3.4	23.0	1.4	2.0	4.8	25.0
1965	4.0	24.9	2.2	3.0	6.2	28.0
1970	4.8	25.0	2.7	4.2	7.5	29.2
1975	4.7	23.1	2.7	5.2	7.5	28.2
1980	4.1	20.3	2.6	5.3	6.8	25.6
1985	4.0	18.8	2.7	5.1	6.7	24.0
1990	4.5	18.4	3.0	5.4	7.5	24.0
1994	4.6	19.1	3.0	5.5	7.5	24.6

SOURCE: National Center for Education Statistics. (1995). *Digest of Education Statistics.* Washington, DC: U.S. Government Printing Office.

centage of the total population attending elementary and secondary schools. Enrollment at this level peaked in 1970 at 25.0 percent. It subsequently declined to 18.4 percent in 1990.

The percentage of GDP spent on colleges and universities rose from 1.4 percent in 1959 to 2.7 percent in 1970. Between 1970 and 1985, it ranged from 2.6 percent to 2.7 percent. In contrast to the percentage spent on elementary and secondary schools, it has risen since then to a record high of 3.0 percent. Actual enrollments in postsecondary education rose from 3,640,000 in 1959 to 8,581,000 in 1970. They have continued to increase and are now over 12,000,000. The percentage of the population enrolled in higher education was 2.0 percent in 1959. It has steadily increased since then and stood at 5.5 percent in 1994.

With respect to external efficiency, as already noted, rate-of-return studies suggest that advanced countries, including the United States, are probably spending at or near the optimal rate for educational services, given the existing state of educational technology. If the rate of investment in education were to be increased, it could probably best be justified at the preschool and elementary levels. The percentage of GDP allocated to education

may continue to fluctuate along with the percentage of the population engaged in formal schooling.

INTERNAL EFFICIENCY

We now turn to consideration of the efficiency with which resources allocated to schools are used to educate children. The ability of such resources to improve individual and societal welfare will be enhanced or diminished depending on the efficiency with which they are used. If our tentative policy conclusion of the previous section is correct and the United States (along with other advanced nations) is spending about the optimal amount on education given current instructional technology, then we can improve the educational performance of American students primarily by improving the internal efficiency of schools and school systems rather than by adding more resources.

Fuller and Clarke (1994) divide educators and researchers into two camps with respect to defining and studying school effectiveness and efficiency: policy mechanics and classroom culturalists. Policy mechanics, working from a production-function metaphor, attempt to identify instructional inputs and uniform teaching practices that yield higher achievement, that is, their focus is on economic efficiency. They search for universal determinants of effective schools that can be manipulated by central agencies (for example, state education departments) and assume that the same instructional materials and practices will produce similar results across diverse settings. The classroom culturalists reject this orientation. They "focus on the normative socialization that occurs within classrooms: the value children come to place on individualistic versus cooperative work, legitimated forms of adult authority and power, and acquired attitudes toward achievement and modern forms of status" (p. 120). The classroom culturalists tend to ignore narrower forms of cognitive achievement and have not been particularly interested in antecedent inputs and classroom rules that are manipulable by central authority. Although they do not normally use the term, their focus is on what economists refer to as technical efficiency. Fuller and Clarke concluded:

> The classroom culturalists have advanced researchers' understanding of how motivated learning occurs within particular social contexts, like classrooms. The production function gurus continue to hold comparative advantage in empirically linking classroom tools to achievement. But this advantage will only be retained if these inputs and teaching practices are awarded real cultural meaning—within a particular content which is energized by variable forms of teacher authority, social participation, and classroom tasks. (p. 143)

In this section, we review the findings of both camps. We begin by examining production-function studies of economic efficiency done by *policy mechanics.* We then consider research and applications relating to technical efficiency that were done by educational psychologists, effective school advocates, and others. We review findings from comparison studies of public and private schools. We study the impact of economies and dis-

economies of scale. Finally, we discuss policy implications for improving the internal efficiency of schools.

Economic Efficiency

Studies of the economic efficiency of schooling that relate outcomes to inputs have been classified by several terms: educational production functions, input-output analysis, and cost-quality studies. Researchers from a variety of disciplines have pursued such research in an effort to improve educational productivity. In this section we refer to them by the economic classification, *production function.*

A production function may be conceptualized as a set of relations among possible inputs and a corresponding set of outputs for a firm or industry—in this case, schools and education (Burkhead, 1967, p. 18). According to Hanushek (1987), "A firm's production possibilities are assumed to be governed by certain technical relationships, and the production function describes the maximum feasible output that can be obtained from a set of inputs" (p. 33). Monk (1989, p. 31) states that a production function tells what is currently possible: "It provides a standard against which practice can be evaluated on productivity grounds." Monk goes on to identify two traditions with respect to the study of the production of education services. The first attempts to estimate the parameters of the educational production function. The second uses the production function as a metaphor, allowing for application of broader economic theories and reasoning that can be used to guide inquiry.

An educational production function may be expressed simply as output *(O)* being a function of inputs consisting of student characteristics *(S),* schooling inputs *(I),* and instructional processes *(P):*

$$O = f(S,I,P).$$

Outputs *(O)* include behavioral and attitudinal changes in pupils induced through school activities. Outputs are usually measured by standardized test scores. But they occasionally include other measures such as high school graduation rate, attendance rate, and percentage of graduates continuing on to postsecondary education. Student characteristics *(S)* range from socioeconomic status of family and student IQ to previous achievement. Schooling inputs *(I)* include expenditures, teacher characteristics, class size, characteristics of buildings, and so forth. Instructional processes *(P)* include student time on task, teaching methods, student-teacher interactions, and so forth.

If indeed there is an educational production function, there must also be a common underlying technology of education. This assumption may come as a surprise to many educators, because production technologies in education are inexact. Nevertheless, the sameness of American schools (and schools around the world for that matter) lend credibility to an assumption of an implicit technology. School buildings are typically arranged with classrooms and certain ancillary spaces such as libraries, auditoriums, and gymnasiums. Usually one teacher presides over each classroom. And teachers organize and manage their classrooms in very similar ways.

Klitgaard and Hall (1975) first tested the assumption of a common technology. They examined the distributions of residual student achievement once the effects of socioeconomic status had been controlled statistically. They hypothesized that if there were schools functioning under different pedagogical assumptions (that is, different production functions), the distribution of residuals would be multimodal. Although their findings were not definitive, they concluded that it is reasonable to assume that all schools, including highly effective ones, function under the same pedagogical technology.

James Coleman (1966) conducted one of the first production-function studies ever attempted for education. It remains one of the largest. It involved over a half-million students in four thousand schools and thousands of teachers. The unit of analysis was the school. This is perhaps the best known and most controversial of all the input-output studies. Its conclusion that schooling had little potential for closing the achievement gap between white and minority students was controversial. So was the methodology used. Among the critics were Bowles and Levin (1968), Mostellar and Moynihan (1972), and Cain and Watts (1970). Benson (1988) summarized the shortcomings of the early studies:

> They used achievement scores at one point in time. The unit of analysis was the school, or even the school district, and the consequent averaging of results weakened the power of the findings. Each variable on the right-hand side of the regression (independent and control variables) was treated as wholly independent of the other variables. In considering the effects of teacher characteristics on achievement, no account was taken of the fact that the child's progress in school is not determined by his or her current teacher alone but is the result of the cumulative actions of all the teachers in the child's school career. (p. 365)

Criticisms of Coleman (1966) led to more sophisticated studies and conceptualizations of the problem (Bridge, Judd, & Moock, 1979; Dreeben & Thomas, 1980; Madaus, Airasian, & Kellaghan, 1980; Murnane, 1975; Rutter, Maughan, Mortimore, & Ouston, 1979; and Summers & Wolfe, 1975). Murnane (1983) discussed what was learned about methodology from more than fifteen years of controversy. This included the importance of using the individual child as the unit of observation rather than the school or school district. In estimating educational effectiveness, Murnane recommended that a child's progress be measured by growth in achievement over a period of time instead of the student's achievement level at a point in time. School resources should be measured according to what is available to a specific child and not according to the average resources present in the school or school district. Murnane also pointed out that the types of resources examined had broadened and had become more sophisticated. Early studies focused on factors that were easy to quantify, such as school size, the number of books in the library, and student-to-teacher ratios. More recent studies focused on the quality and intensity of student-teacher interaction, student time on task, and characteristics of teachers and classmates. Certainly, production-function studies being conducted today have overcome many of the shortcomings identified by Benson. But the recommendations of Murnane remain more an ideal than a reality.

A most significant finding of the production-function studies, beginning with the Coleman (1966) study, is the very strong relationship between family background and pupil achievement. The relationship is so strong that the findings of these studies have frequently been misinterpreted to mean that schools have relatively little impact on pupil achievement. It is well documented that schools have not been very effective in closing achievement gaps among racial and ethnic groups and among socioeconomic classes. Nevertheless, schools do have enormous impacts on the development of all children.

Even the most gifted of children learn—or at least develop—their basic academic skills in schools. Most children come into schools as non-readers and leave with varying levels of literacy skills. Similar statements could be made about mathematics, writing, and other academic skills, as well as about knowledge and attitudinal development. Mayeski et al. (1972) stated it very well in a reanalysis of the Coleman (1966) data: "Schools are indeed important. It is equally clear, however, that their influence is bound up with that of the student's background" (p. ix). Very little influence of schools can be separated from the social backgrounds of their students. And very little of the influence of social background on learning can be separated from the influence of the schools. Dealing with the colinearity of variables is a major challenge to researchers making production-function analyses in education.

Hanushek (1986, 1991) conducted one of the most influential studies involving production-function research. On the basis of a meta-analysis of 187 production-function studies published in thirty-eight articles or books, he concluded: *"There is no systematic relationship between school expenditures and student performance"* (1991, p. 425, emphasis in original).

Hedges, Laine, and Greenwald have bitterly challenged Hanushek's methodology and conclusion (1994a & 1994b; also Greenwald, Hedges, & Laine, 1994). They claim that while the methods that Hanushek used were accepted as adequate when he began his research more than fifteen years ago, they "are now regarded as inadequate synthesis procedures. When examined using more adequate methods, the data upon which his finding is based support exactly the opposite inference: the amount of resources are positively related to the accomplishments of students" (Greenwald, Hedges, & Laine, 1994, p. 2). Because of more stringent standards for including studies in their reanalysis, it involved fewer cases than did Hanusek's original study. Also, Hanushek employed an analytic method known as vote counting, while Greenwald et al. used combined significance tests and combined estimation methods.

In a rebuttal to the challenge of Greenwald et al., Hanushek (1994) retorted that the challengers had made the larger error in asking the wrong question. According to Hanushek, the challengers posed the fundamental issue as one of using the right statistical method. He saw it as one of identifying correct policies: "It is important that the policy significance not be lost in the technical details. . . . Most importantly, the policy interpretations do not depend really on the statistical issues" (p. 5). Some credence is given to Hanushek's rebuttal in the conclusion of Greenwald et al. (1994, p. 20) that:

Even if the conclusions drawn from the studies analyzed in this paper are correct, we would not argue that "throwing money at schools" is the most efficient method of increasing educational achievement. It certainly is not. Greater emphasis must be placed on the manner in which resources are utilized, not simply the provision of those resources.

A number of attempts have been made to overcome the weaknesses of production-function studies. One of the major weaknesses of multiple regression analysis—the principal statistical tool in production-function analysis—is that it permits the analysis of a set of independent variables (input and control) against only one dependent variable (output) at a time. As we noted in Chapter 1, schools affect many outputs simultaneously. It is usually not clear how much of a given input is involved in influencing a given output. Crampton (1994) used canonical analysis to enable the inclusion of more than one output in any given analysis. Canonical analysis allows examination of the influence of a set of independent and control variables on multiple dependent variables. Brewer (1994) attempted to address the problem of multiple outputs by using a cost-minimizing model of school district behavior. Engert (1995) turned to data envelopment analysis (DEA), which also allows the specification of inputs and outputs in monetary and nonmonetary terms, eliminating the need for price/cost data.

Ferguson (1991) has completed a most promising study of a large and particularly rich data source that he assembled for the state of Texas. The data included information on nearly 900 school districts serving over 2.4 million students and employing 150,000 teachers. The database included the scores achieved by all teachers on the Texas Examination of Current Administrators and Teachers (TECAT); other measures of school quality, such as teacher characteristics and pupil-to-teacher ratios; measures of school spending; student reading and math scores from the Texas Educational Assessment of Minimum Skills (TEAMS); characteristics of the region surrounding a school district; and census data and other socioeconomic background and context measures.

Ferguson used multiple regression analysis, as have other production-function studies. But, what set his study apart, besides the richness of the data, was the systematic preparation that preceded the final analysis. For example, threshold analysis revealed that some factors are important up to a point, but not beyond. He took this into account in scoring such factors. Also, he traced the flow of influences. As a result of these refinements, Ferguson found a much larger school effect than had been found in similar studies. Ferguson explained between one-quarter and one-third of the variation among Texas school districts in students' scores on the TEAMS reading examination by school effects—primarily teachers' scores on the TECAT. A major weakness of the Ferguson study is that data were aggregated at the district level.

The power of teachers' TECAT scores to predict student achievement is of particular interest. It is in keeping with the findings of other studies, beginning with Coleman (1966). The studies found that the strongest school effect on pupil achievement was teachers' verbal ability. Using threshold analysis, Ferguson found that class size matters as well. Reducing the number of students per teachers in districts to eighteen—which approximates an average class size of twenty-three—is very important for performance in the primary grades. Dropping the ratio below the threshold of eighteen had no influence on test scores.[1] He also found a threshold effect for teacher experience. Up to five years of experience at the primary level and up to nine years at the secondary level have a positive influence on student performance. He found no upper limit for the positive effect of teachers' TECAT scores, however. He concluded:

> The teacher supply results, when combined with the results for student test scores, demonstrate that hiring teachers with stronger literacy skills, hiring more teachers (when students-per-teacher exceeds eighteen), retaining experienced teachers, and attracting more teachers with advanced training are all measures that produce higher test scores in exchange for more money. (Ferguson, 1991, p. 485)

On the basis of his findings, Ferguson makes the policy recommendation that apart from the common focus by states on equalizing spending per pupil, a serious equalization policy should equalize the most important of all schooling inputs, teacher quality. Similar recommendations were made in the equity studies of New York City (Berne & Stiefel, 1994) and Dade County, Florida (Owens, 1994) reviewed in Chapter 12. To do this would require state-enforced salary differentials that would result in the highest salaries being paid to teachers working in communities characterized by lower socioeconomic populations.

King and MacPhail-Wilcox (1994) recently reviewed the literature on educational production functions. They summarized the prevailing thinking about the relationships between school inputs and outputs: "A safe conclusion is that the way in which schools, teachers, and students take advantage of whatever materials are available matters as much or more than the actual human, physical and fiscal resources present in schools" (p. 47). According to Hanushek (1991), most economists would readily accept that differences in spending would be directly related to the quality of education, *if* schools were operating efficiently. While some schools are operating close to the efficiency frontier (Engert, 1995), most are not.

Monk (1989) criticized the direction that school effectiveness research has taken. According to Monk, the estimation approach to education production functions is with a few exceptions void of economic content, because analysts have been forced to make so many simplifying assumptions. Instead of becoming further involved in increasingly sophisticated applications of econometrics that hold very limited value for educational policy makers, Monk encouraged using the production function as an analogy in the application of economic reasoning to education problems.

While we are learning more about the relationships between educational inputs and outputs, the causal relationships between school inputs and processes on pupil achievement are largely unknown. This high degree of ignorance has serious policy implications for deploying strategies to improve student equity. It places in serious question the efficacy of the provision in the 1994 Educate America Act encouraging states to develop opportunity-to-learn standards (see Chapter 10). At this point, the posture of the classroom culturalists looks quite wise. They are focusing on the normative socialization that occurs within classrooms. There is not sufficient knowledge to specify one best way for the organization, management, and operation of schools from the center, whether it is the state or the federal government.

Technical Efficiency

Effective-Schools Research.   Effective-schools research constituted a reaction to the finding of Coleman (1966) and other production-function studies that schools had little impact on closing the gap between minority and majority pupil achievement. While education production-function research takes a normative approach in studying school efficiency, effective-schools research focuses on exceptions to the norm. It consists largely of case studies of schools and classrooms that have unusually positive effects on pupil achievement. It tries to identify practices that might cause or contribute to that effectiveness (Brookover & Lezotte, 1979; Edmonds, 1979; Jackson, Logsdon, & Taylor, 1983; Reed, 1985; Venezky & Winfield, 1980; Weber, 1971). Effective-schools research usually ignores cost considerations. Thus, its findings relate more to technical efficiency than to economic efficiency.

Effective schools are characterized by effective classroom teaching practices that include high teacher expectations, good classroom management techniques, and more time on task than one would find in most schools. These schools are also characterized by strong leadership, usually in the person of the principal, who provides for the coordination of the instructional program at the building level in a manner that is tightly coupled, but not bureaucratic. The principal appears to be a key factor in establishing a common school culture and sense of community consisting of "shared goals; high expectations for student performance; mechanisms to sustain motivation and commitment; collegiality among teachers, students, and the principal; and a school-wide focus on continuous improvement" (Odden & Webb, 1983, p. xiv). Given current assumptions about schooling, effective-schools research is identifying some ways that schools can make more efficient use of the resources they already have.

Monk (1989) referred to effective-schools research as "backwards-looking." He called effective schools "sites of excellence . . . making exemplary use of traditional, labor intensive instructional technologies" (p. 38). According to him, effective schools accept all the parameters of the present system, and the methodology condemns them only to refine the current system's very labor-intensive and expensive organization and practice rather than permitting them to break through into the discovery and use of new technologies.

Evaluation Studies. Evaluation studies of schooling also have important implications for the technical efficiency of schools. For the most part, like effective-schools research, evaluation studies do not take into account the price of inputs. Evaluation studies have produced results that provide grounds for greater optimism about the impact of schools on pupil achievement than do those conducted by economists and sociologists.

Walberg (1984) analyzed nearly 3,000 investigations of the productive factors in learning conducted during the 1970s. Table 13.4 summarizes his synthesis of the effects of various approaches to improving teaching and learning. Relationships between achievement and socioeconomic status (0.25) and peer groups (0.24) are relatively small when compared to many of the instructional interventions reported in Table 13.4.

Reinforcement (1.17) and instructional cues and feedback (0.97), both of which are psychological components of mastery learning, ranked first and third in effect. Acceleration programs (1.00), which provide advanced activities to high-achieving students, ranked second. Also ranking third was reading training (0.97), which involves skimming, comprehension, finding answers to questions, and adjusting reading speeds. Other highly effective techniques included cooperative learning (0.76), graded homework (0.79), and various approaches to individualized instruction. High teacher expectations (0.28) had a moderate impact,

as did time on task, advanced organizing techniques, morale or climate of the classroom, and home interventions. Reduced class size had little impact. Walberg (1984) concluded:

> Synthesis of educational and psychological research in ordinary schools shows that improving the amount and quality of instruction can result in vastly more effective and efficient academic learning. Educators can do even more by also enlisting families as partners and engaging them directly and indirectly in their efforts. (p. 26)

Most of the techniques identified by Walberg as effectively improving student achievement require few, if any, new resources. Rather they require a redirection of already committed resources.

School Reform Networks. A number of organizational strategies intended to make schools more effective have been developed over the past decade. Slavin (1994) pointed out that classroom-level change cannot be dictated from above. However, not every school must reinvent the wheel. School staffs and community representatives can select among a variety of existing, well-designed methods and materials that have been shown to be effective with children. Schools subscribing to a given set of organizing principles frequently form networks, usually under the direction of the model designer. We describe a few such networks.

The Comer School Development Program is such a network. Psychiatrist James Comer began the program in 1968 as a joint effort of the Child Study Center at Yale University and the New Haven Public Schools. His concepts have now received national attention. Comer's (1988) approach emphasizes connecting families with schools, helping school staffs appreciate and incorporate the values and perspectives of minority families into their teaching, and increasing student self-esteem. The program does not have an explicit approach to curriculum. But it does provide a process for making curricular decisions. The process involves systematic identification of a school's

TABLE 13.4. Walberg's Syntheses of Effects on Learning

Method	Effect	Size
Reinforcement	1.17	xxxxxxxxxxx
Acceleration	1.00	xxxxxxxxxx
Reading Training	.97	xxxxxxxxxx
Cues and Feedback	.97	xxxxxxxxxx
Science Mastery Learning	.81	xxxxxxxx
Graded Homework	.79	xxxxxxxx
Cooperative Learning	.76	xxxxxxxx
Class Morale	.60	xxxxxx
Reading Experiments	.60	xxxxxx
Personalized Instruction	.57	xxxxxx
Home Interventions	.50	xxxxx
Adaptive Instruction	.45	xxxxx
Tutoring	.40	xxxx
Instructional Time	.38	xxxx
Individualized Science	.35	xxxx
Higher-Order Questions	.34	xxx
Diagnostic Prescriptive Methods	.33	xxx
Individualized Instruction	.32	xxx
Individualized Mathematics	.32	xxx
New Science Curricula	.31	xxx
Teacher Expectations	.28	xxx
Computer Assisted Instruction	.24	xx
Sequenced Lessons	.24	xx
Advance Organizers	.23	xx
New Mathematics Curricula	.18	xx
Inquiry Biology	.16	xx
Homogeneous Groups	.10	x
Class Size	.09	x
Programmed Instruction	−.03	−.
Mainstreaming	−.12	−x.

Note: The x symbols represent the sizes of effects in tenths of standard deviations.
SOURCE: H. J. Walberg. (1984). Improving the Productivity of America's Schools. *Educational Leadership, 41* (8), Figures 3–4, p. 24. © 1984 by ASCD.

goals, planning, regular assessment of effort and progress, followed by design modifications as necessary. Three guiding principles are no-fault problem solving, consensus decision making, and collaboration. All staff members and parents are involved at every level of school activity.

Another network has formed around William Glasser's *The Quality School* (1992). The concept of the quality school is based on control theory and reality therapy. Control theory holds that all human beings are born with five basic needs built into their genetic structure: survival, love, power, fun, and freedom. People's behavior is always their best attempt at the time to do what they believe will best satisfy one or more of those needs. The school operates under a philosophy of noncoercive leadership.

The focus of the quality school is on student outcomes. Careful attention is paid to alignment between schoolwide, grade-level, and student goals. Students are expected to assume much of the responsibility for managing their own learning. Considerable effort is given to helping students understand the worth of what they are doing and the contribution it can make to their personal and career goals. The curriculum stresses the skills of speaking, writing, calculating, and problem solving, both as individuals and in groups. The quality school uses cooperative groups extensively in teaching academic subjects.

The quality school closely watches internal and external research and data on students and the school. It carefully monitors student progress using authentic and performance-based means. It bases corrective action (for individual student, classroom, and school) on analysis of the data collected. It does not stress formal grading but only accepts work that is regarded as of high quality by teachers and students. All of these efforts are enhanced through a targeted training program that equips students, teachers, and administrators with precisely those skills they believe they need to function effectively in their work.

Theodore Sizer's (1992) Coalition of Essential Schools is a national network of over 900 secondary schools. The schools make no attempt to be comprehensive but rather focus on helping adolescents to use their minds well. The achievement goals apply to all students, although the school individualizes the specific approach for each student. The governing metaphor is "student as worker" as contrasted with the more typical metaphor of "teacher as deliverer of instructional services." Students progress and ultimately graduate by demonstrating mastery of subjects. The school uses neither a system of strict age grading nor of credit accumulation. It perceives the principal and teachers as generalists first and specialists second. It expects staff members to have multiple obligations and commitment to the entire school. Ideally, the total student load per teacher should not exceed eighty. Substantial time should be allowed for planning by teachers.

The central thrust of the Accelerated Schools network is academic acceleration for at-risk students. Henry Levin (1994) developed this schooling model in the mid-1980s. Now over five hundred elementary and middle schools are implementing the model in thirty-three states. In a radical restructuring of school to create productive efficiency, accelerated schools were designed to bring at-risk students into the educational mainstream so that they are academically able and capable of benefiting from a high-quality and high-content school experience. Accelerated schools challenge the common practice among most public schools of remediation for at-risk children. The schools' strategy is based on the belief that such children must learn at a faster—not slower—rate than other children. Three central principles guide the strategy: unity of purpose, school-site empowerment, and building on the strengths of at-risk children rather than being preoccupied with their deficiencies (Hopfenberg et al., 1993).

Robert Slavin's Success for All network involves fifty-nine school districts in twenty states. It is a comprehensive program for elementary schools serving disadvantaged children. The program incorporates research-based prekindergarten and kindergarten programs; one-to-one tutoring for first-graders experiencing difficulties in reading; extensive use of cooperative learning in grades 1–5 for reading, writing, and language arts; and an active family-support program. A building facilitator coordinates ongoing professional development and monitors an eight-week assessment program to make sure all students are making adequate progress (Slavin, 1994; Slavin, Madden, Karweit, Dolan & Wasik, 1992).

One of the newest networks is built around Ernest Boyer's *The Basic School* (1995). Boyer developed the concept of the school model with funding from the Carnegie Foundation for the Advancement of Teaching. A grant from the Ewing Marion Kauffman Foundation is supporting the network. The model is a comprehensive approach to school renewal that pulls together the findings of extensive national and international studies of what actually works well in schools. It is built around four priorities: community, curriculum coherence, climate, and character.

The school is united as a community with a shared vision that emphasizes purpose, communication, justice, discipline, caring, and celebration. Teachers are leaders by inspiration rather than directive. Parents are considered full partners and are recognized and respected as the child's first and most important teachers. The curriculum is carefully coordinated through a core of eight commonalities, with language and literacy being the first and most essential goal. Academic standards are established in language and the core commonalities with benchmarks to monitor student achievement. In a commitment to the whole child, the school develops a climate for promoting learning through making connections between generations, providing adequate resources, and acknowledging that a student's physical, social, and emotional well-being also relates to learning. The school addresses the ethical and moral dimensions of a child's life through core virtues such as respect, compassion, and perseverance. It teaches these virtues through the curriculum, through the school climate, and through service.

Efficiency Comparisons between Public and Private Schools

Coleman returned to center stage of school policy controversy with his comparison of public and private high schools (Coleman, Hoffer, & Kilgore, 1981). His methodology involved multiple regression similar to that of Coleman (1966) and other production-function studies. Data for this study were from High School and Beyond, an ongoing national study of achievement and other high school outcomes, sponsored by the National Center for Education Statistics and carried out by the National Opinion Research Center. More than 50,000 students in over 1,000 schools participated in the initial data collection in 1980. The schools included approximately eighty Catholic and twenty-five other private high schools. Because of the small number of "other" private high schools, the study drew few conclusions concerning them. Longitudinal data became available in 1984 and are updated periodically.

The researchers found greater achievement growth in verbal and mathematical skills between the sophomore and senior years among students in Catholic high schools than in public high schools when they used statistical controls for differences in student background characteristics (Coleman & Hoffer, 1987). The magnitude of the differences

was equivalent to one grade on average. It was greater for minority, low socioeconomic status, and other at-risk students than for other students. They found no differences in science knowledge and civics. Coleman's conclusions have been challenged but not refuted by others (Alexander, 1987; Alexander & Pallas, 1987; and Willms, 1987). The challenges reinforce our understanding of the subjectivity of even quantitative research. In reviewing Coleman's work and the challenges to it, Haertel (1987) concluded:

> Given our present state of knowledge, all of the authors' different choices are defensible. They are dictated by different *conceptions* of school policy, of the sources of individual differences in learning, of what is taught during the last two years of high school, and of appropriate public policy. (p. 16; emphasis added)

Haertel also pointed out that none of the challengers found public school achievement to be superior to that in Catholic schools. The argument was over the size of the Catholic school advantage and whether or not it was significant from a policy perspective. The Hoffer, Greeley, and Coleman (1987) analysis pointed out that Catholic high schools succeeded in obtaining higher student achievement despite the fact that their class sizes were larger, teachers held fewer advanced degrees and were less likely to be state certified, resources were more limited, and per pupil costs were far smaller than those characteristic of public high schools. As a result, Catholic high schools could be said to be functioning at greater technical and economic efficiency than were public high schools on average.

Hoffer, Greeley, and Coleman (1987) attributed the greater success of the Catholic schools to their higher demands on students. These schools place larger percentages of their students in the academic track, including many who would be relegated to general or vocational tracks in public high schools. Catholic high schools also demand more course work, more advanced course work, and better discipline. The researchers found that at-risk pupils did especially well in Catholic schools, and that the productive characteristics of this school climate could be successfully replicated in public schools:

> Catholic schools are especially beneficial to the least advantaged students: minorities, poor, and those whose initial achievement is low. For these students, the lack of structure, demands, and expectations found in many public schools is especially harmful. *Our analyses show that those public schools which make the same demands as found in the average Catholic school produce comparable achievement.* (p. 87, emphasis added)

The description of the average Catholic high school culture sounds very much like that characterized by "effective" public schools and many of the reform network schools.

Coleman and Hoffer (1987) attributed the ability of Catholic high schools to make greater demands on their students to their greater "social capital." Social capital, discussed in Chapter 7 in the context of partnerships and volunteerism, consists of the relationships between people. Social capital provides norms and sanctions which in turn "depend both on social relations and the closure of networks created by these relations" (p. 222). The religious communities surrounding Catholic schools provide the social capital that is not found in most public and independent schools today.

In a simpler time, according to Coleman and Hoffer, public schools were part of a functioning community. This is still the case in many rural areas, where achievement tends to be unexpectedly high given the relatively low average socioeconomic status of rural communities and the low investment of economic resources. But functional communities in metropolitan areas, where most Americans live, are no longer based on residence as are most public school attendance boundaries. Functional communities have been replaced by value communities. Residential proximity is no

longer the source of dense interaction in metropolitan areas. It is thus incapable of providing public schools organized around residential proximity with norms, sanctions, and networks in support of the schools' educational missions. To bring significant amounts of social capital to public schools, Coleman and Hoffer urged choice among schools built around value communities: "Policies which would bring about expansion of choice should contain provisions that encourage the growth of social structures that can provide the social capital important to a school" (p. 243).

Chubb and Moe (1985, 1990) expanded the database used by Coleman et al. (1981) to include organizational and environmental information. In their analyses, they attributed the generally poor achievement of American public school pupils to the institutions of direct democratic control by which schools have been governed traditionally. Like Coleman et al., they recommended that public schools be built around parent-student choice and school autonomy that would induce marketlike competition among schools. Their findings, those of Coleman et al., and others are discussed at length in Chapter 14 with reference to school-based management and in Chapter 15 with reference to family choice.

Economies and Diseconomies of Scale

If we assume a universal educational production function, economies of scale are realized when average production costs decline as more units are produced or serviced. Conversely, there are diseconomies of scale when average production costs increase as more units are produced or serviced. These are important concepts in the efficient organization of educational enterprises.

Policies concerning school district consolidation are directed toward realizing economies of scale. Policies decentralizing large city school districts, on the other hand, are directed toward avoiding diseconomies of scale. Likewise, during periods of declining enrollments, closing underutilized buildings is a strategy for minimizing operating costs. Reorganizing very large schools into "houses" or "schools within schools" is a strategy for realizing the benefits of both large and small units while minimizing their disadvantages. Interest in scale economies derives from concern over economic efficiency.

Policy implications drawn from studies of relationships between school and district size, pupil achievement, and cost have taken a dramatic turn in recent years. From the beginning of this century through the 1960s, the overwhelming evidence seemed to support large schools and school districts in terms of economies and the higher number, diversity, and caliber of professional and administrative personnel that they could attract. These early studies were concerned primarily with inputs (costs). They gave little attention, if any, to outputs and ratios of outputs to inputs. As researchers began to take into account total cost and the socioeconomic status of pupils, and as they began to include measures of output such as achievement, pupil self-image, and success in college, economies of scale evaporated at relatively low numbers of pupils, and the disadvantages of large size became readily apparent.

The new emphases in research on the relationships between size and quality of schooling may have been a by-product of the disenchantment with large city schools in recent years. City educational systems had served through the 1950s as the standard for measuring the quality of educational opportunities. Beginning in the 1960s and continuing through the present, evidence of low cognitive achievement, low attendance rates, and high dropout rates has surfaced in urban school systems. This, coupled with these schools' inability to use substantial federal and state funds to raise significantly the achievement levels of most disadvantaged children, severely marred the images of urban schools. It now appears that, given present assumptions about how schools (and school districts) should organize, the relationships between size and quality of schooling are curvilinear. The benefits brought by larger enrollments increase to an optimal point and then decline following an inverted *U*-shaped curve (Engert, 1995; Fox, 1981; Riew, 1981, 1986).

Scale research has two foci: the district and the school. For very small districts, these are the same thing. Large districts have choices, however. They may operate schools over a wide range of sizes. Thus, a large district may operate small schools as a matter of district policy. But most do not. Large districts may also formulate most policy centrally. Or they may empower schools to make policy within general parameters the center establishes. A large school can operate as a single unit. Or it can organize schools within schools to secure the advantages inherent in both large and small schools.

What size should a school be? Barker and Gump (1964) were not specific. But they provided a useful guide as they concluded their classical work with these words:

> The data of this research and our own educational values tell us that a school should be sufficiently small that all of its students are needed for its enterprises. A school should be small enough that students are not redundant. (p. 202)

Barker and Gump (1964) concluded that large school size has an undesirable influence on the development of certain personal attributes of students. Specifically, they found that in most large schools, just a few students dominate leadership. In small schools, proportionally more students take an active part in school programs. The actual percentage of students who participated in extracurricular activities and the satisfaction of students with their schooling clearly supported small local schools over large centralized ones.

More varieties of subjects are available to students in large schools. Baker and Gump observed, however, that a given pupil participates in proportionally fewer of these electives than do students in small schools. They concluded: "if versatility of experience is preferred over opportunity for specialization, a smaller school is better than a larger one; if specialization is sought, the larger school is the better" (p. 201).

A 1986 study by the U.S. Department of Education updated the Barker and Gump analysis. This study reported that participation rates in extracurricular activities were consistently greater in small high schools (200 or fewer seniors) than for larger ones. Small schools also compared favorably with larger schools with respect to course credits taken by students, hours of homework, test scores and grade average, and involvement in extracurricular activities (Sweet, 1986). Lindsay (1982) did another replication of Barker and Gump using a representative national sample of 328 elementary schools. He found higher participation in extracurricular activities, student satisfaction, and attendance in small schools (fewer than 100 in each grade level).

Newman (1981) reported that the optimum size of secondary schools falls in the range of 500 to 1,200 pupils. Student participation in school activities and general interaction were greatest and vandalism and delinquency were lowest in that range.

> The opportunity that small schools provide for sustained contact among all members is a significant safeguard against alienation. The larger the school, the more difficult it is to achieve clear, consensual goals, to promote student participation in school management, and to create positive personal relations among students and staff. (p. 552)

In a similar vein, Rogers (1992) pointed to the disaffectedness and disconnectedness of many of today's youth of all types.

> When kids belong, they are engaged, they are "available" to learn and be taught. However, behind the pedagogical justification which argues for small schools where kids can be easily known, there is a psychological advantage as well. Adolescence is a time of craving acceptance, ways to fit in, a sense of *belonging*. In a large school where anonymity is the rule, kids go to what we might consider fool-

ish lengths in order to gain attention and acceptance. . . . The lack of connection that leads some kids to join gangs is frighteningly pervasive, invading even those communities we think of as "safe." (pp. 103–105)

New York City found the value of small schools combined with parental choice and community involvement in its Central Park East Project in East Harlem, one of the poorest sections of the city. Over thirty small schools of choice were created. The concept is now being replicated throughout the city. Rather than trying to fit all students into a standard school, a variety of schools have been designed so that there is a school to fit every student (Fliegel, 1993; Meier, 1995a, 1995b).

Goodlad (1984), in his comprehensive national study of *A Place Called School,* observed:

> Most of the schools clustering in the top group of our sample on major characteristics were small, compared with the schools clustering near the bottom. It is not impossible to have a good large school; it is simply more difficult. What are the defensible reasons for operating an elementary school of more than a dozen teachers and 300 boys and girls? I can think of none. (p. 309)

With respect to secondary school size, Goodlad wrote:

> Clearly we need sustained, creative efforts designed to show the curricular deficits incurred in very small high schools, the curricular possibilities of larger schools, and the point where increased size suggests no curricular gain. . . . The burden of proof, it appears to me, is on large size. Indeed, I would not want to face the challenge of justifying a senior, let alone a junior, high of more than 500 to 600 students (unless I were willing to place arguments for a strong football team ahead of arguments for a good school, which I am not). (p. 310)

Current research clearly suggests that small schools have the edge over large schools. Berlin and Cienkus (1989), after coediting an issue of *Education and Urban Society* devoted to the subject of size of school districts, schools, and classrooms, concluded that "smaller seems to be better."

Why does smaller seem to work better? . . . The literature on educational change repeats the answer. That is, people seem to learn, to change, and to grow in situations in which they feel that they have some control, some personal influence, some efficacy. Those situations in which parents, teachers and students are bonded together in pursuit of learning are likely to be the most productive. Small size by itself can only aid the complex process (p. 231)

In reporting the Carnegie Foundation's study *High School,* Boyer (1983) noted that research over the past several decades has suggested that small schools provide greater opportunity for student participation and greater emotional support than larger ones. Acknowledging the difficulty of knowing the exact point at which a high school becomes too large, he proposed that schools enrolling 1,500 to 2,000 students were good candidates for reorganizing into smaller units (using a school-within-a-school concept). Turning to the issue of the small high school, Boyer raised the question:

Can a small school provide the education opportunities to match the social and emotional advantages that may accompany smallness? We believe the preferred arrangement is to have bigness *and* smallness—a broad education program with supportive social arrangements. (p. 235)

Economist Ronald Coase (1988) developed a theory of "transaction costs" to explain such phenomena in organizations in general. For this research he received the Nobel Prize in economics in 1991. Transaction costs are costs of communication, coordination, and deciding. Eventually, expansion of an organization (for example, school or district) can lead to diseconomies and higher unit costs because of the managerial problems that are characteristic of large operations. Conventional estimates of economies of scale have vastly underestimated transactional costs. Peters and Waterman (1982), in their study of "America's best-run companies," found that divisions, plants, and branches were smaller than any cost analysis would suggest they should be. Decentralization of function was practiced where classic economics would ordain otherwise. "The excellent companies understand that beyond a certain surprisingly small size, *diseconomies* of scale seem to set in with a vengeance" (p. 112).

Optimum school and district size is a function of desired standards, available technology, and governing structures. The criteria defining these have changed over time and will continue to do so. In the past, providing diversity in curriculum and support services at an affordable cost were the primary justifications for large urban schools and rural school consolidation. Now, the disadvantages of bigness and the virtues of smallness have been well documented. Additionally, technological advances characteristic of the information age have made it possible for any individual in almost any place to access curricular diversity easily. These developments combine to impel a reassessment of the large school policies of central cities and of state school consolidation policies for rural areas. Fowler (1989) concluded:

It is apparent that public school size and district size both influence schooling outcomes, and although other evidence of this relationship has accumulated, policy makers seem to ignore the finding and its significance. Much litigation has been undertaken to equalize expenditures per pupil, or to assure equivalent staff characteristics in an effort to increase learning; however, it appears that keeping schools relatively small might be more efficacious. (p. 21)

Based on an extensive review of the literature, Walberg and Walberg (1994) tested the hypotheses that states with large districts, large schools, and large state shares of within-state funding can be expected to achieve poorly. They found support for all three hypotheses with respect to mathematics achievement. On the average, states whose eighth-grade students scored higher on the National Assessment of Educational Progress mathematics examination had smaller districts, smaller schools, and smaller state shares of school financial aid. They concluded that many of the prominent new reforms may be interpreted as countervailing responses to problems of size and remote government. The more radical of these reforms devolve governing authority and financial control to small groups of lay citizens as educational consumers rather than educational producers. They include the school governing councils of Chicago and the United Kingdom, New York City's community boards, and proposals to break up the Los Angeles Unified School District into many freestanding, smaller districts.

Schools of any size, but especially small schools, require support services that they cannot provide themselves in a cost-effective manner. In rural areas, such services are increasingly being provided through intermediate districts and other cooperative arrangements. This trend needs to be greatly accelerated if rural schools are to keep up with modern demands. But outright consolidation is no longer necessary for districts having at least one hundred pupils per grade.

Creation of regional service units greatly lowers the minimum functional size of schools and school districts. It does this by making it possible for a number of small schools and districts to provide jointly selected services none could provide alone. Occupational education and education of the severely disabled are examples that involve relatively small percentages of enrollments. Regional centers also provide technological services of educational television, interactive video, and computer-assisted instruction.

By enlarging the domain of decision making at the building level and reducing the domain of decision making at the district level, central offices of large urban districts may begin to take on the characteristics of intermediate districts. In this respect, it is interesting to note that Illinois has radically changed the governance of education in the city of Chicago (Hess, 1994). The new arrangement limits the authority of the citywide Board of Education and places control of schools in the hands of school councils consisting of parents, other local residents, and teachers. Day-to-day authority resides in the hands of principals who are selected by the councils. The councils also have authority to set the budget and to dismiss incompetent teachers. We see this as a precursor of things to come.

SUMMARY AND POLICY IMPLICATIONS

In this chapter, we have looked at evidence concerning the economic efficiency of elementary and secondary schools. We concluded that in terms of external efficiency, the United States, along with most other advanced nations, devotes about the optimal percentage of its resources (GDP) to education given our current understanding of educational technology. If there are to be improvements in educational outcomes, those improvements will be primarily a result of improvements in internal efficiency. They will not be through the application of additional resources. Studies relating to the efficiency of public schools indicate consistently, however, that many—perhaps most—schools are not using their resources to full advantage. Given current organization and practice, the problem is not so much the lack of resources as the nature of the available resources and the way they are being used.

Elmore (1994) argues that we need to get educators and those who influence them to think differently about resources and how they are applied to student learning:

So at the core of the problem of adequacy, I would argue, is a problem of productivity and incentives. And behind the problem of productivity and incentives is a problem of knowledge and practice. There is virtually nothing in the background and preparation of educators that prepares them to confront the difficult and messy problems involved with using existing resources, or new resources, to cause dramatic shifts in student performance. Furthermore, there are many factors in the environment of schools that encourage educators not to think systematically about resources: categorical policies that "solve" the resource allocation problem for schools by mandating staffing patterns and ratios; collective bargaining contracts that set limits on the ability of schools to use resources flexibly; line-item budgeting practices; and the like. Most of the factors that limit the capacity of educators to pay attention to resource and output problems are either deeply ingrained in their background and prior experience or hard-wired in the organizational and policy context in which they work. (p. 457)

The evaluation and scale studies, school reform networks, effective-schools research, and comparisons with private schools have identified instructional and organizational interventions that do positively affect student achievement in cost-effective ways. Most, if not all, of these interventions require few new resources. Rather they require a redirection of existing resources.

The effective-schools research, scale studies, and the Coleman work point to the importance of the social climate of schools. Coleman found that the building of supportive climates is facilitated when schools are organized around value communities to which the families of children subscribe rather than around residential areas. This suggests that the prevailing neighborhood school attendance policy should be replaced with a policy of schools of choice. District governance should yield to greater involvement of parents and teachers in policy making and operation at the school level.

Relationships between size and effectiveness and economy appear to be curvilinear. While there are disadvantages in being very small, there are also disadvantages in being very large. There is little agreement on an optimal size. Optimal size appears to be a function of circumstances. The challenge before us is to provide stimulating learning environments with the broad educational programs that are characteristic of large schools along with the supportive social structure that is characteristic of small schools.

In Part V, we analyze the financial implications of proposals for the fundamental restructuring of the organization, governance, and delivery of educational services. In Chapter 16 we examine personnel remuneration policies in relation to teacher supply and demand and to teacher quality and motivation. In Chapter 17 we look at the potential of educational technology in terms of relative prices, substitution effects, and trade-offs. Chapters 14 and 15 examine the financial implications of policies directed toward injecting marketlike incentives in the provision of educational services. We look at school-based decision making in Chapter 14 and permitting choice of school by parents in Chapter 15.

NOTE

1. The evidence on class size is conflicting. According to Hanushek (1986), of 112 studies investigating student-to-teacher ratios, only 9 found positive, statistically significant relationships with achievement. On the other hand, a meta-analysis by Glass and Smith (1979) found little relationship between class size and achievement over the normal range of classes. In small classes *where instruction was individualized,* better achievement was found. Unless the mode of teaching was individualized, however, the potential of small classes was not realized. Finn and Achilles (1990), in a major study conducted in Tennessee

schools, found that small classes (13–17 students per teacher) were definitely related to higher achievement in the primary grades in reading and mathematics.

ACTIVITIES

1. Has the investment in your own education paid off? Estimate in current dollars the cost of your education beyond high school. Include the income forgone in acquiring your education. Find the present values of your investments by compounding annually each cost from the time it was incurred at a 10 percent rate of interest. Now estimate the earning differentials in current dollar values between the positions you have held (and are likely to hold over your lifetime) and the positions you would likely have held if you had terminated your education at high school graduation. Estimate the present value by discounting the differentials from the times they were incurred at a 10 percent rate of interest. Is the present value of the sum of the earnings differentials as large as, or larger than, the present value of the sum of the costs? If so, you have at least broken even. If not, from an economic standpoint, it would have made more sense if you had entered the workforce directly after high school or pursued another career.

2. List and discuss arguments for and against using the educational production function as a paradigm for analyzing resource allocations within public schools.

3. In this chapter we have concluded that the United States is already devoting an adequate percentage of its resources to formal education and that any improvements in education will have to come from using those resources more wisely (more efficiently). Do you agree with this position? List and discuss arguments supporting it and some that do not.

4. Using the information provided in the *Internal Efficiency* section, devise a configuration for using public school resources that may be more efficient than those typically used now.

5. Visit a large school and a small school serving the same grade levels. Look for answers to the questions that follow. Alternatively, form a study group made up of persons with experience in different-size schools and compare your experiences as you discuss the questions below.
   a. Do you find any differences between schools that can be attributed to their differences in size?
   b. What are the advantages and disadvantages of being large? Of being small?
   c. What strategies might best neutralize the effects of school size?

6. Elmore (1994) is quoted as saying that there is little likelihood that professional educators are capable of designing new methods of delivering instruction that would result in dramatic positive shifts in student performance. Further, he characterizes the schooling bureaucracy as being hamstrung with organizational limitations that make fundamental reform unlikely. These limiting factors include mandated staffing patterns and ratios, collective bargaining contracts that limit flexibility in the use of resources, and incremental budgeting.
   a. Do you agree with Elmore's observations? Why or why not?
   b. What, if anything, can be done to correct the situation?
   c. If educators cannot reform schooling, are there any other likely sources of reform?

 **COMPUTER SIMULATION**

Objectives of This Activity

- *To further understanding of the statistical concepts behind educational production functions*

- *To introduce the procedure of multiple regression analysis using a spreadsheet*

This simulation explores the concept of educational production functions and regression analysis. Thorough study and application of these topics are well beyond the means of spreadsheet software. Therefore, these simulations have been designed only to introduce readers to some of the basic principles, techniques, and difficulties that characterize regression analysis and the design of educational production functions. To facilitate more comprehensive coverage of the topics, it is recommended that those persons having access to a standard statistical package such as the Statistical Package for the Social Sciences (SPSS-PC) and a larger database than we have provided for these simulations use them to do a parallel set of analyses. (Even with the application of more sophisticated statistical applications, only the most powerful relationships are statistically significant with a database of ten as used in these exercises; a larger database is likely to yield more interesting results.)

Simulation 13.1: *Education Production-Function*

Part 1. Regression of Pupil Achievement on a Measure of Pupil Socioeconomic Status

a. Retrieve the file PROFUN. This file contains selected data from the hypothetical state database to illustrate the concept of an educational production function. The three variables, EXPEND PER PUPIL, PERM CERT, and MASTER PLUS, represent school district spending levels, and the proportion of teachers having earned permanent certification and master's degrees. These variables are commonly used as measures of inputs to the schooling process. FREE LUNCH is a representative measure of the socioeconomic status (SES) of the pupils in the districts. GRADE 4 READING is a representative measure of schooling outputs.

b. In Lotus 1-2-3, use the /, Data, Regression command sequence to begin the first regression analysis. In Microsoft Excel, use the Options, Analysis Tools, Regression command sequence.

c. Select the X-Ranges from the column that contains data for the independent variable, FREE LUNCH.

d. Select the Y-Range in the column that con-

tains data for the dependent variable, GRADE 4 READING.

e. Select the Output-Range cell in the left-most column below the data table.

f. Execute the "Go" (Lotus) or "OK" (Excel) command. Note: Reference to an F-Test indicates that both the "R Squared" (proportion of the Y variance shared with the variance of the X variable) and the X coefficient are statistically significant, that is, there is little likelihood that the true relationship is zero.

g. Print the results.

h. What do the results indicate about the relationship between student SES and achievement as measured by the variables used?

Part 2. Regression of Pupil Achievement on Selected School Characteristics

a. For Lotus 1-2-3, use the /, Data, Regression command sequence to begin a multiple regression analysis that includes more than one independent variable. For Microsoft Excel, use the Options, Analysis Tools, Regression command sequence.

b. Select the X-Ranges in the columns that contain data for the following independent variables that represent schooling inputs: EXPEND PER PUPIL, PERM CERT, and MASTER PLUS.

c. Select the Y-Range in the column that contains data for the dependent variable, GRADE 4 READING.

d. Select an Output-Range cell in the left-most column below the last Output-Range.

e. Execute the "Go" (Lotus) or "OK" (Excel) command. Note: The R Squared for Part 2 is much smaller than for Part 1. An F-Test shows that it is not statistically significant, that is, we have no confidence that the true relationship is not zero. The X coefficients for the independent variables are not statistically significant either.

f. Print the results.

g. What do these findings suggest about the relationship between school inputs and pupil achievement?

Part 3. Multiple Regression of Pupil Achievement on Pupil and School Characteristics (Simulation of an Educational Production Function)

a. For Lotus 1-2-3, use the /, Data, Regression command sequence to begin a second multiple regression analysis. For Microsoft Excel, use the Options, Analysis Tools, Regression command sequence.

b. Select the X-Ranges using the independent variables used in Parts 1 and 2—EXPEND PER PUPIL, PERM CERT, MASTER PLUS, and FREE LUNCH.

c. Select the Y-Range in the column that contains data for the dependent variable, GRADE 4 READING.

d. Select an Output-Range cell in the left-most column below the last Output-Range.

e. Execute the "Go" (Lotus) or "OK" (Excel) command. Note: Reference to an F-Test indicates that the R Square and the X coefficient for the FREE LUNCH independent variable are statistically significant. But the X coefficients for the schooling input variables are not. Based on this information, which variable or set of variables has the largest statistical relationship with pupil achievement?

This is a typical outcome of educational production-function analysis; the influence of socioeconomic status on student achievement tends to be much stronger than the influence of schooling inputs. With a larger sample, some of the schooling input variables would be statistically significant. But the relative explanatory power of student achievement by socioeconomic status and schooling inputs would be approximately the same.

f. Print the results.

g. ***Further activity.*** Obtain a data set that includes measures of SES, school inputs, and pupil achievement for school districts in a state or region/metropolitan area. Design several multiple regression analyses of possible factors affecting pupil achievement and compare the results with the production-function analyses described in this chapter.

REFERENCES

Alexander, K. L. (1987). Cross-sectional comparisons of public and private school effectiveness: A review of the evidence and issues. In E. H. Haertel, T. James, & H. M. Levin (Eds.), *Comparing public and private schools: Volume 2, School achievement* (pp. 33–66). New York: Falmer.

Alexander, K. L., & Pallas, A. M. (1987). School sector and cognitive performance: When is a little a little? In E. H. Haertel, T. James, & H. M. Levin (Eds.), *Comparing public and private schools: Volume 2, School achievement* (pp. 89–112). New York: Falmer.

Barker, R. G., & Gump, P. V. (1964). *Big school, small school.* Stanford, CA: Stanford University Press.

Becker, G. S. (1960). Underinvestment in college education? *American Economic Review* (Papers and proceedings), *50,* 345–354.

Becker, G. S. (1964). *Human capital: A theoretical and empirical analysis, with special reference to education.* New York: National Bureau of Economic Research.

Benson, C. S. (1978). *The economics of public education* (3rd ed.). Boston: Houghton Mifflin.

Benson, C. S. (1988). Economics of education: The U.S. experience. In N. J. Boyan (Ed.), *Handbook of research on educational administration* (pp. 355–372). New York: Longman.

Berlin, B., & Cienkus, R. (1989). Size: The ultimate educational issue? *Education and Urban Society, 21,* 228–231.

Berne, R., & Stiefel, L. (1994). Measuring equity at the school level: The finance perspective. *Educational Evaluation and Policy Analysis, 16,* 405–421.

Bowles, S. S., & Levin, H. M. (1968). The determinants of scholastic achievement: An appraisal of recent findings. *Journal of Human Resources, 3:* 3–24.

Boyer, E. L. (1983). *High school: A report on secondary education in America.* New York: Harper and Row.

Boyer, E. L. (1995). *The basic school: A community for learning.* Princeton, NJ: Carnegie Foundation for the Advancement of Teaching.

Brewer, D. J. (1994). *School district productivity, efficiency, and resource allocation: Evidence from New York.* Paper presented at the annual conference of the American Education Finance Association, Nashville, TN.

Bridge, R. G., Judd, C. M., & Moock, P. R. (1979). *The determinants of educational outcomes: The impact of families, peers, teachers, and schools.* Cambridge, MA: Ballinger.

Brookover, W., & Lezotte, L. (1979). *Changes in school characteristics coincident with changes in student achievement.* East Lansing, MI: State University, College of Urban Development.

Burkhead, J. (1967). *Input and output in large-city high schools.* Syracuse, NY: Syracuse University Press.

Cain, G. G., & Watts, H. W. (1970). Problems in making policy inferences from the Coleman report. *American Sociological Review, 35,* 228–252.

Chubb, J. E., & Moe, T. M. (1985). *Politics, markets, and the organization of schools.* Stanford, CA: Institute for Research on Educational Finance and Governance, School of Education, Stanford University.

Chubb, J. E., & Moe, T. M. (1990). *Politics, markets, and America's schools.* Washington, DC: Brookings Institution.

Coase, R. H. (1988). *The firm, the market, and the law.* Chicago: University of Chicago Press.

Coleman, J. S. (1966). *Equality of educational opportunity.* Washington, DC: U.S. Government Printing Office.

Coleman, J. S., & Hoffer, T. (1987). *Public and private high schools: The impact of communities.* New York: Basic Books.

Coleman, J. S., Hoffer, T., & Kilgore, S. (1981). *Public and private high schools.* Washington, DC: National Center for Education Statistics.

Comer, J. (1988). Educating poor minority children. *Scientific American, 259,* 42–48.

Crampton, F. E. (1994). *Beyond the production function: A new look at the relationship of educational inputs and student outcomes.* Paper presented at the annual conference of the American Education Finance Association, Nashville, TN.

Dreeben, R., & Thomas, J. A. (1980). *The analysis of educational productivity, Volume I: Issues in microanalysis.* Cambridge, MA: Ballinger.

Edmonds, R. (1979). Effective schools for the urban poor. *Educational Leadership, 37,* 15–24.

Elmore, R. F. (1994). Thoughts on program equity: Productivity and incentives for performance in education. *Educational Policy, 8,* 453–459.

Engert, F. (1995). *Efficiency analysis of school districts using multiple inputs and outputs: An application of data envelopment analysis.* Unpublished doctoral dissertation, State University of New York at Buffalo.

Ferguson, R. F. (1991). Paying for public education: New evidence on how and why money matters. *Harvard Journal on Legislation, 28,* 465–498.

Finn, J. D., & Achilles, C. M. (1990). Answers and questions about class size: A statewide experiment. *American Educational Research Journal, 27,* 557–577.

Fliegel, S. (1993). *Miracle in East Harlem: The fight for choice in public education.* New York: Random House.

Fowler, W. J., Jr. (1989). *School size, school characteristics, and school outcomes.* Paper presented at the annual meeting of the American Educational Research Association, San Francisco.

Fox, W. F. (1981). Reviewing economies of size in education. *Journal of Education Finance, 6,* 273–296.

Fuller, B., & Clarke, P. (1994). Raising school effects while ignoring culture? Local conditions and the influence of classroom tools, rules, and pedagogy. *Review of Educational Research, 64* (1), 119–157.

Glass, G. V., & Smith, M. L. (1979). Meta-analysis of research on the relationship of class-size and achievement. *Educational Evaluation and Policy Analysis, 1,* 2–16.

Glasser, W. (1992). *The quality school* (2d ed.). New York: Harper Perennial, HarperCollins.

Goodlad, J. I. (1984). *A place called school: Prospects for the future.* New York: McGraw-Hill.

Greenwald, R., Hedges, L. V., & Laine, R. D. (1994). When reinventing the wheel is not necessary: A case study in the use of meta-analysis in education finance. *Journal of Education Finance, 20,* 1–20.

Haertel, E. H. (1987). Comparing public and private schools using longitudinal data from the HSB study. In E. H. Haertel, T. James, & H. M. Levin (Eds.), *Comparing public and private schools: Volume 2, School achievement* (pp. 9–32). New York: Falmer.

Hanushek, E. A. (1986). The economics of schooling: Production and efficiency in public schools. *Journal of Economic Literature, 24,* 1141–1177.

Hanushek, E. A. (1987). Education production functions. In G. Psacharopoulos (Ed.), *Economics of education: Research and studies* (pp. 33–42). Oxford, England: Pergamon.

Hanushek, E. A. (1991). When school finance "reform" may not be good policy. *Harvard Journal on Education, 28,* 423–456.

Hanushek, E. A. (1994). Money might matter somewhere: A response to Hedges, Laine, and Greenwald. *Educational Researcher, 23* (4), 5–8.

Hedges, L. V., Laine, R. D., & Greenwald, R. (1994a). Does money matter? A meta-analysis of studies of the effects of differential school inputs on student outcomes. *Educational Researcher, 23* (3), 5–14.

Hedges, L. V., Laine, R. D., & Greenwald, R. (1994b). Money does matter somewhere: A reply to Hanushek. *Educational Researcher, 23* (4), 9–10.

Hess, G. A., Jr. (Ed.). (1994). *Education and Urban Society* (Special issue on Outcomes of Chicago School Reform), *26,* (3).

Hoffer, T., Greeley, A. M., & Coleman, J. S. (1987). Catholic high school effects on achievement growth. In E. H. Haertel, T. James, & H. M. Levin (Eds.), *Comparing public and private schools: Volume 2, School achievement* (pp. 67–88). New York: Falmer.

Hopfenberg, W., Levin, H. M., Chase, C., Christensen, S. G., Moore, M., Soler, P., Brunner, I., Keller, B., & Rodriguez, G. (1993). *The accelerated schools resource guide.* San Francisco: Jossey-Bass.

Jackson, S., Logsdon, D., & Taylor, N. (1983). Instructional leadership behaviors: Differentiating effective from ineffective low-income urban schools. *Urban Education, 18,* 59–70.

King, R. A., & MacPhail-Wilcox, B. (1994). Unraveling the production equation: The continuing quest for resources that make a difference. *Journal of Education Finance, 20,* 47–65.

Klitgaard, R. E., & Hall, G. R. (1975). Are there unusually effective schools? *Journal of Human Resources, 10,* 90–106.

Levin, H. M. (1994). The necessary and sufficient conditions for achieving educational equity. In R. Berne & L. O. Picus (Eds.), *Outcome equity in education.* Thousand Oaks, CA: Corwin Press.

Lindsay, P. (1982). The effect of high school size on student participation, satisfaction, and attendance. *Educational Evaluation and Policy Analysis, 4,* 57–65.

Madaus, G. F., Airasian, P. W., & Kellaghan, T. (1980). *School effectiveness: A reassessment of the evidence.* New York: McGraw-Hill.

Mayeski, G. W., Wisler, C. E., Beaton, A. E., Jr., Weinfeld, F. D., Cohen, W. M., Okada, T., Proshek, J. M., & Tabler, K. A. (1972). *A study of our nation's schools.* Washington, DC: U.S. Government Printing Office.

Meier, D. (1995a). How our schools could be. *Phi Delta Kappan, 76,* 369–373.

Meier, D. (1995b). *The power of their ideas: Lessons for America from a small school in Harlem.* Boston: Beacon.

Monk, D. H. (1989). The education production function: Its evolving role in policy analysis. *Educational Evaluation and Policy Analysis, 11,* 31–45.

Mostellar, F., & Moynihan, D. P. (1972). *On equality of educational opportunity.* New York: Vintage Press.

Murnane, R. J. (1975). *The impact of school resources on the learning of inner city children.* Cambridge, MA: Ballinger.

Murnane, R. J. (1980). *Interpreting the evidence on school effectiveness* (Working Paper No. 830). New Haven, CT: Yale University, Institution for Social and Policy Studies.

Murnane, R. J. (1983). Quantitative studies of effective schools: What have we learned? In A. Odden & L. D. Webb (Eds.), *School finance and school improvement: Linkages for the 1980s* (pp. 193–209). Cambridge, MA: Ballinger.

Murphy, K., & Welch, F. (1989). Wage premiums for college graduates: Recent growth and possible explanations. *Educational Researcher, 18* (4), 17–26.

National Center for Education Statistics. (1991). *Condition of education, 1991.* Vol. 1. Washington, DC: U.S. Department of Education.

National Center for Education Statistics. (1995). *Digest of education statistics.* Washington, DC: U.S. Government Printing Office.

Newman, F. M. (1981). Reducing student alienation in high schools: Implications of theory. *Harvard Education Review, 51,* 546–564.

Odden, A., & Webb, L. D. (1983). Introduction: The linkages between school finance and school improvement. In A. Odden & L. D. Webb (Eds.), *School finance and school improvement: Linkages for the 1980s* (pp. xiii–xxi). Cambridge, MA: Ballinger.

Owens, J. T., Jr. (1994). *Interdistrict resource allocation in Dade County Florida: An analysis of equity of educational opportunity.* Paper delivered at the annual meeting of the American Educational Finance Association, Nashville, TN.

Paquette, J. (1991). Why should I stay in school? Quantizing private educational returns. *Journal of Education Finance, 16,* 458–477.

Peters, T. J., & Waterman, R. H., Jr. (1982). *In search of excellence: Lessons from America's best-run companies.* New York: Warner Books.

Psacharopoulos, G. (1973). *Returns to education: An international comparison.* Amsterdam: Elsevier.

Psacharopoulos, G. (1981). Returns to education: An updated international comparison. *Comparative Education, 17,* 321–341.

Psacharopoulos, G. (1985). Returns to education: A further international update and implications. *Journal of Human Resources, 20,* 583–604.

Reed, L. (1985). *An inquiry into the specific school-based practices involving principals that distinguish unusually effective elementary schools from effective elementary schools.* Unpublished doctoral dissertation, State University of New York at Buffalo.

Riew, J. (1981). Enrollment decline and school reorganization: A cost efficiency analysis. *Economics of Education Review, 1,* 53–73.

Riew, J. (1986). Scale economies, capacity utilization, and school costs: A comparative analysis of secondary and elementary schools. *Journal of Education Finance, 11,* 433–446.

Rogers, B. (1992). Small is beautiful. In D. Durrett & J.

Nathan (Eds.), *Source book on school and district size, cost, and quality.* Minneapolis, MN: North Central Regional Educational Laboratory.

Rutter, M., Maughan, B., Mortimore, P., & Ouston, J. (1979). *Fifteen thousand hours: Secondary schools and their effects on children.* London, England: Open Books.

Sizer, T. R. (1992). *Horace's school: Redesigning the American high school.* Boston: Houghton-Mifflin.

Slavin, R. E. (1994). Statewide finance reform: Ensuring educational adequacy for high-poverty schools. *Educational Policy, 8,* 425–434.

Slavin, R. E., Madden, N. A., Karweit, N. L., Dolan, L., & Wasik, B. A. (1992). Success for all: A relentless approach to prevention and early intervention in elementary schools. Arlington, VA: Educational Research Service.

Smith, T. M., & Phelps, R. P. (1995). Educational finance indicators: What can we learn from comparing states and nations. In W. J. Fowler, Jr. (Ed.), *Developments in school finance.* Washington, DC: National Center for Educational Statistics, pp. 99–107.

Summers, A. A., & Wolfe, B. L. (1975). *Equality of educational opportunity quantified: A production function approach.* Philadelphia, PA: Federal Reserve Bank of Philadelphia, Department of Research.

Sweet, D. A. (1986). Extracurricular activity participants outperform other students. *Office of Educational Research and Improvement Bulletin* (CS 85-2136), September.

U.S. Department of Education. (1990). Shortchanging education: A case study of flawed economics. In Committee on Education and Labor, House of Representatives, *Hearings on education funding* (Serial No. 101-86) (pp. 59–67). Washington, DC: U.S. Government Printing Office.

Venezsky, R., & Winfield, L. (1980). *Schools that exceed beyond expectations in the teaching of reading: Studies on education, technical report no. 1.* Newark, DE: University of Delaware.

Verstegen, D. (1992). International comparisons of education spending: A review and analysis of reports. *Journal of Education Finance, 17,* 257–276.

Walberg, H. J. (1984). Improving the productivity of America's schools. *Educational Leadership, 41* (May), 19–27.

Walberg, H. J., & Walberg, H. J., III. (1994). Losing local control. *Educational Researcher, 23* (5), 19–26.

Weber, G. (1971). *Inner city children can be taught to read: Four successful schools.* Washington, DC: Council for Basic Education.

Willms, J. D. (1987). Patterns of academic achievement in public and private schools: Implications for public policy and future research. In E. H. Haertel, T. James, & H. M. Levin (Eds.), *Comparing public and private schools: Volume 2, School achievement* (pp. 113–134). New York: Falmer.

Woodhall, M. (1987). Human capital concepts. In G. Psacharopoulos (Ed.), *Economics of education: Research and studies* (pp. 21–24). Oxford, England: Pergamon.

PART FIVE

Reforming the Governance, Finance, and Delivery of Schooling

Part III featured strategies for improving the equity of funding among school districts. But evidence presented in Part IV showed how badly these well-intended strategies had failed. Inequities in the distribution of resources among and within school districts remained despite many attempts to remove them. Further, the evidence strongly suggested that bringing about equity in the distribution of funding would not produce equity in student achievement unless efficiency of the education system was improved. There are those who blame the very structure of schooling and its governance for the system's poor performance.

In Part V we examine some of the major reform proposals to improve the functioning of the education system and their implications for school finance policy. Two chapters (14 and 15) are devoted to arguments for changing the governance of education by inducing marketlike forces into the process for making decisions about matters related to education. Chapter 14 focuses on expanding the authority of professional educators in designing and governing schools through school-based decision making and budgeting. Chapter 15 focuses on expanding the authority of parents in making decisions about which schools their children should attend.

Chapters 16 and 17 look at more microissues, exploring opportunities for improving efficiency in the use of resources. Chapter 16 suggests new ways for rewarding teachers and other educators for the services they render. These rewards would improve the quality of those attracted to the profession and provide salary incentives linked to student outcomes. Chapter 17 approaches the issue of improved efficiency by addressing the mix of labor and technology used in schooling and strategies for improving the quality of both.

CHAPTER 14

School-Based Decision Making: Provider Sovereignty

Primary Issues Explored in This Chapter:

- *Definition:* What is school-based decision making (SBDM)? Why is SBDM being seriously considered as a possible reform of education governance?
- *Privatization:* Can SBDM contribute to the stimulation of marketlike forces in the public provision of education services?

- *Experience with SBDM:* What have been the effects of SBDM? What has been its impact on students, educators, and the quality of service?
- *School-based budgeting:* What kind of financial infrastructure is required to support SBDM?

There are a growing number of critics of public education who believe that it is the school governance structure itself that is the cause of the inequities and inefficiencies in the education system. This posture views the education policy-making process from the perspective of institutionalism (see Chapter 1). These critics initiated the second wave of education reforms beginning in the mid-1980s. They can be divided into advocates of administrative decentralization (school-based decision making), advocates of market solutions involving parental choice of schools, and advocates of systemic reform involving greater centralization of some functions (especially finance and the setting of curricular and achievement standards) and decentralization of other functions (notably the organization and operations of schools) (Elmore, 1993).

Two fundamental questions are associated with radically reforming the governance of educa-

tion. The first is the extent to which parents and students should be empowered to choose among schools or among programs within schools. Elmore (1988) called this the "demand side" question. "It poses the question of whether the consumers of education should be given the central role in deciding what kind of education is appropriate for them" (p. 79). Chapter 15 focuses on this issue with respect to market concepts.

The second question is the extent to which educators should be empowered to organize and manage schools, to design educational programs, and to receive public funds for providing education to students. Elmore referred to this as the "supply side" question. "It poses the issue of whether the providers of education should be given the autonomy and flexibility to respond to differences in judgments of consumers about appropriate education" (p. 79). We address the supply-side issue in this chapter by considering proposals for school-based decision making and budgeting as strategies for stimulating alternative means of combining schooling inputs to obtain desired outputs.

In this chapter, we examine arguments for, and experiences with, the decentralization of educational governance to the school level. SBDM, when coupled with family choice of schools, can be part of a strategy intended to simulate in public schools many of the perceived organizational advantages of private schools. Therefore we review a study that contrasts public and private school organizations and environments. We report actual experiences implementing SBDM in the United States and elsewhere. The chapter closes with a discussion of school-based budgeting and cost accounting.

SCHOOL-BASED DECISION MAKING (SBDM) DEFINED

School-based decision making as a strategy of reform is founded on the premise that the school is the fundamental decision-making unit within the education system; its administrators, teachers, and other professional staff constitute a natural decision-making and management team. Each school is considered a relatively autonomous unit with the principal in the role of chief executive officer. Shifting decision-making responsibilities from central administrative offices to schools means a redistribution of power among principals, teachers, parents, and community. This is done under the assumption that involving key stakeholders in the decision-making process will make schools more responsive to the unique needs of local conditions. It is also assumed that SBDM will more effectively harness stakeholders' knowledge, creativity, and energy. SBDM is the product of decentralizing strategies, beginning in the 1970s with the concept of school-based management and budgeting. In the 1990s this trend has led to self-governing charter schools.

Structures for making policy at the school level vary. Authority may be placed with the prin-

cipal alone. Or the responsibility may be shared in some combination among administrators, teachers, parents, community representatives, and upper-grade students (Lindelow, 1981). Some manifestations of SBDM place authority with a school-based governing board dominated by laypersons, for example, in Chicago and England. When power is placed with lay boards, specific provision is usually made for formal professional involvement in the decision-making process.

Under SBDM, school authorities may develop the budget, select staff, and refine the school's curriculum to meet specific needs of its pupils within legal constraints set by the school district or higher levels of government (Cawelti, 1989; United States General Accounting Office, 1994). The school district continues to set general priorities within which all schools must function, develop overarching educational objectives and the basic curriculum for meeting those objectives, allocate lump sums of money to schools based on student needs, negotiate labor contracts, and provide facilities and other support services such as transportation, payroll, and accounting.

In actuality, there is little evidence that SBDM leads directly to improved pupil achievement (Conway, 1984; Malen, Ogawa, & Kranz, 1990; Smylie, 1994; Wohlstetter, Smyer, & Mohrman, 1994). Therefore, we must view SBDM as an element of systemic reform if we are to make a connection with improved pupil achievement. Other elements need to involve higher performance expectations, more directed pedagogical demands, and clear accountability systems (Hannaway & Carnoy, 1993). They may include such reforms as national and state curricula, performance standards, and assessment; national teacher certification; and family choice of schools.

It has been suggested that SBDM and other decentralizing initiatives are implemented largely for political rather than educational reasons (Elmore, 1993; Malen, 1994; Malen, Ogawa, & Kranz, 1990; Weiler, 1993). Although not linked directly to improvement in student outcomes, SBDM is credited with being an efficacious means of addressing conflicts over the distribution of scarce resources and enhancing the legitimacy of institutions authorized to make those decisions.

> The bottom line is that school based management is not an end in itself, although research indicates that it can help foster an improved school culture and higher quality decisions. School based management is, however, a potentially valuable tool for engaging the talents and enthusiasm of far more of a school's stake-holders than traditional, top-down governance systems. Moreover, once in place, school based management holds the promise of enabling schools to better address students' needs. (Wohlstetter & Mohrman, 1994, p. 1)

ARGUMENTS FOR ADMINISTRATIVE DECENTRALIZATION

Sizer (1985) claimed that hierarchical bureaucracy is paralyzing American education. "The structure is getting in the way of children's learning" (p. 206). Sizer's first imperative for better schools was to give room to teachers and students to work and learn in their own, appropriate ways. He saw decentralized authority as allowing teachers and principals to adapt their schools to the needs, learning styles, and learning rates of students individually. Sizer did not deny the need to upgrade the overall quality of the educating profession. But he believed that, if empowered, there were enough fine teachers and administrators to lead a renaissance of American schools.

Goodlad (1984) identified the school as the unit for improvement. Goodlad considered the most promising approach to educational reform to be the one "that will seek to cultivate the capacity of schools to deal with their own problems, to become largely self-renewing" (p. 31). He did not see the schools as being "cut loose" but rather as being linked to the hub (district office) and to each other in a network. State officials should be responsible for developing "a common framework for schools within which there is room for some

differences in interpretation at the district level and for some variations in schools resulting from differences in size, location, and perspective" (p. 275). According to Goodlad, the district should concern itself with the balance in curricula presented, the processes employed in planning, and the equitable distribution of funds. "What I am proposing is genuine decentralization of authority and responsibility to the local school within a framework designed to assure school-to-school equity and a measure of accountability" (p. 275).

Boyer (1983) also saw heavy doses of bureaucracy as "stifling creativity in too many schools, and preventing principals and their staffs from exercising their best professional judgement on decisions that properly should be made at the local level" (p. 227). For Boyer, "Rebuilding excellence in education means reaffirming the importance of the local school and freeing leadership to lead" (p. 316). Among his recommendations for accomplishing this were that:

> Principals and staff at the local school should have more control over their own budgets, operating within the guidelines set by the district office. Further, every principal should have a School Improvement Fund, discretionary money to provide time and materials for program development and for special seminars and staff retreats. Principals should also have more control over the selection and rewarding of teachers. Acting in consultation with their staffs, they should be given responsibility for the final choice of teachers for their schools. (p. 316)

Cuban (1988) argued that the bureaucratic organization of schooling is responsible for the lack of professional leadership. Autonomy is the necessary condition for leadership to arise.

> Without choice, there is no autonomy. Without autonomy, there is no leadership. . . . Schools as they are presently organized press teachers, principals, and superintendents toward managing rather than leading, toward

maintaining what is rather than moving to what can be. The structures of schooling and the incentives buried within them produce a managerial imperative. (pp. xx–xxi)

Cuban also recognized the need for federal, state, and district regulations and their accompanying forms of accountability. He called for balanced procedures that permit sufficient discretion to those delivering a service while allowing prudent monitoring by higher levels of authority. Such procedures would focus "less on control through regulation and more on vesting individual schools and educators with the independence to alter basic organizational arrangements (if necessary) to reach explicit goals and standards" (p. 248).

One of the first proposals for SBDM was made by New York State's Fleischmann Commission (1973), along with a companion proposal for full state funding. Referring to studies by the Committee for Economic Development (1970) and the Urban Institute (1972), the commission concluded that:

centralization and decentralization are not inconsistent concepts and that it is quite possible to have financing at one level and policy making and other kinds of control at another, with the implication that state financing is not inconsistent with decentralized operating units.

The Commission strongly urges greater powers of decision making in the *local school*. . . . The effective point for expression of citizen and parent-citizen interest in education is the school, not the school district, for the school is the basic operating unit and cost center in the provision of educational services. (pp. 86–87)

In order to facilitate citizen involvement in the educational process, the commission called for a Parent Advisory Council (PAC) for every public school in the state. The PACs would participate in the selection of principals and would provide criteria for the employment of teaching staffs. The principal would be responsible for the final selection of staff, however (Fleischmann, 1972). These com-

mission recommendations were never implemented in New York State. They are remarkably similar, however, to reforms made in Chicago, Kentucky, England, Australia, New Zealand, and elsewhere.

A decade later, the National Governors' Association (1986) renewed the call of the Fleischmann Commission for SBDM. Their Task Force on Leadership and Management recommended that states provide districts with incentives and technical assistance to promote school site management and improvement. They proposed the identification and removal of legal and organizational barriers and the encouragement of local experimentation in school-based budgeting, school-based hiring of teachers, and provision of discretionary resources at the school level. Lamar Alexander, governor of Tennessee and chairman of the association at the time the report was issued, commented that if schools and school districts were held accountable for results, "Then, we're ready to give up a lot of state regulatory control" (National Governors' Association, 1986, p. 4).

Is it possible that SBDM in public schools can reduce the complexity of pressures from external authorities on the schools? Or might SBDM create even greater conflict among principals, teachers, and community representatives—conflicts that they can ignore or push off to the school district for resolution under current arrangements? In the next section we look for clues to the answers for these questions by reviewing the results of some SBDM experiences.

EXPERIENCES WITH SCHOOL-BASED DECISION MAKING

Edmonton

Edmonton, Alberta, Canada, has been functioning under a SBDM configuration since 1976. It is an urban district serving 80,000 students in 205 schools. Decisions related to the allocation of resources have been decentralized to schools for teaching and nonteaching staff, maintenance, utilities, equipment, and supplies. But the point of accountability has been clearly placed with the principal. Funds are allocated to schools on the basis of a per child amount. This is weighted according to student characteristics such as poverty, disability, or gifted-and-talented status (United States General Accounting Office, 1994). School administrators and teachers develop their budgets on the basis of priorities established in an annual school plan. They submit the budget to the superintendent and school board for approval. Schools contract for consultant and other services as needed from district providers or outside vendors. The district also operates a professional development program that derives its funds by charging school-based budgets.

Brown (1990) reported a survey of Edmonton principals and teachers that revealed that principals saw flexibility, efficiency, and staff involvement in decision making as strongly positive attributes of SBDM. Resource allocation was a problem for some. But they viewed time demands and stress accompanying decentralization as its major disadvantages. Teacher involvement appeared to be primarily consultative. Seventy-nine percent of the principals would recommend that other districts consider SBDM.

Teachers in Edmonton identified flexibility and staff involvement in decision making as being the major advantages of SBDM. As with the principals, teachers saw the primary weakness of SBDM as the time demand. This was followed by problems with the allocation of resources, heightened stress, and the increased authority of the principal.

The Edmonton school district has instituted formal procedures for monitoring SBDM. In addition to standardized tests administered on a regular basis, the district surveys parents, students, and staff to measure their level of satisfaction with matters affecting them. The school reports results with district averages indicated. Satisfaction among the three groups has steadily improved under SBDM. The growth in satisfaction has been particularly strong among parents and students at the secondary level (Brown, 1990).

The Edmonton program was implemented gradually. It began as a pilot project involving seven volunteer schools that represented the variety in the district. Community support for the concept grew. In 1979 the Board of Education voted to implement the idea districtwide.

Dade County

Dade County, Florida, which includes the City of Miami, began implementing its school governance experiment, School Based Management/Shared Decision Making (SBM/SDM) during the 1987–1988 school year. Dade County has approximately 300,000 students and 300 schools.

SBM/SDM was conceived and initiated as part of a cooperative initiative that involved the superintendent, the school board, and the teachers' union, to promote teacher professionalism. It began as a pilot program in thirty-three schools and has been expanded on a voluntary basis to include most schools in the district. To participate in the program, a school or group of schools must submit a proposal to the district office carrying the approval of the principal, union steward, and two-thirds of the faculty. Technical assistance in developing proposals is available from the district office. Proposal assessment criteria include educational impact/accountability; collegial process; shared decision-making model; targeted changes; feasibility for implementation; rationale; community involvement; school climate; and replication.

Schools selected for participation are granted significantly increased flexibility in both budgeting and staffing. Many decisions that were traditionally made at the district and intermediate levels on how to allocate funds, as well as how to organize instructional plans, are placed with SBM/SDM schools. Parents and other community representatives may participate in the school's decision-making process as advisors and as supportive and helpful partners. SBM/SDM schools report directly to the central office, bypassing midlevel management. School board rules, teacher labor contract provisions, and State Department of Education regulations may be waived. Upon request, the school board has suspended requirements regarding maximum class size, length of school day, number of minutes per subject, and distribution of report cards. The union has allowed teachers to give up planning periods, work longer hours for no additional pay, and engage in peer evaluation programs (Mojkowski & Fleming, 1988).

Under district guidelines, the participating schools receive the same level of funds as non–SBM/SDM schools. The district develops the initial budgets for all schools. Administrators of SBM/SDM schools decide whether or not to change the allocation of funds recommended by the district. The district allocates funds to SBM/SDM schools on the basis of a per staff amount. Allocations for personnel are based on the number of teachers and other staff a school is entitled to have as determined by student size and characteristics. This number is multiplied by the sum of the average district salary for the appropriate personnel category and the corresponding cost of benefits. By allocating funds for benefits to schools, the district encourages schools to hire part-time teachers, paid by the hour, because they receive less costly benefits (United States General Accounting Office, 1994). The district can then use these savings for other purposes. Schools can also convert allocated professional and staff positions into equivalent dollar amounts to be used for other purposes. Equivalent dollars for the special services that once were available only through area or district offices are distributed to participating schools. The schools may use such funds to purchase these services from the district or private vendors as determined by the school or converted to staff positions.

Alternative arrangements proposed by schools vary considerably. Some schools have opened on Saturdays. Others have added programs before and after school. Several have modified staffing patterns by hiring aides in place of assistant principals, employing teachers by the hour, and creating new positions (Mojkowski & Fleming, 1988).

Evaluations of the initiative have been generally positive. Collins (1988) reported the results of a survey of staff of SBM/SDM schools in which

teachers indicated a shift in their attitudes in favor of a collegial approach to school operation. Principals believed that SBM/SDM had a favorable impact on the school environment. They saw SBM/SDM as facilitating the generation of instructional ideas and the design of specific interventions. They also saw it as a vehicle for feedback. Principals acknowledged that SBM/SDM was more time-consuming than management methods they had previously used. They acknowledged that it made their jobs more complex. Teachers in general said they had been increasingly involved in decision-making activities usually considered management prerogatives. But teachers serving on school planning teams that were interviewed by staff of the United States General Accounting Office (1994) reported that they were seldom involved in determining budget allocations and lacked knowledge about their school's budget authority.

Timar (1989) linked the Dade County experience with state actions dating back to 1971. At that time Governor Ruben Askew appointed the Citizens' Committee on Education. Among other things, the committee recommended that decision making be placed at the level of instruction. Enabling legislation was subsequently adopted that made the Dade County initiative possible. Within the district, the school board, administration, and teachers' union have cooperated fully in the development and implementation of SBM/SDM. According to Timar, "Restructuring was not something that one side wanted and the other resisted; hence it could not be held hostage and used as a bargaining chip" (p. 272). Timar sees in the Dade County experience cause for optimism that genuine restructuring is possible.

Chicago

One of the most ambitious attempts at school-based governance is in Chicago. The Chicago school system was alleged to contain the worst schools in the country. The Illinois legislature adopted the plan in December 1988 in a desperate attempt to reform the system by realigning its incentives and power structure (Hess, 1990). The plan was phased in over a five-year period. The act identified ten goals. But the primary goals were to raise student achievement, attendance rates, and graduation rates to national norms for all schools.

The Chicago reform, perhaps more than any other in the United States, is based mainly on the theory that schools can be improved by strengthening democratic control at the school-community level (Hess, 1993). The keys for achieving the goals of the act are Local School Councils (LSCs) composed of six parents, two community representatives, two teachers, and the principal. For high schools, councils also include one nonvoting student. Except for teacher representatives and the principal, employees of the system may not serve as members of LSCs. District employees are also barred from voting in elections of parent and community representatives. This configuration was designed to give parents a major voice in the education decisions affecting their children and to avoid the problems encountered in New York City. In New York, employees have been able to dominate elections to the thirty-two Community Boards of Education that govern elementary and middle schools (Hess, 1990).

Each council has the responsibility for adopting a School Improvement Plan, developing a budget for spending its discretionary funds, and selecting and evaluating the school's principal. In recognition of the authority of these new semiautonomous LSCs, the powers of the city board of education were redefined from *management of* to *jurisdiction over* the public education and the public school system of the city (Hess, 1990).

Unlike most other school-based plans, the Chicago plan places greater responsibility with parents and community representatives than with teachers. The importance of staff participation in decision making was recognized in the legislation, however. The plan establishes a Professional Personnel Advisory Committee (PPAC) in each school for the purpose of advising the principal and the LSC on the educational program. The PPAC is composed of teachers and other professional personnel in the school.

Although never stated explicitly, the Chicago School Reform Act is built on the assumption that the principal is the chief instruction leader in each school (Hess, 1990). Principals are given the right to select teachers, aides, counselors, clerks, hall guards, and any other instructional program staff for vacant or newly created positions. Principals are responsible for initiating a needs assessment and a School Improvement Plan in consultation with the LSC and the PPAC. They are also responsible for drafting a budget for amendment or adoption by the LSC. Principals hold no tenure rights in the position other than those they hold as teachers.

In addition to restructuring the governance of Chicago schools, the legislation was intended to correct improprieties in the allocation of resources among schools and district administration. Before reform, the Chicago Panel (1988) revealed that one-third of targeted funds (state and federal categorical aids) were being misappropriated into supporting central office bureaucratic positions. Further, compensatory funds were being used to provide basic services in schools with high percentages of children from low-income families. Thus, schools serving children from middle-income families had greater access to financial support for basic programs. Implementation of the reforms has corrected these inequities. As a result, during the 1993–1994 school year, the average elementary school had $491,000 in discretionary funds. The average high school had $849,000 (Rosenkranz, 1994). Unlike the authority distribution in Edmonton and Dade County, LSCs in Chicago do not have discretion over personnel allocations, except for personnel that may be employed with discretionary funds.

By year 4 of the reforms, 1,755 district- and subdistrict-level administrative positions had been eliminated and 4,594 new positions had been created in schools. When the reform began, 88.5 percent of the system's staff were budgeted to schools. The percentage grew to 93.1 percent by 1992–1993 (Rosenkranz, 1994). Initially, schools used their discretionary funds to take care of support needs by adding more clerks and aides than teachers. By year 4, schools began focusing their discretionary resources on direct student services through the addition of teaching positions.

The overall district fiscal situation, however, is quite troubled for support of basic programs. Following the reform legislation, the city's school board entered into contracts with employee unions that included wage increases that the board could not fund. By 1995, the board had accumulated a $150,000,000 deficit. Responding to the district's ongoing financial crises, the Illinois legislature passed a law in 1995 that dissolved the fifteen-member Chicago Board of Education and subdistrict councils. The district is now governed by a five-member board appointed by the mayor. The board is charged with establishing "system-wide curriculum objectives and standards which reflect the multi-cultural diversity of the city." The mayor was also granted authority to name the district's superintendent of schools. A new position was authorized to improve the financial efficiency of the district and to oversee privatization of district services.

Nothing in the 1995 law limited the authority of school councils. Principals were granted much-desired authority over custodial and food service workers and setting work schedules (Harp, 1995b). The law limited the items that may be negotiated with employee unions. It also placed a moratorium on strikes for eighteen months. Managerial employees were barred from union membership.

Bryk, Deabster, Easton, Luppescu, and Thum (1994) concluded that the systemwide trends in student achievement through the third year of reform had shown no significant gains. They did not think that this was a fair evaluation of the potential of the reform, however, because it was being implemented gradually. Hess (1994) also thought that it was too early to measure the full effects on student achievement.

Hess (1994) observed that the Chicago experiment is not a perfect testing of the SBDM strategy of school reform. This is because the devolution of authority to the schools was tentative and was characterized by resistance during much of the initial implementation effort. In addition, the school system was floundering through a persistent fiscal crisis. The experiment was based on the effective schools literature. Hess concluded that the experiment was plowing the ground of more plebeian incremental change and restructuring. But given the context of the reform effort, it has produced unprecedented change in Chicago schools.

A survey sponsored by the Consortium on Chicago School Research (Easton, Bryk, Driscoll, Kotsakis, Sebring, & Van der Ploeg, 1991) found the overall reaction of teachers to the impact of reform on them and their schools was moderately positive. Teachers in sixty-two schools said the reform was working very well. However, more than half of the district's teachers responding to the survey said that reform had not affected their classroom practices.

Reform brought a substantial change in the characteristics of principals. About half were new to the job, although they were not new employees of the district. Ninety-four percent of the newly appointed principals had had no previous experience as principal. Over half were African American. Nearly 60 percent were women. The average age dropped from fifty-two before reform to forty-six after reform. New principals were most often found in racially isolated schools. They were likely to be matched racially or ethnically with the majority of their school's population.

In 1992, the Consortium on Chicago School Research surveyed elementary and secondary school principals (Bennett, Bryk, Easton, Kerbow, Luppescu, & Sebring, 1992). That survey found that principals generally thought that SBDM had given them increased flexibility and discretion to deal with school issues. Over three-quarters believed that their schools were getting better. Two-thirds were even more optimistic about the future. There was genuine concern, however, over the lack of time to complete all of the tasks associated with school reform. Principals reported working almost sixty hours per week. Yet their most critical worry was that their ability to provide curricular leadership was threatened by managerial demands. A substantial majority of principals thought that their LSCs were making important contributions to academic improvements and that they were effective policy-making bodies.

Kentucky

In 1990, the state of Kentucky enacted sweeping legislation transforming its entire educational governance structure. This action was precipitated by a decision of the Kentucky Supreme Court ruling that the total school governance and finance systems of the state were in violation of the state's constitutional requirement of an "efficient system of common schools" (see Chapter 11). The Kentucky reforms are considered by some to be a blueprint for change nationally (Danzberger, Kirst, & Usdan, 1992). The reforms involve both centralizing and decentralizing features.

Student achievement is the centerpiece of the new system in Kentucky. It focuses on outcomes, not inputs. It expects that every child will learn and that the education system will become driven by performance and oriented by results. A state Council on School Performance Standards was established to set learning goals and definitions of what students were expected to learn.

Each school is governed by a school council made up of three teachers, two parents, and the principal. Councils are empowered to adopt curriculum, select instructional materials, set policies for discipline and classroom management, oversee extracurricular activities, and assign students and staff. A council can select staff, including the principal, from a list of candidates recommended by its district's superintendent of schools.

The Kentucky Instructional Results Information System (KIRIS) has been established to provide evidence on the attainment of the six broad learning goals set forth in the reform act. There are three components to the accountability strand of assessment: performance measurements (heavily weighted in terms of cognitive achievement), portfolio tasks, and transitional items and tasks.

Schools that show significant improvements in KIRIS results receive financial awards to be distributed as determined by a majority of teachers in each school receiving the award. Schools that fail to improve or decline are subject to sanctions.

Accountability assessments are made over two-year cycles based on evaluations at grades four, eight, and twelve. Baseline data were obtained in 1992. The Kentucky State Board for Elementary and Secondary Education established a threshold for each school. The threshold achievement levels are expected to be met by the end of the following biennium. If a school drops more than 5 percent below its baseline during the biennium, it becomes a *school in crisis*. As such, it is required to develop a school improvement plan in consultation with a Kentucky Distinguished Educator (KDE) assigned to work with the school. The KDE must also evaluate the school staff within six months and determine the future employment status of all certified staff in the school. Parents of children in an affected school must be notified of its status and granted the right to transfer their children to other schools (Kifer, 1994; Trimble, 1994). The state makes supplementary school improvement funds available.

The instructional staffs of schools that exceed their threshold amounts by 1 percent or more qualify for financial bonuses provided by the state. The first of these awards was distributed to staff of 480 schools in 1995. Awards ranged from $1,300 to $2,600 per teacher (Harp, 1995a). Awards can be shared with noncertified staff or used for other purposes at the discretion of the teachers. A school that reaches its threshold is considered successful. But it does not qualify for a financial award. Schools between those that meet their threshold and those in crisis face varying degrees of sanctions. The program is under continual revision.

Two years into a five-year study of SBDM in Kentucky, David (1994) found that it has been a major force in communicating the importance and seriousness of the reform effort and in forging a critical link between schools and their communities. Teachers especially welcomed the opportunity to select their principals. Parents appreciate having an official voice in making school policy.

Typically, school districts have not granted to school councils discretion over the staffing portions of school budgets in the initial stages of reform implementation. This is expected to change, however. Councils are permitted to carry over unspent funds to subsequent years. The biggest problem with the allocation process is that districts have inadequate accounting systems to track all expenditures to the school level and to permit schools on-line access to the status of their accounts (David, 1994).

England

Probably no country has had more experience in school-based decision making than England. In Chapter 2, we described the nature of the English reforms in general. The reader may wish to refer back to that description for context. We now focus specifically on English reforms related to SBDM— or, as the English call it, local management of schools (LMS).

Before the 1980s, approximately 95 percent of English children were educated in a national system of state schools that were administered by local education authorities (LEAs). These authorities were part of the local governance structure similar to that of fiscally dependent school districts in the United States. The LEAs exercised considerable political and bureaucratic control over schools within their jurisdictions. They provided them with significant professional and ancillary support. There was (and continues to be) much greater equity in the distribution of human and fiscal resources among schools in the English system than is characteristic of the American system.

Since coming to power in 1979, the Conservative government has enacted reforms of a privatizing nature. These include the following with reference to local management of schools.

Reformed Governing Bodies.   Before the reforms of the Conservative Party, all schools had govern-

ing bodies with limited powers and with the majority of the membership of each body appointed by the LEA. The 1986 Education Act removed majority control by LEA-designated membership and increased the representation of parents and local business interests.

Local Management of Schools (LMS).   The Education Act of 1988 gave to school governing bodies control over their own budgets and day-to-day management of operations. Schools remaining under LEA jurisdiction receive funds according to a formula that insures that 80 percent of a school's budget is determined directly by the number and ages of its pupils. That is, the money follows the child. The amount allocated to schools includes teachers' salaries and teachers are de facto employees of a school's governing body. Previously, LEAs set the budgets for each school. They could positively discriminate to counter pupil disadvantage or for any other reason. Between 80 and 85 percent of the funding for schools is provided to the general local governing agency by the national government and the balance by the local agency.

City Technology Colleges (CTC).   City Technology Colleges are secondary inner-city schools chartered by the national government beginning in 1986. They are run by independent trusts with business sponsors that provide some capital funding. The national government provides recurrent funding and net capital costs directly to the schools' boards of trustees. Their curricula emphasize science and technology. CTCs are totally outside the control of any LEA.

Grant Maintained Schools (GMS).   The 1988 Education Reform Act established a procedure whereby state schools (grant maintained schools [GMS]) could opt out of their LEAs and run themselves with direct funding from the national government. Parameters governing a school are set forth in a charter negotiated by school authorities and the national government.

Under these reforms, parents have gained in representation on school-governing bodies and have freedom of choice of schools that are not oversubscribed. In the case of oversubscribed schools, each school determines criteria for selection with the approval of the LEA or the Department for Education. Schools have gained control over their own budgets. They are able to decide matters previously decided by LEAs, such as staff deployment, personnel selection, and employee remuneration within national guidelines. Schools are also permitted to contract for services directly, including building maintenance, accounting, purchasing, payroll, insurance, and auditing.

There is no doubt that LMS is the most popular of the English reforms. The support is so broad that LMS is likely to withstand any change in government. Even persons who were highly critical of Tory policy generally have become supporters of LMS. A survey conducted by Fitz and Halpin (1994) found no head teacher in a GMS or LMS school who wished to return to the former system of LEA control.

A study by Mortimore and Mortimore (1992) found that LMS had greatly spurred innovation, providing increased opportunities for rethinking existing staffing practices. They concluded that giving budgetary authority to school heads had in most instances enhanced their powers.

A study sponsored by the National Association of Head Teachers was broadly positive. It conceded, however, that direct evidence of the influence of self-management on learning was elusive (Bullock & Thomas, 1994). The initial survey revealed that school heads thought that LMS allowed them to make more effective use of a school's resources. But they also thought that they spent more of their own time on administrative matters. This diverted their attention from matters related to student learning (Arnott, Bullock, & Thomas, 1992).

It should be noted that the relatively few classroom teachers who were interviewed in the Bullock and Thomas study were more cautious in their assessment of its benefits for pupil learning and overall standards. A study by Marren and Levacic (1994) also found teachers were less positive in their assessment of self-management than were school governors or head teachers.

In England collective (societal) rights and responsibilities are competing with private rights and responsibilities. LMS and other reforms were initially proposed and implemented by the political right. The political left has heavily criticized the reforms because there is evidence that they are re-creating a selective school system that is highly inequitable to the lower socioeconomic classes and immigrant groups. The political right argues that the reforms encourage the growth of different types of schools, responsive to needs of particular communities and interest groups. The right's arguments appeal to those subscribing to concepts of multiple identities and radical pluralism. Whitty (1994) did a study of educational reforms in the United Kingdom, Australia, New Zealand, and the United States. He recommended seeking a balance between these views by creating new forms of association to counterbalance the prerogative of the state and to act as a generator of new ideas. "[P]art of the challenge must be to move away from atomized decision making to the reassertion of collective responsibility without recreating the very bureaucratic systems whose shortcomings have helped to legitimate the current tendency to treat education as a private good rather than a public responsibility" (p. 18).

Multidistrict Analyses of SBDM

Of the situations studied by Timar (1989), only Dade County had state, district, and union authorities working in concert. In contrast to Dade County, he studied schools in suburban Seattle, Washington, and Jefferson County, Kentucky (prior to reform) where SBDM had not been so successful. For successful implementation, Timar underscored the importance of a policy climate that fosters an integrated and organizationally coherent response to restructuring—one that redefines the roles and responsibilities of just about every party connected with schools: teachers, administrators, professional organizations, policy makers, parents, students, and colleges and universities. He concluded that an integrated response to restructuring at the school level is not likely to occur in politically Balkanized and programmatically fragmented districts and states.

Wohlstetter, Smyer, and Mohrman (1994) stressed the importance of expanding the boundaries of SBDM beyond the involvement of school-level people in organizational decision making. It should also include increased professional development, access to information required for making wise decisions, and a reward system that motivates and reinforces efforts to produce high performance. They confirmed the importance of the first three factors (power, development of knowledge and skills, and access to information) in their comparisons of actively restructuring and struggling schools. Neither group of schools did much with respect to providing tangible rewards for successful performance. The authors questioned whether change activities can be sustained over the long term in the absence of an incentive structure that recognizes the additional demands placed on participants.

Wohlstetter et al. (1994) also found that teachers in most restructuring schools were not as interested in being involved in managing the schools' daily operations as in decisions related to the schools' performance and in finding new approaches to improving performance. Their findings also confirmed the importance of combining SBDM reforms with ambitious curriculum and instruction reforms (see also Hannaway, 1993; Smylie, 1994).

Brown (1990) analyzed the implementation of SBDM in five districts, including Edmonton, Alberta, and Cleveland, Ohio. The other districts were Langley (a suburb of Vancouver, British Columbia) and two rural districts in British Columbia. He interviewed district personnel in SBDM districts and five selected centralized districts and examined district documents. We will use his extensive findings and conclusions as a summary of this section.

Brown (1990) identified two main processes as part of the structure of SBDM: the mechanism by which resources are allocated to schools and the budgeting process within the school. Schools received the bulk of their allocations by multiplying their enrollments by a district-established amount such that, "The money follows the child." Adjustments were made for special programs and for school attributes. Districts provided schools with systemwide goals and objectives. Schools responded with their own curricular plans and budgets for implementation that are mostly absorbed by personnel costs. Typically schools purchased teachers from the district at a uniform rate (rather than on an actual cost basis). Teachers not located in a particular school were placed within the district pool for selection.

Brown's (1990) analysis found that the SBDM school boards became more concerned with policy matters than with the administration of schools. Under SBDM, the district hierarchy was sharpened. Each person had only one supervisor. Nonline central office staff assumed a strictly advisory, on-call relationship with school-level personnel. "Most importantly, authority and responsibility are largely brought together, particularly for the school principal, but also for others in the administrative structure" (Brown, 1990, p. 2).

Still, Brown found that many things remained the same as before SBDM. He detected little change in the accountability model employed under SBDM. Ultimate authority still came from the electorate and was directed through school boards and administrators. Thus the school board was still responsible for establishing the general direction for the district through the setting of goals. The district remained the reservoir of funds, whether they came from local sources such as the property tax or from the state or federal governments. Collective bargaining remained a district prerogative. The district continued to provide financial and other support services. The district retained responsibility for monitoring and evaluating school performance.

Under SBDM, specific budgetary and personnel decisions were made at the school level. But the school board set the general parameters by which the school's lump-sum allocation was determined. The school board had to answer such questions as

What should the size of the pupil allocation be? Should it vary according to type of program, for example, elementary, secondary, vocational? Should the allocation vary according to the characteristics of the children served, for example, socioeconomic status, learning-disabled, gifted? Should the allocation vary according to characteristics of the school, for example, size and complexity of services offered? In many respects, decisions made by school boards under SBDM were similar to those made by the state government in apportioning funds to school districts.

By the same token, many of the decisions made at the school level under SBDM were similar to those made by school boards operating under a centralized model. School-level authority approached that of a single-building rural district. The primary differences were that the SBDM schools did not control the size of their budgets (they had no authority to levy taxes or to charge tuition) and they could not set wage scales. The role of principal took on aspects of that of a superintendent of a small district (David, 1989; Jacobson, 1988). While SBDM introduced substantial procedural changes at the district level, the changes were revolutionary at the school level.

Brown (1990) found that under SBDM, schools were better able to adapt resources and procedures to student needs as school personnel perceived them. He reported that SBDM may be a viable avenue for school improvement because of the flexibility it accords schools. But it did not appear to be a key stimulus for innovation. In the five SBDM districts, Brown observed tradeoffs between personnel and material. Examples of personnel-related decisions included more dollars for professional development, teacher choice of school, swaps of personnel, and increases in personnel allocations for specific learning tasks.

Principals strongly favored SBDM in the five districts studied. They believed that it enhanced their ability to be educational leaders. Teachers were less positive in their endorsement. Teachers and principals agreed that the primary strength of SBDM was greater flexibility at the school level. They agreed that the greatest weakness was the additional time that it required. Brown found that most school staff were consulted during the budgeting process. But they did not control the planning process or school decision making. Some teachers and support staff wanted to be involved in the process, while others did not. Parents were only tangentially involved, if at all.

Brown found through surveys that SBDM was not intended as a vehicle to cut costs in the districts studied. Staff commonly offered illustrations, however, to show that funds were being used more effectively under SBDM than they were before it. For example, they thought the practice of permitting schools to accumulate surpluses led to more efficient use of funds than spending just to meet financial deadlines. Hoarding of supplies had been common under centralized management. But this was no longer necessary under SBDM. There was also some evidence that central office staffs were slightly smaller in SBDM districts. Interviewees generally believed that school staffs were more aware of costs and tried to reduce unnecessary ones. They thought the allocation rule allowing the dollar to follow the child provided a more equitable distribution of resources among children than previous centralized procedures.

The experiences of SBDM districts clearly showed that SBDM is no trivial change from traditional centralized decision making. It involves new relationships between the district and the school and among people within the school itself. Brown found that district interest in SBDM was usually stimulated by one person. After the adoption decision, leadership from other sources became very important. The reported experience of other districts with SBDM appeared to be a primary consideration in making the adoption decision. Extensive preparations were required for successful implementation of SBDM, including several years of pilot experiments. Despite the difficulties entailed in implementing SBDM, Brown observed little tendency to recentralize once SBDM was fully implemented. In a national survey, however, Ornstein (1989) found a trend among large districts to recentralize after an initial experience with decentralization.

CHARTER SCHOOLS

Another approach to school-based decision making is charter schools. Laws governing charter schools permit teachers, parents, private companies, or combinations of these to apply to a public governing body for a charter permitting them to operate a school or schools with public financial support. The charter specifies the terms under which the schools may operate and the student outcomes they are expected to achieve. Charter schools are legal entities. The state, district, or other governmental agency issuing a charter becomes a purchaser of educational services from these entities. It assumes responsibility for assessing results, appraising costs and educational benefits, and choosing among competitors for charters.

Charter schools may be exempted from local and state policies, hire their own staff, determine their own curriculum, receive funding directly from the state, and control their own budgets. Charter schools are supposed to encourage innovative teaching, promote performance-based accountability, expand choices in types of available public schools, create new professional opportunities for teachers, improve student learning, and promote community involvement (United States General Accounting Office, 1995). Charter holders must account for public funds they receive, and they are accountable for meeting the educational performance standards set forth in their charters.

Twenty states had enacted legislation authorizing charter schools between 1991 and 1995. The Michigan law was declared unconstitutional in November of 1994 by a lower court on the basis of a very narrow definition of *public school* in the Michigan constitution. One of the plaintiffs in the case was the state's largest teachers' union. Elsewhere, as of January 1995, fourteen additional states were considering charter school legislation and 134 charter schools had been approved. Eighty-five of these approvals were new schools and forty-nine were conversions of existing schools. The Improving America's Schools Act passed by Congress in 1994, reauthorizing and amending the Elementary and Secondary Educa-

tion Act of 1965, included a new federal grant program to support the design and implementation of charter schools (United States General Accounting Office, 1995; also see the related discussion in Chapter 10).

Specific legislation varies considerably from state to state. Most charters are issued by a school district or the state board of education. But some states allow other institutions, such as public universities, community colleges, and intermediate school districts, to issue charters. In some states, charter schools are legally independent of the school districts in which they are located. In other states, they must be part of a local school district that is responsible for its operations. The degree to which charter schools are constrained by regulations affecting other public schools differs among states. Funding is provided directly by the state in some cases. In others it is subject to negotiation with the school districts that approve the charters.

SCHOOL-BASED DECISION MAKING AND PRIVATIZATION

Some have argued that SBDM can introduce into public schools some of the incentives for productivity and client satisfaction that are believed to be more prevalent in private than public schools. But it still protects the public interest through limited regulation and control. The debate over the relative effectiveness of public and private schools stimulated by the Coleman, Hoffer, and Kilgore (1981) study was introduced in Chapter 13. Chubb and Moe (1985, 1989, 1990) applied a different analysis to the data used by Coleman et al. but arrived at similar conclusions.

Like the Coleman et al. study that preceded it, the Chubb and Moe study generated a lot of controversy and criticism. Lee and Bryk (1993) and Sukstorf, Wells, and Crain (1993) challenged on technical grounds the Chubb and Moe conclusion about the generally superior effectiveness of private schools compared with public schools. The critics found the most serious fault to be the way in which Chubb and Moe measured student achievement and the way they structured their sample. Chubb and Moe (1993) defended their methodology and pointed out that the weakness of theories in the social sciences with respect to their ability to explain cause-and-effect relationships leads to disagreement about what the critical factors are, how they should be measured, what data should be collected, and what adequate tests look like. As a result, legitimate controversies arise, as in this case and those described in Chapter 13 with respect to the Coleman study and to education production-function analysis generally. In any event, the controversy over the Chubb and Moe study relates to the relative effectiveness of public and private schools and not to the differences between them in characteristics as we will discuss.

Chubb and Moe (1985, 1989, 1990) supplemented the High School and Beyond (HSB) database used by Coleman et al. (1981) with a new survey aimed at organizational and environmental factors. They administered the survey to the principal and thirty teachers, among others, in nearly five hundred of the HSB schools, including more than one hundred private schools. Their findings are instructive with respect to operational differences between bureaucratically organized public schools and private schools where decisions are for the most part made at the school level.

Chubb and Moe (1985) described the very different environments in which public and private schools exist. The former is characterized by politics, hierarchy, and authority, and the latter by markets, competition, and volunteerism. They hypothesized, however, that the differences these environments make for school organization may not be due entirely, or even primarily, to qualities that are inherently public or private. Rather, they suggest that organizational differences may derive from environmental characteristics such as control, constraint, and complexity that differentiate among school environments regardless of sector. Thus, like Coleman and Hoffer (1987), Chubb and Moe concluded that through organizational redesign, the strengths characteristic of schools in one sector may be incorporated into schools in the other.

As expected, Chubb and Moe found that outside authority exerts much stronger influence on public schools than on private schools. Because of strong external influences, public school personnel have less freedom to choose how to respond to their more difficult environments since they are more constrained by formal rules and regulations and informal norms than are private school personnel. Unexpectedly, however, the external influence on Catholic schools was even less than that experienced by other private schools. This is true although unlike other private schools, Catholic schools are part of a rather substantial hierarchy. This last finding supported their conclusion that bureaucracy need not necessarily be the stultifying force it often becomes.

Among their other findings: Teachers in private schools rated their principals as better all-around leaders than did teachers in public schools. Private school teachers also rated their principals as being more helpful than their counterparts in the public sector. Further, private school teachers rated the goals of their schools as clearer and more clearly communicated by the principal than did public school teachers. Teachers in private schools were also more likely to rate their principals as encouraging, supportive, and reinforcing. "Private school principals are likely to be in a position to lead their organizations. They may not succeed, but they should have the tools and the flexibility to do what leaders need to do. Public school principals, on the other hand, are systematically denied much of what it takes to lead" (Chubb and Moe, 1990, p. 56).

Chubb and Moe found that public school principals are likely to take on the roles of manager and representative. This is consistent with what Cuban (1988) found; the external pressures on the public school principal demand it. Private school principals appear to have greater freedom to pursue the role of leader and to direct their schools according to their best professional judgments.

Chubb and Moe found that private schools delegate significantly more discretion to their teachers and are more likely to involve them in school-level policy decisions than are public schools. Private schools also seemed to do a better job of relieving teachers of routine and paperwork. There was a higher level of collegiality among private school staff. Teachers were more likely to know what their colleagues were teaching and to coordinate the content of their courses. Private school teachers spent more time meeting to discuss curriculum and students and observing each other's classes. Private school teachers believed that they had more influence over school policies governing student behavior, pupil assignment to classes, curriculum, and in-service programs. Within their classrooms, private school teachers believed that they had more control than did public school teachers over text selection, course content, teaching techniques, and student discipline. Private school teachers even thought that they had more influence over hiring and firing practices than did public school teachers.

Of all the potential barriers to hiring excellent teachers, not one barrier was rated higher by private school principals than by their public school counterparts. Public school principals regarded "central office control" and "excessive transfers from other schools" as particularly onerous. They also faced substantially greater obstacles in dismissing teachers for poor performance than did private school principals. The complexity of formal dismissal procedures was the highest barrier to firing cited by public school principals. For private school principals, it was "a personal reluctance to fire."

Public school pupils were less likely to know what school policy comprised than were students in private schools. Public school students also regarded their school policies as less fair and effective. Parents were much more involved and cooperative in private schools. In public schools, parents were more likely to be required to communicate with school officials through formal channels. And school officials had less flexibility in addressing reasonable grievances of parents.

Chubb and Moe (1985) concluded that the external environment placed complex and conflicting expectations on public school principals:

Public schools relative to private, live in environments that are complex, demanding, powerful, constraining, and uncooperative. As a result, their policies, procedures, and personnel are more likely to be imposed from the outside. Public principals make the best of this environment by blending two roles, the middle manager and the politician. Like the middle manager, he consolidates whatever power is given him and guards the school's few prerogatives against the influence of a staff over which he has inadequate control. In the same role he emphasizes efficient administration as a safe way to please the administrative hierarchy of which he is a part. But the principal must also deal with a more complex and less friendly environment than the private principal—an environment that is politicized by school boards, state politicians, superintendents, local communities, and last but not least, parents. To do so, he plays the role of a politician, campaigning for the support of his school from a host of sometime hostile constituencies. (p. 41)

The sources of the signals to which private school principals must respond is clear: They are the school clients and the school trustees. The sources of signals to which public school principals must respond are varied and the messages are frequently conflicting and ambiguous. This makes a coherent response difficult.

SCHOOL-BASED BUDGETING AND INFORMATION SYSTEMS

To be effective, school-based decision making requires extensive information at the school level to facilitate making wise decisions, monitoring the implementation of those decisions, and adjusting those decisions on the basis of experience gained in implementation and on changing conditions. School personnel need easy access to information directly related to students' learning and about the resources required to provide an infrastructure in support of student learning. Information related to students' learning includes the school's mission and goals, the learning objectives of the school, curricular material organized according to learning objectives, student characteristics, and student accomplishments with respect to learning objectives. Information related to the school's infrastructure in support of learning includes material and human resources that must be purchased, such as teachers, support personnel, buildings, buses, computers, and books.

School personnel cannot make meaningful curricular decisions without the authority to also make the necessary resource commitment decisions that enable the implementation of those curricular decisions. School-based decision making must include school-based budgeting as an integral component. The degree of empowerment of school staff is directly related to the proportion of the school budget under its control. In this section we focus on issues related to school-based budgeting (SBB).

In her study of the implementation of education reforms in Kentucky, David (1994) found that the biggest problem with the process of allocation to schools was the lack of appropriate accounting systems and technological support by school districts. England faced a similar problem in moving to its system of local management of schools. Before districts can make financial allocations to schools, they need to know what the total resource requirement of schools is. Most current school accounting procedures are incapable of providing such information. Except for minor portions of the budget such as instructional supplies, our accounting procedures do not link expenditures to buildings, programs, or classrooms. Computer and accounting technology permit such linkages. Our ability to trace all expenditures to the school level will improve as the practice of SBDM spreads.

In Chapter 12 we referred to a new dimension of equity studies, the intradistrict dimension. Such studies have become possible because information on spending at the building level is available in some places. Berne and Stiefel (1994) found general equity in the distribution of funds to school buildings in New York City. But they also found that only $2,550 per pupil was allocated to schools out of a district average expenditure per pupil of nearly $7,000. The discretionary money now available to Chicago schools, as discussed above, is the result of redistribution to schools of funds previously held for general administration.

Other intradistrict studies referred to in Chapter 12 were those by Owens (1994) of the distribution of resources to elementary schools in Dade County, Florida, and by Hertert (1994) of the distribution of resources among unified school districts in California with enrollments in excess of 2,500. Both found a great deal of variation in the amount of resources available at the school level. In the California study, Hertert did not find correlates (for example, school size or ethnicity) with the variation. In Dade County, low expenditure was related to high percentages of African American and low-income students and large schools. Until information is routinely available on resource allocation to schools, such inequities will be masked by district averages.

Wohlstetter and Buffett (1992) have described the differences between traditional centralized budgeting at the district level and school-based budgeting. Regardless of the level at which it takes place, the budgeting process involves formulation, adoption, and monitoring. Under the traditional mode, all three are accomplished at the district level with minimal involvement of school personnel. Human and physical resources are then assigned to schools for use in district-specified areas. Schools are usually given discretionary control over a small allocation, primarily for purchasing instructional supplies and providing student enrichment experiences.

Where budgetary authority is decentralized, the district still forecasts the resources that will be available at the district level. But from that point on, the procedures become quite different. Decentralized districts must first determine the extent of budgetary authority to be extended to schools. The primary issue is the degree of control to be granted to schools over personnel expenditures that account for between 60 and 80 percent of school and district budgets. Of the cases described in a previous section, schools in Edmonton and England are granted a lump-sum allocation covering virtually all costs encountered by schools, with no specific amount designated for personnel or for any other expenditure category. In Dade County, schools are allocated staff units. But these units may be exchanged for a monetary amount to be used for other purposes. Chicago schools do not have control over the resources assigned to the basic program. But they do have authority over funds provided by categorical aids in support of students. These funds may be used to purchase human or physical resources at the discretion of the school's council. Kentucky districts are still working out these decisions. David (1994) found that only small parts of the budgets were being allocated to schools at this stage of the Kentucky reform. For example, staffing decisions are still typically made at the district level. She expected that schools will be allowed more resource decisions as the reform progresses.

The second district-level decision is how much to allocate to schools and according to what unit. Some districts make their allocations by pupil units and others by staff units. In either case, the number of students in a school, their characteristics, and the nature of the school (for example, grade levels served and the presence of special programs) are primary determinants of the size of the school's allocation.

Once an estimate of a school's allocation is determined by the district, school authorities devise a detailed plan for using the funds within the constraints established by higher authority. Whatever procedure is followed, budget building should be done within the context of a school's curricular plan.

With respect to budget adoption, the procedure is similar in centralized and decentralized districts. In either case the board of education gives the final approval. Wohlstetter and Buffett (1992)

pointed out that the main difference is in the flow. While centralized districts may consult with school authorities, in the decentralized mode the school develops the budget and recommends its adoption to district officials. District review of school budgets is in terms of compliance with district and other legal constraints and not in terms of educational substance, philosophy, and so forth.

Both district and school personnel need to monitor expenditures. The district role in the decentralized mode is primarily to provide information to the schools and to ensure that schools do not exceed their spending authorizations. In Chicago, Dade County, and Edmonton, the district provides budgetary information to school personnel on a regular basis. Edmonton school officials have the option of being on-line to access financial information held in computer memory at any time and have the flexibility of establishing their own accounting codes within the constraints of the district code structure.

While most accounting systems can be adapted to SBDM, national models are available for guidance. Cooper and Sarrel (1993) developed a cascade model to analyze funding of New York City's 123 high schools. The cascade model tracks funds from the district to the school to the classroom. The model fails to provide a detailed accounting of funds spent at the district office level, however. And it gives the impression that money that does not reach the classroom is unnecessary and wasted. With a grant from the Lilly Foundation, Cooper, Sarrel, and the Center for Workforce Preparation developed a Micro-Finance Model to overcome the weaknesses of the cascade model. The Micro-Finance Model has been used in over 2,200 schools in over fifty districts in fourteen states. Coopers and Lybrand, L.L.P., joined the effort to refine the Micro-Finance Model into an analytical tool known as the Finance Analysis Model.

The Finance Analysis Model is a technology-based management information tool that operates on a standard personal computer. The model consists of a series of multidimensional spreadsheets that compile information on district and school expenditures. The three basic dimensions of the model are functional, program, and grade level (Finance Analysis Model, 1995). The functional dimension is divided into five components: instruction, instructional support, operations, other commitments, and leadership. The program dimension is flexible and may include such programs as special education, bilingual education, gifted and talented, Title/Chapter 1, summer school, and so forth. The model requires the time of persons working in more than one site to be prorated according to the amount of time they spend at each site. Salaries and fringe benefits are then prorated to the respective sites accordingly. Likewise, utility bills and other expenditures that are not normally distributed to cost centers are so prorated under this model. The components of the model are illustrated in Figure 14.1.

The type of resource allocation and expenditure distribution information provided by the finance analysis model is critical to the successful functioning of SBDM (Speakman, Cooper, Sampieri, May, Holsomback, & Glass, 1996). Nevertheless, as Monk and King (1993) remind us, conventional cost analysis is facilitated by clear measures of the economic values of resources and a good understanding of the technical properties of the relevant processes. Neither of these conditions holds for education. The Finance Analysis Model improves our knowledge of cost of resources. But it does not by itself advance our understanding of the underlying technical relationships between costs of inputs and outcomes.

Monk and King proposed that until we have a better understanding of both conditions, it is better to use the concept of cost analysis metaphorically. Using cost analysis in this way:

> places less emphasis on generating questionable numerical estimates of costs and more emphasis on understanding the origins of costs. It also recognizes that costs matter and seeks to understand their influence on how people behave in educational settings. As a

consequence, it has the potential to generate considerable insight into the functioning of educational production processes and may even give rise to an improved understanding of how resources are transformed into educational outcomes. (p. 147)

Tracing resource demands to the school and classroom level is essential for informed decision making in a SBDM environment. It also holds the potential, with appropriate analysis, for advancing our understanding of the influences of inputs on educational outcomes.

SUMMARY

In this chapter, we have addressed the supply-side question of education provision: To what extent should providers of education be given the autonomy and flexibility to respond to differences in the judgments of consumers about appropriate education? School-based decision making is a strategy for granting education professionals greater autonomy in this respect. We defined SBDM and reviewed the rationale for its adoption through the words of some of its advocates. We described several instances of the implementation of SBDM. Since SBDM, along with family choice of schools, is intended to simulate, in part, private sector conditions within the public sector, we reviewed in some detail the studies by Chubb and Moe (1985, 1989, 1990) of organization and environmental attributes of public and private schools. We described the Finance Analysis Model to illustrate the type of financial information that is required at school and district levels to support SBDM.

In the next chapter, we address the demand-side question of education provision. That is, to what extent should consumers of education be given a central role in deciding what kind of education is appropriate for them? We examine the implications of family choice proposals for school finance policy and the continuing need for some governmental regulation.

Total Actual or Budgeted Expenditures

Function	Sub-Functions	Detail Functions
Instruction	Face-to-Face Teaching	Instructional Teachers
		Substitutes
		Instructional Paraprofessionals
	Classroom Materials	Pupil-Use Technology & Software
		Instructional Materials, Tests & Supplies
Instructional Support	Pupil Support	Guidance & Counseling
		Library & Media
		Extracurricular
		Student Health & Services
	Teacher Support	Curriculum Development
		In-Service, Staff Development & Support
		Sabbaticals
	Program Support	Program Development
		Therapists, Psychologists, Evaluators, Personal Attendants, Social Workers
Operations	Non-Instructional Pupil Services	Transportation
		Food Service
		Safety
	Facilities	School Buildings, Utilities & Maintenance
		Non-School Buildings, Utilities & Maintenance
	Business Services	Data Processing
		Business Operations
Other Commitments	Contingencies	Budgeted Contingencies
		Debt Service
	Capital	Capital Projects
		Parochial, Private & Charter School Pass-Throughs
	Out-of-District Obligations	Retiree Benefits & Other
		Enterprise & Community Service Operations
	Legal Obligations	Claims and Settlements
Leadership	School Management	Principals
		Assistant Principals
	Program & Operations Management	Deputies, Senior Administrators, Research & Program Evaluators
	District Management	Superintendent & School Board

Figure 14.1. Finance Analysis Model for Education
SOURCE: Copyright 1994 Coopers & Lybrand L.L.P.

ACTIVITIES

1. Imagine a policy board for each public school composed of the principal, serving as the chief executive officer, and representatives of teachers, parents, and students.
   - What are the advantages and disadvantages of such an arrangement?
   - Would you add representation from any other group?
   - Would you eliminate representation of any group?
   - Assuming each representative has one vote, how many representatives should there be from each group?
   - What constraints, if any, would you place on the decision-making powers of the board?
   - Provide your rationale for each response.
2. Within the context of the decision matrix presented in Figure 1.7 of Chapter 1, what educational decisions are best placed with professional educators at the school level? What safeguards need to be implemented to protect societal and family interests? Give your rationale for each response.
3. In what ways can the public interest be protected without the bureaucratization of schools? Explain the rationale supporting your answer.
4. To what extent, if any, should public control and regulation follow public finance? Give examples of alternative patterns of providing publicly financed support of the provision of educational services and the levels of control and regulation accompanying each.
5. Under a school-based budgeting scheme, what factors should be taken into account in determining the amount of a school's lump-sum distribution?

🖫 COMPUTER SIMULATIONS

Objective of This Activity

- *To understand the construction and management of a site-based budget*

Simulation 14.1: *Site-Based Budget*

By adapting and expanding the budget format provided in this simulation, a building principal or site-based management team is able to monitor all funds under the school's control. The initial spreadsheet includes selected objects of expenditure by five cost areas: Principal's Office, Pupil Services, Instruction, Media Center, and Building and Grounds. Each cost area has several objects of expenditure listed for illustrative purposes; both the cost areas and line items should be expanded as appropriate for actual use in a school.

For each of the objects listed, there is a corresponding budget code, the initial budget for the school year, previous and current month expenditures, encumbrances, and the remaining balance available. Students who are not familiar with basic concepts of budgeting and accounting should refer to a text on school business management or budgeting (e.g., Hartman, 1988).

The budget code includes seven digits in this simulation: the first two indicate the school (33), the next two show the department or other division, and the last three reveal the object. These codes may be replaced by those actually used by a school district or state. The initial budget for each cost and object is reduced by expenditures and encumbrances (i.e., funds already committed but not yet expended) to compute the remaining balance.

a. Retrieve the file BUDGET.

b. Create a formula in the TOTAL expenditure column that will add the PREVIOUS amount spent and the CURRENT MONTH's expenditures. Copy this formula down the column for each of the objects.

c. Create a formula in the UNENCUMBERED BALANCE column that will reduce the INITIAL BUDGET by the TOTAL expenditures and the ENCUMBRANCES. Copy this formula down the column for each of the objects.

d. Add a row at the bottom of the worksheet that will report the TOTAL of all cost areas. Create a formula to find the sum of all columns except the first two.

e. Save and print the budget. How much of the school's budget is already committed or spent, and how much remains?

Simulation 14.2: *Recision*

Assume that the state told the district of a recision that will require budget reductions. Such reductions require careful consideration and mediation through the district's political and personnel structures. In order to prepare for discussions, create a worksheet that illustrates the effect a $50,000 shortfall would have on each item in the school's budget if it were allocated in the percentage of initial budgetary amounts.

a. Copy the first three columns of your completed worksheet to the spreadsheet area below.

b. Copy the UNENCUMBERED BALANCE heading down to the new column next to the INITIAL BUDGET column. In this new column on the CERTIFIED PERSONNEL row, type the cell reference of the corresponding cell in the completed worksheet. Copy the formula all the way down through the column.

c. In the column next to the UNENCUMBERED BALANCE column, create a new heading: INITIAL PORTION. In this column on the CERTIFIED PERSONNEL row, create a formula that indicates the proportion of the TOTAL INITIAL BUDGET that was dedicated to this particular budget item.

d. Edit the formula to make the TOTAL INITIAL BUDGET cell an "absolute cell reference," and copy the formula for all objects of expenditure.

e. Print the worksheet produced in step d.

f. In the next column, create a new heading: $50,000 RECISION (make sure that $50,000 is in a cell by itself as a numeric value). In this column on the CERTIFIED PERSONNEL row, create a formula that multiplies the INITIAL PORTION by the cell which contains $50,000.

g. Edit the formula to make the $50,000 cell an "absolute cell reference," and copy the formula for all objects of expenditure.

h. In the next column, create a new heading: TEMP BALANCE (because this is the column to be used *temporarily* by decision makers to allocate the budget shortfall). In this column on the CERTIFIED PERSONNEL row, create a formula that subtracts the $50,000 SHORTFALL amount from the UNENCUMBERED BALANCE amount. Copy the formula through the column.

i. Copy the TOTAL row formula across the new columns. Save your file and print the revised table.

j. **Further Activities.** Does the temporary balance make sense? Is this method of allocating the shortfall appropriate to this district? What recommendations would you make, given that none of the budget items may have a negative balance? Prepare a spreadsheet that reflects your recommended adjustments to the temporary budget.

Simulation 14.3: *Additions*

Assume that the district has been awarded a $25,000 federal grant for staff development. The grant money may be allocated to any cost area as long as the line item is staff development. Also assume that the district has been awarded a $25,000 grant from the local business community that must be dedicated to instructional equipment. Prepare a worksheet that illustrates the effect of the grants on the budget if the STAFF DEVELOPMENT money were allocated in the proportion of initial budgetary amounts, and the instructional

EQUIPMENT money were allocated in equal shares.

a. Copy the first three columns of your completed worksheet to the spreadsheet area below.

b. Copy the UNENCUMBERED BALANCE heading down to the column next to the INITIAL BUDGET column. In this new column on the CERTIFIED PERSONNEL row, type the cell reference of the corresponding cell in the completed worksheet. Copy the formula all the way down through the column.

c. Copy the TEMP BALANCE heading down to the column next to the UNENCUMBERED BALANCE column. In this new column on the CERTIFIED PERSONNEL row, type the cell reference of the corresponding cell in the completed worksheet. Copy the formula through the column.

d. In the column next to the TEMP BALANCE column, create a new heading: $25,000 STAFF GRANT (make sure that $25,000 is in a cell by itself as a numeric value). In this column on each of the four STAFF DEVELOPMENT item lines, create a formula that will allocate the grant in the proportion of initial budgetary amounts (out of the total $21,000 allocated to Staff Development).

e. In the column next to the $25,000 STAFF GRANT column, create a new heading: $25,000 EQUIPMENT GRANT (make sure

that $25,000 is in a cell by itself as a numeric value). In this column on three of the four EQUIPMENT item lines (excluding PRINCIPAL'S OFFICE EQUIPMENT), create a formula that will allocate the grant in thirds.

f. In the column next to the $25,000 EQUIPMENT GRANT column, create a new heading: NEW TEMP BALANCE. In this column on the CERTIFIED PERSONNEL row, create a formula that adds the $25,000 STAFF GRANT amount and the $25,000 EQUIPMENT GRANT amount to the TEMP BALANCE amount. Copy the formula through the column.

g. Copy the TOTAL row formula across the new columns.

h. Save and print the worksheet produced in step g.

i. **Further Activities.** Does the new temporary balance make sense? Is this method of allocating the grant monies and shortfall appropriate to this district? What recommendations would you make, given that none of the budget items may have a negative balance and that the categorical grants must be spent for the designated purposes? Prepare a spreadsheet that reflects your recommended adjustments to the temporary budget.

REFERENCES

Arnott, M., Bullock, A., & Thomas, H. (1992). *Consequences of local management: An assessment by head teachers.* Paper presented to the ERA Research Network, February 12.

Bennett, A. L., Bryk, A. S., Easton, J. Q., Kerbow, D., Luppescu, S., & Sebring, P. A. (1992). *Charting reform: The principals' perspective.* Chicago: Consortium on Chicago School Research.

Berne, R., & Stiefel, L. (1994). Measuring equity at the school level: The finance perspective. *Educational Evaluation and Policy Analysis, 16,* 405–421.

Boyer, E. L. (1983). *High school: A report on secondary education in America.* New York: Harper and Row.

Brown, D. J. (1990). *Decentralization and school-based management.* London: Falmer Press.

Bryk, A. S., Deabster, P. E., Easton, J. Q., Luppescu, S., & Thum, Y. M. (1994). Measuring achievement gain in the Chicago public schools. *Education and Urban Society, 26,* 306–319.

Bullock, A., & Thomas, H. (1994). *The impact of local management of schools: Final report.* Birmingham, England: University of Birmingham.

Cawelti, G. (1989). Key elements of site-based management. *Educational Leadership, 46,* 46.

Chicago Panel on Public School Policy and Finance. (1988). *Illegal use of State Chapter I funds.* Chicago: Author.

Chubb, J. E., & Moe, T. M. (1985). *Politics, markets, and the organization of schools.* Stanford, CA: Institute for Research on Educational Finance and Governance, School of Education, Stanford University.

Chubb, J. E., & Moe, T. M. (1989). Effective schools and equal opportunity. In N. E. Devins (Ed.), *Public values, private schools* (pp. 161–183). London, England: Falmer Press.

Chubb, J. E., & Moe, T. M. (1990). *Politics, markets, and America's schools.* Washington, DC: Brookings Institution.

Chubb, J. E., & Moe, T. M. (1993). The forest and the trees: A response to our critics. In E. Rasell & R. Rothstein (Eds.), *School choice: Examining the evidence.* Washington, DC: Economic Policy Institute.

Coleman, J. S., & Hoffer, T. (1987). *Public and private high schools: The impact of communities.* New York: Basic Books.

Coleman, J. S., Hoffer, T., & Kilgore, S. (1981). *Public and private schools.* Final report to the National Center for Education Statistics, Contract No. 300-78-0208. Chicago: National Opinion Research Center.

Collins, R. A. (1988). *Interim evaluation report, school-based management/shared decision making project, 1987–88, project-wide findings.* Miami, FL: Dade County Public Schools, Office of Educational Accountability.

Committee for Economic Development. (1970). *Reshaping government in metropolitan areas.* New York: The Committee.

Conway, J. A. (1984). The myth, mystery, and mastery of participative decision making in education. *Educational Administration Quarterly, 20* (3), 11–40.

Cooper, B. S., & Sarrel, R. (1993). Managing for school efficiency and effectiveness. *National Forum of Educational Administration and Supervision Journal, 8, 3,* 3–38.

Cuban, L. (1988). *The managerial imperative and the practice of leadership in schools.* Albany, NY: State University of New York Press.

Danzberger, J. P., Kirst, M. W., & Usdan, M. D. (1992). *Governing public schools: New times, new requirements.* Washington, DC: Institute for Educational Leadership.

David, J. L. (1989). Synthesis of research on school-based management. *Educational Leadership, 46,* 45–53.

David, J. L. (1994). School-based decision making: Kentucky's test of decentralization. *Phi Delta Kappan, 75,* 706–712.

Easton, J. Q., Bryk, A. S., Driscoll, M. E., Kotsakis, J. G., Sebring, P. A., & Van der Ploeg, A. J. (1991). *Charting reform: The teachers' turn.* Chicago: Consortium on Chicago School Research.

Elmore, R. F. (1988). Choice in public schools. In W. L. Boyd & C. T. Kerchner (Eds.), *The politics of excellence and choice in education* (pp. 79–98). New York: Falmer Press.

Elmore, R. F. (1993). School decentralization: Who gains? Who loses? In J. Hannaway & M. Carnoy (Eds.), *Decentralization and school improvement: Can we fulfill the promise?* San Francisco: Jossey-Bass.

Finance Analysis Model, The (1995). Chicago: Coopers & Lybrand, L.L.P., and Center for Workforce Preparation.

Fitz, J., & Halpin, D. (1994). *Grant-maintained schools: Problems and prospects of school autonomy.* Paper presented at the annual meeting of the Politics of Education Association, Philadelphia, October 27–28.

Fleischmann, M. (1972). *Report of the New York State Commission on the Quality, Cost, and Financing of Elementary and Secondary Education,* Vol. 3. Albany, NY: The Commission.

Fleischmann, M. (1973). *The Fleischmann report on the quality, cost, and financing of elementary and secondary education in New York State,* Vol. 1. New York: Viking Press.

Goodlad, J. I. (1984). *A place called school: Prospects for the future.* New York: McGraw-Hill.

Guthrie, J. W., Garms, W. I., & Pierce, L. C. (1988). *School finance and education policy: Enhancing educational efficiency, equality and choice.* Englewood Cliffs, NJ: Prentice-Hall.

Hannaway, J. (1993). Decentralization in two districts: Challenging the standard paradigm. In J. Hannaway & M. Carnoy (Eds.), *Decentralization and school improvement: Can we fulfill the promise?* San Francisco, CA: Jossey-Bass.

Hannaway, J., & Carnoy, M. (1993). Preface. In J. Hannaway & M. Carnoy (Eds.). *Decentralization and school improvement: Can we fulfill the promise?* San Francisco, CA: Jossey-Bass.

Harp, L. (1995a). Ky. schools put on the line bonus budgeting. *Education Week, 14* (31), 1:9.

Harp, L. (1995b). Governor signs bill putting mayor in control of Chicago schools. *Education Week, 14* (37), 11.

Hartman, W. T. (1988). *School district budgeting.* Englewood Cliffs, NJ: Prentice-Hall.

Hertert, L. (1994). *Equalizing dollars across schools: A study of district- and school-level fiscal equity in California.* Paper delivered at the annual meeting of the American Education Finance Association, Nashville, TN.

Hess, G. A., Jr. (1990). *Chicago school reform: What it is and how it came to be.* Chicago: Chicago Panel on Public School Policy and Finance.

Hess, G. A., Jr. (1993). Decentralization and community control. In S. L. Jacobson & R. Berne, *Reforming education: The emerging systemic approach* (pp. 66–86). Thousand Oaks, CA: Corwin.

Hess, G. A., Jr. (1994). School-based management as a vehicle for school reform. *Education and Urban Society, 26,* 203–219.

Jacobson, S. L. (1988). The rural superintendency: Reconsidering the administrative farm system. *Research in Rural Education, 5* (2), 37–42.

Kifer, E. (1994). Development of the Kentucky Instructional Results Information System (KIRIS). In T. R. Guskey (Ed.), *High stakes performance assessment: Perspectives on Kentucky's educational reform* (pp. 7–18). Thousand Oaks, CA: Corwin.

Lee, V. E., & Bryk, A. S. (1993). Science or policy argument? A review of the quantitative evidence in Chubb's and Moe's *Politics, Markets, and America's Schools.* In E. Rasell & R. Rothstein (Eds.), *School choice: Examining the evidence.* Washington, DC: Economic Policy Institute.

Lindelow, J. (1981). School-based management. In S. C. Smith, J. A. Mazzarella, & P. K. Piele (Eds.), *School leadership: Handbook for survival* (pp. 94–129). Eugene, OR: Clearinghouse on Educational Management, University of Oregon.

Malen, B. (1994). Enacting site-based management: A political utilities analysis. *Educational Evaluation and Policy Analysis, 16,* 249–267.

Malen, B., Ogawa, R. T., & Kranz, J. (1990). What do we know about school-based management? A case study of the literature—A call for research. In W. H. Clune & J. F. Witte (Eds.), *Choice and control in American education, Vol. 2, The practice of choice, decentralization, and school restructuring* (pp. 289–342). New York: Falmer Press.

Marren, E., & Levacic, R. (1994). Senior management, classroom teacher, and governor responses to local management of schools. *Educational Management and Administration, 22* (1), 39–53.

Mojkowski, C., & Fleming, D. (1988). *School-site management: Concepts and approaches.* Andover, MA: The Regional Laboratory for Educational Improvement of the Northeast and Islands.

Monk, D. H., & King, J. A. (1993). Cost analysis as a tool for education reform. In S. L. Jacobson & R. Berne, *Reforming education: The emerging systemic approach* (pp. 131–150). Thousand Oaks, CA: Corwin.

Mortimore, P., & Mortimore, J. (1992). *The innovative use of non-teaching staff in primary and secondary schools project.* London: University of London, Institute of Education.

National Governors' Association. (1986). *Time for results: The Governors' 1991 report on education.* Washington, DC: National Governors' Association.

Ornstein, A. C. (1989). Centralization and decentralization of large public school districts. *Urban Education, 24,* 233–235.

Owens, J. T., Jr. (1994). *Intradistrict resource allocation in Dade County, Florida: An analysis of equality of educational opportunity.* Paper delivered at the annual meeting of the American Education Finance Association, Nashville, TN.

Peters, T. J., & Waterman, R. H. (1982). *In search of excellence: Lessons from America's best-run companies.* New York: Warner Books.

Rosenkranz, T. (1994). Reallocating resources: Discretionary funds provide engine for change. *Education and Urban Society, 26,* 264–284.

Sizer, T. R. (1985). *Horace's compromise: The dilemma of the American high school.* Boston: Houghton Mifflin.

Smylie, M. A. (1994). Redesigning teachers' work: Connections to the classroom. *Review of Research in Education, 20,* 129–177.

Speakman, S. T., Cooper, B. S., Sampieri, R., May, J., Holsomback, H., & Glass, B. (1996). Bringing money to the classroom: A systemic resource allocations model applied to the New York City public schools. In L. O. Picus & J. L. Wattenbarger (Eds.), *Where does the money go? Resource allocation in elementary and secondary schools* (pp. 106–131). Thousand Oaks, CA: Corwin Press.

Sukstorf, A., Wells, A., & Crain, R. L. (1993). A reexamination of Chubb and Moe's *Politics, Markets, and America's Schools.* In E. Rasell & R. Rothstein (Eds.), *School choice: Examining the evidence.* Washington, DC: Economic Policy Institute.

Timar, T. (1989). The politics of school restructuring. *Phi Delta Kappan, 71,* 4, 265–275.

Trimble, C. S. (1994). Ensuring educational accountability. In T. R. Guskey (Ed.), *High stakes performance assessment: Perspectives on Kentucky's educational reform* (pp. 7–18). Thousand Oaks, CA: Corwin.

United States General Accounting Office (GAO). (1994). *Education reform: School-based management results in changes in instruction and budgeting.* Washington, DC: GAO.

United States General Accounting Office (GAO). (1995). *Charter schools: New model for public schools provides opportunity and challenges.* Washington, DC: GAO.

Urban Institute, The (1972). *Public school finance: Present disparities and fiscal alternatives.* A report to the President's Commission on School Finance, Vol. 1, Chap. 5. Washington, DC: U.S. Government Printing Office.

Weiler, H. N. (1993). Control versus legitimation: The politics of ambivalence. In J. Hannaway & M. Carnoy (Eds.), *Decentralization and school improvement: Can we fulfill the promise?* San Francisco: Jossey-Bass.

Whitty, G. (1994). *Consumer rights versus citizen rights in contemporary education policy.* Paper presented to a conference on Education, Democracy and Reform at the University of Auckland, August 13–14.

Wohlstetter, P., & Buffett, T. M. (1992). Promoting school based management: Are dollars decentralized too? In A. R. Odden (Ed.), *Rethinking school finance: An agenda for the 1990s* (pp. 128–165). San Francisco: Jossey-Bass.

Wohlstetter, P., & Mohrman, S. A. (1994). School-based management: Promise and process. *CPRE Finance Briefs,* December.

Wohlstetter, P., Smyer, R., & Mohrman, S. A. (1994). New boundaries for school-based management: The high involvement model. *Educational Evaluation and Policy Analysis, 16,* 268–286.

CHAPTER 15

Family Choice of Schooling: Consumer Sovereignty

Primary Issues Explored in This Chapter:

- *Definition:* What is meant by "family choice of schooling"? Why is it being considered as a possible reform of education governance?
- *Relationships between choice and student achievement:* How does the effectiveness of schools in the private and public sectors compare? How likely is it that a policy of choice would lead to general improvement in school quality?
- *Criteria:* What criteria do parents use in choosing schools? Are there any relationships between the criteria used and socioeconomic status or eth-

nicity? Would a policy of choice lead to greater social stratification among schools?
- *Alternative policies for implementing choice:* How well have policies of open enrollment worked in the United States and elsewhere? How might education voucher plans be designed to protect equity? How might religiously affiliated schools be included in a publicly funded choice plan? Should religiously affiliated schools be included if they could be?
- *Systemic Reform:* How do school-choice plans relate to other education reform proposals?

On no issue do the values of liberty come into sharper conflict with those of equity and fraternity than on the issue of family choice of schooling. Yet because policymakers are aware of the social consequences of choice, unlike elsewhere, in the United States policy makers have tried to design choice policies that are socially just (OECD, 1994). In the debate over policies of choice, there are political and educational contexts directed toward school improvement. But there is also an important philosophical and moral subtext about values, identity, and freedom (Cookson, 1992).

People see school choice as a means of increasing the influence of consumers of educational services over what goes on in schools and of reducing the control of government, professional administrators, and educators. Major objectives of school choice include:

- Providing affordable options among desirable schools to those who do not currently enjoy such options
- Enhancing the efficiency of the education enterprise by improving student achievement at little or no increase in expense
- Accommodating cultural pluralism and diversity in values and philosophies

Critics of choice fear that it will weaken the social cohesion of communities and increase ethnic and class polarization. When choice options include private schools, they worry that public schools will be supported less and their quality will be harmed. Critics claim that choices will be made mostly by privileged persons, and that popular schools will begin to choose students. This will lead to greater stratification of students according to socioeconomic characteristics and academic ability. Critics believe that rather than promoting innovation, choice will make school leaders more conservative. They will tailor their curriculum to what will ensure a dependable clientele.

About 11 percent of American children are being educated outside the public sector, at the choice of their parents and at the parents' expense (see Table 3.7). The middle class and more affluent persons frequently make the quality of education in a community a criterion for deciding to live there. Once in a school district, children attending public schools are typically assigned to their school by public officials. For growing numbers, however, a degree of discretion is being allowed. Where they exist, choice structures are of three basic types: choice of public schools within the district of residence; choice of public schools within the state; choice among public and private schools.

In this chapter, we examine the nature of existing choice policies. We review studies of possible linkages between student achievement and choice. We assess whether the criteria used by parents in selecting schools are likely to bring greater efficiency in the schooling system or encourage greater inequities. We examine the implications of extending public funding through vouchers to private and religious schools through the experiences of other nations and some states and cities in the United States. Finally we bring together the arguments and evidence concerning decentralized administration of schools and choice. We propose that we need systemic reform that combines school-based decision making and choice with social controls such as a required common core curriculum, standards, and assessments.

RELATIONSHIPS BETWEEN CHOICE AND STUDENT ACHIEVEMENT

Much of the debate over school choice has revolved around comparing student achievement in public schools with that in private schools. Measured achievement is usually better among private school students. But much of the difference can be explained by the higher socioeconomic status of private school students and by differences between the two types of schools in organizational characteristics (such as size). Two major studies suggest that private schools are more effective than public schools when proper control is made for corelationships (Chubb & Moe, 1990; Coleman & Hoffer, 1987). Many have criticized both of these studies on technical grounds as well as for their policy recommendations. The criticisms are sufficient to suggest caution when using the results for policy formulation. But critics have failed to discredit the merit of the studies. The Coleman and Hoffer findings were discussed in Chapter 13 along with the critics' challenges. Chubb and Moe's study is treated in Chapter 16.

In reviewing studies globally, the Organization for Economic Cooperation and Development (OECD, 1994) concluded that research is unlikely to prove or disprove a relationship between school choice or competition on the one hand and improvement in the quality or effectiveness of schools on the other. This is because of the intractable corelationships involved. Nevertheless, the evidence does point to certain characteristics of schools of choice (in both the public and private sectors) that are associated with higher achievement and effectiveness. These include small size, caring communities with focused values, coherent curriculum, high academic standards, and lack of tracking (Bryk, Lee, & Smith, 1990; Chubb, 1990; Cohen, 1990).

Smallness

We discussed economies and diseconomies of scale in Chapter 13. We concluded that relationships between school size and school effectiveness are curvilinear. While there are disadvantages in very small schools, there are also disadvantages in very large schools. We describe two settings in which strategies of small schools and choice have been deliberately linked for the purpose of improving the academic achievement of at-risk and inner-city youth.

Referring to the schools she founded in New York City's District Four, Deborah Meier (1995) wrote: "It would have been impossible to create these successful experiments without choice. Choice was a necessary prerequisite—not an end in itself, but a tool for effecting change" (p. 93). She also noted that choice may be the only way to create schools that can experiment with radically new pedagogical practices. The most efficient strategy for rapid change is undercutting the natural layers of resistance—going with the willing and the able and not trying to bludgeon people into accepting changes for which they may not be ready.

Meier (1995) stressed the importance of smallness for the success of the pedagogical innovations being implemented. She recommended a maximum size for elementary schools of 300 pupils and for high schools of 400. She contended that small and focused educational communities enhance the climate of trust between families and schools. Only in a small school can deep discussion go on in ways that produce change and involve the entire faculty. Small schools enable the faculty to know students and their work individually. They permit adults to play a significant role in the development of a positive school culture. They more easily provide for the physical safety of all and are more readily made accountable to parents and to the public.

Fine (1993) saw large schools as promoting a general rather than a particularistic perspective on students. "They encourage passivity rather than participation, and they stress, by definition, the need to control students rather than to engage them critically" (p. 273). To address the concerns of Philadelphia school officials over low student achievement and high dropout rates, big secondary schools are being broken up into charter schools of 200–400 students and ten to twelve core faculty

working with students from ninth grade through graduation. By this restructuring they aim to care for the emotional and social needs and wants of students and to engage the intellects and passions of educators and scholars. Accomplishing these goals is much more difficult in a large setting.

Caring and Focused Value Communities

Bryk, Lee, and Smith (1990) pointed out that caring and individual commitment are the basic ground of the teaching act. They believed that the voluntary nature of Catholic schools and their shared communal theology and values were central to their success—especially with at-risk children.

> In the case of Catholic schools, field research describes strong institutional norms directly linked to basic religious beliefs about the dignity of each person and a shared responsibility for advancing a just, caring society. Not surprisingly, the educational philosophy that derives from these ideals is well aligned with social equity aims. When such understandings meld to a coherent organizational structure, desirable academic and social consequences appear to result. (p. 191)

Bryk, Lee, and Smith observed that much of what happens in schools involves discretionary action. In the bureaucratic structure of public schooling, great effort is required to secure agreement on issues that are intrinsically judgmental. Under a choice system, the effort expended on fostering such agreements can be redirected to the actual work of the school.

In a similar vein, Coleman and Hoffer (1987) referred to parochial schools as "value communities." One factor they offered in explanation of the relatively high achievement of students enrolled in parochial schools, even after controlling for differences in social background, was their "social capital." Social capital (see Chapter 13) consists of the interrelationships between children and youth and the adults most proximate to them, first and most prominently the family, and second, a surrounding community of adults. In simpler times, the social capital of schools came from functional communities that served the residential, economic, commercial, cultural, and spiritual needs of their inhabitants. Except in some rural towns, villages, and small cities, schools are no longer related to functional communities. Instead they are related to residential communities. As a result, the public schools serving residential communities in metropolitan areas no longer interact intensively with a surrounding community of adults. Coleman and Hoffer suggested that in order to increase the social capital currently available to public schools, we must abandon the practice of organizing public schools around residential areas. Instead we must organize them around voluntary value communities, as private schools do, especially parochial schools. For this we need a policy of choice among public schools.

Bryk, Lee, and Smith (1990) observed that the effectiveness of parochial schools—especially with respect to at-risk children—is not always realized in other private schools. Therefore, they doubt that market-driven schools would excel in the way that Catholic schools have. Walberg, however, argued that self-interest can compel caring for others, as it has in psychiatry, nursing, and other serving professions (Walberg, 1993). There is little reason to believe that competition for pupils would not encourage a posture of caring when this is a characteristic sought by potential clients.

Academic Focus and High Standards

Bryk, Lee, and Smith (1990) asserted unequivocally that any view of the school as a community must be integrated with a view of the school as a formal organization that seeks to rationally, effectively, and efficiently promote student learning. Their review of research found that most of the differences in achievement between pupils enrolled in public and private schools can be attributed to the different academic opportunities afforded by schools in each sector.

The extant research strongly supports the conclusion that the curricular organization of high

schools (including course-taking requirements, guidance functions, and policies affecting the assignment of students and teachers to schools and classes within schools) is the primary mechanism influencing both the average level of student achievement and how that achievement is distributed with regard to background characteristics such as race and class. (p. 187)

Walberg (1993) supported the concept that a common core of rigorous academic courses best promotes achievement and college readiness. Further, he referred to studies suggesting that non-college-bound youth are also best prepared for employment by such courses.

In summary, there is evidence that schools operated in the private sector—especially parochial schools—have a slight edge over public schools in effectiveness. Several researchers argue, however, that the small difference can be attributed to organizational factors and not to the public-private dichotomy. Chubb (1990) countered by asking why these facilitating organizational factors are more common among private than public schools. Chubb proposed that the answer is in the fundamental nature of public institutions and their politics. To get a more complete answer, we need a theory of government that can explain how public authority actually gets exercised in the governance of schools. No such theory currently exists. But Chubb and Moe's (1990) work (see Chapter 14) marks the beginning of the development of such a theory. We now look at the criteria parents use in choosing schools for their children and the implications of these criteria for equity in the distribution of schooling opportunities and efficiency in the operation of schools.

CRITERIA PARENTS USE IN CHOOSING SCHOOLS

Advocates argue that policies of school choice as a means of school improvement will succeed because parents value high achievement. Critics say that parents choose schools for many reasons that are unrelated to their effectiveness. Further, critics fear that the choosers would come disproportionately from the higher-income and better-educated classes if a voucher or other publicly financed plan were instituted. In this section, we examine the reasons people give for choosing a particular school and the relationships, if any, those reasons have with their background characteristics.

Bauch and Small (1986) developed a topology with four dimensions for categorizing the reasons parents give for choosing private schools: academic/curriculum, discipline/safety, religion, and values. Academic reasons are overwhelmingly the most common responses (Bauch & Goldring, 1995; Martinez, Thomas, & Kemerer, 1994; Slaughter & Schneider, 1986; Witte, 1993).

In a national study, Kutner, Sherman, and Williams (1986) found that the most common reasons public school parents give for choosing the schools they did were: it was the school assigned (28 percent), transportation (24 percent), and academic quality (17 percent). The most common reasons given by private school parents for exercising choice included academic quality (42 percent), religious instruction (30 percent), and discipline (12 percent). Nearly half of the children in the study attending private schools had once attended public schools, and 17 percent of those attending public schools had once attended private schools. Reasons given for switching from private to public schools included cost (24 percent), change of residence (21 percent), and availability of public alternatives (17 percent). Reasons for switching from public to private schools included academics (27 percent), discipline (25 percent), religious instruction or values orientation (25 percent), and quality of teachers (12 percent). In the Kutner et al. (1986) study, respondents with a child in private school tended to be better educated, earn a higher income, be Catholic, have attended private schools themselves, and live in large or medium-size cities. Parents sending their children to public schools were more likely to live in nonmetropolitan environs and to have attended only public schools themselves.

Kutner et al. concluded that for any given level of funding, "access and choice would be expanded most for low-income and minority families by increasing the proportion of tuition eligible" (p. 80).

Zhang (1995) studied the attitudes of parents who had switched their children among public neighborhood schools, public magnet schools, and parochial schools. He solicited information on attitudes about curriculum, school-parent relationships, and values in schooling. He found significant differences in opinion only with respect to the latter classification. Parents transferring their children from public to parochial schools placed greater importance on curricula stressing moral values and religion. Parents transferring their children from parochial to public schools placed greater importance on cultural diversity.

Darling-Hammond and Kirby (1988) and Erickson (1986) found similar differences in preferences among public and private school parents in surveys in Minnesota and British Columbia, respectively. Erickson also found that among parents with children in private schools:

> the preferential differences were much more pronounced among school types (i.e., Catholic, Calvinistic, and high-tuition) than among social class strata. The data suggest that private school types, rather than being mere vehicles of social stratification, attracted parents with different preferences, with limited regard to social class. The schools were products, as it were, of different preference structures. (pp. 95–96)

Bauch and Goldring (1995), in a study of metropolitan high schools of choice in Chicago, Washington, DC, and Chattanooga, Tennessee, found that parents usually had multiple reasons for selecting a particular school. While Catholics placed high priority on a school's academic reputation, they were also concerned about moral development and discipline. The value profile of parents choosing single-focus magnet schools was similar to that of parents choosing Catholic schools, except they didn't give such high priority to moral development. Multifocus magnet schools were chosen most frequently by minority families. Their primary motivation for choice was academic considerations. But they also transferred schools for career and transportation/proximity reasons.

Lee, Croninger, and Smith (1994) studied the attitudes of parents in the Detroit metropolitan area. They found some support for the contention that choice would reduce socioeconomic stratification in that socially disadvantaged adults were the strongest supporters of the policy. Favorable attitudes toward choice were inversely related to the quality rating respondents gave to their local schools. This latter finding was a paradox, however. Persons in districts of perceived quality were less interested in choice and less likely to give persons seeking choice an opportunity to choose their districts. The researchers raised the question: "Are those who favor choice likely to actually gain access to better schools?" They concluded: "Although disadvantaged families see choice (in theory) as a vehicle for better education for their children, and although the exercise of such choice could benefit a few children and their families, . . . the overall effect of implementation of a choice plan would be to increase, rather than decrease social stratification in education" (p. 450).

The Massachusetts legislature passed a law in 1991 permitting children to attend schools outside their home districts. The law provided that the state would pay the cost of tuition to the districts that enrolled nonresident students and deduct the amount from allocations to districts that lost students. The law did not require a school district to accept students from another district. But the incentives were high for doing so. Fossey (1994) studied the nature of student flow after the first year. He found that parents switched their children to schools with higher expenditure levels and student achievement in communities with higher-socioeconomic-status populations. His findings also lend credence to the conclusion of Lee, Croninger, and Smith (1994) reported above. Only about 15 percent of the state's school districts accepted school-choice students. No suburban district within convenient commuting distance of

Boston participated. Consequently, only fifteen Boston students out of sixty thousand transferred under this program. Only 4 percent of the three thousand school-choice students were African American or Hispanic. Even in districts with large minority populations, most of the students who transferred were white. Fossey concluded that families seemed to be making rational decisions when transferring their children out of their home communities. They were not making decisions for reasons of mere convenience. The Massachusetts choice plan was improving the schooling options of a few students. But it was not effective in increasing the mixing of ethnic groups.

Witte (1993) did a study of the characteristics of children and families participating in Milwaukee's voucher program. He found that the students came from poor, often single-parent households. They were not doing well in the Milwaukee Public Schools (MPS), and their parents expressed dissatisfaction with the schools their children had previously attended. Despite all this, choice families were smaller than those with children in MPS. Voucher parents (especially mothers) were more educated, had higher educational expectations for their children, were more likely to work at home with their children on education-related problems, and had participated in their children's previous public schools at higher rates than the average MPS parent.

Martinez, Thomas, and Kemerer (1994) studied the characteristics of families that chose and their rationales for exercising choice in Minnesota, San Antonio, Milwaukee, and Indianapolis. They found that parents overwhelmingly picked educational quality or learning climate as their number-one reason for choosing a school for their children. They also rated discipline and general atmosphere in the schools highly. Families that chose were quite different from nonchoosing families in that both the education level of parents and parents' educational expectations for their children were higher. They also found that some low-income minority families were not aware that school-choice programs were available. This was a formidable obstacle to their participation.

In weighing the evidence of numerous studies, Levin (1990) concluded that the empirical evidence supported the interpretation that choice schemes, whether market or public, will tend to favor more-advantaged families. Cohen (1990) put it this way:

[P]art of the appeal of choice and decentralization is their promise to improve schooling by opening it to greater influence from parents. But both reforms would thus only be effective to the extent that parents mobilized to take advantage of the opportunities that new market or political organization offered. Some parents would make good use of these opportunities, but many others would not. And those parents with the greatest need for improved education would have the greatest difficulty taking advantage of the reforms. (p. 378)

Cohen's conclusion is supported by the findings of Ambler (1994) in an analysis of school-choice plans in Britain, France, and the Netherlands. He found that school choice increased the educational gap between the privileged and the underprivileged, primarily because students from higher socioeconomic backgrounds were more likely to exercise the prerogative of choice. When subsidies are provided to private education, higher-income families derive even greater benefits.

In a study of the exercise of choice in Scotland, Adler, Petch, and Tweedie (1989) found that parents across the social-class spectrum requested transfers and not predominantly a middle-class minority. Ball, Bode, and Gars (1992), however, detected two distinct discourses of school choice in England that were class related. The working-class discourse was dominated by practical and immediate considerations such as convenience in location of the school. The middle class used the school strategically for the furtherance of social mobility. If this is true, the belief that choice will serve significantly to reduce disparities in the delivery of educational services is seriously challenged.

The study by Adler et al. (1989) of Scotland, which has had a relatively long experience with choice, found that the policy had a greater impact on secondary schools than on primary schools. The arrangement clearly led to the widening of educational inequalities and to the reemergence of a selective system of schooling in the big cities. Most of the schools that lost large numbers of pupils were situated in the least-prosperous housing neighborhoods. Most of the schools that gained were located in mixed inner-city areas. Pupils transferred from schools with poor examination results and higher dropout rates to schools with better examination results and lower dropout rates. Choice exaggerated the problems of schools that lost pupils. Willms and Echols (1993) arrived at similar conclusions in a later study in Scotland.

Adler (1993) did not recommend abandoning the choice scheme altogether, however. Rather he called for "a better balance between the rights of parents to choose schools for their children and the duties of education authorities to promote the education of all children." He called for procedures whereby all parents, with the assistance of teachers, would be able to make more informed choices in the selection of schools that would best promote their children's learning. At the same time the procedures should protect legitimate collective policy concerns that have been eclipsed by the construction of a "quasi-market." An OECD (1994) study of choice policies in England, Australia, the Netherlands, New Zealand, Sweden, and the United States made similar recommendations.

In summary, American studies of the criteria parents use in selecting schools for their children clearly show that academic, moral, and religious concerns dominate. When given a choice, parents tend to select schools that are better than the ones their children attended previously. These findings support the claims by market advocates that a policy of school choice will be a force for improving the quality of schools generally.

Parents living in areas served by poor schools (usually low-income) want choice more than parents living in areas served by good schools (generally high-income). The latter are not particularly willing to open their good schools to others. Because of this, market opponents worry that a choice policy would make an already inequitable system even more inequitable. This fear is further supported by studies in other countries where choice of schools has been the norm for generations. In applying international studies to the United States, however, we must keep in mind that any publicly supported system in the United States must function under the equal protection provisions of the Fifth and Fourteenth Amendments to the United States Constitution. Such protection is generally not available in other countries where school choice is national policy. As noted earlier, OECD (1994) has observed that the United States, unlike most other nations, has made explicit attempts to design choice policies that are socially just.

INCLUDING PRIVATE AND RELIGIOUS SCHOOLS IN FAMILY-CHOICE SCHEMES

Educational Vouchers and Tax Credits

Educational Vouchers.   An educational voucher is an entitlement extended to an individual by a government permitting that individual to receive educational services up to the maximum dollar amount specified. The holder can normally redeem the voucher according to preference at any institution or enterprise approved by the granting agency. According to Guthrie, Garms, and Pierce (1988):

> Regardless of operating details, voucher plans possess a common fundamental principle. Their intent is to enfranchise households as the basic decision-making unit. Vouchers do not eliminate government interest in education. Rather, voucher plans retain the prospect of government responsibility for financing and otherwise maintaining a marketplace of education providers, which would require regulation. (p. 356)

In Chapter 1 we discussed the differences between the public and private sectors in making decisions about resource allocation. Each household can maximize its satisfaction, within its purchasing power, in the private sector, because multiple decisions are allowed. In the public sector, however, a single decision is generally required. This tends to reflect the opinion of the average voter. This in turn makes it difficult for households that deviate substantially from the average to match their tastes with their resources optimally.

Noting that the quality of public schooling is the worst where parents have the fewest options, or none, Friedman (1962) argued that equity and fraternal goals, as well as libertarian goals and efficiency, would be better served through government-financed vouchers. Vouchers would separate the nexus between public support of education, place of residence, and the public ownership of educational enterprises. Under the Friedman scheme, parents sending their children to private schools would be paid a sum equal to the estimated cost of educating a child in a public school, provided that at least that amount was spent on education in an approved school. If the cost of the private school were greater, the parent would have to make up the difference. Such a plan, Friedman argued (Friedman & Friedman, 1980), would greatly expand educational options available to poor families.

> One way to achieve a major improvement, to bring learning back into the classroom, especially for the currently most disadvantaged, is to give all parents greater control over their children's schooling, similar to that which those of us in the upper-income classes now have. Parents generally have both greater interest in their children's schooling and more intimate knowledge of their capacities and needs than anyone else. Social reformers, and educational reformers in particular, often self-righteously take for granted that parents, especially those who are poor and have little education themselves, have little interest in their children's education and no competence to choose for them. This is a gratuitous insult. (p. 150)

Critics of the Friedman plan argue that unregulated vouchers would merely enable private schools to raise their tuition. They would still be out of reach of low-income families. At the same time, unregulated vouchers would make private schools more accessible to higher-income families. This would encourage them to abandon the public schools, which would become havens for the poor. This, they claim, would further stratify society. Some critics do see merit in the general concept of vouchers, however. They propose modifications to the Friedman plan that they believe would overcome perceived inequities while retaining what they consider to be its more attractive features.

Coons and Sugarman (1978) approached family choice through a plan designed to promote variety in the quality of schools rather than uniformity. Their plan has been called both family power equalizing (FPE) and the quality choice model (QCM). QCM would allow schools to charge whatever tuition they wanted within a very broad, but specified, range. Tuition would be paid partly by the parents and partly by the state. State subsidies would be based on the tuition charged and on family income. Thus poorer parents, in some meaningful sense, could afford high-priced schools as easily as the rich. The actual formula would work similarly to district power equalization (see Chapter 8), with families being the focus of wealth equalization rather than school districts. Even the poorest family would have to pay something to establish a personal stake in the choice. Families with more than one child in school would need to pay no additional charge. After the first child, the state would fully subsidize tuition. The financial obligation of families sending their children to differently priced schools would be based on the average tuition charged. Open access to participating schools would be assured by having oversubscribed schools make selections of students on a random basis.

Coons and Sugarman (1978) acknowledged social science research that questions the relationship between cost and quality in schooling. They projected that QCM "would encourage families to exercise their own judgement about the efficacy of extra school purchases compared to other goods and services" (p. 200). Enactment of this plan would constitute a marked departure from the current financing of public schools in that for the first time in this century, such schools would charge tuition. (Tuition and "rate bills" were commonly charged by public schools in the nineteenth century; see Chapter 4.) This could significantly alter the educational burden between users and nonusers.

The Center for the Study of Public Policy (CSPP, 1970) did one of the most comprehensive studies of vouchers. It analyzed the potential impact of seven voucher models, including Friedman's unregulated market model. The report concluded that regulations were required to ensure more equitable distribution of resources over the system of neighborhood schools. But the regulations themselves would likely generate greater segregation in the schools by ability or income than currently exists. Only their regulated compensatory model (described below) was judged likely to give the poor a larger share of the nation's educational resources. In addition to lotteries and quota systems, economic incentives that encourage schools to accept disadvantaged and handicapped students would be needed to give such students a reasonable chance of getting into the schools of their choice. They reported that the fundamental political and pedagogic danger posed by most voucher plans was that at least a few publicly managed schools would become dumping grounds for the students that oversubscribed public and private schools did not want. Oversubscribed schools under an unregulated model would become sanctuaries of privilege.

CSPP's Regulated Compensatory Voucher Model.
We describe here in some detail the regulated compensatory voucher model developed by the Center for the Study of Public Policy (CSPP, 1970) as one that provides the benefits of educational vouchers while protecting societal concerns over equity and fraternity. According to this model, every child would receive a voucher roughly equivalent to the cost of the public schools in the area. A supplement would be paid for children who were in some way

disadvantaged because of poverty or physical, psychological, or other learning disabilities. The receiving school would not necessarily have to spend the supplement exclusively on the child for whom it was given. For example, it could use the supplement to reduce class size in general throughout a school. No school could charge tuition beyond the voucher amount awarded for a given student. Schools wishing to increase their revenue beyond the voucher amount could seek subventions from such sponsors as churches and businesses or from special-purpose grants from the federal government and foundations. They could also enhance income by proportionally increasing the enrollment of disadvantaged students. Schools would have considerable latitude in developing their curricula and in setting their expenditure levels (by admitting larger numbers of students qualifying for supplements). Parents desiring high-expenditure programs would be able to find them only in schools accommodating significant numbers of disadvantaged children. Thus, under the plan parents would have the basic choice between schools with high financial resources or with more able students. Parents could continue to fully finance their children's education at schools not participating in the voucher plan.

As previously noted, the report of the CSPP (1970) concluded that equal access to schools for disadvantaged students could not be insured by financial incentives alone. Regulations would also need to limit application, admission, and transfer procedures. The regulated compensatory voucher model provides for regulations designed to facilitate social equity.

Any marketlike plan for distributing educational services depends on parents making informed choices in selecting schools for their children. Parents must be able to obtain accurate, relevant, and comprehensive information about the advantages and disadvantages of all available alternatives. In the absence of a public initiative, private information sources would likely develop, as with higher education, but such sources are likely to charge fees for services and would therefore not be readily available to the poor. Hence, providing a public information system must become a respon-

sibility of a coordinating public agency. The CSPP (1970) proposed that such responsibilities should include:

- Collecting information about each school on matters of social and parental concern
- Compiling information in clear and comprehensible printed formats
- Providing counselors who can explain the printed information to those who do not understand it
- Monitoring information provided to parents, protecting them against misleading advertising claims
- Investigating claims of fraud, discrimination, and deception and taking appropriate remedial action where these claims are verified (pp. 62–63)

CSPP recommended a procedure whereby parents would have to appear personally at an office of the coordinating agency to fill out the necessary voucher-application forms. At that time a voucher counselor would provide information on available options and review the procedures for making application. Individual schools would likely establish their own recruiting procedures.

The CSPP (1970) found the most promising device for preventing discrimination in admissions by oversubscribed schools was some kind of lottery for at least half of their admissions. In recognition that there needs to be some correlation between the curriculum of a school and the characteristics of its students, they built a case for allowing schools some discretionary admissions so long as their criteria do not reinforce patterns of invidious discrimination.

> The idea of favoring cellists over pianists, for example, seems harmless because it does not aggravate any of the more general problems of the educational system. The idea of favoring Spanish-speaking or black applicants seems acceptable to us for the same reason. The idea of discriminating against children against whom everyone else also discriminates is less acceptable. (p. 77)

There are other reasons justifying discretionary admissions. Families with one child already in a school, for a number of very good reasons, would probably want to enroll younger brothers and sisters in the same school. To encourage new schools that would enhance variety, parents establishing schools would need to be guaranteed a place for their children in recognition of their efforts. So long as the number of founders was limited to a reasonable number, and so long as all founders were listed when the school was incorporated, the CSPP saw no serious difficulty in this procedure.

According to the model, either the school or the parent initiates transfers. A parent may become dissatisfied with a school or may find, with experience, that the school has not lived up to expectations. In either case, parents should have the option to withdraw their children from a school at any time as long as they can continue to meet compulsory attendance laws by enrolling them in other schools. Admission counselors should be available to them.

Schools also enroll students they would rather not have. Private schools may persuade such children to withdraw. Public schools are constrained by compulsory attendance laws but deal with the situation by placing problem children in special schools or programs, by removing them through suspension or expulsion, or by encouraging them to drop out. Private schools have a great deal of flexibility in eliminating misfits. But public schools must follow formal bureaucratic procedures. The CSPP could see no justification for providing publicly and privately managed schools with the same amount of money and then allowing the private schools to shirk the responsibilities that public schools have. They recommended that the constraints placed on public schools in these matters be extended to private schools receiving vouchers. Normally it should be assumed that once a child is admitted to a school and surrenders a voucher, the school is obliged to provide for the education of that child until the child has completed the course of study or elects to transfer. If a school finds it necessary to expel a child, evidence supporting such action should be submitted to an impartial arbitrator. Both the school and the parents of the child should have access to professional consultation. Parents should also have access to the services of an educational ombudsman to ensure their rights are protected.

The Boston public schools use procedures similar to those proposed in the CSPP model in administering their universal program of choice among the city's public schools (OECD, 1994). All parents are required to list their school preferences before their children enter grades one, six, and nine. The schools make selections to satisfy as many choices as possible consistent with racial integration. Parent information centers help parents to make informed choices. Approximately 94 percent of children are placed in their first- or second-choice school. The schools avoid having the best-informed parents select a handful of socially favored schools by forcing everyone to choose, spreading information as evenly as possible to all parents, and making it virtually impossible for the most privileged to manipulate the system. Most parents do not select the school closest to their residence. It appears, moreover, that white flight from the system has been stemmed. Similar plans are functioning in Cambridge, Massachusetts, and White Plains, New York (Yanofsky & Young, 1992).

Milwaukee's Voucher Scheme and Others.   Milwaukee provides the only state-financed private school-choice program in the country. Under the program enacted by the Wisconsin legislature in 1990, up to 1,500 low-income Milwaukee families are eligible for $3,200 state tuition grants to send their children to any private, nonreligious school in the state. *Low income* is defined as not exceeding 1.75 times the nationally defined poverty line. The program is expected to be expanded to allow participation by schools having religious affiliations. Participating schools may not receive the subsidy for more than 49 percent of their students. And they must use random selection to admit students if their rolls are oversubscribed.

As described earlier, although poor, the parents who chose private schools in Milwaukee were better educated and had been more active in the school system than those parents who kept their children in public schools. Early evaluations of the academic gains of students participating in the choice program were mixed. Choice parents had very positive attitudes toward their private schools, however. And parents became even more involved than they had been in their previous public schools (Witte, 1993).

In a privately financed choice program, low-income Indianapolis families can qualify for partial tuition payments to any private school (religious or sectarian). These subsidies are provided by the Educational Choice Charitable Trust, which is underwritten by the Golden Rule Insurance Company. The single criterion for student participation is financial need. No limitations are placed on receiving schools. In the first year of operation (1991), the program enabled 774 students to attend fifty-eight different private schools (Martinez, Thomas, & Kemerer, 1994).

Several private corporations in San Antonio support a similar scholarship program under the name of Children's Educational Opportunity (CEO). Half of the CEO scholarships go to students who previously attended public schools. The other half go to financially eligible students already enrolled in private schools. In 1992, 967 students received scholarships to attend seventy-six private schools (Martinez et al., 1994). These choice programs supported by private contributions seem to be growing in number throughout the country.

Tuition Tax Credits and Deductions. Another approach to aiding persons attending private schools is by giving tax credits and deductions rather than subsidizing the schools directly. A tax credit reduces the amount of the tax (usually an income tax) owed up to a specified sum. Tuition payments (or a percentage of them, depending on how the law is written) can be subtracted from the computed tax amount owed. No federal or state tax credits are currently available for educational purposes.

Tax deductions apply to income taxes exclu-sively. They are not as favorable for qualifying tax-payers as tax credits. Tax deductions, similar to those for medical expenses (see Chapter 5), reduce the amount of taxable income. Thus the reduction in tax liability is only a percentage (the marginal tax rate) of tuition payments. Such deductions are allowed in Minnesota. The Minnesota law allows parents with children in public and private schools to deduct from their taxable income educational expenses of up to $650 per elementary school child and $1000 per secondary school child. Expenses eligible for deduction include tuition and the cost of secular textbooks, transportation, school supplies, and fees. With marginal tax rates in Minnesota ranging from 1.6 percent to 16 percent, the maximum reduction in tax liability per secondary school child ranges from nothing, for nontaxpayers, to $160. The Minnesota law has been reviewed at all levels of the court system and was upheld by the United States Supreme Court in 1983 (*Mueller v. Allen*).

Opponents of tax credits and deductions argue that the benefits flow disproportionally to high-income persons. To qualify for either a credit or a deduction, a person has to incur a tax liability and file a return. Thus, the very poorest would not benefit. Poor parents could be brought into a tax credit scheme through refundability provisions. That is, the government would reimburse to the individual the amount of the credit. This would still require the person to file a tax return.

Proposals usually contain civil rights guarantees based on school eligibility requirements. Credits and deductions would only be allowed for expenditures incurred in schools that had received governmental approval.

Including Religious Schools

Constitutional Constraints. There appear to be no constitutional restrictions on family choice among public schools as long as the civil rights (for example, nondiscrimination) of children are not violated in the process. This is probably also true with respect to independent private schools. Direct government aid to religiously affiliated private schools, however, is a different matter. Here there is potential conflict with the First Amendment to the United States Constitution, which bars governmental actions "respecting the establishment of religion." Several state constitutions have even more restrictive terminology that bars any form of public assistance to religious institutions. It remains to be determined whether aid to parents through vouchers or tax credits that may be used in religious or other schools is constitutional. We noted above that courts have determined that state income tax deductions for tuition and other educational expenses for both public and private school children are constitutional (*Mueller* v. *Allen,* 1983).

In *Lemon* v. *Kurtzman* (1970), the Supreme Court established a three-point test to determine whether statutes violate the establishment clause: (1) the statute must have a secular legislative purpose; (2) its principal or primary effect must be one that neither advances nor hinders religion; and (3) the statute must not foster an excessive government entanglement with religion. Applications of this test to various forms of governmental aid preclude direct subsidy of religiously affiliated private schools. Thus, the constitutional amendment that protects the right of parents to select a private school for their children under the free exercise clause virtually prohibits direct aid to the most common type of private school under the establishment clause.

Aid to parents may be another matter, however. Anthony (1987) detected a change in position by the U.S. Supreme Court on this issue. Ten years before their *Mueller* v. *Allen* decision, the Court had found deductions unconstitutional in a New York case (*Levitt* v. *Committee for Public Education and Religious Liberty,* 1973). According to the Court, a critical difference in the two cases is that in the Minnesota statute, all parents could take advantage of the deduction. In the New York case, on the other hand, only parents paying tuition to private schools could benefit.

Anthony related the change in this and other interpretations to the shift in the composition of the Supreme Court from liberal domination to conservative domination during the Reagan administration. She saw a softening in the Court's position on parochial aid as a result. She drew on the *Mueller* decision in particular in support of her position. First, she noted the majority's unsolicited endorsement of Minnesota's efforts to defray costs for parents of parochial school children. Because of the heavy burden borne by parents in educating their children in parochial schools, the majority found, "whatever unequal effect may be attributed to the statutory classification can fairly be regarded as a rough return for the benefits . . . provided to the state and all taxpayers by parents sending their children to parochial schools" (at 3070).

As a second piece of evidence of the Court's softening position, Anthony referred to the majority's opinion concerning the Founding Fathers' interpretation of the Establishment Clause.

> Here, again, Rehnquist [writing for the majority] suggests that the Court no longer needs to be concerned about the separation of church and state. Thus he writes, "At this point in the 20th century we are quite far removed from the dangers that prompted the Framers to include the Establishment Clause in the Bill of Rights. . . . The risk of significant religious or denominational control over our democratic processes—or even of deep political division along religious lines—is remote" (at 3069). (p. 599)

Anthony concluded that the application of the "original intent" doctrine to future parochial school aid is likely to result in decisions that hold public funding of parochial schools as constitutional. "However, due to the tendency of conservative jurists to uphold precedent, one can expect a gradual chipping away at previous parochial aid decisions rather than a total renunciation of those rulings" (p. 604).

Doyle (1992) interpreted statements made by Justice Lewis Powell in his concurring opinion to the U.S. Supreme Court's 1985 decision in *Aguilar v. Felton* as inviting Congress to devise a voucher program for poor children. The Court's decision overturned a twenty-year practice whereby poor children could receive educational services in parochial schools supported by Title One of the Elementary and Secondary Education Act. Powell's statement to which Doyle referred reads:

> [T]he court has never foreclosed the possibility that some types of aid to parochial schools could be valid under the Establishment Clause. . . . If, for example, the Congress should fashion a program of evenhanded financial assistance to both public and private schools that could be administered, with government supervision in the private schools, so as to prevent the diversion of the aid for secular purposes, we would be presented with a different question. (Cited in Doyle, 1992, p. 516)

The Reagan administration unsuccessfully attempted to overcome the restrictions on aid to poor children attending religious schools imposed by the *Aguilar* decision by proposing to Congress that the then more than $3 billion provided annually through Chapter One of the Education Consolidation and Improvement Act for supplementary educational services for educationally disadvantaged children be distributed through "minivouchers." Under the Reagan proposal, states and local school districts would give low-income parents vouchers to spend on their children's education to enable choice among public schools within or outside their home district or at private schools.

Coleman (1990) contended that by excluding public funds to religious schools, an opportunity is lost to strengthen the strongest asset a child has: a parent's interest, involvement, and attention to the child's growth.

> Religious involvement is and has been stronger on average for those who are less advantaged, white and black, than for those who are more advantaged. And it is the children of the less advantaged who are most at risk of being harmed by drugs, crime, alcohol, delinquency. The possibility of having their children under the care of a church-related school offers a far greater benefit to these parents than to those whose children are less at risk. And it does so because the church constitutes a basis for community that builds upon, reinforces, and extends the most worthy of the values the parent holds and would transmit to the child. (p. xx)

Cibulka (1989) noted that in many nations it would not be necessary to fashion a philosophical defense of private schooling because the distinction between public and private is not so sharply drawn. Outside the United States, it is not common to think of the government-run schools as public and all others as private. Private schools are assumed to serve a public purpose and are frequently aided by public funds. Doyle (1992) argued that providing vouchers for at-risk children in the United States is a known policy remedy for the shortcomings of inner-city schools and that failure to implement such policies is not due to constitutional restrictions, but to "the intransigence of public school advocates" (p. 518).

Impact on Diversity. Although the intent of vouchers and tax credits is to provide parents with more educational options for their children, some evidence suggests that there is actually a narrowing in range of choice—but more people may participate in that narrower range. Currently, with no governmental aid and with only a small percentage of the population attending private schools, there is very little governmental regulation or oversight of private schools in the United States. Adoption of increased fiscal support of private schools could come only as a result of extensive political compromises that recognize other objectives such as equality and fraternity. Greater aid and greater participation would thus, undoubtedly, be accompanied by greater governmental control and regulation over private schools to address equity and fraternal considerations. This would restrict the flexibility of private schools. It would make them more acceptable to the average voter but not necessarily to their original clientele.

Policies on the support of public, private, and religious schools in Canada vary markedly from province to province. Thus Canada provides an excellent setting for the empirical study of the impact of alternative policies. Erickson (1986) reported on a series of studies beginning in 1975 that involved interviews of persons associated with Catholic school systems in Alberta, Saskatchewan, and Ontario, where Catholic schools were fully supported with public funds, and in Manitoba and British Columbia, where they were not. Evidence from the interviews convinced Erickson that:

> the lengthy period of total support has significantly "deprivatized" Catholic schools in Alberta, Saskatchewan, and Ontario, attenuating or obliterating numerous characteristics which elsewhere distinguished Catholic schools from public schools. (pp. 99–100)

In 1978, British Columbia embarked on a new policy of partial support of private schools by providing most private schools with a grant per pupil equal to 30 percent of the per pupil public school operating cost. Regulations that would protect the public interest were held to a minimum to avoid homogenizing the private schools. Erickson subsequently launched a follow-up to his 1975 study in British Columbia.

In Catholic elementary schools in British Columbia, dramatic declines were detected in teacher commitment as perceived by parents, and in parent commitment as perceived by teachers. The most pronounced negative consequences of increased public assistance were found in the Catholic secondary schools. At this level:

> there was a notable decline in the sense among parents that their schools needed their help, in the extent to which parents viewed their schools as responsive, in teacher commitment as perceived by both parents and students, in parent commitment as perceived by

teachers, in student affection toward teachers and classes, and in the perception by students that their schools, rather than being just like public schools, were doing something special. (p. 102)

Erickson concluded that the Canadian examples do not lend much credence to efforts to encourage educational diversity by extending public funds to private schools.

> In one important sense, what the British Columbia government is attempting to do is far from unusual. Faced with the evidence of what they have done to bias the marketplace, governments have often attempted to rectify the situation by returning to the citizens, for their unbiased use, some of the funds previously extracted from them through taxation. It soon turns out, unfortunately, that the money has been transformed by passing through the public pipeline. It cannot be freely used. It has become a political instrument, laden with constraints produced by the anxieties, pressures, and concerns of public officials. (p. 106)

Erickson suspected that the negative effects would not have been nearly so great if the aid had been provided directly to parents in the form of vouchers, tax credits, or tax deductions. Such strategies would encourage less centralization and less loss of parental influence.

James (1986) came to remarkably similar conclusions in a study of school finance and control in the Netherlands. There private schools have been almost wholly supported by public funds for most of this century. At the primary level, 31 percent of the children are enrolled in public schools, 28 percent in Protestant schools, 38 percent in Catholic schools, and 3 percent in other schools (p. 118). At the secondary level, the corresponding percentages are 28 percent, 27 percent, 39 percent, and 6 percent.

Families are free to choose the school or schools their children attend. Teachers are prorated to schools on the basis of school enrollments.

Teacher salaries in all schools are fully paid by the central government. Private schools may supplement neither the staffing levels nor teacher salaries. Buildings are provided by municipal governments for both public and private schools. A small fund for operating expenses is allocated to each school, public or private. The school may use this fund according to its discretion for such items as maintenance, cleaning, heating, libraries, and instructional supplies. Private schools have severely limited rights to supplement the fund with student fees. Public schools do not have such rights. James comments, "Both society in choosing its system, and private schools, in choosing where they fit into the system, would then face a trade-off between autonomy and more funds" (p. 122).

James (1986) concluded that private schools sacrifice their individuality when they accept public support:

> Cultural heterogeneity often generates a demand for private education and for government subsidies to help cover the associated costs. The subsidies facilitate private sector growth, but they also allow government to impose regulations, particularly over inputs and other behavioral characteristics. Thus, the initial demand for differentiation, if successful, sets in motion forces which make the private sector quasi-governmental; subsidized private sectors are very much like public sectors. If we [in the United States] institute a voucher scheme or other privatization policies, we may end up with a private sector which is larger but less distinctive than the one we have now. (p. 135)

Hill (1993) contended that you cannot have an unregulated system that uses public money. The reason that public money is spent on education is to satisfy a public interest in ensuring a minimum school experience for all children. Public interest will drive legislatures to regulate schools that accept public funds—even private schools accepting vouchers. Hill, an advocate of Catholic schools, warns Catholic audiences that if they want to have Catholic schools, they should not take public money. "In the long run, schools in a publicly funded choice system will be public because they'll be regulated" (p. 248).

Hirschoff (1986), after a thorough review of the legal structure of schooling in the United States, found that a significant degree of choice already exists. She cautioned that the expansion of family choice brought by increased public funding of private schools has to be weighed against the increased governmental regulation that is sure to follow and the resultant loss of flexibility. She closed her analysis with the observation: "Particularly with regard to fiscal change, then, one might conclude that the present legal structure of the mixed system—with perhaps minor adjustments—maximizes parental choice more than would the major changes on which public discussion usually focuses" (p. 52).

CURRENT CHOICE POLICIES AND PRACTICE

Whereas public schools are financed through taxation and are tuition free, private schools depend primarily upon tuition, donations, and volunteer or low-priced labor. Some public assistance is provided to students enrolled in private schools. To a small degree this makes family choice possible in that sector. Many states provide public support of transportation, health services, testing and remedial services, and textbooks to children enrolled in private schools. In addition, governments provide assistance to nonprofit private schools, sectarian and independent alike, through exemption from property taxation (see Chapter 6). As an incentive to private contributors, the contributors may deduct donations to nonprofit private schools from their taxable income.

Traditionally, parents have been able to choose between free public and tuition-supported private schools. But even this option was seriously challenged during the 1920s. In 1925, the United

States Supreme Court in its landmark decision in *Pierce* v. *Society of Sisters* (1925) ruled that the Constitution protected the right of private schools to exist as an alternative to public schools. In so doing, the Court recognized parental rights to direct the education and upbringing of their own children, foreclosing the possibility of a public monopoly. On the other hand, *Pierce* and other decisions permit reasonable regulation of private schooling by government without requiring public subsidization of the choice of private schooling.

Without subsidization, schooling costs can become very expensive. They force most parents out of the private school market. In the absence of public support, it is primarily religious groups that have the financial capacity, organization, and motivation to sponsor nongovernment schooling that is a feasible option for many families. Table 3.7 in Chapter 3 shows that 11 percent of elementary and secondary pupils attend private schools. Table 3.8 indicates that of those enrolled in private schools, 88 percent attend religiously affiliated schools and 48 percent attend Roman Catholic schools. The percentages in private schools and the percentages in religiously affiliated schools have remained quite stable over the years. But the nature of religious affiliation is rapidly changing from being almost exclusively Catholic to a heterogeneous mixture of denominations.

At the federal level, until 1965, the issue of aid to private schools—or the lack of it—often led to the defeat of proposals for aid for public schools. The Elementary and Secondary Education Act (ESEA) was the first federal program that required federally funded services to be provided to elementary and secondary private school children. Compromise was reached among contending interest groups over a child-benefit approach to federal aid that focused on educationally disadvantaged children wherever they were enrolled. Services that were provided to children enrolled in private schools on site remained under public control and supervision. Subsequently, assurances were extended to make services purchased through federal funds equitably available to private school students

for vocational education, bilingual education, education of children with disabilities, and instructional and library materials. It was estimated that in 1980 about 25 percent of school districts provided services to students in private schools that had less than 4 percent of total private school enrollments (Jung, 1982). Enactment of the Education Consolidation and Improvement Act in 1981 brought substantially greater support for programs serving private school children. Recent court decisions, however, have placed severe constraints on the manner in which such services may be delivered to children attending private schools (*Aguilar* v. *Felton*, 1985; *Pulido* v. *Cavazos*, 1989). Now services must be provided at public sites, including publicly owned portable classrooms adjacent to private schools. This, in turn, has affected the number being served.

Within the public sector, there is also a degree of choice. The most widespread choice is selection of courses at the high school level. Here choice is so extensive that Powell, Farrar, and Cohen (1985) likened the high school curriculum to the availability of goods and services in a shopping mall.

Choice through Selecting Place of Residence

The most common means of school choice in the public sector is the selection of a residence. Tiebout (1956) presented a theory for the existence of local governments. He argued that they permit people with similar tastes for public services to cluster together within jurisdictions. Variety in local government offers households arrays of public services that are significantly different in type and quality. Choice of residence becomes equivalent to consumer choice in the market. It becomes a middle ground between a free market and centralized governmental control. This appears to be what has happened with respect to educational services. In metropolitan areas persons with high demands for educational services cluster in specific suburbs—usually affluent. Persons with low demands or who cannot afford high levels of service cluster in central cities and other suburbs—usually blue-collar.

In a random survey of the attitudes of Minnesota residents about educational choice, Darling-Hammond and Kirby (1988) found impressive evidence of the Tiebout effect. Households that had considered the quality of public schools in deciding where to live were less likely to express interest in private schools even with governmental subsidies. They believed that their educational needs were already well served by the public schools of the communities they had selected. Murnane (1986) also pointed to compelling evidence that families pay premiums for housing in school districts with reputations for good schools.

Kutner, Sherman, and Williams (1986) reported on a survey of a national random sample of approximately 1,200 households with school-age children. About half of the parents indicated that the public schools their children would attend influenced their choice of a place to live; 18 percent said that it was the most important factor in their choice of residence.

The Balkanization of local government and of school districts in particular does advance libertarian objectives to a limited extent. But it also creates serious inequities and impedes the realization of fraternal objectives. This was illustrated in Table 3.3 using data drawn from the New York City metropolitan area. Balkanization works to the advantage of a rich or upper-middle-class household because such a household has sufficient resources to choose a community whose array of services includes those it most desires. These households have sufficient resources that if the community provides additional services to which they are indifferent this is not an insurmountable economic barrier to living there. This is not the case with poor households. Those with a strong desire for education might be able to afford a high level of service by sacrificing in other areas, such as housing and transportation. But if educational services depend on residence, this is not possible because high levels of educational services usually go together with high housing costs and the lack of public transportation. This may account for the

strong interest in choice plans by racial and ethnic minorities (Elam & Gallup, 1989).

Other Forms of Public School Choice

More than half the states have passed laws permitting other forms of public school choice, and other states are considering such laws (Elam & Rose, 1995). For many years, students in Vermont school districts that do not operate high schools have been able to choose among public and nonsectarian private schools at public expense. In 1987, Minnesota established the first statewide plan permitting parents to enroll their children in virtually any public school district they choose (Nathan, 1989; OECD, 1994; Pearson, 1989). Since then, numerous other state legislatures have adopted some form of public school choice as statewide policy (Rothstein, 1993). For over a quarter of a century, Massachusetts has encouraged and financed interdistrict transfer of pupils to improve racial balance (Glenn, 1986). In 1991, the state broadened its choice policy by enacting open enrollment legislation permitting all schoolchildren to attend public schools outside their home districts. Similarly, Saint Louis city and county school districts voluntarily exchange students to improve racial balance as part of a court-ordered desegregation plan.

A number of large cities have developed open enrollment plans within their districts, frequently to improve racial and ethnic balance in schools. For generations, New York City has operated a variety of specialty schools, including the prestigious Bronx High School of Science, that draw their students from throughout the city. The Boston Latin School dates to Colonial times. Boston also operates a universal form of public school enrollment choice (OECD, 1994) as an alternative to the forced busing imposed by the courts to remedy racial imbalances in the district. The Boston plan includes decentralized decision making and school-based management. At least a dozen other large cities have used a variety of choice plans to end racial segregation. One of the most successful has been the magnet school program in Buffalo.

Elmore (1988) estimated that about one-third of big-city school districts offer school choice in the form of magnet or specialty schools.

District Four in New York City's East Harlem has received much attention in recent years for the academic success of its students and its open enrollment policies (Fliegel & MacGuire, 1993; Meier, 1995). The district serves a generally poor population with 80 percent of its 14,000 students eligible for free or reduced lunch. Ninety-five percent of its students are from minority populations with Hispanics constituting the majority of the enrollment. The district's achievements in conventional terms are not as impressive in recent years as they were ten years ago, but continue to surpass those of similar low-income districts (Meier, 1995). The accomplishments in District Four cannot be attributed to choice alone, as was noted in a previous section. Meier (1995) observed that choice was enacted as a means of attracting pupils to educational innovations generated by teachers and that it was the innovations that were directly responsible for the achievement gains.

Public Opinion about School Choice

The annual Gallup polls of the public's attitudes toward schools, sponsored by Phi Delta Kappa, have since 1989 tracked the issue of giving parents the choice of the public schools their children attend regardless of where they live. Sentiment has consistently favored this form of choice. The support has grown from 60 percent in favor in 1989 to 69 percent in favor in 1995 (Elam & Rose, 1995). The support by parents with children in public school was 69 percent and by parents with children in private schools was 78 percent. The 1989 report broke the responses down by ethnic and age groups (Elam & Gallup, 1989). Support at that time was stronger among nonwhites: 67 percent, than among whites: 59 percent. It was stronger among younger persons than older persons: 67 percent of the 18–29 age group, 64 percent of those between 30 and 49, and 51 percent of those over 50. Regionally, support for choice was least in the East, where it was

53 percent, and strongest in the West, where it was 64 percent.

Opinion about public support of choice involving public, private, and religious schools was a different matter, however (Elam & Rose, 1995). Although opposition to the proposition is dropping, 65 percent of the respondents in 1995 were opposed compared with 74 percent in 1993. Seventy-three percent believe that private schools accepting government funds should be accountable to public authorities. In the 1994 poll, 54 percent of the population saw charter schools as a good thing for education and 39 percent saw them as a bad thing (Elam, Rose, & Gallop, 1994). Those aged between eighteen and twenty-nine supported charter schools by a margin of more than two to one; the majority of those over fifty opposed them.

THE NEED FOR SYSTEMIC REFORM

Now that we have examined the evidence, we can see that neither school-based decision making (SBDM) nor family choice enables schools to educate children more effectively than the current system. Neither policy is directly linked to significant improvement in scholastic achievement. But both facilitate practices that are so linked. Both policies, however, may be part of a multifaceted solution. The basic question remains: How can society provide good schools universally?

At the heart of the debate over choice and SBDM is the need to satisfy societal interests in education while permitting choice in those areas that confer private benefits and are of particular interest to families. Meier (1995) observed that Americans have long supported two levels of schooling:

> Whether schools are public or private, the social class of the students has been and continues to be the single most significant factor in determining how a school works and the intellectual values it promotes. The higher the student body's economic status, the meatier

the curriculum, the more open-ended the discussion, the less rote and rigid the pedagogy, the more respectful the tone, the more rigorous the expectation, the greater the staff autonomy. . . . What we need are strategies for giving to everyone what the rich always valued. The rich, after all, have had both good public schools and good private schools. The good public ones looked a lot like the good private ones. (pp. 97–98)

Bureaucratization of public schools and Balkanization of communities seem to be the greatest barriers to school reform. SBDM may at least diminish the power of the center by placing authority over the design and implementation of learning systems in the hands of practicing professionals. This frees practicing professionals to tailor programs to the needs and interests of their student clients, if they so desire, and if parents wish to have their children exposed to the innovations designed by teachers. This second *if* makes parental choice of schools necessary to balance parental interest against professional expertise (Hill, 1993):

Once you create good schools, choice is inevitable. A good school has a definite purpose. Staff has the opportunity to collaborate on that purpose. A good school can sustain itself by the way it selects and socializes staff. It can make demands on students, telling them what they have to do in order to stay in school. A school can't be good if it has to satisfy all demands. It can say from the beginning what demands it will satisfy. A public school system as a whole can satisfy all demands, but no one school can do so.

Likewise, good schools can't be constrained by staff members who say, "I'm not doing it your way. I'm a senior teacher. You can't boot me out, and I'll be damned if I'll change the way I teach." Where you have good schools, questions of fit, not just competence, have to be considered in the assignment of staff. (p. 249).

A good school has a coherent and sharply defined curriculum, although the focus may differ among schools. When schools are different, choice becomes a necessity because both teachers and students in a given school must fit and subscribe to its focus. Choice and SBDM policies alone do not create good schools. However, good schools are more likely to develop in a climate of SBDM and choice.

But actually, under policies of SBDM and choice, most schools are likely to remain as they are, because of professional inertia and parental disinterest. Choice will work only if parents take full advantage of their new freedoms. Some parents will make good use of these new opportunities, but many others will not. Unfortunately, the parents of children with the greatest need for improved education would experience the greatest difficulty in taking advantage of a choice policy. A choice policy would do little to improve the inequalities of the current system and could lead to even worse inequalities. To provide equity in a choice system, government intervention is required to provide mechanisms for informing and guiding parents who desire—or need—assistance in making their choices. Regulation of school admissions would also be necessary to insure that oversubscribed schools do not use socially discriminatory criteria when selecting students. The CSPP regulated voucher model we discussed is one way to do this. To protect schools from professional inertia—or incompetence—external standards are also needed in the form of curricular guides and uniform assessments (Bauch, 1989; Cookson, 1992; Elmore, 1990; Glenn, 1990; Lee, Croninger, & Smith, 1994; Levin, 1990; OECD, 1994).

In other words, policies of SBDM and choice, by themselves, are unlikely to produce the kind of improvement in student achievement that is desired. They are very important elements in a strategy of systemic reform, however. The strategy should also include governmental oversight and regulation of information systems supporting parental choice, pupil selection procedures used by schools, curricular guidelines, and uniform assessment and reporting procedures.

SUMMARY

One of the most controversial issues on the school reform agenda is family choice of schooling. In this chapter, we have looked at the implications for school finance policy of possible mechanisms for enhancing choice. We considered choice within the public sector, education vouchers, tax credits, and tax deductions. The latter three strategies extend public funding to private schools. Mechanisms for choice among public schools include magnet schools and open enrollment plans. Drawing upon international studies, we looked at the probable loss of flexibility and diversity in the private school sector that would result from public regulation. Regulation would in all likelihood accompany funding of private schools. We considered potential constitutional barriers to the use of tax monies in support of religiously affiliated schools in light of the changing legal interpretations of the issue initiated by the new conservative majority controlling the United States Supreme Court. We concluded that policies of SBDM and school choice are not sufficient to bring about the degree of educational reform needed, especially in our worst schools. They can be highly important elements, however, in an overall strategy of systemic reform.

This chapter concludes our evaluation of possible changes in the governance structure of education by inducing market-like forces into making decisions about matters related to education. Chapter 16 and 17 look at more micro issues in the quest for improving efficiency in the use of resources in education. The next chapter focuses on teacher remuneration strategies, and Chapter 17 addresses the mix of labor and technology used in schooling and explores strategies for improving both.

ACTIVITIES

1. Within the context of the decision matrix presented in Figure 1.7, what educational decisions might best be placed with parents? What safeguards need to be implemented to protect legitimate social and professional interests? Provide rationales for your responses.
2. If parents are free to choose the schools their children attend, how might their interests best be represented in the designing of educational programs (assuming school-based decision making)?
3. Do you believe that education vouchers issued directly to parents would violate the prohibitions of the First Amendment of the United States Constitution against the establishment of religion if some parents chose to enroll their children in religiously affiliated schools? Why?
4. Examine the provisions of the laws of a state or another nation governing church-state relationships. Compare them to the provisions in the United States Constitution. In what ways are the provisions of this state or nation more or less restrictive with respect to making public monies available to support children attending religiously affiliated schools? What arrangements might be advanced to modify a specific provision, or court interpretation of constitutional language, to either advance or restrict family choice of schooling?
5. Discuss the advantages and disadvantages of alternative arrangements for expanding diversity through these approaches:
   - Free publicly financed and operated schools with direct aid to private schools prohibited, but allowing supporting services that benefit children attending private schools
   - Education vouchers, with options among public and private schools
   - Tax deductions for tuition and other expenses incurred in public and private education
   - Tax credits that rebate the cost of tuition up to a specified amount
   - Direct aid to private schools, for example, the Netherlands' plan
   - Open enrollment among public schools without public aid for private schools
6. Design a voucher scheme that would enhance family choice of schools while protecting equity considerations.

REFERENCES

Adler, M. (1993). An alternative approach to parental choice. *NCE Briefing No. 13*. London, England: The National Commission on Education.

Adler, M., Petch, A., & Tweedie, J. (1989). *Parental choice and educational policy*. Edinburgh, Scotland: Edinburgh University Press.

Aguilar v. *Felton*. 473 U.S. 402 (1985).

Ambler, J. S. (1994). Who benefits from educational choice? Some evidence from Europe. *Journal of Policy Analysis and Management, 13,* 454–476.

Anthony, P. (1987). Public monies for private schools: The Supreme Court's changing approach. *Journal of Education Finance, 12,* 592–605.

Ball, S. J., Bode, R., & Gars, S. (1992). *Circuits of schooling: A sociological exploration of parental choice of school in social class contexts*. London, England: Centre for Educational Studies, King's College.

Bauch, P. A. (1989). Can poor parents make wise educational choices? In W. L. Boyd & J. G. Cibulka (Eds.), *Private schools and public policy: International perspectives* (pp. 285–314). Philadelphia: Falmer.

Bauch, P. A., & Goldring, E. B. (1995). Parent involvement and school responsiveness: Facilitating the home-school connection in schools of choice. *Educational Evaluation and Policy Analysis, 17,* 1–21.

Bauch, P.A., & Small, T. W. (1986). *Parents' reasons for school choice in four inner-city Catholic high schools: Their relationship to education, income, and ethnicity*. Paper presented at the annual meeting of the American Educational Research Association.

Bryk, A. S., Lee, V. E., & Smith, J. L. (1990). High school organization and its effects on teachers and students: An interpretive summary of the research. In W. H. Clune & J. F. Witte (Eds.), *Choice and control in American education: Volume 1—The theory of choice and control in education* (pp. 135–226). Philadelphia: Falmer.

Chubb, J. E. (1990). Political institutions and school organization. In W. H. Clune & J. F. Witte (Eds.), *Choice and control in American education: Volume 1—The theory of choice and control in education* (pp. 227–234). Philadelphia: Falmer.

Chubb, J. E., & Moe, T. M. (1990). *Politics, markets, and America's schools*. Washington, DC: Brookings Institution.

Cibulka, J. G. (1989). Rationales for private schools: A commentary. In W. L. Boyd & J. G. Cibulka (Eds.), *Private schools and public policy: International perspectives*. Philadelphia: Falmer.

Cohen, D. K. (1990). Governance and instruction: The promise of decentralization and choice. In W. H. Clune & J. F. Witte (Eds.), *Choice and control in American education: Volume 1—The theory of choice and control in education* (pp. 337–386). Philadelphia: Falmer.

Coleman, J. S. (1990). Choice, community, and future schools. In W. H. Clune & J. F. Witte (Eds.), *Choice and control in American education: Volume 1—The theory of choice and control in education* (pp. ix–xxii). Philadelphia: Falmer.

Coleman, J. S., & Hoffer, T. (1987). *Public and private high schools: The impact of communities*. New York: Basic Books.

Cookson, P. W., Jr. (1992). Introduction. *Educational Policy, 6,* 99–104.

Coons, J. E., & Sugarman, S. D. (1978). *Education by choice: The case for family control*. Berkeley: University of California Press.

CSPP (Center for the Study of Public Policy). (1970). *Education vouchers: A report on financing education by grants to parents*. Cambridge, MA: The Center.

Darling-Hammond, L., & Kirby, S. N. (1988). Public policy and private choice: The case of Minnesota. In T. James & H. M. Levin (Eds.), *Comparing public and private schools: Volume 1, Institutions and organizations* (pp. 243–267). New York: Falmer Press.

Doyle, D. P. (1992). The challenge, the opportunity. *Phi Delta Kappan, 73,* 512–520.

Elam, S. M., & Gallup, A. M. (1989). The 21st annual Gallup poll of the public's attitudes toward the public schools. *Phi Delta Kappan, 71* (1), 41–54.

Elam, S. M., & Rose, L. C. (1995). The 27th annual Phi Delta Kappa Gallup poll of the public's attitude toward the public schools. *Phi Delta Kappan, 77,* 41–56.

Elam, S. M., Rose, L. C., & Gallup, A. M. (1994). The 26th annual Phi Delta Kappa Gallup poll of the public's attitude toward the public schools. *Phi Delta Kappan, 76,* 41–56.

Elmore, R. F. (1988). Choice in public education. In W. L. Boyd & C. T. Kerchner (Eds.), *The politics of excellence and choice in education* (pp. 79–98). New York: Falmer Press.

Elmore, R. F. (1990). Choice as an instrument of public policy: Evidence from education and health care. In W. H. Clune & J. F. Witte (Eds.), *Choice and control in American education: Volume 1—The theory of choice and control in education* (pp. ix–xxii). Philadelphia: Falmer.

Erickson, D. A. (1986). Choice and private schools. In D. C. Levy (Ed.), *Private education: Studies in choice and public policy* (pp. 57–81). New York: Oxford University Press.

Fine, M. (1993). Democratizing choice: Reinventing, not retreating from, public education. In E. Rasell & R. Rothstein (Eds.), *School choice: Examining the evidence* (pp. 269–300). Washington, DC: Economic Policy Institute.

Fliegel, S., & MacGuire, J. (1993). *Miracle in East Harlem: The fight for choice in public education.* New York: Times Books, Random House.

Fossey, R. (1994). Open enrollment in Massachusetts: Why families choose. *Educational Evaluation and Policy Analysis, 16,* 320–334.

Friedman, M. (1962). *Capitalism and freedom.* Chicago: University of Chicago Press.

Friedman, M., & Friedman, R. (1980). *Free to choose: A personal statement.* New York: Avon.

Glenn, C. L. (1986). The Massachusetts experience with public school choice. *Time for results: The governors' 1991 report on education, Supporting works, Task Force on Parent Involvement and Choice.* Washington, DC: National Governors' Association.

Glenn, C. L. (1990). Parent choice: A state perspective. In W. H. Clune & J. F. Witte (Eds.), *Choice and control in American education: Volume 1—The theory of choice and control in education* (pp. ix–xxii). Philadelphia: Falmer.

Guthrie, J. W., Garms, W. I., & Pierce, L. C. (1988). *School finance and education policy: Expanding educational efficiency, equity, and choice.* Englewood Cliffs, NJ: Prentice-Hall.

Hill, P. (1993). Comments and general discussion. In E. Rasell & R. Rothstein (Eds.), *School choice: Examining the evidence* (pp. 247–249). Washington, DC: Economic Policy Institute.

Hirschoff, M. U. (1986). Public policy toward private schools: A focus on parental choice. In D. C. Levy (Ed.), *Private education: Studies in choice and public policy* (pp. 33–56). New York: Oxford University Press.

James, E. (1986). Public subsidies for private and public education: The Dutch case. In D. C. Levy (Ed.), *Private education: Studies in choice and public policy* (pp. 113–137). New York: Oxford University Press.

Jung, R. (1982). *Nonpublic school students in Title I ESEA programs; A question of "equal" services.* McLean, VA: Advanced Technology.

Kutner, M. A., Sherman, J. D., & Williams, M. F. (1986). Federal policies for public schools. In D. C. Levy (Ed.), *Private education: Studies in choice and public policy* (pp. 57–81). New York: Oxford University Press.

Lee, V. E., Croninger, R. G., & Smith, J. B. (1994). Parental choice of schools and social stratification in education: The paradox of Detroit. *Educational Evaluation and Policy Analysis, 16,* 434–457.

Lemon v. *Kurtzman,* 403 U.S. 602 (1970).

Levin, H. M. (1990). The theory of choice applied to education. In W. H. Clune & J. F. Witte (Eds.), *Choice and control in American education: Volume 1— The theory of choice and control in education* (pp. ix–xxii). Philadelphia: Falmer.

Levitt v. *Committee for Public Education and Religious Liberty,* 413 U.S. 472 (1973).

Martinez, V., Thomas, K., & Kemerer, F. R. (1994). Who chooses and why: A look at five school choice plans. *Phi Delta Kappan, 75,* 678–681.

Meier, D. (1995). *The power of their ideas: Lessons for America from a small school in Harlem.* Boston: Beacon Press.

Mueller v. *Allen,* 463 U.S. 388 (1983).

Murnane, R. J. (1986). Comparisons of private and public schools: The critical role of regulations. In D. C. Levy (Ed.), *Private education: Studies in choice and public policy* (pp. 138–152). New York: Oxford University Press.

Nathan, J. (1989). Helping all children, empowering all educators: Another view of school choice. *Phi Delta Kappan, 71,* 304–307.

OECD (Organization for Economic Cooperation and Development). (1994). *School: A matter of choice.* Paris: OECD.

Pearson, J. (1989). Myths of choice: The governor's new clothes? *Phi Delta Kappan, 70,* 821–823.

Pierce v. *Society of Sisters,* 268 U.S. 510 (1925).

Powell, A. G., Farrar, E., & Cohen, D. K. (1985). *The shopping mall high school: Winners and losers in the educational marketplace.* Boston: Houghton Mifflin.

Pulido v. *Cavazos,* 728 F. Supp. 574 (1989).

Rothstein, R. (1993). Introduction. In E. Rasell & R. Rothstein (Eds.), *School choice: Examining the evidence* (pp. 1–25). Washington, DC: Economic Policy Institute.

Slaughter, D., & Schneider, B. (1986). *Newcomers: Blacks in private schools. Final report to the National Institute of Education. Volumes I & II.* (Contract No. NIE-G-82-0040). Northwestern University, ERIC Documents ED 274 768 & ED274 769.

Tiebout, C. M. (1956). A pure theory of local expenditures. *Journal of Political Economy, 64* (5), 416–424.

Walberg, H. J. (1993). Comments and general discussion. In E. Rasell & R. Rothstein (Eds.), *School choice: Examining the evidence* (pp. 301–303). Washington, DC: Economic Policy Institute.

Willms, J. D., & Echols, F. H. (1993). The Scottish experience of parental school choice. In E. Rasell & R. Rothstein (Eds.), *School choice: Examining the evidence* (pp. 49–68). Washington, DC: Economic Policy Institute.

Witte, J. F. (1993). The Milwaukee parental choice program. In E. Rasell & R. Rothstein (Eds.), *School choice: Examining the evidence* (pp. 49–68). Washington, DC: Economic Policy Institute.

Yanofsky, S. M., & Young, L. (1992). A successful parents' choice program. *Phi Delta Kappan, 73,* 476–479.

Zhang, Z. (1995). *A comparative study of parental attitudes towards public and parochial schools.* Unpublished doctoral dissertation, State University of New York at Buffalo.

CHAPTER 16

Reforms to Improve Teacher Quality and Remuneration

Primary Issues Explored in This Chapter:

- *The labor market:* How do private and public sectors differ with respect to the ways that economic and social considerations influence people's movement among job markets and influence the wages or salaries paid?
- *Teacher demand and supply:* What social and economic factors affect the need for additional teachers or influence people's decisions to enter and continue in the profession?

- *Strengthening teacher quality:* Do some policy options offer the potential for increasing the supply of highly capable teachers?
- *Compensating teachers:* What are the underlying premises of the single salary schedule? Are there strategies to strengthen the relationship between remuneration, responsibilities, and performance?

Because labor is the most critical and the most costly resource for education, the recent educational reform movement has paid much attention to strategies to improve personnel quality and remuneration. Discussions of efficiency in education quickly focus on how many teachers, administrators, and other support staff are employed and their responsibilities. The public desires improvements in student performance at the same or lower cost of instruction. Educators desire additional investments in personnel. They believe that fair compensation in line with that of other professions will attract and retain excellent classroom teachers. Those who advance reform proposals realize that efforts to restructure other aspects of schools as

organizations will be less effective if personnel policies are not altered (Firestone, 1994).

The importance of labor in the educational production function (see Chapter 13) and the large commitment of resources to purchase personnel services warrant our expanded discussion of personnel issues in this chapter and the next. We begin by discussing the broader labor market and factors that influence demand and supply for workers generally and for teachers specifically. We then discuss reforms that are designed to increase the supply of teachers to satisfy schools' demands for capable personnel. These reforms may alter compensation by linking salaries with teachers' responsibilities and performance measures.

THE LABOR MARKET FOR TEACHERS' SERVICES

We introduced the concepts of supply and demand (Chapter 1) in the context of the flow of resources between households and producers in a market-oriented society. Households purchase products and offer labor. Businesses hire workers for production processes. This creates the supply-and-demand sides of product and labor markets. In this section, we differentiate the teacher labor market from the operation of the larger economy. We discuss the conditions of demand and supply that affect the applicant pool for teaching positions.

The Private Sector Labor Market

Conditions of supply and demand in a free-market economy influence the level at which equilibrium is reached for prices of goods and services (see Figure 1.2). The prevailing wage for labor is the amount of money necessary to ensure that there are enough qualified applicants (supply) for the available jobs (demand). Wage differentials move workers to occupations in which the demand for labor is the greatest and away from those occupations where the demand is the least (Butler, 1963). Differentials exist among job assignments within a given enterprise, among different business firms within a given industry, and among the many industries employing people of the same occupation.

Setting wages in the private sector assumes that consumers exercise free choice among available products and that employers exercise choice among similarly skilled laborers. Workers are presumed to be free and willing to move among jobs and geographic locations in response to conditions of labor surplus and shortages. In reality, such a perfect free-market economy does not exist. Workers are not uniform in motivation, attitudes, ability, and mobility, nor do they have information about all the alternatives in their labor market choices (Kreps, Somers, & Perlman, 1974). In our mixed economy, the government intervenes in the marketplace by setting minimum wages and specifying such benefits as social security and unemployment

insurance. The public sector also influences wages in the private sector by its ability to attract labor into public employment. The private sector similarly influences the wages that must be paid to attract and retain public sector workers.

Personal and economic considerations influence the supply of labor that households are willing to provide to private and public sector employers. The desire for income is balanced with individual and family decisions about alternative uses of their talents. Alternatives may include working within the household, obtaining additional education, and volunteering time and effort in any number of pursuits. Employers decide how much compensation to offer and the working conditions. They use these monetary and nonmonetary benefits to entice people to enter the workforce and to prepare for particular occupations. Not all individuals who are willing and able to perform a given job, however, find satisfactory employment. A ready supply of willing workers does not elicit a demand for their services on the part of employers. Rather, the demand for workers with particular skills depends on the public's consumption of related goods and services and on opportunities to alter the mix of labor and capital required in production processes. The goal of maximizing profits encourages private sector businesses to increase workers' productivity and to substitute capital for labor in production processes.

These characteristics of the private sector labor market do not accurately describe the market that exists for teachers' services.

The Labor Market for Teachers

Teachers and other certified personnel constitute a labor market that operates somewhat differently from the larger economy, but not independently. Public schools produce a service that is not marketed at a price to their clients. It is difficult to determine how much an individual teacher or administrator contributes to this product. Legislatures and school boards determine compensation levels and working conditions through processes of political compromise. In most states teachers' unions influence salary models and working conditions through collective bargaining.

State policies often restrict teachers' mobility and the supply of potential school employees. Licensure or certification requirements define the minimum qualifications needed to enter the profession. But short-term exceptions are readily granted. In addition, state-determined minimum salary schedules may influence levels of compensation offered teachers. The salaries and benefits may deter some candidates from seeking positions. This is particularly true when there are suitable employment opportunities in other fields offering relatively higher wages. Tenure statutes and state retirement systems, as well as personal and family preferences, restrict teachers' ability to respond to changes in labor markets.

Changes in social attitudes and behaviors further influence supply conditions. These include the exodus of women and minorities from teaching to other professions during the past several decades. The number of teachers seeking employment varies greatly among subject fields and geographic areas. Furthermore, social and economic factors influence the quality of teacher candidates. This assumes that higher-ability teachers are more responsive to changes in the wages paid in various types of employment (Thangaraj, 1985).

The demand for teachers also differs from free-market assumptions. In many states and labor markets within states, there is not a large number of buyers (school systems) demanding teachers' services. There may be less competition among public and private schools, or between schools and other sectors of society, than in other labor markets. For these reasons, teachers' salaries are less responsive to market conditions than are wages paid to other workers. The teacher labor market approaches that described by Fleisher and Kniesner (1980) as a *monopsony*. A monopsony is a market in which there is one effective demander of labor. In such restricted markets, wages tend to be lower than they might be in competitive marketplaces. However, there are some salary differentials among districts, particularly as wealthy districts compete for excellent teachers. Policies that permit greater student choice and mobility among public schools, and perhaps between public and private schools (see Chapter 15), may induce larger wage differentials in the future. Schools in competitive markets may find it necessary to improve compensation packages to attract high-quality teachers (e.g., those having the National Board certificates discussed later) in other schools. Schools may then find salary enhancements and improved working conditions essential to retain such teachers.

The public sector labor market does not operate in isolation from the broader labor market. There is competition for employees between the two sectors of the economy. The supply curve in Figure 1.2 suggests that as salaries increase, more individuals prepare for careers in teaching and more people in the reserve pool of certified teachers reenter the profession. Once this larger supply meets the demand, salaries stabilize at a new equilibrium level. The demand curve suggests that as society requires additional teachers to serve more children, reduce class size, or expand offerings, the equilibrium price rises to attract people from other careers (assuming supply remains the same). The converse is also true. Lower salaries are possible when demand is lower.

When the supply of teachers differs from demand, instabilities in the marketplace result in shortages and surpluses. The labor market is slow to respond to these changes. This is because it takes a long time for the demand for teachers in particular subject fields to increase, for individuals to select different college majors, and for new entrants to the profession to graduate. Periods of high teacher demand, such as that existing in the 1950s, 1960s, and 1990s, lead to aggressive recruitment and relatively higher salaries. Eventually there is an oversupply. This occurred in the 1970s, when enrollments rapidly declined. Salaries stabilize or decrease in terms of purchasing power.

Predicting supply and demand in the teacher labor market is complex, given difficulties such as those identified by Fox (1988). First, demand depends not only on assumptions about pupils to be served but also on policy decisions regarding class size and the number of supplementary teachers needed. For example, growth in birthrates, particularly in low-income households, and the expansion of public school offerings for preschool children stimulate demand for teachers.

Second, newly certified or licensed people do not necessarily begin their teaching careers immediately, nor do they remain in classrooms until retirement. It is therefore more difficult to determine the supply of educators than for another professions. The number of teacher candidates depends on the number of college students who prepare to teach and the number in the reserve pool of people who are qualified to teach but are not actively seeking a teaching position. The number enrolled in teacher preparation programs fell steadily between the early 1970s and the mid 1980s along with a lower demand for teachers. The demand for teachers increased in the 1990s. Then somewhat improved financial incentives and working conditions, along with a generally slowed economy that diminished other employment opportunities in many regions of the nation, positively influenced the teacher supply (NCES, 1992, p. 6).

Third, definitions of teacher quality influence projections. It is desirable to attract and retain a teaching force of sufficient quantity and quality. But there is little agreement about defining *sufficient*. An inadequate supply of quality teachers is reflected in the percentage assigned to teach classes outside their area of expertise and in analyses of their academic abilities. Overall in 1987–1988, 23 percent of all teachers taught in fields in which they did not major. This inadequacy is more pronounced in some fields. Over 40 percent of teachers in bilingual education, computer science, and mathematics did not have these college majors (Bobbitt & McMillen, 1990). A number of researchers have found that prospective teachers score lower on tests of academic ability than individuals preparing for other professions. Furthermore, those who abandoned the profession were often the academically most able (Fox, 1984; Murnane, Singer, Willet, Kemple, & Olsen, 1991; Sykes, 1983; Vance & Schlechty, 1982).

Reforms examined in this chapter—including changes in states' statutes governing licensure, in teacher preparation programs, and in working conditions and remuneration strategies—are designed to alter these conditions and thus to improve the supply of qualified candidates to meet schools' needs and improve pupil performance. Clearly, people's decisions to seek employment in public education are shaped by a number of factors. One of them is the positions available. We examine this demand for teachers next.

The Demand for Teachers and Support Personnel

The demand for classroom teachers and personnel who support instruction may be stated simply in terms of the number of children enrolled. However, districts' employment requirements are greatly influenced by decisions to expand offerings and reduce class size. We discuss trends in teacher employment in relation to all district personnel. Then we discuss changes in pupil : teacher ratios and pupils' educational needs as influences on the demand for teachers.

Employment of Instructional and Noninstructional Personnel.   Table 16.1 gives the number of full-time-equivalent (FTE) teachers and support personnel employed in public education between 1959 and 1993. The growing demand for educators over these years more than doubled the total number employed, from 2.1 million in the 1959–1960 school year to 4.8 million in the fall of 1993. There has been steady growth in the number of classroom teachers. This is evidenced in the 79 percent increase from about 1.4 million to 2.5 million teachers over these decades. However, there was a more substantial demand for support personnel in schools and central offices. The number of personnel other than classroom teachers expanded from 736,000 in 1959–1960 to 2.4 million in 1993. This was a 226 percent increase.

The number of school employees grew rapidly during the 1960s. There was a 60.9 percent increase, from 2.1 million to 3.4 million employees. At this time student enrollments also expanded. Even though there was a decline in the number of students enrolled in public schools during the 1970s (from 46.6 million in 1971 to a low of 39.3 in 1983; see Table 3.7), there was not a commensurate decline in the number of employees. Policies at the federal, state, and local levels resulted in programs to meet the educational needs of disadvantaged and disabled students. These policies permitted a reduction in the ratio of pupils to teachers. They also continued to create demands for additional personnel. In fact, there was a 24.0 percent increase during the 1970s, from 3.4 million to 4.2 million employees. The rate of growth slowed in the 1980s. But there was still a 15.2 percent increase in employees between 1980 and 1993. Some of this increase reflects the increase in student enrollments (from 40.9 million in 1980 to

42.7 million in 1992). The demand for teachers and support personnel is likely to continue to grow in the future, because enrollments are projected to increase to 49.7 million in 2005 (see Table 3.7).

The demand for support personnel in relation to classroom teachers is evident in the percentage of all employees in various groups (see Table 16.1). The percentage of employees who were classroom teachers declined from 64.8 percent to 52.2 percent during the three decades. Decisions to involve paraprofessionals in classrooms are reflected in the large increase in instructional aides, from 1.7 percent of all employees in 1969–1970 to 9.4 percent in 1993. The percentage of counselors increased slightly. The percentage of employees who were librarians declined in the 1970s and 1980s. The

TABLE 16.1. Full-Time-Equivalent Personnel Employed in Public Schools

Type of Personnel	1959– 1960	1969– 1970	Fall 1980	Fall 1987	Fall 1993
Number (in thousands)					
Instructional staff	1,449	2,256	2,729	2,860	3,210
Classroom teachers	1,353	2,016	2,184	2,279	2,505
Instructional aides	c	57	326	336	451
Principals/assistant principals	64	91	107	126	121
Counselors	15	49	64	70	83
Librarians	17	43	48	48	50
Support staff[a]	598	1,040	1,361	1,378	1,513
District administrative staff[b]	42	65	79	74	80
Total	2,089	3,361	4,168	4,312	4,803
Percentage distribution					
Instructional staff	69.4	67.1	65.5	66.3	66.8
Classroom teachers	64.8	60.0	52.4	52.9	52.2
Instructional aides	c	1.7	7.8	7.8	9.4
Principals/assistant principals	3.0	2.7	2.6	2.9	2.5
Counselors	0.7	1.5	1.5	1.6	1.7
Librarians	0.8	1.3	1.2	1.1	1.1
Support staff[a]	28.6	31.0	32.6	32.0	31.5
District administrative staff[b]	2.0	1.9	1.9	1.7	1.7
Total	100.0	100.0	100.0	100.0	100.0

Note: Data for 1987 and 1993 may not be directly comparable to that of previous years because of classification revisions. Totals are rounded.
[a]Includes secretarial, transportation, food service, operation and maintenance, health, psychological, and media personnel.
[b]Includes superintendents, assistant superintendents, and instruction coordinators.
[c]Included in the number (and percentage) of teachers.
SOURCE: NCES. (1995b). *Digest of Education Statistics, 1995*. Washington, DC: U.S. Government Printing Office, Table 81, p. 89.

percentages of principals and assistant principals fluctuated between 3.0 percent in 1959–1960 and 2.5 percent in 1993. The percentage of people employed in noninstructional support roles at school and central office levels (particular positions are listed in the table's footnotes) increased from 30.6 percent in 1959–1960 to 33.2 percent in 1993. In response to concerns with the proliferation of support personnel, the percentage declined from the high of 34.5 percent in 1980. Even with this decline, the percentage of personnel in classroom teaching roles remained about the same, 52 percent of the total, between 1980 and 1993.

Not all regions of the nation will experience the same enrollment growth or demand for additional personnel in the future. Districts located in the western and southern states, where enrollments are expected to rise by 26 and 15 percent, respectively, should experience the largest need for teachers (Gerald & Hussar, 1995). Growth will also occur, but at a slower pace, in northeastern (9 percent) and midwestern (7 percent) states. High schools will experience greater growth (25 percent) than elementary (11 percent) schools, and there will be secondary enrollment increases of over 40 percent in Alaska, California, Nevada, and Washington. Thus, the demand for teachers is anticipated to rise substantially through 2005. The need for secondary teachers will increase at a faster rate than that for elementary teachers.

In addition to increases in the number of teachers and support personnel required in schools, there is an increasing demand for people with special skills. Just as the 1970s saw a sharp increase in special education teachers, today's changing student population puts pressure on school boards to employ teachers who can work effectively with racial and ethnic minorities. The projected 15 percent increase in African American schoolchildren and 28 percent increase in Hispanic schoolchildren between 1992 and 2000 will create a large demand for such teachers in some cities and regions of the country (Snyder, 1993). In addition, the growing percentage of children living in poverty and the national concern for quality educational and day-care services for preschool children raises the demand for other types of specially trained teachers (Anthony, 1988). Increases in the number of single-parent homes and the number of women in the workforce bring opportunities for schools to provide care for students before and after school. In addition to these external pressures to add personnel, internal decisions to restructure school organizations, for example, by altering grade levels served within smaller facilities, may also require additional professionals.

Pupil : Teacher Ratio. In Chapter 3 we discussed trends in pupil : teacher ratios (PTRs) in public elementary and secondary schools. Data presented in Table 3.9 indicated a steady decline from twenty-six pupils per teacher to seventeen pupils per teacher between 1960–1961 and 1994–1995. However, large variations in class sizes among states illustrate differing beliefs about internal efficiencies of schools. PTR in 1991–1992 ranged from about fourteen pupils per teacher in Connecticut, Maine, New Jersey, and Vermont to over twenty in California, Utah, and Washington (see Table 3.1).

Snyder (1993) questioned whether class sizes have actually decreased, as is implied in such reports. For example, the addition of specialty teachers and support personnel to serve limited numbers of students (e.g., disabled, disadvantaged, English-language-deficient) for short time periods, rather than smaller classes for all students, contributed to the apparent decline in PTR. Snyder reported that class size averaged twenty-six pupils in secondary schools and twenty-four pupils in elementary schools in 1990–1991—a decline of only one student per classroom since 1970. Statistical reports do not always clearly identify whether ratios pertain to pupils per classroom teacher (PTR), per professional (PPR) personnel including all certified or licensed persons, or per adult (PAR), including all noncertified staff members employed by the district.

The decline in reported PTR in the United States is similar to that in other industrialized nations. Table 16.2 presents an international comparison of staffing practices in public and private schools. PTRs were smaller in six of the twelve countries providing recent data than the seventeen pupils per teacher listed for the United States. The PTR profiles ranged from a low of fourteen to one in Australia, France, and Poland to a high of thirty-four to one in Nigeria. Like the United States, all nations except Nigeria had reduced class size between 1970 and 1990. PTRs are substantially larger in elementary than secondary schools in each of these countries. This perhaps indicates a worldwide belief that secondary education requires more professional staff. These data show that other nations have reduced class size. Schools in the United States are not likely to raise pupil : teacher ratios as numbers of students enrolled rise in the future. Thus, the demand for teachers will rise.

Increasing enrollments and changing pupils' needs that require specially trained teachers require additional personnel. However, Darling-Hammond and Berry (1988) observed that this increased demand will occur at a time when schools will face large numbers of teacher retirements. They antici-pated that the supply of graduating teacher candidates would satisfy only 60 percent of this demand.

The Supply of Teacher Candidates

There are not always personnel ready to meet the changing requirements of school systems. Varied social and economic conditions often depress the supply of candidates for the available positions. The source of new entrants to the profession indicates that school systems must look beyond recent college graduates for new hires. And the decisions of current teachers to remain or depart from the classroom reveal that the best-quality teachers are often the first to leave. These conditions require policies and working conditions to attract capable teacher candidates.

Social and Economic Influences. Fluctuating birthrates bring cycles of growth and decline. They create shortages of teacher candidates qualified to

TABLE 16.2. Pupils per Teacher in Public and Private Schools in Selected Countries, 1970 to 1990

Country	Elementary			Secondary			All Schools		
	1970	1980	1990	1970	1980	1990	1970	1980	1990
Australia	28	19	17	NA	13	12	NA	16	14
Canada	23	NA	15	17	NA	14	21	NA	15
France	26	24	16[a]	16	20	12[a]	20	21	14[a]
Germany (former West)	26	17	18[a]	12	NA	14[a]	19	NA	15[a]
Italy	22	16	12[a]	12	10	9[a]	16	12	10[a]
Japan	26	25	21[a]	18	17	17[a]	22	21	19[a]
Korea	57	48	34[b]	37	39	24[b]	50	44	28[b]
Mexico	46	39	31	15	18	17	35	30	24
Nigeria	34	37	39[b]	21	29	22[b]	32	36	34[b]
Poland	23	20	16[c]	10	12	11[c]	18	17	14[c]
Spain	34	28	23	22	21	20	29	24	21
United Kingdom	23	19	18	16	NA	NA	20	NA	NA
United States	25	21	18	20	17	16	22	19	17
USSR	11	9	8	20	NA	NA	NA	NA	NA
Yugoslavia	27	24	23	22	19	17	24	20	18

NA, Not available.
[a]Data from 1989.
[b]Data from 1991.
[c]Data from 1988.
SOURCE: NCES. (1993c). *Digest of Education Statistics, 1993.* Washington, DC: U.S. Government Printing Office, Table 283.

teach some grade levels while other levels have short-term surpluses. Population shifts from cities to suburbs and from northern states to southern and western states have produced oversupplies of teachers in some districts and shortages in others. Furthermore, other factors influence the attractiveness of careers in education: racial conflicts, drug abuse, violence, the lack of parental involvement, diminished public support for taxation, teachers' salaries compared to those in other occupations, the prestige of teaching, attitudes toward teachers' unions, and teachers' work conditions.

Competition for college graduates depresses the number and quality of teacher applicants. Minorities and women historically sought careers in teaching because they were denied access to other fields. But they have more diverse career opportunities available to them now than in the past. College graduates with such majors as physics, chemistry, mathematics, and computer science have readily available employment alternatives. Furthermore, teachers in these fields tend to leave education careers more rapidly than those in other subject areas (Darling-Hammond, 1984; Murnane et al., 1991, p. 67).

Sources of Teacher Candidates. It is difficult to determine current supplies of teachers or predict future supplies because many graduates of teacher preparation programs do not enter the profession immediately or do not enter at all. Many of those who do become teachers interrupt their careers to raise their families or pursue further education or other career opportunities. Despite the 11 percent increase in the number of newly qualified teachers between 1987 and 1991 (Gray et al., 1993), there is little assurance that these individuals will pursue careers in education.

Table 16.3 lists the supply sources for public school teachers in 1988 and 1991. Fewer than one-half of new teachers in 1991 were first-time teachers (42 percent). However, this source supplied considerably more new teachers than in 1988 (31 percent). At the same time, the proportion of newly hired teachers who were reentrants from the reserve pool of former teachers declined from 33

percent in 1988 to 24 percent in 1991. The remaining supply source, transfers among districts or from private schools, also declined, from 37 percent to 34 percent during this brief period.

Somewhat fewer new teachers came directly from college in 1991 than three years earlier (see Table 16.3). The majority (58 percent) of first-time teachers in 1991 were most recently in college, a decline from 67 percent in 1988. Many new hires were working as substitute teachers (18 percent). Only 10 percent were late entrants who had delayed their teaching careers to work in other fields. Even fewer had pursued family responsibilities (4 percent). Of those who had reentered the profession in 1991, many were substitute teachers (24 percent) or working in other education roles (19 percent). Fewer new teachers in 1991 were most recently involved in family responsibilities (19 percent) than in 1988 (28 percent).

Reentrants offer districts more teaching experience and professional preparation. They also earn higher salaries than recent college graduates. However, first-time teachers, and those under age 30, have higher attrition rates (Murnane et al., 1991; NCES, 1995a, p. 164). Districts must look beyond recent college graduates for supplies of new teachers to meet the growing demand we identified earlier. And they must balance the advantages of hiring mature personnel who may remain in the profession for more years against the lower cost of first-time teachers.

Teacher Retention. Decisions of current employees to remain in the classroom also affect supply and demand. Bobbitt (1992) observed that the teaching force had been quite stable in recent years, with 94 percent remaining in the classroom between 1987–1988 and 1990–1991. Retention was anticipated to improve even more. A somewhat larger percentage of teachers (35 percent) responded in 1991 that they planned to stay in teaching as long as they could than in 1988 (31 percent).

Despite this report that teachers tend to remain in the profession, a study of teacher attrition provides insights into the characteristics of teach-

TABLE 16.3. Distribution of Newly Hired Teachers, 1988 and 1991

Source and Previous Year Activity	Percentage of New Teachers	
	1988	1991
Supply source		
First-time teachers	30.6	41.7
Transfers	36.6	34.3
Reentrants	32.8	24.0
Total	100.0	100.0
Previous year activity		
First-time teachers		
College	66.5	58.4
Work outside education	11.0	10.0
Work in education	5.7	5.2
Homemaking/childrearing	3.6	4.4
Other	13.2	22.0
Substitute teaching	NA	18.0
Total	100.0	100.0
Reentrants		
Homemaking/childrearing	27.8	19.3
Work in education	10.3	19.1
Work outside education	17.4	17.9
College	18.0	10.4
Other	26.5	33.3
Substitute teaching	NA	23.8
Total	100.0	100.0

Note: Newly hired teachers are defined as regular teachers who teach half-time or more and who in the previous year did not hold regular teaching positions in that public school district.
SOURCE: NCES. (1994a). *The Condition of Education, 1994.* Washington, DC: U.S. Government Printing Office, p. 158.

ers who choose to leave. Teachers are most likely to leave during their early years in the profession. White teachers are more likely to leave than African American teachers. Secondary school teachers leave earlier in their careers than elementary school teachers. Chemistry and physics teachers are the most likely to leave. Teachers with high scores on standardized tests have shorter careers in teaching than those with low scores. And teachers who are paid the least leave most quickly (Murnane et al., 1991, pp. 59–60).

The anticipated increase in demand for teachers and the social and economic factors that depress the supply of candidates suggest states and school systems should develop policies and incentives to attract new teachers. Furthermore, the findings of retention studies challenge schools to keep capable teachers, particularly in subject fields with fewer candidates for available positions.

Reforms to Improve Teacher Quality

Just as policy changes over the years increased the demand for teachers, reforms within states, school systems, and institutions of higher education attempt to increase the initial supply of capable teachers and reduce their attrition. The educational reforms of the past several decades were designed to address many of the root causes of the decrease in high-quality teachers (MacPhail-Wilcox & King, 1988). We explore several options that promise to strengthen the quality of beginning and experienced teachers: raising entry standards for first-time teachers and professional certification of career teachers, strengthening preparation of teachers, and improving salaries and working conditions.

Entry Standards and Professional Certification. Assessments of knowledge of specialized subjects and demonstrations of particular skills, which are prerequisites to entry into other professions, have been adopted by states to raise the quality of newly hired teachers. In 1975 Georgia and Mississippi were the first to require written competency tests for licensure. By 1990, a total of forty-three states and the District of Columbia had made passing at least one of the following a condition for initial certification or licensure: basic skills (27 states), professional skills (24 states), content knowledge (25 states), in-class observation (18 states) (NCES, 1994b, p. 151).

Merely requiring a test of knowledge of the field is not sufficient, especially when there are concerns about the content validity and predictive validity of the competency tests for initial licensure, as well as about the role of these tests in defining the professional knowledge base (Darling-Hammond, 1986; Madaus & Pullin, 1987). To address these limitations, Shulman (1987) urged simulations, assessment center exercises, and closely supervised field experiences to enrich the measures of knowledge and skills of potential teachers. By 1988, twenty-five states had initiated induction or beginning teacher programs, and eighteen of these states required new entrants to pass a formal performance assessment before qualifying for permanent certification (Darling-Hammond & Berry, 1988). For example, California, Indiana, and West Virginia fund stipends for mentor teachers, and Ohio's entry-year program enables mentor training and ongoing professional support for first-year teachers (Gold, Smith, & Lawton, 1995, pp. 152, 250, 503, 655).

Alternative routes to licensure increase the supply of applicants by permitting people who have not completed formal teacher education programs before their employment to teach full-time. Parker (1993) reported that thirty-nine states had established such alternatives, and that 10 percent of first-time teachers entered the profession by this route. In the New Jersey lateral entry program, for example, applicants holding a bachelor's degree and thirty credit hours or equivalent work experience in the subject field they intend to teach must pass a subject field exam, do a year-long paid internship, and receive 200 contact hours of formal instruction in education during the first year of teaching. School systems assign these new teachers to a team (consisting of an administrator, a peer teacher, a college faculty member, and a curricular specialist) that assists their development and evaluates their performance.

Initial state licensure to enforce minimal standards differs from professional certification. This was initially recommended by the Carnegie Forum (1986). Following the guidelines in the Carnegie report, a National Board for Professional Teaching Standards was created to develop high standards for professional competence and to certify teachers who meet those standards. Performance-based assessments using videotapes of teaching, portfolios of student work, on-site observations, structured interviews, and simulations began in 1993 for selected middle-school teachers. This voluntary system of national certification was designed to be fully operational by the 1998–1999 school year. Then certificates would be awarded in more than thirty fields. However, the cost of developing initial assessments forced the board to scale back the timeline for creating assessments in additional fields (Bradley, 1995).

Teacher Preparation. Recommendations for changes in traditional teacher preparation promise future supplies of applicants with greater subject matter expertise. And financial incentives encourage college students to earn teacher certification or licensure.

Reports of several highly visible consortia recommended a fifth year of professional education beyond a four-year liberal arts degree. The most influential among these were recommendations of the Carnegie Forum (1986), which consisted of public, business, and educational leaders, and the Holmes Group (1986), which comprised deans of selected colleges of education. The Holmes Group urged an "integrated extended" program over five or more years, including an intensively supervised and reflective internship. However, there were concerns that the additional investment in preparation without the promise of commensurate future compensation would diminish the profession's attractiveness. Thus, reports of the Consortium for Excellence in Teacher Education (Travers & Sacks, 1987) and the Association of American Colleges (1989) contended that four-year undergraduate programs could successfully integrate the liberal arts with professional studies.

The 1995 report of the Holmes Group challenged teacher training institutions to raise their quality standards and make changes in their curricula, faculty, the location of much of their work, and their student bodies. The curriculum should focus on the learning needs of the young and the development of educators across their careers. The faculty of education schools should work as effectively in the public schools and professional development schools as they would on a university campus. The changing population of public school students would necessitate a more diverse cadre of school teachers, administrators, counselors, and university faculty.

Financial aid programs and forgiven loans provide incentives for financially less able students to prepare for teaching careers. Very often this assistance expands career opportunities for capable students who might otherwise not be able to afford college and increases the supply of capable minority group teacher candidates. For example, statewide initiatives such as Massachusetts' payment of college expenses in exchange for future teaching within the state, the Governor's Teaching Scholarship program in New Jersey, and North Carolina's teaching fellows program were designed to attract capable candidates to teaching careers.

Salaries and Working Conditions. It is not clear that raising salaries will affect the quality of the labor pool positively. Jacobson (1990) reported that salaries paid beginning teachers have the potential to lure the most highly educated candidates away from neighboring districts. However, other researchers found that raising salaries overall, without increasing entrance standards, would have minimal influence on the quality of candidates even if the size of the pool itself were expanded (Manski, 1985; Murnane et al., 1991). In contrast, the importance of improving compensation is evident in Hawley's (1986) conclusion that many reform strategies, including tests and other screening devices to control entry, would not attract better-qualified people because they fail to alter rewards.

Policies that restructure the workplace by giving greater responsibility, fostering collegiality, and maximizing the time teachers teach are low-cost reforms that offer potentially positive benefits in terms of recruitment and improved teacher effectiveness. Darling-Hammond and Berry (1988) observed that the emphasis of reform proposals had shifted in 1986 toward decentralizing decision making and professionalizing teaching. They argued that rigorous preparation, licensing, and selection processes to ensure teaching competence would be acceptable trade-offs for fewer rules prescribing what would be taught, when, and how. Darling-Hammond (1984) had previously claimed that the bureaucratic orientation of public schools negatively affected teacher retention: "Lack of input into professional decision making, overly restrictive bureaucratic controls, and inadequate administrative supports for teaching contribute to teacher dissatisfaction and attrition, particularly among the most highly qualified members of the teaching force" (p. v).

It appears that several strategies offer promise for increasing both the supply and the quality of teachers. Raising entrance standards through valid and reliable assessments, redesigning teacher preparation programs, financing incentives for capable college students to prepare for teaching careers, and improving teachers' working conditions should contribute to attracting and keeping capable teachers and improving their skills. We next explore the limitations of the traditional salary schedule and the promises that compensation systems that recognize teachers' responsibilities and performance can effectively motivate and retain excellent teachers.

STRATEGIES FOR IMPROVING TEACHERS' REMUNERATION

Among the most important aspects of personnel policies are the nature of the compensation packages offered to employees and the relationship that people's skills, responsibilities, and job performance have to remuneration. The presumption that these factors affect the internal efficiencies of schools and the future supplies of capable teachers makes them the subject of educational reform proposals.

The National Commission on Excellence (1983) stated that maintaining current levels of salaries would not be sufficient to attract and retain high-quality teachers: "Salaries for the teaching profession should be increased and should be professionally competitive, market-sensitive, and performance-based" (p. 30). In this section we discuss the competitiveness of teachers' salaries in relation to the cost of living and to wages paid other workers. We explore structures of salary schedules, beginning with the single salary schedule and the presumed relationship between teachers' experience and training and teachers' skills. Finally, we examine merit pay, career ladders, and other strategies that relate compensation to responsibilities or performance.

Salaries and Fringe Benefits

Salaries are indicators of the economic health of the profession and of teachers' status in the community (Salmon, 1988). They therefore influence people's career choices and the number of college graduates who pursue teaching as a career (Murnane et al., 1991). Trends in teachers' salaries over several decades, comparisons with salaries paid in other nations and with other occupations, and the fringe benefits provided teachers clarify the eco-

nomic health and competitiveness of teaching. Salaries are generally low relative to those in comparison groups.

Changes in salaries reveal dramatic increases in absolute dollars over time. But teachers have not always maintained their economic positions relative to the cost of living. Trends in teachers' salaries were depicted in Figure 3.3. Figure 3.3 traced fluctuations in salaries from 1960 through 1994 after accounting for inflation. Teachers lost purchasing power in the 1970s. But by 1988 they had recouped their position relative to the cost of living. The value of the average salary earned in 1981 had declined to $28,577 (expressed in 1992 dollars), which was a loss of $4,768 in purchasing power from that of 1973. The average teacher's salary in 1992 ($34,934) represented an increase of $6,357 in constant dollars over the 1981 level. The average beginning salary was $23,054 in 1992. This was an increase of 20 percent from the 1980 salary of $19,260 (NCES, 1993b, p. 150). By 1993–1994 the average salary earned by teachers was $35,958 (NCES, 1994b, p. 84).

Salaries vary greatly among regions in the nation, as do rates of change over time. Data presented in Table 16.4, which lists regions according to average salaries paid in 1993–1994, reveal a range of $15,039—from $30,484 in the southwestern states to $45,523 in the mideast region. The largest increase in average salaries, adjusted for inflation, between 1980–1981 and 1993–1994 occurred in the New England states (49.7 percent). Here salaries increased relative to those in the nation as a whole (20.7 percent). The smallest increase occurred in the Rocky Mountain region. Here growth was only 7.0 percent. Some of the variation among regions might be explained by differences in the cost of living. However, Nelson and O'Brien (1993, p. 121) found a wide salary range among states, from $26,237 in South Dakota to $43,677 in Michigan during 1991–1992, after adjustments were made for such differences.

International comparisons show that teachers in the United States are not compensated at the same level as their counterparts in other nations.

TABLE 16.4. Average Teachers' Salaries by Region, 1980–1981 and 1993–1994 (in 1994 dollars)

Region	1980–1981	1993–1994	Percentage Increase 1981–1994
Mideast	33,562	45,523	35.6
New England	27,502	41,169	49.7
Far West	36,529	39,679	8.6
Great Lakes	31,660	39,324	24.2
Plains	26,186	32,291	23.3
Rocky Mountains	28,973	31,007	7.0
Southeast	25,763	30,817	19.6
Southwest	27,510	30,484	10.8
50 states and the District of Columbia	30,226	36,495	20.7

SOURCE: NCES. (1995a). *The Condition of Education, 1995.* Washington, DC: U.S. Government Printing Office, p. 158.

Nelson (1995) reported teachers' salaries in nineteen economically advanced nations. When midcareer secondary teachers' salaries were compared in terms of U.S. dollars and in terms of purchasing power in various nations during 1991 or 1992, the average paid in the United States ($34,213) ranked eighth (p. 122, errata sheet). Teachers earned a high of over $48,000 in Switzerland and a low of $21,566 in Italy. Primary-level teachers fared somewhat better relative to their counterparts in other nations (p. 120). The average starting salaries of beginning teachers in Switzerland, Germany, Canada, and Spain were higher than those paid in the United States ($22,171). Nelson related the generally low salaries to the quality of teacher candidates: "The low relative pay of U.S. teachers coincides with the general notion that low pay for teachers in the United States makes it difficult to recruit teachers who graduate in the top half of their college graduating classes" (p. 126).

Comparisons of teachers' salaries with those of other occupations in the United States also indicate the relatively low economic status of educators. One ranking placed teachers last among professions in both 1979–1980 and 1985–1986 (Salmon, 1988, pp. 255–256). Salaries paid teachers were more comparable to those of technical occupations than to those of professions. However, during these six years, teachers had moved from the midpoint among technical occupations to the top of this group. Feistritzer (1986) found teachers to be twenty-sixth of thirty-five occupations. Of the ten ranked below teachers, only two (social worker and priest) demanded a college degree. When the Carnegie Forum (1986) compared salaries of twelve selected occupations, only plumbers, airline ticket agents, and secretaries earned less than teachers. Beginning teachers' salaries in 1990–1991 ($19,913) were higher than those of beginning salaries in communications ($19,584) and public affairs/social services ($19,227), but lower than those of five other fields that ranged from biology ($21,325) to computer science ($30,419) (NCES, 1993a). Schlechty (1987) noted the effect of the relatively low career earnings: "Thus, the longer one stays in teaching, the greater the economic cost to the teacher. Such a condition certainly discourages careerism [and] probably discourages those who stay in teaching from maintaining a high commitment to outstanding performance" (p. 6).

The amount of salaries, the most visible reward for work, overshadows the diversity of fringe benefits offered and the proportion of their cost paid by school districts. Yet the total compensation package may affect school districts' competitiveness, both among school systems and in the broader marketplace, for certified/licensed personnel and for classified secretarial and custodial staff.

Rebore (1987) defined a fringe benefit as "a service made available to employees as a direct result of a fiscal expenditure by the school district" (p. 298). Individual employees and school districts contribute to the cost of federally sponsored social security and workmen's compensation plans (see Chapter 5). Most also share the expense of statewide teachers' retirement programs and group health, dental, disability, and life insurance plans. School boards bear the cost of liability insurance to protect themselves and their employees from negligence suits.

The labor intensity of schooling is apparent in the large percentage of budgets devoted to personnel costs, including fringe benefits. This is generally between 85 percent and 90 percent. Of the $128.4 billion total expended in the nation for instruction in elementary and secondary schools in 1991–1992, $95.0 billion (74 percent) was spent on salaries and another $23.6 billion (18 percent) financed the state portion of their benefits (NCES, 1994b, p. 162). Nelson and O'Brien (1993) noted that the 13 to 21 percent of salaries paid by teachers in the United States as their individual contributions for retirement, social security, and health care was the highest for any of the nineteen nations. Swedish teachers had no deductions for benefits (but a very high income tax rate to contribute to social services). But teachers contributed 8.1 percent of their salaries in Italy, 11.2 percent in Japan, and 12.6 percent in France (p. 2).

Several additional benefits are available to certified personnel in the United States. Favorable income tax policies enable teachers to invest funds for retirement in annuities that shelter tax obligations until they can take advantage of lower tax brackets. School districts bear the cost of substitute teachers when health, personal, and extended sabbatical leaves are granted. In some districts, a "sick leave incentive cash payment plan" (Candoli, Hack, Ray, & Stollar, 1984, p. 367) accumulates unused leave to a maximum number of days over a career, providing teachers large payments upon retirement or departure from the profession. Other districts enable employees to choose from a number of benefits in a cafeteria approach in order to make compensation more attractive to employees who do not require standard family-oriented benefit packages.

Programs to increase the future supplies of capable teachers and improve the internal efficiencies of schools through compensation must consider more than merely salaries and fringe benefits. We next scrutinize the factors used in determining salaries.

The Two Dimensions of the Single Salary Schedule

A uniform salary schedule for all teachers in a school district emerged early in the twentieth century in response to inequities. At that time, wages differed according to such factors as elementary and secondary grade levels, subjects taught, gender, number of dependents, political affiliations, and bargaining between individual teachers and school boards. The principle of equal pay for equal qualifications called for the same salary for teachers of equal training and experience.

Salaries of all teachers employed by a given school board were to follow one schedule. There would be minimal differentiations in pay resulting only from such extra services as coaching teams and overseeing extracurricular activities. By 1990–1991, over one-third of all teachers benefited from supplemental contracts. Pay increased by an average of $1,942 for 788,215 out of the 2.3 million teachers. In addition, 393,215 teachers (17 percent) earned $1,993 for supplementary work during the summer (NCES, 1994b, p. 82). Nevertheless, the base pay for teachers continues to be determined by two objective criteria in most school systems.

The two-dimensional structure of the single salary schedule typically differentiates teachers' pay according to years of experience (longevity) and advanced preparation (training). The first dimension brings annual step increases that raise salaries for a stated maximum number of years of teaching experience. The number of years of out-of-district experience that can be credited for previous teaching in other school systems is generally restricted. And longevity raises occur for only between ten and twenty years. Nelson's (1995) analysis of primary-level teachers revealed that it took longer for thirteen of the nineteen nations than the average of sixteen years it took for teachers in the United States to achieve maximum longevity increases. It took between ten and forty-three years in other countries to achieve the maximum salary. Interestingly, Lawton (1988) commented that pay scales with fifteen steps or fewer were limited to countries with historical connections to Great Britain. Other countries used scales with twenty or more steps, including forty years in Italy and forty-three years in Spain. The practice of rewarding nearly all teachers for longevity was premised initially on the presumption that seniority equates with improvements in instructional quality and pupil learning. This assumption has been challenged in recent years (see Chapter 13).

The second dimension included in salary schedules rewards and encourages continued preparation in professional education and the subject fields taught. Four to six training categories typically range from having no college degree to earning a doctoral degree. Teachers advance along this continuum upon completion of advanced degrees or specified numbers of graduate hours.

The effect of these experience and training dimensions is generally to double salaries from the initial cell of the matrix (e.g., first-year teacher with a bachelor's degree) to the last cell (e.g., teacher with sixteen years of experience and a doc-

toral degree). In addition to these increments, actual annual increases in salaries, including those of experienced teachers who are frozen on the top step, depend upon legislative or school board actions. All cells of the matrix are changed, reflecting increases in the cost of living, state legislative appropriations, results of negotiations between boards of education and teachers' associations, and other factors.

Trends in the experience and preparation of teachers between 1961 and 1991—see Table 16.5—reveal a more experienced and highly educated teaching force in recent years. The median number of years in teaching declined from eleven to eight in the 1960s. During this period many inexperienced teachers were hired to meet the demands of increased enrollments and program expansions. This trend reversed through 1991, when the typical teacher had fifteen years of experience. The declining percentage of first-year teachers, from 9.1 percent in 1971 to 3.0 percent in 1991, reflected declining enrollments, tenure and retirement policies, and conditions of the general economy that discouraged new hires and limited turnover among veteran teachers. At the same time, the length of academic preparation increased. The percentages of teachers without a bachelor's degree declined from 15 percent in 1961 to less than 1 percent in 1991. The percentage of teachers with only a bachelor's degree dropped from 70 percent in 1971 to 46 percent two decades later. The percentage of teachers with advanced preparation in-

TABLE 16.5. Teachers' Experience and Training, 1961–1991

	1961	1971	1981	1991
Experience				
Median years of experience	11.0	8.0	12.0	15.0
Percentage teaching for first year	8.0	9.1	2.4	3.0
Training: highest degree held (%)				
Less than bachelor's	14.6	2.9	0.4	0.6
Bachelor's	61.9	69.6	50.1	46.3
Master's or specialist	23.1	27.1	49.3	52.6
Doctor's	0.4	0.4	0.3	0.5

SOURCE: NCES. (1994b). *Digest of Education Statistics*, 1994. Washington, DC: U.S. Government Printing Office, Table 69.

creased substantially, from under a quarter in 1961 to over one-half of all teachers holding a graduate degree in 1991.

Advances in these mean experience and training levels translate into substantial increases in average salaries under schedules that depend on these two dimensions. A more experienced teaching force today appears to be paid higher average salaries than a decade ago. But the average teacher is only marginally better off in terms of purchasing power (see Figure 3.3). Larger average salaries reflect movements on salary schedules and general increases provided by state legislatures or school boards. But these increases have not compensated teachers for cost-of-living changes.

In response to calls for altering teacher compensation policies, the National Education Association (1985, p. 19) argued that a single salary schedule:

- promotes positive working relationships among teachers and between teachers and administrators;
- is a relatively inexpensive and unburdened system for allocating pay when compared with other systems;
- has minimal impacts on productive school processes, such as teachers' intrinsic motivations to perform and principals' decisions for effectively using skills of teachers; and
- avoids racial, ethnic and gender discrimination among teachers.

The American Federation of Teachers also contended that the only fair procedure for paying teachers was "by the use of an adequate single salary schedule based upon training and experience" which would "permit the experienced teachers to perform their services in an atmosphere of dignity and personal satisfaction" (Magel, 1961).

On the other hand, the single salary schedule offers little opportunity for teachers to be given monetary recognition for their performance. Rather than giving salary increases on the basis of individual or school productivity, teachers' pay is subject to collective decision made by groups external to

school districts. This occurs with statewide salary schedules. Or it occurs within districts by means of negotiations between teachers' associations and boards of education in states that permit or mandate collective bargaining. The structure of the schedule itself rewards the number of years teachers have taught rather than their skills or performance. It rewards the number of graduate courses or continuing education units completed rather than their usefulness or relevance to the subjects taught. These dimensions permit little recognition of teachers' initiative, enthusiasm, efficiency, innovation, cooperation, ability, or improvements in performance. These factors may affect teachers' decisions to leave the profession voluntarily or school boards' decisions to dismiss teachers for poor classroom teaching. But they are not direct determinants of annual salaries.

An important goal of processes that reward and compensate individuals is to improve the quality of teachers (Castetter, 1986, p. 427; Rebore, 1987, p. 238). Determining salaries by criteria of training and experience is most defensible if these characteristics are related to the quality of instruction or pupil performance. We challenged these assumed relationships in Chapter 13. Policy makers are giving greater consideration to alternative compensation plans that relate remuneration to measures of performance or redefined job responsibilities.

Performance-Based Pay and Career Ladders

Rewarding meritorious work performance and differentiating the responsibilities of teachers are the most visible strategies advanced for improving teachers' compensation and productivity. The National Commission on Excellence in Education (1983) urged performance-based salaries and the development of career ladders that would distinguish among beginning, experienced, and master teachers (pp. 30–31). Rather than two-dimensional salary schedules, these compensation systems relate salary to performance, as measured by gains in pupil achievement or by supervisors' or peers' evaluations of teaching abilities, or to clearly differentiated roles.

Merit pay, career ladder, and other performance-based compensation plans are visible initiatives that present an aura of accountability to the public. Furthermore, these reforms may increase the supply of teachers who seek careers in which their efforts can be recognized. We present theoretical bases for these policies, discuss their potential and limitations, and describe the current status of states' initiatives for relating teachers' compensation to skills and performance.

Theoretical Perspectives. There are several theoretical bases for developing policies that link compensation to teachers' performance. Offering rewards to alter workers' behaviors follows Skinner's (1974) view that people are basically passive and must be motivated by carrots and other incentives in the environment. Incentives for meritorious performance must be seen as being valuable, according to Vroom's (1964) expectancy theory, which suggests that people work harder when they anticipate valued rewards. Merit pay is also based on equity theory. Equity theory proposes that dissatisfaction results when individuals perceive that they are unjustly compensated in relation to others (Frohreich, 1988). A single salary schedule that does not differentiate and reward individual accomplishments may bring dissatisfaction. Alternatively, a merit plan that rewards some teachers in ways that others believe are not warranted may also bring dissatisfaction. Career ladders and other differentiated staffing patterns rest on the assumption that productivity is improved when there is job enrichment, such as when teachers' responsibilities become more varied and challenging throughout their careers.

The nature of the rewards entailed in compensation systems may make a difference in job satisfaction and in teachers' motivations to improve their performance. A merit pay policy assumes that external and material rewards motivate teachers to be more productive. These extrinsic incentives may include salary increases, additions to instructional material accounts, or travel funds for professional meetings. Alternatively, they may bring nonmonetary benefits such as relief from assigned duties. Extrinsic rewards may not, however, be sufficient motivators.

Herzberg, Mausner, and Snyderman (1959) suggested that extrinsic rewards, including monetary incentives, play an important role in inducing dissatisfaction among workers. Inadequate salaries and work conditions may lead to decisions to leave teaching careers. Thus, compensation strategies must be more attentive to intrinsic rewards if they are to improve teacher performance (Jacobson, 1988). Career ladders considerably expand the range of motivators to include intrinsic, or internal and intangible, rewards such as recognition, responsibility, variety in work tasks, and a sense of achievement. Lawler (1981) contended that career ladders offer stronger potential for changing behaviors and for retaining capable teachers because they provide both intrinsic and extrinsic rewards.

Merit pay and career ladder strategies permit teachers to increase their salaries or responsibilities without abandoning teaching roles. They offer opportunities and incentives for professional growth, improved teaching skills, and increased productivity in upgrading student performance (Poston & Frase, 1991). They also presume that opportunities for extra compensation will enrich the overall quality of the applicant pool and effectively motivate teacher behavior throughout careers. We discuss the potential of each approach in greater detail in the following sections.

Merit Pay. Merit-based pay is an alternative compensation plan that awards bonuses to those teachers who demonstrate particular effectiveness through some form of performance assessment. Salary incentive plans generally grant a one-time pay bonus based on superior performance. Policies typically do not advance teachers on the salary matrix, because this would effectively raise salaries into the future for past performance.

The push for merit recognition is cyclical. It became popular in the early 1960s after *Sputnik* raised concerns about the productivity of schools. It has reappeared in the most recent context of educational reform. Murnane and Cohen (1986, p. 2) observed that "while interest in paying teachers according to merit endures, attempts to use merit pay do not." Astuto (1985) found that very few school districts (4 percent) had any form of pay for performance. More districts that had tried merit pay had dropped their plans than had retained this compensation strategy. Districts with plans invested very little money in merit awards, in many cases less than the cost of a single teacher's salary. The majority of approaches to determining merit assessed input data (e.g., subject knowledge, evidence of preparation) to evaluate teachers. Less than 20 percent of the plans linked merit pay to student achievement or other performance measures. Advocates of merit pay for teachers argue that:

- Performance-based pay provides a competitive environment with higher pay for effective teachers
- Teachers are held accountable, bringing public support to schools that pay teachers in accordance with performance
- Evaluation processes improve, and more individuals become involved in the appraisal and improvement of instruction
- Intrinsic recognition of the value of outstanding teaching motivates as much as monetary rewards do
- Merit compensation helps to attract and retain effective teachers while discouraging ineffective ones from continuing in the profession (Frohreich, 1988; Herndon, 1985; National Education Association, 1984).

Recent reports attest that merit pay can be successfully implemented. Murnane and Cohen (1986) characterized successful merit plans as those that supplemented already high salaries and good working conditions and that compensated teachers for extra responsibilities outside classrooms, rather than determining the relative abilities of teachers within classrooms. Ballou and Podgursky (1993) analyzed data from the 1987–1988 Schools and Staffing Survey of 56,000 public

school teachers and concluded that teachers in districts with merit pay were not demoralized or hostile toward the compensation plan, and that teachers of disadvantaged and low-achieving pupils supported merit pay. Farnsworth, Debenham, and Smith (1991, p. 321) described a successful plan in one district and concluded that "merit pay, when properly administered and funded, can increase teaching effectiveness."

In contrast to these reports of success, merit pay has serious shortcomings, particularly when the goal of a compensation plan is to improve teaching and learning. Merit pay's critics contend that:

- There is no clear agreement on what constitutes effective teaching or on which teacher qualities influence pupil achievement.
- Most evaluation systems do not provide valid or comprehensive indicators of teaching abilities, and teachers resist evaluation systems that are linked to compensation.
- There is no evidence that incentives contribute to student achievement. It is difficult to separate an individual teacher's contributions to pupils' successes from other school (e.g., previous teachers') or nonschool (e.g., families') influences.
- Competition for bonuses may be counterproductive, lowering morale and decreasing cooperation among colleagues.
- Like the abuses in the operation of many local governments, the selection of deserving teachers can be driven more by political forces (including nepotism, racism, sexism, and cronyism) than by professional considerations.
- Plans may punish average teachers while only minimally motivating those deemed productive.
- Schools may lack financial support to enable merit awards in addition to cost-of-living adjustments.
- Plans are expensive to initiate and maintain.

The cost and time necessary to develop and implement an effective plan detract from more critical responsibilities (Astuto, 1985; Ballou & Podgursky, 1993; Johnson, 1985).

These criticisms focus on the structure and cost of merit pay plans as well as the difficulty of developing valid and objective criteria to measure performance. The failure of merit plans to motivate teachers may be rooted in the theoretical assumptions underlying this incentive system. We stated above that merit plans assume that financial rewards can effectively change people's behavior and motivate them to improve their performance. This premise was challenged by Kohn (1993). He found rewards were deficient in several ways: People focus on the reward and are less interested in the quality of the task. Improvements occur for only a short period of time. Intrinsic motivation is eroded by extrinsic motivators. Rewards rupture relationships among workers. And rewards are instruments of control that reinforce hierarchy. Herzberg, Mausner, and Snyderman (1959) placed money among the factors that demotivate and dissatisfy workers. Furthermore, Deming (1982) argued that pay is not a motivator and that competition and fear work against organizational goals.

A career ladder approach changes the nature of teacher work more comprehensively and is developed locally with teacher involvement. This approach offers greater potential for effectively differentiating compensation. Yet career ladders also have limitations in school improvement efforts, because individual rather than group accomplishments are rewarded.

Career Ladder.   A career ladder is an alternative compensation plan that differentiates levels of responsibility, status, and salary. Unlike merit pay, which does not assign formal status distinctions, career ladders and other differentiated staffing approaches restructure salary schedules along with a hierarchy of job classifications.

The Holmes Group (1986) called for three levels within a staged career that would create and reward formal distinctions based on responsibilities and degrees of autonomy. The first-level *instructor* would teach for several years under the supervision of experienced teachers. The majority of autonomous classroom teachers would hold the title of *professional teacher.* The highest level, the *career professional,* includes teachers who are capable of using their pedagogical expertise to improve other teachers' work. A four-step model advanced by the Association of Teacher Educators (1985) included teacher, associate teacher, senior teacher, and master teacher. The Carnegie Forum (1986) called for more responsibilities to be given to board-certified teachers who would serve in the role of *lead teacher.*

Schlechty (1987) urged states and districts to adopt career ladders because of their potential for encouraging and developing high-quality teaching performance. He argued that an effective compensation system must provide increased rewards, including money, status, and responsibility, over a long period of time. A career ladder inspires high-quality performance and encourages long-term commitment from teachers who perform at high levels. The strength of career ladders is in their potential for:

- Recognizing, rewarding, and encouraging increased responsibilities, as well as improved performance, as teachers grow in the profession
- Enabling the advancement of teachers who no longer need to leave the classroom to gain intrinsic and extrinsic rewards
- Increasing teacher efficacy and self-fulfillment as the honor of a promotion is recognized by colleagues and the public
- Improving instructional conditions schoolwide by encouraging students to learn and mentoring beginning or struggling teachers

A number of limitations of this compensation strategy contrast with these advantages. Like merit pay, career ladders are expensive to initiate and maintain. They presume to recognize excellence within teaching roles, but often the added responsibilities remove teachers from classrooms into quasi-administrative positions. Responsibilities may be difficult to distinguish at different levels of careers. But pay and status differentials create divisions among teachers. Limited funds may restrict the number of teachers who are paid for added responsibilities, which may be assumed by others who do not receive recognition and salary increases. Quotas and poor morale may result from the public's perception that there are unwarranted advancements on the ladder solely for salary gains. Decisions about career advancement, like merit awards, may rest on subjective evaluations and thus breed similar concerns with unfairness (Firestone & Bader, 1992).

States and school systems incur many monetary and nonmonetary costs under career ladder programs (Smith, 1987; Weeks & Cornett, 1985). Developing the plan itself is costly in teacher and administrator time. A new evaluation system may be required, along with instruments for testing basic skills, content knowledge of the subject field, professional knowledge, and classroom performance. The process of performance assessment itself is costly, because multiple observers (including colleague teachers) and conferences mean released time and evaluator training. The incentives must be sufficiently large to encourage teachers to achieve the standards for advancement. Many nonsalary costs must also be recognized in planning and implementing an effective career ladder, including the fears and concerns of teachers and administrators about the fairness of the system. Even public recognition of career advancement and performance awards can bring pain for those not advancing and embarassment for those who receive them (Hatry, Greiner, & Ashford, 1994).

The first career ladders advanced teachers according to traditional measures of experience and advanced preparation, along with evaluations of teaching abilities. For example, a standardized appraisal system to assess classroom performance was an important aspect of the career ladders in Tennessee and North Carolina. However, there was not a reasonable and valid way to distinguish good from excellent teachers in these plans. More teachers than anticipated qualified for advancement (Cornett, 1985). In addition, the large investment for development, implementation, and evaluation in addition to salary supplements and fringe benefits required long-term commitments from states and districts. Furthermore, career ladders were found to breed suspicion, aggressive and circumventing behavior, and poor morale among teachers in many districts (MacPhail-Wilcox & King, 1988). Because of these limitations, some states placed a cap on participation, as occurred in Arizona. Or they withdrew funding entirely. By 1990, Alabama, Florida, Nebraska, North Carolina, and Wisconsin had terminated state-sponsored career ladder programs.

Only four states—Arizona, Missouri, Tennessee, and Utah—supported career ladders in 1994 (Cornett & Gaines, 1994). The Tennessee and Utah plans were the oldest continually operating career ladders. Since enactment of the Comprehensive Education Reform Act in 1984, Tennessee teachers were eligible to participate in a three-step ladder. This plan was fully funded by the state and in 1993–1994 offered salary supplements of between $1,000 and $7,000, depending on status and contract length. The Utah program offered several options to districts. These included a performance bonus that rewarded excellence by individuals or teams of teachers, a job enlargement plan to provide additional pay for extra work, extended contract days that enabled teachers to earn more for nonteaching days beyond the school year, and the career ladder.

The Arizona pilot program grew from 14 districts in 1988–1989 to 29 districts in 1993–1994. Teachers had the option of participating or continuing on the traditional salary schedule. Eligible teachers in all Missouri districts could participate in the Career Development and Teacher Excellence Plan that began in 1986–1987. At that time, 63 districts participated, in comparison with about 229 districts in 1993–1994. Teachers were eligible after their fifth year. Participants assumed additional responsibilities in professional growth, school and community involvement, and faculty collaboration. Funds for the plan were equalized by the state, such that districts received between 35 percent and 90 percent of the salary supplements for the career ladder's three stages.

Improved teaching performance is not a key feature of career ladders. They place the emphasis on differentiated responsibilities and salaries through the expansion or redesign of teaching roles. Although promotion to one of the designated levels may depend upon performance, differentiated pay typically reflects additional responsibilities rather than job performance. For example, in Utah when school boards, administrators, teachers, and parents were given latitude to cooperatively develop programs around the incentives listed above, the career ladders that included job expansion or redesign were found to be superior to those based on merit pay (Malen, Murphy, & Hart, 1988). Astuto (1985) also concluded that career ladders are more effective than traditional merit pay. She encouraged states to support local districts' experiments with diverse approaches.

Poston and Frase (1991) identified five factors that characterized successful career ladders: no legislative involvement or restrictive outside funding; teacher cooperation in planning; clear and attainable objectives that are creatively designed to meet local needs; freedom to determine the form of rewards, including both extrinsic and intrinsic incentives to improve skills; and sound and valid performance measures. Hawley (1985) and Hatry, Greiner, and Ashford (1994) recognized the importance of involving teachers in the development and implementation of plans. Firestone and Pennell (1993) concluded that increased participation, collaboration, and feedback contributed to teachers' commitment to this compensation strategy.

The primary limitation of career ladders, like that of merit pay plans, is their practice of rewarding individual teacher responsibilities and performance in ways that divide teachers. Other strategies recognize teachers' skills without dif-ferentiating rewards and provide incentives for group accomplishments.

Performance-Based Structures that Focus on Skills. Other career development plans enable continuous professional growth and the refinement of teaching skills without status differentiation. Like career ladders, these career development systems recognize that teachers have different skills and abilities depending on their stage of growth as professionals. However, increases in salary follow a uniform salary schedule according to experience and advanced preparation. For example, the Collegial Research Consortium offered a *career lattice* (Pipho, 1988) of roles, including mentor, peer coach, and knowledge producer, from which teachers design individual professional development plans appropriate to their stages in the career cycle. This career lattice stresses intrinsic rewards in giving greater job satisfaction, varied responsibilities, and a voice in decision making without differentiating pay. Hatry, Greiner, and Ashford (1994) investigated nonmonetary performance-by-objective plans that involved target setting by teachers early in the year and later measurement of performance. They concluded that this low-cost strategy can stimulate improved performance if properly designed and implemented. At the same time it avoids the difficulties associated with monetary incentives.

Odden and Conley (1992) offered a redesigned compensation structure that parallels efforts to improve schools and upgrade teacher quality by rewarding productivity. They urged educators to develop plans that would be linked to student outcomes; to focus on providing teachers with the knowledge and skills necessary to help students to learn; to support continuous development of professional expertise; to incorporate high-involvement management techniques, including participation in decision making; and to create norms of continuous improvement, collegiality, and teacher involvement in schoolwide issues. Their recommendations were comprehensive. They called for fellowships to attract capable students into teacher preparation, beginning salaries competitive with those earned by all college graduates, salary increments tied to growth in knowledge and skills, pay for performance, and flexible benefit packages. Conley and Odden (1995) subsequently recommended a compensation system based on several career stages in which advancement would depend on a rigorous assessment of specified skill and knowledge areas, with identified high standards that the teacher must meet to qualify (p. 232).

Group Performance Incentives.   Rewarding meritorious schools is still another approach that states have adopted to encourage schoolwide improvement efforts (see the discussion of incentives in funding plans in Chapter 9). These collective or group performance incentives address many of the limitations of merit and career ladder plans that reward individual teachers.

Rosenholtz (1987) noted that the competition evident in merit pay and career ladder plans does not foster teamwork and collegiality. Hawley (1985) identified this deficiency in performance-based pay (PBP) plans that reward individual achievements: "Indeed, some types of PBP systems are likely to reduce the collegial and supervisory support that research has shown to be related to teacher effectiveness" (p. 6). Group performance incentives use intrinsic rewards to motivate teachers to reach common goals: Because the teachers share their fate, the competitiveness and divisiveness of individual incentive plans are avoided. Moreover, when teachers collaborate and participate in decision making, the intrinsic incentives increase their motivation and commitment (Firestone, 1994, p. 561).

School-based group performance incentives may be a preferred strategy in the future, particularly as restructured schools increasingly rely upon collaborative efforts.

Status of Incentive Programs.   Table 16.6 shows the extent of state sponsorship of incentive programs, including reforms in individual teachers' compensation and rewards for improved school performance. Cornett and Gaines (1994) reported that eighteen states had local initiatives going on, nineteen states supported state-financed or state-assisted pilot projects, twenty-two states fully implemented incentives (but several programs are not funded), and sixteen states are developing incentive programs.

Twenty-two states were implementing or developing mentor teacher programs to reward or provide released time for exemplary teachers who assist new and other experienced teachers. Seventeen states have teacher incentives, including various plans to tie compensation to performance measures. Thirteen states have local efforts and four have full implementation (one of which was not funded). Sixteen states have career ladders piloted or fully implemented statewide. Another state had school district initiatives. Five states encouraged professional growth without status differentiation through local or state-financed career development programs. Several other states adopted differentiated pay or tiered certification or licensure to recognize career progression. Incentives tied additional school resources to productivity measures, including student achievement, in eleven states. Resources were available or proposed for staff development, school improvement, or a form of restructuring in five states.

The experiences of states and school systems during the past decade teach a number of lessons. Cornett and Gaines (1994) observed the following in their analyses of career ladders and other incentive plans:

- programs that fundamentally alter pay structures based on performance can produce fundamental change;
- comprehensive evaluation of incentive programs has occurred in only a few states;
- actions to fund, not fund, or disband programs are rarely based on real knowledge of programs and effects on students;
- changes in leadership at local and state levels have meant programs move away

from the original intent, never become implemented as intended, or are not given enough time to work;

- most teachers, when given a chance, choose to receive additional pay for more work, rather than for demonstrating high performance;
- teachers who participate in incentive programs are positive about the programs; those who do not are negative;
- teacher evaluation has changed, becoming more comprehensive and using teachers to evaluate teachers;
- individual pilot incentive programs designed at the district level without a guiding vision or support from the state have resulted in few fundamental changes or programs that last;
- fundamental change in structures has occurred in very few schools across the nation because of the incentive programs; and
- comprehensive incentive programs that alter fundamentally the ways teachers work and are paid have promise for improving results for students.

There is little doubt that state and district policies governing teachers' compensation will play important roles in efforts to improve teachers' performance and school productivity.

SUMMARY

There are several important differences between the teacher labor market and that of the private sector. Traditional economic assumptions about supply and demand do not adequately describe the setting of wages in the public sector. A host of social and political considerations influence the availability of teachers (supply), school systems' need for teachers (demand), and teachers' salaries.

Improving the efficiency of schools depends in large part on reforms in personnel policies, including compensation systems and teachers' responsibilities as professionals. Policies that address the following issues are designed to attract and retain highly capable teachers: raising initial qualifications, increasing the level of compensation relative to that of other professions, relating remuneration to individual and team performance, expanding professional roles and opportunities for growth, and improving working conditions.

Restructured compensation plans are supposed to improve education by influencing teachers' motivation and performance. Unlike the single salary schedule which rewards limited but easily measured characteristics of teachers, merit pay and career ladder programs strive to relate remuneration to actual teaching performance and responsibilities. These performance-based plans presume that teachers are motivated by financial rewards. But there is evidence that pay works as a dissatisfier and demotivator. These individual teacher rewards also have severe shortcomings related to the quality of performance assessments. And they interfere with cooperative working relationships. Until the nature of teachers' work is substantially changed in ways that strengthen schools' capacities to improve teaching and learning, the reform of compensation systems alone is not likely to have dramatic impacts on the supply of teachers or student performance.

Policy changes that affect the number and qualifications of personnel directly influence school finance policy because of the high cost of labor relative to total school budgets. Effective performance-based compensation systems, as one aspect of systemic reform, are costly strategies. However, improved working conditions and teaching skills promise to enhance the internal efficiency of schools. Chapter 17 continues this discussion of educational production by examining the potential of the increased use of information technologies as teachers' responsibilities change in the future.

TABLE 16.6. Status of Teacher and School Incentive Programs, 1993

State	Type of Program	Local Initiative	State-funded or -assisted Pilots	Full Implementation of State Program	State Program under Development
Alabama	NA			X	
Alaska	Teacher incentive	X			
Arizona	School restructuring		X		
	Career ladder			X	
Arkansas	Mentor teacher				X
California	Mentor teacher			X	
Colorado	Teacher incentive	X			
	Teacher/school incentive				X[a]
	Tiered licensing				X
Connecticut	Mentor teacher			X	
	Career development				X[a]
Florida	School improvement/ accountability			X	
Georgia	School incentive			X	
	Mentor teacher			X	
Hawaii	Mentor teacher				X
Idaho	Mentor teacher			X[a]	
	Career compensation				X[a]
Illinois	Teacher incentive	X			
Indiana	Career ladder/development	X			
	Mentor teacher			X	
	School incentive			X	
Iowa	Teacher incentive/ school transformation			X	
Kansas	Teacher incentive	X			
Kentucky	School incentive				X
Louisiana	Career options		X[a]		
	School incentive				X[a]
	Mentor teacher		X		
Maine	Tiered certification			X	
Maryland	Career development	X			
Massachusetts	Tiered certification				X
	Mentor teacher				X
Michigan	Teacher incentive	X			
Minnesota	Teacher incentive	X			
	Mentor teacher		X		
Missouri	Career ladder			X	
Montana	Teacher incentive	X			
	Mentor teacher		X		
New Hampshire	Teacher incentive	X			
New Jersey	Teacher incentive			X[a]	
	Mentor teacher				X
New Mexico	Tiered licensing			X	
	Mentor teacher			X	
New York	Mentor teacher	X			
	Teacher incentive			X	
	Staff development			X	
	School incentive				X
North Carolina	Career ladder		X		
	Differentiated pay			X	
North Dakota	Career development	X			

TABLE 16.6. Status of Teacher and School Incentive Programs, 1993 (*Continued*)

State	Type of Program	Local Initiative	State-funded or -assisted Pilots	Full Implementation of State Program	State Program under Development
Ohio	Career ladder		X		
Oklahoma	Teacher incentive	X			
Oregon	School restructuring				X
Pennsylvania	Career development			X	
	Mentor teacher			X	
	School incentive			X[a]	
Rhode Island	Mentor teacher		X		
South Carolina	School incentive			X	
	Campus incentive				X
South Dakota	Mentor teacher	X			X
Tennessee	Career ladder			X	
	School/teacher incentive				X
Texas	School incentive			X	
Utah	Career ladder			X	
Virginia	Teacher incentive	X			
	Mentor teacher		X		
Washington	School incentive		X		
	Mentor teacher			X	
West Virginia	Mentor teacher			X	
Wisconsin	Mentor teacher	X			
	Teacher incentive	X			
Wyoming	Teacher incentive	X			

[a]Reform called for but not funded.

SOURCE: L. M. Cornett & G. F. Gaines. (1994). Reflecting on Ten Years of Incentive Programs: The 1993 SREB Career Ladder Clearinghouse Survey. *Career Ladder Clearinghouse.* Atlanta, GA: Southern Regional Education Board.

ACTIVITIES

1. Examine teacher supply and demand conditions in a given state, region, or school district. Construct a chart or spreadsheet that compares the number of applicants for teaching positions with the number of personnel hired for different grade levels and subject areas over a ten-year period. Interview state and local officials about the trends evidenced and the steps that had been taken or might be taken to stimulate supply, particularly in high-demand subject areas.

2. Interview principals and teachers, including, if possible, one who has earned certification through the National Board for Professional Teaching Standards, to learn about the potential benefits and costs of encouraging teachers to seek this national recognition. Should school districts provide incentives for teachers to participate in assessments? Should there be pay differentials to attract and retain board-certified teachers?

3. Research and debate the advantages of merit pay plans that condition additional compensation on an individual teacher's performance, career ladder programs that differentiate salaries in accordance with the responsibilities of redefined positions, and collective incentive programs that reward team accomplishments. Is there empirical evidence that any of these approaches is effective in improving job satisfaction, teachers' skills, or pupil performance?

COMPUTER SIMULATIONS

Objectives of This Activity

- *To develop an understanding of the structures of traditional and performance-based teacher salary models.*

- *To conduct "what if" analyses on teacher salary models using spreadsheets.*

These simulations present two approaches to paying teachers. We begin with a traditional single salary schedule having two dimensions—years of experience and professional preparation. We then introduce a model for basing annual salaries on teachers' satisfaction of criteria for advancement in professional status and for annual performance reviews. In each of these approaches, the spreadsheet determines the cost implications of the model given the number of teachers at each level and permits those engaged in negotiations to ask "what if" questions as modifications are anticipated.

Simulation 16.1: *Single Salary Schedule*

In this simulation, the Lake County School District compensates its certified teachers according to the number of years of teaching experience (24 increments) and the degrees earned (6 advancements for blocks of semester hours and degrees).

a. Retrieve the file SALARY_1. Note that there are three worksheets contained in the file: the salary schedule itself, the number of teachers within each cell, and a calculation of the total cost of salaries.

b. Beginning with the base salary of $22,035 for a first-year teacher with a Bachelor's degree, determine the amount of salary for others with a BA. Create and copy a formula through the 17th year such that there is an increment of $480 over the previous year. The schedule does not include increments for teachers having over 17 years' experience.

c. Return to the base salary, and create formulas to reward first-year teachers $850 for having 15 semester hours of graduate study beyond the BA and to provide increments in this column of $650 through the 17 years and on obtaining 20 years' experience (there is no additional increment for 24 years' experience).

d. Continue in like manner to create and copy formulas in columns such that teachers are rewarded: (1) $900 for BA + 36 OR MA column over the BA + 15 column and $900 for each annual increment including the 20th and 24th anniversaries; (2) $850 for MA + 15 and $900 for annual increments in this column; (3) $900 for having 36 hours beyond the MA or Ed.S. diploma (MA + 36 ED.S.) and $900 for each additional year of experience; and (4) $1,000 for an earned DOCTORATE and $950 for each year of experience. (**Note:** An accurate schedule will show a salary of $43,635 for a teacher having a doctorate and at least 24 years' experience.)

e. Print the worksheet for step d.

f. The number of teachers at each salary level of the schedule is listed in the second worksheet. Create formulas in the TOTAL row to add the number of teachers in each column and, in the last column on the GRAND TOTAL row, create a formula to report the number of teachers in the district. **Handy Hint:** The correct GRAND TOTAL of teachers is 260.

g. Print the worksheet produced in step f.

h. The final worksheet in this part enables calculation of the cost of the salary schedule given the configuration of teachers. Create a formula in the cell for the first-year BA teacher which will multiply the salary in the first cell of the salary schedule by the number of teachers at that level (**Note:** Be sure to enter the cell references in the formula rather than $22,035 or 16 teachers. Copy this formula into all other cells of this third worksheet, except for the TOTAL, GRAND TOTAL, and AVERAGE SALARY rows.)

i. Create formulas in the TOTAL row to add the salaries paid in each column; in the last column of the GRAND TOTAL row, create a formula to report the amount of salaries paid all teachers in the district. In the last column of the AVERAGE SALARY row, create a formula to determine the mean salary paid.

j. Print a copy of the worksheet produced in step i.

k. Assume that the Board of Education is considering a proposal to provide an additional $100 for all movements on the schedule according to semester hour and degree advancements and $50 for each experience step. Assume also that the second worksheet represents the experience levels and degrees of teachers in the year for which this projection is desired. Retain the current base and make these dollar changes in the formulas that were entered in the first worksheet, and note the changes in the last worksheet.

Helpful Hints: The $100 education adjustments require the editing of all formulas on the first row of the salary schedule except for the formula in the BA column. All other formulas on this row have the following edit: +100. For example, in the BA + 15 column on the first row, the edited formula is +B10+850+100 for Lotus and =B10+850+100 for Excel. The $50 experience adjustments require editing of formulas on the second row of the salary schedule. All formulas on this row have the following edit: +50. For example, in the BA column on the second row, the edited formula is +B10+480+50 for Lotus and =B10+480+50 for Excel.

l. Print a copy of the worksheets produced in step k. Compare your printouts and answer the following questions: What is the overall cost of these changes in the schedule? What

are the percentage increases in the overall salary commitment and in the average salary paid?

m. Negotiations between the board and the Teachers' Association have reached a tentative agreement that the original schedule be retained, but that the base salary be increased by a three percent (3%) "cost-of-living" factor [modify only the base salary by a factor of 1.03, increasing it to $22,696]. Assume that the experience levels and degrees of teachers remain the same as in step g.

n. Print a copy of the worksheet produced in step m. Compare your printouts and determine the cost impacts of this percentage change in the base. Which teachers (according to experience levels) are most advantaged in actual dollar changes under this proposal? What are some of the arguments that the board and the Teachers' Association might use to advance or defeat this proposal?

o. **Further Activities.** Modify the spreadsheets in a way to illustrate another possible proposal for changing the salary schedule, such as a different cost-of-living adjustment, and develop a rationale for presenting these modifications before the board and teachers.

Simulation 16.2: *Performance-Based Salary Model*

In this continuation of the Lake County salary simulation, differentiations in salaries are based on four professional statuses, including "Provisional" for initially certified teachers and three "Career" levels as teachers grow in professional responsibilities. In addition to these statuses, an annual determination of performance brings one-year increments above any negotiated cost-of-living (COL) allowance that applies to all teachers.

An initially certified/licensed teacher enters the model according to the highest degree earned; subsequent years' salaries are determined by (1) the shift in the model induced by COL increases and (2) annual performance reviews that *may* result in an "Above Standard" or "Outstanding" rating and thus raise salaries for one year at a time above the base. For example, a second- (or fifth-) year teacher with a Master's degree who has not achieved Career Status I would be paid $27,096 if the prior year's performance review was "Above Standard." A teacher could remain at this level only in those years for which positive reviews had occurred the previous year.

A large increase in salary accompanies movements in professional status. Advancement to Career I, II, and III depends on criteria in negotiated contracts, and each successive professional status carries greater responsibilities (see discussion of career ladders in this chapter). Again, a teacher who remains at any one status for one, several, or all years of a career receives increments for positive performance reviews for selected (or all) years in addition to COL increases. Note that Career II status is not available to teachers who hold only a Bachelor's degree and that advancement to Career III is open only to those teachers who have 36 hours beyond a Master's degree or an earned doctorate.

a. Retrieve the file SALARY_2. Note that there are two worksheets located within the file. The first worksheet is the Model itself, and all columns except the OUTSTANDING columns already have either the rate of increase or calculated salary amount. The second worksheet, which determines the cost of the model given the number of teachers at each professional status and performance level, does not yet include salary or total amounts.

b. Assume that the Board of Education has agreed to award increases above the CURRENT BASE for OUTSTANDING performance as follows: .09 for PROVISIONAL BA, .078 for PROVISIONAL MA, .064 for CAREER I BA, .058 for CAREER I MA, .051

for CAREER II MA, .045 for CAREER II MA plus 36 hours, .041 for CAREER III MA plus 36 hours, and 0.37 for CAREER III DOCTORATE. Enter these rates of increase and create formulas that will calculate salaries in the $ column relative to the CURRENT BASE salary for each professional status in the model.

c. In the second worksheet, which reports the number of teachers and accumulated salaries paid, create formulas to:

(1) calculate in the TOTAL row the numbers of teachers who are actually paid salaries according to the base, above standard, and outstanding performance levels; in the TOTAL column the number at each professional status/degree level; and the total number of teachers in the district.

(2) determine the amount of total salaries paid to all teachers at each performance level. **Helpful Hint:** Multiply the number of teachers times respective salary from the model.

(3) compute the TOTAL salary paid at each professional status in the last column and the TOTAL of all teachers' salaries.

d. Print the worksheet created in step c.

e. How does the total salary commitment under this performance-based model compare to that of the last negotiated single salary schedule of Simulation 16.1, step m? What modifications in the performance-based model might ease the extra cost of moving to this system?

f. Modify the first worksheet model for a year in which the board and Teachers' Association agree to increase the PRIOR YEAR BASE using the following COL adjustments: PROVISIONAL by .04, CAREER I by .038, CAREER II by .036, and CAREER III by .034. The ABOVE STANDARD and OUTSTANDING rates should be changed to zero. Note the overall increase in total salaries paid under this revised model from the former model.

g. Print the worksheet created in step f.

h. What are the strengths and limitations of the model resulting from the changes in steps c and f in relation to the criticisms of traditional salary schedules?

i. **Further Activities.** Describe and defend one or more recommendations you would make to the board and/or Teachers' Association to improve this performance-based pay model. Prepare a revised model and cost implications to accompany one of these recommendations.

REFERENCES

Anthony, P. (1988). Teachers in the economic system. In K. Alexander & D. H. Monk (Eds.), *Attracting and compensating America's teachers* (pp. 1–20). Cambridge, MA: Ballinger.

Association of American Colleges. (1989). *Those who can: Undergraduate programs to prepare arts and sciences majors for teaching.* Washington, DC: Association of American Colleges.

Association of Teacher Educators. (1985). *Developing career ladders in teaching.* Reston, VA: Author.

Astuto, T. A. (1985). *Merit pay for teachers: An analysis of state policy options.* Educational Policy Studies Series. Bloomington, IN: Indiana University.

Ballou, D., & Podgursky, M. (1993). Teachers' attitudes toward merit pay: Examining conventional wisdom. *Industrial and Labor Relations Review, 47,* 50–61.

Bobbitt, S. A. (1992). *Trends in schools and staffing: 1987–88 to 1990–91.* Washington, DC: National Center for Education Statistics. ERIC Document, ED 363 661.

Bobbitt, S. A., & McMillen, M. M. (1990). *Teacher training, certification, and assignment.* Paper presented at the annual meeting of the American Educational Research Association, Boston. ERIC Document, ED 322 138.

Bradley, A. (1995). Overruns spur teacher board to alter plans. *Education Week, 14* (1), 12.

Butler, A. D. (1963). *Labor economics and institutions.* New York: Macmillan.

Candoli, I. C., Hack, W. G., Ray, J. R., & Stollar, D. H. (1984). *School business administration: A planning approach* (3rd. ed.). Boston, MA: Allyn and Bacon.

Carnegie Forum. (1986). *A nation prepared: Teachers for the twenty-first century.* New York: Carnegie Forum on Education and the Economy.

Castetter, W. B. (1986). *The personnel function in educational administration* (4th ed.). New York: Macmillan.

Conley, S., & Odden, A. (1995). Linking teacher compensation to teacher career development. *Educational Evaluation and Policy Analysis, 17,* 219–237.

Cornett, L. M. (1985). Trends and emerging issues in career ladder plans. *Educational Leadership, 43,* 6–10.

Cornett, L. M., & Gaines, G. F. (1994). Reflecting on ten years of incentive programs: The 1993 SREB career ladder clearinghouse survey. *Career ladder clearinghouse.* Atlanta, GA: Southern Regional Education Board.

Darling-Hammond, L. (1984). *Beyond the commission reports: The coming crisis in teaching.* R-3177-RC. Santa Monica, CA: Rand Corporation.

Darling-Hammond, L. (1986). Teaching knowledge: How do we test it? *American Educator, 10,* 18–21, 46–47.

Darling-Hammond, L., & Berry, B. (1988). *The evolution of teacher policy.* JRE-01. Center for Policy Research in Education. Santa Monica, CA: Rand Corporation.

Deming, W. E. (1982). *Quality, productivity, and competitive position.* Cambridge, MA: Center for Advanced Engineering Study, Massachusetts Institute of Technology.

Farnsworth, B., Debenham, J., & Smith, G. (1991). Designing and implementing a successful merit pay program for teachers. *Phi Delta Kappan, 73,* 320–325.

Feistritzer, C. E. (1986). *Profile of teachers in the U.S.* Washington, DC: National Center for Education Information.

Firestone, W. A. (1994). Redesigning teacher salary systems for educational reform. *American Educational Research Journal, 31,* 549–574.

Firestone, W. A., & Bader, B. D. (1992). *Redesigning teaching: Professionalism or bureaucracy?* Albany: State University of New York Press.

Firestone, W. A., & Pennell, J. R. (1993). Teacher commitment, working conditions, and differential incentive policies. *Review of Educational Research, 63,* 489–525.

Fleisher, B. M., & Kniesner, T. J. (1980). *Labor economics: Theory, evidence, and policy.* Englewood Cliffs, NJ: Prentice-Hall.

Fox, J. M. (1984). Restructuring the teacher work force to attract the best and the brightest. *Journal of Education Finance, 10,* 214–237.

Fox, J. M. (1988). The supply of U.S. teachers: Quality for the twenty-first century. In K. Alexander & D. H. Monk (Eds.), *Attracting and compensating America's teachers* (pp. 49–68). Cambridge, MA: Ballinger.

Frohreich, L. E. (1988). Merit pay: Issues and solutions. In K. Alexander & D. H. Monk (Eds.), *Attracting and compensating America's teachers* (pp. 143–160). Cambridge, MA: Ballinger.

Gerald, D. E., & Hussar, W. J. (1995). *Projections of education statistics to 2005.* Washington, DC: National Center for Education Statistics.

Gold, S. D., Smith, D. M., & Lawton, S. B. (Eds.). (1995). *Public school finance programs of the United States and Canada, 1993–94.* Albany, NY: American Education Finance Association and the Center for the Study of the States.

Gray, L., Cahalan, M., Hein, S., Litman, C., Severynse, J., Warren, S., & Wisan, G. (1993). *New teachers in the job market, 1991 update.* Washington, DC: National Center for Educational Statistics.

Hatry, H. P., Greiner, J. M., & Ashford, B. G. (1994). *Issues and case studies in teacher incentive plans.* Washington, DC: Urban Institute Press.

Hawley, W. D. (1985). The limits and potential of performance-based pay as a source of school improvement. In H. C. Johnson (Ed.), *Merit, money and teachers' careers: Studies on merit pay and career ladders for teachers* (pp. 3–22). Lanham, MD: University Press of America.

Hawley, W. D. (1986). Toward a comprehensive strategy for addressing the teacher shortage. *Phi Delta Kappan, 67,* 712–718.

Herndon, T. (1985). Merit pay and the concerns of the teaching profession. In H. C. Johnson (Ed.), *Merit, money and teachers' careers: Studies on merit pay and career ladders for teachers* (pp. 93–98). Lanham, MD: University Press of America.

Herzberg, F., Mausner, B., & Snyderman, B. (1959). *The motivation to work.* New York: John Wiley.

Holmes Group. (1986). *Tomorrow's teachers: A report of the Holmes Group.* East Lansing, MI: Holmes Group.

Holmes Group. (1995). *Tomorrow's schools of education: A report of the Holmes Group* (Final Draft). East Lansing, MI: Holmes Group.

Jacobson, S. L. (1988). Merit pay and teaching as a career. In K. Alexander & D. H. Monk (Eds.), *Attracting and compensating America's teachers* (pp. 161–177). Cambridge, MA: Ballinger.

Jacobson, S. L. (1990). Change in entry-level salary and the recruitment of novice teachers. *Journal of Education Finance, 15,* 408–413.

Johnson, H. C. (Ed.). (1985). *Merit, money and teachers' careers: Studies on merit pay and career ladders for teachers.* Lanham, MD: University Press of America.

Johnson, S. M. (1986). Incentives for teachers: What motivates, what matters? *Educational Administration Quarterly, 22,* 54–79.

Kohn, A. (1993). *Punished by rewards: The trouble with gold stars, incentive plans, As, praise, and other bribes.* Boston: Houghton Mifflin.

Kreps, J. M., Somers, G. G., & Perlman, R. (1974). *Contemporary labor economics: Issues, analysis, and policies.* Belmont, CA: Wadsworth.

Lawler, E. E. (1981). *Pay and organization development.* Reading, MA: Addison-Wesley.

Lawton, S. B. (1988). Teachers' salaries: An international perspective. In K. Alexander & D. H. Monk (Eds.), *Attracting and compensating America's teachers* (pp. 69–89). Cambridge, MA: Ballinger.

MacPhail-Wilcox, B., & King, R. A. (1988). Personnel reforms in education: Intents, consequences, and fiscal implications. *Journal of Education Finance, 14,* 100–134.

Madaus, G. F., & Pullin, D. (1987). Teacher certification tests: Do they really measure what we need to know? *Phi Delta Kappan, 69,* 31–38.

Magel, C. J. (1961). Merit rating is unsound. *Phi Delta Kappan, 42,* 154–156.

Malen, B., Murphy, M. J., & Hart, A. W. (1988). Restructuring teacher compensation systems: An analysis of three incentive strategies. In K. Alexander & D. H. Monk (Eds.), *Attracting and compensating America's teachers* (pp. 91–142). Cambridge, MA: Ballinger.

Manski, C. F. (1985). *Academic ability, earnings, and the decision to become a teacher: Evidence from the national longitudinal study of the high school class of 1972*, Working Paper No. 1539. Cambridge, MA: National Bureau of Economic Research.

Murnane, R. J., & Cohen, D. K. (1986). Merit pay and the evaluation problem: Why most merit pay plans fail and a few survive. *Harvard Educational Review, 56,* 1–17.

Murnane, R. J., Singer, J. D., Willet, J. B., Kemple, J. J., & Olsen, R. J. (1991). *Who will teach? Policies that matter.* Cambridge, MA: Harvard University Press.

National Commission on Excellence in Education. (1983). A *nation at risk: The imperative for educational reform.* Washington, DC: U.S. Department of Education.

National Education Association. (1984). *Merit pay: Promises and facts.* Washington, DC: NEA.

National Education Association. (1985). *The single salary schedule.* Washington, DC: NEA.

NCES (National Center for Education Statistics). (1992). *Historical trends: State education facts, 1969–1989.* Washington, DC: U.S. Government Printing Office.

NCES (National Center for Education Statistics). (1993a). Teacher salaries—Are they competitive? *Issue Brief.* Washington, DC: U.S. Department of Education.

NCES (National Center for Education Statistics). (1993b). *The condition of education: Elementary and secondary education, 1993* (Vol. 1). Washington, DC: U.S. Government Printing Office.

NCES (National Center for Education Statistics). (1993c). *Digest of education statistics, 1993.* Washington, DC: U.S. Government Printing Office.

NCES (National Center for Education Statistics) (1994a). *The condition of education, 1994.* Washington, DC: U.S. Government Printing Office.

NCES (National Center for Education Statistics). (1994b). *Digest of education statistics, 1994.* Washington, DC: U.S. Government Printing Office.

NCES (National Center for Education Statistics). (1995a). *The condition of education, 1995.* Washington, DC: U.S. Government Printing Office.

NCES (National Center for Education Statistics). (1995b). *Digest of education statistics, 1995.* Washington, DC: U.S. Government Printing Office.

Nelson, F. H. (1995). International comparison of teacher salaries and conditions of employment. In W. J. Fowler (Ed.), *Developments in school finance* (pp. 109–127). Washington, DC: U.S. Government Printing Office.

Nelson, F. H., & O'Brien, T. (1993). *How U.S. teachers measure up internationally: A comparative study of teacher pay, training, and conditions of service.* Washington, DC: American Federation of Teachers, AFL-CIO.

Odden, A. R., & Conley, S. (1992). Restructuring teacher compensation systems. In A. R. Odden (Ed.), *Rethinking school finance: An agenda for the 1990s* (pp. 41–96). San Francisco: Jossey-Bass.

Parker, F. (1993). *Reforming U.S. teacher education in the 1990s.* ERIC Document, ED 358 084.

Pipho, C. (1988). Career ladders are changing. *Phi Delta Kappan, 69,* 550–551.

Poston, W. K., & Frase, L. E. (1991). Alternative compensation programs for teachers: Rolling boulders up the mountain of reform. *Phi Delta Kappan, 73,* 317–320.

Rebore, R. W. (1987). *Personnel administration in education: A management approach* (2nd ed.). Englewood Cliffs, NJ: Prentice-Hall.

Rosenholtz, S. J. (1987). Education reform strategies: Will they increase teacher commitment? *American Journal of Education, 92,* 352–389.

Salmon, R. G. (1988). Teacher salaries: Progress over the decade. In K. Alexander & D. H. Monk (Eds.), *Attracting and compensating America's teachers* (pp. 249–261). Cambridge, MA: Ballinger.

Schlechty, P. C. (1987). The concept of career ladders. In P. R. Burden (Ed.), *Establishing career ladders in teaching: A guide for policy makers* (pp. 4–16). Springfield, IL: Charles C Thomas.

Shulman, L. S. (1987). Assessment for teaching: An initiative for the profession. *Phi Delta Kappan, 69,* 38–44.

Skinner, B. F. (1974). *About behaviorism.* New York: Knopf.

Smith, G. N. (1987). Costs for a career ladder. In P. R. Burden (Ed.), *Establishing career ladders in teaching: A guide for policy makers* (pp. 216–225). Springfield, IL: Charles C Thomas.

Snyder, T. D. (1993). *Trends in education.* ERIC Document, ED 362 970.

Sykes, G. (1983). Public policy and the problem of teacher quality: The need for screens and magnets. In L.S. Shulman & G. Sykes (Eds.), *Handbook of teaching and policy* (pp. 97–125). New York: Longman.

Thangaraj, E. P. (1985). *The impact of teacher labor market forces on characteristics of the teacher aspirant pool.* Unpublished doctoral dissertation, State University of New York at Buffalo.

Travers, E. F., & Sacks, S. R. (1987). *Teacher education and the liberal arts: The position of the Consortium for Excellence in Teacher Education.* Swarthmore, PA: Swarthmore College.

Vance, V. S., and Schlechty, P. C. (1982). The distribution of academic ability in the teaching force: Policy implications. *Phi Delta Kappan, 64,* 22–27.

Vroom, V. H. (1964). *Work and motivation.* New York: John Wiley.

Weeks, K., & Cornett, L. M. (1985). Planning career ladders: Lessons from the states. *Career Ladder Clearinghouse.* Atlanta, GA: Southern Regional Education Board.

CHAPTER 17

Integrating Educational Technology into Instructional Systems

Primary Issues Explored in This Chapter:

- *Education and technology:* What are the relationships between education and technology?
- *Contrasting information age and industrial age schools:* What are the implications of current technological innovations for the organization of schooling?

- *Information age schools:* What do information age schools look like?
- *Politics of innovation:* What forces are impeding the widespread implementation of information age schools? How can these impeding forces be overcome?

We introduced the concepts of education production functions and input-output analysis in Chapter 13 in reference to the internal efficiency of educational enterprises. In Chapter 16, we examined the possibilities for incorporating efficiency incentives into remuneration policies for teachers. In this chapter we continue our analysis of efficiency. But now we focus on enhancing the efficiency of schools through changing the mix of inputs into the instructional process—specifically, labor and capital. While productivity and efficiency may be improved by achieving better outcomes, economic efficiency can also be improved through lower costs at a given level of productivity. Any rearrangement of inputs that lowers total cost without changing the quality of education delivered is an increase in efficiency. The resulting decreases in total cost represent decreases in the amount of real resources (human and nonhuman) that society must commit to current educational processes. This frees

resources to satisfy other human aspirations or permits investment in new educational pursuits.

We begin with a general discussion of education and technology. We then describe some of the current initiatives for integrating technology into schools and thereby revolutionizing the conceptualization of schooling. We conclude with a discussion of the politics of technological change in education and the implications for school administration and finance.

TECHNOLOGICAL CHANGE AND EDUCATION

Technology is the application of science to control the material environment for human benefit by using tools and the intellect. When used prudently, technologies allow society to produce more and better goods and services from a fixed amount of resources. Advances in technology have permitted mankind to live longer and more comfortably. But they have also led to undesirable results including environmental degradation, unemployment, and even the capacity for total human annihilation.

Educational technology is the application of scientific knowledge, including learning theory, to the solution of problems in education. Education and technology are both cause and effect. Technological developments place continuing pressure on educators to keep curriculum and instructional methods up to date. At the same time, educational institutions are essential to the generation and assimilation of new technology.

Although society in general has tended toward enhanced technological sophistication and increased capital intensity, the education sector still has a traditional, labor-intensive, craft-oriented technology (Bolton, 1994; Butzin, 1992; Cuban, 1988; Goodlad, 1984; Murphy, 1993). This conservatism creates both sociological and economic problems. From an economic standpoint, labor-intensive education is unnecessarily expensive. In general, it does not produce a workforce with the attitudes and skills needed for a rapidly changing workplace. From a sociological standpoint, technologically unsophisticated schools are losing their credibility and thereby their effectiveness with pupils because they are no longer congruent with the larger societal context.

We have referred to the growing labor intensity of education. Figure 3.2 showed the dramatic increases between 1971 and 1995 in expenditures per pupil in constant dollar purchasing power. The fivefold increase—from $960 to $5,149 (National Center for Education Statistics, 1993) in 1993 dollars—was sufficient to allow for significant program expansion in terms of smaller class sizes, more specialists, more electives, and new programs for gifted children and children with physical and learning disabilities. We discussed the growing labor intensiveness of education further in Chapter 16. For the American economy as a whole, approximately 66 percent of total product cost is for labor. But for education it ranges between 85 percent and 90 percent. Most schools and school districts allocate less than 1 percent of their budgets to the purchase of electronic technology. In comparison, most low-tech industries devote between 5 and 10 percent of their budgets to such technologies. High-tech firms devote as much as 40 percent (Mecklenburger, 1994a).

Nonservice industries, for example, manufacturing, generally understand that technological structure is not inalterably fixed, especially under competitive market conditions. Instead, there is an ongoing search for alternative, more efficient productive methods that require different mixes of human and nonhuman resources. Industries judge these alternatives by their potential costs and effectiveness. Education, however, is largely a state monopoly with weak market incentives for efficiency. It appears to be locked into one labor-intensive mode of production. Even when parents enter the educational marketplace, they choose among public and private schools that differ in size and philosophies but are remarkably similar in the teaching technologies they use.

In response to the education reform movement, expenditures per pupil in inflation-adjusted dollars increased by 48 percent during the 1980s. But the pattern of allocation of resources has not changed on average. Picus (1995) observed that "the effect of new money on student achievement may be limited by the fact that new resources are used in the same way as existing resources, limiting the potential effectiveness of those new dollars" (p. 2).

Baumol (1967) argued that "inherent in the technological structure" of such service industries as education "are forces working almost unavoidably for progressive and cumulative increases in the real costs incurred in supplying them" (p. 415). If productivity is to be enhanced in education (and other service industries), industries must be willing to develop alternative means of providing services, including modifications in their technological structures. The purpose of technology is to make labor go further by replacing it, to the extent possible, with mechanical devices and more efficient organization in order to produce a better product or service or to reduce the costs of production (Benson, 1961).

Educators tend to think of instructional technology as being very expensive. But this is the case only when technology is used as an add-on and not as a substitute for labor. One of the most telling shortcomings of leadership in the public schools is its failure to understand the role of technology. Using new technologies has only one purpose: to increase productivity. This is why most of the rest of the economy spends billions of dollars annually on new technological devices in order to remain competitive by keeping unit production costs low. Public schools need to learn from the practice of other organizations and squarely address the issue of productivity (Doyle, 1994).

Even allowing for substantial increases in teacher salaries, Willett, Swanson, and Nelson (1979) estimated that the cost per pupil of an instructional system that optimally integrated human and machine capabilities would be well below that of the existing system. They assumed that there would be fewer teachers (although with higher qualifications). The information transfer function would be provided largely through use of instructional technology. The system would make extensive use of relatively low-cost paraprofessionals under the supervision of teachers. And it would make extensive use of community resources. Because the cost of instructional technology is even lower today relative to other costs and the sophistication of the technology is much greater than when Willett et al. made their analysis, cost comparisons would be even more favorable now.

Contrast in your mind, for example, what $2,000 buys today compared to a decade ago. That amount of money now buys a computer with a high-resolution color monitor, 200+ MB hard disk and a double-speed CD-ROM drive, 33 MHz or faster processing time, 8 MB or more of random-access memory, and the ability to display audio and video. A decade ago, $2,000 would buy a fuzzy monochrome monitor, a 10 MB hard disk, 6 MHz processing time, 0.6 MB of random-access mem-

ory, and no audio or video capability (Mecklenburger, 1994a). Furthermore, instructional software was very limited in the 1980s. Since then there has been a dramatic increase in its variety, sophistication, and capabilities.

The Waterford Institute compared the cost of tutorial reading programs for first-grade children and individualized instructional programs using computer technology (Heuston, 1994). The tutorial program required one teacher for every eight or ten pupils and cost between $5,000 and $8,000 per child per year. In contrast, a well-run technology program could produce similar results at a cost of $250 to $300 per pupil per year.

The National Governors' Association (1986) found that, "despite extensive purchase and high expectations, most American schools have not become significantly more cost-effective or more efficient because of technology. The structure of most schools has not changed significantly because technology is available" (p. 123). A 1987 report by the National School Boards Association (Perelman, 1987) criticized the school reform movement because it failed to address the issue of increasing efficiency in education. This report anticipated an inevitable technological transformation of teaching and learning in the United States and elsewhere in the world.

According to Levin and Meister (1985), educational technologies have been characterized by promise rather than realization of that promise. During this century, the educational potential of new inventions such as radio, motion pictures, television, video cassettes, compact disks, and computers has been praised. But the praise was followed by disappointment as the invention remained ancillary to traditional instructional procedures. These authors diagnosed the generic failure of educational technologies as being due largely "to a misplaced obsession with the hardware and neglect of software, other resources, and instructional setting that are necessary to successful implementation" (p. 9). They pointed out that the purchase of equipment should be only about 10 percent of the total cost of an innovation, if that innovation is to be effective.

To improve the situation, Levin and Meister (1985, p. 38) proposed three initiatives: (1) more coordinated market information, (2) improved decision mechanisms in schools, and (3) large-scale institutional approaches to software development and funding. They proposed a decision mechanism that would provide districtwide coordination of the purchase and installation of technology, integration of software into district curricular objectives and materials, and training of professional and support staff in the use of hardware and software (p. 43).

In a similar vein, a report by the Office of Technology Assessment (1982) of the United States Congress concluded that information technologies can best be applied to tasks when they are well integrated into their institutional environments. This is not the way technology has been used in schools, however. The most commonly proposed reforms to improve public education continue to be heavily labor intensive.

It isn't that schools have totally neglected new technologies. We are concerned about the way in which schools have chosen to accommodate them. Technological devices have been used as add-ons to assist or supplement teacher efforts rather than as integral parts of new learning systems that combine the capabilities and energy of students and teachers with those devices to achieve results superior to what could be achieved without them or equal results at a lower cost. When technology is used as an add-on or as enrichment, costs are increased and efficiency is decreased unless there is evidence of greatly improved outcomes (Butzin, 1992).

Using technology in school as an add-on is not a recent phenomenon. In a 1972 study, Vaizey, Norris, and Sheehan noted that teacher costs accounted for at least half of all school costs. They said that unless increases in pupil : teacher ratios took place as a result of the use of the new technologies, new technologies would necessarily add to total costs. The authors accurately predicted that increases in pupil : teacher ratios would not happen:

[I]t seems unlikely that any teacher substitution will occur—certainly none has yet taken place. Thus for new methods to be used on a wider scale, the decision will have to be taken that the educational benefits are worth the resulting increases in costs. (p. 234)

But in a few places that are scattered widely across the United States and the developed world, we are beginning to see schools that are fundamentally redesigned to reform the learning experiences of students. In the next sections, we contrast the conceptualizations of these new schools with those of the typical industrial age school. We describe interpretations of the new philosophy in actual practice.

CONTRASTING INDUSTRIAL AGE SCHOOLS WITH THE EMERGING INFORMATION AGE SCHOOLS

In an increasingly literate and sophisticated society, we are finding ways to meet the unique needs of individual students at current or reduced costs. No longer are these two goals mutually exclusive. They are being obtained concurrently in new schools designed for the information age. These schools (1) place the learner in a role of active participant, (2) restructure the ratio of human and capital inputs in the schooling process, and (3) take advantage of existing information and communication technologies.

The move from the nineteenth-century American common school to mass education in the twentieth century appears to have been at least partly dictated by the new least-cost combinations of inputs that made larger schools economically viable. Likewise, the present technological changes in information processing, transmission, and retrieval make it necessary for us to reexamine the relative prices of educational inputs and reconsider the design of educational production functions. A number of production possibilities exist in any educational situation. It would be rare to have an improvement in resource allocation without having a resulting positive effect on both unit cost and productivity.

The Curriculum

Our system of schooling began to develop 150 years ago to make book learning available to every person. Most of the schools we have today are remnants of the industrial age when we lived in communities that were nearly self-contained, served by local newspapers, local merchants, and locally owned factories (Mecklenburger, 1994a). The ideas of that period about how the industrial world worked were adapted to schooling. Those industrial concepts of standardization and economies of scale continue to dominate thinking about the organization and administration of schools (Callahan, 1962), even though modern technology has rendered them virtually irrelevant. Many still believe large schools are necessary to enable variety in course offerings and specialization. This industrial age thinking has made today's schools so rigid that they cannot respond adequately to the individual differences of students or to the changing environment. We developed this point more fully when we discussed economies of scale in Chapter 13.

In our current school organization, we give too little recognition to the fact that learning is primarily a function of the interest, motivation, and hard work of the student (Levin, 1994). We frequently assume that students learn best in the physical presence of a teacher to guide and supervise the learning activities from moment to moment. The practical effect of this assumption has been to claim that in order for a child to learn, we must establish a course. More critically, that course requires a certified teacher. And cost considerations require approximately twenty or more pupils per class. Under these assumptions, individualization requires many courses, many teachers, and many students.

Contemporary schooling is too often rigidified and standardized in ways that actually thwart learning and fail to educate young people for productive lives in a society now facing accelerating change and diversity. Rather than create self-directed learners who can function independently and interpret change, the school has continued to create teacher-dependent role players. The industrial age school assumes that students are raw materials to be processed by schools according to specifications dictated by schedules, programs, courses, and exit tests (Darling-Hammond, 1993). The school further assumes that children are passive rather than active, incapable rather than capable, directed rather than self-directed, acquiescent rather than assertive, and dependent rather than independent (Des Dixon, 1994).

Only a handful of entirely new schools are actually in operation. A number of these schools, along with other individuals, schools, and school districts that are involved in designing schools for the information age, have affiliated with the Global Village School Institute. Affiliates of the institute believe that it is not possible to reform existing industrial age schools. Instead they week to invent an entirely new school. It is the institute's position (Mecklenburger, 1994b) that "pioneering educators, schools, school districts, and institutions in America must begin an earnest and public dialogue that takes the nation and its educators and policy makers far beyond the current politically driven, well meaning but limited 'reform' drumbeat of national goals, outcomes, standards, assessment, and accountability" (p. 18). The institute defines an educated person as follows:

> Because we now live in an information age and electronic networks are linking the world into a global village, an educated person is becoming one who has the ability to find what is known, to reflect upon changes in what is known, to explore, to share, to debate, to question, to compare and contrast, to solve problems—to engage in what today's educators sometimes call "higher order thinking skills" and even to contribute to what is known. (p. 19)

Darling-Hammond (1993) described emerging information age schools as assuming that students are not standardized and that teaching is not routine:

> [T]his view acknowledges that effective teaching techniques will vary for students

with different learning styles, with differently developed intelligences, or at different stages of cognitive and psychological development; for different subject areas; and for different instructional goals. Far from following standardized instructional packages, teachers must base their judgements on knowledge of learning theory and pedagogy, of child development and cognition, and of curriculum and assessment. They must then connect this knowledge to the understandings, dispositions, and conceptions that individual students bring with them to the classroom. (p. 758)

The emerging schools provide regimens and instructional methods that are flexible enough to provide students with programs and content that are individualized according to their learning abilities and personal interests. A constructivist view of learning has replaced a positivist view. These schools no longer consider learning a linear process. Rather, they recognize that stimuli are received largely at random and the role of the teacher is to help the learner develop procedures for processing the stimuli and for constructing meaning (Butzin, 1992; Mecklenburger, 1994a). School curricula are becoming interrelated across subject boundaries in order to permit the integration of ideas and to emphasize the interrelatedness of problems.

New Roles for Teachers

In an information-rich society, the teacher's role as purveyor of information is rapidly becoming obsolete. Communication and computer technologies provide the means whereby any students, knowing how to read and to use these resources, can obtain most of the information they need in a way that is at least as effective as today's typical teaching (Butzin, 1992). This portends new roles for education professionals. In the information age schools, teachers—if we continue to call them that (the emerging schools described below tend to label them with more appropriate titles)—become

experts in managing information resources and in designing learning experiences for individual students that are relevant to their needs, growth, and development. Teachers are primarily involved in diagnosing individual learning needs, prescribing individualized learning experiences (that is, curriculum design), motivating each student, and evaluating the results (Levin, 1994). In carrying out these functions, teachers primarily interact with students on a one-to-one basis, in essence eliminating the classroom as we have known it.

The emerging schools focus on learning rather than teaching. With the nearly unlimited accounting capabilities of computer networks, they can emphasize *continuous* rather than discontinuous learning that is *individualized* to capitalize on student strengths and to remedy student weaknesses as these are diagnosed. For nearly three decades, it has been the law of the land that children with learning disabilities and other disabling conditions receive individual diagnoses and education prescriptions. Information age schools treat all children this way.

A multimedia approach to learning does not eliminate traditional teaching. But traditional teaching becomes only one of many methods. Other media include books, drill, computer-assisted instruction (CAI), videodisk enhanced by computer, audiodisk, lecture (large group), discussion (small group), drama, chorus, band, athletic teams, tutors (teacher, aide, volunteer, or other student), collaborative learning, laboratory, and field experiences (Halal & Liebowitz, 1994).

The learning experience is viewed as a function of all life experiences, not just those in school. A school building is viewed as a *place* of learning, but not the *center* of learning. In emerging schools, student-to-teacher ratios are relevant only where particular group sizes can be shown to contribute to greater efficiency in the learning process.

Combining teacher assessments of individual student needs with a multimedia approach to instruction makes possible the development of an individualized education plan for each student. But simultaneously the individualization of instruction increases the problems of scheduling, monitoring, assessing, and record keeping. Nevertheless, instructional management software can handle these complexities.

In order to take full advantage of available technology, information age schools rely on computers for their complete range of capabilities. But these machines are subject to human direction, planning, and control. Teachers are still absolutely essential, but their role is changed from director, leader, and final authority to diagnostician, prescriber, motivator, facilitator, and evaluator. Teachers, students, and aides are seen as multidimensional human resources leading to specialization and division of labor, breaking the self-contained classroom mold of today's schools. Tasks requiring professional judgment are separated from those that are routine. High-cost, professionally trained persons are assigned to the former and lower-cost paraprofessionals are assigned to the latter. The pupil-to-teacher ratio is likely to increase over time. But the pupil-to-adult ratio is likely to remain the same or even decline from current levels as more paraprofessionals assume routine tasks.

Staffing

Intelligent direction for these emerging schools depends upon the professional educators associated with them. School-based decision making is the norm for them (see also Chapter 14). Their teachers have become experts in learning theory, curriculum design, motivational techniques, and developmental procedures. They have highly specialized skills in diagnosing the strengths and weaknesses of individual students with various intellectual skills and backgrounds and in prescribing the best combinations of the available learning experiences and resources (Darling-Hammond, 1993; Des Dixon, 1994).

Student assistants (Johnson & Johnson, 1987; Lippitt, 1975) and paraprofessional adults have become valuable staff members in these schools. The roles of both are arranged to complement and supplement that of the highly trained professionals who have the prime responsibility for guiding student instruction. The use of these two ancillary groups results in distinct advantages to the professional personnel. Each professional can specialize in the areas of expertise to which that individual is best suited by personality and training. The required omniscience in the classroom assumed under the present system as necessary for the professional is relaxed.

For a long time, the supply of teachers was so abundant and teacher salaries were so low that little attention was given to maximizing the time available for teachers to make decisions that required professional discretion. As a result, teachers have been expected to assume such assignments as collecting lunch money, typing worksheets, and monitoring cafeterias, lavatories, and hallways. These could be done as well or better by persons without professional teacher training. With a growing shortage of well-qualified teachers and salaries that are reaching professional levels in some districts, it becomes imperative that teachers' time be concentrated on tasks requiring professional discretion. Less-expensive persons can carry out clerical and routine tasks.

Graduate study at the doctoral level could easily be justified for teachers functioning in the above mode. Such teachers need to be truly "reflective practitioners" (Schon, 1983). Differentiated staffing and multimedia instructional delivery systems can release resources sufficient to enable salaries to be raised to a level competitive with other professions, especially those of teachers who supervise a number of paraprofessionals and community volunteers.

EXAMPLES OF INFORMATION AGE SCHOOLS

As schools have been conceptualized for the industrial age, teachers are the workers and pupils are the raw materials to be shaped. In the reconceptualized model of the information age schools, learning is the mission and students are the workers.

Teachers are there along with other human and material resources to facilitate students' learning. These schools are student-centered and children are active participants in their own education. The new schools are designed to eliminate mediators of information. They thus free children to interact fully with their environments and to explore them and the abstract world of knowledge. Information and communication technologies are integral and critical parts of their design, and teachers assume new roles.

Williston Central School

Based on the district's essential learning behaviors, each student in Williston, Vermont,[1] has a personal education plan that is developed jointly by the student (referred to as "learner") and a mentor in consultation with the learner's parents and other educators. The school's philosophy expresses a belief that every learner can master the behaviors, skills, and knowledge essential for becoming a contributing member of a diverse and changing world. The school assumes that curricula can be developed in which learning is a constant and time a variable. It considers innovation an ongoing process.

Williston redefined the role of the professional. It initiates a continuous cycle of learning improvement with the diagnosis of learner weaknesses and strengths. The professional is charged with the task of designing curricula that can best meet the identified needs. Throughout the learning-teaching program, professional response and facilitation are key behaviors as the professional encourages learners to strive for outstanding accomplishments. The professional is also responsible for evaluation in terms of both achievement and feedback into the diagnostic-prescriptive process.

The school district believes that technology can enhance learning opportunities. Through the use of a Personalized Educational Management System, the school is able to implement its ideal of an individualized program for every child. Technology supports a significant part of the learning process. Learners produce written and visual products using technology. Portfolios that document student achievement are stored on computers and other appropriate technologies such as videotape. Learners regularly access databases, manipulate information, and make presentations using state-of-the-art technology. Library catalogs are computerized and learners have access to numerous other information bases. Learners, faculty, and parents communicate both inside and outside the school using a variety of telecommunication instruments.

The Williston School is organized according to a house system of professional teams with multiaged groupings of approximately ninety learners, each including learners with disabling conditions. Learners normally remain in a house until they graduate. Professionals, called "facilitators," are responsible for making educational decisions and authorized to make them. The individualized programs for learners allow for flexibility of time, permit a variety of learning experiences, and demand high performance as evidence of mastery. The programs are process oriented within the context of common fields of knowledge. Outcomes are assessed by a variety of authentic methods. Instruction for learners moves from transmission of information to the discovery of knowledge. It shifts from an emphasis on knowing to an emphasis on searching. Learners are expected to synthesize what they learn and place value on it.

The school enrolls approximately 1,000 learners in grades one through eight. It is served by 79 professionals, 71 support staff, and 2 administrators. A fiber optic network links 300 workstations through a Novell Netware 3.1 system, providing each with access to 300 different software programs.

The ACT Academy

The ACT Academy[2] is a demonstration project funded by the McKinney, Texas, Independent School District and the U.S. Department of Education. Its mission is to establish a twenty-first-century school by breaking the mold of conventional teaching strategies and providing instruction that results in superior academic performance. The school serves 250 students aged five through eighteen in a nongraded environment. Students represent a cross-section of the district's population.

Eleven learning facilitators provide instruction and use technology as a tool to leverage learning. They are assisted by a project director, two project specialists, and an office manager. Staff members and students in the twelve–eighteen-year-old team have their own portable computers. In the seven–eleven age grouping, one portable computer is available for every two students. And for the five–six-year-old group, there are fixed docking stations. In addition, students and staff have access to multimedia computers, printers, CD-ROMs, laserdiscs, VCRs, camcorders, still video cameras, distance learning, cable television, on-line services, and telephones. Through electronic and nonelectronic methods, learning moves beyond the walls of the school building into the local, national, and international communities.

The building is a renovated elementary school. Its design reflects the academy's philosophy. It contains both open and closed learning spaces for maximum flexibility. The hallways and outdoor courtyard as well as classrooms and media centers have been wired for access to the building's communication network. This allows for flexibility in the use of computers and other technologies.

The curricular foundation of the academy is based on six tenets:

- Students are active learners who construct knowledge on the basis of previous experiences, values, and beliefs.
- Learning must move beyond factual recall to deep conceptual understanding of topics.
- Students bring to the learning process their own notions, myths, and ideas of particular concepts. They must identify and value them, with opportunities provided for them to evaluate, modify, and strengthen them on the basis of new experience.
- Learning extends beyond the four walls of the classroom through the use of technology, mentorships, internships, and local and national resources.

- Assessments and evaluations are embedded in the learning process. They are an integral component of all activities and projects. Student growth and learning are measured against a standard, not against other students.
- Curriculum development is a dynamic and ongoing process based on major concepts and consisting of an elaboration of students' interests and needs.

Learning opportunities are developed using both single-discipline and interdisciplinary approaches. The school takes care to balance tension between what students want to know and what they need to know. The staff uses alternative forms of assessment including portfolio systems and creative-performance tasks.

Belle Valley Elementary School

Known as "The School of the Future," Belle Valley Elementary School[3] is located in the Millcreek Township School District. It serves a suburban area of Erie, Pennsylvania. The building, which opened in 1990, was designed to serve 1,000 children in six major cluster areas or houses. Each house has six semiflexible teaching/learning environments and a central area that contains a family room to accommodate a variety of student activities.

The school was designed to accommodate the growth of technology in education. Kindergartens and first-grade clusters each share twenty to thirty Macintosh LC or SE computers located in their respective family rooms. Grades two through four have eight to ten computers in each classroom for a ratio of three students per computer. Each student in fifth grade has a Macintosh LC computer on his or her desk. All teachers have personal computers assigned to them. The school is part of an alliance with Apple Computer.

The school views computers as tools for learning. Technology has been integrated into all areas of study. Students use computers for learning to write, to prepare presentations, and to communicate with other students in the school and around the world. They use them to locate information, create their own databases, and access visual, auditory, and written information. The school's library and media center catalog and selected compact disk information are electronically accessible from any classroom and from the homes of teachers and students. According to school officials, the computer encourages the student to become an active participant in the learning process. It creates new excitement as teachers and students become partners in discovery and learning.

Teachers working in the school must demonstrate an ability to work in a team framework with other educators. Each coordinates an area of the curriculum for a teaching team. Teachers are expected to confer with parents, other teachers, and administrators to develop, discuss, and explain the ideas of the school. They must be able to use computer technology as a part of regular classroom instruction. They must also be able to work on a regular basis with the mildly disabled children who are included in the regular classroom. Teachers are provided with frequent staff development programs. Time is scheduled for the members of a teaching team to meet on a regular basis for curriculum planning and coordination.

McArthur Elementary School

The McArthur Elementary School[4] is a Florida Model Technology School in Pensacola. The school has 680 students, 45 teachers, 1 media specialist, 1 technology facilitator, 1 guidance counselor, 1 resource teacher, and 1 curriculum coordinator. Grade levels include kindergarten through grade five. A large percentage of the students (42 percent) qualify for free or reduced-price lunches.

The school seeks to create relationships among teachers and children that give each the freedom to innovate, experiment, and use creativity to improve teaching and learning. The goals of instruction are to teach students how to get information, how to use it, and how to present it. The curriculum is built around four major concepts: thematic, real-world, integrated content; problem solving and higher-order thinking; whole language

instruction; and teamwork. The curriculum has a global thrust, reflecting the world's interdependence and the diversity found in the American economy, polity, demography, and culture. It stresses electronic information gathering, observation skills, research skills, and discussion skills.

Technology becomes a tool to help integrate different curriculum strands into thematic units. It provides ways for students to explore knowledge in a real-life manner. It allows teachers new ways to manage and evaluate units. Computers, laserdiscs, videos, digitized sound, and graphics enable interactive programs to help to individualize learning situations. Satellite dish, cable TV, and the Internet are resources for two-way communication with others. Students use probeware for data collection, databases for charting observations, telecommunications for sharing strategies and multiple solutions with other students, and word processing for desktop publishing. Laserdisc and digitized video add visual emphasis to presentations and reports. Camcorders, television production hardware, and telecommunications offer opportunities for sharing student work with classes across town and around the world.

A locally networked computer database program records every aspect of the curriculum in order to maintain quality control. The software (a set of relational databases from Learning Technology Systems) allows teachers to increase the richness of the curriculum while storing data from all activity, resource, and student variables to produce a history over time of each curricular element. The instructional management software allows for impromptu entry of lesson plans, permitting interests of individual students to be pursued.

Each teacher has a workstation, networked to the schoolwide server, with e-mail and calendar. Each classroom has three or four computers for student use, and the school operates a supplementary computer lab. Each grade level has one videodisk player, one CD-ROM drive computer, and one videotape player. The school has closed-circuit television capable of sending four different signals simultaneously and a studio for live programs. A satellite dish is available for downloading both student and staff development programs. The multimedia center has an online electronic catalog and multimedia computers. The school has a home-school communicator that enables parents to dial in to receive announcements, classroom news, assignments, and other information.

The school governance group is composed of the School Improvement Team (composed of one teacher from each grade level or area), one representative from custodial and food services, and the PTA president. Action teams are set up to design and implement new program and policy initiatives (for example, whole language, problem-solving, cooperative learning, and thematic units).

The Edison Project

The Edison Project[5] is a private for-profit group, established in 1992, that operates public schools under contract with states and local school districts and a small number of private, tuition-charging schools. Its goal is "to create the best school system in America with an educational program that will work for all children, and to do so for approximately the same cost per pupil as the average public school" (Hechinger, 1994, p. 214). The project opened its first four schools in August 1995 in Boston, Massachusetts, Mount Clemens, Michigan, Sherman, Texas, and Wichita, Kansas. It is too early to evaluate their effectiveness.

The basic design calls for six small schools-within-a-school of 200 to 300 students each, called academies. Each academy serves a range of students divided as follows: prekindergarten, kindergarten through grade two, grades three through five, grades six through eight, grades nine and ten, and grades eleven and twelve. There is no age or ability grouping within academies (Edison Project, 1994a, 1994b).

One of the most interesting aspects of the Edison school design is its use of technology to enhance productivity, efficiency, creative expression, communication, and access to information. All teachers have their own portable computers and classrooms are equipped with computers and other video-display technology as well as books and other traditional materials. Classrooms are elec-

tronically linked with others around the country. And teachers and students can access an array of educational databases. Teachers share offices that are well equipped with telephones, copiers, and fax machines.

Every member of the school community is served by an easy-to-use communication system that facilitates teaching and learning. The networked system permits students to work together at school, permits teachers to assign and evaluate student work, permits students in one project school to work with students in another, permits teachers to share insights across the nation, and permits parents and teachers to communicate with one another. The network includes two tools to support and enhance instruction and assessment. An electronic markup database gives teachers multiple views and ways to assess and review student work. An interactive curriculum frameworks database helps administrators and teachers find or develop lessons and plan curriculum.

Most decisions are made on-site by teachers and principals. Project schools can draw upon external support through the project's nationwide education system which provides ongoing research and development, access to an array of resources and instructional materials that allow teachers to customize their teaching, extensive professional development, and administrative systems designed to expedite simple record keeping, reporting, and ordering.

To ensure equal access, the project is committed to placing a computer in every student's home at an age- and ability-appropriate level. In addition to use by students, the home computer provides families with a way of keeping up with their children's activities, of communicating easily with teachers, and of taking part in the life of the school community. Parents can also get in touch with teachers through voice mail.

"Break-the-Mold" Schools

Late in 1992 the eleven first-round winners of the New American Schools Development Corporation (NASDC) competition for funds to finance the design of "break-the-mold" schools were announced. NASDC was proposed by President George Bush and was funded by contributions from the private sector—especially from American businesses. The purpose was to identify and put into practice the best school restructuring ideas it could find. Eight of the successful proposals highlighted strategies for integrating information technologies into the instructional process. A number of these proposals indicated coalitions with computer and information businesses, including Apple Computer, IBM, AT&T, NYNEX, Lotus Development Corporation, Massachusetts Corporation for Education Telecommunications, and Xerox Corporation (Mecklenburger, 1992).

STRATEGIES FOR IMPLEMENTATION

Redesigning educational systems to make optimal use of technology and the time of professionals, students, and support staff can contribute to the solution of a number of current policy problems, including upgrading teaching roles to professional levels, paying teachers professionally competitive salaries, and making the system more effective and more efficient.

The arguments we have given in support of redesigning elementary and secondary schooling through the use of technology are derived from both economic and pedagogical considerations. However, the decision to modernize or not to modernize is political, in that 90 percent of elementary and secondary schooling is provided through the public sector. Because of the highly decentralized structure for policy making in education and because of the incremental nature of democratic policy development, modernization is likely to come about as a series of decisions over an extended period of time made in a variety of legislative forums.

Any strategy for change will have to take into account two factors that tend to perpetuate the status quo. The first is the strong and articulate constituency of professional and auxiliary employees of public schools who have a vested interest in

maintaining the current arrangements (Mirel, 1994). The second is that even with their recognized shortcomings, elementary and secondary schools as presently constituted are familiar. The emerging schools are still largely unknown and unfamiliar. A new system could be better, but it could be worse. Under such circumstances, the prudent person is likely to opt for the known until there is convincing evidence of the merit of the proposed. That is why prototypes such as those we have described are so essential.

Reforms will be accomplished most quickly if they can be done in collaboration with professional organizations. Obtaining collaboration will require a recognition on the part of state and local officials that the proposed innovations pose threats to the psychological and economic security of employees and their associations. An incremental strategy of implementation would allow time for building a base of experience and alleviating the fear of the unknown (Lindblom, 1968).

The costs and benefits for the present members of the teaching profession are mixed. For teachers of the future, the benefits should far exceed the cost. But for those currently teaching, significant changes in their professional duties would be required as the role of teacher is redefined, and some might face the possibility of losing their positions. Both possibilities can cause an inordinate amount of personal trauma. Movements of labor are essential if society is to improve its productivity through technological change. But it does not follow that it needs to be a financial burden to those directly concerned. The public will have to bear start-up costs to offset economic losses to individuals due to early retirement and to cover costs of retraining and relocating younger education personnel. Providing fair guarantees of economic security to present teachers represents a major challenge to teacher organizations, local school leadership, and the state and federal governments.

On the positive side, a general reorganization of schools along the lines described would help realize proposed reforms in personnel policies as discussed in Chapter 16. Those remaining in teaching would have substantially higher salaries. The possibility of more interesting job definitions that are wholly professional in nature and the possibility of career advancement without leaving the field of teaching would help to recruit and retain capable teachers.

The implications for administrators at both the district and school levels are significant. Change requires professional leadership. At the initial stages this is most likely to come from professionally alert principals and central office administrators. At the central office level, a strategic plan needs to be developed and implemented for moving from the status quo to the desired future states. The board of education, the professional staff, and the community need to be convinced of the merits of the plan and its strategy. Tough negotiations can be expected with the unions representing teachers and other personnel, especially if there are to be cutbacks in personnel and redefinitions of duties. Extensive staff development programs have to be initiated. Political action and strategic planning at the state and federal levels are necessary to secure essential technological infrastructures, human support systems, and start-up financing.

The most dramatic change in roles will be at the school level. High-caliber and highly trained teachers need to be responsible for curricular and instructional decisions made at the school. Principals and lead teachers need to stimulate and coordinate the redesign process and establish and maintain wholesome school environments. They also need to provide properly functioning support systems. These changes are of such magnitude that they cannot be mandated. Nor is it reasonable to expect that all school staffs are motivated or able to undertake such changes. The changes cannot be incremental within a school. But they can be incremental in a state or district, school by school, by encouraging school staffs that are willing and able to make the desirable changes to do so, while allowing the others to operate traditional schools— at least in the short term.

School leaders of the future must first and foremost be visionaries. They also need to be politically astute, diplomats, planners, negotiators, and trainers.

SUMMARY

There is a recursive relationship between education and technological innovation. Technological innovations place social and economic pressures on educational institutions to change. Educational institutions are the means by which scientists, engineers, planners, and designers get the underlying knowledge base from which they create new technological innovations.

The world is currently going through a basic shift in its techno-economic paradigm from manufacturing to information processing. This is affecting the very structure and conditions of production and distribution for almost all sectors of the economy. This paradigm shift is manifesting itself in educational institutions in what has been called the "educational reform movement." An educational system designed for an industrial age is being replaced very slowly with schools designed to meet the requirements of the information age. Instead of making better use of traditional labor-intensive technologies, as Monk (1989) says has been the predominant mode of educational reform, all schools of the future need to develop very different strategies in their uses of labor and capital. These strategies must be in harmony with trends in the larger society.

This chapter has described several information age schools that blend human and technological resources into the learning process. Such schools efficiently integrate information and communication technologies, making schooling compatible with a technologically sophisticated world. This integration transforms the role of elementary and secondary teachers from purveyors of information to facilitators of learning. The role of student is changed from passive participant to active learner. Increasing numbers of paraprofessionals are used in the instructional process. To implement such changes, school leaders are needed who are visionaries, planners, coordinators, and negotiators. They must be able to serve as liaison with the community and other levels of government.

NOTES

1. For additional information, contact the Chittenden South School District, P. O. Box 127, Shelburne, VT 05482. Telephone: (802)482–3885.
2. For additional information, contact the ACT Academy, 510 Heard Street, McKinney, TX 75069. Telephone: (214)569-6455. FAX: (214)542-2924.
3. For additional information, contact The Principal, Belle Valley Elementary School, Millcreek Township School District, 5300 Henderson Road, Erie, PA 16506.
4. For further information, contact The Principal, McArthur Model Technology School, 330 East Ten Mile Road, Pensacola, FL 32354. Telephone: (904)484-5115.
5. For more information, contact The Edison Project, 529 Fifth Avenue, 12th Floor, New York, NY 10017. Telephone: (212) 309-1600. FAX: (212) 309-1604.

ACTIVITIES

1. Describe an educational system that maximizes the utilization of human and machine capabilities as is suggested in the following statement:

   In order to take full advantage of available technology, schools rely on computers for their complete range of capabilities; but these machines are subject to human direction, planning, and control.

2. Information age schools as described in this chapter may have important implications for other reform proposals such as the raising of academic expectations and standards, the professionalization of teaching, school-site management, and family choice of schooling. Describe potential interrelationships among these reforms and indicate whether technology is likely to facilitate or inhibit each of the reforms.

REFERENCES

Baumol, W. J. (1967). Macroeconomics of unbalanced growth: The anatomy of urban crisis. *American Economic Review, 57* (3), 415–426.

Benson, C. (1961). *The economics of public education.* Boston: Houghton Mifflin.

Bolton, W. R. (1994). *Factors that may influence the use of computer technology in the teaching and learning process.* Unpublished doctoral dissertation, State University of New York at Buffalo.

Butzin, S. M. (1992). Integrating technology into the classroom: Lessons from the Project CHILD experience. *Phi Delta Kappan, 74,* 330–333.

Callahan, R. (1962). *Education and the cult of efficiency: A study of the social forces that have shaped the administration of the public schools.* Chicago: University of Chicago Press.

Cuban, L. (1988). *The managerial imperative and the practice of leadership in schools.* Albany: State University of New York Press.

Darling-Hammond, L. (1993). Reframing the school reform agenda: Developing capacity for school transformation. *Phi Delta Kappan, 74,* 752–761.

Des Dixon, R. G. (1994). Future schools: How to get there from here. *Phi Delta Kappan, 75,* 360–365.

Doyle, D. P. (1994). The role of private sector management in public education. *Phi Delta Kappan, 76,* 128–132.

Edison Project, The. (1994a). *An invitation to public school partnership: Executive summary.* New York: Edison Project.

Edison Project, The. (1994b). *Partnership school design.* New York: Edison Project.

Goodlad, J. I. (1984). *A place called school: Prospects for the future.* New York: McGraw-Hill.

Halal, W. E., & Liebowitz, J. (1994). Telelearning: The multimedia revolution in education. *The Futurist, 28* (6), 21–26.

Hechinger, N. (1994). Technology in the Edison School. In C. E. Finn, Jr., & H. J. Walberg (Eds.), *Radical education reforms.* Berkeley, CA: McCutchan.

Heuston, D. H. (1994). Technology in school improvement. In C. E. Finn, Jr., & H. J. Walberg (Eds.), *Radical education reforms.* Berkeley, CA: McCutchan.

Johnson, D. W., & Johnson, R. (1987). *Learning together and alone: Cooperative, competitive, and individualistic learning* (2nd ed.). Englewood Cliffs, NJ: Prentice-Hall.

Levin, B. (1994). Improving educational productivity: Putting students at the center. *Phi Delta Kappan, 75,* 758–760.

Levin, H., & Meister, G. (1985). *Educational technology and computers: Promises, promises, always promises* (Project Report No. 85-A13). Stanford, CA: Stanford University, Stanford Education Policy Institute.

Lindblom, C. S. (1968). *The public policy-making process.* Englewood Cliffs, NJ: Prentice-Hall.

Lippitt, P. (1975). *Students teach students.* Bloomington, IN: Phi Delta Kappa Educational Foundation.

Mecklenburger, J. A. (1992). The breaking of the "break-the-mold" express. *Phi Delta Kappan, 74,* 280–289.

Mecklenburger, J. A. (1994a). Thinking about schooling in the Global Village: We can see into the future of schooling, now. And its name is not just "reform." *Inventing Tomorrow's Schools, 4* (2), 2–9.

Mecklenburger, J. A. (1994b). To start a dialog: The next generation of American schools. *Inventing Tomorrow's Schools, 4* (2), 18–20.

Mirel, J. (1994). School reform unplugged: The Bensenville New American School project, 1991–1993. *American Educational Research Journal, 31,* 481–518.

Monk, D. H. (1989). The education production function: Its evolving role in policy analysis. *Educational Evaluation and Policy Analysis, 11,* 31–45.

Murphy, J. (1993). What's in? What's out? American education in the nineties. *Phi Delta Kappan, 74,* 641–646.

National Center for Education Statistics. (1993). *Digest of education statistics.* Washington, DC: U.S. Government Printing Office.

National Governors' Association. (1986). *Time for results: The governors' 1991 report on education.* Washington, DC: Center for Policy Research and Analysis, National Governors' Association.

Office of Technology Assessment, Congress of the United States. (1982). *Informational technology and its impact on American education.* Washington, DC: U.S. Government Printing Office.

Perelman, L. (1987). *Technology and the transformation of schools.* Alexandria, VA: National School Boards Association.

Picus, L. O. (1995). *Does money matter in education? A policymaker's guide.* Paper delivered at the annual meeting of the American Education Finance Association, Savannah, GA.

Schon, D. A. (1983). *The reflective practitioner: How professionals think in action.* New York: Basic Books.

Vaizey, J., Norris, K., & Sheehan, J. (1972). *The political economy of education.* New York: John Wiley & Sons.

Willett, E., Swanson, A., & Nelson, E. (1979). *Modernizing the little red schoolhouse: The economics of improved schooling.* Englewood Cliffs, NJ: Educational Technology Publications.

PART SIX

Charting New Directions in School Finance Policy

We hope that this journey through the concepts and issues of the field of school finance has been an enlightening one for you. It is our purpose in Part VI to bring together the themes of this book in an integrated discussion of the problems that must be addressed in the years immediately ahead and to identify some of the more promising alternatives before us.

CHAPTER 18

Implications of Educational Restructuring for School Finance Policy

Primary Issues Explored in This Chapter:

- *The level of investment in education:* What percentage of United States resources should be invested in education?
- *Setting goals and objectives for education:* What is the optimum allocation of authority for setting education goals and objectives?
- *Recipients of educational services:* Who should be educated? What services should be available to people of varying characteristics?

- *The organization of schooling:* How can society ensure that schools operate so as to use resources efficiently?
- *Guides for applying state resources to the educational process:* How should states distribute resources to districts and schools in a way that facilitates the efficient operation of schools while promoting societal interests and protecting the rights and concerns of individuals?

As the first edition of this text went to press (in 1991), school finance policy debates were still focused on inputs and their distribution, as they had been for decades. This was despite the public outcry since the early 1980s over poor academic achievement by students in public school. Five years later, there has been a dramatic shift in attention to schooling outcomes and standards. Critics now view reforms of curricular, finance, and governance structures as being systemically related to each other and the outcomes of the schooling process. They now link school finance and school improvement in a quest for equity along with efficiency and adequacy (Clune, 1994; Odden, 1994). They believe there is little benefit in changing financial policies if the performance of students does not improve.

Linking student performance with inputs makes enormous sense conceptually. It is very difficult, however, to develop school finance policies on the basis of student performance. Research has found no evidence of strong and dependable causal relationships between schooling inputs and outcomes. The lack of such identifiable relationships has supported the conclusion of many that schools are functioning inefficiently. Consequently, we see improving understanding of these relationships as the most important educational issue before us. We hope in this way to help to improve the internal efficiency of schools.

Lack of equity in the distribution of resources for schooling purposes is also a serious problem. It may be related to the inequities in the distribution of desired schooling outcomes. We place this problem second only because the evidence is very strong that the persons most affected by the inefficiencies of the education system are children and youth who are at risk. Simply providing more resources for them will not improve their achievements unless we make the instructional system itself more effective. Middle- and upper-class students in general appear to have sufficient nonschool support systems to compensate for most of the shortcomings of the schools.

Thus, we must direct school finance policy toward improving (1) the efficiency of the school system by acquiring a better understanding of the relationships between its inputs and outcomes; (2) the equity of the distribution of opportunities to learn and the quality of student achievement. We must clearly understand, however, that developing school finance policy is largely a political process. We make decisions about the provision of elementary and secondary education primarily in the public sector. But the public sector functions within a market economy in which two-thirds of the nation's GNP is allocated through decisions made by individuals. Thus, we must study the impact of political decisions about financing education using economic paradigms. We assume here that school finance policy is made within a political-economic context.

Figure 1.8 in Chapter 1 provided a model of the political-economic system of education policy development. It divided education policies into five groups: determining levels of investment, setting goals and objectives, distributing services, producing services, and allocating resources. In this chapter, we discuss each of the five types of educational policy issues in terms of policy alternatives we considered in earlier chapters and in terms of the peculiar interests of society, the teaching profession, and family clients. We also discuss where there appears to be evidence about the effectiveness of a particular alternative.

DETERMINING THE LEVEL OF INVESTMENT IN POPULATION QUALITY

In Chapter 13, we reviewed a number of studies of the external efficiency of expenditures for education. This is an important consideration in determining what percentage of a society's resources should be allocated to educational services. Because of the heavy involvement of government in elementary and secondary education, the level of investment in schooling is largely a political decision. It is supplemented marginally by decisions made by individuals through the market.

We showed that a person's formal education is directly and strongly correlated with expected earnings. Education increases the value of one's labor by increasing the cache of knowledge at one's command and by honing one's occupational skills. The anticipation of higher incomes persuades individuals to invest some of their own resources in further education, especially at the postsecondary level. By the same token, the more sophisticated the technological development of a country, the greater is the demand for highly skilled workers. Thus, we see that the percentage of a nation's resources that it allocates to education increases along with the sophistication of its technology.

Rate-of-return studies have shown that the United States, along with most other developed countries, is investing in education at an appropriate level given the current organization of elementary and secondary schools. In terms of the amount spent on education and the proportion of the gross domestic product invested, the United States ranks among the highest when compared with other large industrialized countries (Smith & Phelps, 1995). Unlike other developed countries, however, the United States has a highly decentralized education system. While the overall statistics for the United States look good, the internal distribution of investment is very uneven. As a result, the United States has some of the best- and worst-financed schools in the developed world.

To maintain its level of investment in education, the United States has increased expenditures per pupil at an average rate of 2.2 percent in inflation-adjusted dollars over the past thirty years (Odden, 1994). There are indications at all levels of government that this rate of growth will no longer be maintained. The federal government appears to be making a genuine effort to balance the budget early in the next century without resorting to higher taxes. This means a reduction in federal spending—especially for domestic programs, including education. At the local level, people have strongly reacted to incessant increases in property taxes, the major source of support for public education at the elementary and secondary level. Local taxes have been the fastest growing revenue source in the country since 1985. They have outpaced both state and federal taxes. Most of the increase has gone to schools (Odden, 1994). To reduce dependence on property taxation and to control spending of local school boards, most states have assumed greater responsibility for financing schools. In Chapter 8 we saw evidence that per pupil revenues tend to be lower as the percentage of state financing increases.

Some strategies have been proposed for infusing more nontax dollars into elementary and secondary education through such means as equalized vouchers, by which wealthy parents pay part of the school tuition; establishment of school foundations and partnerships with businesses and industries; and the use of volunteers. Further privatization of schooling, however, would likely result in increased investment by upper-income families in the education of their children and less investment by parents of children from lower-income families. Thus, improving equity in the distribution of resources directed toward schooling will continue to depend on public funds. Given that financial support for public schools will experience, at best, historically low growth in the near future, improving the achievements of school children will depend largely on improving the efficiency of school operations.

SETTING GOALS AND OBJECTIVES FOR THE EDUCATIONAL ENTERPRISE

The history of public education in the United States has been a history of centralization of authority. Compulsory school attendance legislation in the nineteenth century was one of the first acts of centralization. It removed the right of parents to decide *not* to educate their children. The establishment of the common school with the use of public funds relegated the setting of educational goals and objectives to school districts. For the most part, these were very small and easily controlled by family constituents.

At the same time, parents continued to have the privilege of enrolling their children in private schools at their own expense, if they so desired. This was an important accommodation for those whose value orientations were not satisfied by the philosophy and orientation of the public schools or who were dissatisfied with the quality of the public schools. The combination of compulsory attendance laws, publicly financed and operated schools, and privately financed private schools was intended to improve the societal objectives of fraternity and equality of educational opportunity within, but not among, school districts. The intention was also to minimize the diminution of liberty for family clients. This political compromise balanced the interests of society with those of parents.

During the first half of the twentieth century, the growth of cities and the policy of consolidating rural and suburban school districts weakened control over the direction of schools by family clients and strengthened the authority of the teaching profession. Teachers and administrators received much better professional preparation during that period than they had previously. The efficiency of schools was enhanced at the expense of liberty for the 90 percent of parents that sent their children to public schools.

Immediately following World War II, the state and federal governments began to play a larger role in shaping public schooling through legislation and litigation. Increasing numbers of young people found it necessary to complete secondary school in order to qualify for satisfactory employment. This increased the cost of education beyond what most communities could support through the property tax alone. It magnified the disparities among school districts in their ability to finance educational services and in the quality of their services. Most states responded by gradually assuming a greater percentage of the financial support of public schools. In the process, states got more control over them. States sought equality, efficiency, and economic growth at the expense of the liberty of family clients, of local communities, and of the profession.

In the pursuit of equality and fraternal objectives, in the 1950s and 1960s litigants successfully challenged through federal courts the practices of segregating schools by race, and in the 1970s of discriminating by gender and disabilities. Court-ordered desegregation, racial and gender hiring preferences, limits on the disciplinary discretion of educators, and curricular change resulted. Disparities in spending due to reliance on local property taxes within and supplemental to state school aid formulas were also successfully challenged in several states. State and federal legislation often reenforced the holdings of courts, making specific decisions universal. Little discretion was left to family clients within public schools. The discretion of independent teaching professionals was severely constrained by bureaucratic rules and regulations and compounded by collective bargaining. The objectives of fraternity and equality came into sharp conflict with those of efficiency and client liberty.

Greater centralization of decision making continued with the first wave of educational reform in the 1980s. This reform responded to national concerns for global economic competitiveness. In an effort to increase student achievement (efficiency), states instituted more rigorous curricula, more stringent high school graduation requirements, statewide standardized testing, and higher certification standards for teachers and administrators.

Centralization of authority did not always produce the results desired. By the mid 1980s, people realized that it might be necessary to differentiate among those decisions that were appropriate to centralize and those that were not. From the mid-1950s through the early 1980s, efficiency and equity had been pursued through centralizing authority. Policy implementation studies of that period showed that state and federal governments are particularly effective in dealing with issues of equity and access. But those governments appear to be ineffective in dealing with matters of efficiency and "production," that is, how a school is organized and operated. We have learned from our experience and there is now a growing movement to pursue efficiency through decentralized authority and equity through centralized authority.

School-based decision making (discussed in Chapter 14) and family choice (discussed in Chapter 15) represent important tactics in an overall strategy of decentralization. These tactics return some decision-making authority to professional educators and to parents in order to induce market-like forces into the public school sector to increase its efficiency. In responding to the issue of who should set goals and objectives for educational enterprises, these chapters concluded that extreme centralization had sapped public schooling of much of its vitality and efficiency and had alienated a significant proportion of its family clients. Notwithstanding, we recognized that society has important interests that have to be protected through intervention by state and federal governments in matters of equity and fraternity. People have legitimate and varying concerns about the goals and objectives of education at all levels of the sociopolitical hierarchy. Our task is to achieve an acceptable balance among legitimate interests. While state and federal authorities can best make decisions concerning equity and access, teaching professionals hold the technical expertise of schooling. Parents are the guardians of the interests and needs of individual children. The family, in general, knows and cares most about the child. It is through the family that the child's voice can best be heard (see Chapter 15).

A pattern is emerging in the United States and other postindustrialized nations of dividing the responsibility for setting goals and objectives for the educational enterprise among interested parties as appropriate. At the national level, the federal government is cooperating with state governments and professional associations in setting voluntary curricular frameworks, achievement standards for students, and certification standards for teachers. These frameworks and standards are only *guides* to policy; it is up to each state and school district to determine if and how these guides are to be incorporated into state and local policy. States are assuming greater responsibility for finance, curriculum, and setting and enforcing student achievement standards. In many states, the education profession is getting greater authority to develop policy at the school building level. In some cases this authority is shared with parents, community members, and students. More and more parents are enjoying the right to select schools whose philosophies and expectations match their own as charter schools, magnet schools, inter- and intradistrict choice plans, and vouchers for low-income children become more pervasive. Choice of schools enhances the influence of parents in setting goals and objectives for the education enterprise.

DETERMINING WHO SHOULD RECEIVE WHICH EDUCATIONAL SERVICES

Except for those few who are able to exercise private options, determining for whom educational services will be provided has been largely a societal decision. Over the years, society has expanded the availability of schooling until virtually all people between the ages of five and eighteen now have access to some form of publicly funded instruction.

Expansion is frequently the result of intensive lobbying on the part of special interest groups, such as those promoting educational opportunities for children with disabilities. Recognizing the differences in the quality of preschool experiences among children, and to ensure that all children

begin school ready to learn (the first of the eight national education goals), growing numbers of publicly financed preschool programs, such as Head Start, are available for at-risk children. The private sector is also rapidly developing preschools, nursery schools, and after-school centers to meet the demand of families with all parents working. At the other end of the spectrum, a postsecondary education is essential for most people desiring to maintain a traditional middle-class lifestyle. The first four years of college are becoming an integral part of basic education. This is suggested by the often-made reference to the *pre-k through 16* system of education. In the middle, grades K–12, the percentage of children educated in the public and private sectors, respectively, has remained relatively steady for generations. About 90 percent are in the public sector and 10 percent in the private sector. The characteristics of children attending private schools, however, have changed quite dramatically during the past two decades. Both public and private sector forces are working to expand educational opportunities.

Although people generally recognize the value of education to the individual, they have different opinions about the philosophy, content, and context appropriate for specific individuals. Differences in educational tastes create social tension over the orientation of services to be offered through the public sector. This is especially true because the philosophical choices available have narrowed recently. As the implementation of school-based decision making (SBDM) spreads, different organizational patterns for schools will develop. But this can serve to increase tensions further unless clients are permitted to choose freely among them.

Once the bureaucratic uniformity among schools is broken, it is difficult to justify district assignment of pupils to schools. Family choice of schooling permits the matching of child characteristics and family preferences to school characteristics. It also provides a monitoring mechanism that assures society that each public school is satisfactorily providing a service desired by a sufficiently large clientele. Choice enhances the policy objectives of liberty and efficiency. Unfettered choice, however, could violate the objectives of equality and fraternity. This can be avoided with social controls like those exercised through the magnet school concept or the regulated compensatory voucher model described in Chapter 15.

SBDM frees the producers of educational services to use their professional knowledge, experience, insights, and imagination to design learning systems to fit specific situations. Family choice of schooling permits clients to select the options that they think are best for their children and family circumstances. When a money-follows-the-child strategy is used for allocating resources to schools, marketlike forces make producers more sensitive to the needs of clients and potential clients. Producers also become more aware of alternative uses of available resources to maximize the positive impact of those resources. A dissatisfied client who leaves takes resources from a school. Likewise, each new client attracted brings additional resources.

In the new order, society (through government) will continue to exert the primary influence in determining the range of educational services to be provided. School-based decision making will enlarge the role of professional educators in designing those services. School choice will enhance the voice of parents in determining what kind of education is appropriate for their own children.

DETERMINING THE MEANS BY WHICH EDUCATIONAL SERVICES ARE PROVIDED

For over a decade, reports of national assessments of educational progress have provided strong evidence that the public schools, in general, are not living up to societal—or individual—expectations. We looked at this evidence in detail in Part IV. Chapter 11 looked at the issues of equality and efficiency from the perspective of the judiciary. Chapter 12 examined the issues of equality and frater-

nity from the perspective of policy analysts. Using economic paradigms in Chapter 13, we concluded that schools were inadequate more because of inefficient use of economic resources already available to most schools than because the available resources were inadequate.

In Part V, we examined some of the major reform proposals for enabling the education system to function within societal expectations. We examined the possibilities of injecting marketlike incentives into public school organizations through school-based decision making and through family choice of schooling in Chapters 14 and 15, respectively. In Chapter 16 we discussed personnel matters, including remuneration and professional growth strategies for teachers that would increase the efficiency of using labor resources. Also to promote efficiency, Chapter 17 argued for integrating electronic and communication technologies into the teaching/learning process, restructuring the role of teacher, and totally reorganizing the school to focus on the individual child as learner.

Throughout those chapters, there is a consistent theme that the school, rather than the district or classroom, is the place where students learn and that the major decisions of operation should be placed at that level. School-based decision making (SBDM) provides teaching professionals with authority to make decisions of production that require technical expertise. It enables schools to adapt to unique local and individual circumstances. Given the lack of knowledge about the causal relationships between schooling inputs and outputs, SBDM enables organizations to use a variety of instructional delivery systems. Careful evaluation of the diversity of schools should contribute to a better understanding of what educational practices work best under specific circumstances. Systematic evaluation would thereby contribute to improved operational efficiency. But to ensure equity, SBDM must function within a state and federal framework that permits professional discretion and parental choice among schools. At the same time it must allow prudent monitoring by higher levels of authority.

Increasing the authority of schools at a time when states are assuming greater responsibility for defining curriculum and setting achievement standards for pupils raises serious question about the future viability of school districts as they are currently organized. In Chapter 13, we suggested that large city school districts will gradually take on the characteristics of service units, similar to those of intermediate districts serving rural and suburban areas in a number of states. But they will have the added responsibility of acting as a funding conduit for schools. This has already happened in Chicago.

In rural areas, except for very small districts with graduating classes of under one hundred students, pressures for the consolidation of districts are likely to subside. In many respects, rural school districts already embody many of the characteristics of school-based decision making. They consist of one school (or very few schools) with a self-governing board of education. On the other hand, county or regional units can more efficiently assume responsibilities currently exercised by rural districts for providing services to schools like levying taxes and furnishing financial and personnel support. Some states may attempt to dissolve school districts, dividing their current responsibilities between regional or county units and school-level authorities.

Recent studies of economies of scale in schools show that there is a certain beauty in small schools. Small schools provide for sustained contact among all members of the learning community. This serves as a safeguard against the alienation found in many large schools. Compared to large schools, small schools provide greater opportunity for student participation and greater educational and personal support. These influences appear to be especially beneficial for at-risk students. The primary advantage of large schools is in their en-riched curricular offerings. But advances in electronic and communication technologies are rapidly bringing such variety to small schools as well. A challenge of the next decade is to design arrangements that combine the advantages of big schools and small schools in one setting, while eliminating their disadvantages. This is taking place in New York City, Philadelphia, and other major cities. Large, impersonal, bureaucratic schools are being divided into independent schools of choice with no more than 400 students each within a shared building. The reported beneficial effects on students are gratifying (Fliegel, 1993; Meier, 1995).

As suggested above, technological advances can assist in correcting some of the shortcomings of present-day schools. Computers facilitate individualized instruction and provide a mechanism for continuously and patiently monitoring individual progress. CD-ROM and other video technologies are now linked to the personal computer and provide for instructional enrichment that cannot be matched by words alone—written or spoken. Communication technology makes the world's information resources available to any person in almost any place.

Integrating technology into the instructional process facilitates reduction of the number of professionally trained personnel needed and more extensive use of lower-cost paraprofessionals. This in turn facilitates the upgrading of the teaching profession, permitting teachers to concentrate on activities in which professional discretion is essential. Differentiated staffing allows for more professional career options and, because there will be fewer of them, salaries of those professional teachers remaining could be made competitive with those of other professions.

Putting all these factors together, production decisions are best made at the school building level with support services provided at district, intermediate, and state levels and through the private sector. Reforming the structure of schools through the integration of technology into teacher/learning processes brings about a redefinition of the role of teaching and its rewards so as to make the profession more attractive to persons with exceptional skills. Available technology can improve the efficiency of schooling through enabling students, teachers, and support personnel to use their time and talents more productively and through upgrading the competence of those attracted into the teaching profession.

ALLOCATING RESOURCES TO AND AMONG EDUCATIONAL SERVICES

Two basic policy decisions must be made concerning the allocation of resources to education:

- Should there be governmental intervention?
- If there is to be governmental intervention, what should be the nature and extent of that intervention?

In Chapters 1 and 2, we developed the case for governmental involvement in the financing of education. Such involvement ensures that societal interests in a literate citizenry are satisfied and promotes equality of educational opportunity within the population. The current practice of public ownership and operation of schools, however, is only one form of intervention. Other public policy options include aid to privately owned and operated schools and direct aid to parents in the form of education vouchers. Nevertheless, we believe that the most likely scenario for the immediate future is a continuation of the near public monopoly of the ownership and operation of elementary and secondary schools. Accommodation of efficiency and liberty concerns are more likely to be made through incremental adjustments to the current system through innovations like school-based decision making, open enrollment among public schools, and charter schools than through more radical reforms that would privatize ownership of schools.

Growing state involvement in school finance makes the structuring of mechanisms for distributing state resources an even more important policy consideration than it was in the past (see Chapters 8 and 9). Flat grant and foundation programs of state aid to school districts that permit significantly large local leeway are inequitable to students and taxpayers in property-poor districts that need to spend beyond the established aid levels. Unfettered tax base equalizing schemes remove the inequitable effects of variations in the distribution of property wealth. But they do not remove the inequitable effects of variations among school districts in the priority they give to education and therefore their willingness to tax themselves to provide educational services. Full state funding is equitable in that it treats all alike. But the cost to liberty is high. The difficulty of determining what level of support is adequate may impinge upon efficiency and adequacy.

Of all financing strategies, full state funding most clearly recognizes that providing for the basic educational needs of citizens is a responsibility of the state as required by state constitutions. Full state funding does not necessarily eliminate the possibility of decentralized decisions about how schools are organized and operated, however. Further, full state funding does not preclude the recognition that some children require more expensive educations than do other children (see Chapter 9).

The greatest difficulty with full state funding arises in defining the level of funding, that is, in determining adequacy. It assumes that state legislatures are fully competent to determine unilaterally an adequate standard of finance for education—a role currently filled in most states by local school boards and state legislatures jointly. Equally distributed resources that are inadequate are of little value to anyone. They would certainly encourage all who are able to abandon public schools. On the other hand, no state can afford uniform opulence. Substantial financial support of public schools generated by school districts has enabled most state legislatures to avoid fully facing the issue of funding adequacy.

Full state funding replaces many independent decisions of local districts about the level of financial adequacy for schools with a single state-level decision. On the surface, this appears to be the height of equity and efficiency—if only we knew the technical relationships between schooling inputs and outcomes and if state legislatures were not distracted by concerns other than education. Unfortunately, we do not fully understand the relationships, and state legislatures must compromise among multiple demands. School districts have a singular focus. But they are also drawn in many directions by a variety of special interests. Unwise decisions made by school districts affect only a small portion of a state's population, except for major city districts. The law of averages works to dilute the bad decisions. And we can learn from both good and bad decisions. This is not to suggest that we condone the resulting inequities, but rather that we accept them within limits as political trade-offs between equity and efficiency.

The pattern of finance operating in most states assumes a partnership between state and local authorities. Local authorities define financial requirements based on constituent demands for schooling, educational program needs, and the availability of resources from locally generated revenue and intergovernmental transfers. State aid to education represents a series of political compromises within the economic constraints inherent in a state's tax-collecting capacity. Legislators and governors forge compromises in response to pressures generated by advocates of the public schools, including school district officials, advocates of all other functions of state government, and those who would reduce public services and taxes.

Since in most states the level of state support lags behind actual expenditures by school districts, the definition of an adequate level of financial support is actually made by each school district. A district does this through its regular planning and budgeting processes, which primarily involve school-related groups and individuals. In seeking funds at the state level, the advocates of high-quality educational services have greatly enhanced the effectiveness of their arguments in the past by their ability to draw upon data generated from independent decisions of many school districts. To remove all local discretion in establishing expenditure levels would be to remove a very important experience test in determining the adequacy of state support levels. It would leave resource allocation decisions to be made largely on the basis of state politics and would reduce the impact of input from an educational perspective.

Permitting variation in expenditures also enhances the ability to accommodate local preferences. With no absolute pedagogical principles to guide educational decision makers, valuable empirical evidence is gained through encouraging a variety of educational programs and expenditure levels. From a political standpoint, such a procedure holds the potential for reducing social stress as long as local resource bases are equalized. This is because there are fewer interest groups that must be satisfied within any substate jurisdiction than for the state as a whole. A limited amount of local discretion in setting expenditure levels enables authorities to meet higher costs because of unique local conditions or aspirations without unduly complicating a state aid formula with technical corrections and special categorical aids (see Chapter 9).

Growing out of the above discussion, we recommend the following as guides for structuring a state school finance program.

1. The state has the overall constitutional responsibility for establishing and maintaining a system of schools within which all of the children and youth of the state may be educated.
2. The state may establish a range of per pupil expenditures that defines minimum and maximum district/school spending in the light of state resources. But it should not set an absolute level of expenditure for all jurisdictions or unnecessarily restrict the use of those resources.
   2.1. Given societal interest in equality of educational opportunities, wide variation in educational expenditures cannot be justified.
   2.2. Economic, social, and environmental variations within most states preclude the establishment of a single expenditure level for the entire state. Local authorities are in the best position to fine-tune expenditure levels, but they need some degree of leeway to do so and financial assistance to attain their program goals.
   2.3. Since there is no absolute standard of an adequate educational program, limited local discretion provides state authorities

with data critical to the establishment of a realistic range of expenditure levels.

3. Within established constraints, the financial capacity of each local authority should be the same throughout the state. For example, a given tax rate in any jurisdiction should produce as much, but no more, revenue per pupil as the same tax rate levied against all the state's property. State revenue should guarantee a defined level of adequacy by supplying the difference between a desired spending level and what can be raised locally with a given level of effort. The state should recapture the amounts raised above this level. (See the discussion of tax-based equalization in Chapter 8.)

4. State governments should gradually increase the percentage of educational costs they provide through nonproperty taxes to about 60 percent of all spending levels combined.

5. Any aid formula should automatically adjust to changes in costs of delivering education, pupils' educational needs, and local financial capacity.

6. Aid for meeting extraordinary pupil needs should be separate from aid to correct for the uneven distribution of wealth among local authorities and to relieve the burden on the property tax.

7. The cost of meeting extraordinary pupil needs should be financed solely from state and federal funds.

The guides presented above could be made operational with a state finance program that includes the following features:

- A first-tier foundation program that is sufficient for supporting a generally acceptable educational program below which no local authority (for example, school district or intermediate unit) may spend, and that is financed from the state's general fund including a state-levied property tax.
- A second-tier fully equalized discretionary range of expenditure (not to exceed 20% of the foundation program) that is supported by state and local funds according to one of

the alternative methods for implementing a tax base equalizing concept, including a recapture provision (see Chapter 8).

- Special state and federal financial assistance for meeting extraordinary educational needs.

The objectives of the foundation program, the discretionary range of expenditures, and the maximum support level are to make available to every child in a state educational services adequate to meet the needs of a typical child, to equalize the property tax ability at chosen levels of effort, and to distribute schooling costs equitably between property and nonproperty taxes. The objective of special aids is to provide adequate educational services for children with extraordinary needs.

School-based management casts school districts into new roles. They now become conduits of funds rather than direct procurors of human and material resources. In keeping with these new roles, school districts will have to develop formulas for the equitable distribution of resources to schools. They will have to develop accounting and information systems appropriate for the new decision-making environment. They will have to develop school assessment and reporting procedures and new sets of rewards and sanctions.

A SYSTEMIC APPROACH TO REFORMING SCHOOL FINANCE POLICY

A decade of reforms followed release of *A Nation at Risk*. In a first wave of reform, state policy addressed academic requirements, curriculum revisions, standardized testing, teacher certification, and work conditions. School-level changes framed a second wave of reform in which school-based management and decision making gave control over curriculum, budgets, and pupil assessments to principals, teachers, and parents in an effort to improve instruction and learning. The complexity and lack of coherence in these many educational and financial policies at school, district, state, and federal levels—with their conflicting expectations for teacher performance to improve student learning—are giving rise to a third wave: systemic reform. Systemic reform attempts to coordinate state policies with restructured school and district governance. The promise is to improve the performance of the whole school, treating all students as if they can meet high expectations and increasing the coherence of teachers' and students' engagement in learning by closely coordinating various elements of the policy infrastructure around outcome expectations.

The challenge is for policy makers and educators to rethink the most effective ways of integrating policies and structuring organizations in support of core teaching-learning activities. State policy makers need to alter government structures and oversight and to change allocation mechanisms in ways that will reduce turf protection among public agencies. Public finance policy can encourage systemic reform by:

1. financing high-quality instructional programs and technologies that successfully help students achieve challenging outcomes;
2. redesigning compensation systems to reward teacher skills and performance;
3. financing professional development at a level adequate to enable teachers to design better instructional systems in relation to new pupil learning expectations; and,
4. directly funding community-based groups to better focus public programs on needs of children and families and to support school-level decisions.

These multiple waves of reform and the increasing competition for state and local resources mean greater political pressure from policy makers for evidence of positive results from education spending. National goals and parallel state policies urge schools to evaluate organizational structures and educational practices in terms of their relationships with student learning. It is anticipated that state finance reform in the coming decade will emphasize incentives for school improvement and financial links among state standards and goals,

spending for programs and personnel, and pupil outcomes. We see school-based decision making and family choice of schools playing facilitating roles in these changes.

The apparent emphasis on efficiency, accountability, and economic growth that drives many of these reforms does not diminish the importance of goals of equality, fraternity, and liberty. Systemic reform efforts will need to embrace these values or the necessary policy changes will not receive the broad political support necessary to ensure their success. Systemic reform will need to demonstrate concern for improving education for children of all backgrounds and learning abilities, for drawing together diverse groups within caring communities, and for enabling parents and students to choose among school structures and philosophies that reach expected outcomes despite their differences. The various values that frame the issues and debate must not be seen as antagonistic but as challenges to policy makers and educators as they strive to construct finance policies and practices that support school improvements in education for a continually changing society.

SUMMARY

The greatest challenge facing policy makers today in the field of public school finance is designing systems for financing schools that encourage improvement in their efficiency. The second-most-important challenge is improving the equity of the distribution of resources to schools whereby all children may have access to good facilities, competent instruction, and state-of-the-art learning materials. These challenges must be addressed systemically.

The primary barriers to the implementation of reforms directed toward making the educational system more efficient appear to be the bureaucratic nature of its current organization and the Balkanization of school districts. Federal and state categorical aids along with court interventions and state regulation have contributed significantly to this condition. To counter its bureaucratic nature, decision making concerning the organization and operation of schools and the allocation of resources within schools needs to be devolved to persons at the school level. To provide incentives for making school personnel more sensitive to the demands of family clients and more concerned about the quality of service provided, the assurance of school funding needs to be removed and to be linked to the quality of school performance. One way of accomplishing this is by permitting parents to select the schools their children are to attend, ignoring school district boundaries, and by linking the flow of resources to the flow of children. School finance strategies facilitating such arrangements are school-based decision making, open enrollment among public schools, and educational vouchers. The latter are appropriate only if private schools are brought within the purview of the publicly supported system.

To safeguard legitimate societal concerns, especially concern for equal educational opportunities, and to overcome inequities created by small and diverse school districts, school-based decision making and family choice among public schools must function within a framework of state and federal finance, coordination, and supervision. Societal controls may well include a required basic curriculum, protection of the rights of minorities and children with disabling conditions to attend their schools of choice, monitoring standards and

progress through formal systems of evaluation, and a system of information and counseling available to parents to assist them in enrolling their children in the most appropriate schools. The percentage of school funding from state resources must continue to increase, and it is entirely conceivable that more states will formally take over the taxation of property for school purposes. The rate of growth in per pupil expenditures is likely to decline.

Equity demands that states require the maintenance of a level of support commensurate with the cost of an adequate basic education program and that a cap, fractionally above the defined level of adequacy, be placed on spending. The current linkages between per pupil expenditure levels, the wealth of school districts, and the priorities given to education by constituents of school districts must be broken. With the centralization of some decisions at the state and federal levels, and with the decentralization of many decisions to school personnel and to parents, the future viability of school districts as currently organized is in question.

The new millennium will see dramatic changes in the financing of elementary and secondary schools as part of a series of systemic reforms that will also include governance, curriculum, standards, and assessment. The problems are sufficient to challenge the best and the brightest of policy analysts and policy makers.

ACTIVITIES

1. Develop your own recommendations for school finance policies in your state during the next decade. Present your rationale for those recommendations.
2. Give your recommendations a reality check by discussing them with a local or state-level policy maker. Revise your recommendations as appropriate.
3. Identify those issues on which you agree with the authors and those issues on which you disagree. Reflect on areas of disagreement and possible reasons for them.

REFERENCES

Clune, W. H. (1994). The shift from equity to adequacy in school finance. *Educational policy, 8,* 376–394.

Fliegel, S. (1993). *Miracle in East Harlem: The fight for choice in public education.* New York: Random House.

Meier, D. (1995). *The power of their ideas: Lessons from a small school in Harlem.* Boston: Beacon Press.

Odden, A. (1994). Including school finance in systemic reform strategies: A commentary. *CPRE Finance Briefs.* Rutgers, State University of New Jersey: Consortium for Policy Research in Education.

Smith, T. M., & Phelps, R. P. (1995). Education finance indicators: What can we learn from comparing states and nations? In W. J. Fowler, Jr. (Ed.), *Developments in school finance* (pp. 99–107). Washington: National Center for Educational Statistics.

Index